AF690974

This work: "Innovations in Derivatives Markets: Fixed Income Modeling, Valuation Adjustments, Risk Management, and Regulation", was originally published by Springer Nature and is being sold pursuant to a Creative Commons license permitting commercial use. All rights not granted by the work's license are retained by the author or authors.

*Cover Image Credit/Copyright Attribution: IIIerlok_Xolms/Shutterstock*

Kathrin Glau · Zorana Grbac
Matthias Scherer · Rudi Zagst
Editors

# Innovations in Derivatives Markets

## Fixed Income Modeling, Valuation Adjustments, Risk Management, and Regulation

*Editors*
Kathrin Glau
Lehrstuhl für Finanzmathematik
Technische Universität München
Garching-Hochbrück
Germany

Matthias Scherer
Lehrstuhl für Finanzmathematik
Technische Universität München
Garching-Hochbrück
Germany

Zorana Grbac
LPMA
Université Paris–Diderot (Paris 7)
Paris Cedex 13
France

Rudi Zagst
Lehrstuhl für Finanzmathematik
Technische Universität München
Garching-Hochbrück
Germany

DOI 10.1007/978-3-319-33446-2

Library of Congress Control Number: 2016939102

© The Editor(s) (if applicable) and The Author(s) 2016. This book is published open access.
**Open Access** This book is distributed under the terms of the Creative Commons Attribution 4.0 International License (http://creativecommons.org/licenses/by/4.0/), which permits use, duplication, adaptation, distribution, and reproduction in any medium or format, as long as you give appropriate credit to the original author(s) and the source, a link is provided to the Creative Commons license, and any changes made are indicated.
The images or other third party material in this book are included in the work's Creative Commons license, unless indicated otherwise in the credit line; if such material is not included in the work's Creative Commons license and the respective action is not permitted by statutory regulation, users will need to obtain permission from the license holder to duplicate, adapt or reproduce the material.
The use of general descriptive names, registered names, trademarks, service marks, etc. in this publication does not imply, even in the absence of a specific statement, that such names are exempt from the relevant protective laws and regulations and therefore free for general use.
The publisher, the authors and the editors are safe to assume that the advice and information in this book are believed to be true and accurate at the date of publication. Neither the publisher nor the authors or the editors give a warranty, express or implied, with respect to the material contained herein or for any errors or omissions that may have been made.

# Preface

The financial crisis of 2007–2009 swallowed billions of dollars and caused many corporate defaults. Massive monetary intervention by the US and European central bank stabilized the global financial system, but the long-term consequences of this low interest rate/high government debt policy remain unclear. To avoid such crises scenarios in the future, better regulation was called for by many politicians. The market for portfolio credit derivatives has almost dried out in the aftermath of the crisis and has only recently recovered. Banks are not considered default free anymore, their CDS spreads can tell the story. This has major consequences for OTC derivative transactions between banks and their clients, since the risk of a counterparty credit default cannot be neglected anymore. Concerning interest rates, it has become unclear if there are risk-free rates at all, and if so, how these should be modeled. On top, we have observed negative interest rates for government bonds of countries like Switzerland, Germany, and the US—a feature not captured by many stochastic models.

The conference *Innovations in Derivatives Markets—Fixed income modeling, valuation adjustments, risk management, and regulation*, March 30–April 1, 2015 at the Technical University of Munich shed some light on the tremendous changes in the financial system. We gratefully acknowledge the support by the *KPMG Center of Excellence in Risk Management*, which allowed us to bring together leading experts from fixed income markets, credit modeling, banking, and financial engineering. We thank the contributing authors to this volume for presenting the state of the art in postcrisis financial modeling and computational tools. Their contributions reflect the enormous efforts academia and the financial industry have invested in adapting to a new reality.

The financial crisis made evident that changes in risk attitude are imperative. It is therefore fortunate that postcrisis mathematical finance has immediately accepted to go the path of critically reflecting its old paradigms, identifying new rules, and, finally, implementing the necessary changes. This renewal process has led to a paradigm shift characterized by a changed attitude toward—and a reappraisal of—liquidity and counterparty risk. We are happy that we can invite the reader to gather insight on these changes, to learn which assumptions to trust and which ones to replace, as well as to enter into the discussion on how to overcome the current difficulties of a practical implementation.

Among others, the plenary speakers Damiano Brigo, Stéphane Crépey, Ernst Eberlein, John Hull, Wolfgang Runggaldier, Luis Seco, and Wim Schoutens are represented with articles in this book. The process of identifying and incorporating key features of financial assets and underlying risks is still in progress, as the reader can discover in the form of a vital panel discussion that complements the scientific contributions of the book. The book is divided into three parts. First, the vast field of counterparty credit risk is discussed. Second, FX markets and particularly multi-curve interest-rate models are investigated. The third part contains innovations in financial engineering with diverse topics from dependence modeling, measuring basis spreads, to innovative fee structures for hedge funds.

We thank the *KPMG Center of Excellence in Risk Management* for the opportunity to publish this proceedings volume with online open access and acknowledge the fruitful collaboration with Franz Lorenz, Matthias Mayer, and Daniel Sommer. Moreover, we thank all speakers, visitors, the participants of the panel discussion—Damiano Brigo, Christian Fries, John Hull, Daniel Sommer, and Ralf Werner—and the local supporting team—Bettina Haas, Mirco Mahlstedt, Steffen Schenk, and Thorsten Schulz—who helped to make this conference a success.

Garching-Hochbrück, Germany Kathrin Glau
Paris Cedex 13, France Zorana Grbac
Garching-Hochbrück, Germany Matthias Scherer
Garching-Hochbrück, Germany Rudi Zagst

# Foreword

The conference "Innovations in Derivatives Markets—Fixed Income Modelling, Valuation Adjustments, Risk Management, and Regulation" was held on the campus of Technical University of Munich in Garching-Hochbrück (Munich) from March 30, until April 1, 2015. Thanks to the great efforts of the organizers, the scientific committee, the keynote speakers, contributors, and all other participants, the conference was a huge success, bringing together academics and practitioners to learn about and to discuss state-of-the-art derivatives valuation and mathematical finance. More than 200 participants (35 % of whom were academics, 60 % practitioners, and 5 % students) had many fruitful discussions and exchanges during three days of talks.

The conference "Innovations in Derivatives Markets" and this book are part of an initiative that was founded in 2012 as a cooperation between the Chair of Mathematical Finance at the Technical University of Munich and KPMG AG Wirtschaftsprüfungsgesellschaft. This cooperation is based on three pillars: first strengthening a scientifically challenging education of students that at the same time addresses real-world topics, second supporting research with particular focus on young researchers, and third, bringing together academic researchers with practitioners from the financial industry in the areas of trading, treasury, financial engineering, risk management, and risk controlling in order to develop trendsetting and viable improvements in the effective management of financial risks.

The main focus of the conference was the topic of derivatives valuation which is a subject of great importance for the financial industry, specifically the rise of new valuation adjustments commonly referred to as "XVAs". These XVAs have gained significant attention ever since the financial crisis in 2008 when banks suffered tremendous losses due to counterparty credit risk reflected in derivatives valuation via the credit valuation adjustment, CVA. A debate on the incorporation of funding costs in derivatives valuation starting in 2012 introduced a new letter to the XVA alphabet, the so-called funding valuation adjustment, FVA, together with its specific impact in banks' profit and loss statements. With the conference, we intended to discuss these topics in the light of market evolutions, regulatory change, and state-of-the-art research in financial mathematics by bringing together renowned scientists, practitioners, and ambitious young researchers.

Over the first two days of the conference, several keynote speeches and invited talks addressed various aspects of derivatives valuation. Topics included the fundamental change of moving from one interest rate curve to a multiple curve environment, taking into account counterparty credit risk and funding into derivatives valuation, new approaches to modeling negative interest rates, and also presenting other advances in mathematical finance. The panel discussion on the first day brought together the views of renowned representatives from academia and the financial industry on the necessity, reasonableness and, to some extent, the future of derivatives valuation and XVAs. The conference was rounded out by a day of contributed talks, giving young researchers the opportunity to present and discuss their results in front of a broad audience. All in all, the topics presented during the conference covered a large spectrum, ranging from market developments and the management of derivative valuation adjustments to theoretical advances in financial mathematics.

We would like to thank everyone who contributed to make this event a great success. In particular, we express our gratitude to the scientific committee, namely Kathrin Glau, Zorana Grbac, Matthias Scherer, and Rudi Zagst, the organizational team, namely Kathrin Glau, Bettina Haas, Mirco Mahlstedt, Matthias Scherer, Steffen Schenk, Thorsten Schulz, and Rudi Zagst, the keynote speakers, the moderator and participants of the panel discussion, all speakers of invited and contributed talks, and, last but not least, all participants that attended the conference.

We are convinced that this book will help you to gain insights about state-of-the-art research in the area of mathematical finance and to broaden your horizon on the use of mathematical concepts to the fields of derivatives valuation and risk management.

Dr. Matthias Mayer
Dr. Daniel Sommer
Franz Lorenz
KPMG AG Wirtschaftsprüfungsgesellschaft

# Contents

**Part I Valuation Adjustments**

**Nonlinearity Valuation Adjustment** . . . 3
Damiano Brigo, Qing D. Liu, Andrea Pallavicini and David Sloth

**Analysis of Nonlinear Valuation Equations Under Credit and Funding Effects** . . . 37
Damiano Brigo, Marco Francischello and Andrea Pallavicini

**Nonlinear Monte Carlo Schemes for Counterparty Risk on Credit Derivatives** . . . 53
Stéphane Crépey and Tuyet Mai Nguyen

**Tight Semi-model-free Bounds on (Bilateral) CVA** . . . 83
Jördis Helmers, Jan-J. Rückmann and Ralf Werner

**CVA with Wrong-Way Risk in the Presence of Early Exercise** . . . 103
Roberto Baviera, Gaetano La Bua and Paolo Pellicioli

**Simultaneous Hedging of Regulatory and Accounting CVA** . . . 117
Christoph Berns

**Capital Optimization Through an Innovative CVA Hedge** . . . 133
Michael Hünseler and Dirk Schubert

**FVA and Electricity Bill Valuation Adjustment—Much of a Difference?** . . . 147
Damiano Brigo, Christian P. Fries, John Hull, Matthias Scherer, Daniel Sommer and Ralf Werner

**Part II Fixed Income Modeling**

**Multi-curve Modelling Using Trees** . . . 171
John Hull and Alan White

**Derivative Pricing for a Multi-curve Extension of the Gaussian, Exponentially Quadratic Short Rate Model** . . . . . . . . . . . . . . . . . . . . . . 191
Zorana Grbac, Laura Meneghello and Wolfgang J. Runggaldier

**Multi-curve Construction** . . . . . . . . . . . . . . . . . . . . . . . . . . . . . . 227
Christian P. Fries

**Impact of Multiple-Curve Dynamics in Credit Valuation Adjustments** . . . . . . . . . . . . . . . . . . . . . . . . . . . . . . . . . . . . . 251
Giacomo Bormetti, Damiano Brigo, Marco Francischello and Andrea Pallavicini

**A Generalized Intensity-Based Framework for Single-Name Credit Risk** . . . . . . . . . . . . . . . . . . . . . . . . . . . . . . . . . . . . . . . . . 267
Frank Gehmlich and Thorsten Schmidt

**Option Pricing and Sensitivity Analysis in the Lévy Forward Process Model** . . . . . . . . . . . . . . . . . . . . . . . . . . . . . . . . . . . . 285
Ernst Eberlein, M'hamed Eddahbi and Sidi Mohamed Lalaoui Ben Cherif

**Inside the EMs Risky Spreads and CDS-Sovereign Bonds Basis** . . . . . . 315
Vilimir Yordanov

**Part III Financial Engineering**

**Basket Option Pricing and Implied Correlation in a One-Factor Lévy Model** . . . . . . . . . . . . . . . . . . . . . . . . . . . . . . . . . . . . . 335
Daniël Linders and Wim Schoutens

**Pricing Shared-Loss Hedge Fund Fee Structures** . . . . . . . . . . . . . . . . 369
Ben Djerroud, David Saunders, Luis Seco and Mohammad Shakourifar

**Negative Basis Measurement: Finding the Holy Scale** . . . . . . . . . . . . . 385
German Bernhart and Jan-Frederik Mai

**The Impact of a New CoCo Issuance on the Price Performance of Outstanding CoCos** . . . . . . . . . . . . . . . . . . . . . . . . . . . . . . . . 405
Jan De Spiegeleer, Stephan Höcht, Ine Marquet and Wim Schoutens

**The Impact of Cointegration on Commodity Spread Options** . . . . . . . . 421
Walter Farkas, Elise Gourier, Robert Huitema and Ciprian Necula

**The Dynamic Correlation Model and Its Application to the Heston Model** . . . . . . . . . . . . . . . . . . . . . . . . . . . . . . . . . . . . . . 437
L. Teng, M. Ehrhardt and M. Günther

# Part I
# Valuation Adjustments

# Nonlinearity Valuation Adjustment

## Nonlinear Valuation Under Collateralization, Credit Risk, and Funding Costs

**Damiano Brigo, Qing D. Liu, Andrea Pallavicini and David Sloth**

**Abstract** We develop a consistent, arbitrage-free framework for valuing derivative trades with collateral, counterparty credit risk, and funding costs. Credit, debit, liquidity, and funding valuation adjustments (CVA, DVA, LVA, and FVA) are simply introduced as modifications to the payout cash flows of the trade position. The framework is flexible enough to accommodate actual trading complexities such as asymmetric collateral and funding rates, replacement close-out, and re-hypothecation of posted collateral—all aspects which are often neglected. The generalized valuation equation takes the form of a forward–backward SDE or semi-linear PDE. Nevertheless, it may be recast as a set of iterative equations which can be efficiently solved by our proposed least-squares Monte Carlo algorithm. We implement numerically the case of an equity option and show how its valuation changes when including the above effects. In the paper we also discuss the financial impact of the proposed valuation framework and of nonlinearity more generally. This is fourfold: First, the valuation equation is only based on observable market rates, leaving the value of a derivatives transaction invariant to any theoretical risk-free rate. Secondly, the presence of funding costs makes the valuation problem a highly recursive and nonlinear one. Thus, credit and funding risks are non-separable in general, and despite common practice in banks, CVA, DVA, and FVA cannot be treated as purely additive adjustments without running the risk of double counting. To quantify the valuation error that can be attributed to double counting, we introduce a "nonlinearity valuation adjustment" (NVA) and show that its magnitude can be significant under asymmetric funding rates and replacement close-out at default. Thirdly, as trading

D. Brigo (✉) · Q.D. Liu · A. Pallavicini
Department of Mathematics, Imperial College London, London, UK
e-mail: damiano.brigo@imperial.ac.uk

Q.D. Liu
e-mail: daphne.q.liu@gmail.com

A. Pallavicini
Banca IMI, largo Mattioli 3, Milan 20121, Italy
e-mail: andrea.pallavicini@imperial.ac.uk

D. Sloth
Rate Options & Inflation Trading, Danske Bank, Copenhagen, Denmark
e-mail: dap@danskebank.com

© The Author(s) 2016

K. Glau et al. (eds.), *Innovations in Derivatives Markets*, Springer Proceedings in Mathematics & Statistics 165, DOI 10.1007/978-3-319-33446-2_1

parties cannot observe each others' liquidity policies nor their respective funding costs, the bilateral nature of a derivative price breaks down. The value of a trade to a counterparty will not be just the opposite of the value seen by the bank. Finally, valuation becomes aggregation-dependent and portfolio values cannot simply be added up. This has operational consequences for banks, calling for a holistic, consistent approach across trading desks and asset classes.

**Keywords** Nonlinear valuation · Nonlinear valuation adjustment NVA · Credit risk · Credit valuation adjustment CVA · Funding costs · Funding valuation adjustment FVA · Consistent valuation · Collateral

## 1 Introduction

Recent years have seen an unprecedented interest among banks in understanding the risks and associated costs of running a derivatives business. The financial crisis in 2007–2008 made banks painfully aware that derivative transactions involve a number of risks, e.g., credit or liquidity risks that they had previously overlooked or simply ignored. The industry practice for dealing with these issues comes in the form of a series of price adjustments to the classic, risk-neutral price definition of a contingent claim, often coined under mysteriously sounding acronyms such as CVA, DVA, or FVA.[1] The credit valuation adjustment (CVA) corrects the price for the expected costs to the dealer due to the possibility that the counterparty may default, while the so-called debit valuation adjustment (DVA) is a correction for the expected benefits to the dealer due to his own default risk. Dealers also make adjustments due to the costs of funding the trade. This practice is known as a liquidity and funding valuation adjustment (LVA, FVA). Recent headlines such as J.P. Morgan taking a hit of \$1.5 billion in its 2013 fourth-quarter earnings due to funding valuation adjustments underscores the sheer importance of accounting for FVA.

In this paper we develop an arbitrage-free valuation approach of collateralized as well as uncollateralized trades that consistently accounts for credit risk, collateral, and funding costs. We derive a general valuation equation where CVA, DVA, collateral, and funding costs are introduced simply as modifications of payout cash flows. This approach can also be tailored to address trading through a central clearing house (CCP) with initial and variation margins as investigated in Brigo and Pallavicini [6]. In addition, our valuation approach does not put any restrictions on the banks' liquidity policies and hedging strategies, while accommodating asymmetric collateral and funding rates, collateral rehypothecation, and risk-free/replacement close-out conventions. We present an invariance theorem showing that our valuation equa-

[1] Recently, a new adjustment, the so-called KVA or capital valuation adjustment, has been proposed to account for the capital cost of a derivatives transaction (see e.g. Green et al. [26]). Following the financial crisis, banks are faced by more severe capital requirements and leverage constraints put forth by the Basel Committee and local authorities. Despite being a key issue for the industry, we will not consider costs of capital in this paper.

tions do not depend on some unobservable risk-free rates; valuation is purely based on observable market rates. The invariance theorem has appeared first implicitly in Pallavicini et al. [33], and is studied in detail in Brigo et al. [15], a version of which is in this same volume.

Several studies have analyzed the various valuation adjustments separately, but few have tried to build a valuation approach that consistently takes collateralization, counterparty credit risk, and funding costs into account. Under unilateral default risk, i.e., when only one party is defaultable, Brigo and Masetti [4] consider valuation of derivatives with CVA, while particular applications of their approach are given in Brigo and Pallavicini [5], Brigo and Chourdakis [3], and Brigo et al. [8]; see Brigo et al. [11] for a summary. Bilateral default risk appears in Bielecki and Rutkowski [1], Brigo and Capponi [2], Brigo et al. [9] and Gregory [27] who price both the CVA and DVA of a derivatives deal. The impact of collateralization on default risk has been investigated in Cherubini [20] and more recently in Brigo et al. [7, 12]. Assuming no default risk, Piterbarg [36] provides an initial analysis of collateralization and funding risk in a stylized Black–Scholes economy. Morini and Prampolini [31], Fries [25] and Castagna [19] consider basic implications of funding in presence of default risk. However, the most comprehensive attempts to develop a consistent valuation framework are those of Burgard and Kjaer [16, 17], Crépey [21–23], Crépey et al. [24], Pallavicini et al. [33, 34], and Brigo et al. [13, 14].

We follow the works of Pallavicini et al. [34], Brigo et al. [13, 14], and Sloth [37] and consider a general valuation framework that fully and consistently accounts for collateralization, counterparty credit risk, and funding risk when pricing a derivatives trade. We find that the precise patterns of funding-adjusted values depend on a number of factors, including the asymmetry between borrowing and lending rates. Moreover, the introduction of funding risk creates a highly recursive and nonlinear valuation problem. The inherent nonlinearity manifests itself in the valuation equations by taking the form of semi-linear PDEs or BSDEs.

Thus, valuation under funding risk poses a computationally challenging problem; funding and credit costs do not split up in a purely additive way. A consequence of this is that valuation becomes aggregation-dependent. Portfolio values do not simply add up, making it difficult for banks to create CVA and FVA desks with separate and clear-cut responsibilities. Nevertheless, banks often make such simplifying assumptions when accounting for the various price adjustments. This can be done, however, only at the expense of tolerating some degree of double counting in the different valuation adjustments.

We introduce the concept of nonlinearity valuation adjustment (NVA) to quantify the valuation error that one makes when treating CVA, DVA, and FVA as separate, additive terms. In particular, we examine the financial error of neglecting nonlinearities such as asymmetric borrowing and lending funding rates and by substituting replacement close-out at default by the more stylized risk-free close-out assumption. We analyze the large scale implications of nonlinearity of the valuation equations: non-separability of risks, aggregation dependence in valuation, and local valuation measures as opposed to universal ones. Finally, our numerical results confirm that

NVA and asymmetric funding rates can have a non-trivial impact on the valuation of financial derivatives.

To summarize, the financial implications of our valuation framework are fourfold:

- Valuation is invariant to any theoretical risk-free rate and only based on observable market rates.
- Valuation is a nonlinear problem under asymmetric funding and replacement close-out at default, making funding and credit risks non-separable.
- Valuation is no longer bilateral because counterparties cannot observe each others' liquidity policies nor their respective funding costs.
- Valuation is aggregation-dependent and portfolio values can no longer simply be added up.

The above points stress the fact that we are dealing with values rather than prices. By this, we mean to distinguish between the unique *price* of an asset in a complete market with a traded risk-free bank account and the *value* a bank or market participant attributes to the particular asset. Nevertheless, in the following, we will use the terms price and value interchangeably to mean the latter. The paper is organized as follows. Section 2 describes the general valuation framework with collateralized credit, debit, liquidity, and funding valuation adjustments. Section 3 derives an iterative solution of the pricing equation as well as a continuous-time approximation. Section 4 introduces the nonlinearity valuation adjustment and provides numerical results for specific valuation examples. Finally, Sect. 5 concludes the paper.

## 2 Trading Under Collateralization, Close-Out Netting, and Funding Risk

In this section we develop a general risk-neutral valuation framework for OTC derivative deals. The section clarifies how the traditional pre-crisis derivative price is consistently adjusted to reflect the new market realities of collateralization, counterparty credit risk, and funding risk. We refer to the two parties of a credit-risky deal as the investor or dealer ("I") on one side and the counterparty or client ("C") on the other.

We now introduce the mathematical framework we will use. We point out that the focus here is not on mathematics but on building the valuation framework. Full mathematical subtleties are left for other papers and may motivate slightly different versions of the cash flows, see for example Brigo et al. [15]. More details on the origins of the cash flows used here are in Pallavicini et al. [33, 34].

Fixing the time horizon $T \in \mathbb{R}_+$ of the deal, we define our risk-neutral valuation model on the probability space $(\Omega, \mathscr{G}, (\mathscr{G}_t)_{t\in[0,T]}, \mathbb{Q})$. $\mathbb{Q}$ is the risk-neutral probability measure ideally associated with the locally risk-free bank account numeraire growing at the risk-free rate $r$. The filtration $(\mathscr{G}_t)_{t\in[0,T]}$ models the flow of information of the whole market, including credit, such that the default times of the investor $\tau_I$ and the counterparty $\tau_C$ are $\mathscr{G}$-stopping times. We adopt the notational convention that $\mathbb{E}_t$ is the risk-neutral expectation conditional on the information $\mathcal{G}_t$. Moreover, we exclude the possibility of simultaneous defaults for simplicity and define the time of the first default event among the two parties as the stopping time

$$\tau \triangleq (\tau_I \wedge \tau_C).$$

In the sequel we adopt the view of the investor and consider the cash flows and consequences of the deal from her perspective. In other words, when we price the deal we obtain the value of the position to the investor. As we will see, with funding risk this price will not be the value of the deal to the counterparty with opposite sign, in general.

The gist of the valuation framework is conceptually simple and rests neatly on the classical finance disciplines of risk-neutral valuation and discounting cash flows. When a dealer enters into a derivatives deal with a client, a number of cash flows are exchanged, and just like valuation of any other financial claim, discounting these cash in- or outflows gives us a price of the deal. Post-crisis market practice includes four (or more) different types of cash flow streams occurring once a trading position has been entered: (i) Cash flows coming directly from the derivatives contract, such as payoffs, coupons, dividends, etc. We denote by $\pi(t, T)$ the sum of the discounted cash flows happening over the time period $(t, T]$ without including any credit, collateral, and funding effects. This is where classical derivatives valuation would usually stop and the price of a derivative contract with maturity $T$ would be given by

$$V_t = \mathbb{E}_t\left[\pi(t, T)\right].$$

This price assumes no credit risk of the parties involved and no funding risk of the trade. However, present-day market practice requires the price to be adjusted by taking further cash-flow transactions into account: (ii) Cash flows required by collateral margining. If the deal is collateralized, cash flows happen in order to maintain a collateral account that in the case of default will be used to cover any losses. $\gamma(t, T; C)$ is the sum of the discounted margining costs over the period $(t, T]$ with $C$ denoting the collateral account. (iii) Cash flows exchanged once a default event has occurred. We let $\theta_\tau(C, \varepsilon)$ denote the on-default cash-flow with $\varepsilon$ being the residual value of the claim traded at default. Lastly, (iv) cash flows required for funding the deal. We denote the sum of the discounted funding costs over the period $(t, T]$ by $\varphi(t, T; F)$ with $F$ being the cash account needed for funding the deal. Collecting the terms we obtain a consistent price $\bar{V}$ of a derivative deal taking into account counterparty credit risk, margining costs, and funding costs

$$\begin{aligned}\bar{V}_t(C, F) = \mathbb{E}_t\big[&\pi(t, T\wedge\tau) + \gamma(t, T\wedge\tau; C) + \varphi(t, T\wedge\tau; F) \\ &+\mathbf{1}_{\{t<\tau<T\}} D(t, \tau)\theta_\tau(C, \varepsilon)\big],\end{aligned} \tag{1}$$

where $D(t, \tau) = \exp(-\int_t^\tau r_s ds)$ is the risk-free discount factor.

By using a risk-neutral valuation approach, we see that only the payout needs to be adjusted under counterparty credit and funding risk. In the following paragraphs we expand the terms of (1) and carefully discuss how to compute them.

## 2.1 Collateralization

The ISDA master agreement is the most commonly used framework for full and flexible documentation of OTC derivative transactions and is published by the International Swaps and Derivatives Association (ISDA [29]). Once agreed between two parties, the master agreement sets out standard terms that apply to all deals entered into between those parties. The ISDA master agreement lists two tools to mitigate counterparty credit risk: *collateralization* and *close-out netting*. Collateralization of a deal means that the party which is out-of-the-money is required to post collateral—usually cash, government securities, or highly rated bonds—corresponding to the amount payable by that party in the case of a default event. The credit support annex (CSA) to the ISDA master agreement defines the rules under which the collateral is posted or transferred between counterparties. Close-out netting means that in the case of default, all transactions with the counterparty under the ISDA master agreement are consolidated into a single net obligation which then forms the basis for any recovery settlements.

Collateralization of a deal usually happens according to a margining procedure. Such a procedure involves that both parties post collateral amounts to or withdraw amounts from the collateral account $C$ according to their current exposure on prefixed dates $\{t_1, \dots, t_n = T\}$ during the life of the deal, typically daily. Let $\alpha_i$ be the year fraction between $t_i$ and $t_{i+1}$. The terms of the margining procedure may, furthermore, include independent amounts, minimum transfer amounts, thresholds, etc., as described in Brigo et al. [7]. However, here we adopt a general description of the margining procedure that does not rely on the particular terms chosen by the parties.

We consider a collateral account $C$ held by the investor. Moreover, we assume that the investor is the collateral taker when $C_t > 0$ and the collateral provider when $C_t < 0$. The CSA ensures that the collateral taker remunerates the account $C$ at an accrual rate. If the investor is the collateral taker, he remunerates the collateral account by the accrual rate $c_t^+(T)$, while if he is the collateral provider, the counterparty remunerates the account at the rate $c_t^-(T)$.[2] The effective accrual collateral rate $\tilde{c}_t(T)$ is defined as

$$\tilde{c}_t(T) \triangleq c_t^-(T)\mathbf{1}_{\{C_t<0\}} + c_t^+(T)\mathbf{1}_{\{C_t>0\}}. \tag{2}$$

[2]We stress the slight abuse of notation here: A plus and minus sign does not indicate that the rates are positive or negative parts of some other rate, but instead it tells which rate is used to accrue interest on the collateral according to the sign of the collateral account.

More generally, to understand the cash flows originating from collateralization of the deal, let us consider the consequences of the margining procedure to the investor. At the first margin date, say $t_1$, the investor opens the account and posts collateral if he is out-of-the-money, i.e. if $C_{t_1} < 0$, which means that the counterparty is the collateral taker. On each of the following margin dates $t_k$, the investor posts collateral according to his exposure as long as $C_{t_k} < 0$. As collateral taker, the counterparty pays interest on the collateral at the accrual rate $c^-_{t_k}(t_{k+1})$ between the following margin dates $t_k$ and $t_{k+1}$. We assume that interest accrued on the collateral is saved into the account and thereby directly included in the margining procedure and the close-out. Finally, if $C_{t_n} < 0$ on the last margin date $t_n$, the investor closes the collateral account, given no default event has occurred in between. Similarly, for positive values of the collateral account, the investor is instead the collateral taker and the counterparty faces corresponding cash flows at each margin date. If we sum up all the discounted margining cash flows of the investor and the counterparty, we obtain

$$\gamma(t, T \wedge \tau; C) \triangleq \sum_{k=1}^{n-1} \mathbf{1}_{\{t \leqslant t_k < (T \wedge \tau)\}} D(t, t_k) C_{t_k} \left(1 - \frac{P_{t_k}(t_{k+1})}{P^{\tilde{c}}_{t_k}(t_{k+1})}\right), \tag{3}$$

with the zero-coupon bond $P^{\tilde{c}}_t(T) \triangleq [1 + (T - t)\tilde{c}_t(T)]^{-1}$, and the risk-free zero coupon bond, related to the risk-free rate $r$, given by $P_t(T)$. If we adopt a first order expansion (for small $c$ and $r$), we can approximate

$$\gamma(t, T \wedge \tau; C) \approx \sum_{k=1}^{n-1} \mathbf{1}_{\{t \leqslant t_k < (T \wedge \tau)\}} D(t, t_k) C_{t_k} \alpha_k \left(r_{t_k}(t_{k+1}) - \tilde{c}_{t_k}(t_{k+1})\right), \tag{4}$$

where with a slight abuse of notation we call $\tilde{c}_t(T)$ and $r_t(T)$ the continuously (as opposed to simple) compounded interest rates associated with the bonds $P^{\tilde{c}}$ and $P$. This last expression clearly shows a cost of carry structure for collateral costs. If $C$ is positive to "I", then "I" is holding collateral and will have to pay (hence the minus sign) an interest $c^+$, while receiving the natural growth $r$ for cash, since we are in a risk-neutral world. In the opposite case, if "I" posts collateral, $C$ is negative to "I" and "I" receives interest $c^-$ while paying the risk-free rate, as should happen when one shorts cash in a risk-neutral world.

A crucial role in collateral procedures is played by rehypothecation. We discuss rehypothecation and its inherent liquidity risk in the following.

**Rehypothecation**

Often the CSA grants the collateral taker relatively unrestricted use of the collateral for his liquidity and trading needs until it is returned to the collateral provider. Effectively, the practice of rehypothecation lowers the costs of remuneration of the provided collateral. However, while without rehypothecation the collateral provider can expect to get any excess collateral returned after honoring the amount payable on the deal, if rehypothecation is allowed the collateral provider runs the risk of losing a fraction or all of the excess collateral in case of default on the collateral taker's part.

We denote the recovery fraction on the rehypothecated collateral by $R'_I$ when the investor is the collateral taker and by $R'_C$ when the counterparty is the collateral taker. The general recovery fraction on the market value of the deal that the investor receives in the case of default of the counterparty is denoted by $R_C$, while $R_I$ is the recovery fraction received by the counterparty if the investor defaults. The collateral provider typically has precedence over other creditors of the defaulting party in getting back any excess capital, which means $R_I \leqslant R'_I \leqslant 1$ and $R_C \leqslant R'_C \leqslant 1$. If no rehypothecation is allowed and the collateral is kept safe in a segregated account, we have that $R'_I = R'_C = 1$.

## 2.2 *Close-Out Netting*

In case of default, all terminated transactions under the ISDA master agreement with a given counterparty are netted and consolidated into a single claim. This also includes any posted collateral to back the transactions. In this context the close-out amount plays a central role in calculating the on-default cash flows. The close-out amount is the costs or losses that the surviving party incurs when replacing the terminated deal with an economic equivalent. Clearly, the size of these costs will depend on which party survives so we define the close-out amount as

$$\varepsilon_\tau \triangleq \mathbf{1}_{\{\tau=\tau_C<\tau_I\}}\varepsilon_{I,\tau} + \mathbf{1}_{\{\tau=\tau_I<\tau_C\}}\varepsilon_{C,\tau}, \tag{5}$$

where $\varepsilon_{I,\tau}$ is the close-out amount on the counterparty's default priced at time $\tau$ by the investor and $\varepsilon_{C,\tau}$ is the close-out amount if the investor defaults. Recall that we always consider the deal from the investor's viewpoint in terms of the sign of the cash flows involved. This means that if the close-out amount $\varepsilon_{I,\tau}$ as measured by the investor is positive, the investor is a creditor of the counterpaty, while if it is negative, the investor is a debtor of the counterparty. Analogously, if the close-out amount $\varepsilon_{C,\tau}$ to the counterparty but viewed from the investor is positive, the investor is a creditor of the counterparty, and if it is negative, the investor is a debtor to the counterparty.

We note that the ISDA documentation is, in fact, not very specific in terms of how to actually calculate the close-out amount. Since 2009, ISDA has allowed for the possibility to switch from a risk-free close-out rule to a replacement rule that includes the DVA of the surviving party in the recoverable amount. Parker and McGarry[35] and Weeber and Robson [40] show how a wide range of values of the close-out amount can be produced within the terms of ISDA. We refer to Brigo et al. [7] and the references therein for further discussions on these issues. Here, we adopt the approach of Brigo et al. [7] listing the cash flows of all the various scenarios that can occur if default happens. We will net the exposure against the pre-default value of the collateral $C_{\tau-}$ and treat any remaining collateral as an unsecured claim.

If we aggregate all these cash flows and the pre-default value of collateral account, we reach the following expression for the on-default cash-flow

$$\theta_\tau(C,\varepsilon) \triangleq \mathbf{1}_{\{\tau=\tau_C<\tau_I\}}\left(\varepsilon_{I,\tau} - \mathrm{LGD}_C(\varepsilon^+_{I,\tau} - C^+_{\tau-})^+ - \mathrm{LGD}'_C(\varepsilon^-_{I,\tau} - C^-_{\tau-})^+\right) \quad (6)$$
$$+ \mathbf{1}_{\{\tau=\tau_I<\tau_C\}}\left(\varepsilon_{C,\tau} - \mathrm{LGD}_I(\varepsilon^-_{C,\tau} - C^-_{\tau-})^- - \mathrm{LGD}'_I(\varepsilon^+_{C,\tau} - C^+_{\tau-})^-\right).$$

We use the short-hand notation $\mathscr{X}^+ := \max(\mathscr{X}, 0)$ and $\mathscr{X}^- := \min(\mathscr{X}, 0)$, and define the loss-given-default as $\mathrm{LGD}_C \triangleq 1 - R_C$, and the collateral loss-given-default as $\mathrm{LGD}'_C \triangleq 1 - R'_C$. If both parties agree on the exposure, namely $\varepsilon_{I,\tau} = \varepsilon_{C,\tau} = \varepsilon_\tau$, when we take the risk-neutral expectation in (1), we see that the price of the discounted on-default cash-flow,

$$\mathbb{E}_t[\mathbf{1}_{\{t<\tau<T\}}D(t,\tau)\theta_\tau(C,\varepsilon)] = \mathbb{E}_t[\mathbf{1}_{\{t<\tau<T\}}D(t,\tau)\,\varepsilon_\tau] - \mathrm{CVA}(t,T;C) + \mathrm{DVA}(t,T;C), \quad (7)$$

is the present value of the close-out amount reduced by the positive collateralized CVA and DVA terms

$$\Pi_{\mathrm{CVAcoll}}(s) = \left(\mathrm{LGD}_C(\varepsilon^+_{I,s} - C^+_{s-})^+ + \mathrm{LGD}'_C(\varepsilon^-_{I,s} - C^-_{s-})^+\right) \geq 0,$$
$$\Pi_{\mathrm{DVAcoll}}(s) = -\left(\mathrm{LGD}_I(\varepsilon^-_{C,s} - C^-_{s-})^- + \mathrm{LGD}'_I(\varepsilon^+_{C,s} - C^+_{s-})^-\right) \geq 0,$$

and

$$\mathrm{CVA}(t,T;C) \triangleq \mathbb{E}_t\left[\mathbf{1}_{\{\tau=\tau_C<T\}}D(t,\tau)\Pi_{\mathrm{CVAcoll}}(\tau)\right],$$
$$\mathrm{DVA}(t,T;C) \triangleq \mathbb{E}_t\left[\mathbf{1}_{\{\tau=\tau_I<T\}}D(t,\tau)\Pi_{\mathrm{DVAcoll}}(\tau)\right]. \quad (8)$$

Also, observe that if rehypothecation of the collateral is not allowed, the terms multiplied by $\mathrm{LGD}'_C$ and $\mathrm{LGD}'_I$ drop out of the CVA and DVA calculations.

## 2.3 *Funding Risk*

The hedging strategy that perfectly replicates the no-arbitrage price of a derivative is formed by a position in cash and a position in a portfolio of hedging instruments. When we talk about a derivative deal's funding, we essentially mean the cash position that is required as part of the hedging strategy, and with funding costs we refer to the costs of maintaining this cash position. If we denote the cash account by $F$ and the risky asset account by $H$, we get

$$\bar{V}_t = F_t + H_t.$$

In the classical Black–Scholes–Merton theory, the risky part $H$ of the hedge would be a delta position in the underlying stock, whereas the locally risk-free (cash) part $F$ would be a position in the risk-free bank account. If the deal is collateralized, the margining procedure is included in the deal definition insuring that funding of

the collateral is automatically taken into account. Moreover, if rehypothecation is allowed for the collateralized deal, the collateral taker can use the posted collateral as a funding source and thereby reduce or maybe even eliminate the costs of funding the deal. Thus, we have the following two definitions of the funding account:
If rehypothecation of the posted collateral is allowed,

$$F_t \triangleq \bar{V}_t - C_t - H_t, \tag{9}$$

and if such rehypothecation is forbidden, we have

$$F_t \triangleq \bar{V}_t - H_t. \tag{10}$$

By implication of (9) and (10) it is obvious that if the funding account $F_t > 0$, the dealer needs to borrow cash to establish the hedging strategy at time $t$. Correspondingly, if the funding account $F_t < 0$, the hedging strategy requires the dealer to invest surplus cash. Specifically, we assume the dealer enters a funding position on a discrete time-grid $\{t_1, \ldots, t_m\}$ during the life of the deal. Given two adjacent funding times $t_j$ and $t_{j+1}$, for $1 \le j \le m-1$, the dealer enters a position in cash equal to $F_{t_j}$ at time $t_j$. At time $t_{j+1}$ the dealer redeems the position again and either returns the cash to the funder if it was a long cash position and pays funding costs on the borrowed cash, or he gets the cash back if it was a short cash position and receives funding benefits as interest on the invested cash. We assume that these funding costs and benefits are determined at the start date of each funding period and charged at the end of the period.

Let $P_t^{\tilde{f}}(T)$ represent the price of a borrowing (or lending) contract measurable at $t$ where the dealer pays (or receives) one unit of cash at maturity $T > t$. We introduce the effective funding rate $\tilde{f}_t$ as a function: $\tilde{f}_t = f(t, F, H, C)$, assuming that it depends on the cash account $F_t$, hedging account $H_t$, and collateral account $C_t$. Moreover, the zero-coupon bond corresponding to the effective funding rate is defined as

$$P_t^{\tilde{f}}(T) \triangleq [1 + (T-t)\tilde{f}_t(T)]^{-1},$$

If we assume that the dealer hedges the derivatives position by trading in the spot market of the underlying asset(s), and the hedging strategy is implemented on the same time-grid as the funding procedure of the deal, the sum of discounted cash flows from funding the hedging strategy during the life of the deal is equal to

$$\begin{aligned}
&\varphi(t, T \wedge \tau; F, H) \\
&\quad = \sum_{j=1}^{m-1} \mathbf{1}_{\{t \leqslant t_j < (T \wedge \tau)\}} D(t, t_j) \left( F_{t_j} - (F_{t_j} + H_{t_j}) \frac{P_{t_j}(t_{j+1})}{P_{t_j}^{\tilde{f}}(t_{j+1})} + H_{t_j} \frac{P_{t_j}(t_{j+1})}{P_{t_j}^{\tilde{f}}(t_{j+1})} \right) \\
&\quad = \sum_{j=1}^{m-1} \mathbf{1}_{\{t \leqslant t_j < (T \wedge \tau)\}} D(t, t_j) F_{t_j} \left( 1 - \frac{P_{t_j}(t_{j+1})}{P_{t_j}^{\tilde{f}}(t_{j+1})} \right).
\end{aligned} \tag{11}$$

This is, strictly speaking, a discounted payout and the funding cost or benefit at time $t$ is obtained by taking the risk-neutral expectation of the above cash flows. For a trading example giving more details on how the above formula for $\varphi$ originates, see Brigo et al. [15].

As we can see from Eq. (11), the dependence of hedging account dropped off from the funding procedure. For modeling convenience, we can define the effective funding rate $\tilde{f}_t$ faced by the dealer as

$$\tilde{f}_t(T) \triangleq f_t^-(T)\mathbf{1}_{\{F_t<0\}} + f_t^+(T)\mathbf{1}_{\{F_t>0\}}. \tag{12}$$

A related framework would be to consider the hedging account $H$ as being perfectly collateralized and use the collateral to fund hedging, so that there is no funding cost associated with the hedging account.

As with collateral costs mentioned earlier, we may rewrite the cash flows for funding as a first order approximation in continuously compounded rates $\tilde{f}$ and $r$ associated to the relevant bonds. We obtain

$$\varphi(t, T\wedge\tau; F) \approx \sum_{j=1}^{m-1} \mathbf{1}_{\{t\leqslant t_j<(T\wedge\tau)\}} D(t,t_j) F_{t_j} \alpha_j \left( r_{t_j}(t_{j+1}) - \tilde{f}_{t_j}(t_{j+1}) \right), \tag{13}$$

We should also mention that, occasionally, we may include the effects of repo markets or stock lending in our framework. In general, we may borrow/lend the cash needed to establish $H$ from/to our treasury, and we may then use the risky asset in $H$ for repo or stock lending/borrowing in the market. This means that we could include the funding costs and benefits coming from this use of the risky asset. Here, we assume that the bank's treasury automatically recognizes this benefit or cost at the same rate $\tilde{f}$ as used for cash, but for a more general analysis involving repo rate $\tilde{h}$ please refer to, for example, Pallavicini et al. [34], Brigo et al. [15].

The particular positions entered by the dealer to either borrow or invest cash according to the sign and size of the funding account depend on the bank's liquidity policy. In the following we discuss two possible cases: One where the dealer can fund at rates set by the bank's treasury department, and another where the dealer goes to the market directly and funds his trades at the prevailing market rates. As a result, the funding rates and therefore the funding effect on the price of a derivative deal depends intimately on the chosen liquidity policy.

**Treasury Funding**

If the dealer funds the hedge through the bank's treasury department, the treasury determines the funding rates $f^{\pm}$ faced by the dealer, often assuming average funding costs and benefits across all deals. This leads to two curves as functions of maturity; one for borrowing funds $f^+$ and one for lending funds $f^-$. After entering a funding position $F_{t_j}$ at time $t_j$, the dealer faces the following discounted cash-flow

$$\Phi_j(t_j, t_{j+1}; F) \triangleq -N_{t_j} D(t_j, t_{j+1}),$$

with

$$N_{t_j} \triangleq \frac{F^-_{t_j}}{P^{f^-}_{t_j}(t_{j+1})} + \frac{F^+_{t_j}}{P^{f^+}_{t_j}(t_{j+1})}.$$

Under this liquidity policy, the treasury—and not the dealer himself—is in charge of debt valuation adjustments due to funding-related positions. Also, being entities of the same institution, both the dealer and the treasury disappear in case of default of the institution without any further cash flows being exchanged and we can neglect the effects of funding in this case. So, when default risk is considered, this leads to following definition of the funding cash flows

$$\bar{\Phi}_j(t_j, t_{j+1}; F) \triangleq \mathbf{1}_{\{\tau > t_j\}} \Phi_j(t_j, t_{j+1}; F).$$

Thus, the risk-neutral price of the cash flows due to the funding positions entered at time $t_j$ is

$$\mathbb{E}_{t_j}\left[\,\bar{\Phi}_j(t_j, t_{j+1}; F)\,\right] = -\mathbf{1}_{\{\tau > t_j\}} \left( F^-_{t_j} \frac{P_{t_j}(t_{j+1})}{P^{f^-}_{t_j}(t_{j+1})} + F^+_{t_j} \frac{P_{t_j}(t_{j+1})}{P^{f^+}_{t_j}(t_{j+1})} \right).$$

If we consider a sequence of such funding operations at each time $t_j$ during the life of the deal, we can define the sum of cash flows coming from all the borrowing and lending positions opened by the dealer to hedge the trade up to the first-default event

$$\begin{aligned} \varphi(t, T \wedge \tau; F) &\triangleq \sum_{j=1}^{m-1} \mathbf{1}_{\{t \leqslant t_j < (T \wedge \tau)\}} D(t, t_j) \left( F_{t_j} + \mathbb{E}_{t_j}\left[\,\bar{\Phi}_j(t_j, t_{j+1}; F)\,\right] \right) \qquad (14) \\ &= \sum_{j=1}^{m-1} \mathbf{1}_{\{t \leqslant t_j < (T \wedge \tau)\}} D(t, t_j) \left( F_{t_j} - F^-_{t_j} \frac{P_{t_j}(t_{j+1})}{P^{f^-}_{t_j}(t_{j+1})} - F^+_{t_j} \frac{P_{t_j}(t_{j+1})}{P^{f^+}_{t_j}(t_{j+1})} \right). \end{aligned}$$

In terms of the effective funding rate, this expression collapses to (11).

**Market Funding**

If the dealer funds the hedging strategy in the market—and not through the bank's treasury—the funding rates are determined by prevailing market conditions and are often deal-specific. This means that the rate $f^+$ the dealer can borrow funds at may be different from the rate $f^-$ at which funds can be invested. Moreover, these rates may differ across deals depending on the deals' notional, maturity structures, dealer-client relationship, and so forth. Similar to the liquidity policy of treasury funding, we assume a deal's funding operations are closed down in the case of default. Furthermore, as the dealer now operates directly on the market, he needs to include a DVA due to his funding positions when he marks-to-market his trading books. For simplicity, we assume that the funder in the market is default-free so no funding CVA needs to be accounted for. The discounted cash-flow from the borrowing or lending position between two adjacent funding times $t_j$ and $t_{j+1}$ is given by

$$\begin{aligned}\bar{\Phi}_j(t_j, t_{j+1}; F) \triangleq \mathbf{1}_{\{\tau > t_j\}} \mathbf{1}_{\{\tau_I > t_{j+1}\}} \Phi_j(t_j, t_{j+1}; F) \\ - \mathbf{1}_{\{\tau > t_j\}} \mathbf{1}_{\{\tau_I < t_{j+1}\}} (\mathrm{LGD}_I \varepsilon^-_{F,\tau_I} - \varepsilon_{F,\tau_I}) D(t_j, \tau_I),\end{aligned}$$

where $\varepsilon_{F,t}$ is the close-out amount calculated by the funder on the dealer's default

$$\varepsilon_{F,\tau_I} \triangleq -N_{t_j} P_{\tau_I}(t_{j+1}).$$

To price this funding cash-flow, we take the risk-neutral expectation

$$\mathbb{E}_{t_j}\big[\, \bar{\Phi}_j(t_j, t_{j+1}; F) \,\big] = -\mathbf{1}_{\{\tau > t_j\}} \left( F^-_{t_j} \frac{P_{t_j}(t_{j+1})}{P^{f^-}_{t_j}(t_{j+1})} + F^+_{t_j} \frac{P_{t_j}(t_{j+1})}{\bar{P}^{f^+}_{t_j}(t_{j+1})} \right).$$

Here, the zero-coupon funding bond $\bar{P}^{f^+}_t(T)$ for borrowing cash is adjusted for the dealer's credit risk

$$\bar{P}^{f^+}_t(T) \triangleq \frac{P^{f^+}_t(T)}{\mathbb{E}^T_t\big[\, \mathrm{LGD}_I \mathbf{1}_{\{\tau_I > T\}} + R_I \,\big]},$$

where the expectation on the right-hand side is taken under the $T$-forward measure. Naturally, since the seniority could be different, one might assume a different recovery rate on the funding position than on the derivatives deal itself (see Crépey [21]). Extensions to this case are straightforward.

Next, summing the discounted cash flows from the sequence of funding operations through the life of the deal, we get a new expression for $\varphi$ that is identical to (14) where the $P^{f^+}_t(T)$ in the denominator is replaced by $\bar{P}^{f^+}_t(T)$. To avoid cumbersome notation, we will not explicitly write $\bar{P}^{f^+}$ in the sequel, but just keep in mind that when the dealer funds directly in the market then $P^{f^+}$ needs to be adjusted for *funding DVA*. Thus, in terms of the effective funding rate, we obtain (11).

## 3 Generalized Derivatives Valuation

In the previous section we analyzed the discounted cash flows of a derivatives trade and we developed a framework for consistent valuation of such deals under collateralized counterparty credit and funding risk. The arbitrage-free valuation framework is captured in the following theorem.

**Theorem 1** (Generalized Valuation Equation)
*The consistent arbitrage-free price $\bar{V}_t(C, F)$ of a contingent claim under counterparty credit risk and funding costs takes the form*

$$\bar{V}_t(C,F) = \mathbb{E}_t\big[\pi(t,T\wedge\tau) + \gamma(t,T\wedge\tau;C) + \varphi(t,T\wedge\tau;F) \\ + \mathbf{1}_{\{t<\tau<T\}} D(t,\tau)\theta_\tau(C,\varepsilon)\big], \tag{15}$$

*where*

1. *$\pi(t,T\wedge\tau)$ is the discounted cash flows from the contract's payoff structure up to the first-default event.*
2. *$\gamma(t,T\wedge\tau;C)$ is the discounted cash flows from the collateral margining procedure up to the first-default event and is defined in (3).*
3. *$\varphi(t,T\wedge\tau;F)$ is the discounted cash flows from funding the hedging strategy up to the first-default event and is defined in (11).*
4. *$\theta_\tau(C,\varepsilon)$ is the on-default cash-flow with close-out amount $\varepsilon$ and is defined in (6).*

Note that in general a nonlinear funding rate may lead to arbitrages since the choice of the martingale measure depends on the funding/hedging strategy (see Remark 4.2). One has to be careful in order to guarantee that the relevant valuation equation admits solutions. Existence and uniqueness of solutions in the framework of this paper are discussed from a fully mathematical point of view in Brigo et al. [15], a version of which, from the same authors, appears in this volume.

In general, while the valuation equation is conceptually clear—we simply take the expectation of the sum of all discounted cash flows of the trade under the risk-neutral measure—solving the equation poses a recursive, nonlinear problem. The future paths of the effective funding rate $\tilde{f}$ depend on the future signs of the funding account $F$, i.e. whether we need to borrow or lend cash on each future funding date. At the same time, through the relations (9) and (10), the future sign and size of the funding account $F$ depend on the adjusted price $\bar{V}$ of the deal which is the quantity we are trying to compute in the first place. One crucial implication of this nonlinear structure of the valuation problem is the fact that FVA is generally not just an additive adjustment term, as often assumed. More importantly, we see that the celebrated conjecture identifying the DVA of a deal with its funding benefit is not fully general. Only in the unrealistic setting where the dealer can fund an uncollateralized trade at equal borrowing and lending rates, i.e. $f^+ = f^-$, do we achieve the additive structure often assumed by practitioners. If the trade is collateralized, we need to impose even further restrictions as to how the collateral is linked to the price of the trade $\bar{V}$. It should be noted here that funding DVA (as referred to in the previous section) is similar to the DVA2 in Hull and White [28] and the concept of "windfall funding benefit at own default" in Crépey [22, 23]. In practice, however, funds transfer pricing and similar operations conducted by banks' treasuries clearly weaken the link between FVA and this source of DVA. The DVA of the funding instruments does not regard the bank's funding positions, but the derivatives position, and in general it does not match the FVA mainly due to the presence of funding netting sets.

*Remark 1* (*The Law of One Price.*)
On the theoretical side, the generalized valuation equation shakes the foundation of the celebrated Law of One Price prevailing in classical derivatives pricing. Clearly, if we assume no funding costs, the dealer and counterparty agree on the price of

the deal as both parties can—at least theoretically—observe the credit risk of each other through CDS contracts traded in the market and the relevant market risks, thus agreeing on CVA and DVA. In contrast, introducing funding costs, they will not agree on the FVA for the deal due to asymmetric information. The parties cannot observe each others' liquidity policies nor their respective funding costs associated with a particular deal. As a result, the value of a deal position will not generally be the same to the counterparty as to the dealer just with opposite sign.

Finally, as we adopt a risk-neutral valuation framework, we implicitly assume the existence of a risk-free interest rate. Indeed, since the valuation adjustments are included as additional cash flows and not as ad-hoc spreads, all the cash flows in (15) are discounted by the risk-free discount factor $D(t, T)$. Nevertheless, the risk-free rate is merely an instrumental variable of the general valuation equation. We clearly distinguish market rates from the theoretical risk-free rate avoiding the dubious claim that the over-night rates are risk free. In fact, as we will show in continuous time, if the dealer funds the hedging strategy of the trade through cash accounts available to him—whether as rehypothecated collateral or funds from the treasury, repo market, etc.—the risk-free rate vanishes from the valuation equation.

## 3.1 Discrete-Time Solution

Our purpose here is to turn the generalized valuation equation (15) into a set of iterative equations that can be solved by least-squares Monte Carlo methods. These methods are already standard in CVA and DVA calculations (Brigo and Pallavicini [5]). To this end, we introduce the auxiliary function

$$
\begin{aligned}
\bar{\pi}(t_j, t_{j+1}; C) \triangleq\; & \pi(t_j, t_{j+1} \wedge \tau) + \gamma(t_j, t_{j+1} \wedge \tau; C) \\
& + \mathbf{1}_{\{t_j < \tau < t_{j+1}\}} D(t_j, \tau) \theta_\tau(C, \varepsilon)
\end{aligned}
\tag{16}
$$

which defines the cash flows of the deal occurring between time $t_j$ and $t_{j+1}$ adjusted for collateral margining costs and default risks. We stress the fact that the close-out amount used for calculating the on-default cash flow still refers to a deal with maturity $T$. If we then solve valuation equation (15) at each funding date $t_j$ in the time-grid $\{t_1, \ldots, t_n = T\}$, we obtain the deal price $\bar{V}$ at time $t_j$ as a function of the deal price on the next consecutive funding date $t_{j+1}$

$$
\begin{aligned}
\bar{V}_{t_j} =\; & \mathbb{E}_{t_j}\big[\, \bar{V}_{t_{j+1}} D(t_j, t_{j+1}) + \bar{\pi}(t_j, t_{j+1}; C) \,\big] \\
& + \mathbf{1}_{\{\tau > t_j\}} \left( F_{t_j} - F^-_{t_j} \frac{P_{t_j}(t_{j+1})}{P^{f^-}_{t_j}(t_{j+1})} - F^+_{t_j} \frac{P_{t_j}(t_{j+1})}{P^{f^+}_{t_j}(t_{j+1})} \right),
\end{aligned}
$$

where, by definition, $\bar{V}_{t_n} \triangleq 0$ on the final date $t_n$. Recall the definitions of the funding account in (9) if no rehypothecation of collateral is allowed and in (10) if rehypothecation is permitted, we can then solve the above for the positive and negative parts of the funding account. The outcome of this exercise is a discrete-time iterative solution of the recursive valuation equation, provided in the following theorem.

**Theorem 2** (Discrete-time Solution of the Generalized Valuation Equation)
*We may solve the full recursive valuation equation in Theorem 1 as a set of backward-iterative equations on the time-grid* $\{t_1, \ldots, t_n = T\}$ *with* $\bar{V}_{t_n} \triangleq 0$. *For* $\tau < t_j$, *we have*

$$\bar{V}_{t_j} = 0,$$

*while for* $\tau > t_j$, *we have*

*(i) if rehypothecation is forbidden:*

$$\left(\bar{V}_{t_j} - H_{t_j}\right)^{\pm} = P_{t_j}^{\tilde{f}}(t_{j+1}) \left(\mathbb{E}_{t_j}^{t_{j+1}}\left[\bar{V}_{t_{j+1}} + \frac{\bar{\pi}(t_j, t_{j+1}; C) - H_{t_j}}{D(t_j, t_{j+1})}\right]\right)^{\pm},$$

*(ii) if rehypothecation is allowed:*

$$\begin{aligned}(\bar{V}_{t_j} - C_{t_j} - H_{t_j})^{\pm} \\ &= P_{t_j}^{\tilde{f}}(t_{j+1}) \left(\mathbb{E}_{t_j}^{t_{j+1}}\left[\bar{V}_{t_{j+1}} + \frac{\bar{\pi}(t_j, t_{j+1}; C) - C_{t_j} - H_{t_j}}{D(t_j, t_{j+1})}\right]\right)^{\pm},\end{aligned}$$

*where the expectations are taken under the* $\mathbb{Q}^{t_{j+1}}$*-forward measure.*

The $\pm$ sign in the theorem is supposed to stress the fact that the sign of the funding account, which determines the effective funding rate, depends on the sign of the conditional expectation. Further intuition may be gained by going to continuous time, which is the case we will now turn to.

## 3.2 *Continuous-Time Solution*

Let us consider a continuous-time approximation of the general valuation equation. This implies that collateral margining, funding, and hedging strategies are executed in continuous time. Moreover, we assume that rehypothecation is allowed, but similar results hold if this is not the case. By taking the time limit, we have the following expressions for the discounted cash flow streams of the deal

$$\begin{aligned}\pi(t, T \wedge \tau) &= \int_t^{T\wedge\tau} \pi(s, s + ds) D(t, s), \\ \gamma(t, T \wedge \tau; C) &= \int_t^{T\wedge\tau} (r_s - \tilde{c}_s) C_s D(t, s) ds,\end{aligned}$$

$$\varphi(t, T \wedge \tau; F) = \int_t^{T\wedge\tau} (r_s - \tilde{f}_s) F_s D(t, s) ds,$$

where as mentioned earlier $\pi(t, t + dt)$ is the pay-off coupon process of the derivative contract and $r_t$ is the risk-free rate. These equations can also be immediately derived by looking at the approximations given in Eqs. (4) and (13).

Then, putting all the above terms together with the on-default cash flow as in Theorem 1, the recursive valuation equation yields

$$\begin{aligned} \bar{V}_t = & \int_t^T \mathbb{E}_t\Big[ \big(\mathbf{1}_{\{s<\tau\}}\pi(s, s+ds) + \mathbf{1}_{\{\tau\in ds\}}\theta_s(C, \varepsilon)\big)\, D(t, s) \Big] \\ & + \int_t^T \mathbb{E}_t\big[ \mathbf{1}_{\{s<\tau\}}(r_s - \tilde{c}_s) C_s D(t, s) \big] ds \\ & + \int_t^T \mathbb{E}_t\Big[ \mathbf{1}_{\{s<\tau\}}(r_s - \tilde{f}_s) F_s \Big] D(t, s) ds. \end{aligned} \tag{17}$$

By recalling Eq. (7), we can write the following

**Proposition 1** *The value $\bar{V}_t$ of the claim under credit gap risk, collateral, and funding costs can be written as*

$$\bar{V}_t = V_t - CVA_t + DVA_t + LVA_t + FVA_t \tag{18}$$

*where $V_t$ is the price of the deal when there is no credit risk, no collateral, and no funding costs; LVA is a liquidity valuation adjustment accounting for the costs/benefits of collateral margining; FVA is the funding cost/benefit of the deal hedging strategy, and CVA and DVA are the familiar credit and debit valuation adjustments after collateralization. These different adjustments can be obtained by rewriting (17). One gets*

$$V_t = \int_t^T \mathbb{E}_t\Big\{ D(t, s) 1_{\{\tau>s\}} \Big[ \pi(s, s+ds) + 1_{\{\tau\in ds\}} \varepsilon_s \Big] \Big\} \tag{19}$$

*and the valuation adjustments*

$$\begin{aligned} CVA_t &= -\int_t^T \mathbb{E}\Big\{ D(t, s) 1_{\{\tau>s\}} \big[ -\mathbf{1}_{\{s=\tau_C<\tau_I\}} \Pi_{CVAcoll}(s) \big] \Big\} du \\ DVA_t &= \int_t^T \mathbb{E}\Big\{ D(t, s) 1_{\{\tau>s\}} \big[ \mathbf{1}_{\{s=\tau_I<\tau_C\}} \Pi_{DVAcoll}(s) \big] \Big\} du \\ LVA_t &= \int_t^T \mathbb{E}_t\Big\{ D(t, s) 1_{\{\tau>s\}} (r_s - \tilde{c}_s) C_s \Big\} ds \\ FVA_t &= \int_t^T \mathbb{E}\Big\{ D(t, s) 1_{\{\tau>s\}} \big[ (r_s - \tilde{f}_s) F_s \big] \Big\} ds \end{aligned}$$

*As usual, CVA and DVA are both positive, while LVA and FVA can be either positive or negative. Notice that if $\tilde{c}$ equals the risk-free rate, LVA vanishes. Similarly, FVA vanishes if the funding rate $\tilde{f}$ is equal to the risk-free rate.*

We note that there is no general consensus on our definition of LVA and other authors may define it differently. For instance, Crépey [21–23] refers to LVA as the liquidity component (i.e., net of credit) of the funding valuation adjustment.

We now take a number of heuristic steps. A more formal analysis in terms of FBSDEs or PDEs is, for example, provided in Brigo et al. [15]. For simplicity, we first switch to the default-free market filtration $(\mathscr{F}_t)_{t\geq 0}$. This step implicitly assumes a separable structure of our complete filtration $(\mathscr{G}_t)_{t\geq 0}$. We are also assuming that the basic portfolio cash flows $\pi(0,t)$ are $\mathscr{F}_t$-measurable and that default times of all parties are conditionally independent, given filtration $\mathscr{F}$.

Assuming the relevant technical conditions are satisfied, the Feynman–Kac theorem now allows us to write down the corresponding pre-default partial differential equation (PDE) of the valuation problem (further details may be found in Brigo et al. [13, 14], and Sloth [37]). This PDE could be solved directly as in Crépey [22]. However, if we apply the Feynman–Kac theorem again—this time going from the pre-default PDE to the valuation expectation—and integrate by parts, we arrive at the following result

**Theorem 3** (Continuous-time Solution of the Generalized Valuation Equation) *If we assume collateral rehypothecation and delta-hedging, we can solve the iterative equations of Theorem 2 in continuous time. We obtain*

$$\bar{V}_t = \int_t^T \mathbb{E}^{\tilde{f}}\{D(t,u;\tilde{f}+\lambda)[\pi_u + \lambda_u\theta_u + (\tilde{f}_u - \tilde{c}_u)C_u]|\mathscr{F}_t\}du \tag{20}$$

*where $\lambda_t$ is the first-to-default intensity, $\pi_t\,dt$ is shorthand for $\pi(t,t+dt)$, and the discount factor is defined as $D(t,s;\xi) \triangleq e^{-\int_t^s \xi_u du}$. The expectations are taken under the pricing measure $\mathbb{Q}^{\tilde{f}}$ for which the underlying risk factors grow at the rate $\tilde{f}$ when the underlying pays no dividend.*

Theorem 3 decomposes the deal price $\bar{V}$ into three intuitive terms. The first term is the value of the deal cash flows, discounted at the funding rate plus credit. The second term is the price of the on-default cash-flow in excess of the collateral, which includes the CVA and DVA of the deal after collateralization. The last term collects the cost of collateralization. At this point it is very important to appreciate once again that $\tilde{f}$ depends on $F$, and hence on $V$.

*Remark 2* (*Deal-dependent Valuation Measure, Local Risk-neutral Measures*). Since the pricing measure depends on $\tilde{f}$ which in turn depends on the very value $\bar{V}$ we are trying to compute, we have that the valuation measure becomes deal/portfolio-dependent. Claims sharing a common set of hedging instruments can be priced under a common measure.

Finally, we stress once again a very important invariance result that first appeared in Pallavicini et al. [34] and studied in detail in a more mathematical setting in Brigo et al. [15]. The proof is immediate by inspection.

**Theorem 4** (Invariance of the Valuation Equation wrt. the Short Rate $r_t$).
*Equation (20) for valuation under credit, collateral, and funding costs is completely governed by market rates; there is no dependence on a risk-free rate $r_t$. Whichever initial process is postulated for $r$, the final price is invariant to it.*

## 4 Nonlinear Valuation: A Numerical Analysis

This section provides a numerical case study of the valuation framework outlined in the previous sections. We investigate the impact of funding risk on the price of a derivatives trade under default risk and collateralization. Also, we analyze the valuation error of ignoring nonlinearties of the general valuation problem. Specifically, to quantify this error, we introduce the concept of a nonlinearity valuation adjustment (NVA). A generalized least-squares Monte Carlo algorithm is proposed inspired by the simulation methods of Carriere [18], Longstaff and Schwartz [30], Tilley [38], and Tsitsiklis and Van Roy [39] for pricing American-style options. As the purpose is to understand the fundamental implications of funding risk and other nonlinearities, we focus on trading positions in relatively simple derivatives. However, the Monte Carlo method we propose below can be applied to more complex derivative contracts, including derivatives with bilateral payments.

### *4.1 Monte Carlo Pricing*

Recall the recursive structure of the general valuation: The deal price depends on the funding decisions, while the funding strategy depends on the future price itself. The intimate relationship among the key quantities makes the valuation problem computationally challenging.

We consider $K$ default scenarios during the life of the deal—either obtained by simulation, bootstrapped from empirical data, or assumed in advance. For each first-to-default time $\tau$ corresponding to a default scenario, we compute the price of the deal $\bar{V}$ under collateralization, close-out netting, and funding costs. The first step of our simulation method entails simulating a large number of sample paths $N$ of the underlying risk factors $X$. We simulate these paths on the time-grid $\{t_1, \ldots, t_m = T^*\}$ with step size $\Delta t = t_{j+1} - t_j$ from the assumed dynamics of the risk factors. $T^*$ is equal to the final maturity $T$ of the deal or the consecutive time-grid point following the first-default time $\tau$, whichever occurs first. For simplicity, we assume the time periods for funding decisions and collateral margin payments coincide with the simulation time grid.

Given the set of simulated paths, we solve the funding strategy recursively in a dynamic programming fashion. Starting one period before $T^*$, we compute for each simulated path the funding decision $F$ and the deal price $\bar{V}$ according to the set of backward-inductive equations of Theorem 2. Note that while the reduced formulation of Theorem 3 may look simpler at first sight, avoiding the implicit recursive structure of Theorem 2, it would instead give us a forward–backward SDE problem to solve since the underlying asset now accrues at the funding rate which itself depends on $\bar{V}$. The algorithm then proceeds recursively until time zero. Ultimately, the total price of the deal is computed as the probability-weighted average of the individual prices obtained in each of the $K$ default scenarios.

The conditional expectations in the backward-inductive funding equations are approximated by across-path regressions based on least squares estimation similar to Longstaff and Schwartz [30]. We regress the present value of the deal price at time $t_{j+1}$, the adjusted payout cash flow between $t_j$ and $t_{j+1}$, the collateral account and funding account at time $t_j$ on basis functions $\psi$ of realizations of the underlying risk factors at time $t_j$ across the simulated paths. To keep notation simple, let us assume that we are exposed to only one underlying risk factor, e.g. a stock price. Specifically, the conditional expectations in the iterative equations of Theorem 2, taken under the risk-neutral measure, are equal to

$$\mathbb{E}_{t_j}\left[\Xi_{t_j}(\bar{V}_{t_{j+1}})\right] = \theta'_{t_j}\,\psi(X_{t_j}), \tag{21}$$

where we have defined $\Xi_{t_j}(\bar{V}_{t_{j+1}}) \triangleq D(t_j, t_{j+1})\bar{V}_{t_{j+1}} + \bar{\pi}(t_j, t_{j+1}; C) - C_{t_j} - H_{t_j}$. Note the $C_{t_j}$ term drops out if rehypothecation is not allowed. The usual least-squares estimator of $\theta$ is then given by

$$\hat{\theta}_{t_j} \triangleq \left[\psi(X_{t_j})\psi(X_{t_j})'\right]^{-1}\psi(X_{t_j})\,\Xi_{t_j}(\bar{V}_{t_{j+1}}). \tag{22}$$

Orthogonal polynomials such as Chebyshev, Hermite, Laguerre, and Legendre may all be used as basis functions for evaluating the conditional expectations. We find, however, that simple power series are quite effective and that the order of the polynomials can be kept relatively small. In fact, linear or quadratic polynomials, i.e. $\psi(X_{t_j}) = (\mathbf{1}, X_{t_j}, X_{t_j}^2)'$, are often enough.

Further complexities are added, as the dealer may—realistically—decide to hedge the full deal price $\bar{V}$. Now, the hedge $H$ itself depends on the funding strategy through $\bar{V}$, while the funding decision depends on the hedging strategy. This added recursion requires that we solve the funding and hedging strategies simultaneously. For example, if the dealer applies a delta-hedging strategy we can write, heuristically,

$$H_{t_j} = \left.\frac{\partial\bar{V}}{\partial X}\right|_{t_j} X_{t_j} \approx \frac{\bar{V}_{t_{j+1}} - (1 + \Delta t_j \tilde{f}_{t_j})\bar{V}_{t_j}}{X_{t_{j+1}} - (1 + \Delta t_j \tilde{f}_{t_j})X_{t_j}}\,X_{t_j}, \tag{23}$$

and we obtain, in the case of rehypothecation, the following system of nonlinear equations

$$\begin{cases} F_{t_j} - \frac{P_{t_j}^{\tilde{f}}(t_{j+1})}{P_{t_j}(t_{j+1})} \mathbb{E}_{t_j} \left[ \Xi_{t_j}(\bar{V}_{t_{j+1}}) \right] = 0, \\ H_{t_j} - \frac{\bar{V}_{t_{j+1}} - (1+\Delta t_j \tilde{f}_{t_j}) \bar{V}_{t_j}}{X_{t_{j+1}} - (1+\Delta t_j \tilde{f}_{t_j}) X_{t_j}} X_{t_j} = 0, \\ \bar{V}_{t_j} = F_{t_j} + C_{t_j} + H_{t_j}, \end{cases} \tag{24}$$

where all matrix operations are on an element-by-element basis. An analogous result holds when rehypothecation of the posted collateral is forbidden.

Each period and for each simulated path, we find the funding and hedging decisions by solving this system of equations, given the funding and hedging strategies for all future periods until the end of the deal. We apply a simple Newton–Raphson method to solve the system of nonlinear equations numerically, but instead of using the exact Jacobian, we approximate it by finite differences. As initial guess, we use the Black–Scholes delta position

$$H_{t_j}^0 = \Delta_{t_j}^{BS} X_{t_j}.$$

The convergence is quite fast and only a small number of iterations are needed in practice. Finally, if the dealer decides to hedge only the risk-free price of the deal, i.e. the classic derivative price $V$, the valuation problem collapses to a much simpler one. The hedge $H$ no longer depends on the funding decision and can be computed separately, and the numerical solution of the nonlinear equation system can be avoided altogether.

In the following we apply our valuation framework to the case of a stock or equity index option. Nevertheless, the methodology extends fully to any other derivatives transaction. For instance, applications to interest rate swaps can be found in Pallavicini and Brigo [32] and Brigo and Pallavicini [6].

## 4.2 Case Outline

Let $S_t$ denote the price of some stock or equity index and assume it evolves according to a geometric Brownian motion $dS_t = rS_t dt + \sigma S_t dW_t$ where $W$ is a standard Brownian motion under the risk-neutral measure. The risk-free interest rate $r$ is 100 bps, the volatility $\sigma$ is 25 %, and the current price of the underlying is $S_0 = 100$. The European call option is in-the-money and has strike $K = 80$. The maturity $T$ of the deal is 3 years and, in the full case, we assume that the investor delta-hedges the deal according to (23). The usual default-free funding-free and collateral-free Black–Scholes price $V_0$ of the call option deal is given by

$$V_t = S_t \Phi(d_1(t)) - Ke^{-r(T-t)} \Phi(d_2(t)), \;\; d_{1,2} = \frac{\ln(S_t/K) + (r \pm \sigma^2/2)(T-t)}{\sigma\sqrt{T-t}},$$

and for $t = 0$ we get

$$V_0 = 28.9$$

with our choice of inputs. As usual, $\Phi$ is the cumulative distribution function of the standard normal random variable. In the usual setting, the hedge would not be (23) but a classical delta-hedging strategy based on $\Phi(d_1(t))$.

We consider two simple discrete probability distributions of default. Both parties of the deal are considered default risky but can only default at year 1 or at year 2. The localized joint default probabilities are provided in the matrices below. The rows denote the default time of the investor, while the columns denote the default times of the counterparty. For example, in matrix $D_{\text{low}}$ the event $(\tau_I = 2yr, \tau_C = 1yr)$ has a 3 % probability and the first-to-default time is 1 year. Simultaneous defaults are introduced as an extension of our previous assumptions, and we determine the close-out amount by a random draw from a uniform distribution. If the random number is above 0.5, we compute the close-out as if the counterparty defaulted first, and vice versa.

For the first default distribution, we have a low dependence between the default risk of the counterparty and the default risk of the investor

$$D_{\text{low}} = \begin{array}{c} \\ 1yr \\ 2yr \\ n.d. \end{array} \begin{array}{c} \begin{array}{ccc} 1yr & 2yr & n.d. \end{array} \\ \begin{pmatrix} 0.01 & 0.01 & 0.03 \\ 0.03 & 0.01 & 0.05 \\ 0.07 & 0.09 & 0.70 \end{pmatrix} \end{array}, \qquad \tau_K(D_{\text{low}}) = 0.21 \tag{25}$$

where $n.d.$ means no default and $\tau_K$ denotes the rank correlation as measured by Kendall's tau. In the second case, we have a high dependence between the two parties' default risk

$$D_{\text{high}} = \begin{array}{c} \\ 1yr \\ 2yr \\ n.d. \end{array} \begin{array}{c} \begin{array}{ccc} 1yr & 2yr & n.d. \end{array} \\ \begin{pmatrix} 0.09 & 0.01 & 0.01 \\ 0.03 & 0.11 & 0.01 \\ 0.01 & 0.03 & 0.70 \end{pmatrix} \end{array}, \qquad \tau_K(D_{\text{high}}) = 0.83 \tag{26}$$

Note also that the distributions are skewed in the sense that the counterparty has a higher default probability than the investor. The loss, given default, is 50 % for both the investor and the counterparty and the loss on any posted collateral is considered the same. The collateral rates are chosen to be equal to the risk-free rate. We assume that the collateral account is equal to the risk-free price of the deal at each margin date, i.e. $C_t = V_t$. This is reasonable as the dealer and client will be able to agree on this price, in contrast to $\bar{V}_t$ due to asymmetric information. Also, choosing the collateral this way has the added advantage that the collateral account $C$ works as a control variate, reducing the variance of the least-squares Monte Carlo estimator of the deal price.

### 4.3 *Preliminary Valuation Under Symmetric Funding and Without Credit Risk*

To provide some ball-park figures on the effect of funding risk, we first look at the case without default risk and without collateralization of the deal. We compare our Monte Carlo approach to the following two alternative (simplified) approaches:

(a) The Black–Scholes price where both discounting and the growth of the underlying happens at the symmetric funding rate

$$V_t^{(a)} = \left(S_t \Phi(g_1(t)) - K e^{-\hat{f}(T-t)} \Phi(g_2(t))\right),$$
$$g_{1,2} = \frac{\ln(S_t/K) + (\hat{f} \pm \sigma^2/2)(T-t)}{\sigma\sqrt{T-t}}.$$

(b) We use the above FVA formula in Proposition 1 with some approximations. Since in a standard Black–Scholes setting $F_t = -Ke^{-r(T-t)}\Phi(d_2(t))$, we compute

$$\begin{aligned}\mathrm{FVA}^{(b)} =& (r - \hat{f}) \int_0^T \mathbb{E}_0\left\{e^{-rs}[F_s]\right\} ds \\ =& (\hat{f} - r) K e^{-rT} \int_0^T \mathbb{E}_0\left\{\Phi(d_2(s))\right\} ds\end{aligned}$$

We illustrate the two approaches for a long position in an equity call option. Moreover, let the funding valuation adjustment in each case be defined by $\mathrm{FVA}^{(a,b)} = V^{(a,b)} - V$. Figure 1 plots the resulting funding valuation adjustment with credit and collateral switched off under both simplified approaches and under the full valuation approach. Recall that if the funding rate is equal to the risk-free rate, the value of the call option collapses to the Black–Scholes price and the funding valuation adjustment is zero.

*Remark 3* (*Current Market Practice for FVA*).
Looking at Fig. 1, it is important to realize that at the time of writing this paper, most market players would adopt a methodology like (a) or (b) for a simple call option. Even if borrowing or lending rates were different, most market players would average them and apply a common rate to borrowing and lending, in order to avoid nonlinearities. We notice that method (b) produces the same results as the quicker method (a) which simply replaces the risk-free rate by the funding rate. In the simple case without credit and collateral, and with symmetric borrowing and lending rates, we can show that this method is sound since it stems directly from (20). We also see that both methods (a) and (b) are quite close to the full numerical method we adopt. Overall both simplified methods (a) and (b) work well here, and there would be no need to implement the full machinery under these simplifying assumptions. However, once collateral, credit, and funding risks are in the picture, we have to abandon approximations like (a) or (b) and implement the full methodology instead.

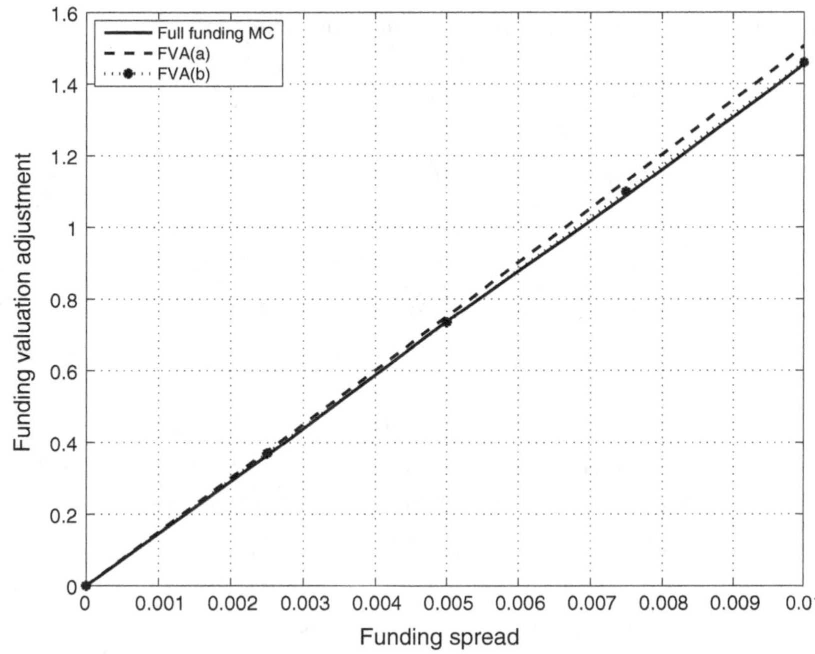


**Fig. 1** Funding valuation adjustment of a long call position as a function of symmetric funding spreads $s_f := \hat{f} - r$ with $\hat{f} := f^+ = f^-$. The adjustments are computed under the assumption of no default risk nor collateralization

## 4.4 *Complete Valuation Under Credit Risk, Collateral, and Asymmetric Funding*

Let us now switch on credit risk and consider the impact of asymmetric funding rates. Due the presence of collateral as a control variate, the accuracy is quite good in our example even for relatively small numbers of sample paths. Based on the simulation of 1,000 paths, Tables 1 and 2 report the results of a ceteris paribus analysis of funding risk under counterparty credit risk and collateralization. Specifically, we investigate how the value of a deal changes for different values of the borrowing (lending) rate $f^+$ ($f^-$) while keeping the lending (borrowing) rate fixed to 100 bps. When both funding rates are equal to 100 bps, the deal is funded at the risk-free rate and we are in the classical derivatives valuation setting.

*Remark 4* (*Potential Arbitrage*).
Note that if $f^+ < f^-$ arbitrage opportunities might be present, unless certain constraints are imposed on the funding policy of the treasury. Such constraints may look unrealistic and may be debated themselves from the point of view of arbitrageability, but since our point here is strictly to explore the impact of asymmetries in the funding equations, we will still apply our framework to a few examples where $f^+ < f^-$.

Table 1 reports the impact of changing funding rates for a call position when the posted collateral may not be used for funding the deal, i.e. rehypothecation is not allowed. First, we note that increasing the lending rate for a long position has a much

**Table 1** Price impact of funding with default risk and collateralization

| Funding[a] (bps) | Default risk, low[b] | | Default risk, high[c] | |
|---|---|---|---|---|
| | Long | Short | Long | Short |
| *Borrowing rate* $f^+$ | | | | |
| 100 | 28.70 (0.15) | −28.72 (0.15) | 29.06 (0.21) | −29.07 (0.21) |
| 125 | 28.53 (0.17) | −29.37 (0.18) | 28.91 (0.21) | −29.70 (0.20) |
| 150 | 28.37 (0.18) | −30.02 (0.22) | 28.75 (0.22) | −30.34 (0.20) |
| 175 | 28.21 (0.20) | −30.69 (0.27) | 28.60 (0.22) | −30.99 (0.21) |
| 200 | 28.05 (0.21) | −31.37 (0.31) | 28.45 (0.22) | −31.66 (0.25) |
| *Lending rate* $f^-$ | | | | |
| 100 | 28.70 (0.15) | −28.72 (0.15) | 29.06 (0.21) | −29.07 (0.21) |
| 125 | 29.35 (0.18) | −28.56 (0.17) | 29.69 (0.20) | −28.92 (0.21) |
| 150 | 30.01 (0.22) | −28.40 (0.18) | 30.34 (0.20) | −28.76 (0.22) |
| 175 | 30.68 (0.27) | −28.23 (0.20) | 31.00 (0.21) | −28.61 (0.22) |
| 200 | 31.37 (0.32) | −28.07 (0.39) | 31.67 (0.25) | −28.46 (0.22) |

Standard errors of the price estimates are given in parentheses
[a]Ceteris paribus changes in one funding rate while keeping the other fixed to 100 bps
[b]Based on the joint default distribution $D_{\text{low}}$ with low dependence
[c]Based on the joint default distribution $D_{\text{high}}$ with high dependence

**Table 2** Price impact of funding with default risk, collateralization, and rehypothecation

| Funding[a] (bps) | Default risk, low[b] | | Default risk, high[c] | |
|---|---|---|---|---|
| | Long | Short | Long | Short |
| *Borrowing rate* $f^+$ | | | | |
| 100 | 28.70 (0.15) | −28.73 (0.15) | 29.07 (0.22) | −29.08 (0.22) |
| 125 | 28.55 (0.17) | −29.56 (0.19) | 28.92 (0.22) | −29.89 (0.20) |
| 150 | 28.39 (0.18) | −30.40 (0.24) | 28.77 (0.22) | −30.72 (0.20) |
| 175 | 28.23 (0.20) | −31.26 (0.30) | 28.63 (0.22) | −31.56 (0.23) |
| 200 | 28.07 (0.22) | −32.14 (0.36) | 28.48 (0.22) | −32.43 (0.29) |
| *Lending rate* $f^-$ | | | | |
| 100 | 28.70 (0.15) | −28.73 (0.15) | 29.07 (0.22) | −29.08 (0.22) |
| 125 | 29.53 (0.19) | −28.57 (0.17) | 29.07 (0.22) | −28.93 (0.22) |
| 150 | 30.38 (0.24) | −28.42 (0.18) | 32.44 (0.29) | −28.78 (0.22) |
| 175 | 31.25 (0.30) | −28.26 (0.20) | 36.19 (0.61) | −28.64 (0.22) |
| 200 | 32.14 (0.37) | −28.10 (0.22) | 32.44 (0.29) | −28.49 (0.22) |

Standard errors of the price estimates are given in parentheses
[a]Ceteris paribus changes in one funding rate while keeping the other fixed to 100 bps
[b]Based on the joint default distribution $D_{\text{low}}$ with low dependence
[c]Based on the joint default distribution $D_{\text{high}}$ with high dependence

larger impact than increasing the borrowing rate. This is due to the fact that a call option is just a one-sided contract. Recall that $F$ is defined as the cash account needed as part of the derivative replication strategy or, analogously, the cash account required to fund the hedged derivative position. To hedge a long call, the investor goes short in a delta position of the underlying asset and invests excess cash in the treasury at $f^-$. Correspondingly, to hedge the short position, the investor enters a long delta position in the stock and finances it by borrowing cash from the treasury at $f^+$, so changing the lending rate only has a small effect on the deal value. Finally, due to the presence of collateral, we observe an almost similar price impact of funding under the two different default distributions $D_{\text{low}}$ and $D_{\text{high}}$.

Finally, assuming cash collateral, we consider the case of rehypothecation and allow the investor and counterparty to use any posted collateral as a funding source. If the collateral is posted to the investor, this means it effectively reduces his costs of funding the delta-hedging strategy. As the payoff of the call is one-sided, the investor only receives collateral when he holds a long position in the call option. But as he hedges this position by short-selling the underlying stock and lending the excess cash proceeds, the collateral adds to his cash lending position and increases the funding benefit of the deal. Analogously, if the investor has a short position, he posts collateral to the counterparty and a higher borrowing rate would increase his costs of funding the collateral he has to post as well as his delta-hedge position. Table 2 reports the results for the short and long positions in the call option when rehypothecation is allowed. Figures 2 and 3 plot the values of collateralized long and short positions in the call option as a function of asymmetric funding spreads. In addition, Fig. 4

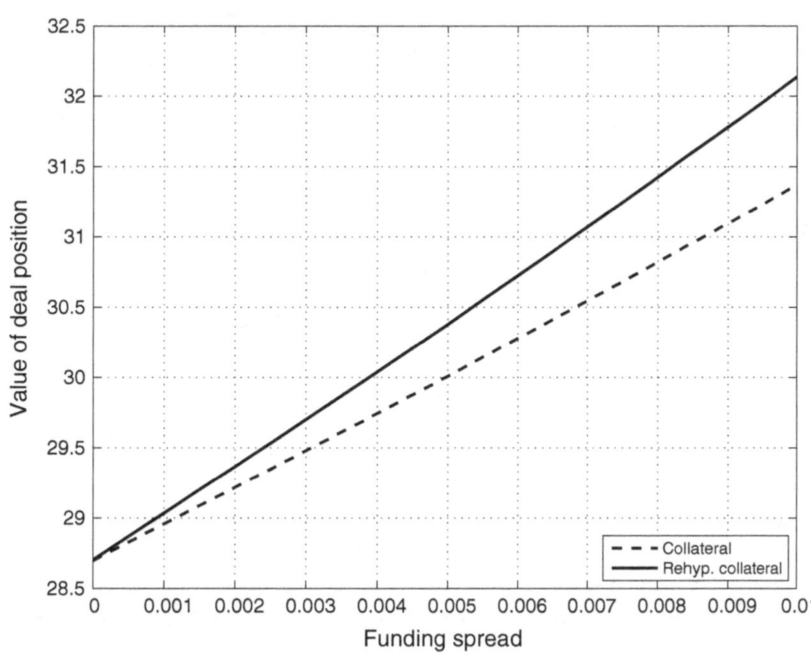


**Fig. 2** The value of a long call position for asymmetric funding spreads $s_f^- = f^- - r$, i.e. fixing $f^+ = r = 0.01$ and varying $f^- \in (0.01, 0.0125, 0.015, 0.0175, 0.02)$

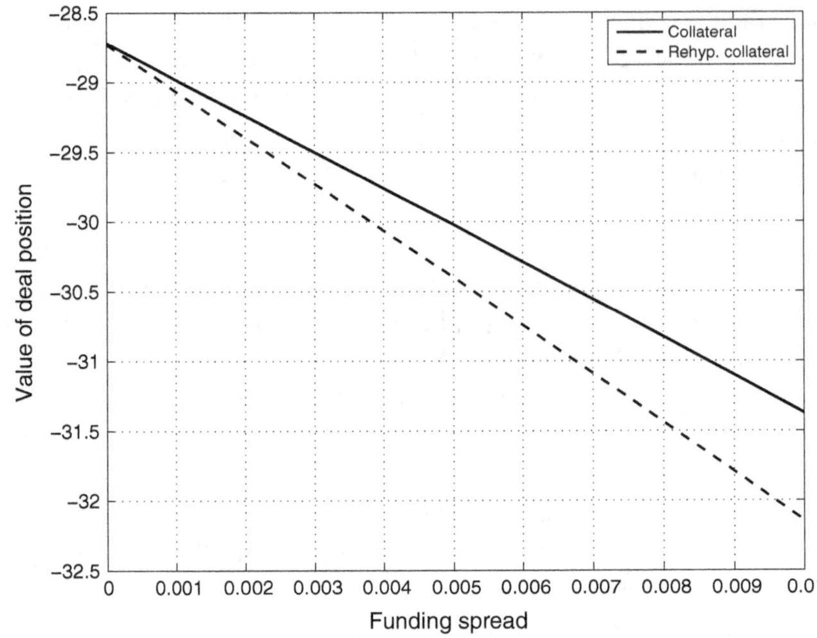


**Fig. 3** The value of a short call position for asymmetric funding spreads $s_f^+ = f^+ - r$, i.e. fixing $f^- = r = 0.01$ and varying $f^+ \in (0.01, 0.0125, 0.015, 0.0175, 0.02)$

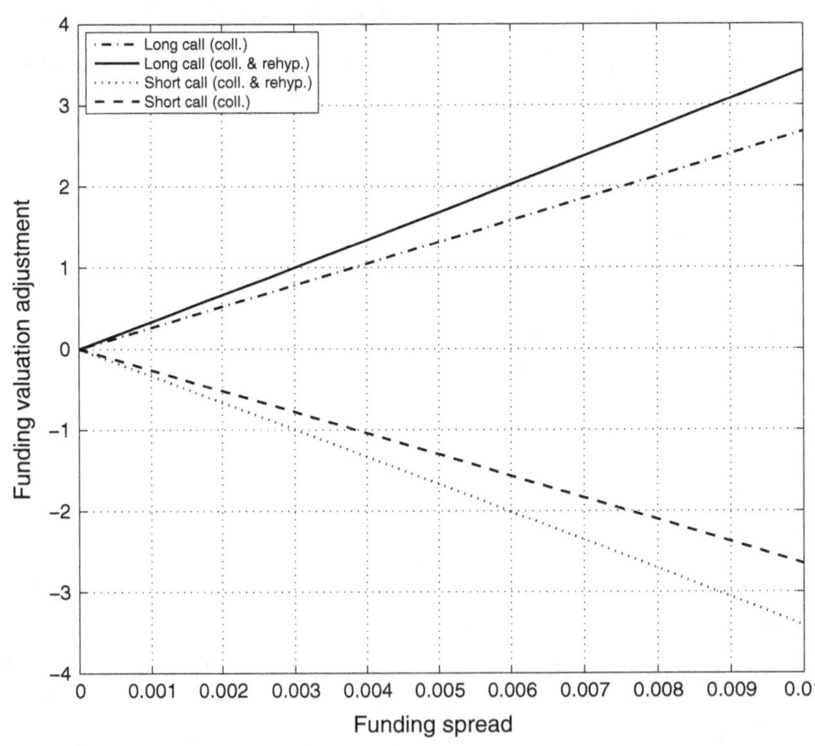


**Fig. 4** Funding valuation adjustment as a function of asymmetric funding spreads. The adjustments are computed under the presence of default risk and collateralization

reports the FVA with respect to the magnitude of the funding spreads, where the FVA is defined as the difference between the full funding-inclusive deal price and the full deal price, but symmetric funding rates equal to the risk-free rate. Recall that the collateral rates are equal to the risk-free rate, so the LVA collapses to zero in these examples.

This shows that funding asymmetry matters even under full collateralization when there is no repo market for the underlying stock. In practice, however, the dealer cannot hedge a long call by shorting a stock he does not own. Instead, he would first borrow the stock in a repo transaction and then sell it in the spot market. Similarly, to enter the long delta position needed to hedge a short call, the dealer could finance the purchase by lending the stock in a reverse repo transaction. Effectively, the delta position in the underlying stock would be funded at the prevailing repo rate. Thus, once the delta hedge has to be executed through the repo market, there is no funding valuation adjustment (meaning any dependence on the funding rate $\tilde{f}$ drops out) given the deal is fully collateralized, but the underlying asset still grows at the repo rate. If there is no credit risk, this would leave us with the result of Piterbarg [36]. However, if the deal is not fully collateralized or the collateral cannot be rehypothecated, funding costs enter the picture even when there is a repo market for the underlying stock.

## 4.5 Nonlinearity Valuation Adjustment

In this last section we introduce a nonlinearity valuation adjustment, and to stay within the usual jargon of the business, we abbreviate it NVA. The NVA is defined by the difference between the true price $\bar{V}$ and a version of $\bar{V}$ where nonlinearities have been approximated away through blunt symmetrization of rates and possibly a change in the close-out convention from replacement close-out to risk-free close-out. This entails a degree of double counting (both positive and negative interest). In some situations the positive and negative double counting will offset each other, but in other cases this may not happen. Moreover, as pointed out by Brigo et al. [10], a further source of double counting might be neglecting the first-to-default time in bilateral CVA/DVA valuation. This is done in a number of industry approximations.

Let $\hat{V}$ be the resulting price when we replace both $f^+$ and $f^-$ by $\hat{f} := (f^+ + f^-)/2$ and adopt a risk-free close-out at default in our valuation framework. A further simplification in $\hat{V}$ could be to neglect the first-to-default check in the close-out. We have the following definition

**Definition 1** (*Nonlinearity Valuation Adjustment, NVA*)
NVA is defined as

$$\text{NVA}_t \triangleq \bar{V}_t - \hat{V}_t$$

where $\bar{V}$ denotes the full nonlinear deal value while $\hat{V}$ denotes an approximate linearized price of the deal.

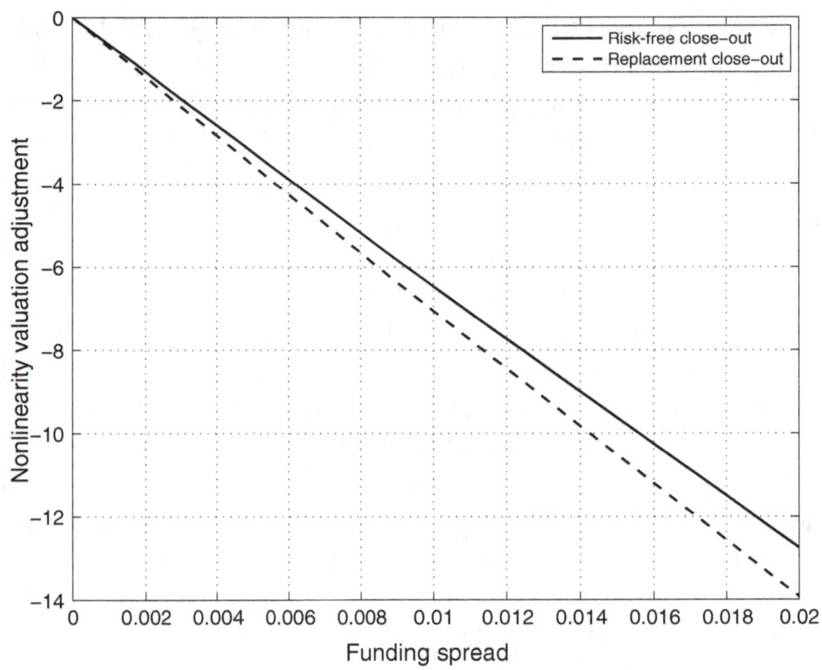


**Fig. 5** Nonlinearity valuation adjustment (in percentage of $\hat{V}$) for different funding spreads $s_f^+ = f^+ - f^- \in (0, 0.005, 0.01, 0.015, 0.02)$ and fixed $\hat{f} = (f^+ + f^-)/2 = 0.01$

As an illustration, we revisit the above example of an equity call option and analyze the NVA in a number of cases. The results are reported in Figs. 5 and 6.

In both figures, we compare NVA under risk-free close-out and under replacement close-out. We can see that, depending on the direction of the symmetrization, NVA may be either positive or negative. As the funding spread increases, NVA grows in absolute value. In addition, adopting the replacement close-out amplifies the presence of double counting. The NVA accounts for up to 15 % of the full deal price $\bar{V}$ depending on the funding spread—a relevant figure in a valuation context.

Table 3 reports (a) $\%\widehat{\text{NVA}}$ denoting the fraction of the approximated deal price $\hat{V}$ explained by NVA, and (b) %NVA denoting the fraction of the full deal price $\bar{V}$ (with symmetric funding rates equal to the risk-free rate $r$) explained by NVA. Notice that for those cases where we adopt a risk-free close-out at default, the results primarily highlight the double-counting error due to symmetrization of borrowing and lending rates. We should point out that close-out nonlinearities play a limited role here, due to absence of wrong way risk. An analysis of close-out nonlinearity under wrong way risk is under development.

Finally, it should be noted that linearization may in fact be done in arbitrarily many ways by playing with the discount factor, hence taking the average of two funding rates as in our definition of NVA is not necessarily the best one. However, we postpone further investigations into this interesting topic for future research.

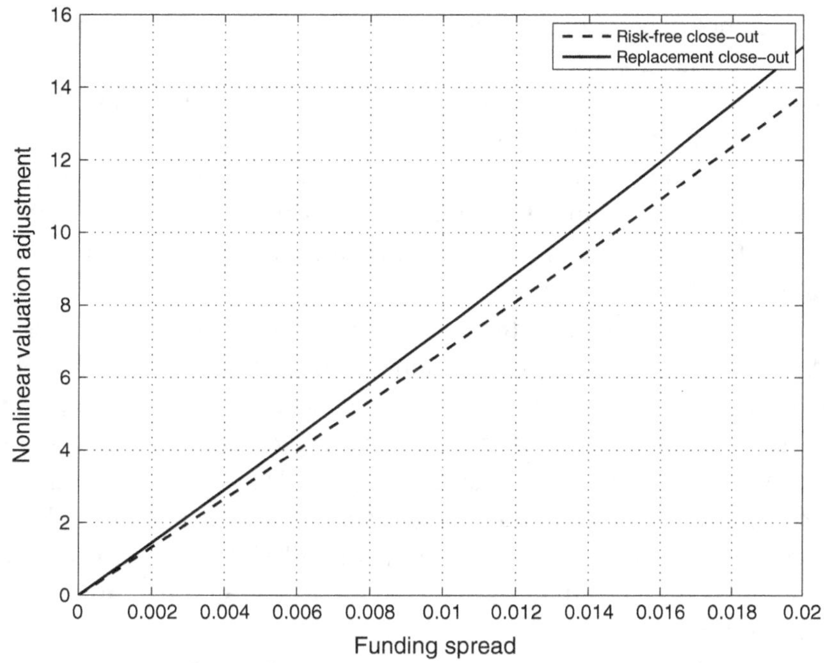


**Fig. 6** Nonlinearity valuation adjustment (in percentage of $\hat{V}$) for different funding spreads $s_f^- = f^- - f^+ \in (0, 0.005, 0.01, 0.015, 0.02)$ and fixed $\hat{f} = (f^+ + f^-)/2 = 0.01$

**Table 3** %NVA with default risk, collateralization and rehypothecation

| Funding rates | | Risk free | | Replacement | |
|---|---|---|---|---|---|
| | | $\%\widehat{\text{NVA}}$ | %NVA | $\%\widehat{\text{NVA}}$ | %NVA |
| $s_f^{\text{b}}$ (bps) | $\hat{f}$ (bps) | | | | |
| 0 | 100 | 0 % | 0 % | 0 % | 0 % |
| 25 | 112.5 | 1.65 % | 1.67 % | 1.79 % | 1.81 % |
| 50 | 125 | 3.31 % | 3.39 % | 3.58 % | 3.68 % |
| 75 | 137.5 | 5.02 % | 5.19 % | 5.39 % | 5.61 % |
| 100 | 150 | 6.70 % | 7.01 % | 7.24 % | 7.62 % |

[a]Funding spread $s_f = f^- - f^+$
[b]The prices of the call option are based on the joint default distribution $D_{\text{high}}$ with high dependence

## 5 Conclusions and Financial Implications

We have developed a consistent framework for valuation of derivative trades under collateralization, counterparty credit risk, and funding costs. Based on no arbitrage, we derived a generalized pricing equation where CVA, DVA, LVA, and FVA are introduced by simply modifying the payout cash flows of the trade. The framework is flexible enough to accommodate actual trading complexities such as asymmetric collateral and funding rates, replacement close-out, and rehypothecation of posted collateral. Moreover, we presented an invariance theorem showing that the valuation framework does not depend on any theoretical risk-free rate, but is purely based on observable market rates.

The generalized valuation equation under credit, collateral, and funding takes the form of a forward–backward SDE or semi-linear PDE. Nevertheless, it can be recast as a set of iterative equations which can be efficiently solved by a proposed least-squares Monte Carlo algorithm. Our numerical results confirm that funding risk as well as asymmetries in borrowing and lending rates have a significant impact on the ultimate value of a derivatives transaction.

Introducing funding costs into the pricing equation makes the valuation problem recursive and nonlinear. The price of the deal depends on the trader's funding strategy, while to determine the funding strategy we need to know the deal price itself. Credit and funding risks are in general non-separable; this means that FVA is not an additive adjustment, let alone a discounting spread. Thus, despite being common practice among market participants, treating it as such comes at the cost of double counting. We introduce the "nonlinearity valuation adjustment" (NVA) to quantify the effect of double counting and we show that its magnitude can be significant under asymmetric funding rates and replacement close-out at default.

Furthermore, valuation under funding costs is no longer bilateral as the particular funding policy chosen by the dealer is not known to the client, and vice versa. As a result, the value of the trade will generally be different to the two counterparties.

Finally, valuation depends on the level of aggregation; asset portfolios cannot simply be priced separately and added up. Theoretically, valuation is conducted under deal or portfolio-dependent risk-neutral measures. This has clear operational consequences for financial institutions; it is difficult for banks to establish CVA and FVA desks with separate, clear-cut responsibilities. In theory, they should adopt a consistent valuation approach across all trading desks and asset classes. A trade should be priced on an appropriate aggregation-level to quantify the value it actually adds to the business. This, of course, prompts to the old distinction between price and value: Should funding costs be charged to the client or just included internally to determine the profitability of a particular trade? The relevance of this question is reinforced by the fact that the client has no direct control on the funding policy of the bank and therefore cannot influence any potential inefficiencies for which he or she would have to pay.

While holistic trading applications may be unrealistic with current technology, our valuation framework offers a unique understanding of the nature and presence of nonlinearities and paves the way for developing more suitable and practical linearizations. The latter topic we will leave for future research.

**Acknowledgements** The KPMG Center of Excellence in Risk Management is acknowledged for organizing the conference "Challenges in Derivatives Markets - Fixed Income Modeling, Valuation Adjustments, Risk Management, and Regulation".

**Open Access** This chapter is distributed under the terms of the Creative Commons Attribution 4.0 International License (http://creativecommons.org/licenses/by/4.0/), which permits use, duplication, adaptation, distribution and reproduction in any medium or format, as long as you give appropriate credit to the original author(s) and the source, a link is provided to the Creative Commons license and any changes made are indicated.

The images or other third party material in this chapter are included in the work's Creative Commons license, unless indicated otherwise in the credit line; if such material is not included in the work's Creative Commons license and the respective action is not permitted by statutory regulation, users will need to obtain permission from the license holder to duplicate, adapt or reproduce the material.

## References

1. Bielecki, T., Rutkowski, M.: Credit Risk: Modeling, Valuation and Hedging. Springer, Berlin (2002)
2. Brigo, D., Capponi, A.: Bilateral counterparty risk with application to CDSs. Working Paper, pp. 241–268 (2008)
3. Brigo, D., Chourdakis, K.: Counterparty risk for credit default swaps: impact of spread volatility and default correlation. Int. J. Theor. Appl. Financ. **12**(07), 1007–1026 (2009)
4. Brigo, D., Masetti, M.: Risk neutral pricing of counterparty risk. In: Pykhtin, M. (ed.) Counterparty Credit Risk Modeling: Risk Management, Pricing and Regulation, Risk Books (2005)
5. Brigo, D., Pallavicini, A.: Counterparty risk under correlation between default and interest rates. In: Miller, J., Edelman, D., Appleby, J. (eds.) Numerical Methods for Finance, Chapman Hall (2007)
6. Brigo, D., Pallavicini, A.: Nonlinear consistent valuation of CCP cleared or CSA bilateral trades with initial margins under credit, funding and wrong-way risks. J. Financ. Eng. **1**(1), 1–60 (2014)
7. Brigo, D., Capponi, A., Pallavicini, A., Papatheodorou, V.: Collateral margining in arbitrage-free counterparty valuation adjustment including re-hypotecation and netting. Working Paper (2011)
8. Brigo, D., Morini, M., Tarenghi, M.: Equity return swap valuation under counterparty risk. In: Bielecki, T., Brigo, D., Patras, F. (eds.) Credit Risk Frontiers: Sub-prime Crisis, Pricing and Hedging, CVA, MBS, Ratings and Liquidity, pp. 457–484. Wiley (2011)
9. Brigo, D., Pallavicini, A., Papatheodorou, V.: Arbitrage-free valuation of bilateral counterparty risk for interest-rate products: impact of volatilities and correlations. Int. J. Theor. Appl. Financ. **14**(6), 773–802 (2011)
10. Brigo, D., Buescu, C., Morini, M.: Counterparty risk pricing: impact of closeout and first-to-default times. Int. J. Theor. Appl. Financ. **15**, 1250039–1250039 (2012)
11. Brigo, D., Morini, M., Pallavicini, A.: Counterparty Credit Risk. Collateral and Funding with Pricing Cases for All Asset Classes. Wiley, Chichester (2013)
12. Brigo, D., Capponi, A., Pallavicini, A.: Arbitrage-free bilateral counterparty risk valuation under collateralization and re-hypothecation with application to CDS. Math. Financ. **24**(1), 125–146 (2014)
13. Brigo, D., Liu, Q., Pallavicini, A., Sloth, D.: Nonlinear Valuation Under Margining and Funding Costs With Residual Credit Risk: A Unified Approach. Handbook in Fixed-Income Securities. Wiley, New Jersey (2014)
14. Brigo, D., Liu, Q., Pallavicini, A., Sloth, D.: Nonlinear valuation under collateral, credit risk and funding costs: a numerical case study extending Black-Scholes. arXiv preprint arXiv:1404.7314 (2014)
15. Brigo, D., Francischello, M., Pallavicini, A.: Invariance, existence and uniqueness of solutions of nonlinear valuation PDEs and FBSDEs inclusive of credit risk, collateral and funding costs. arXiv preprint arXiv:1506.00686. A refined version of this paper appears in the present volume (2015)

16. Burgard, C., Kjaer, M.: Partial differential equation representations of derivatives with counterparty risk and funding costs. J. Credit Risk **7**(3), 1–19. www.ssrn.com/abstract=1605307 (2011)
17. Burgard, C., Kjaer, M.: In the balance. Risk Mag. (2011)
18. Carriere, J.F.: Valuation of the early-exercise price for options using simulations and nonparametric regression. Insur. Math. Econ. **19**(1), 19–30 (1996)
19. Castagna, A.: Funding, liquidity, credit and counterparty risk: links and implications. Working Paper. www.ssrn.com (2011)
20. Cherubini, U.: Counterparty risk in derivatives and collateral policies: the replicating portfolio approach. In: Tilman, L. (ed.) ALM of Financial Institutions. Institutional Investor Books (2005)
21. Crépey, S.: A BSDE approach to counterparty risk under funding constraints. Working Paper. www.grozny.maths.univ-evry.fr/pages_perso/crepey (2011)
22. Crépey, S.: Bilateral counterparty risk under funding constraints Part I: Pricing. Math. Financ. **25**(1), 1–22 (2012a)
23. Crépey, S.: Bilateral counterparty risk under funding constraints Part II: CVA. Math. Financ. **25**(1), 23–50 (2012b)
24. Crépey, S., Bielecki, T., Brigo, D.: Counterparty Risk and Funding: A Tale of Two Puzzles. Taylor & Francis, Abingdon (2014)
25. Fries, C.: Discounting revisited: valuation under funding, counterparty risk and collateralization. Working Paper. www.ssrn.com (2010)
26. Green, A.D., Kenyon, C., Dennis, C.R.: KVA: capital valuation adjustment. Risk (2014)
27. Gregory, J.K.: Being two faced over counterparty credit risk. Risk Mag. **22**, 86–90 (2009)
28. Hull, J., White, A.: The FVA debate. Risk Mag. **8**, (2012)
29. ISDA. ISDA close-out amount protocol. Working Paper (2009). www.isda.com
30. Longstaff, F.A., Schwartz, E.S.: Valuing American options by simulation: a simple least-squares approach. Rev. Financ. Stud. **14**(1), 113–147 (2001)
31. Morini, M., Prampolini, A.: Risky funding: a unified framework for counterparty and liquidity charges. Risk Mag. (2011)
32. Pallavicini, A., Brigo, D.: Interest-rate modelling in collateralized markets: multiple curves, credit-liquidity effects, CCPs. arXiv:1212.2383, ssrn.com (2013)
33. Pallavicini, A., Perini, D., Brigo, D.: Funding Valuation Adjustment: FVA consistent with CVA, DVA, WWR. Netting and re-hyphotecation. arXiv.org, ssrn.com, Collateral (2011)
34. Pallavicini, A., Perini, D., Brigo, D.: Funding, collateral and hedging: uncovering the mechanics and the subtleties of funding valuation adjustments. arXiv preprint arXiv:1210.3811 (2012)
35. Parker, E., McGarry, A.: The isda master agreement and csa: close-out weaknesses exposed in the banking crisis and suggestions for change. Butterworths J. Int. Bank. Law **1** (2009)
36. Piterbarg, V.: Funding beyond discounting: collateral agreements and derivatives pricing. Risk Mag. **2**, 97–102 (2010)
37. Sloth, D.: A Journey into the Dark Arts of Quantitative Finance. Aarhus University, Department of Economics and Business (2013)
38. Tilley, J.A.: Valuing American options in a path simulation model. Trans. Soc. Actuar. **45**(83), 104 (1993)
39. Tsitsiklis, J.N., Van Roy, B.: Regression methods for pricing complex American-style options. IEEE Trans. Neural Netw. **12**(4), 694–703 (2001)
40. Weeber, P., Robson, E.S.: Market practices for settling derivatives in bankruptcy. ABI J. **34–35**(9), 76–78 (2009)

# Analysis of Nonlinear Valuation Equations Under Credit and Funding Effects

**Damiano Brigo, Marco Francischello and Andrea Pallavicini**

**Abstract** We study conditions for existence, uniqueness, and invariance of the comprehensive nonlinear valuation equations first introduced in Pallavicini et al. (Funding valuation adjustment: a consistent framework including CVA, DVA, collateral, netting rules and re-hypothecation, 2011, [11]). These equations take the form of semi-linear PDEs and Forward–Backward Stochastic Differential Equations (FBSDEs). After summarizing the cash flows definitions allowing us to extend valuation to credit risk and default closeout, including collateral margining with possible re-hypothecation, and treasury funding costs, we show how such cash flows, when present-valued in an arbitrage-free setting, lead to semi-linear PDEs or more generally to FBSDEs. We provide conditions for existence and uniqueness of such solutions in a classical sense, discussing the role of the hedging strategy. We show an invariance theorem stating that even though we start from a risk-neutral valuation approach based on a locally risk-free bank account growing at a risk-free rate, our final valuation equations do not depend on the risk-free rate. Indeed, our final semi-linear PDE or FBSDEs and their classical solutions depend only on contractual, market or treasury rates and we do not need to proxy the risk-free rate with a real market rate, since it acts as an instrumental variable. The equations' derivations, their numerical solutions, the related XVA valuation adjustments with their overlap, and the invariance result had been analyzed numerically and extended to central clearing and multiple discount curves in a number of previous works, including Brigo and Pallavicini (J. Financ. Eng. 1(1):1–60 (2014), [3]), Pallavicini and Brigo (Interest-rate modelling in collateralized markets: multiple curves, credit-liquidity effects, CCPs, 2011, [10]), Pallavicini et al. (Funding valuation adjustment: a consistent framework including cva, dva, collateral, netting rules and re-hypothecation, 2011, [11]), Pallavicini et al. (Funding, collateral and hedging: uncovering the mechanics and the subtleties of

D. Brigo (✉) · M. Francischello
Imperial College London, London SW7 2AZ, UK
e-mail: damiano.brigo@imperial.ac.uk

M. Francischello
e-mail: m.francischello14@imperial.ac.uk

A. Pallavicini
Banca IMI, Largo Mattioli 3, Milan 20121, Italy
e-mail: andrea.pallavicini@imperial.ac.uk

© The Author(s) 2016

K. Glau et al. (eds.), *Innovations in Derivatives Markets*, Springer Proceedings in Mathematics & Statistics 165, DOI 10.1007/978-3-319-33446-2_2

funding valuation adjustments, 2012, [12]), and Brigo et al. (Nonlinear valuation under collateral, credit risk and funding costs: a numerical case study extending Black–Scholes, [5]).

**Keywords** Counterparty credit risk · Funding valuation adjustment · Funding costs · Collateralization · Nonlinearity valuation adjustment · Nonlinear valuation · Derivatives valuation · Semi-linear PDE · FBSDE · BSDE · Existence and uniqueness of solutions

## 1 Introduction

This is a technical paper where we analyze in detail invariance, existence, and uniqueness of solutions for nonlinear valuation equations inclusive of credit risk, collateral margining with possible re-hypothecation, and funding costs. In particular, we study conditions for existence, uniqueness, and invariance of the comprehensive nonlinear valuation equations first introduced in Pallavicini et al. (2011) [11]. After briefly summarizing the cash flows definitions allowing us to extend valuation to default closeout, collateral margining with possible re-hypothecation and treasury funding costs, we show how such cash flows, when present-valued in an arbitrage-free setting, lead straightforwardly to semi-linear PDEs or more generally to FBSDEs. We study conditions for existence and uniqueness of such solutions.

We formalize an invariance theorem showing that even though we start from a risk-neutral valuation approach based on a locally risk-free bank account growing at a risk-free rate, our final valuation equations do not depend on the risk-free rate at all. In other words, we do not need to proxy the risk-free rate with any actual market rate, since it acts as an instrumental variable that does not manifest itself in our final valuation equations. Indeed, our final semi-linear PDEs or FBSDEs and their classical solutions depend only on contractual, market or treasury rates and contractual closeout specifications once we use a hedging strategy that is defined as a straightforward generalization of the natural delta hedging in the classical setting.

The equations' derivations, their numerical solutions, and the invariance result had been analyzed numerically and extended to central clearing and multiple discount curves in a number of previous works, including [3, 5, 10–12], and the monograph [6], which further summarizes earlier credit and debit valuation adjustment (CVA and DVA) results. We refer to such works and references therein for a general introduction to comprehensive nonlinear valuation and to the related issues with valuation adjustments related to credit (CVA), collateral (LVA), and funding costs (FVA). In this paper, given the technical nature of our investigation and the emphasis on nonlinear valuation, we refrain from decomposing the nonlinear value into valuation adjustments or XVAs. Moreover, in practice such separation is possible only under very specific assumptions, while in general all terms depend on all risks due to nonlinearity. Forcing separation may lead to double counting, as initially analyzed through the Nonlinearity Valuation Adjustment (NVA) in [5]. Separation is discussed in the CCP setting in [3].

The paper is structured as follows.

Section 2 introduces the probabilistic setting, the cash flows analysis, and derives a first valuation equation based on conditional expectations. Section 3 derives an FBSDE under the default-free filtration from the initial valuation equation under assumptions of conditional independence of default times and of default-free initial portfolio cash flows. Section 4 specifies the FBSDE obtained earlier to a Markovian setting and studies conditions for existence and uniqueness of solutions for the non-linear valuation FBSDE and classical solutions to the associated PDE. Finally, we present the invariance theorem: when adopting delta-hedging, the solution does not depend on the risk-free rate.

## 2 Cash Flows Analysis and First Valuation Equation

We fix a filtered probability space $(\Omega, \mathscr{A}, \mathbb{Q})$, with a filtration $(\mathscr{G}_u)_{u\geq 0}$ representing the evolution of all the available information on the market. With an abuse of notation, we will refer to $(\mathscr{G}_u)_{u\geq 0}$ by $\mathscr{G}$. The object of our investigation is a portfolio of contracts, or "contract" for brevity, typically a netting set, with final maturity $T$, between two financial entities, the investor $I$ and the counterparty $C$. Both $I$ and $C$ are supposed to be subject to default risk. In particular we model their default times with two $\mathscr{G}$-stopping times $\tau_I, \tau_C$. We assume that the stopping times are generated by Cox processes of positive, stochastic intensities $\lambda^I$ and $\lambda^C$. Furthermore, we describe the *default-free* information by means of a filtration $(\mathscr{F}_u)_{u\geq 0}$ generated by the price of the underlying $S_t$ of our contract. This process has the following dynamic under the measure $\mathbb{Q}$:

$$dS_t = r_t S_t dt + \sigma(t, S_t) dW_t$$

where $r_t$ is an $\mathscr{F}$-adapted process, called the *risk-free* rate. We then suppose the existence of a risk-free account $B_t$ following the dynamics

$$dB_t = r_t B_t dt.$$

We denote $D(s, t, x) = e^{-\int_s^t x_u du}$, the discount factor associated to the rate $x_u$. In the case of the risk-free rate, we define $D(s, t) := D(s, t, r)$.

We further assume that for all $t$ we have $\mathscr{G}_t = \mathscr{F}_t \vee \mathscr{H}_t^I \vee \mathscr{H}_t^C$ where

$$\mathscr{H}_t^I = \sigma(1_{\{\tau_I \leq s\}},\ s \leq t),$$
$$\mathscr{H}_t^C = \sigma(1_{\{\tau_C \leq s\}},\ s \leq t).$$

Again we indicate $(\mathscr{F}_u)_{u\geq 0}$ by $\mathscr{F}$ and we will write $\mathbb{E}_t^{\mathscr{G}}[\cdot] := \mathbb{E}[\cdot|\mathscr{G}_t]$ and similarly for $\mathscr{F}$. As in the classic framework of Duffie and Huang [8], we postulate the default times to be *conditionally independent* with respect to $\mathscr{F}$, i.e. for any $t > 0$ and $t_1, t_2 \in [0, t]$, we assume $\mathbb{Q}\{\tau_I > t_1, \tau_C > t_2 | \mathscr{F}_t\} = \mathbb{Q}\{\tau_I > t_1 | \mathscr{F}_t\}\mathbb{Q}\{\tau_C > t_2 | \mathscr{F}_t\}$. Moreover, we indicate $\tau = \tau_I \wedge \tau_C$ and with these assumptions we have that $\tau$ has intensity $\lambda_u = \lambda_u^I + \lambda_u^C$. For convenience of notation we use the symbol $\bar{\tau}$ to indicate the minimum between $\tau$ and $T$.

*Remark 1* We suppose that the measure $\mathbb{Q}$ is the so-called *risk-neutral* measure, i.e. a measure under which the prices of the traded non-dividend-paying assets discounted at the risk-free rate are martingales or, in equivalent terms, the measure associated with the numeraire $B_t$.

## 2.1 The Cash Flows

To price this portfolio we take the conditional expectation of all the cash flows of the portfolio and discount them at the risk-free rate. An alternative to the explicit cash flows approach adopted here is discussed in [4].

To begin with, we consider a collateralized hedged contract, so the cash flows generated by the contract are:

- The payments due to the contract itself: modeled by an $\mathscr{F}$-predictable process $\pi_t$ and a final cash flow $\Phi(S_T)$ payed at maturity modeled by a Lipschitz function $\Phi$. At time $t$ the cumulated discounted flows due to these components amount to

$$1_{\{\tau > T\}} D(0, T)\Phi(S_T) + \int_t^{\bar{\tau}} D(t, u)\pi_u du.$$

- The payments due to default: in particular we suppose that at time $\tau$ we have a cash flow due to the default event (if it happened) modeled by a $\mathscr{G}_\tau$-measurable random variable $\theta_\tau$. So the flows due to this component are

$$1_{\{t < \tau < T\}} D(t, \tau)\theta_\tau = 1_{\{t < \tau < T\}} \int_t^T D(t, u)\theta_u d1_{\{\tau \leq u\}}.$$

- The payments due to the collateral account: more precisely we model this account by an $\mathscr{F}$-predictable process $C_t$. We postulate that $C_t > 0$ if the investor is the collateral taker, and $C_t < 0$ if the investor is the collateral provider. Moreover, we assume that the collateral taker remunerates the account at a certain interest rate (written on the CSA); in particular we may have different rates depending on who the collateral taker is, so we introduce the rate

$$c_t = 1_{\{C_t > 0\}} c_t^+ + 1_{\{C_t \leq 0\}} c_t^- , \tag{1}$$

where $c_t^+$, $c_t^-$ are two $\mathscr{F}$-predictable processes. We also suppose that the collateral can be re-hypothecated, i.e. the collateral taker can use the collateral for funding purposes. Since the collateral taker has to remunerate the account at the rate $c_t$, the discounted flows due to the collateral can be expressed as a cost of carry and sum up to

$$\int_t^{\bar{\tau}} D(t,u)(r_u - c_u)C_u du.$$

- We suppose that the deal we are considering is to be hedged by a position in cash and risky assets, represented respectively by the $\mathcal{G}$-adapted processes $F_t$ and $H_t$, with the convention that $F_t > 0$ means that the investor is borrowing money (from the bank's treasury for example), while $F < 0$ means that $I$ is investing money. Also in this case to take into account different rates in the borrowing or lending case we introduce the rate

$$f_t = 1_{\{V_t - C_t > 0\}} f_t^+ + 1_{\{V_t - C_t \leq 0\}} f_t^- . \tag{2}$$

The flows due to the funding part are

$$\int_t^{\bar{\tau}} D(t,u)(r_u - f_u)F_u du.$$

For the flows related to the risky assets account $H_t$ we assume that we are hedging by means of repo contracts. We have that $H_t > 0$ means that we need some risky asset, so we borrow it, while if $H < 0$ we lend. So, for example, if we need to borrow the risky asset we need cash from the treasury, hence we borrow cash at a rate $f_t$ and as soon as we have the asset we can repo lend it at a rate $h_t$. In general $h_t$ is defined as

$$h_t = 1_{\{H_t > 0\}} h_t^+ + 1_{\{H_t \leq 0\}} h_t^- . \tag{3}$$

Thus we have that the total discounted cash flows for the risky part of the hedge are equal to

$$\int_t^{\bar{\tau}} D(t,u)(h_u - f_u)H_u du.$$

The last expression could also be seen as resulting from $(r - f) - (r - h)$, in line with the previous definitions. If we add all the cash flows mentioned above we obtain that the value of the contract $V_t$ must satisfy

$$\begin{aligned} V_t =& \mathbb{E}_t^{\mathcal{G}}\left[\int_t^{\bar{\tau}} D(t,u)(\pi_u + (r_u - c_u)C_u + (r_u - f_u)F_u - (f_u - h_u)H_u)du\right] \\ &+ \mathbb{E}_t^{\mathcal{G}}\left[1_{\{\tau > T\}} D(t,T)\Phi(S_T) + D(t,\tau)1_{\{t < \tau < T\}}\theta_\tau\right]. \end{aligned} \tag{4}$$

If we further suppose that we are able to replicate the value of our contract using the funding, the collateral (assuming re-hypothecation, otherwise $C$ is to be omitted from the following equation) and the risky asset accounts, i.e.

$$V_u = F_u + H_u + C_u, \tag{5}$$

we have, substituting for $F_u$:

$$\begin{aligned} V_t =&\mathbb{E}_t^{\mathcal{G}}\left[\int_t^{\bar{\tau}} D(t,u)(\pi_u + (f_u - c_u)C_u + (r_u - f_u)V_u - (r_u - h_u)H_u)du\right] \\ &+ \mathbb{E}_t^{\mathcal{G}}\left[1_{\{\tau>T\}}D(t,T)\Phi(S_T) + D(t,\tau)1_{\{t<\tau<T\}}\theta_\tau\right]. \end{aligned} \tag{6}$$

*Remark 2* In the classic no-arbitrage theory and in a complete market setting, without credit risk, the hedging process $H$ would correspond to a delta hedging strategy account. Here we do not enforce this interpretation yet. However, we will see that a delta-hedging interpretation emerges from the combined effect of working under the default-free filtration $\mathcal{F}$ (valuation under partial information) and of identifying part of the solution of the resulting BSDE, under reasonable regularity assumptions, as a sensitivity of the value to the underlying asset price $S$.

## 2.2 *Adjusted Cash Flows Under a Simple Trading Model*

We now show how the adjusted cash flows originate assuming we buy a call option on an equity asset $S_T$ with strike $K$. We analyze the operations a trader would enact with the treasury and the repo market in order to fund the trade, and we map these operations to the related cash flows. We go through the following steps in each small interval $[t, t+dt]$, seen from the point of view of the trader/investor buying the option. This is written in first person for clarity and is based on conversations with traders working with their bank treasuries.

Time $t$:

1. I wish to buy a call option with maturity $T$ whose current price is $V_t = V(t, S_t)$. I need $V_t$ cash to do that. So I borrow $V_t$ cash from my bank treasury and buy the call.
2. I receive the collateral amount $C_t$ for the call, that I give to the treasury.
3. Now I wish to hedge the call option I bought. To do this, I plan to repo-borrow $\Delta_t$ stock on the repo-market.
4. To do this, I borrow $H_t = \Delta_t S_t$ cash at time $t$ from the treasury.
5. I repo-borrow an amount $\Delta_t$ of stock, posting cash $H_t$ as a guarantee.
6. I sell the stock I just obtained from the repo to the market, getting back the price $H_t$ in cash.
7. I give $H_t$ back to treasury.
8. My outstanding debt to the treasury is $V_t - C_t$.

Time $t + dt$:

9. I need to close the repo. To do that I need to give back $\Delta_t$ stock. I need to buy this stock from the market. To do that I need $\Delta_t S_{t+dt}$ cash.
10. I thus borrow $\Delta_t S_{t+dt}$ cash from the bank treasury.
11. I buy $\Delta_t$ stock and I give it back to close the repo and I get back the cash $H_t$ deposited at time $t$ plus interest $h_t H_t$.
12. I give back to the treasury the cash $H_t$ I just obtained, so that the net value of the repo operation has been

$$H_t(1 + h_t\, dt) - \Delta_t S_{t+dt} = -\Delta_t\, dS_t + h_t H_t\, dt$$

Notice that this $-\Delta_t dS_t$ is the right amount I needed to hedge $V$ in a classic delta hedging setting.

13. I close the derivative position, the call option, and get $V_{t+dt}$ cash.
14. I have to pay back the collateral plus interest, so I ask the treasury the amount $C_t(1 + c_t\, dt)$ that I give back to the counterparty.
15. My outstanding debt plus interest (at rate $f$) to the treasury is $V_t - C_t + C_t(1 + c_t\, dt) + (V_t - C_t)f_t\, dt = V_t(1 + f_t\, dt) + C_t(c_t - f_t\, dt)$. I then give to the treasury the cash $V_{t+dt}$ I just obtained, the net effect being

$$V_{t+dt} - V_t(1 + f_t\, dt) - C_t(c_t - f_t)\, dt = dV_t - f_t V_t\, dt - C_t(c_t - f_t)\, dt$$

16. I now have that the total amount of flows is:

$$-\Delta_t\, dS_t + h_t H_t\, dt + dV_t - f_t V_t\, dt - C_t(c_t - f_t)\, dt$$

17. Now I present-value the above flows in $t$ in a risk-neutral setting.

$$\begin{aligned}
&\mathbb{E}_t[-\Delta_t\, dS_t + h_t H_t\, dt + dV_t - f_t V_t\, dt - C_t(c_t - f_t)\, dt] \\
&\quad = -\Delta_t(r_t - h_t)S_t\, dt + (r_t - f_t)V_t\, dt - C_t(c_t - f_t)\, dt - d\varphi(t) \\
&\quad = -H_t(r_t - h_t)\, dt + (r_t - f_t)(H_t + F_t + C_t)\, dt - C_t(c_t - f_t)\, dt - d\varphi(t) \\
&\quad = (h_t - f_t)H_t\, dt + (r_t - f_t)F_t\, dt + (r_t - c_t)C_t\, dt - d\varphi(t)
\end{aligned}$$

This derivation holds assuming that $\mathbb{E}_t[dS_t] = r_t S_t\, dt$ and $\mathbb{E}_t[dV_t] = r_t V_t\, dt - d\varphi(t)$, where $d\varphi$ is a dividend of $V$ in $[t, t + dt)$ expressing the funding costs. Setting the above expression to zero we obtain

$$d\varphi(t) = (h_t - f_t)H_t\, dt + (r_t - f_t)F_t\, dt + (r_t - c_t)C_t\, dt$$

which coincides with the definition given earlier in (6).

## 3 An FBSDE Under $\mathscr{F}$

We aim to switch to the default free filtration $\mathscr{F} = (\mathscr{F}_t)_{t\geq 0}$, and the following lemma (taken from Bielecki and Rutkowski [1] Sect. 5.1) is the key in understanding how the information expressed by $\mathscr{G}$ relates to the one expressed by $\mathscr{F}$.

**Lemma 1** *For any $\mathscr{A}$-measurable random variable $X$ and any $t \in \mathbb{R}_+$, we have:*

$$\mathbb{E}_t^{\mathscr{G}}[1_{\{t<\tau\leq s\}}X] = 1_{\{\tau>t\}}\frac{\mathbb{E}_t^{\mathscr{F}}[1_{\{t<\tau\leq s\}}X]}{\mathbb{E}_t^{\mathscr{F}}[1_{\{\tau>t\}}]}. \tag{7}$$

*In particular we have that for any $\mathscr{G}_t$-measurable random variable $Y$ there exists an $\mathscr{F}_t$-measurable random variable $Z$ such that*

$$1_{\{\tau>t\}}Y = 1_{\{\tau>t\}}Z.$$

What follows is an application of the previous lemma exploiting the fact that we have to deal with a stochastic process structure and not only a simple random variable. Similar results are illustrated in [2].

**Lemma 2** *Suppose that $\phi_u$ is a $\mathscr{G}$-adapted process. We consider a default time $\tau$ with intensity $\lambda_u$. If we denote $\bar{\tau} = \tau \wedge T$ we have:*

$$\mathbb{E}_t^{\mathscr{G}}\left[\int_t^{\bar{\tau}} \phi_u du\right] = 1_{\{\tau>t\}}\mathbb{E}_t^{\mathscr{F}}\left[\int_t^T D(t,u,\lambda)\widetilde{\phi}_u du\right]$$

*where $\widetilde{\phi_u}$ is an $\mathscr{F}_u$ measurable variable such that $1_{\{\tau>u\}}\widetilde{\phi_u} = 1_{\{\tau>u\}}\phi_u$.*

*Proof*

$$\mathbb{E}_t^{\mathscr{G}}\left[\int_t^{\bar{\tau}} \phi_u du\right] = \mathbb{E}_t^{\mathscr{G}}\left[\int_t^T 1_{\{\tau>t\}}1_{\{\tau>u\}}\phi_u du\right] = \int_t^T \mathbb{E}_t^{\mathscr{G}}\left[1_{\{\tau>t\}}1_{\{\tau>u\}}\phi_u\right] du$$

then by using Lemma 1 we have

$$= \int_t^T 1_{\{\tau>t\}}\frac{\mathbb{E}_t^{\mathscr{F}}\left[1_{\{\tau>t\}}1_{\{\tau>u\}}\phi_u\right]}{\mathbb{Q}[\tau > t\,|\mathscr{F}_t]}du = 1_{\{\tau>t\}}\int_t^T \mathbb{E}_t^{\mathscr{F}}\left[1_{\{\tau>u\}}\phi_u\right]D(0,t,\lambda)^{-1}du$$

now we choose an $\mathscr{F}_u$ measurable variable such that $1_{\{\tau>u\}}\widetilde{\phi_u} = 1_{\{\tau>u\}}\phi_u$ and obtain

$$= 1_{\{\tau>t\}}\int_t^T \mathbb{E}_t^{\mathscr{F}}\left[\mathbb{E}_u^{\mathscr{F}}\left[1_{\{\tau>u\}}\right]\widetilde{\phi_u}\right]D(0,t,\lambda)^{-1}du$$

$$= 1_{\{\tau>t\}}\int_t^T \mathbb{E}_t^{\mathscr{F}}\left[D(0,u,\lambda)\widetilde{\phi_u}\right]D(0,t,\lambda)^{-1}du = 1_{\{\tau>t\}}\mathbb{E}_t^{\mathscr{F}}\left[\int_t^T D(t,u,\lambda)\widetilde{\phi}_u du\right]$$

where the penultimate equality comes from the fact that the default times are conditionally independent and if we define $\Lambda_X(u) = \int_0^u \lambda_s^X ds$ with $X \in \{I, C\}$ we have that $\tau_X = \Lambda_X^{-1}(\xi_X)$ with $\xi_X$ mutually independent exponential random variables independent from $\lambda^X$.[1] A similar result will enable us to deal with the default cash flow term. In fact we have the following (Lemma 3.8.1 in [2])

**Lemma 3** *Suppose that $\phi_u$ is an $\mathscr{F}$-predictable process. We consider two conditionally independent default times $\tau_I, \tau_C$ generated by Cox processes with $\mathscr{F}$-intensity rates $\lambda_t^I, \lambda_t^C$. If we denote $\tau = \tau_C \wedge \tau_I$ we have:*

$$\mathbb{E}_t^{\mathscr{G}}\left[1_{\{t<\tau<T\}}1_{\{\tau_I<\tau_C\}}\phi_\tau\right] = 1_{\{\tau>t\}}\mathbb{E}_t^{\mathscr{F}}\left[\int_t^T D(t,u,\lambda^I+\lambda^C)\lambda_u^I\phi_u du\right].$$

Now we postulate a particular form for the default cash flow, more precisely if we indicate $\widetilde{V}_t$ the $\mathscr{F}$-adapted process such that

$$1_{\{\tau>t\}}\widetilde{V}_t = 1_{\{\tau>t\}}V_t$$

then we define

$$\theta_t = \epsilon_t - 1_{\{\tau_C<\tau_I\}}LGD_C(\epsilon_t - C_t)^+ + 1_{\{\tau_I<\tau_C\}}LGD_I(\epsilon_t - C_t)^-.$$

Where $LGD$ indicates the loss given default, typically defined as $1 - REC$, where $REC$ is the corresponding recovery rate and $(x)^+$ indicates the positive part of $x$ and $(x)^- = -(-x)^+$. The meaning of these flows is the following, consider $\theta_\tau$:

- at first to default time $\tau$ we compute the close-out value $\epsilon_\tau$;
- if the counterparty defaults and we are net debtor, i.e. $\epsilon_\tau - C_\tau \leq 0$ then we have to pay the whole close-out value $\varepsilon_\tau$ to the counterparty;
- if the counterparty defaults and we are net creditor, i.e. $\epsilon_\tau - C_\tau > 0$ then we are able to recover just a fraction of our credits, namely $C_\tau + REC_C(\varepsilon_\tau - C_\tau) = REC_C\varepsilon_\tau + LGD_C C_\tau = \varepsilon_\tau - LGD_C(\varepsilon_\tau - C_\tau)$ where $LGD_C$ indicates the loss given default and is equal to one minus the recovery rate $REC_C$.

A similar reasoning applies to the case when the Investor defaults.

If we now change filtration, we obtain the following expression for $V_t$ (where we omitted the tilde sign over the rates, see Remark 3):

[1] See for example Sect. 8.2.1 and Lemma 9.1.1 of [1].

$$
\begin{aligned}
V_t =& 1_{\{\tau>t\}}\mathbb{E}_t^{\mathscr{F}}\left[\int_t^T D(t,u,r+\lambda)((f_u-c_u)C_u+(r_u-f_u)\widetilde{V}_u-(r_u-h_u)\widetilde{H}_u)du\right] \\
&+1_{\{\tau>t\}}\mathbb{E}_t^{\mathscr{F}}\left[D(t,T,r+\lambda)\Phi(S_T)+\int_t^T D(t,u,r+\lambda)\pi_u du\right] \\
&+1_{\{\tau>t\}}\mathbb{E}_t^{\mathscr{F}}\left[\int_t^T D(t,u,r+\lambda)\widetilde{\theta}_u du\right],
\end{aligned}
\tag{8}
$$

where, if we suppose $\epsilon_t$ to be $\mathscr{F}$-predictable, we have (using Lemma 3):

$$
\widetilde{\theta}_u = \epsilon_u\lambda_u - LGD_C(\epsilon_u - C_u)^+\lambda_u^C + LGD_I(\epsilon_u - C_u)^-\lambda_u^I. \tag{9}
$$

*Remark 3* From now on we will omit the tilde sign over the rates $f_u$, $h_u$. Moreover, we note that if a rate is of the form

$$
x_t = x^+ 1_{\{g(V_t,H_t,C_t)>0\}} + x^- 1_{\{g(V_t,H_t,C_t)\leq 0\}}
$$

then on the set $\{\tau > t\}$ it coincides with the rate

$$
\widetilde{x}_t = \widetilde{x}^+ 1_{\{g(\widetilde{V}_t,\widetilde{H}_t,C_t)>0\}} + \widetilde{x}^- 1_{\{g(\widetilde{V}_t,\widetilde{H}_t,C_t)\leq 0\}}
$$

because $1_{\{\tau>t\}}x^+ 1_{\{g(V_t,H_t,C_t)>0\}} = \widetilde{x}^+ 1_{\{\tau>t\}} 1_{\{g(V_t,H_t,C_t)>0\}}$, and on $\{\tau > t\}$ we have $V_t = \widetilde{V}_t$ and $H_t = \widetilde{H}_t$, and hence $g(V_t, H_t, C_t) > 0 \iff g(\widetilde{V}_t, \widetilde{H}_t, C_t) > 0$.

We note that this expression is of the form $V_t = 1_{\{\tau>t\}}\Upsilon$ meaning that $V_t$ is zero on $\{\tau \leq t\}$ and that on the set $\{\tau > t\}$ it coincides with the $\mathscr{F}$-measurable random variable $\Upsilon$. But we already know a variable that coincides with $V_t$ on $\{\tau > t\}$, i.e. $\widetilde{V}_t$. Hence we can write the following:

$$
\begin{aligned}
\widetilde{V}_t =& \mathbb{E}_t^{\mathscr{F}}\left[\int_t^T D(t,u,r+\lambda)(\pi_u+(f_u-c_u)C_u+(r_u-f_u)\widetilde{V}_u-(r_u-h_u)\widetilde{H}_u)du\right] \\
&+\mathbb{E}_t^{\mathscr{F}}\left[D(t,T,r+\lambda)\Phi(S_T)+\int_t^T D(t,u,r+\lambda)\widetilde{\theta}_u du\right].
\end{aligned}
\tag{10}
$$

We now show a way to obtain a BSDE from Eq. (10), another possible approach (without default risk) is shown for example in [9]. We introduce the process

$$
\begin{aligned}
X_t =& \int_0^t D(0,u,r+\lambda)\pi_u du + \int_0^t D(0,u,r+\lambda)\widetilde{\theta}_u du \\
&+ \int_0^t D(0,u,r+\lambda)\left[(f_u-c_u)C_u+(r_u-f_u)\widetilde{V}_u-(r_u-h_u)\widetilde{H}_u\right]du.
\end{aligned}
\tag{11}
$$

Now we can construct a martingale summing up $X_t$ and the discounted value of the deal as in the following:

$$D(0,t,r+\lambda)\widetilde{V}_t + X_t = \mathbb{E}_t^{\mathscr{F}}[X_T + D(0,T,r+\lambda)\Phi(S_T)].$$

So differentiating both sides we obtain:

$$\begin{aligned}&-(r_u+\lambda_u)D(0,u,r+\lambda)\widetilde{V}_u du + D(0,u,r+\lambda)d\widetilde{V}_u + dX_u\\ &= d\mathbb{E}_u^{\mathscr{F}}[X_T + D(0,T,r+\lambda)\Phi(S_T)].\end{aligned}$$

If we substitute for $X_t$ we have that the expression:

$$d\widetilde{V}_u + \left[\pi_u - (r_u+\lambda_u)\widetilde{V}_u + \widetilde{\theta}_u + (f_u - c_u)C_u + (r_u - f_u)\widetilde{V}_u - (r_u - h_u)\widetilde{H}_u\right]du$$

is equal to;

$$\frac{d\mathbb{E}_u^{\mathscr{F}}[X_T + D(0,T,r+\lambda)\Phi(S_T)]}{D(0,u,r+\lambda)}.$$

The process $(\mathbb{E}_t^{\mathscr{F}}[X_T + D(0,T,r+\lambda)\Phi(S_T)])_{t\geq 0}$ is clearly a closed $\mathscr{F}$-martingale, and hence

$$\int_0^t D(0,u,r+\lambda)^{-1} d\mathbb{E}_u^{\mathscr{F}}[X_T + D(0,T,r+\lambda)\Phi(S_T)]$$

is a local $\mathscr{F}$-martingale. Then, being

$$\int_0^t D(0,u,r+\lambda)^{-1} d\mathbb{E}_u^{\mathscr{F}}[X_T + D(0,T,r+\lambda)\Phi(S_T)]$$

adapted to the Brownian-driven filtration $\mathscr{F}$, by the martingale representation theorem we have

$$\int_0^t D(0,u,r+\lambda)^{-1} d\mathbb{E}_u^{\mathscr{F}}[X_T + D(0,T,r+\lambda)\Phi(S_T)] = \int_0^t Z_u dW_u$$

for some $\mathscr{F}$-predictable process $Z_u$. Hence we can write:

$$d\widetilde{V}_u + \left[\pi_u - (f_u+\lambda_u)\widetilde{V}_u + \widetilde{\theta}_u + (f_u - c_u)C_u - (r_u - h_u)\widetilde{H}_u\right]du = Z_u dW_u. \quad (12)$$

## 4 Markovian FBSDE and PDE for $\widetilde{V}_t$ and the Invariance Theorem

As it is, Eq. (12) is way too general, thus we will make some simplifying assumptions in order to guarantee existence and uniqueness of a solution. First we assume a Markovian setting, and hence we suppose that all the processes appearing in (12) are deterministic functions of $S_u$, $\widetilde{V}_u$ or $Z_u$ and time. More precisely we assume that:

- the dividend process $\pi_u$ is a deterministic function $\pi(u, S_u)$ of $u$ and $S_u$, Lipschitz continuous in $S_u$;
- the rates $r, f^{\pm}, c^{\pm}, \lambda^I, \lambda^C$ are deterministic bounded functions of time;
- the rate $h_t$ is a deterministic function of time, and does not depend on the sign of $H$, namely $h^+ = h^-$, hence there is only one rate relative to the repo market of assets;
- the collateral process is a fraction of the process $\widetilde{V}_u$, namely $C_u = \alpha_u \widetilde{V}_u$, where $0 \le \alpha_u \le 1$ is a function of time;
- the close-out value $\epsilon_t$ is equal to $\widetilde{V}_t$ (this adds a source of nonlinearity with respect to choosing a risk-free closeout, see for example [6] and [5]);
- the diffusion coefficient $\sigma(t, S_t)$ of the underlying dynamic is Lipschitz continuous, uniformly in time, in $S_t$;
- we consider a delta-hedging strategy, and to this extent we choose $\widetilde{H}_t = S_t \frac{Z_t}{\sigma(t,S_t)}$; this reasoning derives from the fact that if we suppose $\widetilde{V}_t = V(t, S_t)$ with $V(\cdot, \cdot) \in C^{1,2}$ applying Ito's formula and comparing it with Eq. (12), we have that $\sigma(t, S_t)\, \partial_S V(t, S_t) = Z_t$.[2]

Under our assumptions, Eq. (12) becomes the following FBSDE:

$$
\begin{aligned}
dS_t &= r_t S_t dt + \sigma(t, S_t) dW_t \\
S_0 &= s \\
d\widetilde{V}_t &= -\underbrace{\left[\pi_t + \widetilde{\theta}_t - \lambda_t \widetilde{V}_t + f_t \widetilde{V}_t(\alpha_t - 1) - c_t(\alpha_t \widetilde{V}_t) - (r_t - h_t) S_t \frac{Z_t}{\sigma(t, S_t)}\right]}_{B(t,S_t,\widetilde{V}_t,Z_t)} dt + Z_t dW_t \\
V_T &= \Phi(S_T)
\end{aligned}
\tag{13}
$$

We want to obtain existence and uniqueness of the solution to the above-mentioned FBSDE and a related PDE. A possible choice is the following (see J. Zhang [15] Theorem 2.4.1 on page 41):

[2]At this stage the assumption we made on $V$ is not properly justified, see Theorem 3 and Remark 4 for details.

**Theorem 1** *Consider the following FBSDE on* $[0, T]$*:*

$$\begin{aligned} dX_t^{q,x} &= \mu(t, X_t^{q,x})dt + \sigma(t, X_t^{q,x})dW_t \quad q < t \le T \\ X_t &= x \quad 0 \le t \le q \\ dY_t^{q,x} &= -f(t, X_t^{q,x}, Y_t^{q,x}, Z_t^{q,x})dt + Z_t^{q,x}dW_t \\ Y_T^{q,x} &= g(X_T^{q,x}) \end{aligned} \tag{14}$$

*If we assume that there exists a positive constant K such that*

- $\sigma(t, x)^2 \ge \frac{1}{K}$;
- $|f(t, x, y, z) - f(t, x', y', z')| + |g(x) - g(x')| \le K(|x - x'| + |y - y'| + |z - z'|)$;
- $|f(t, 0, 0, 0)| + |g(0)| \le K$;

*and moreover the functions* $\mu(t, x)$ *and* $\sigma(t, x)$ *are* $C^2$ *with bounded derivatives, then Eq.* (14) *has a unique solution* $(X_t^{q,x}, Y_t^{q,x}, Z_t^{q,x})$ *and* $u(t, x) = Y_t^{t,x}$ *is the unique* classical *(i.e.* $C^{1,2}$*) solution to the following semilinear PDE*

$$\begin{aligned} \partial_t u(t, x) + \frac{1}{2}\sigma(t, x)^2\partial_x^2 u(t, x) + \mu(t, x)\partial_x u(t, x) + f(t, x, u(t, x), \sigma(t, x)\partial_x u(t, x)) &= 0 \\ u(T, x) &= g(x) \end{aligned} \tag{15}$$

We cannot directly apply Theorem 1 to our FBSDE because $B(t, s, v, z)$ is not Lipschitz continuous in $s$ because of the hedging term. But, since the hedging term is linear in $Z_t$ we can move it from the drift of the backward equation to the drift of the forward one. More precisely consider the following:

$$\begin{aligned} dS_t^{q,s} &= h_t S_t^{q,s}dt + \sigma(t, S_t^{q,s})dW_t \quad q < t \le T \\ S_q &= s_q \quad 0 \le t \le q \\ dV_t^{q,s} &= -\underbrace{\left[\pi_t + \theta_t - \lambda_t V_t^{q,s} + f_t V_t^{q,s}(\alpha_t - 1) - c_t(\alpha_t V_t^{q,s})\right]}_{B'(t, S_t^{q,s}, V_t^{q,s})} dt + Z_t^{q,s}dW_t \\ V_T^{q,s} &= \Phi(S_T^{q,s}). \end{aligned} \tag{16}$$

Indeed, one can check that the assumptions of Theorem 1 are satisfied for this equation:

**Theorem 2** *If the rates* $\lambda_t$, $f_t$, $c_t$, $h_t$, $r_t$ *are bounded, then* $|B'(t, s, v) - B'(t, s', v')| \le K(|s - s'| + |v - v'|)$ *and* $|B'(t, 0, 0)| + \Phi(0) \le K$*. Hence if* $\sigma(t, s)$ *is a positive* $C^2$ *function with bounded derivatives, then the assumptions of Theorem 1 are satisfied and so Eq.* (16) *has a unique solution, and moreover* $V_t^{t,s} = u(t, s) \in C^{1,2}$ *and satisfies the following semilinear PDE:*

$$\partial_t u(t,s) + \frac{1}{2}\sigma(t,s)^2\partial_s^2 u(t,s) + h_t s\partial_s u(t,s) + B'(t,s,u(t,s)) = 0 \qquad (17)$$
$$u(T,s) = \Phi(s)$$

*Proof* We start by rewriting the term

$$B'(t,s,v) = \pi_t(s) + \theta_t(v) + (f_t(\alpha_t - 1) - \lambda_t - c_t\alpha_t)v.$$

Since the sum of two Lipschitz functions is itself a Lipschitz function we can restrict ourselves to analyzing the summands that appear in the previous formula. The term $\pi_t$ is Lipschitz continuous in $s$ by assumption. The $\theta$ term and the $(f_t(\alpha_t - 1) - \lambda_t - c_t\alpha_t)v$ term are continuous and piece-wise linear, hence Lipschitz continuous and this concludes the proof.

Note that the $S$-dynamics in (16) has the repo rate $h$ as drift. Since in general $h$ will depend on the future values of the deal, this is a source of nonlinearity and is at times represented informally with an expected value $\mathbb{E}^h$ or a pricing measure $\mathbb{Q}^h$, see for example [5] and the related discussion on operational implications for the case $h = f$.

We now show that a solution to Eq. (13) can be obtained by means of the classical solution to the PDE (17). We start considering the following forward equation which is known to have a unique solution under our assumptions about $\sigma(t,s)$.

$$dS_t = r_t S_t dt + \sigma(t,S_t)dW_t \quad S_0 = s. \qquad (18)$$

We define $V_t = u(t,S_t)$ and $Z_t = \sigma(t,S_t)\partial_s u(t,S_t)$. By Theorem 2 we know that $u(t,s) \in C^{1,2}$ and by applying Ito's formula and (17) we obtain:

$$\begin{aligned}
dV_t &= du(t,S_t) \\
&= \left(\partial_t u(t,S_t) + r_t S_t \partial_s u(t,S_t) + \frac{1}{2}\sigma(t,S_t)^2\partial_s^2 u(t,S_t)\right) dt + \sigma(t,S_t)\partial_s u(t,S_t)dW_t \\
&= \left((r_t - h_t)S_t\partial_s u(t,S_t) - B'(t,S_t,u(t,S_t))\right) dt + \sigma(t,S_t)\partial_s u(t,S_t)dW_t \\
&= \left((r_t - h_t)S_t\frac{Z_t}{\sigma(t,S_t)} - \pi_t(S_t) - \theta_t(V_t) - (f_t(\alpha_t - 1) - \lambda_t - c_t\alpha_t)V_t)\right) dt + Z_t dW_t
\end{aligned}$$

Hence we found the following:

**Theorem 3** (Solution to the Valuation Equation) *Let $S_t$ be the solution to Eq. (18) and $u(t,s)$ the classical solution to Eq. (17). Then the process $(S_t, u(t,S_t), \sigma(t,S_t)$ $\partial_s u(t,S_t))$ is the unique solution to Eq. (13).*

*Proof* From the reasoning above we found that $(S_t, u(t,S_t), \sigma(t,S_t)\partial_s u(t,S_t))$ solves Eq. (13). Finally from the seminal result of [14] we know that if there exist $K > 0$ and $p \geq \frac{1}{2}$ such that:

- $|\mu(t,x) - \mu(t,x')| + |\sigma(t,x) - \sigma(t,x')| \leq K|x - x'|$

- $|\mu(t,x)| + |\sigma(t,x)| \leq K(1+|x|)$
- $|f(t,x,y,z) - f(t,x,y',z')| \leq K(|y-y'| + |z-z'|)$
- $|g(x)| + |f(t,x,0,0)| \leq K(1+|x|^p)$

then the FBSDE (14) has a unique solution. Since we have to check the Lipschitz continuity just for $y$ and $z$ we can verify that Eq. (13) satisfies the above-mentioned assumptions and hence has a unique solution.

*Remark 4* Since we proved that $V_t = u(t, S_t)$ with $u(t,s) \in C^{1,2}$, the reasoning we used, when saying that $\widetilde{H}_t = S_t \frac{Z_t}{\sigma(t,S_t)}$ represented choosing a delta-hedge, it is actually more than a heuristic argument.

Moreover, since (17) does not depend on the risk-free rate $r_t$ so we can state the following:

**Theorem 4** (Invariance Theorem) *If we are under the assumptions at the beginning of Sect. 4 and we assume that we are backing our deal with a delta hedging strategy, then the price $V_t$ can be calculated via the semilinear PDE (17) and does* not *depend on the risk-free rate $r(t)$.*

This invariance result shows that even when starting from a risk-neutral valuation theory, the risk-free rate disappears from the nonlinear valuation equations. A discussion on consequences of nonlinearity and invariance on valuation in general, on the operational procedures of a bank, on the legitimacy of fully charging the nonlinear value to a client, and on the related dangers of overlapping valuation adjustments is presented elsewhere, see for example [3, 5] and references therein.

**Acknowledgements** The opinions here expressed are solely those of the authors and do not represent in any way those of their employers. We are grateful to Cristin Buescu, Jean-François Chassagneux, François Delarue, and Marek Rutkowski for helpful discussion and suggestions that helped us improve the paper. Marek Rutkowski and Andrea Pallavicini visits were funded via the EPSRC Mathematics Platform grant EP/I019111/1.
The KPMG Center of Excellence in Risk Management is acknowledged for organizing the conference "Challenges in Derivatives Markets - Fixed Income Modeling, Valuation Adjustments, Risk Management, and Regulation".

**Open Access** This chapter is distributed under the terms of the Creative Commons Attribution 4.0 International License (http://creativecommons.org/licenses/by/4.0/), which permits use, duplication, adaptation, distribution and reproduction in any medium or format, as long as you give appropriate credit to the original author(s) and the source, a link is provided to the Creative Commons license and any changes made are indicated.

The images or other third party material in this chapter are included in the work's Creative Commons license, unless indicated otherwise in the credit line; if such material is not included in the work's Creative Commons license and the respective action is not permitted by statutory regulation, users will need to obtain permission from the license holder to duplicate, adapt or reproduce the material.

## References

1. Bielecki, T.R., Rutkowski, M.: Credit Risk: Modeling, Valuation and Hedging. Springer, Heidelberg (2002)
2. Bielecki, T.R., Jeanblanc-Picqué, M., Rutkowski, M.: Credit Risk Modeling. Osaka University Press, Osaka (2009)
3. Brigo, D., Pallavicini, A.: Nonlinear consistent valuation of CCP cleared or CSA bilateral trades with initial margins under credit, funding and wrong-way risks. J. Financ. Eng. **1**(1), 1–60 (2014)
4. Bielecki, T.R., Rutkowski, M.: Valuation and hedging of contracts with funding costs and collateralization. arXiv preprint arXiv:1405.4079 (2014)
5. Brigo, D., Liu, Q., Pallavicini, A., Sloth, D.: Nonlinear valuation under collateral, credit risk and funding costs: a numerical case study extending Black–Scholes. arXiv preprint at arXiv:1404.7314. A refined version of this report by the same authors is being published in this same volume
6. Brigo, D., Morini, M., Pallavicini, A.: Counterparty Credit Risk, Collateral and Funding with Pricing Cases for all Asset Classes. Wiley, Chichester (2013)
7. Delarue, F.: On the existence and uniqueness of solutions to FBSDEs in a non-degenerate case. Stoch. Process. Appl. **99**(2), 209–286 (2002)
8. Duffie, D., Huang, M.: Swap rates and credit quality. J. Financ. **51**(3), 921–949 (1996)
9. Nie, T., Rutkowski, M.: A bsde approach to fair bilateral pricing under endogenous collateralization. arXiv preprint arXiv:1412.2453 (2014)
10. Pallavicini, A., Brigo, D.: Interest-rate modelling in collateralized markets: multiple curves, credit-liquidity effects, CCPs. arXiv preprint arXiv:1304.1397 (2013)
11. Pallavicini, A., Perini, D., Brigo, D.: Funding valuation adjustment: a consistent framework including CVA, DVA, collateral, netting rules and re-hypothecation. arXiv preprint arXiv:1112.1521 (2011)
12. Pallavicini, A., Perini, D., Brigo, D.: Funding, collateral and hedging: uncovering the mechanics and the subtleties of funding valuation adjustments. arXiv preprint arXiv:1210.3811 (2012)
13. Pardoux, E., Peng, S.: Adapted solution of a backward stochastic differential equation. Syst. Control Lett. **14**(1), 55–61 (1990)
14. Pardoux, E., Peng, S.: Backward stochastic differential equations and quasilinear parabolic partial differential equations. In: Rozovskii, B., Sowers, R. (eds.) Stochastic Differential Equations and their Applications. Lecture Notes in Control and Information Sciences, vol. 176, pp. 200–217. Springer, Berlin (1992)
15. Zhang, J.: Some fine properties of backward stochastic differential equations, with applications. Ph.D. thesis, Purdue University. http://www-bcf.usc.edu/~jianfenz/Papers/thesis.pdf (2001)

# Nonlinear Monte Carlo Schemes for Counterparty Risk on Credit Derivatives

**Stéphane Crépey and Tuyet Mai Nguyen**

**Abstract** Two nonlinear Monte Carlo schemes, namely, the linear Monte Carlo expansion with randomization of Fujii and Takahashi (Int J Theor Appl Financ 15(5):1250034(24), 2012 [9], Q J Financ 2(3), 1250015(24), 2012, [10]) and the marked branching diffusion scheme of Henry-Labordère (Risk Mag 25(7), 67–73, 2012, [13]), are compared in terms of applicability and numerical behavior regarding counterparty risk computations on credit derivatives. This is done in two dynamic copula models of portfolio credit risk: the dynamic Gaussian copula model and the model in which default dependence stems from joint defaults. For such high-dimensional and nonlinear pricing problems, more standard deterministic or simulation/regression schemes are ruled out by Bellman's "curse of dimensionality" and only purely forward Monte Carlo schemes can be used.

**Keywords** Counterparty risk · Funding · BSDE · Gaussian copula · Marshall–Olkin copula · Particles

## 1 Introduction

Counterparty risk is a major issue since the global credit crisis and the ongoing European sovereign debt crisis. In a bilateral counterparty risk setup, counterparty risk is valued as the so-called credit valuation adjustment (CVA), for the risk of default of the counterparty, and debt valuation adjustment (DVA), for own default risk. In such a setup, the classical assumption of a locally risk-free funding asset used for both investing and unsecured borrowing is no longer sustainable. The proper accounting of the funding costs of a position leads to the funding valuation adjustment (FVA). Moreover, these adjustments are interdependent and must be computed jointly

S. Crépey (✉) · T.M. Nguyen
Laboratoire de Mathématiques et Modélisation, Université d'Évry
Val d'Essonne, 91037 Évry Cedex, France
e-mail: stephane.crepey@univ-evry.fr

T.M. Nguyen
e-mail: tuyetmai.nguyen@univ-evry.fr

© The Author(s) 2016 
K. Glau et al. (eds.), *Innovations in Derivatives Markets*, Springer Proceedings in Mathematics & Statistics 165, DOI 10.1007/978-3-319-33446-2_3

through a global correction dubbed total valuation adjustment (TVA). The pricing equation for the TVA is nonlinear due to the funding costs. It is posed over a random time interval determined by the first default time of the two counterparties. To deal with the corresponding backward stochastic differential equation (BSDE), a first reduced-form modeling approach has been proposed in Crépey [3], under a rather standard immersion hypothesis between a reference (or market) filtration and the full model filtration progressively enlarged by the default times of the counterparties. This basic immersion setup is fine for standard applications, such as counterparty risk on interest rate derivatives. But it is too restrictive for situations of strong dependence between the underlying exposure and the default risk of the two counterparties, such as counterparty risk on credit derivatives, which involves strong adverse dependence, called wrong-way risk (for some insights of related financial contexts, see Fujii and Takahashi [11], Brigo et al. [2]). For this reason, an extended reduced-form modeling approach has been recently developed in Crépey and Song [4–6]. With credit derivatives, the problem is also very high-dimensional. From a numerical point of view, for high-dimensional nonlinear problems, only purely forward simulation schemes can be used. In Crépey and Song [6], the problem is addressed by the linear Monte Carlo expansion with randomization of Fujii and Takahashi [9, 10].

In the present work, we assess another scheme, namely the marked branching diffusion approach of Henry-Labordère [13], which we compare with the previous one in terms of applicability and numerical behavior. This is done in two dynamic copula models of portfolio credit risk: the dynamic Gaussian copula model and the dynamic Marshall–Olkin model in which default dependence stems from joint defaults.

The paper is organized as follows. Sections 2 and 3 provide a summary of the main pricing and TVA BSDEs that are derived in Crépey and Song [4–6]. Section 4 exposes two nonlinear Monte Carlo schemes that can be considered for solving these in high-dimensional models, such as the portfolio credit models of Sect. 5. Comparative numerics in these models are presented in Sect. 6. Section 7 concludes.

## 2 Prices

### 2.1 Setup

We consider a netted portfolio of OTC derivatives between two defaultable counterparties, generally referred to as the contract between a bank, the perspective of which is taken, and its counterparty. After having bought the contract from its counterparty at time 0, the bank sets up a hedging, collateralization (or margining), and funding portfolio. We call the funder of the bank a third party, possibly composed in practice of several entities or devices, insuring funding of the bank's strategy. The funder, assumed default-free for simplicity, plays the role of lender/borrower of last resort after the exhaustion of the internal sources of funding provided to the bank through its hedge and collateral.

For notational simplicity we assume no collateralization. All the numerical considerations, our main focus in this work, can be readily extended to the case of collateralized portfolios using the corresponding developments in Crépey and Song [6]. Likewise, we assume hedging in the simplest sense of replication by the bank and we consider the case of a fully securely funded hedge, so that the cost of the hedge of the bank is exactly reflected by the wealth of its hedging and funding portfolio.

We consider a stochastic basis $(\Omega, \mathscr{G}_T, \mathscr{G}, \mathbb{Q})$, where $\mathscr{G} = (\mathscr{G}_t)_{t\in[0,T]}$ is interpreted as a risk-neutral pricing model on the primary market of the instruments that are used by the bank for hedging its TVA. The reference filtration $\mathscr{F}$ is a subfiltration of $\mathscr{G}$ representing the counterparty risk-free filtration, not carrying any direct information about the defaults of the two counterparties. The relation between these two filtrations will be pointed out in the condition (C) introduced later. We denote by:

- $\mathbb{E}_t$, the conditional expectation under $\mathbb{Q}$ given $\mathscr{G}_t$,
- $r$, the risk-free short rate process, with related discount factor $\beta_t = e^{-\int_0^t r_s ds}$,
- $T$, the maturity of the contract,
- $\tau_b$ and $\tau_c$, the default time of the bank and of the counterparty, modeled as $\mathscr{G}$ stopping times with $(\mathscr{G}, \mathbb{Q})$ intensities $\gamma^b$ and $\gamma^c$,
- $\tau = \tau_b \wedge \tau_c$, the first-to-default time of the two counterparties, also a $\mathscr{G}$ stopping time, with intensity $\gamma$ such that $\max(\gamma^b, \gamma^c) \le \gamma \le \gamma^b + \gamma^c$,
- $\bar{\tau} = \tau \wedge T$, the effective time horizon of our problem (there is no cashflow after $\bar{\tau}$),
- $D$, the contractual dividend process,
- $\Delta = D - D_-$, the jump process of $D$.

## 2.2 Clean Price

We denote by $P$ the reference (or clean) price of the contract ignoring counterparty risk and assuming the position of the bank financed at the risk-free rate $r$, i.e. the $\mathscr{G}$ conditional expectation of the future contractual cash-flows discounted at the risk-free rate $r$. In particular,

$$\beta_t P_t = \mathbb{E}_t \left[ \int_t^{\bar{\tau}} \beta_s dD_s + \beta_{\bar{\tau}} P_{\bar{\tau}} \right], \ \forall t \in [0, \bar{\tau}]. \tag{1}$$

We also define $Q_t = P_t + \mathbb{1}_{\{t=\tau<T\}} \Delta_\tau$, so that $Q_\tau$ represents the clean value of the contract inclusive of the promised dividend at default (if any) $\Delta_\tau$, which also belongs to the "debt" of the counterparty to the bank (or vice versa depending on the sign of $Q_\tau$) in case of default of a party. Accordingly, at time $\tau$ (if $< T$), the close-out cash-flow of the counterparty to the bank is modeled as

$$\mathscr{R} = \mathbb{1}_{\{\tau=\tau_c\}} \left(R_c Q_\tau^+ - Q_\tau^-\right) - \mathbb{1}_{\{\tau=\tau_b\}} \left(R_b Q_\tau^- - Q_\tau^+\right) - \mathbb{1}_{\{\tau_b=\tau_c\}} Q_\tau, \tag{2}$$

where $R_b$ and $R_c$ are the recovery rates of the bank and of the counterparty to each other.

### 2.3 All-Inclusive Price

Let $\Pi$ be the all-inclusive price of the contract for the bank, including the cost of counterparty risk and funding costs. Since we assume a securely funded hedge (in the sense of replication) and no collateralization, the amounts invested and funded by the bank at time $t$ are respectively given by $\Pi_t^-$ and $\Pi_t^+$. The all-inclusive price $\Pi$ is the discounted conditional expectation of all effective future cash flows including the contractual dividends before $\tau$, the cost of funding the position prior to time $\tau$ and the terminal cash flow at time $\tau$. Hence,

$$\beta_t \Pi_t = \mathbb{E}_t \left[ \int_t^{\bar{\tau}} \beta_s \mathbb{1}_{s<\tau} dD_s - \int_t^{\bar{\tau}} \beta_s \bar{\lambda}_s \Pi_s^+ ds + \beta_{\bar{\tau}} \mathbb{1}_{\tau<T} \mathscr{R} \right], \tag{3}$$

where $\bar{\lambda}$ is the funding spread over $r$ of the bank toward the external funder, i.e. the bank borrows cash from its funder at rate $r + \bar{\lambda}$ (and invests cash at the risk-free rate $r$). Since the right hand side in (3) depends also on $\Pi$, (3) is in fact a backward stochastic differential equation (BSDE). Consistent with the no arbitrage principle, the gain process on the hedge is a $\mathbb{Q}$ martingale, which explains why it does not appear in (3).

## 3 TVA BSDEs

The total valuation adjustment (TVA) process $\Theta$ is defined as

$$\Theta = Q - \Pi. \tag{4}$$

In this section we review the main TVA BSDEs that are derived in Crépey and Song [4–6]. Three BSDEs are presented. These three equations are essentially equivalent mathematically. However, depending on the underlying model, they are not always amenable to the same numerical schemes or the numerical performance of a given scheme may differ between them.

### 3.1 Full TVA BSDE

By taking the difference between (1) and (3), we obtain

$$\beta_t \Theta_t = \mathbb{E}_t \left[ \int_t^{\bar{\tau}} \beta_s f\!va_s(\Theta_s) ds + \beta_{\bar{\tau}} \mathbb{1}_{\tau<T} \xi \right], \ \forall t \in [0, \bar{\tau}], \tag{5}$$

where $fva_t(\vartheta) = \bar{\lambda}_t(P_t - \vartheta)^+$ is the funding coefficient and where

$$\xi = Q_\tau - \mathscr{R} = \mathbb{1}_{\{\tau=\tau_c\}}(1 - R_c)(P_\tau + \Delta_\tau)^+ - \mathbb{1}_{\{\tau=\tau_b\}}(1 - R_b)(P_\tau + \Delta_\tau)^- \quad (6)$$

is the exposure at default of the bank. Equivalent to (5), the "full TVA BSDE" is written as

$$\Theta_t = \mathbb{E}_t\left[\int_t^{\bar{\tau}} f_s(\Theta_s)ds + \mathbb{1}_{\tau<T}\xi\right],\ 0 \le t \le \bar{\tau}, \quad \text{(I)}$$

for the coefficient $f_t(\vartheta) = fva_t(\vartheta) - r_t\vartheta$.

### 3.2 *Partially Reduced TVA BSDE*

Let $\hat{\xi}$ be a $\mathscr{G}$-predictable process, which exists by Corollary 3.23 2 in He et al. [12], such that $\hat{\xi}_\tau = \mathbb{E}[\xi|\mathscr{G}_{\tau-}]$ on $\tau < \infty$ and let $\bar{f}$ be the modified coefficient such that

$$\bar{f}_t(\vartheta) + r_t\vartheta = \underbrace{\gamma_t\hat{\xi}_t}_{cdva_t} + \underbrace{\bar{\lambda}_t(P_t - \vartheta)^+}_{fva_t(\vartheta)}. \quad (7)$$

As easily shown (cf. [4, Lemma 2.2]), the full TVA BSDE (I) can be simplified into the "partially reduced BSDE"

$$\bar{\Theta}_t = \mathbb{E}_t\left[\int_t^{\bar{\tau}} \bar{f}_s(\bar{\Theta}_s)ds\right],\ 0 \le t \le \bar{\tau}, \quad \text{(II)}$$

in the sense that if $\Theta$ solves (I), then $\bar{\Theta} = \Theta\mathbb{1}_{[0,\tau)}$ solves (II), while if $\bar{\Theta}$ solves (II), then the process $\Theta$ defined as $\bar{\Theta}$ before $\bar{\tau}$ and $\Theta_{\bar{\tau}} = \mathbb{1}_{\tau<T}\xi$ solves (I). Note that both BSDEs (I) and (II) are $(\mathscr{G}, \mathbb{Q})$ BSDEs posed over the random time interval $[0, \bar{\tau}]$, but with the terminal condition $\xi$ for (I) as opposed to a null terminal condition (and a modified coefficient) for (II).

### 3.3 *Fully Reduced TVA BSDE*

Let

$$\hat{f}_t(\vartheta) = \bar{f}_t(\vartheta) - \gamma_t\vartheta = cdva_t + fva_t(\vartheta) - (r_t + \gamma_t)\vartheta.$$

Assume the following conditions, which are studied in Crépey and Song [4–6]:

**Condition (C).** There exist:

**(C.1)** a subfiltration $\mathscr{F}$ of $\mathscr{G}$ satisfying the usual conditions and such that $\mathscr{F}$ semimartingales stopped at $\tau$ are $\mathscr{G}$ semimartingales,

**(C.2)** a probability measure $\mathbb{P}$ equivalent to $\mathbb{Q}$ on $\mathscr{F}_T$ such that any $(\mathscr{F}, \mathbb{P})$ local martingale stopped at $(\tau-)$ is a $(\mathscr{G}, \mathbb{Q})$ local martingale on $[0, T]$,

**(C.3)** an $\mathscr{F}$ progressive "reduction" $\widetilde{f}_t(\vartheta)$ of $\hat{f}_t(\vartheta)$ such that $\int_0^{\cdot} \hat{f}_t(\vartheta)dt = \int_0^{\cdot} \widetilde{f}_t(\vartheta)dt$ on $[0, \bar{\tau}]$.

Let $\widetilde{\mathbb{E}}_t$ denote the conditional expectation under $\mathbb{P}$ given $\mathscr{F}_t$. It is shown in Crépey and Song [4–6]) that the full TVA BSDE (I) is equivalent to the following "fully reduced BSDE":

$$\widetilde{\Theta}_t = \widetilde{\mathbb{E}}_t \left[ \int_t^T \widetilde{f}_s(\widetilde{\Theta}_s)ds \right], \quad t \in [0, T], \tag{III}$$

equivalent in the sense that if $\Theta$ solves (I), then the "$\mathscr{F}$ optional reduction" $\widetilde{\Theta}$ of $\Theta$ ($\mathscr{F}$ optional process that coincides with $\Theta$ before $\tau$) solves (III), while if $\widetilde{\Theta}$ solves (III), then $\Theta = \widetilde{\Theta}\mathbb{1}_{[0,\tau)} + \mathbb{1}_{[\tau]}\mathbb{1}_{\tau<T}\xi$ solves (I).

Moreover, under mild assumptions (see e.g. Crépey and Song [6, Theorem 4.1]), one can easily check that $\bar{f}_t(\vartheta)$ in (7) (resp. $\widetilde{f}_t(\vartheta)$) satisfies the classical BSDE monotonicity assumption

$$\big(\bar{f}_t(\vartheta) - \bar{f}_t(\vartheta')\big)(\vartheta - \vartheta') \le C(\vartheta - \vartheta')^2$$

(and likewise for $\widetilde{f}$), for some constant $C$. Hence, by classical BSDE results nicely surveyed in Kruse and Popier [14, Sect. 2 (resp. 3)], the partially reduced TVA BSDE (II), hence the equivalent full TVA BSDE (I) (resp. the fully reduced BSDE (III)), is well-posed in the space of $(\mathscr{G}, \mathbb{Q})$ (resp. $(\mathscr{F}, \mathbb{P})$) square integrable solutions, where well-posedness includes existence, uniqueness, comparison and BSDE standard estimates.

### *3.4 Marked Default Time Setup*

In order to be able to compute $\gamma\hat{\xi}$ in $\bar{f}$, we assume that $\tau$ is endowed with a mark $e$ in a finite set $E$, in the sense that

$$\tau = \min_{e \in E} \tau_e, \tag{8}$$

where each $\tau_e$ is a stopping time with intensity $\gamma_t^e$ such that $\mathbb{Q}(\tau_e \neq \tau_{e'}) = 1$, $e \neq e'$, and

$$\mathscr{G}_\tau = \mathscr{G}_{\tau-} \vee \sigma(\varepsilon),$$

where $\varepsilon = \text{argmin}_{e\in E}\tau_e$ yields the "identity" of the mark. The role of the mark is to convey some additional information about the default, e.g. to encode wrong-way and gap risk features. The assumption of a finite set $E$ in (8) ensures tractability of the setup. In fact, by Lemma 5.1 in Crépey and Song [6], there exists $\mathscr{G}$-predictable processes $\widetilde{P}_t^e$ and $\widetilde{\Delta}_t^e$ such that

$$P_\tau = \widetilde{P}_\tau^e \text{ and } \Delta_\tau = \widetilde{\Delta}_\tau^e \text{ on the event } \{\tau = \tau_e\}.$$

Assuming further that $\tau_b = \min_{e\in E_b} \tau_e$ and $\tau_c = \min_{e\in E_c} \tau_e$, where $E = E_b \cup E_c$ (not necessarily a disjoint union), one can then take on $[0, \bar{\tau}]$:

$$\gamma_t\hat{\xi}_t = (1 - R_c) \sum_{e\in E_c} \gamma_t^e \left(\widetilde{P}_t^e + \widetilde{\Delta}_t^e\right)^+ - (1 - R_b) \sum_{e\in E_b} \gamma_t^e \left(\widetilde{P}_t^e + \widetilde{\Delta}_t^e\right)^- ,$$

where the two terms have clear respective CVA and DVA interpretation. Hence, (7) is rewritten, on $[0, \bar{\tau}]$, as

$$\begin{aligned}\bar{f}_t(\vartheta) + r_t\vartheta = &\underbrace{(1 - R_c) \sum_{e\in E_c} \gamma_t^e \left(\widetilde{P}_t^e + \widetilde{\Delta}_t^e\right)^+}_{\text{CVA coefficient } (cva_t)} - \underbrace{(1 - R_b) \sum_{e\in E_b} \gamma_t^e \left(\widetilde{P}_t^e + \widetilde{\Delta}_t^e\right)^-}_{\text{DVA coefficient } (dva_t)} \\ &+ \underbrace{\bar{\lambda}_t(P_t - \vartheta)^+}_{\text{FVA coefficient } (fva_t(\vartheta))} .\end{aligned} \tag{9}$$

If the functions $\widetilde{P}_t^e$ and $\widetilde{\Delta}_t^e$ above not only exist, but can be computed explicitly (as will be the case in the concrete models of Sects. 5.1 and 5.2), once stated in a Markov setup where

$$\bar{f}_t(\vartheta) = \bar{f}(t, X_t, \vartheta), \; t \in [0, T], \tag{10}$$

for some $(\mathscr{G}, \mathbb{Q})$ jump diffusion $X$, then the partially reduced TVA BSDE (II) can be tackled numerically. Similarly, once stated in a Markov setup where

$$\widetilde{f}_t(\vartheta) = \widetilde{f}(t, \widetilde{X}_t, \vartheta), \; t \in [0, T], \tag{11}$$

for some $(\mathscr{F}, \mathbb{P})$ jump diffusion $\widetilde{X}$, then the fully reduced TVA BSDE (III) can be tackled numerically.

# 4 TVA Numerical Schemes

## 4.1 Linear Approximation

Our first TVA approximation is obtained replacing $\Theta_s$ by 0 in the right hand side of (I), i.e.

$$\Theta_0 \approx \mathbb{E}\left[\int_0^{\bar{\tau}} f_s(0)ds + \mathbb{1}_{\tau<T}\xi\right] = \mathbb{E}\left[\int_0^{\bar{\tau}} \bar{\lambda}_s P_s^+ ds + \mathbb{1}_{\tau<T}\xi\right]. \tag{12}$$

We then approximate the TVA by standard Monte-Carlo, with randomization of the integral to reduce the computation time (at the cost of a small increase in the variance). Hence, introducing an exponential time $\zeta$ of parameter $\mu$, i.e. a random variable with density $\phi(s) = \mathbb{1}_{s\geq 0}\,\mu\, e^{-\mu s}$, we have

$$\mathbb{E}\left[\int_0^{\bar{\tau}} f_s(0)ds\right] = \mathbb{E}\left[\int_0^{\bar{\tau}} \phi(s)\frac{1}{\mu}e^{\mu s} f_s(0)ds\right] = \mathbb{E}\left[\mathbb{1}_{\zeta<\bar{\tau}}\frac{e^{\mu\zeta}}{\mu} f_\zeta(0)\right]. \tag{13}$$

We can use the same technic for (II) and (III), which yields:

$$\Theta_0 = \bar{\Theta}_0 \approx \mathbb{E}\left[\int_0^{\bar{\tau}} \bar{f}_s(0)ds\right] = \mathbb{E}\left[\mathbb{1}_{\zeta<\bar{\tau}}\frac{e^{\mu\zeta}}{\mu}\bar{f}_\zeta(0)\right], \tag{14}$$

$$\Theta_0 = \widetilde{\Theta}_0 \approx \widetilde{\mathbb{E}}\left[\int_0^{T} \widetilde{f}_s(0)ds\right] = \widetilde{\mathbb{E}}\left[\mathbb{1}_{\zeta<T}\frac{e^{\mu\zeta}}{\mu}\widetilde{f}_\zeta(0)\right]. \tag{15}$$

## 4.2 Linear Expansion and Interacting Particle Implementation

Following Fujii and Takahashi [9, 10], we can introduce a perturbation parameter $\varepsilon$ and the following perturbed form of the fully reduced BSDE (III):

$$\widetilde{\Theta}_t^\varepsilon = \widetilde{\mathbb{E}}_t\left[\int_t^T \varepsilon \widetilde{f}_s(\widetilde{\Theta}_s^\varepsilon)ds\right], \quad t \in [0, T], \tag{16}$$

where $\varepsilon = 1$ corresponds to the original BSDE (III). Suppose that the solution of (16) can be expanded in a power series of $\varepsilon$:

$$\widetilde{\Theta}_t^\varepsilon = \widetilde{\Theta}_t^{(0)} + \varepsilon\widetilde{\Theta}_t^{(1)} + \varepsilon^2\widetilde{\Theta}_t^{(2)} + \varepsilon^3\widetilde{\Theta}_t^{(3)} + \cdots. \tag{17}$$

The Taylor expansion of $f$ at $\widetilde{\Theta}^{(0)}$ reads

$$\begin{aligned}\widetilde{f}_t(\widetilde{\Theta}^{\varepsilon}_t) &= \widetilde{f}_t(\widetilde{\Theta}^{(0)}_t) + (\varepsilon\widetilde{\Theta}^{(1)}_t + \varepsilon^2\widetilde{\Theta}^{(2)}_t + \cdots)\partial_\vartheta \widetilde{f}_t(\widetilde{\Theta}^{(0)}_t) \\ &+ \frac{1}{2}(\varepsilon\widetilde{\Theta}^{(1)}_t + \varepsilon^2\widetilde{\Theta}^{(2)}_t + \cdots)^2\partial^2_{\vartheta^2}\widetilde{f}_t(\widetilde{\Theta}^{(0)}_t) + \cdots\end{aligned}$$

Collecting the terms of the same order with respect to $\varepsilon$ in (16), we obtain $\widetilde{\Theta}^{(0)}_t = 0$, due to the null terminal condition of the fully reduced BSDE (III), and

$$\begin{aligned}\widetilde{\Theta}^{(1)}_t &= \widetilde{\mathbb{E}}_t\left[\int_t^T \widetilde{f}_s(\widetilde{\Theta}^{(0)}_s)ds\right], \\ \widetilde{\Theta}^{(2)}_t &= \widetilde{\mathbb{E}}_t\left[\int_t^T \widetilde{\Theta}^{(1)}_s\partial_\vartheta\widetilde{f}_s(\widetilde{\Theta}^{(0)}_s)ds\right], \\ \widetilde{\Theta}^{(3)}_t &= \widetilde{\mathbb{E}}_t\left[\int_t^T \widetilde{\Theta}^{(2)}_s\partial_\vartheta\widetilde{f}_s(\widetilde{\Theta}^{(0)}_s)ds\right],\end{aligned} \tag{18}$$

where the third order term should contain another component based on $\partial^2_{\vartheta^2}\widetilde{f}$. But, in our case, $\partial^2_{\vartheta^2}\widetilde{f}$ involves a Dirac measure via the terms $(P_t - \vartheta)^+$ in $fva_t(\vartheta)$, so that we truncate the expansion to the term $\widetilde{\Theta}^{(3)}_t$ as above. If the nonlinearity in (III) is sub-dominant, one can expect to obtain a reasonable approximation of the original equation by setting $\varepsilon = 1$ at the end of the calculation, i.e.

$$\widetilde{\Theta}_0 \approx \widetilde{\Theta}^{(1)}_0 + \widetilde{\Theta}^{(2)}_0 + \widetilde{\Theta}^{(3)}_0.$$

Carrying out a Monte Carlo simulation by an Euler scheme for every time $s$ in a time grid and integrating to obtain $\widetilde{\Theta}^{(1)}_0$ would be quite heavy. Moreover, this would become completely unpractical for the higher order terms that involve iterated (multivariate) time integrals. For these reasons, Fujii and Takahashi [10] have introduced a particle interpretation to randomize and compute numerically the integrals in (18), which we call the FT scheme. Let $\eta_1$ be the interaction time of a particle drawn independently as the first jump time of a Poisson process with an arbitrary intensity $\mu > 0$ starting from time $t \geq 0$, i.e., $\eta_1$ is a random variable with density

$$\phi(t,s) = \mathbb{1}_{s\geq t}\,\mu\, e^{-\mu(s-t)}. \tag{19}$$

From the first line in (18), we have

$$\widetilde{\Theta}^{(1)}_t = \widetilde{\mathbb{E}}_t\left[\int_t^T \phi(t,s)\frac{e^{\mu(s-t)}}{\mu}\widetilde{f}_s(\widetilde{\Theta}^{(0)}_s)ds\right] = \widetilde{\mathbb{E}}_t\left[\mathbb{1}_{\eta_1<T}\frac{e^{\mu(\eta_1-t)}}{\mu}\widetilde{f}_{\eta_1}(\widetilde{\Theta}^{(0)}_{\eta_1})\right]. \tag{20}$$

Similarly, the particle representation is available for the higher order. By applying the same procedure as above, we obtain

$$\widetilde{\Theta}_t^{(2)} = \widetilde{\mathbb{E}}_t\left[\mathbb{1}_{\eta_1<T}\widetilde{\Theta}_{\eta_1}^{(1)}\frac{e^{\mu(\eta_1-t)}}{\mu}\partial_\vartheta\widetilde{f}_{\eta_1}(\widetilde{\Theta}_{\eta_1}^{(0)})\right],$$

where $\widetilde{\Theta}_{\eta_1}^{(1)}$ can be computed by (20). Therefore, by using the tower property of conditional expectations, we obtain

$$\widetilde{\Theta}_t^{(2)} = \widetilde{\mathbb{E}}_t\left[\mathbb{1}_{\eta_2<T}\frac{e^{\mu(\eta_2-\eta_1)}}{\mu}\widetilde{f}_{\eta_2}(\widetilde{\Theta}_{\eta_2}^{(0)})\frac{e^{\mu(\eta_1-t)}}{\mu}\partial_\vartheta\widetilde{f}_{\eta_1}(\widetilde{\Theta}_{\eta_1}^{(0)})\right], \tag{21}$$

where $\eta_1$, $\eta_2$ are the two consecutive interaction times of a particle randomly drawn with intensity $\mu$ starting from $t$. Similarly, for the third order, we get

$$\widetilde{\Theta}_t^{(3)} = \widetilde{\mathbb{E}}_t\left[\mathbb{1}_{\eta_3<T}\frac{e^{\mu(\eta_3-\eta_2)}}{\mu}\widetilde{f}_{\eta_3}(\widetilde{\Theta}_{\eta_3}^{(0)})\frac{e^{\mu(\eta_2-\eta_1)}}{\mu}\partial_\vartheta\widetilde{f}_{\eta_2}(\widetilde{\Theta}_{\eta_2}^{(0)})\frac{e^{\mu(\eta_1-t)}}{\mu}\partial_\vartheta\widetilde{f}_{\eta_1}(\widetilde{\Theta}_{\eta_1}^{(0)})\right], \tag{22}$$

where $\eta_1, \eta_2, \eta_3$ are consecutive interaction times of a particle randomly drawn with intensity $\mu$ starting from $t$. In case $t = 0$, (20), (21) and (22) can be simplified as

$$\begin{aligned}
\widetilde{\Theta}_0^{(1)} &= \widetilde{\mathbb{E}}\left[\mathbb{1}_{\zeta_1<T}\frac{e^{\mu\zeta_1}}{\mu}\widetilde{f}_{\zeta_1}(\widetilde{\Theta}_{\zeta_1}^{(0)})\right]\\
\widetilde{\Theta}_0^{(2)} &= \widetilde{\mathbb{E}}\left[\mathbb{1}_{\zeta_1+\zeta_2<T}\frac{e^{\mu\zeta_1}}{\mu}\partial_\vartheta\widetilde{f}_{\zeta_1}(\widetilde{\Theta}_{\zeta_1}^{(0)})\frac{e^{\mu\zeta_2}}{\mu}\widetilde{f}_{\zeta_1+\zeta_2}(\widetilde{\Theta}_{\zeta_1+\zeta_2}^{(0)})\right]\\
\widetilde{\Theta}_0^{(3)} &= \widetilde{\mathbb{E}}\left[\mathbb{1}_{\zeta_1+\zeta_2+\zeta_3<T}\frac{e^{\mu\zeta_1}}{\mu}\partial_\vartheta\widetilde{f}_{\zeta_1}(\widetilde{\Theta}_{\zeta_1}^{(0)})\frac{e^{\mu\zeta_2}}{\mu}\partial_\vartheta\widetilde{f}_{\zeta_1+\zeta_2}(\widetilde{\Theta}_{\zeta_1+\zeta_2}^{(0)})\frac{e^{\mu\zeta_3}}{\mu}\widetilde{f}_{\zeta_1+\zeta_2+\zeta_3}(\widetilde{\Theta}_{\zeta_1+\zeta_2+\zeta_3}^{(0)})\right]
\end{aligned} \tag{23}$$

where $\zeta_1, \zeta_2, \zeta_3$ are the elapsed time from the last interaction until the next interaction, which are independent exponential random variables with parameter $\mu$.

Note that the pricing model is originally defined with respect to the full stochastic basis $(\mathscr{G}, \mathbb{Q})$. Even in the case where there exists a stochastic basis $(\mathscr{F}, \mathbb{Q})$ satisfying the condition (C), $(\mathscr{F}, \mathbb{Q})$ simulation may be nontrivial. Lemma 8.1 in Crépey and Song [6] allows us to reformulate the $\mathbb{Q}$ expectations in (23) as the following $\mathbb{Q}$ expectations, with $\bar{\Theta}^{(0)} = 0$:

$$\begin{aligned}
\widetilde{\Theta}_0^{(1)} &= \bar{\Theta}_0^{(1)} = \mathbb{E}\left[\mathbb{1}_{\zeta_1<\bar{\tau}}\frac{e^{\mu\zeta_1}}{\mu}\bar{f}_{\zeta_1}(\bar{\Theta}_{\zeta_1}^{(0)})\right]\\
\widetilde{\Theta}_0^{(2)} &= \bar{\Theta}_0^{(2)} = \mathbb{E}\left[\mathbb{1}_{\zeta_1+\zeta_2<\bar{\tau}}\frac{e^{\mu\zeta_1}}{\mu}\partial_\vartheta\bar{f}_{\zeta_1}(\bar{\Theta}_{\zeta_1}^{(0)})\frac{e^{\mu\zeta_2}}{\mu}\bar{f}_{\zeta_1+\zeta_2}(\bar{\Theta}_{\zeta_1+\zeta_2}^{(0)})\right]\\
\widetilde{\Theta}_0^{(3)} &= \bar{\Theta}_0^{(3)} = \mathbb{E}\Big[\mathbb{1}_{\zeta_1+\zeta_2+\zeta_3<\bar{\tau}}\frac{e^{\mu\zeta_1}}{\mu}\partial_\vartheta\bar{f}_{\zeta_1}(\bar{\Theta}_{\zeta_1}^{(0)})\frac{e^{\mu\zeta_2}}{\mu}\partial_\vartheta\bar{f}_{\zeta_1+\zeta_2}(\bar{\Theta}_{\zeta_1+\zeta_2}^{(0)})\\
&\qquad\times\frac{e^{\mu\zeta_3}}{\mu}\bar{f}_{\zeta_1+\zeta_2+\zeta_3}(\bar{\Theta}_{\zeta_1+\zeta_2+\zeta_3}^{(0)})\Big],
\end{aligned} \tag{24}$$

which is nothing but the FT scheme applied to the partially reduced BSDE (II). The tractability of the FT schemes (23) and (24) relies on the nullity of the terminal condition of the related BSDEs (III) and (II), which implies that $\bar{\Theta}^{(0)} = \widetilde{\Theta}^{(0)} = 0$. By contrast, an FT scheme would not be practical for the full TVA BSDE (5) with terminal condition $\xi \neq 0$. Also note that the first order in the FT scheme (23) (resp. (24)) is nothing but the linear approximation (15) (resp. (14)).

## 4.3 Marked Branching Diffusion Approach

Based on an old idea of McKean [16], the solution $u(t_0, x_0)$ to a PDE

$$\partial_t u + \mathscr{L}u + \mu(F(u) - u) = 0, \quad u(T, x) = \Psi(x), \tag{25}$$

where $\mathscr{L}$ is the infinitesimal generator of a strong Markov process $X$ and $F(y) = \sum_{k=0}^{d} a_k y^k$ is a polynomial of order $d$, admits a probabilistic representation in terms of a random tree $\mathscr{T}$ (branching diffusion). The tree starts from a single particle ("trunk") born from $(t_0, x_0)$. Subsequently, every particle born from a node $(t, x)$ evolves independently according to the generator $\mathscr{L}$ of $X$ until it dies at time $t' = (t + \zeta)$ in a state $x'$, where $\zeta$ is an independent $\mu$-exponential time (one for each particle). Moreover, in dying, a particle gives birth to an independent number of $k'$ new particles starting from the node $(t', x')$, where $k'$ is drawn in the finite set $\{0, 1, \ldots, d\}$ with some fixed probabilities $p_0, p_1, \ldots, p_d$. The marked branching diffusion probabilistic representation reads

$$\begin{aligned} u(t_0, x_0) &= \mathbb{E}_{t_0,x_0}\left[\prod_{\{\text{inner nodes } (t,x,k) \text{ of } \mathscr{T}\}} \frac{a_k}{p_k} \prod_{\{\text{states } x \text{ of particles alive at } T\}} \Psi(x)\right] \\ &= \mathbb{E}_{t_0,x_0}\left[\prod_{k=0}^{d} \left(\frac{a_k}{p_k}\right)^{n_k} \prod_{l=1}^{\nu} \Psi(x_l)\right], \end{aligned} \tag{26}$$

where $n_k$ is the number of branching with $k$ descendants up on $(0, T)$ and $\nu$ is the number of particles alive at $T$, with corresponding locations $x_1, \ldots, x_\nu$.

The marked branching diffusion method of Henry-Labordère [13] for CVA computations, dubbed PHL scheme henceforth, is based on the idea that, by approximating $y^+$ by a well-chosen polynomial $F(y)$, the solution to the PDE

$$\partial_t u + \mathscr{L}u + \mu(u^+ - u) = 0, \quad u(T, x) = \Psi(x), \tag{27}$$

can be approximated by the solution to the PDE (25), hence by (26). We want to apply this approach to solve the TVA BSDEs (I), (II) or (III) for which, instead of fixing the approximating polynomial $F(y)$ once for all in the simulations, we need a state-dependent polynomial approximation to $g_t(y) = (P_t - y)^+$ (cf. (7)) in a suitable range for $y$. Moreover, (I) and (II) are BSDEs with random terminal time $\bar{\tau}$, equivalently written in a Markov setup as Cauchy–Dirichlet PDE problems, as opposed to the pure Cauchy problem (27). Hence, some adaptation of the method is required. We show how to do it for (II), after which we directly give the algorithm in the similar case of (I) and in the more classical (pure Cauchy) case of (III). Assuming $\tau$ given in terms of a $(\mathscr{G}, \mathbb{Q})$ Markov factor process $X$ as $\tau = \inf\{t > 0 : X_t \notin \mathscr{D}\}$ for some domain $\mathscr{D}$, the Cauchy–Dirichlet PDE used for approximating the partially reduced BSDE (II) reads:

$$(\partial_t + \mathscr{A})\bar{u} + \mu\left(\bar{F}(\bar{u}) - \bar{u}\right) = 0 \text{ on } [0, T] \times \mathscr{D}, \quad \bar{u}(t, x) = 0 \text{ for } t = T \text{ or } x \notin \mathscr{D}, \tag{28}$$

where $\mathscr{A}$ is the generator of $X$ and $\bar{F}_{t,x}(y) = \sum_{k=0}^{d} \bar{a}_k(t, x)y^k$ is such that

$$\mu(\bar{F}_{t,x}(y) - y) \approx \bar{f}(t, x, y), \text{ i.e. } \bar{F}_{t,x}(y) \approx \frac{\bar{f}(t, x, y)}{\mu} + y. \tag{29}$$

Specifically, in view of (9), one can set

$$\bar{F}_{t,x}(y) = \frac{1}{\mu}\left(cdva(t, x) + \bar{\lambda}pol\big(P(t, x) - y\big) - ry\right) + y = \sum_{k=0}^{d} \bar{a}_k(t, x)y^k, \tag{30}$$

where $pol(r)$ is a $d$-order polynomial approximation of $r^+$ in a suitable range for $r$. The marked branching diffusion probabilistic representation of $\bar{u}(t_0, x_0) \in \mathscr{D}$ involves a random tree $\overline{\mathscr{T}}$ made of nodes and "particles" between consecutive nodes as follows. The tree starts from a single particle (trunk) born from the root $(t_0, x_0)$. Subsequently, every particle born from a node $(t, x)$ evolves independently according to the generator $\mathscr{L}$ of $X$ until it dies at time $t' = (t + \zeta)$ in a state $x'$, where $\zeta$ is an independent $\mu$-exponential time. Moreover, in dying, if its position $x'$ at time $t'$ lies in $\mathscr{D}$, the particle gives birth to an independent number of $k'$ new particles starting from the node $(t', x')$, where $k'$ is drawn in the finite set $\{0, 1, \ldots, d\}$ with some fixed probabilities $p_0, p_1, \ldots, p_d$. Figure 1 describes such a random tree in case $d = 2$. The first particle starts from the root $(t_0, x_0)$ and dies at time $t_1$, generating two new particles. The first one dies at time $t_{11}$ and generates a new particle, who dies at time $t_{111} > T$ without descendant. The second one dies at time $t_{12}$ and generates two new particles, where the first one dies at time $t_{121}$ without descendant and the second one dies at time $t_{122}$ outside the domain $\mathscr{D}$, hence also without descendant. The blue points represent the inner nodes, the red points the outer nodes and the green points the exit points of the tree out of the time–space domain $[0, T] \times \mathscr{D}$.

The marked branching diffusion probabilistic representation of $\bar{u}$ is written as

$$\bar{u}(t_0, x_0) = \mathbb{E}_{t_0,x_0}\left[\mathbb{1}_{\overline{\mathscr{T}} \subset [0,T]\times\mathscr{D}} \prod_{\{\text{inner nodes } (t,x,k) \text{ of } \overline{\mathscr{T}}\}} \frac{\bar{a}_k(t, x)}{p_k}\right], \quad (t_0, x_0) \in [0, T] \times \mathscr{D}. \tag{31}$$

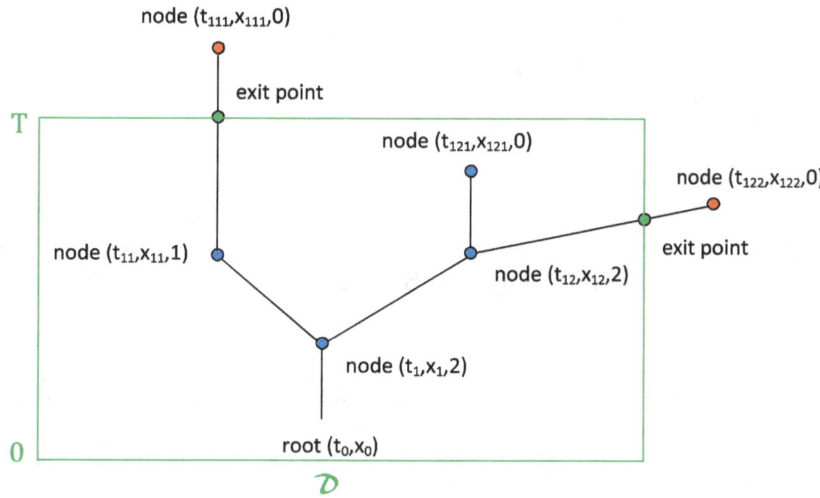


**Fig. 1** PHL random tree

Note that (31) is unformal at that stage, where we did not justify whether the PDE (28) has a solution $\bar{u}$ and in which sense. In fact, the following result could be used for proving that the function $\bar{u}$ defined in the first line is a viscosity solution to (28).

**Proposition 1** *Denoting by $\bar{u}$ the function defined by the right hand side in (31) (assuming integrability of the integrand on the domain $[0, T] \times \mathscr{D}$), the process $Y_t = \bar{u}(t, X_t), 0 \le t \le \bar{\tau}$, solves the BSDE associated with the Cauchy–Dirichlet PDE (28), namely*

$$Y_t = \mathbb{E}_t\left[\int_t^{\bar{\tau}} \mu\Big(\bar{F}_{s,X_s}(Y_s) - Y_s\Big) ds\right], \quad t \in [0, \bar{\tau}] \tag{32}$$

*(which, in view of (29), approximates the partially reduced BSDE (II), so that $Y \approx \bar{\Theta}$ provided $Y$ is square integrable).*

*Proof* Let $(t_1, x_1, k_1)$ be the first branching point in the tree rooted at $(0, X_0)$ and let $\overline{\mathscr{T}}_j$ denote $k_1$ independent trees of the same kind rooted at $(t_1, x_1)$. By using the independence and the strong Markov property postulated for $X$, we obtain

$$\begin{aligned}
\bar{u}(t, X_t) &= \sum_{k_1=0}^{d} \mathbb{E}_{t,X_t}\left[\mathbb{1}_{t_1<T}\, p_{k_1} \frac{a_{k_1}(t_1, x_1)}{p_{k_1}}\right. \\
&\quad \left.\times \prod_{j=1}^{k_1} \mathbb{E}_{t_1,x_1}\left[\mathbb{1}_{\overline{\mathscr{T}}_j \subset [0,T]\times\mathscr{D}\}} \prod_{\{\text{inner node } (s,x,k) \text{ of } \overline{\mathscr{T}}_j\}} \frac{a_k(s,x)}{p_k}\right]\right] \\
&= \mathbb{E}_{t,X_t}\left[\mathbb{1}_{t_1<T} \sum_{k_1=0}^{d} a_{k_1}(t_1, x_1) \prod_{j=1}^{k_1} \mathbb{E}_{t_1,x_1}\left[\mathbb{1}_{\overline{\mathscr{T}}_j \subset [0,T]\times\mathscr{D}} \prod_{\{\text{inner node } (s,x,k) \text{ of } \overline{\mathscr{T}}_j\}} \frac{a_k(s,x)}{p_k}\right]\right] \\
&= \mathbb{E}_{t,X_t}\left[\mathbb{1}_{t_1<T} \sum_{k_1=0}^{d} a_{k_1}(t_1, x_1) \prod_{j=1}^{k_1} \bar{u}(t_1, x_1)\right]
\end{aligned}$$

$$= \mathbb{E}_{t,X_t}\left[\mathbb{1}_{t_1<T}\bar{F}_{t_1,x_1}(\bar{u}(t,X_t^{t_1,x_1}))\right]$$
$$= \mathbb{E}_{t,X_t}\left[\int_t^{\bar{\tau}} \mu(s)e^{-\int_t^s \mu(u)du}\bar{F}_{s,X_s^{t,x}}(\bar{u}(s,X_s^{t,x}))ds\right],\ 0 \le t \le \bar{\tau},$$

i.e. $Y_t = \bar{u}(t, X_t)$ solves (32). □

If $\mathbb{1}_{\tau<T}\xi$ is given as a deterministic function $\Psi(\tau, X_\tau)$, then a similar approach (using the same tree $\overline{\mathscr{T}}$) can be applied to the full BSDE (I) in terms of the Cauchy–Dirichlet PDE

$$(\partial_t + \mathscr{A})u + \mu\,(F(u) - u) = 0 \text{ on } [0,T]\times\mathscr{D},\quad u(t,x) = \Psi(t,x) \text{ for } t = T \text{ or } x \notin \mathscr{D}, \tag{33}$$

where $F_{t,x}(y) = \sum_{k=0}^{d} a_k(t,x)y^k$ is such that

$$\mu(F_{t,x}(y) - y) \approx f(t,x,y), \text{ i.e. } F_{t,x}(y) \approx \frac{f(t,x,y)}{\mu} + y.$$

This yields the approximation formula alternative to (31):

$$\Theta_0 \approx \mathbb{E}\left[\prod_{\{\text{inner node } (t,x,k) \text{ of } \overline{\mathscr{T}}\}} \frac{a_k(t,x)}{p_k} \prod_{\{\text{exit point } (t,x) \text{ of } \overline{\mathscr{T}}\}} \Psi(t,x)\right], \tag{34}$$

where an exit point of $\overline{\mathscr{T}}$ means a point where a branch of the tree leaves for the first time the time–space domain $[0,T]\times\mathscr{D}$. Last, regarding the $(\mathscr{F},\mathbb{Q})$ reduced BSDE (III), assuming an $(\mathscr{F},\mathbb{Q})$ Markov factor process $\widetilde{X}$ with generator $\widetilde{\mathscr{A}}$ and domain $\mathscr{D}$, we can apply a similar approach in terms of the Cauchy PDE

$$(\partial_t + \widetilde{\mathscr{A}})\widetilde{u} + \mu\left(\widetilde{F}_{t,x}(\widetilde{u}) - \widetilde{u}\right) = 0 \text{ on } [0,T]\times\mathscr{D},\quad \widetilde{u}(t,x) = 0 \text{ for } t = T \text{ or } x \notin \mathscr{D}, \tag{35}$$

where $\widetilde{F}_{t,x}(y) = \sum_{k=0}^{d} \widetilde{a}_k(t,x)y^k$ is such that

$$\mu(\widetilde{F}_{t,x}(y) - y) \approx \widetilde{f}(t,x,y), \text{ i.e. } \widetilde{F}_{t,x}(y) \approx \frac{\widetilde{f}(t,x,y)}{\mu} + y.$$

We obtain

$$\Theta_0 = \widetilde{\Theta}_0 \approx \widetilde{\mathbb{E}}\left[\mathbb{1}_{\widetilde{\mathscr{T}}\subset[0,T]\times\mathscr{D}} \prod_{\text{inner node } (t,x,k) \text{ of } \widetilde{\mathscr{T}}} \frac{\widetilde{a}_k(t,x)}{p_k}\right], \tag{36}$$

where $\widetilde{\mathscr{T}}$ is the branching tree associated with the Cauchy PDE (35) (similar to $\widetilde{\mathscr{T}}$ but for the generator $\widetilde{\mathscr{A}}$).

# 5 TVA Models for Credit Derivatives

Our goal is to apply the above approaches to TVA computations on credit derivatives referencing the names in $N^\star = \{1, \dots, n\}$, for some positive integer $n$, traded between the bank and the counterparty respectively labeled as $-1$ and 0. In this section we briefly survey two models of the default times $\tau_i, i \in N = \{-1, 0, 1, \dots, n\}$, that will be used for that purpose with $\tau_b = \tau_{-1}$ and $\tau_c = \tau_0$, namely the dynamic Gaussian copula (DGC) model and the dynamic Marshall–Olkin copula (DMO) model. For more details the reader is referred to [8, Chaps. 7 and 8] and [6, Sects. 6 and 7].

## *5.1 Dynamic Gaussian Copula TVA Model*

### 5.1.1 Model of Default Times

Let there be given a function $\varsigma(\cdot)$ with unit $L^2$ norm on $\mathbb{R}_+$ and a multivariate Brownian motion $\mathbf{B} = (B^i)_{i \in N}$ with pairwise constant correlation $\rho \geq 0$ in its own completed filtration $\mathscr{B} = (\mathscr{B}_t)_{t \geq 0}$. For each $i \in N$, let $h_i$ be a continuously differentiable increasing function from $\mathbb{R}_+^*$ to $\mathbb{R}$, with $\lim_0 h_i(s) = -\infty$ and $\lim_{+\infty} h_i(s) = +\infty$, and let

$$\tau_i = h_i^{-1}(\varepsilon_i), \text{ where } \varepsilon_i = \int_0^{+\infty} \varsigma(u) dB_u^i. \tag{37}$$

Thus the $(\tau_i)_{i \in N}$ follow the standard Gaussian copula model of Li [15], with correlation parameter $\rho$ and with marginal survival function $\Phi \circ h_i$ of $\tau_i$, where $\Phi$ is the standard normal survival function. In particular, these $\tau_i$ do not intersect each other. In order to make the model dynamic as required by counterparty risk applications, the model filtration $\mathscr{G}$ is given as the Brownian filtration $\mathscr{B}$ progressively enlarged by the $\tau_i$, i.e.

$$\mathscr{G}_t = \mathscr{B}_t \vee \bigvee_{i \in N} \big(\sigma(\tau_i \wedge t) \vee \sigma(\{\tau_i > t\})\big), \ \forall t \geq 0, \tag{38}$$

and the reference filtration $\mathscr{F}$ is given as $\mathscr{B}$ progressively enlarged by the default times of the reference names, i.e.

$$\mathscr{F}_t = \mathscr{B}_t \vee \bigvee_{i \in N^\star} \big(\sigma(\tau_i \wedge t) \vee \sigma(\{\tau_i > t\})\big), \ \forall t \geq 0. \tag{39}$$

As shown in Sect. 6.2 of Crépey and Song [6], for the filtrations $\mathscr{G}$ and $\mathscr{F}$ as above, there exists a (unique) probability measure $\mathbb{P}$ equivalent to $\mathbb{Q}$ such that the condition $(C)$ holds. For every $i \in N$, let

$$m_t^i = \int_0^t \varsigma(u) dB_u^i, \ k_t^i = \tau_i \mathbb{1}_{\{\tau_i \leq t\}},$$

and let $\mathbf{m}_t = (m^i_t)_{i \in N}$, $\mathbf{k}_t = (k^i_t)_{i \in N}$, $\widetilde{\mathbf{k}}_t = (\mathbb{1}_{i \in N^\star} k^i_t)_{i \in N}$. The couple $X_t = (\mathbf{m}_t, \mathbf{k}_t)$ (resp. $\widetilde{X}_t = (\mathbf{m}_t, \widetilde{\mathbf{k}}_t)$) plays the role of a $(\mathcal{G}, \mathbb{Q})$ (resp. $(\mathcal{F}, \mathbb{P})$) Markov factor process in the dynamic Gaussian copula (DGC) model.

### 5.1.2 TVA Model

A DGC setup can be used as a TVA model for credit derivatives, with mark $i = -1, 0$ and $E_b = \{-1\}$, $E_c = \{0\}$. Since there are no joint defaults in this model, it is harmless to assume that the contract promises no cash-flow at $\tau$, i.e., $\Delta_\tau = 0$, so that $Q_\tau = P_\tau$. By [8, Propositions 7.3.1 p. 178 and 7.3.3 p. 181], in the case of vanilla credit derivatives on the reference names, namely CDS contracts and CDO tranches (cf. (47)), there exists a continuous, explicit function $\widetilde{P}_i$ such that

$$P_\tau = \widetilde{P}_i(\tau, \mathbf{m}_\tau, \mathbf{k}_{\tau-}), \tag{40}$$

or $\widetilde{P}^i_\tau$ in a shorthand notation, on the event $\{\tau = \tau_i\}$. Hence, (9) yields

$$\bar{f}_t(\vartheta) + r_t\vartheta = (1 - R_c)\gamma^0_t(\widetilde{P}^0_t)^+ - (1 - R_b)\gamma^{-1}_t(\widetilde{P}^{-1}_t)^- + \bar{\lambda}_t(P_t - \vartheta)^+, \quad \forall t \in [0, \bar{\tau}].$$

Assume that the processes $r$ and $\bar{\lambda}$ are given before $\tau$ as continuous functions of $(t, X_t)$, which also holds for $P$ in the case of vanilla credit derivatives on names in $N$. Then the coefficients $\bar{f}$ and in turn $\widetilde{f}$ are deterministically given in terms of the corresponding factor processes as

$$\bar{f}_t(\vartheta) = \bar{f}(t, X_t, \vartheta), \; \widetilde{f}_t(\vartheta) = \widetilde{f}(t, \widetilde{X}_t, \vartheta),$$

so that we are in the Markovian setup where the FT and the PHL schemes are valid and, in principle, applicable.

## 5.2 *Dynamic Marshall–Olkin Copula TVA Model*

The above dynamic Gaussian copula model allows dealing with TVA on CDS contracts. But a Gaussian copula dependence structure is not rich enough for ensuring a proper calibration to CDS and CDO quotes at the same time. If CDO tranches are also present in a portfolio, a possible alternative is the following dynamic Marshall–Olkin (DMO) copula model, also known as the "common shock" model.

### 5.2.1 Model of Default Times

We define a family $\mathscr{Y}$ of "shocks", i.e. subsets $Y \subseteq N$ of obligors, usually consisting of the singletons $\{-1\}, \{0\}, \{1\}, \ldots, \{n\}$, and a few "common shocks" $I_1, I_2, \ldots, I_m$ representing simultaneous defaults. For $Y \in \mathscr{Y}$, the shock time $\eta_Y$ is defined as an i.i.d. exponential random variable with parameter $\gamma_Y$. The default time of obligor $i$ in the common shock model is then defined as

$$\tau_i = \min_{Y \in \mathscr{Y}, i \in Y} \eta_Y. \tag{41}$$

*Example 1* Figure 2 shows one possible default path in a common-shock model with $n = 3$ and $\mathscr{Y} = \{\{-1\}, \{0\}, \{1\}, \{2\}, \{3\}, \{2, 3\}, \{0, 1, 2\}, \{-1, 0\}\}$. The inner oval shows which shocks happened and caused the observed default scenarios at successive default times.

The full model filtration $\mathscr{G}$ is defined as

$$\mathscr{G}_t = \bigvee_{Y \in \mathscr{Y}} \left(\sigma(\eta_Y \wedge t) \vee \sigma(\{\eta_Y > t\})\right), \; \forall t \geq 0.$$

Letting $\mathscr{Y}_\circ = \{Y \in \mathscr{Y};\ -1, 0 \notin Y\}$, the reference filtration $\mathscr{F}$ is given as

$$\mathscr{F}_t = \bigvee_{Y \in \mathscr{Y}_\circ} \left(\sigma(\eta_Y \wedge t) \vee \sigma(\{\eta_Y > t\})\right), \; t \geq 0.$$

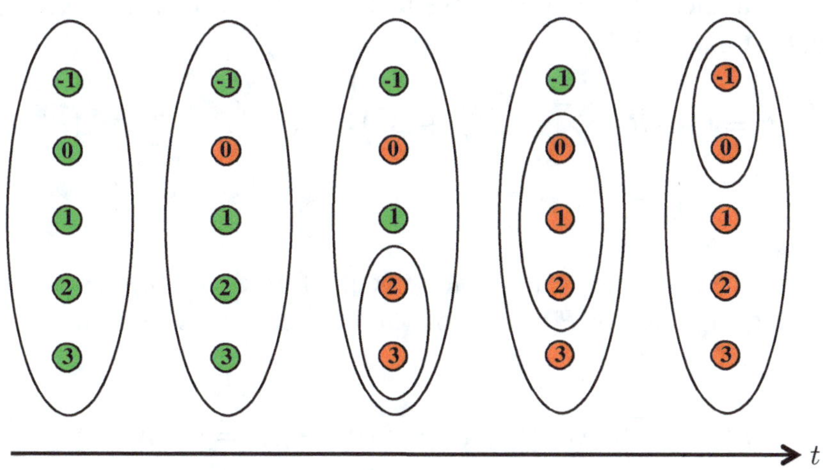


**Fig. 2** One possible default path in the common-shock model with $n = 3$ and $\mathscr{Y} = \{\{-1\}, \{0\}, \{1\}, \{2\}, \{3\}, \{2, 3\}, \{0, 1, 2\}, \{-1, 0\}\}$

As shown in Sect. 7.2 of Crépey and Song [6], in the DMO model with $\mathcal{G}$ and $\mathcal{F}$ as above, the condition (C) holds for $\mathbb{P} = \mathbb{Q}$. Let $J^Y = \mathbb{1}_{[0,\eta_Y)}$. Similar to $(\mathbf{m}, \mathbf{k})$ (resp. $(\mathbf{m}, \widetilde{\mathbf{k}})$) in the DGC model, the process

$$X = (J^Y)_{Y\in\mathscr{Y}} \text{ (resp. } \widetilde{X} = (\mathbb{1}_{Y\in\mathscr{Y}_\circ} J^Y)_{Y\in\mathscr{Y}}) \tag{42}$$

plays the role of a $(\mathcal{G}, \mathbb{Q})$ (resp. $(\mathcal{F}, \mathbb{Q})$) Markov factor in the DMO model.

### 5.2.2 TVA Model

A DMO setup can be used as a TVA model for credit derivatives, with

$$E_b = \mathscr{Y}_b := \{Y \in \mathscr{Y};\ -1 \in Y\},\ E_c = \mathscr{Y}_c := \{Y \in \mathscr{Y};\ 0 \in Y\},\ E = \mathscr{Y}_\bullet := \mathscr{Y}_b \cup \mathscr{Y}_c$$

and

$$\tau_b = \tau_{-1} = \min_{Y\in\mathscr{Y}_b} \eta_Y,\ \tau_c = \tau_0 = \min_{Y\in\mathscr{Y}_c} \eta_Y,$$

hence

$$\tau = \min_{Y\in\mathscr{Y}_\bullet} \eta_Y,\ \gamma = \mathbb{1}_{[0,\tau)}\widetilde{\gamma} \text{ with } \widetilde{\gamma} = \sum_{Y\in\mathscr{Y}_\bullet} \gamma_Y. \tag{43}$$

By [8, Proposition 8.3.1 p. 205], in the case of CDS contracts and CDO tranches, for every shock $Y \in \mathscr{Y}$ and process $U = P$ or $\Delta$, there exists a continuous, explicit function $\widetilde{U}_Y$ such that

$$U_\tau = \widetilde{U}_Y(\tau, X_{\tau-}), \tag{44}$$

or $\widetilde{U}^Y_\tau$ in a shorthand notation, on the event $\{\tau = \eta_Y\}$. The coefficient $\bar{f}_t(\vartheta)$ in (9) is then given, for $t \in [0, \bar{\tau}]$, by

$$\begin{aligned} \bar{f}_t(\vartheta) + r_t\vartheta = (1 - R_c) \sum_{Y\in\mathscr{Y}_c} \gamma^Y_t (\widetilde{P}^Y_t + \widetilde{\Delta}^Y_t)^+ - (1 - R_b) \sum_{Y\in\mathscr{Y}_b} \gamma^Y_t (\widetilde{P}^Y_t + \widetilde{\Delta}^Y_t)^- \\ + \bar{\lambda}_t(P_t - \vartheta)^+. \end{aligned} \tag{45}$$

Assuming that the processes $r$ and $\bar{\lambda}$ are given before $\tau$ as continuous functions of $(t, X_t)$, which also holds for $P$ in case of vanilla credit derivatives on the reference names, then

$$\bar{f}_t(\vartheta) = \bar{f}(t, X_t, \vartheta), \widetilde{f}_t(\vartheta) = \bar{f}_t(\vartheta) - \widetilde{\gamma}\vartheta = \widetilde{f}(t, \widetilde{X}_t, \vartheta) \tag{46}$$

(cf. (43)), so that we are again in a Markovian setup where the FT and the PHL schemes are valid and, in principle, applicable.

### 5.3 Strong Versus Weak Dynamic Copula Model

However, one peculiarity of the TVA BSDEs in our credit portfolio models is that, even though full and reduced Markov structures have been identified, which is required for justifying the validity of the FT and/or PHL numerical schemes, and the corresponding generators $\mathscr{A}$ or $\widetilde{\mathscr{A}}$ can be written explicitly, the Markov structures are too heavy for being of any practical use in the numerics. Instead, fast and exact simulation and clean pricing schemes are available based on the dynamic copula structures.

Moreover, in the case of the DGC model, we lose the Gaussian copula structure after a branching point in the PHL scheme. In fact, as visible in [8, Formula (7.7) p. 175], the DGC conditional multivariate survival probability function is stated in terms of a ratio of Gaussian survival probability functions, which is explicit but does not simplify into a single Gaussian survival probability function. It is only in the DMO model that the conditional multivariate survival probability function, which arises as a ratio of exponential survival probability functions (see [8, Formula (8.11) p. 197 and Sect. 8.2.1.1]), simplifies into a genuine exponential survival probability function. Hence, the PHL scheme is not applicable in the DGC model.

The FT scheme based on (III) is not practical either because the Gaussian copula structure is only under $\mathbb{Q}$ and, again, the (full or reduced) Markov structures are not practical. In the end, the only practical scheme in the DGC model is the FT scheme based on the partially reduced BSDE (II). Eventually, it is only in the DMO model that the FT and the PHL schemes are both practical and can be compared numerically.

## 6 Numerics

For the numerical implementation, we consider stylized CDS contracts and protection legs of CDO tranches corresponding to dividend processes of the respective form, for $0 \leq t \leq T$ :

$$\begin{aligned} D_t^i &= \big((1-R_i)\mathbb{1}_{t\geq\tau_i} - S_i(t\wedge\tau_i)\big)Nom_i \\ D_t &= \Big(\big((1-R)\sum_{j\in N}\mathbb{1}_{t\geq\tau_j} - (n+2)a\big)^+ \wedge (n+2)(b-a)\Big)Nom, \end{aligned} \tag{47}$$

where all the recoveries $R_i$ and $R$ (resp. nominals $Nom_i$ and $Nom$) are set to 40 % (resp. to 100). The contractual spreads $S_i$ of the CDS contracts are set such that the corresponding prices are equal to 0 at time 0. Protection legs of CDO tranches, where the attachment and detachment points $a$ and $b$ are such that $0 \leq a \leq b \leq$ 100 %, can also be seen as CDO tranches with upfront payment. Note that credit derivatives traded as swaps or with upfront payment coexist since the crisis. Unless stated otherwise, the following numerical values are used:

$$r = 0, R_b = 1, R_c = 40\,\%, \bar{\lambda} = 100 \text{ bp} = 0.01, \mu = \frac{2}{T}, m = 10^4.$$

## 6.1 Numerical Results in the DGC Model

First we consider DGC random times $\tau_i$ defined by (37), where the function $h_i$ is chosen so that $\tau_i$ follows an exponential distribution with parameter $\gamma_i$ (which in practice can be calibrated to a related CDS spread or a suitable proxy). More precisely, let $\Phi$ and $\Psi_i$ be the survival functions of a standard normal distribution and an exponential distribution with intensity $\gamma_i$. We choose $h_i = \Phi^{-1} \circ \Psi_i$, so that (cf. (37))

$$\mathbb{Q}(\tau_i \geq t) = \mathbb{Q}\left(\Psi_i^{-1}\left(\Phi\left(\varepsilon_i\right)\right) \geq t\right) = \mathbb{Q}\Big(\Phi\left(\varepsilon_i\right) \leq \Psi_i(t)\Big) = \Psi_i(t),$$

for $\Phi\left(\varepsilon_i\right)$ has a standard uniform distribution. Moreover, we use a function $\varsigma(\cdot)$ in (37) constant before a time horizon $\bar{T} > T$ and null after $\bar{T}$, so that $\varsigma(0) = \frac{1}{\sqrt{\bar{T}}}$ (given the constraint that $\nu^2(0) = \int_0^\infty \varsigma^2(s)ds = 1$) and, for $t \leq \bar{T}$,

$$\nu^2(t) = \int_t^\infty \varsigma^2(s)ds = \frac{\bar{T} - t}{\bar{T}},\ m_t^i = \int_0^t \varsigma(u)dB_u^i = \frac{1}{\sqrt{\bar{T}}}B_t^i,\ \int_0^\infty \varsigma(u)dB_u^i = \frac{1}{\sqrt{\bar{T}}}B_{\bar{T}}^i.$$

In the case of the DGC model, the only practical TVA numerical scheme is the FT scheme (24) based on the partially reduced BSDE (II), which can be described by the following steps:

1. Draw a time $\zeta_1$ following an exponential law of parameter $\mu$. If $\zeta_1 < T$, then simulate $\mathbf{m}_{\zeta_1} = (\frac{1}{\sqrt{\bar{T}}}B_{\zeta_1}^i)_{l \in N} \sim \mathcal{N}(0, \frac{\zeta_1}{\bar{T}}I_n(1,\rho))$, where $I_n(1,\rho)$ is a $n \times n$ matrix with diagonal equal to 1 and all off-diagonal entries equal to $\rho$, and go to Step 2. Otherwise, go to Step 4.
2. Draw a second time $\zeta_2$, independent from $\zeta_1$, following an exponential law of parameter $\mu$. If $\zeta_1 + \zeta_2 < T$, then obtain the vector $\mathbf{m}_{\zeta_1+\zeta_2}$ as $\mathbf{m}_{\zeta_1} + (\mathbf{m}_{\zeta_1+\zeta_2} - \mathbf{m}_{\zeta_1})$, where $\mathbf{m}_{\zeta_1+\zeta_2} - \mathbf{m}_{\zeta_1} = (\frac{1}{\sqrt{\bar{T}}}(B_{\zeta_1+\zeta_2}^i - B_{\zeta_1}^i))_{l \in N} \sim \mathcal{N}(0, \frac{\zeta_2}{\bar{T}}I_n(1,\rho))$, and go to Step 3. Otherwise, go to Step 4.
3. Draw a third time $\zeta_3$, independent from $\zeta_1$ and $\zeta_2$, following an exponential law of parameter $\mu$. If $\zeta_1 + \zeta_2 + \zeta_3 < T$, then obtain the vector $\mathbf{m}_{\zeta_1+\zeta_2+\zeta_3}$ as $\mathbf{m}_{\zeta_1+\zeta_2} + (\mathbf{m}_{\zeta_1+\zeta_2+\zeta_3} - \mathbf{m}_{\zeta_1+\zeta_2})$, where $\mathbf{m}_{\zeta_1+\zeta_2+\zeta_3} - \mathbf{m}_{\zeta_1+\zeta_2} = (\frac{1}{\sqrt{\bar{T}}}(B_{\zeta_1+\zeta_2+\zeta_3}^i - B_{\zeta_1+\zeta_2}^i))_{l \in N} \sim \mathcal{N}(0, \frac{\zeta_3}{\bar{T}}I_n(1,\rho))$. Go to Step 4.

4. Simulate the vector $\mathbf{m}_{\bar{T}}$ from the last simulated vector $\mathbf{m}_t$ ($t = 0$ by default) as $\mathbf{m}_t + (\mathbf{m}_{\bar{T}} - \mathbf{m}_t)$, where $\mathbf{m}_{\bar{T}} - \mathbf{m}_t = (\frac{1}{\sqrt{\bar{T}}}(B^i_{\bar{T}} - B^i_t))_{i\in N} \sim \mathcal{N}(0, \frac{\bar{T}-t}{\bar{T}} I_n(1,\rho))$. Deduce $(B^i_{\bar{T}})_{i\in N}$, hence $\tau_i = \Psi_i^{-1} \circ \Phi\left(\frac{1}{\sqrt{\bar{T}}} B^i_{\bar{T}}\right)$, $i \in N$, and in turn the vectors $\mathbf{k}_{\zeta_1}$ (if $\zeta_1 + \zeta_2 + \zeta_3 < T$), $\mathbf{k}_{\zeta_1+\zeta_2}$ (if $\zeta_1 + \zeta_2 < T$) and $\mathbf{k}_{\zeta_1+\zeta_2+\zeta_3}$ (if $\zeta_1 + \zeta_2 + \zeta_3 < T$).
5. Compute $f_{\zeta_1}, f_{\zeta_1+\zeta_2}$, and $f_{\zeta_1+\zeta_2+\zeta_3}$ for the three orders of the FT scheme.

We perform TVA computations on CDS contracts with maturity $T = 10$ years, choosing for that matter $\bar{T} = T + 1 = 11$ years, hence $\varsigma = \frac{\mathbb{1}_{[0,11]}}{\sqrt{11}}$, for $\rho = 0.6$ unless otherwise stated. Table 1 displays the contractual spreads of the CDS contracts used in these experiments. In Fig. 3, the left graph shows the TVA on a CDS on name 1, computed in a DGC model with $n = 1$ by FT scheme of order 1 to 3, for different levels of nonlinearity represented by the value of the unsecured borrowing spread $\bar{\lambda}$. The right graph shows similar results regarding a portfolio comprising one CDS contract per name $i = 1, \ldots, 10$. The time-0 clean value of the default leg of the CDS in case $n = 1$, respectively the sum of the ten default legs in case $n = 10$, is 4.52, respectively 40.78 (of course $P_0 = 0$ in both cases by definition of fair contractual spreads). Hence, in relative terms, the TVA numbers visible in Fig. 3 are quite high, much greater for instance than in the cases of counterparty risk on interest rate derivatives considered in Crépey et al. [7]. This is explained by the wrong-way risk feature of the DGC model, namely, the default intensities of the surviving names and the value of the CDS protection spike at defaults in this model. When $\bar{\lambda}$ increases (for $\bar{\lambda} = 0$ that's a case of linear TVA where FT higher order terms equal 0), the second (resp. third) FT term may represent in each case up to 5–10 % of the first

**Table 1** Time-0 bp CDS spreads of names −1 (the bank), 0 (the counterparty) and of the reference names 1 to $n$ used when $n = 1$ (*left*) and $n = 10$ (*right*)

| $i$ | -1 | 0 | 1 |
|---|---|---|---|
| $S_i$ | 36 | 41 | 47 |

| $i$ | −1 | 0 | 1 | 2 | 3 | 4 | 5 | 6 | 7 | 8 | 9 | 10 |
|---|---|---|---|---|---|---|---|---|---|---|---|---|
| $S_i$ | 39 | 40 | 47 | 36 | 41 | 48 | 54 | 54 | 27 | 30 | 36 | 50 |

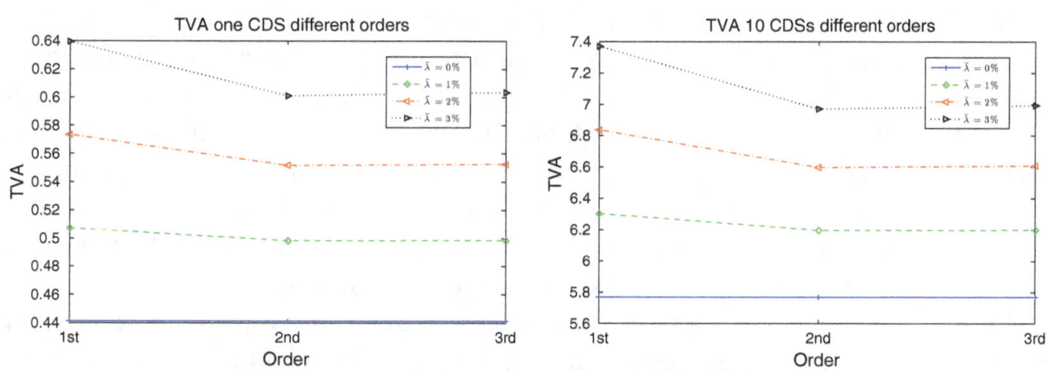


**Fig. 3** *Left* DGC TVA on one CDS computed by FT scheme of order 1–3, for different levels of nonlinearity (unsecured borrowing spread $\bar{\lambda}$). *Right* similar results regarding the portfolio of CDS contracts on ten names

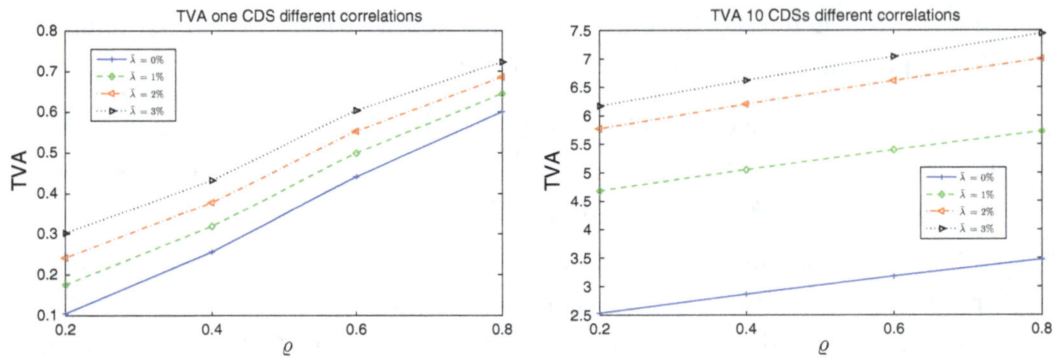


**Fig. 4** *Left* TVA on one CDS computed by FT scheme of order 3 as a function of the DGC correlation parameter $\rho$. *Right* similar results regarding a portfolio of CDS contracts on ten different names

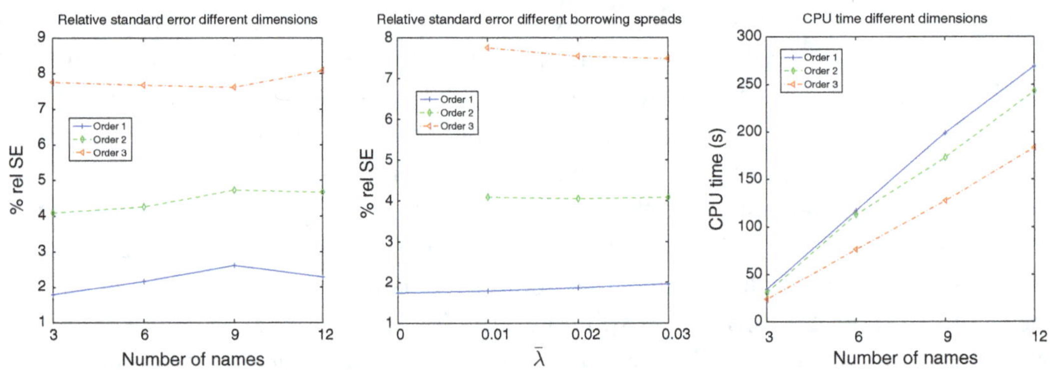


**Fig. 5** *Left* the % relative standard errors of the different orders of the expansions do not explode with the number of names ($\bar{\lambda} = 100$ bp). *Middle* the % relative standard errors of the different orders of the expansions do not explode with the level of nonlinearity represented by the unsecured borrowing spread $\bar{\lambda}$ ($n = 1$). *Right* since FT terms are computed by purely forward Monte Carlo schemes, their computation times are linear in the number of names ($\bar{\lambda} = 100$ bp)

(resp. second) FT term, from which we conclude that the first FT term can be used as a first order linear estimate of the TVA, with a nonlinear correction that can be estimated by the second FT term.

In Fig. 4, the left graph shows the TVA on one CDS computed by FT scheme of order 3 as a function of the DGC correlation parameter $\rho$, with other parameters set as before. The right graph shows the analogous results regarding the portfolio of ten CDS contracts. In both cases, the TVA numbers increase (roughly linearly) with $\rho$, including for high values of $\rho$, as desirable from the financial interpretation point of view, whereas it has been noted in Brigo and Chourdakis [1] (see the blue curve in Fig. 1 of the ssrn version of the paper) that for high levels of the correlation between names, other models may show some pathological behaviors.

In Fig. 5, the left graph shows that the errors, in the sense of the relative standard errors (% rel. SE), of the different orders of the FT scheme do not explode with the dimension (number of credit names that underlie the CDS contracts). The middle graph, produced with $n = 1$, shows that the errors do not explode with the level of nonlinearity represented by the unsecured borrowing spread $\bar{\lambda}$. Consistent with the fact that the successive FT terms are computed by purely forward Monte Carlo schemes, their computation times are essentially linear in the number of names, as visible in the right graph.

To conclude this section, we compare the linear approximation (14) corresponding to the first FT term in (24) (FT1 in Table 2) with the linear approximations (12)–(13) (LA in Table 2). One can see from Table 2 that the LA and FT1 estimates are consistent (at least in the sense of their 95 % confidence intervals, which always intersect each other). But the LA standard errors are larger than the FT1 ones. In fact, using the formula for the intensity $\gamma$ of $\tau$ in FT1 can be viewed as a form of variance reduction with respect to LA, where $\tau$ is simulated. Of course, for $\bar{\lambda} \neq 0$ (case of the right tables where $\bar{\lambda} = 3\,\%$), both linear approximations are biased as compared with the complete FT estimate (with nonlinear correction, also shown in Table 2), particularly in the high dimensional case with 10 CDS contracts (see the bottom panels in Table 2). Figure 6 completes these results by showing the LA, FT1

**Table 2** LA, FT1 and FT estimates: 1 CDS (*top*) and 10 CDSs (*bottom*), with parameters $\bar{\lambda} = 0\,\%$, $\rho = 0.8$ (*left*) and $\bar{\lambda} = 3\,\%$, $\rho = 0.6$ (*right*)

| Method | TVA | 95% CI | Rel. SE | Method | TVA | 95% CI | Rel. SE |
|---|---|---|---|---|---|---|---|
| LA | 0.65 | [0.57,0.73] | 6.08 % | LA | 0.66 | [0.60,0.72] | 4.39% |
| FT1 | 0.61 | [0.59,0.63] | 1.66% | FT1 | 0.62 | [0.59,0.64] | 1.96% |
| FT | 0.60 | [0.58,0.62] | 1.64 % | FT | 0.60 | [0.58,0.63] | 1.84% |

| Method | TVA | 95% CI | Rel. SE | Method | TVA | 95% CI | Rel. SE |
|---|---|---|---|---|---|---|---|
| LA | 6.17 | [5.43,6.92] | 6.03% | LA | 6.81 | [6.16,7.45] | 4.76% |
| FT1 | 6.24 | [5.77,6.72] | 3.78% | FT1 | 7.82 | [7.39,8.25] | 2.73% |
| FT | 6.17 | [5.66,6.68] | 4.15% | FT | 6.99 | [6.67,7.31] | 2.28% |

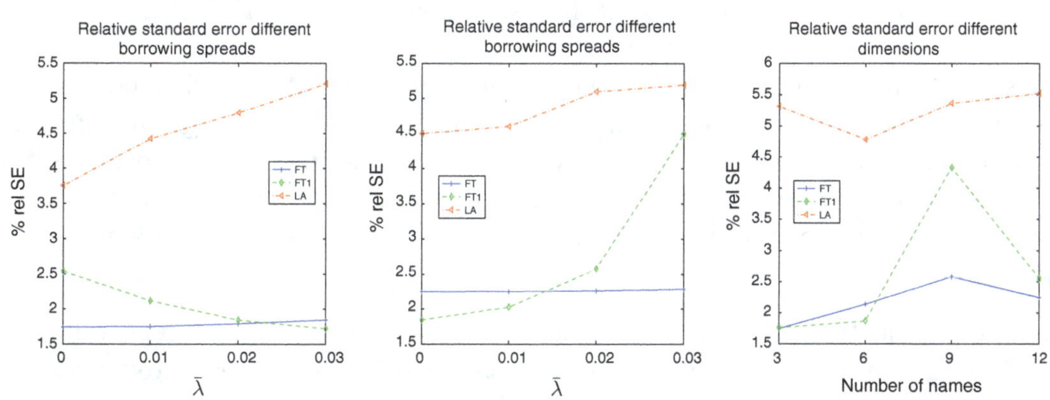


**Fig. 6** The % relative standard errors of the different schemes do not explode with the level of nonlinearity represented by the unsecured borrowing spread $\bar{\lambda}$. *Left* 1 CDS. *Middle* 10 CDSs. *Right* the % relative standard errors of the different schemes (LA, FT1, FT in figures) do not explode with the number of names ($\bar{\lambda} = 100$ bp, $\rho = 0.6$)

and FT standard errors computed for different levels of nonlinearity and different dimensions.

Summarizing, in the DGC model, the PHL is not practical. The FT scheme based on the partially reduced TVA BSDE (II) gives an efficient way of estimating the TVA. The nonlinear correction with respect to the linear approximations (14) or (15) amounts up to 5 % in relative terms, depending on the unsecured borrowing spread $\bar{\lambda}$.

### 6.2 Numerical Results in the DMO Model

In the DMO model, the FT scheme (18) for the fully reduced BSDE (23) can be implemented through following steps:

1. Simulate the time $\eta_Y$ of each (individual or joint) shock following an independent exponential law of parameter $\gamma_Y$, $Y \in \mathscr{Y}$, then retrieve the $\tau_i$ through the formula (41).
2. Draw a time $\zeta_1$ following an exponential law of parameter $\mu$. If $\zeta_1 < T$, compare the default time of each name with $\zeta_1$ to obtain the reduced Markov factor $\widetilde{X}_{\zeta_1}$ as of (42) and in turn $\widetilde{f}_{\zeta_1}$ as of (45)–(46), then go to Step 3. Otherwise stop.
3. Draw a second time $\zeta_2$ following an independent exponential law of parameter $\mu$. If $\zeta_1 + \zeta_2 < T$, compare the default time $\tau_i$ of each name with $\zeta_1 + \zeta_2$ to obtain the Markov factor $\widetilde{X}_{\zeta_1+\zeta_2}$ and $\widetilde{f}_{\zeta_1+\zeta_2}$ then go to Step 4. Otherwise stop.
4. Draw a third time $\zeta_3$ following an independent exponential law of parameter $\mu$. If $\zeta_1 + \zeta_2 + \zeta_3 < T$, compare the default time of each name with $\zeta_1 + \zeta_2 + \zeta_3$ to obtain the Markov factor $\widetilde{X}_{\zeta_1+\zeta_2+\zeta_3}$ and $\widetilde{f}_{\zeta_1+\zeta_2+\zeta_3}$.

We can also consider the PHL scheme (31) based on the partially reduced BSDE (II) with

$$\mathscr{D} = \{x = (x^Y)_{Y \in \mathscr{Y}} \in \{0, 1\}^{\mathscr{Y}} \text{ such that } x^Y = 1 \text{ for } Y \in \mathscr{Y}_{\bullet}\}.$$

To simulate the random tree $\overline{\mathscr{T}}$ in (31), we follow the approach sketched before (31) where, in order to evolve $X$ according to the DMO generator $\mathscr{A}$ during a time interval $\zeta$, a particle born from a node $x = (j_Y)_{Y \in \mathscr{Y}} \in \{0, 1\}^{\mathscr{Y}}$ at time $t$, all one needs is, for each $Y$ such that $j_Y = 1$, draw an independent exponential random variable $\eta_Y$ of parameter $\gamma_Y$ and then set $x' = (j_Y \mathbb{1}_{[0,\eta_Y)}(\zeta))_{Y \in \mathscr{Y}}$. Rephrasing in more algorithmic terms:

1. To simulate the random tree $\overline{\mathscr{T}}$ under the expectation in (31), we repeat the following step (generation of particles, or segments between consecutive nodes of the tree) until a generation of particles dies without children:

   For each node $(t, x = (j_Y)_{Y \in \mathscr{Y}}, k)$ issued from the previous generation of particles (starting with the root-node $(0, X_0, k = 1)$), for each of the $k$ new particles, indexed by

$l$, issued from that node, simulate an independent exponential random variable $\zeta_l$ and set

$$(t'_l, x'_l, k'_l) = (t + \zeta_l, (j_Y \mathbb{1}_{[0,\eta^l_Y)}(\zeta_l))_{Y \in \mathscr{Y}}, \mathbb{1}_{x'_l \in \mathscr{D}} \nu_l),$$

where, for each $l$, the $\eta^l_Y$ are independent exponential-$\gamma_Y$ random draws and $\nu_l$ is an independent draw in the finite set $\{0, 1, \dots, d\}$ with some fixed probabilities $p_0, p_1, \dots, p_d$.

2. To compute the random variable $\Phi$ under the expectation in (31), we loop over the nodes of the tree $\overline{\mathscr{T}}$ thus constructed (if $\overline{\mathscr{T}} \subset [0, T] \times \mathscr{D}$, otherwise $\Phi = 0$ in the first place) and we form the product in (31), where the $\bar{a}_k(t, x)$ are retrieved as in (30).

The PHL schemes (34) based on the full BSDE (I) or (36) based on the fully reduced BSDE (III) can be implemented along similar lines.

We perform TVA computations in a DMO model with $n = 120$, for individual shock intensities taken as $\gamma_{\{i\}} = 10^{-4} \times (100 + i)$ (increasing from $\sim$100 bps to 220 bps as $i$ increases from 1 to 120) and four nested groups of common shocks $I_1 \subset I_2 \subset I_3 \subset I_4$, respectively consisting of the riskiest 3, 9, 21 and 100 % (i.e. all) names, with respective shock intensities $\gamma_{I_1} = 20$ bp, $\gamma_{I_2} = 10$ bp, $\gamma_{I_3} = 6.67$ bp and $\gamma_{I_4} = 5$ bp. The counterparty (resp. the bank) is taken as the eleventh (resp. tenth) safest name in the portfolio. In the model thus specified, we consider CDO tranches with upfront payment, i.e. credit protection bought by the bank from the counterparty at time 0, with nominal 100 for each obligor, maturity $T = 2$ years and attachment (resp. detachment) points are 0, 3 and 14 % (resp. 3 %, 14 % and 100 %). The respective value of $P_0$ (upfront payment) for the equity, mezzanine and senior tranche is 229.65, 5.68, and 2.99. Accordingly, the ranges of approximation chosen for $pol(y) \approx y^+$ in the respective PHL schemes are 250, 200, and 10. We use polynomial approximation of order $d = 4$ with $(p_0, p_1, p_2, p_3, p_4) = (0.5, 0.3, 0.1, 0.09, 0.01)$. We set $\mu = 0.1$ in all PHL schemes and $\mu = 2/T = 0.2$ in all FT schemes.

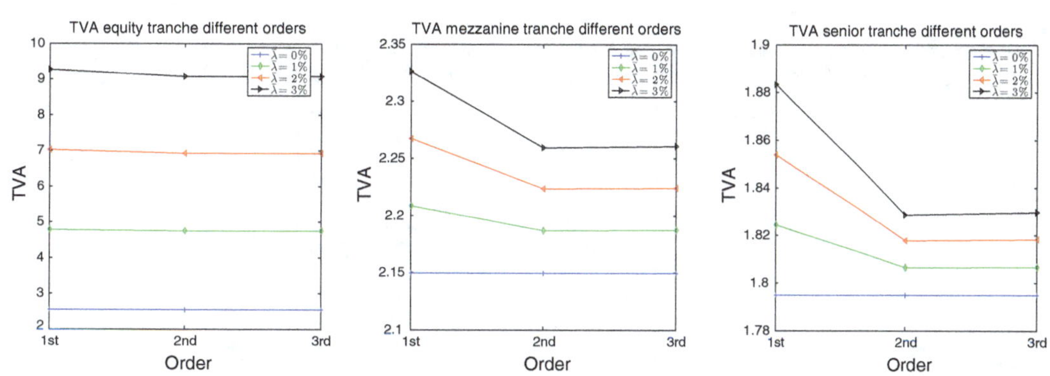


**Fig. 7** TVA on CDO tranches with 120 underlying names computed by FT scheme of order 1–3 for different levels of nonlinearity (unsecured borrowing basis $\bar{\lambda}$). *Left* equity tranche. *Middle* mezzanine tranche. *Right* senior tranche. Originally published in Crépey and Song [6]. Published with kind permission of © Springer-Verlag Berlin Heidelberg 2016. All Rights Reserved. This figure is subject to copyright protection and is not covered by a Creative Commmons License

**Table 3** FT, PHL, $\overline{\text{PHL}}$ and $\widetilde{\text{PHL}}$ schemes applied to the equity (*top*), mezzanine (*middle*), and senior (*bottom*) tranche, for the parameters $\bar{\lambda} = 0\,\%$, $\lambda_{I_j} = 60bp/j$ (*left*) or $\bar{\lambda} = 3\,\%$, $\lambda_{I_j} = 20bp/j$ (*right*)

| Method | TVA | 95% CI | Rel. SE | Method | TVA | 95% CI | Rel. SE |
|---|---|---|---|---|---|---|---|
| FT | 3.13 | [3.10 , 3.16] | 0.48 % | FT | 9.08 | [ 9.00 , 9.16] | 0.46 % |
| $\widetilde{\text{PHL}}$ | 3.07 | [2.87 , 3.28] | 3.35 % | $\widetilde{\text{PHL}}$ | 9.05 | [ 8.40 , 9.70] | 3.58 % |
| $\overline{\text{PHL}}$ | 3.16 | [2.94 , 3.37] | 3.37 % | $\overline{\text{PHL}}$ | 9.28 | [8.63 , 9.94] | 3.51 % |
| PHL | 2.53 | [2.13 , 2.94] | 8.02% | PHL | 12.59 | [6.92 , 18.27] | 22.54% |

| Method | TVA | 95% CI | Rel. SE | Method | TVA | 95% CI | Rel. SE |
|---|---|---|---|---|---|---|---|
| FT | 6.43 | [6.33 , 6.53] | 0.75 % | FT | 2.29 | [2.25 , 2.32] | 0.77 % |
| $\widetilde{\text{PHL}}$ | 6.34 | [5.93 , 6.75 ] | 3.22 % | $\widetilde{\text{PHL}}$ | 2.51 | [2.35 , 2.67] | 3.17 % |
| $\overline{\text{PHL}}$ | 6.34 | [5.93 , 6.75] | 3.25 % | $\overline{\text{PHL}}$ | 2.68 | [2.52 , 2.85] | 3.12 % |
| PHL | 4.86 | [2.84 , 6.89] | 20.82% | PHL | 1.93 | [0.79 , 3.08] | 29.57% |

| Method | TVA | 95% CI | Rel. SE | Method | TVA | 95% CI | Rel. SE |
|---|---|---|---|---|---|---|---|
| FT | 5.32 | [5.24 , 5.40] | 0.75 % | FT | 1.83 | [1.80 , 1.86] | 0.78 % |
| $\widetilde{\text{PHL}}$ | 5.24 | [4.90 , 5.58] | 3.22 % | $\widetilde{\text{PHL}}$ | 1.80 | [1.69 , 1.92] | 3.13 % |
| $\overline{\text{PHL}}$ | 5.25 | [4.90 , 5.58] | 3.25 % | $\overline{\text{PHL}}$ | 1.87 | [1.75 , 1.99] | 3.11 % |
| PHL | 4.01 | [2.32 , 5.70] | 21.03% | PHL | 1.36 | [0.41 , 2.31] | 35.05% |

Figure 7 shows the TVA computed by the FT scheme (23) based on the fully reduced BSDE (III), for different levels of nonlinearity (unsecured borrowing basis $\bar{\lambda}$). We observe that, in all cases, the third order term is negligible. Hence,

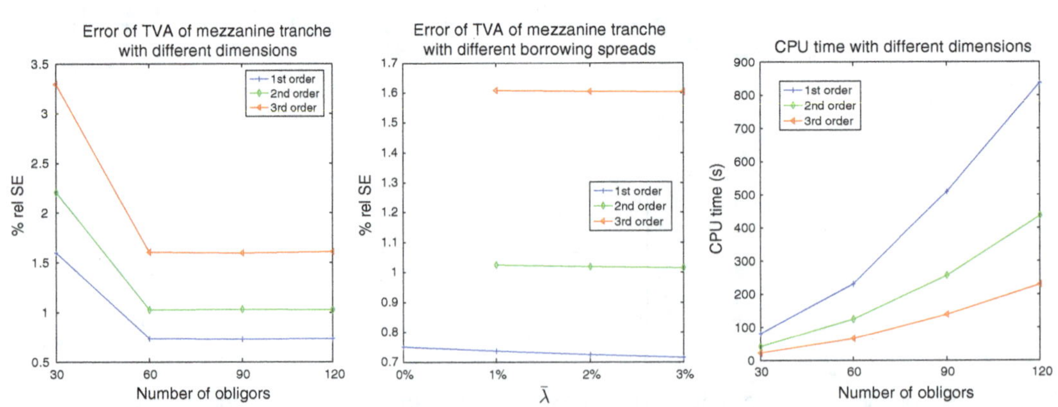


**Fig. 8** Analog of Fig. 5 for the CDO tranche of Fig. 7 in the DMO model ($\bar{\lambda} = 0.01$). Originally published in Crépey and Song [6]. Published with kind permission of © Springer-Verlag Berlin Heidelberg 2016. All Rights Reserved. This figure is subject to copyright protection and is not covered by a Creative Commmons License

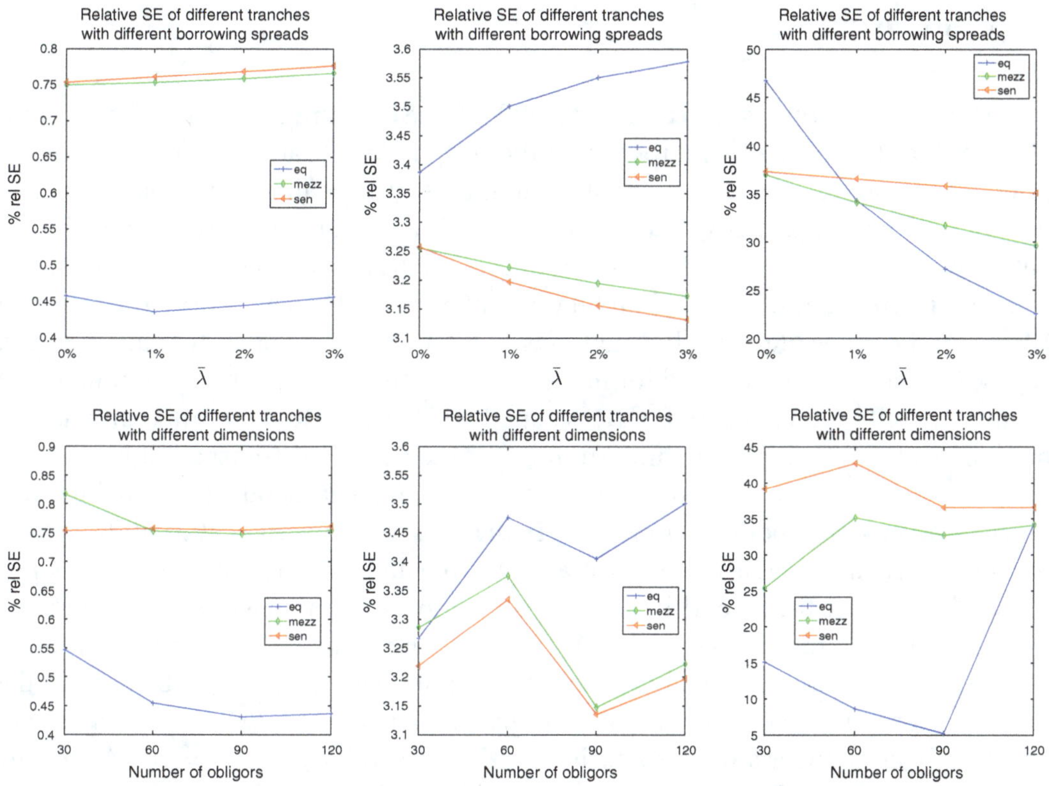


**Fig. 9** *Bottom* the % relative standard errors do not explode with the number of names ($\bar{\lambda} = 100$ bp). *Top* the % relative standard errors do not explode with the level of nonlinearity represented by the unsecured borrowing spread $\bar{\lambda}$ ($n = 120$). *Left* FT scheme. *Middle* $\widetilde{\text{PHL}}$ scheme. *Right* PHL scheme

in further FT computations, we only compute the orders 1 (linear part) and 2 (nonlinear correction) (Fig. 8). Table 3 compares the results of the above FT scheme (23) based on the fully reduced BSDE (III) with those of the PHL schemes (36) based on (III) again ($\widetilde{\text{PHL}}$ in the tables), (31) based on the partially reduced BSDE (II) ($\overline{\text{PHL}}$ in the tables) and (34) based on the full BSDE (I) (PHL in the tables), for the three CDO tranches and two sets of parameters. The three PHL schemes are of course slightly biased, but the first two, based on the BSDEs with null terminal condition (III) or (II), exhibit much less variance than the third one, based on the full BSDE with terminal condition $\xi$. This is also visible in Fig. 9 (note the different scales of the $y$ axes going from left to right in the picture), which also shows that, for any of these schemes, the relative standard errors do not explode with the level of nonlinearity or the number of reference names in the CDO (the results for the $\overline{\text{PHL}}$ scheme are not shown on the figure as very similar to those of the $\widetilde{\text{PHL}}$ scheme). In comparing the TVA values on the left and the right hand side of Table 3, we see that the intensities of the common shocks, which play a role similar to the correlation $\rho$ in the DGC model, have a more important impact on the higher tranches (mezzanine and senior tranche), whereas the equity tranche is more sensitive to the level of the unsecured borrowing spread $\bar{\lambda}$.

## 7 Conclusion

Under mild assumptions, three equivalent TVA BSDEs are available. The original "full" BSDE (I) is stated with respect to the full model filtration $\mathscr{G}$ and the original pricing measure $\mathbb{Q}$. It does not involve the intensity $\gamma$ of the counterparty first-to-default time $\tau$. The partially reduced BSDE (II) is also stated with respect to $(\mathscr{G}, \mathbb{Q})$ but it involves both $\tau$ and $\gamma$. The fully reduced BSDE (III) is stated with respect to a smaller "reference filtration" $\mathscr{F}$ and it only involves $\gamma$. Hence, in principle, the full BSDE (I) should be preferred for models with a "simple" $\tau$ whereas the fully reduced BSDE (III) should be preferred for models with a "simple" $\gamma$. But, in nonimmersive setups, the fully reduced BSDE (III) is stated with respect to a modified probability measure $\mathbb{P}$. Even though switching from $(\mathscr{G}, \mathbb{Q})$ to $(\mathscr{F}, \mathbb{P})$ is transparent in terms of the generator of related Markov factor processes, this can be an issue in situations where the Markov structure is important in the theory to guarantee the validity of the numerical schemes, but is not really practical from an implementation point of view. This is for instance the case with the credit portfolio models that we use for illustrative purposes in our numerics, where the Markov structure that emerges from the dynamic copula model is too heavy and it is only the copula features that can be used in the numerics—copula features under the original stochastic basis $(\mathscr{G}, \mathbb{Q})$, which do not necessarily hold under a reduced basis $(\mathscr{F}, \mathbb{P})$ (especially when $\mathbb{P} \neq \mathbb{Q}$). As for the partially reduced BSDE (II), as compared with the full BSDE (I), its interest is its null terminal condition, which is key for the FT scheme as recalled below. But of course (II) can only be used when one has an explicit formula for $\gamma$.

For nonlinear and very high-dimensional problems such as counterparty risk on credit derivatives, the only feasible numerical schemes are purely forward simulation schemes, such as the linear Monte Carlo expansion of Fujii and Takahashi [9, 10] or the branching particles scheme of Henry–Labordère [13], respectively dubbed "FT scheme" and "PHL scheme" in the paper. In our setup, the PHL scheme involves a nontrivial and rather sensitive fine-tuning for finding a polynomial in $\vartheta$ that approximates the terms $(P_t - \vartheta)^{\pm}$ in $fva_t(\vartheta)$ in a suitable range for $\vartheta$. This fine-tuning requires a preliminary knowledge on the solution obtained by running another approximation (linear approximation or FT scheme) in the first place. Another limitation of the PHL scheme in our case is that it is more demanding than the FT scheme in terms of the structural model properties that it requires. Namely, in our credit portfolio problems, both a Markov structure and a dynamic copula are required for the PHL scheme. But, whereas a "weak" dynamic copula structure in the sense of simulation and forward pricing by copula means is sufficient for the FT scheme, a dynamic copula in the stronger sense that the copula structure is preserved in the future is required in the case of the PHL scheme. This strong dynamic copula property is satisfied by our common-shock model but not in the Gaussian copula model. In conclusion, the FT schemes applied to the partially or fully reduced BSDEs (II) or (III) (a null terminal condition is required so that the full BSDE (I) is not eligible for this scheme) appear as the method of choice on these problems.

An important message of the numerics is that, even for realistically high levels of nonlinearity, i.e. an unsecured borrowing spread $\bar{\lambda} = 3\,\%$, the third order FT correction was always found negligible and the second order FT correction less than 5–10 % of the first order, linear FT term. In conclusion, a first order FT term can be used for obtaining "the best linear approximation" to our problem, whereas a nonlinear correction, if wished, can be computed by a second order FT term.

**Acknowledgements** This research benefited from the support of the "Chair Markets in Transition" under the aegis of Louis Bachelier laboratory, a joint initiative of École polytechnique, Université d'Évry Val d'Essonne and Fédération Bancaire Française.
The KPMG Center of Excellence in Risk Management is acknowledged for organizing the conference "Challenges in Derivatives Markets - Fixed Income Modeling, Valuation Adjustments, Risk Management, and Regulation"

**Open Access** This chapter is distributed under the terms of the Creative Commons Attribution 4.0 International License (http://creativecommons.org/licenses/by/4.0/), which permits use, duplication, adaptation, distribution and reproduction in any medium or format, as long as you give appropriate credit to the original author(s) and the source, a link is provided to the Creative Commons license and any changes made are indicated.

The images or other third party material in this chapter are included in the work's Creative Commons license, unless indicated otherwise in the credit line; if such material is not included in the work's Creative Commons license and the respective action is not permitted by statutory regulation, users will need to obtain permission from the license holder to duplicate, adapt or reproduce the material.

## References

1. Brigo, D., Chourdakis, K.: Counterparty risk for credit default swaps: impact of spread volatility and default correlation. Int. J. Theor. Appl. Financ. **12**(7), 1007–1026 (2008)
2. Brigo, D., Capponi, A., Pallavicini, A.: Arbitrage-free bilateral counterparty risk valuation under collateralization and application to credit default swaps. Math. Financ. **24**(1), 125–146 (2014)
3. Crépey, S.: Bilateral counterparty risk under funding constraints - Part II: CVA. Math. Financ. **25**(1), 23–50 (2012)
4. Crépey, S., Song, S.: Invariant times. hal-01088940v1 (2014)
5. Crépey, S., Song, S.: BSDEs of counterparty risk. Stoch. Process. Appl. **125**(8), 3023–3052 (2014)
6. Crépey, S., Song, S.: Counterparty risk and funding: immersion and beyond. Finance Stoch. **20**(4), 901–930 (2016)
7. Crépey, S., Gerboud, R., Grbac, Z., Ngor, N.: Counterparty risk and funding: the four wings of the TVA. Int. J. Theor. Appl. Financ. **16**(2), 1350006(31 pp.) (2013)
8. Crépey, S., Bielecki, T.R., Brigo, D.: Counterparty Risk and Funding - A Tale of Two Puzzles. Chapman and Hall/CRC Financial Mathematics Series. Chapman and Hall/CRC, Boca Raton (2014)
9. Fujii, M., Takahashi, A.: Analytical approximation for non-linear FBSDEs with perturbation scheme. Int. J. Theor. Appl. Financ. **15**(5), 1250034(24) (2012)
10. Fujii, M., Takahashi, A.: Perturbative expansion of FBSDE in an incomplete market with stochastic volatility. Q. J. Financ. **2**(3), 1250015(24) (2012)
11. Fujii, M., Takahashi, A.: Collateralized credit default swaps and default dependence: implications for the central counterparties. J. Credit Risk **3**(8), 97–113 (2012)

12. He, S.-W., Wang, J.-G., Yan, J.-A.: Semimartingale Theory and Stochastic Calculus. CRC Press Boca Raton (1992)
13. Henry-Labordère, P.: Cutting CVA's complexity. Risk Mag. **25**(7), 67–73 (2012)
14. Kruse, T., Popier, A.: BSDEs with jumps in a general filtration. arXiv:1412.4622 (2014)
15. Li, D.: On default correlation: a copula function approach. J. Fixed Income **9**(4), 43–54 (2000)
16. McKean, H.P.: Application of Brownian motion to the equation of Kolmogorov-Petrovskii-Piskunov. Commun. Pure Appl. Math. **28**(3), 323–331 (1975)

# Tight Semi-model-free Bounds on (Bilateral) CVA

**Jördis Helmers, Jan-J. Rückmann and Ralf Werner**

**Abstract** In the last decade, counterparty default risk has experienced an increased interest both by academics as well as practitioners. This was especially motivated by the market turbulences and the financial crises over the past decade which have highlighted the importance of counterparty default risk for uncollateralized derivatives. After a succinct introduction to the topic, it is demonstrated that standard models can be combined to derive semi-model-free tight lower and upper bounds on bilateral CVA (BCVA). It will be shown in detail how these bounds can be easily and efficiently calculated by the solution of two corresponding linear optimization problems.

**Keywords** Counterparty credit risk · CVA · Tight bounds · Mass transportation problem

## 1 Introduction

Events such as Lehman's default have drawn the attention to counterparty default risk. At the very latest after this default, it has become obvious to all market participants that the credit qualities of both counterparties—usually a client and an investment bank—need to be considered in the pricing of uncollateralized OTC derivatives.

J. Helmers
Finbridge GmbH & Co. KG, Louisenstr. 100, 61348 Bad Homburg, Germany
e-mail: joerdis.helmers@finbridge.de

J.-J. Rückmann
Department of Informatics, University of Bergen,
P.O. Box 7803, 5020 Bergen, Norway
e-mail: Jan-Joachim.Ruckmann@ii.uib.no

R. Werner (✉)
Institut für Mathematik, Universität Augsburg, Universitätsstr. 14,
86159 Augsburg, Germany
e-mail: ralf.werner@math.uni-augsburg.de

© The Author(s) 2016

K. Glau et al. (eds.), *Innovations in Derivatives Markets*, Springer Proceedings in Mathematics & Statistics 165, DOI 10.1007/978-3-319-33446-2_4

Over the past years, several authors have been investigating the pricing of derivatives based on a variety of models which take into account these default risks. Most of these results are covered by a variety of excellent books, for example Pykhtin [16], Gregory [12], or Brigo et al. [7] just to name a few. For a profound discussion on the pros and cons of unilateral versus bilateral counterparty risk let us refer to the two articles by Gregory [11, 13].

In the following exposition, we are concerned with the quantification of the smallest and largest BCVA which can be obtained by any given model with predetermined marginal laws. This takes considerations of Turnbull [21] much further, who first derived weak bounds on CVA for certain types of products. Our approach extends first ideas from Hull and White [15], where the hazard rate determining defaults is coupled to the exposure or other risk factors in either deterministic or stochastic way. Still, Hull and White rely on an explicit choice of the default model and on an explicit coupling. More related is the work by Rosen and Saunders et al. [8, 17], on which we prefer to comment later in Remark 8. As the most related work we note the paper by Cherubini [9] which provided the basis for this semi-model-free approach. There, only one particular two-dimensional copula was used to couple each individual forward swap par rate with the default time. Obviously, a more general approach couples each forward swap par rate with each other and the default time—which is in gist similar to Hull and White [15]. From there the final step to our approach is to observe that the most general approach directly links the whole stochastic evolution of the exposure with both random default times. We will illustrate in the following that these couplings can be readily derived by linear programming. For this purpose the BCVA will be decomposed into three main components: the first component is represented by the loss process, the second component consists of the default indicators of the two counterparties and the third component is comprised of the exposure-at-default of the OTC derivative, i.e. the risk-free present value of the outstanding amount[1] at time of default. This approach takes further early considerations of Haase and Werner [14], where comparable results were obtained from the point of view of generalized stopping problems.

In a very recent working paper by Scherer and Schulz [18], the above idea was analyzed in more detail. It was shown that the computational complexity of the problem is the same, no matter if only marginal distributions of defaults or the joint distribution of defaults are known.

After submission of this paper we became aware of related results by Glasserman and Yang, see [10]. Although the main idea of their exposition is similar in gist, Glasserman and Yang focus on the unilateral CVA instead of bilateral CVA. Besides an analysis of the convergence of finite samples to the continuous setup, their exposition is mainly focused on the penalization of deviation from some *base distribution*. In contrast, our focus is on bilateral CVA, with special attention to numerical solution and to the case that payoffs also depend on the credit quality.

[1] In accordance with the *full two-way payment* rule under ISDA master contracts, see e.g. Bielecki and Rutkowski [2] (Sect. 14.4.4), we assume that the close-out value is determined by the then prevailing risk-free present value.

In summary, this exposition makes the following main contributions:

- First, the three main building blocks of such an adjustment are clearly identified and separated, and it is shown how any coupling of these blocks leads to a feasible adjustment. Unlike Cherubini, who only considered the very specific case of an interest rate swap, all kinds of derivatives (interest rate, FX, commodity, and even credit derivatives) are covered in a unified way—even if the payoff, and thus the present value of the derivative, is explicitly depending on the credit quality of any of the two counterparties.
- Second, by generalizing Cherubini's approach, upper and lower bounds on unilateral and bilateral counterparty value adjustments are derived. It will be demonstrated that these bounds can be efficiently obtained by the solution of linear optimization problems, more specifically, by the solution of balanced transportation problems. In contrast to the approaches of Turnbull [21] or Cherubini [9], both the upper and lower bound derived here are *tight bounds*, i.e. there exists some stochastic model which is consistent with all given market prices in which these bounds are attained.

The rest of the paper is organized as follows. In Sect. 2 a succinct introduction to bilateral counterparty risk is given, before the decomposition of the BCVA into its building blocks is carried out in Sect. 3. In Sect. 4 the two main approaches for the calculation of counterparty valuation adjustments are briefly reviewed. Finally, the tight bounds on CVA are derived in Sect. 5, before the paper concludes.

## 2 Counterparty Default Risk

As usual, to model financial transactions with default risk, let $(\Omega, \mathscr{G}, \mathscr{G}_t, \mathbf{Q})$ be a probability space where $\mathscr{G}_t$ models the flow of information and $\mathbf{Q}$ denotes the risk-neutral measure for a given risk-free numéraire process $N_t > 0$, see e.g. Bielecki and Rutkowski [2] for more details. Further, let the space be endowed with a right-continuous and complete sub-filtration $\mathscr{F}_t$ modeling the flow of information except default, such that $\mathscr{F}_t \subseteq \mathscr{G}_t := \mathscr{F}_t \vee \mathscr{H}_t$ with $\mathscr{H}_t$ being the right-continuous filtration generated by the default events.

Subsequently, we consider a transaction with maturity $T$ between a client $A$ and a counterparty $B$ where both are subject to default. The respective random default times are denoted by $\tau_A$ and $\tau_B$. In order to take into account counterparty default risk we distinguish three cases:

- neither $A$ nor $B$ defaults before $T$: $D_0 := \{\tau_A > T\} \cap \{\tau_B > T\}$,
- $A$ defaults before $B$ and before $T$: $D_A := \{\tau_A \leq T\} \cap \{\tau_A \leq \tau_B\}$,
- $B$ defaults before $A$ and before $T$: $D_B := \{\tau_B \leq T\} \cap \{\tau_B \leq \tau_A\}$.

For simplicity of presentation, we assume in the following that $\mathbf{Q}[\tau_A = T] = \mathbf{Q}[\tau_B = T] = \mathbf{Q}[\tau_A = \tau_B] = 0$. Under this assumption these sets[2] yield a decomposition of one, i.e. it holds

$$\mathbf{1}_{D_0} + \mathbf{1}_{D_A} + \mathbf{1}_{D_B} = 1 \quad \mathbf{Q}\text{-almost-surely.}$$

In the following, let us consider a transaction consisting of cash flows $C(B, A, T_i)$ paid by the counterparty $B$ at times $T_i, i = 1, \ldots, m_B$, and cash flows $C(A, B, T_j)$ paid by the client $A$ at times $T_j, j = 1, \ldots, m_A$. Taking into account default risk of both counterparties, the quantification of the bilateral CVA is summarized in the following well-known theorem, which in essence goes back to Sorensen and Bollier [19].

**Theorem 1** *Conditional on the event $\{t < \min(\tau_A, \tau_B)\}$, i.e. no default has occurred until time $t$, the value $V_A^D(t, T)$ of the transaction under consideration of bilateral counterparty risk at time $t$ is given by*

$$V_A^D(t, T) = V_A(t, T) - CVA_A(t, T) = -\big(V_B(t, T) - CVA_B(t, T)\big) = -V_B^D(t, T)$$

*where the risk-free present value of the transaction is given as*

$$\begin{aligned} V_A(t, T) &= \mathbb{E}\left[\sum_{i=1}^{m_B} \frac{N_t}{N_{T_i}} \cdot C(B, A, T_i) \middle| \mathscr{F}_t\right] - \mathbb{E}\left[\sum_{j=1}^{m_A} \frac{N_t}{N_{T_j}} \cdot C(A, B, T_j) \middle| \mathscr{F}_t\right] \\ &= -V_B(t, T) \end{aligned}$$

*and where the* bilateral counterparty value adjustment *$CVA_A(t, T)$ is defined as*

$$\begin{aligned} CVA_A(t, T) :=& \mathbb{E}\left[ \mathbf{1}_{D_B} \cdot \frac{N_t}{N_{\tau_B}} \cdot L_{\tau_B}^B \cdot \max(0, V_A(\tau_B, T)) \mid \mathscr{G}_t \right] \\ & - \mathbb{E}\left[ \mathbf{1}_{D_A} \cdot \frac{N_t}{N_{\tau_A}} \cdot L_{\tau_A}^A \cdot \max(0, V_B(\tau_A, T)) \mid \mathscr{G}_t \right] \\ =& - CVA_B(t, T). \end{aligned} \tag{1}$$

Here $L_t^i$ denotes the random loss (between 0 and 1) of counterparty $i$ at time $t$.

*Proof* A proof of Theorem 1 can be found in Bielecki and Rutkowski [2], Formula (14.25) or Brigo and Capponi [4], Proposition 2.1 and Appendix A, respectively.

Based on Theorem 1, the general approach for the calculation of the counterparty risk adjusted value $V_A^D(t, T)$ is to determine first the risk-free value $V_A(t, T)$ of the transaction. This can be done by any common valuation method for this kind of transaction. In a second step the counterparty value adjustment $CVA_A(t, T)$ needs to be determined. So far, two main approaches have emerged in the academic literature, which will be briefly reviewed in Sect. 4.

[2]We note that Brigo et al. (in [4, 6]) use different sets to order the default times, which are in essence reducible to the above three events.

## 3 The Main Building Blocks of CVA

Subsequently, let us assume that the default times $\tau_i$ with $i \in \{A, B\}$ can only take a finite number of values $\{\bar{t}_1, \ldots, \bar{t}_K\}$ in the interval $]0, T[$. For continuous time models this assumption can be justified by the *default bucketing* approach, which can, for example, be found in Brigo and Chourdakis [5], if $K$ is chosen sufficiently large. To be able to separate the default dynamics from the market value dynamics, let us introduce the auxiliary time $s$, $s \in [t, T]$ and the discounted market value

$$\widetilde{V}_i^+(t, s, T) := \frac{N_t}{N_s} \cdot \max(0, V_i(s, T)).$$

Then we can rewrite Eq. (1) as:

$$\begin{aligned} CVA_A(t, T) = \mathbb{E}\left[\sum_{k=1}^{K} L_{\bar{t}_k}^B \cdot \mathbf{1}_{D_B} \cdot \mathbf{1}_{\bar{t}_k}(\tau_B) \cdot \widetilde{V}_A^+(t, \bar{t}_k, T) \mid \mathcal{G}_t\right] \qquad (2) \\ -\mathbb{E}\left[\sum_{k=1}^{K} L_{\bar{t}_k}^A \cdot \mathbf{1}_{D_A} \cdot \mathbf{1}_{\bar{t}_k}(\tau_A) \cdot \widetilde{V}_B^+(t, \bar{t}_k, T) \mid \mathcal{G}_t\right]. \end{aligned}$$

Here, $\mathbf{1}_M$ is the indicator function of the set $M$; if $M = \{m\}$ we simply write $\mathbf{1}_m$ instead. Now, collecting all terms relating to the default in the default indicator process $\delta$,

$$\delta_k^i := \mathbf{1}_{D_i} \cdot \mathbf{1}_{\bar{t}_k}(\tau_i),$$

we can rewrite the BCVA in a more compact manner as

$$\begin{aligned} CVA_A(t, T) = \mathbb{E}\left[\sum_{k=1}^{K} L_{\bar{t}_k}^B \cdot \delta_k^B \cdot \widetilde{V}_A^+(t, \bar{t}_k, T) \mid \mathcal{G}_t\right] \qquad (3) \\ -\mathbb{E}\left[\sum_{k=1}^{K} L_{\bar{t}_k}^A \cdot \delta_k^A \cdot \widetilde{V}_B^+(t, \bar{t}_k, T) \mid \mathcal{G}_t\right]. \end{aligned}$$

From Eq. (3) we immediately see that the BCVA at time $t$ is composed of six discrete time[3] processes:

- two *default indicator processes* $\delta_s^A$ and $\delta_s^B$,
- two *loss processes* $L_s^A$ and $L_s^B$, and
- two *discounted exposure processes* $\widetilde{V}_A^+(t, s, T)$ and $\widetilde{V}_B^+(t, s, T)$.

In this way, we are able to separate the default dynamics $\delta$ from the loss process $L$ and the exposure process $\widetilde{V}$. From this decomposition, it becomes obvious that the BCVA is completely determined by the joint distribution of these six processes.

[3] In the following, we replace the time index $\bar{t}_k$ with $k$ for notational convenience.

*Remark 1* We note that in general it is even sufficient to model four processes (loss dynamics and market value dynamics) plus a two-dimensional random variable $(\tau_A, \tau_B)$. However, in the case of finitely many default times, it is more convenient to work with the default indicator process instead.

*Remark 2* For simplicity of the subsequent exposition, we assume that the loss process is actually constant and equals 1: $L_t^i = l^i = 1$. The theory of the remainder of this exposition is not affected by this simplifying assumption, with one notable exception: the resulting two-dimensional transportation problems will become a multi-dimensional transportation problem which renders its numerical solution more complex, but still feasible.

*Remark 3* As we have noted, the default indicator process can only take a finite number of values in the bucketing approach. More exactly, it holds that the joint (i.e. two-dimensional) default indicator process $\delta = (\delta_k)_{k=1,\dots,K} \in \mathbb{R}^{2\times K}$, defined by

$$\delta_k := \begin{pmatrix} \delta_k^A \\ \delta_k^B \end{pmatrix}, \quad k = 1, \dots, K,$$

takes only values in the finite set

$$\mathscr{Y} := \left\{ \gamma \in \mathbb{R}^{2\times K} \mid \gamma_{i,k} \in \{0, 1\}, \sum_{i,k} \gamma_{i,k} \le 1 \right\}$$

which has exactly $2K + 1$ elements. Therefore, the discrete time default indicator process is also a process with a finite state space.

Let us further introduce the joint exposure process in analogy to the above,

$$X_k := \begin{pmatrix} \widetilde{V}_A^+(t, \bar{t}_k, T) \\ \widetilde{V}_B^+(t, \bar{t}_k, T) \end{pmatrix}, \quad k = 1, \dots, K.$$

Then it holds

$$CVA_A(t, T) = \sum_{k=1}^{K} \left( \mathbb{E}\left[ \delta_k^B \cdot X_k^A \mid \mathscr{G}_t \right] - \mathbb{E}\left[ \delta_k^A \cdot X_k^B \mid \mathscr{G}_t \right] \right). \tag{4}$$

To avoid technical considerations for brevity of presentation, we prefer to work with discrete processes (i.e. discrete state space) in discrete time. Thus, it may be necessary to discretize the state space of the remaining discounted exposure process. In general, there exist (at least) two different approaches how a suitable discrete state space version of the process $X$ could be obtained:

- In the first approach—completely similar to the default bucketing approach—the state space $\mathbb{R}^{2\times K}$ for the joint exposure process $X$ is divided into $N$ disjoint components. Then $X$ is replaced by some representative value on this component (usually an average value) on each of the components, and the probabilities of the discretized process are set in accordance with the original probabilities of each component (cf. the default bucketing approach).

- From a computational and practical point of view, a much more convenient approach relies on Monte Carlo simulation: $N$ different scenarios (i.e. realizations) of the process $X$ are used instead of the original process. Each realization is assumed to have probability $1/N$.

For both approaches it is known that they converge at least[4] in distribution to the original process, which is sufficient for our purposes. For more details on the convergence, let us refer to the recent working paper by Glasserman and Yang [10].

## 4 Models for Counterparty Risk

In the last decade two main approaches have emerged in the literature how to model the individual, resp. joint distribution of the processes $\delta$ and $X$:

- The most popular approach is based on the rather strong assumption of independence between exposure and default. Based on this independence assumption, only individual models for $\delta$ and $X$ need to be specified for the CVA calculation. This kind of independence assumption is quite standard in the market, see for example the Bloomberg CVA function (for more details on the Bloomberg model let us refer to Stein and Lee [20]).
- Alternatively, and more recently, a more general approach is based on a joint model (also called *hybrid model*) for the building blocks $\delta$ and $X$ of the CVA calculation, see Sect. 4.3.

### *4.1 Independence of CVA Components*

Let us assume that the exposure process $X$ is independent of the default process $\delta$. Then the expectation inside the summation can be split into two parts:

$$\sum_{k=1}^{K} \mathbb{E}\left[\delta_k^B \cdot X_k^A \mid \mathcal{G}_t\right] = \sum_{k=1}^{K} \mathbb{E}\left[\delta_k^B \mid \mathcal{G}_t\right] \cdot \mathbb{E}\left[X_k^A \mid \mathcal{G}_t\right]. \tag{5}$$

[4]The Monte Carlo approach converges in distribution due to the Theorem of Glivenko–Cantelli. For state space discretization, if for example conditional expectations are used on each bucket, then convergence is in fact almost surely and in $L^1$ due Lévy's 0–1 law.

It is well known that the expected value

$$\mathbb{E}\left[X_k^A \mid \mathscr{G}_t\right] = \mathbb{E}\left[\widetilde{V}_A^+(t, \bar{t}_k, T) \middle| \mathscr{G}_t\right] = \mathbb{E}\left[\frac{N_t}{N_{\bar{t}_k}} \cdot \max(V_A(t, \bar{t}_k, T), 0) \middle| \mathscr{F}_t\right] \tag{6}$$

matches exactly the price of a call option on the basis transaction at time $t$ with strike 0 and exercise time $\bar{t}_k$. The CVA equation can hence be rewritten as

$$CVA_A(t, T) = \sum_{k=1}^{K} \left(\mathbb{E}\left[\delta_k^B \mid \mathscr{G}_t\right] \cdot \mathbb{E}\left[X_k^A \mid \mathscr{G}_t\right] - \mathbb{E}\left[\delta_k^A \mid \mathscr{G}_t\right] \cdot \mathbb{E}\left[X_k^B \mid \mathscr{G}_t\right]\right), \tag{7}$$

and thus the BCVA can be calculated without any further problems as the corresponding default probabilities[5] $\mathbb{E}\left[\delta_k^B \mid \mathscr{G}_t\right] = \mathbf{Q}\left[\tau_B \in \Delta_k, \tau_B \leq \tau_A \mid \mathscr{G}_t\right]$ can be easily computed from any given credit risk model: in order to calculate the probability $\mathbf{Q}\left[\tau_B \in \Delta_k, \tau_B \leq \tau_A \mid \mathscr{G}_t\right]$, the default times $\tau_A$ and $\tau_B$ together with their dependence structure have to be modeled. One of the most popular models for default times in general are intensity models, as for example described in Bielecki and Rutkowsi [2], Part III.

*Remark 4* It has to be noted that a model with deterministic default intensities plus a suitable copula is sufficient for the arbitrary specification of the joint distribution of default times. Stochastic intensities do not add any value in this context. This is true as long as the default risk-free discounted present value is independent of the credit quality of each counterpart. This means that the payoff itself is not allowed to be linked explicitly to the credit quality of any counterparty.

*Remark 5* Let us point out that the intensity model is just one specific example how default times could be modeled. The big advantage of our approach is that any arbitrary credit risk model can be used instead, as only the distribution of the default indicator $\delta$ finally matters. In case only marginal default models are available, we can also take into account the remaining unknown dependence between the default times, however, at the price of a higher dimensional transportation problem.

## 4.2 Modeling Options on the Basis Transaction

Since it could be observed in Eq. (6) that options on the basis transaction need to be priced, a suitable model for this option pricing task needs to be available. Depending on the type of derivative, any model which can be reasonably well calibrated to the market data is sufficient. For instance, for interest rate derivatives, any model ranging from a simple Vasicek or CIR model to sophisticated Libor market models or two-factor Hull–White models could be applied. In case of a credit default swap,

[5] With $\Delta_k := ]\bar{t}_{k-1}, \bar{t}_k]$ if the default bucketing approach has been used, otherwise $\Delta_k := \{\bar{t}_k\}$.

any model which allows to price CDS options, i.e. any model with stochastic credit spread would be feasible. However, for CVA calculations, usually a trade-off between accuracy of the model and efficiency of calculations needs to be made. For this reason, usually simpler models are applied for CVA calculations than for other pricing applications. It needs to be noted that since the financial market usually provides sufficiently many prices of liquid derivatives, any reasonable model can be calibrated to these market prices, and therefore, we can assume in the following that the market implied distribution of the discounted exposure process is fully known and available.

### *4.3 Hybrid Models—An Example*

Another way to calculate the CVA is to use a so-called *hybrid approach* which models all the involved underlying risk factors. Instances of such models can for example be found in Brigo and Capponi [4] for the case of a credit default swap, or Brigo et al. [6] for interest rate derivatives. In Brigo et al. [6], an integrated framework is introduced, where a two-factor Gaussian interest-rate model is set up for a variety of interest rate derivatives[6] in order to deal with the option inherent in the CVA. Further, to model the possible default of the client and its counterparty their stochastic default intensities are given as CIR processes with exponentially distributed positive jumps. The Brownian motions driving those risk factors are assumed to be correlated. Additionally, the defaults of the client and the counterparty are linked by a Gaussian copula.

In summary, the amount of wrong-way risk which can be modeled within such a framework strongly depends on the model choice. If solely correlations between default intensities (i.e. credit spreads) and interest rates are taken into account, only a rather weak relation will emerge between default and the exposure of interest rate derivatives, cf. Brigo et al. [6]. Figure 5 in Scherer and Schulz [18] provides an overview of potential CVA values for different models which illustrates that models can differ quite significantly.

## 5 Tight Bounds on CVA

From the previous section it becomes obvious that hybrid models yield different CVAs depending on the (model and parameter implied) degree of dependence between default and exposure. However, it remains unclear how large the impact of this dependence can be. In other words: *Is it possible to quantify, how small or large the CVA can get for any model, given that the marginal distributions for expo-*

[6]Although this modeling approach is a rather general one, it has to be noted that it links the dependence on tenors of swaption volatilities to the form of the initial yield curve. Therefore, the limits of such an approach became apparent as the yield curve steepened in conjunction with a movement of the volatility surface in the aftermath of the beginning of financial crisis in 2008, when these effects could not be reproduced by such a model.

*sure and default are already given?* In the following, we want to address this question based on our initially given decomposition of the CVA in building blocks.

As mentioned in Sect. 4.2, we can reasonably assume that the distribution of the exposure process $X$ is already completely determined by the available market information. In a similar manner, we have argued that also the distribution of the default indicator process $\delta$ can be assumed to be given by the market. Nevertheless, let us point out that the following ideas and concepts could indeed be generalized to the case that only the marginal distributions of the default times are known. Further, we can even consider the case that the dependence structure between different market risk factors is not known but remains uncertain. However, all these generalizations come at the price that the resulting two-dimensional transportation problem will become multi-dimensional.

For the above reasons, we argue that the following approach is indeed *semi-model-free* in the sense that no model needs to be specified which links the default indicator process with the discounted exposure processes.

## 5.1 *Tight Bounds on CVA by Mass Transportation*

Let us reconsider Eq. (4) and let us highlight the dependence of the BCVA on the measure $\mathbf{P}$.

$$CVA_A^{\mathbf{P}}(t,T) = \sum_{k=1}^{K} \left( \mathbb{E}_{\mathbf{P}}\left[\delta_k^B \cdot X_k^A \mid \mathcal{G}_t\right] - \mathbb{E}_{\mathbf{P}}\left[\delta_k^A \cdot X_k^B \mid \mathcal{G}_t\right] \right).$$

With some abuse of notation, the measure $\mathbf{P}$ denotes the joint distribution of the default process $\delta$ and the exposure process $X$. Since both processes have finite support, $\mathbf{P}$ can be represented as a $(2K+1) \times N$ matrix with entries in $[0, 1]$. We note that the marginals of $\mathbf{P}$, i.e. the distributions of $\delta$ and $X$ (denoted by the probability vectors $\mathbf{p}^{(X)} \in \mathbb{R}^N$ and $\mathbf{p}^{(\delta)} \in \mathbb{R}^{2K+1}$) are already predetermined from the market. Therefore, $\mathbf{P}$ has to satisfy

$$\mathbf{1}^\top \mathbf{P} = \mathbf{p}^{(X)}, \quad \text{and} \quad \mathbf{P}\mathbf{1} = \mathbf{p}^{(\delta)}.$$

*Remark 6* In case of independence between $\delta$ and $X$, $\mathbf{P}$ is given by the product distribution of $\delta$ and $X$, whereas in hybrid models the joint distribution $\mathbf{P}$ is determined by the specification and parametrization of the hybrid model. In the independent case, $\mathbf{P}$ is hence given by the dyadic product

$$\mathbf{P} = \mathbf{p}^{(\delta)} \mathbf{p}^{(X)\top}.$$

Obviously, the smallest and largest CVA which can be obtained by any $\mathbf{P}$ which is consistent with the given marginals, is given by

$$CVA_A^l(t,T) := \min_{\mathbf{P}\in\mathscr{P}} \; CVA_A^{\mathbf{P}}(t,T),$$
$$CVA_A^u(t,T) := \max_{\mathbf{P}\in\mathscr{P}} \; CVA_A^{\mathbf{P}}(t,T),$$

where

$$\mathscr{P} := \{\mathbf{P} \in [0,1]^{(2K+1)\times N} \mid \mathbf{1}^\top \mathbf{P} = \mathbf{p}^{(X)},\ \mathbf{P}\mathbf{1} = \mathbf{p}^{(\delta)}\}.$$

It can be easily noted that the set $\mathscr{P}$ is a convex polytope. Thus, the computation of $CVA_A^l(t,T)$ and $CVA_A^u(t,T)$ essentially requires the solution of a linear program, as the objective functions are linear in $\mathbf{P}$.

*Remark 7* The structure of the above LPs coincides with the structure of so-called *balanced linear transportation problems*. Transportation problems constitute a very important subclass of linear programming problems, see for example Bazaraa et al. [1], Chap. 10, for more details. There exist several very efficient algorithms for the numerical solution of such transportation problems, see also Bazaraa et al. [1], Chaps. 10, 11 and 12.

Let us summarize our results in the following theorem:

**Theorem 2** *Under the given prerequisites, it holds:*

1. $CVA_A^l(t,T) \le CVA_A(t,T) \le CVA_A^u(t,T)$.
2. *These bounds are tight, i.e. they represent the lowest and the highest CVA which can be obtained by any (hybrid) model which is consistent with the market data and there exists at least one model which reaches these bounds.*

The tightness of our bounds is in contrast to Turnbull [21], where only weak bounds were derived. Of course, bounds always represent a best-case and a worst-case estimate only, which may strongly under- and overestimate the true CVA.

*Remark 8* We note that a related approach of coupling default and exposure via copulas was presented by Rosen and Saunders [17] and Crepedes et al. [8]. However, their approach differs from ours in some significant aspects. First, exposure scenarios are sorted by a single number (e.g. effective exposure) to be able to couple exposure scenarios with risk factors of defaults by copulas. Second, risk factors of some credit risk model are employed instead of working with the default indicator directly. Third, their approach is restricted to the real-world setting and does not consider restrictions on the marginal distributions in the coupling process, which is e.g. necessary if stochastic credit spreads should be considered.

### 5.2 An Alternative Formulation as Assignment Problem

For the above setup we have assumed that the probabilities for all possible realizations of the default indicator process could be precomputed from a suitable default model. If for some default model this should not be the case, but only scenarios (with repeated outcomes for the default indicator) could be obtained by a simulation, an alternative LP formulation could be obtained. In such a scenario setting, it is advisable that for both Monte Carlo simulations, the same number $N$ of scenarios is chosen. Then for both given marginal distributions we have $\mathbf{p}_j^{(\delta)} = \mathbf{p}_i^{(X)} = 1/N$. If we apply the same arguments as above we obtain again a transportation problem, however, with probabilites $1/N$ each. If we have a closer look at this problem, we see that the optimization actually runs over all $N \times N$ permutation matrices—since each default scenario is mapped onto exactly one exposure scenario. This means that this problem eventually belongs to the class of assignment problems, for which very efficient algorithms are available, cf. Bazaraa et al. [1]. Nevertheless, please note that although assignment problems can be solved more efficiently than transportation problems, it is still advisable to solve the transportation problem due to its lower dimensionality, as usually $2K + 1 \ll N$ (i.e. time discretization is usually much coarser than exposure discretization). However, if stochastic credit spreads have to be considered, they have to be part of the default simulation and thus assignment problems (with additional linear constraints to guarantee consistency of exposure paths and spreads) become unavoidable.

## 6 Example

### 6.1 Setup

To illustrate these semi-model-free CVA bounds let us give a brief example. For this purpose let us consider a standard payer swap with a remaining lifetime of $T = 4$ years analyzed within a Cox–Ingersoll–Ross (CIR) model at time $t = 0$. The time interval $]0, 4[$ is split up into $K = 8$ disjoint time intervals each covering half a year. For simplicity, the loss process is again assumed to be 1.

#### 6.1.1 Counterparty's Default Modeling

To model the defaults we have chosen the well-known copula approach with constant intensities using the Gaussian copula. For further analyses in this example we will focus on the case of uncorrelated counterparties ($\rho = 0$) and highly correlated counterparties ($\rho = 0.9$). Furthermore, the counterpartys' default intensities are assumed to be deterministic. We will distinguish between symmetric counterparties with identical default intensities and asymmetric counterparties. Thus, four different settings

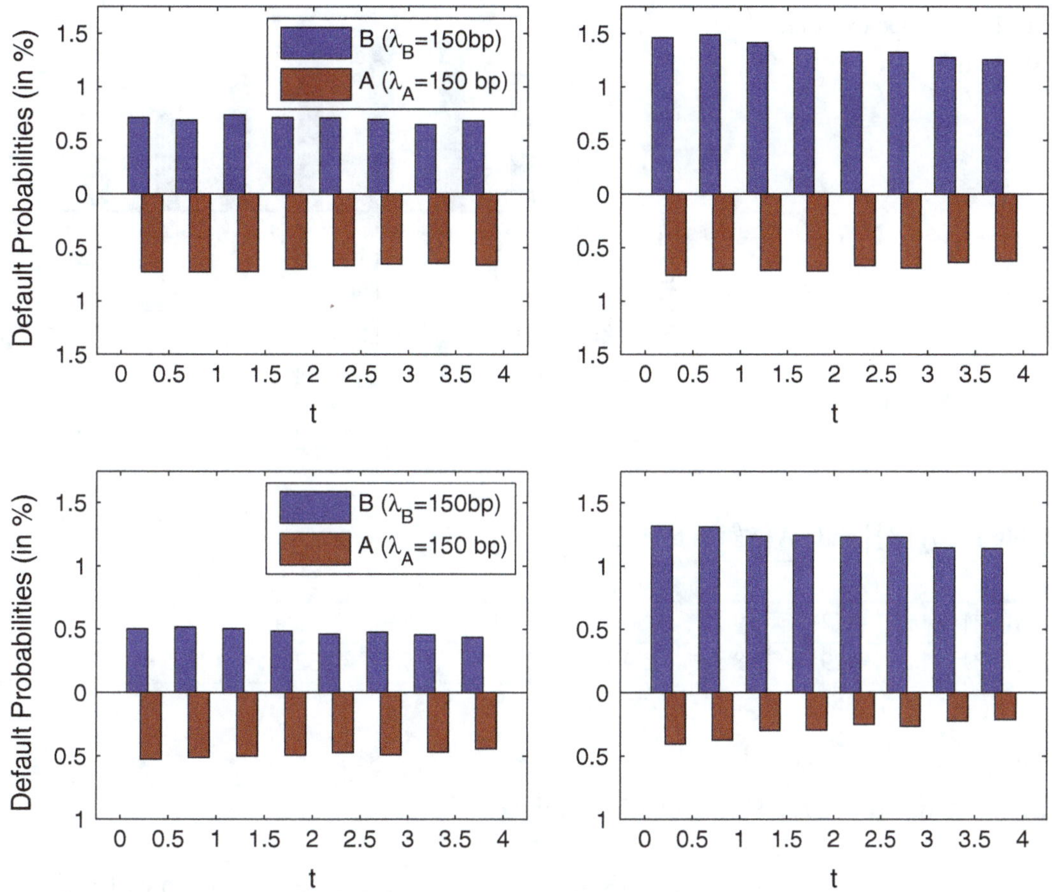


**Fig. 1** Probabilities $\mathbb{E}_{\mathbf{Q}}[\,\delta_k^i]$ in % for Case 1 to Case 4

result: Fig. 1 shows the probabilities $\mathbf{Q}[\,\delta_k^i = 1] = \mathbb{E}_{\mathbf{Q}}[\,\delta_k^i]$ in each of the four cases under the risk-neutral measure $\mathbf{Q}$ implied from the market. To be in line with the following figures, the probabilities for a default of counterparty $B$ in $\Delta_k$, i.e. $\mathbb{E}_{\mathbf{Q}}[\,\delta_k^B]$, correspond to the positive bars and defaults of counterparty $A$ to the negative bars. The left plots show identical counterparties (cases 1 and 2) and the right ones the cases, where counterparty $B$ has a higher default intensity (cases 3 and 4). Furthermore, the upper plots correspond to uncorrelated defaults and for the ones below we have $\rho = 0.9$.

| | | | |
|---|---|---|---|
| Case 1: symmetric, uncorrelated | $\lambda_A = 150$ bps | $\lambda_B = 150$ bps | $\rho = 0$ |
| Case 2: symmetric, correlated | $\lambda_A = 150$ bps | $\lambda_B = 150$ bps | $\rho = 0.9$ |
| Case 3: asymmetric, uncorrelated | $\lambda_A = 150$ bps | $\lambda_B = 300$ bps | $\rho = 0$ |
| Case 4: asymmetric, correlated | $\lambda_A = 150$ bps | $\lambda_B = 300$ bps | $\rho = 0.9$ |

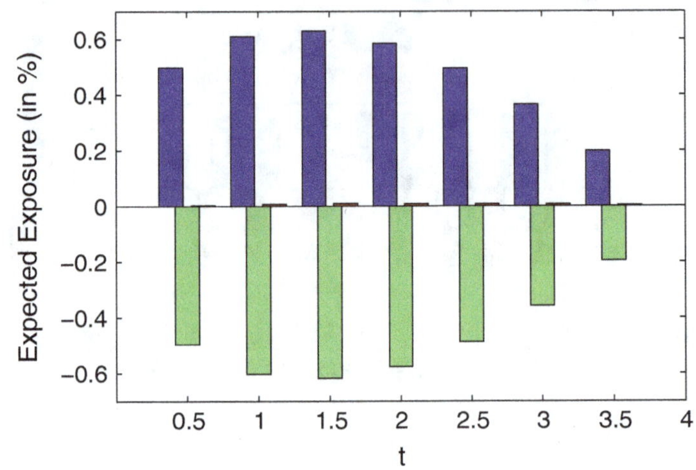


**Fig. 2** Expected exposures $\mathbb{E}_{\mathbf{Q}}\left[X_k^A\right]$, $\mathbb{E}_{\mathbf{Q}}\left[X_k^B\right]$ and $\mathbb{E}_{\mathbf{Q}}[\tilde{V}_A(t_k, T)]$

**Table 1** $\mathbb{E}_{\mathbf{Q}}\left[X_k^A\right]$ and $\mathbb{E}_{\mathbf{Q}}\left[X_k^B\right]$ in basis points

| $k$ | 1 | 2 | 3 | 4 | 5 | 6 | 7 | 8 |
|---|---|---|---|---|---|---|---|---|
| $\mathbb{E}_{\mathbf{Q}}[X_k^A]$ in bp | 49.2 | 59.2 | 60.1 | 55.2 | 45.9 | 33.4 | 17.9 | 0 |
| $\mathbb{E}_{\mathbf{Q}}[X_k^B]$ in bp | 48.9 | 58.5 | 59.1 | 54.2 | 45.1 | 32.6 | 17.5 | 0 |

### 6.1.2 Counterparty Exposure Modeling

As already mentioned, a simple CIR model is applied for the valuation of the payer swap. Since our focus is on the coupling of the default and the exposure model, we have opted for such a simple model for ease of presentation. In the CIR model, the short rate $r_t$ follows the stochastic differential equation

$$dr_t = \kappa(\theta - r_t)dt + \sigma\sqrt{r_t}dW_t$$

where $(W_t)_{t\geq 0}$ denotes a standard Brownian motion. Instead of calibrating the parameters to market data (yield curve plus selected swaption prices) on one specific day, we have set the parameters in the following way

$$\kappa = 0.0156, \quad \theta = 0.0311, \quad \sigma = 0.0313, \quad r_0 = 0.030$$

to obtain an interest rate market which is typical for the last years. Considering now the discounted exposure of each counterparty within the discrete time framework of our example, we can easily compute $\mathbb{E}_{\mathbf{Q}}\left[X_k^i\right]$ as the average of all generated scenarios from a Monte Carlo simulation. Figure 2 illustrates the results of a simulation, which are also given in Table 1. Positive bars correspond to $\mathbb{E}_{\mathbf{Q}}\left[X_k^A\right]$, negative bars to $\mathbb{E}_{\mathbf{Q}}\left[X_k^B\right]$, and the small bars correspond to $\mathbb{E}_{\mathbf{Q}}[\tilde{V}_A(t_k, T)]$. Since payer and receiver swap are not completely symmetric instruments, there remains a residual expectation, as can be observed from Fig. 2.

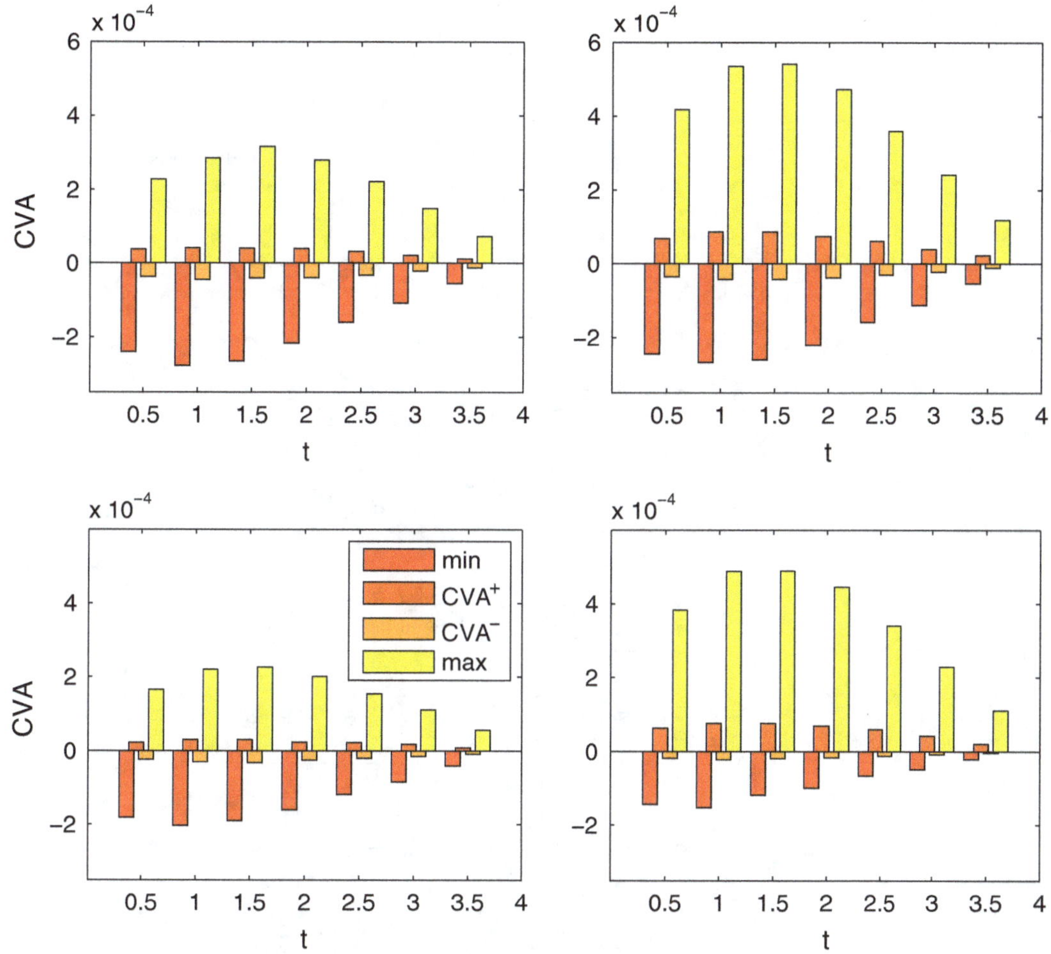


**Fig. 3** Minimal and maximal $CVA_A$, $\mathbb{E}_{\mathbf{Q}_i}\left[\delta_k^B \cdot X_k^A \mid \mathcal{G}_t\right]$ and $-\mathbb{E}_{\mathbf{Q}_i}\left[\delta_k^A \cdot X_k^B \mid \mathcal{G}_t\right]$ in bps

## 6.2 Results

In case of independence between default and exposure, the bilateral CVA is easily obtained by multiplying the default probabilities (as shown in Fig. 1) with the corresponding exposures (as shown in Fig. 2) and summation. Besides the independent $CVA^i$, the minimal and maximal $CVA^l$ and $CVA^u$ have been calculated as well.

The results of these calculations are illustrated in Fig. 3 and Table 2 for each time interval $\Delta_k$. Analogously to Fig. 1 we have for each of the four cases a separate subplot and the left plots belong again to cases 1 and 2. The positive bars now correspond to $\mathbb{E}_{\mathbf{Q}_i}\left[\delta_k^B \cdot X_k^A\right]$ and the negative ones to $\mathbb{E}_{\mathbf{Q}_i}\left[\delta_k^A \cdot X_k^B\right]$. In the case of the minimal *CVA*, $\mathbb{E}_{\mathbf{Q}_l}\left[\delta_k^B \cdot X_k^A\right]$ vanishes, meaning that for counterparty *A* in case of a default of counterparty *B* the exposure is zero, as the present value of the swap at that time is negative from counterparty *A*'s point of view. Contrarily, for the maximal *CVA*, $\mathbb{E}_{\mathbf{Q}_u}\left[\delta_k^A \cdot X_k^B\right]$ is zero. Here, $\mathbf{Q}_u$, $\mathbf{Q}_l$, and $\mathbf{Q}_i$ denote the optimal measures for the maximal, the minimal, and the independent CVA, respectively. As expected there

**Table 2** Minimal and maximal $CVA_A$, $\mathbb{E}_{\mathbf{Q}_i}\left[\delta_k^B \cdot X_k^A \mid \mathscr{G}_t\right]$ and $-\mathbb{E}_{\mathbf{Q}_i}\left[\delta_k^A \cdot X_k^B \mid \mathscr{G}_t\right]$ in bps

| | $k$ | 1 | 2 | 3 | 4 | 5 | 6 | 7 | 8 | $\sum$ |
|---|---|---|---|---|---|---|---|---|---|---|
| Case 1 | min | −2.41 | −2.78 | −2.67 | −2.16 | −1.61 | −1.08 | −0.55 | 0.00 | −13.26 |
| | $\mathbb{E}_{\mathbf{Q}_i}\left[\delta_k^B \cdot X_k^A \mid \mathscr{G}_t\right]$ | 0.37 | 0.41 | 0.41 | 0.40 | 0.32 | 0.22 | 0.12 | 0.00 | 2.24 |
| | $\mathbb{E}_{\mathbf{Q}_i}\left[\delta_k^A \cdot X_k^B \mid \mathscr{G}_t\right]$ | −0.37 | −0.45 | −0.40 | −0.39 | −0.32 | −0.21 | −0.12 | 0.00 | −2.27 |
| | max | 2.28 | 2.85 | 3.16 | 2.80 | 2.21 | 1.48 | 0.73 | 0.00 | 15.51 |
| Case 2 | min | −1.82 | −2.03 | −1.90 | −1.60 | −1.19 | −0.85 | −0.42 | 0.00 | −9.80 |
| | $\mathbb{E}_{\mathbf{Q}_i}\left[\delta_k^B \cdot X_k^A \mid \mathscr{G}_t\right]$ | 0.23 | 0.30 | 0.30 | 0.24 | 0.22 | 0.18 | 0.09 | 0.00 | 1.56 |
| | $\mathbb{E}_{\mathbf{Q}_i}\left[\delta_k^A \cdot X_k^B \mid \mathscr{G}_t\right]$ | −0.24 | −0.31 | −0.34 | −0.25 | −0.20 | −0.15 | −0.09 | 0.00 | −1.57 |
| | max | 1.66 | 2.21 | 2.26 | 2.01 | 1.54 | 1.10 | 0.56 | 0.00 | 11.34 |
| Case 3 | min | −2.45 | −2.68 | −2.60 | −2.21 | −1.58 | −1.13 | −0.54 | 0.00 | −13.19 |
| | $\mathbb{E}_{\mathbf{Q}_i}\left[\delta_k^B \cdot X_k^A \mid \mathscr{G}_t\right]$ | 0.68 | 0.86 | 0.86 | 0.74 | 0.61 | 0.39 | 0.23 | 0.00 | 4.38 |
| | $\mathbb{E}_{\mathbf{Q}_i}\left[\delta_k^A \cdot X_k^B \mid \mathscr{G}_t\right]$ | −0.35 | −0.43 | −0.42 | −0.37 | −0.30 | −0.22 | −0.11 | 0.00 | −2.21 |
| | max | 4.18 | 5.36 | 5.42 | 4.72 | 3.60 | 2.41 | 1.18 | 0.00 | 26.88 |
| Case 4 | min | −1.44 | −1.53 | −1.19 | −1 | −0.67 | −0.49 | −0.21 | 0.00 | −6.53 |
| | $\mathbb{E}_{\mathbf{Q}_i}\left[\delta_k^B \cdot X_k^A \mid \mathscr{G}_t\right]$ | 0.63 | 0.76 | 0.76 | 0.69 | 0.60 | 0.43 | 0.20 | 0.00 | 4.08 |
| | $\mathbb{E}_{\mathbf{Q}_i}\left[\delta_k^A \cdot X_k^B \mid \mathscr{G}_t\right]$ | −0.18 | −0.23 | −0.19 | −0.16 | −0.12 | −0.08 | −0.03 | 0.00 | −1.00 |
| | max | 3.83 | 4.88 | 4.89 | 4.46 | 3.40 | 2.29 | 1.11 | 0.00 | 24.87 |

**Table 3** Computation times for the two-dimensional transportation problem

| $K$ | 10 | 20 | 20 | 20 |
|---|---|---|---|---|
| $N$ | 1024 | 1024 | 2048 | 4096 |
| Time in seconds | 0.2 | 0.5 | 1.5 | 6 |

are large gaps between the lower and the independent CVA, as well as between the independent CVA and the upper bound. This means that wrong-way risk (i.e. higher exposure comes with higher default rates) can have a significant impact on the bilateral CVA. Interestingly, this observation holds true for all four cases, of course, with different significance depending on the specific setup. Although it is clear that our analysis naturally shows more extreme gaps than any hybrid model, it has to be mentioned that these bounds are indeed tight.

## *6.3 Computation Time, Choice of Algorithm, and Impact of Assumptions*

Theoretically, the computation of the bounds boils down to the solution of a linear programming problem. From this it can be expected that state-of-the-art solvers like CPLEX or Gurobi will yield the optimal solution within reasonable computation time. Using CPLEX, we have obtained the following computation times on a standard workstation (Table 3).

It can be observed that the problem can be solved for reasonable discretization levels within decent time. Rather similar computation times have been obtained with an individual implementation of the standard network simplex based on Fibonacci heaps. However, for larger sizes, the performance of standard solvers begins to deteriorate. To dampen the explosion of computation time, we have resorted to a special purpose solver for min cost network flows (which are a general case of the transportation problem) for highly asymmetric problems, as in our case $2K + 1 \ll N$. Based on Brenner's min cost flow algorithm, see Brenner [3], we could still solve problems with $K = 40$ and $N = 8192$ beneath a minute.

If one has to resort to the assignment formulation (to consider credit spreads accordingly), computation times increase due to the fact that now assignment problems have to be solved. Here, a factor 100 compared to the above computation times cannot be avoided.

If the coupling of the two default times is left flexible, the problem becomes a transportation problem with three margins, i.e. of size $K + 1 \times K + 1 \times N$. For these types of problems, no special purpose solver is available and one has to resort to CPLEX. Scherer and Schultz [18] have exploited the structure of this three-dimensional transportation problem to reduce computational complexity. They were able to reduce the problem to a standard two-dimensional transportation problem, hence rendering the computation of bounds similarly easy, no matter if default times are already coupled or not.

## 7 Conclusion and Outlook

In this paper we have shown how tight bounds on unilateral and bilateral counterparty valuation adjustment can be derived by a linear programming approach. This approach has the advantage that simulations of the uncertain loss, of the default times and of the uncertain value of a transaction during her remaining life can be completely separated. Although we have restricted the exposition to the case of two counterparties and one derivative transaction, the model can easily be extended to more counterparties and a whole netting node of trades. Further, as exposure is simulated separately from default, all risk-mitigating components like CSAs, rating triggers, and netting agreements can be easily included in a such a framework.

Interesting open questions for future research include the analogous treatment in continuous time, which requires much more technically involved arguments. Further, this approach yields a new motivation to consider efficient algorithms for transportation or assignment problems with more than two marginals, which did not yet get much attention so far.

**Acknowledgements** The KPMG Center of Excellence in Risk Management is acknowledged for organizing the conference "Challenges in Derivatives Markets - Fixed Income Modeling, Valuation Adjustments, Risk Management, and Regulation".

**Open Access** This chapter is distributed under the terms of the Creative Commons Attribution 4.0 International License (http://creativecommons.org/licenses/by/4.0/), which permits use, duplication, adaptation, distribution and reproduction in any medium or format, as long as you give appropriate credit to the original author(s) and the source, a link is provided to the Creative Commons license and any changes made are indicated.

The images or other third party material in this chapter are included in the work's Creative Commons license, unless indicated otherwise in the credit line; if such material is not included in the work's Creative Commons license and the respective action is not permitted by statutory regulation, users will need to obtain permission from the license holder to duplicate, adapt or reproduce the material.

## References

1. Bazaraa, M.S., Jarvis, J.J., Sherali, H.D.: Linear Programming and Network Flows, 4th edn. Wiley, New Jersey (2010)
2. Bielecki, T.R., Rutkowski, M.: Credit Risk: Modeling, Valuation and Hedging. Springer, Berlin (2002)
3. Brenner, U.: A faster polynomial algorithm for the unbalanced hitchcock transportation problem. Oper. Res. Lett. **36**(4), 408–413 (2008)
4. Brigo, D., Capponi, A.: Bilateral counterparty risk valuation with stochastic dynamical models and application to credit default swaps. Working paper (2009)
5. Brigo, D., Chourdakis, K.: Counterparty risk for credit default swaps: impact of spread volatility and default correlation. Int. J. Theor. Appl. Financ. **12**(7), 1007–1026 (2009)
6. Brigo, D., Pallavicini, A., Papatheodorou, V.: Arbitrage-free valuation of bilateral counterparty risk for interest-rate products: impact of volatilities and correlations. Int. J. Theor. Appl. Financ. **14**(6), 773–802 (2011)

7. Brigo, D., Morini, M., Pallavicini, A.: Counterparty Credit Risk, Collateral and Funding: With Pricing Cases for all Asset Classes. Wiley, New Jersey (2013)
8. Cespedes, J.C.G., Herrero, J.A., Rosen, D., Saunders, D.: Effective modeling of wrong way risk, counterparty credit risk capital and alpha in Basel II. J. Risk Model Valid. **4**(1), 71–98 (2010)
9. Cherubini, U.: Pricing swap credit risk with copulas. EFMA, 2004 Basel Meeting Paper (2004)
10. Glasserman, P., Yang, L.: Bounding wrong-way risk in CVA calculation. Columbia Business School Research Paper No. 15-59. Available at SSRN: http://ssrn.com/abstract=2607649 (2015)
11. Gregory, J.K.: Being two faced over counterparty risk. Risk **22**(2), 86–90 (2009)
12. Gregory, J.K.: Counterparty Credit Risk: The New Challenge for Global Financial Markets. Wiley, New Jersey (2009)
13. Gregory, J.K.: Gaining from your own default—counterparty credit risk and DVA. Working paper (2009)
14. Haase, J., Werner, R.: A generalized stopping problem with application in counterparty risk modelling. In: Piunovsky, A.B. (ed.) Modern Trends in Controlled Stochastic Processes: Theory and Applications, pp. 196–215. Luniver, UK (2010)
15. Hull, J., White, A.: CVA and wrong-way risk. Financ. Anal. J. **68**(5) (2012)
16. Pykhtin, M.: Counterparty Credit Risk Modelling: Risk Management Pricing and Regulation. Risk Books, London (2005)
17. Rosen, D., Saunders, D.: Computing and stress testing counterparty credit risk capital. In: Canabarro, E. (ed.) Counterparty Credit Risk, pp. 245–292. Risk Books, London (2009)
18. Scherer, M., Schulz, T.: Extremal dependence for bilateral credit valuation adjustments. Working paper (2015)
19. Sorensen, E., Bollier, T.: Pricing swap default risk. Financ. Anal. J. **50**(3), 23–33 (1994)
20. Stein, H., Lee, K.P.: Counterparty valuation adjustments. In: Bielecki, T., Brigo, D., Patras, F. (eds.) The Handbook of Credit Derivatives. Wiley, New Jersey (2011)
21. Turnbull, S.M.: The pricing implications of counterparty risk for non-linear credit products. In: Pykhtin, M. (ed.) Counterparty Credit Risk Modeling. Risk Books, London (2005)

# CVA with Wrong-Way Risk in the Presence of Early Exercise

**Roberto Baviera, Gaetano La Bua and Paolo Pellicioli**

**Abstract** Hull–White approach of CVA with embedded WWR (Hull and White, Financ. Anal. J. 68:58-69, 2012, [11]) can be easily applied also to portfolios of derivatives with early termination features. The tree-based approach described in Baviera et al. (Int. J. Financ. Eng. 2015, [1]) allows to deal with American or Bermudan options in a straightforward way. Extensive numerical results highlight the non-trivial impact of early exercise on CVA.

**Keywords** American and Bermudan options · Wrong-way risk · Credit value adjustment

## 1 Introduction

As a direct consequence of the 2008 financial turmoil, counterparty credit risk has become substantial in OTC derivatives transactions. In particular, the credit value adjustment (CVA) is meant to measure the impact of counterparty riskiness on a derivative portfolio value as requested by the current Basel III regulatory framework. Accounting standards (IFRS 13, FAS 157), moreover, require a CVA[1] adjustment as part of a consistent fair value measurement of financial instruments.

CVA is strongly affected by derivative transaction arrangements: exposure depends on collateral and netting agreement between the two counterparties that have written

[1] Even if in this paper we focus on CVA pricing, it is worthwhile to note that accounting standards ask also for a debt value adjustment (DVA) to take into account the own credit risk.

R. Baviera (✉) · G. La Bua
Department of Mathematics, Politecnico di Milano, 32 Piazza Leonardo da Vinci, 20133 Milano, Italy
e-mail: roberto.baviera@polimi.it

G. La Bua
e-mail: gaetano.labua@polimi.it

P. Pellicioli
Intesa Sanpaolo Vita S.p.A., 55/57 Viale Stelvio, 20159 Milano, Italy
e-mail: paolo.pellicioli.guest@intesasanpaolovita.it

© The Author(s) 2016



K. Glau et al. (eds.), *Innovations in Derivatives Markets*, Springer Proceedings in Mathematics & Statistics 165, DOI 10.1007/978-3-319-33446-2_5

the derivative contracts of interest. Despite the increased use of collateral, however, a significant portion of OTC derivatives remains uncollateralized. This is mainly due to the nature of the counterparties involved, such as corporates and sovereigns, without the liquidity and operational capacity to adhere to daily collateral calls. In such cases, an institution must consider the impact of counterparty risk on the overall portfolio value and a correct CVA quantification acquires even more importance. Extensive literature has been produced on the topic in recent years, as for example [5] and [9] that give a comprehensive overview of CVA computation and the more general topic of counterparty credit risk management. It seems, however, that attention has been mainly paid to CVA with respect to portfolios of European-style derivatives. Dealing with derivatives with early exercise features is even more delicate. Indeed, as pointed out in [3], for American- and Bermudan-style derivatives CVA computation becomes path-dependent since we need to take into account the exercise strategy and the fact that exposure falls to zero after the exercise.

A peculiar problem that we encounter in CVA computation is the presence of the so-called wrong-way risk (WWR), that is the non-negligible dependency between the value of a derivatives portfolio and counterparty default probability. In particular we face WWR if a deterioration in counterparty creditworthiness is more likely when portfolio exposure increases. Several attempts have been made to deal with WWR. From a regulatory point of view, the Basel III Committee currently requires to correct by a multiplicative factor $\alpha = 1.4$ the CVA computed under hypothesis of market-credit independence. In this way the impact of WWR is considered equivalent to a 40 % increase in standard CVA. However, the Committee leaves room for financial institutions with approved models to apply for lower multipliers (floored at 1.2). This opportunity opens the way for more sophisticated models in order to reach a more efficient risk capital allocation.

Relevant contributions on alternative approaches to manage WWR include copula-based modeling as in [6], introduction of jumps at default as in [13], the backward stochastic differential equations framework developed in [7], and the stochastic hazard rate approach in [11]. In particular [11] introduces the idea to link the counterparty hazard rate to the portfolio value by means of an arbitrary monotone function. The dependence structure is, then, described uniquely by one parameter that controls the impact of exposures on the hazard rate. Additionally, a deterministic time-dependent function is introduced to match the counterparty credit term structure observed on the market. In this framework CVA pricing in the presence of WWR involves just a small adjustment to the pricing machinery already in place in financial institutions. We only need to take into account the randomness incorporated into the counterparty default probabilities by means of the stochastic hazard rate and price CVA with standard techniques. This is probably the most relevant property of the model: as soon as we associate a WWR parameter to a given counterparty–portfolio combination, we are able to deal with WWR using the same pricing engine underlying standard CVA computation. As pointed out in [14], leveraging as much as possible on existing platforms should be one of the principles an optimal risk model should be shaped on. However, the original approach in [11] relies on a Monte Carlo-based technique to determine the auxiliary deterministic function in order to calibrate the model on the counterparty credit structure. Obtaining this auxiliary function is the trickiest part in the calibration procedure, because it involves a "delicate" path-dependent problem that is difficult to implement for realistic portfolios. In [1], it is shown how it is possible to overcome such a limitation by transforming the path-dependent problem into a recursive one with a considerable reduction in the overall computational complexity. The basic idea is to consider discrete market factor dynamics and induce a change of probability such that the new set of (transition) probabilities are computed recursively in time. We presented a straightforward implementation of our approach via tree methods. Trees are also a straightforward and well understood tool to manage the early termination in derivatives pricing. So combining tree-based dynamic programing and the recursive algorithm in [1] leads to a simple and effective procedure to price CVA with WWR when American or Bermudan features are considered. The paper is organized as follows: in Sect. 2 we review the Hull–White model for CVA in the presence of WWR and the recursive approach in [1]. In Sect. 3 we analyze the effects of early termination on CVA adjustments via numerical tests and in Sect. 4 we study the relevant case of a long position on a Bermudan swaption. Finally Sect. 5 reports some final remarks.

## 2 CVA Pricing and WWR

For a given derivatives portfolio we can define the unilateral CVA[2] as the risk-neutral expectation of the discounted loss that can be suffered over a given period of time

$$CVA = (1 - R) \int_{t_0}^{T} B(t_0, t)\; EE(t)\; PD(dt), \tag{1}$$

where usually $t_0$ is the value date (hereinafter we set $t_0 = 0$ if not stated otherwise) and $T$ is the longest maturity date in the portfolio. Here $R$ is the recovery rate, $PD(dt)$ is the probability density of counterparty default between $t$ and $t + dt$ (with no default before $t$), and $B(t_0, t)EE(t)$ is the discounted expected exposure in $t$. If interest rates are stochastic, the expected exposure is defined

$$B(t_0, t)\; EE(t) \equiv \mathbb{E}[D(t_0, t)\; E(t)],$$

with $\mathbb{E}[\cdot]$ the expectation operator given the information at value date $t_0$, $D(t_0, t)$ the stochastic discount, and $E(t)$ the (stochastic) exposure at time $t$. The latter is inherently defined by the collateral agreement that the parties have in place: for example in uncollateralized transactions, $E(t)$ is simply the max w.r.t. zero of $v(t)$, the portfolio value at time $t$. For practical computation, the integral in (1) is approximated

[2]The party that carries out the valuation is thus considered default-free. Even if it is a restrictive assumption, unilateral CVA is the only relevant quantity for regulatory and accounting purposes. For a detailed discussion on other forms of CVA, see e.g. [9].

by choosing a discretized set of times $\mathscr{T} = \{t_i\}_{i=0,\dots,n}$ with $t_n = T$. In particular, the Basel III standard approach for CVA valuation is

$$CVA = (1 - R) \sum_{i=1}^{n} \frac{B_i \, EE_i + B_{i-1} \, EE_{i-1}}{2} PD_i, \tag{2}$$

with $B_i$ that stands for[3] $B(t_0, t_i)$ and

$$PD_i \equiv SP_{i-1} - SP_i,$$

where $SP_i$ is the counterparty survival probability up to $t_i$. Assuming that the default is modeled by means of a generic intensity-based model, we can link survival probabilities to the so-called hazard rate function $h(t)$, (see e.g. [15]):

$$SP_i = \exp\left( - \int_{t_0}^{t_i} h(t) \, dt \right).$$

A common assumption is to consider $h(t)$ constant between two consecutive dates in the set $\mathscr{T}$. Pricing CVA with (2) holds if there is no "market-credit" dependency. However, in case of wrong-way risk (WWR) a new, more sophisticated, model is needed because exposure and counterparty default probabilities are no more independent: exposure is conditional to default and a positive "market-credit" dependence originates the WWR. Recently Hull and White [11] have proposed an approach to WWR that is financially intuitive: the conditional hazard rate is modeled as a stochastic quantity related to the portfolio value $v(t)$ through a monotonic increasing function. In the following we focus on the specific functional form

$$\tilde{h}(t) = \exp\Big( a(t) + b \, v(t) \Big), \tag{3}$$

where $b \in \Re^+$ is the WWR parameter. However, results still hold for an arbitrary order-preserving function. The function $a(t)$ is a deterministic function of time, chosen in such a way that on each date

$$SP_i = \mathbb{E}\left[ \exp\left( - \int_{t_0}^{t_i} \tilde{h}(t) \, dt \right) \right] \qquad \forall i = 1, \dots, n. \tag{4}$$

Combining (3) and (4) we clearly see that function $a(t)$ depends also on the value specified for the parameter $b$.

The main advantage of this model is that once we know $b$ and $a(t)$, WWR can be implemented easily by means of a simple generalization of (2):

---

[3]From now on we use the notation $x_i$ to represent a discrete-time variable while $x(t)$ indicates its analogous variable in continuous-time. For avoidance of doubt, any other form of dependency $(\cdot)$ does not refer to the temporal one, unless stated otherwise.

$$CVA_W = (1-R)\sum_{i=1}^{n} \mathbb{E}\left[\frac{D_i\, E_i + D_{i-1}\, E_{i-1}}{2}\, \widetilde{PD}_i\right], \tag{5}$$

where $\widetilde{PD}_i$ is the stochastic probability to default between $t_{i-1}$ and $t_i$ defined in terms of $\tilde{h}_i$. We want to stress that expectation in (5) can be computed via any feasible numerical method: this fact implies that, given $b$ and $a(t)$, taking into account WWR just requires a slight modification in the payoff of existing algorithms used for the calculation of CVA.

We now briefly recall the recursive approach presented in [1] that avoids the path dependency in the determination of $a(t)$ so that Eq. (4) is satisfied. Hereinafter we refer to the technique to get such a function as either the calibration of $a(t)$ or the "calibration problem": once the three sets of parameters (the recovery $R$, the default probabilities $PD$s, and the WWR parameter $b$) for dealer's clients are estimated (e.g. with statistical methods) it is the most complicated issue in the calibration of Hull–White model.

Let us assume that the market risk factors underlying the portfolio are discrete and we indicate with $j_i$ the discrete state variable that describes the market at time $t_i$. In this framework market dynamics is described by a Markov chain with

$$q_i(j_{i-1}, j_i) \quad \forall i = 1, \ldots, n$$

the transition probability between $j_{i-1}$ at time $t_{i-1}$ and $j_i$ at time $t_i$. Typical examples where such a discrete approach is natural are lattice models. In particular, in [1], we applied tree methods to the pricing of CVA for linear derivatives portfolios.

Embedding the Hull–White model (3) in our setting, the stochastic survival probability between $t_{i-1}$ and $t_i$ becomes

$$\tilde{P}_i(j) \equiv \exp\left(-(t_i - t_{i-1})\, \tilde{h}_i(j)\right) \equiv P_i\, \eta_i(j) \qquad \forall i = 1, \ldots, n, \tag{6}$$

where

$$P_i \equiv \frac{SP_i}{SP_{i-1}}$$

is the forward survival probability between $t_{i-1}$ and $t_i$ valued in $t_0$. For notational convenience, we also set $\tilde{P}_0(j_0) = \eta_0(j_0) = 1$. The $\eta$ process introduced in (6) can be seen as the driver of the stochasticity in survival probabilities and it plays a key role in circumventing path-dependency in the calibration of $a(t)$, as shown in the following proposition.

**Proposition**

In the model with discrete market risk factors, the calibration problem (4) becomes

$$\sum_{j_i} p_i(j_i)\, \eta_i(j_i) = 1 \qquad \forall i = 1, \ldots, n, \tag{7}$$

where $p_i(j_i)$ are probabilities and they can be obtained via the recursive equation

$$p_i(j_i) = \sum_{j_{i-1}} q_i(j_{i-1}, j_i)\ \eta_{i-1}(j_{i-1})\ p_{i-1}(j_{i-1}) \qquad \forall i = 1, \ldots, n, \tag{8}$$

with the initial condition $p_0(j_0 = 0) = 1$.

*Proof* See [1].

Thus the calibration problem (4) can be solved at each discrete date $t_i$ via (7) by simply exploiting the fact that the process $\eta$, non-path-dependent, is a martingale under the probability measure $p$. Equation (8), in addition, specifies an algorithm to build this new probability measure recursively. In this framework $\widetilde{PD}_i$ can be readily obtained from (6). Let us mention that, although this is just one of the viable approaches to solve (4), it turns out to be, as shown in the next section, a natural way to handle the additional complexity induced by early exercises within the Hull–White approach to WWR modeling.

## 3 The Impact of Early Exercise

As already anticipated in Sect. 1, CVA when early exercise is allowed gives rise to additional features. In this section we want to highlight the differences in CVA figures when both European and American options are considered, implementing the tree-based procedure described in the previous section. It is well known that backward induction and dynamic programing applied on (recombining) trees are, probably, the simplest and most intuitive tool to price derivatives with an early exercise as American options. For these options, indeed, Monte Carlo techniques turn out to be computationally intensive in case of CVA: the exercise date, after which the exposure falls to zero, depends on the path of the underlying asset and on the exercise strategy. In such a case we are asked to describe two random times: the optimal exercise time and the counterparty default time.

### *3.1 The Pricing Problem*

Since our goal is to study the effects of early exercise clauses on CVA, we focus on the case of a dealer that enters into a long position[4] on American-style derivatives with a defaultable counterparty. That is, the dealer is the holder of the option and she has the opportunity to choose the optimal exercise strategy in order to maximize the option value. In particular, following [3], we would need to differentiate between two possible assumptions depending on the effects of counterparty defaultability on

[4]A short option position does not produce any potential CVA exposure.

the exercise strategy. The option holder would or would not take into account the possibility of counterparty default when she chooses whether to exercise or not. In the former case, the continuation value (the value of holding the option until the next exercise date) should be adjusted for the possibility of default. However, following the actual practice in CVA computation, we assume that counterparty defaultability plays no role in defining the exercise strategy of the dealer. This means that the pricing problem (before any CVA consideration) is the classical one for American options in a default-free world.

Let us assume to have a tree for the evolution of market risk factors[5] up to time $T$. Hereinafter, without loss of generality, we can set a constant time step $\Delta t$ and denote the time partition on the tree by means of an index $i$ in $\mathscr{T} = \{t_i\}_{i=0,\dots,n}$ with $t_i = i\,\Delta t$. We further introduce an arbitrary set of $m$ exercise dates $\mathscr{E} = \{e_k\}_{k=1,\dots,m}$ with $\mathscr{E} \subseteq \mathscr{T}$ at which the holder can exercise her rights receiving a payoff $\phi_k$ that could depend on the specific exercise date $e_k$. In this setting we can deal indistinctly with European ($m = 1$), Bermudan ($m \in \mathbb{N}$), and American options ($m \to \infty$). The standard dynamic programing approach then allows us to compute the derivative value at each node of the tree:

$$v_i(j_i) = \begin{cases} \phi_m(j_i) & \text{for } i \text{ s.t. } t_i = e_m = T, \\ \max(c_i(j_i),\ \phi_k(j_i)) & \text{for } i \text{ s.t. } t_i \in \mathscr{E} \setminus \{e_m\}, \\ c_i(j_i) & \text{otherwise.} \end{cases} \tag{9}$$

with $c_i$ the continuation value of the derivative defined as

$$c_i(j_i) = B(i, i+1; j_i) \sum_{j_{i+1}} q_i(j_i, j_{i+1})\, v_{i+1}(j_{i+1}), \tag{10}$$

where the sum must be considered over all possible $t_{i+1}$-nodes connected to $j_i$ at time $t_i$ and $B(i, i+1; j_i)$ is the future discount factor that applies from $t_i$ and $t_{i+1}$ possibly depending on the state variable $j_i$ on the tree.

We describe in detail the simple 1-dimensional tree; however, extensions to the 2-factor case (as, for example, the G2++ model in [4] or the recent dual curve approach in [12]) are straightforward. Once the derivative value is computed for all nodes and the WWR parameter $b$ is specified,[6] we can calibrate the auxiliary function $a(t)$ in (3) by means of the recursive approach in [1]. The advantages of such an approach are, in this case, twofold: we avoid path-dependency in the calibration of $a(t)$, as in any other possible application, and we deal with early exercises via (9) and (10) in a very intuitive way.

[5] If we describe the dynamics of the price of a corporate stock, we assume—for the sake of simplicity—that such entity is not subject to default risk.

[6] We refer the interested reader to the original paper [11] for a heuristic approach to determine the parameter and to [14] for comprehensive numerical tests with market data.

## 3.2 The Plain Vanilla Case

We now want to assess the impact of early termination on CVA in order to understand the potential differences that could arise between European and American options from a counterparty credit risk management perspective.

In the first test we study the plain vanilla option case: we assume that the dealer buys a call option from a defaultable counterparty. Counterparty default probabilities are described in terms of a CDS flat curve at 125 basis points as in [11]. More precisely, with a flat CDS curve we can approximate quite well the survival probability between $t_0$ and $t_i$ as

$$SP_i = \exp\left(-\frac{s_i\, t_i}{1-R}\right),$$

where $s_i$ is the credit spread relative to maturity $t_i$ and $R$ the recovery rate, equal to 40 %. We further assume that trades are fully uncollateralized.[7] The underlying asset is lognormally distributed and represented by means of a Cox-Ross-Rubinstein binomial tree. We can thus apply the dynamic programing approach described above to price options on the tree and calibrate the function $a(t)$ recursively via (7). This procedure turns out to be quite fast: the Matlab coded algorithm takes less than 0.1 second to run on a 3.06 GHz desktop PC with 4 GB RAM when $n = m = 500$. Figure 1 shows CVA profile[8] for both European and American call options as function of WWR parameter $b$ and for different levels of cost of carry. From standard non-arbitrage arguments, we indeed know that the optimality of early exercise for plain vanilla call options is related to the cost of carry (defined as the net cost of holding positions in the underlying asset).[9]

As shown in Fig. 1, CVA profiles are significantly different for European and American options when early exercise can represent the optimal strategy (black and dark gray lines). In particular the impact of WWR is significantly less pronounced for American options compared to the corresponding European ones. On the other hand, when early exercise is no more optimal, the two options are equivalent: light gray lines in Fig. 1 are undistinguishable from each other. In addition, the upward shift in CVA exposures is due to the fact that an increase in cost of carry (e.g. a reduction in the dividend yield) is reflected entirely in an augmented drift of the underlying asset dynamics that makes, *ceteris paribus*, the call option more valuable.

The effect of early exercise on exposure profiles is depicted in Fig. 2 where a possible underlying asset path is displayed along with the optimal exercise boundary

---

[7] Here we are interested in analysing the full exposure profile as function of early exercise opportunities. On the other hand, more realistic collateralization schemes can be taken into account in a straightforward manner within the described framework.

[8] Once $b$ and $a(t)$ are determined we can use whatever numerical technique to compute (5). Here we simply implement a simulation-based scheme that uses the tree as discretization grid. The number of generated paths is $10^5$.

[9] The classical example is an option written on a dividend paying stock. This frame includes also a call option on a commodity whose forward curve is in backwardation or on a currency pair for which the interest rate of the base currency is higher than the one of the reference currency.

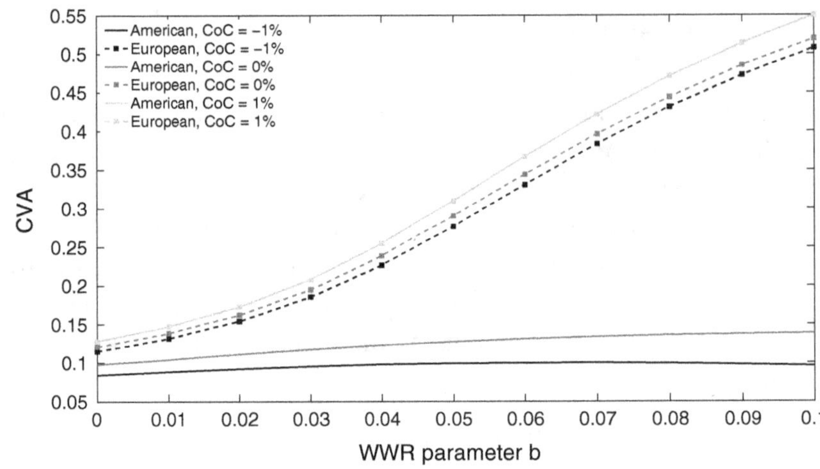


**Fig. 1** CVA profiles for European and American options as function of WWR parameter $b$ for several levels of cost of carry (CoC). Parameters are $S_0 = 100$, $K = 100$, $\sigma = 25\,\%$, $r = 1\,\%$, $T = 1$, $n = m = 500$. Counterparty CDS *curve flat* at 125 basis points

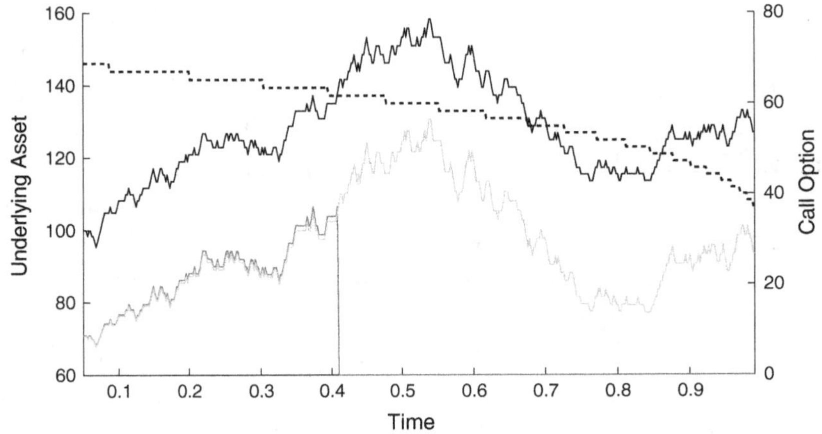


**Fig. 2** The effect of early exercise on exposures. Parameters are $S_0 = 100$, $K = 100$, $\sigma = 25\,\%$, $r = 1\,\%$, CoC $= -2\,\%$, $T = 1$, $n = m = 500$. *Left hand scale* Asset path (*black solid line*) and optimal exercise boundary (*dashed line*). *Right hand scale* European option (*light gray line*) and American option (*dark gray line*)

(reconstructed on the binomial tree) and the corresponding value of European and American options. Until the asset value remains within the continuation region (the area below the dashed line), the two options have a similar value with the only difference given by the early exercise premium embedded in the American style derivative. However, if the asset value reaches or crosses the exercise boundary, the exposure due to the American option falls to zero while the European option remains alive until maturity. From the definition of CVA (1), we can see that early exercise, if optimal, reduces the exposure of the holder to the counterparty default by shortening the life of the option. The effect is even more pronounced when we introduce the WWR: early redemption, indeed, would occur as soon as the portfolio value is large enough with the consequence to eliminate the exposure just when counterparty

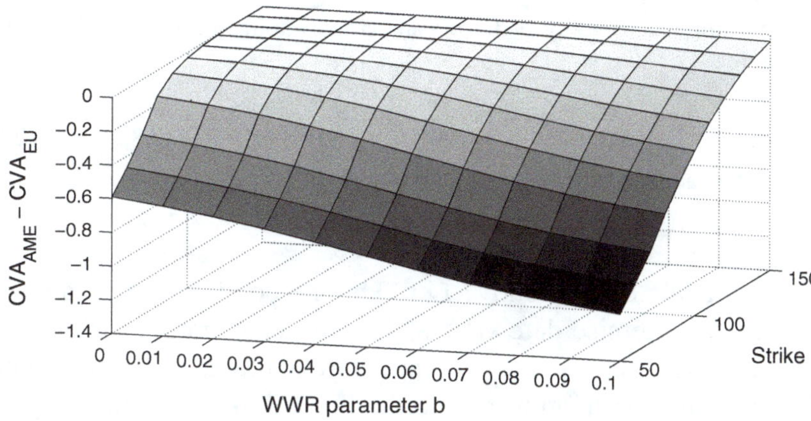


**Fig. 3** Difference in CVA between European and American options as function of WWR parameter $b$ and moneyness. Parameters are $S_0 = 100$, $\sigma = 25\,\%$, $r = 1\,\%$, $\text{CoC} = -2\,\%$, $T = 1$, $n = m = 500$. Counterparty CDS *curve flat* at 125 basis points

default probabilities become more relevant. It is possible, then, to identify in the early termination clause an important mechanism that limits CVA charges, particularly when market-credit dependency is non-negligible as shown in [8] in the case without WWR. Any change that makes early exercise more likely tends to enhance such a mechanism. We see this effect in Fig. 3 where we display the difference in CVA between European and American options as function of WWR parameter and option moneyness. With a given underlying asset dynamics, potential early exercise date is closer for more in the money options: the right of the holder is more likely to be exercised sooner. This shortens the life of the option and reduces both CVA charge (with respect to European options) and WWR sensitivity (with respect to the corresponding European option and the American options with lower moneyness). In this section we have shown that WWR can play a very different role for European and American options. In our opinion, however, WWR should be analyzed on a case-by-case basis in order to determine its magnitude and the adequate capital charge: a 40 % increase in standard CVA could overestimate the losses for an American option that can be optimally exercised in a short period while could be reductive in cases where early termination is less likely.

## 4 The Bermudan Swaption Case

Probably the most relevant case of long position on options with early exercise opportunities in the portfolios of financial institutions is represented by Bermudan swaptions. Such exotic derivatives are, indeed, used by corporate entities to enhance the financial structure related to the issue of callable bonds. Often, by selling a Bermudan receiver swaption to a dealer, the callable bond issuer can reduce its net borrowing cost. Usually the swaption is structured such that exercise dates match

**Table 1** Diagonal implied volatility of European ATM swaptions used to calibrate the 1-factor Hull–White model

| Swaption | 1y9y | 2y8y | 3y7y | 4y6y | 5y5y | 7y3y |
|---|---|---|---|---|---|---|
| Volatility % | 40.4 | 37.6 | 35.1 | 32.8 | 30.8 | 27.7 |

Calibrated parameters are $\hat{a} = 0.0146$ and $\hat{\sigma} = 0.0089$

the callability schedule of the bond.[10] Let $\hat{T}$ be the bond maturity date. The dealer has the right, at any exercise date $e_k \in \mathscr{E} \backslash \{e_m\}$, to enter into an interest rate swap with maturity $\hat{T}$, where she receives the fixed rate $K$ (equal to the fixed coupon rate of the bond) and pays the floating rate to the bond issuer with first payment made on date $e_{k+1}$. In our test we use the Euro interbank market data as of September 13, 2012 as given in [2]. We assume that the dealer buys a 10-year Bermudan receiver swaption where the underlying swap has, for simplicity, both fixed and floating legs with semiannual payments. The swaption can be exercised semiannually and its notional amount is Eur 100 million. We describe interest rates dynamics with a 1-factor Extended Vasicek model on a trinomial tree as in [10]. Model parameters are calibrated to market prices of European ATM swaptions with overall contract maturity equal to 10 years as shown in Table 1. As done in the previous section, we value the Bermudan swaption on the tree via dynamic programing and calibrate the WWR model function $a(t)$. Once again the combined approach on the tree allows to perform both tasks in a negligible amount of time. Figure 4 reports the WWR impact[11] for uncollateralized transactions struck at different levels of moneyness: at the money (swaption strike set equal to the market 10 years spot swap rate) and $\pm 50$ basis points. The upper graph reports the case with no initial lockout period while in the lower one we assume that the option cannot be exercised in the first 2 years. When the option can be exercised with no restrictions, we observe a moderate inverse relationship between moneyness and WWR impact due to the protection mechanism: the opportunity to early exercise when the exposure is large limits the effect of increased counterparty default probabilities. On the other hand, the introduction of a lockout period intensifies the WWR impact. Intuitively, by expanding the lockout period we move toward the limiting case of a European option. In this case the moneyness–WWR effect is reversed: the more in the money the option is, the more relevant the WWR effect becomes. During the lockout period the in-the-money option has a considerably higher exposure to counterparty default that cannot be mitigated via early termination.

[10] Often the bond can be called at any coupon payment date after an initial lockout period.

[11] We define it to be the ratio $CVA_W/CVA$ as given, respectively, by (5) and (2).

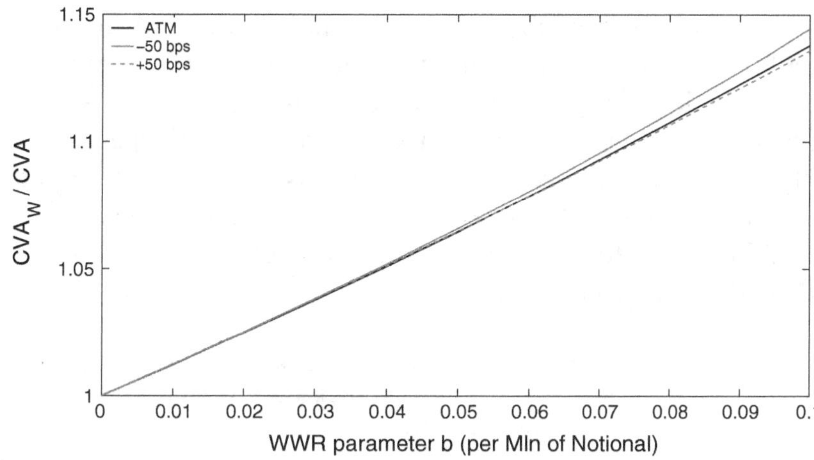


No lockout

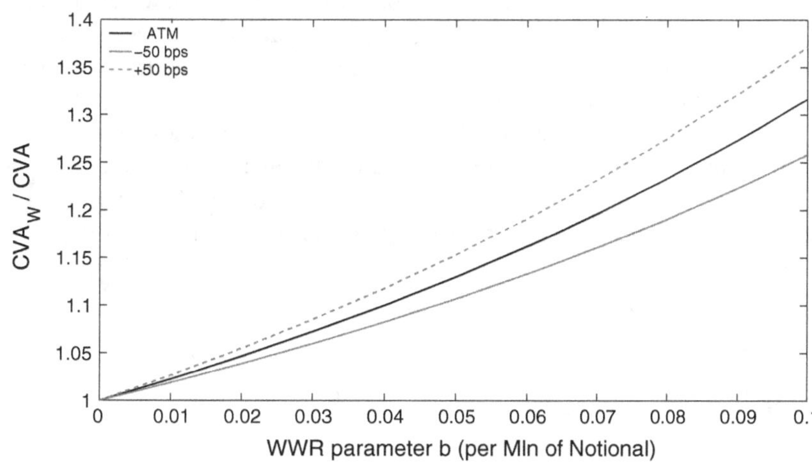


2-year lockout

**Fig. 4** Impact of WWR on Bermudan receiver swaptions as function of WWR parameter $b$ for several levels of moneyness. Market data as of September 13, 2012. Counterparty CDS *curve flat* at 125 basis points

# 5 Concluding Remarks

Nowadays WWR is a crucial concern in OTC derivatives transactions. This is particularly true for uncollateralized trades that a financial institution could have in place with medium-sized corporate clients. The presence of early termination clauses in vulnerable derivatives portfolios makes the CVA computation even more tricky. We have shown a simple and effective approach to deal with calibration and pricing of CVA within the Hull–White framework [11] for American or Bermudan options. We extended the procedure in [1] to the dynamic programing algorithm required to take into account the free boundary problem inherent in the pricing of such derivatives. Numerical tests carried out underline the importance of adequate procedures to differentiate CVA profiles for European and American options. The possibility of early exercise, indeed, plays a remarkable role in mitigating the WWR: an undifferentiated CVA pricing for contingent claims with different exercise styles would then lead to severe misspecification of regulatory capital charges.

An interesting topic for further research would consider the impact of counterparty defaultability in defining the dealer's optimal exercise strategy. Even if intuitive, this poses nontrivial problems mainly due to the interrelation among derivative pricing, WWR, and calibration of function $a(t)$. It is our opinion, however, that the described framework could be extended in this direction.

**Acknowledgements** The KPMG Center of Excellence in Risk Management is acknowledged for organizing the conference "Challenges in Derivatives Markets - Fixed Income Modeling, Valuation Adjustments, Risk Management, and Regulation".

**Open Access** This chapter is distributed under the terms of the Creative Commons Attribution 4.0 International License (http://creativecommons.org/licenses/by/4.0/), which permits use, duplication, adaptation, distribution and reproduction in any medium or format, as long as you give appropriate credit to the original author(s) and the source, a link is provided to the Creative Commons license and any changes made are indicated.

The images or other third party material in this chapter are included in the work's Creative Commons license, unless indicated otherwise in the credit line; if such material is not included in the work's Creative Commons license and the respective action is not permitted by statutory regulation, users will need to obtain permission from the license holder to duplicate, adapt or reproduce the material.

## References

1. Baviera, R., La Bua, G., Pellicioli, P.: A Note on CVA and WWR. Int. J. Financ. Eng. (to appear in 2016)
2. Baviera, R., Cassaro, A.: A note on dual-curve construction: Mr. Crab's Bootstrap. Appl. Math. Financ. **22**, 105–122 (2015)
3. Breton, M., Marzouk, O.: An efficient method to price counterparty risk. https://www.gerad.ca/en/papers/G-2014-29 (2014)
4. Brigo, D., Mercurio, F.: Interest Rate Models: Theory and Practice - With Smile Inflation and Credit. Springer, Heidelberg (2001)
5. Brigo, D., Morini, M., Pallavicini, M.: Counterparty Credit Risk Collateral and Funding: With Pricing Cases for All Asset Classes. Wiley, Chichester (2013)
6. Cespedes, J., Herrero, H., Rosen, D., Saunders, D.: Effective modelling of wrong way risk, counterparty credit risk capital, and alpha in Basel II. J. Risk Model Valid. **4**, 71–98 (2010)
7. Crépey, S., Song, S.: Counterparty risk and funding: immersion and beyond. LaMME preprint (2015)
8. Giada, L., Nordio, C.: Bilateral credit valuation adjustment of an optional early termination clause. http://ssrn.com/abstract=2055251 (2013)
9. Gregory, J.: Counterparty Credit Risk and Credit Value Adjustment: A Continuing Challenge for Global Financial Markets. Wiley, Hoboken (2012)
10. Hull, J., White, A.: Numerical procedures for implementing term structure models I: single-factor models. J Deriv. **2**, 7–16 (1994)
11. Hull, J., White, A.: CVA and wrong way risk. Financ. Analys. J. **68**, 58–69 (2012)
12. Hull, J., White, A.: Multi-curve modeling using trees. http://ssrn.com/abstract=2601457 (2015)

13. Li, M., Mercurio, F.: Jumping with default: wrong-way-risk modeling for credit valuation adjustment. http://ssrn.com/abstract=2605648 (2015)
14. Ruiz, I., Del Boca, P., Pachón, R.: Optimal right- and wrong-way risk from a practitioner standpoint. Financ. Anal. J. **71** (2015)
15. Schönbucher, P.J.: Credit Derivatives Pricing Models: Models Pricing and Implementation. Wiley, Chichester (2003)

# Simultaneous Hedging of Regulatory and Accounting CVA

**Christoph Berns**

**Abstract** As a consequence of the recent financial crisis, Basel III introduced a new capital charge, the CVA risk charge to cover the risk of future CVA fluctuations (CVA volatility). Although Basel III allows for hedging the CVA risk charge, mismatches between the regulatory (Basel III) and accounting (IFRS) rules lead to the fact that hedging the CVA risk charge is challenging. The reason is that the hedge instruments reducing the CVA risk charge cause additional Profit and Loss (P&L) volatility. In the present article, we propose a solution which optimizes the CVA risk charge and the P&L volatility from hedging.

**Keywords** CVA risk charge · Accounting CVA · Hedging · Optimization

## 1 Introduction

Counterparty credit risk is the risk that a counterparty in a derivatives transaction will default prior to expiration of the trade and will therefore not be able to fulfill its contractual obligations. Before the recent financial crisis many market participants believed that some counterparties will never fail ("too big to fail") and therefore counterparty risk was generally considered as not significant. This view changed due to the bankruptcy of Lehman Brothers during the financial crisis and market participants realized that even major banks can fail. For that reason, counterparty risk is nowadays considered to be significant for investment banks. The International Financial Reporting Standards (IFRS) demand that the fair value of a derivative incorporates the credit quality of the counterparty. This is achieved by a valuation adjustment which is commonly referred to as credit valuation adjustment (CVA), see e.g. [3–5]. The CVA is part of the IFRS P&L, i.e. losses (gains) caused by changes of the counterparties credit quality reduce (increase) the balance sheet equity.

Basel III requires a capital charge for future changes of the credit quality of derivatives, i.e. CVA volatility. Banks can either use a standardized approach to

C. Berns (✉)
KPMG AG, Am Flughafen, 60549 Frankfurt am Main, Germany
e-mail: christophberns@kpmg.com

© The Author(s) 2016
K. Glau et al. (eds.), *Innovations in Derivatives Markets*, Springer Proceedings in Mathematics & Statistics 165, DOI 10.1007/978-3-319-33446-2_6

compute this capital charge or an internal model [2]. The latter charge is commonly referred to as CVA risk charge. Many banks have implemented a CVA desk in order to manage actively their CVA risk. CVA desks buy CDS protection on the capital markets to hedge the counterparty credit risk of uncollateralized derivatives which have been bought by the ordinary trading desks. Recognizing that banks actively manage CVA positions, Basel III allows for hedging the CVA risk charge using credit hedges such as single name CDSs and CDS indexes. However, the recognition of hedges is different depending on whether the standardized approach or an internal model is used [2].

Summarizing, we can look at counterparty credit risk from two different perspectives: the regulatory (Basel III) and the accounting (IFRS) one. Depending whether we consider counterparty risk from a regulatory or accounting perspective, different valuation methods are applied for this risk. In general, the regulatory treatment of counterparty risk is more conservative than the accounting one, cf. [6]. The difference between the regulatory and the accounting treatment of counterparty risk causes the following problem in hedging the CVA risk charge: eligible hedge instruments such as CDSs would lead to a reduction of the CVA risk charge. On the other hand, under IFRS, a CDS is recognized as a derivative and thus accounted at fair value through profit and loss and therefore introducing further P&L volatility.

The current accounting and regulatory rules expose banks to the situation that they cannot achieve regulatory capital relief and low P&L volatility simultaneously. Deutsche Bank, for instance, has largely hedged the CVA risk charge in the first half of 2013. The hedging strategy that reduced the CVA risk charge has caused large losses due to additional P&L volatility, cf. [7]. This example illustrates the mismatch between the regulatory and accounting treatment of CVA.[1] The mismatch demands for a trade-off between these two regimes, cf. [8]. For this reason, we propose in this article an approach which leads to an optimal allocation between CVA risk charge reduction and P&L volatility. Our considerations are restricted to the standardized CVA risk charge.

We start with an explanation of the standardized CVA risk charge, i.e. the regulatory treatment of CVA. Afterwards, we show that the standardized CVA charge can be interpreted as a (scaled) volatility/variance of a portfolio of normally distributed positions. This interpretation reveals the modeling assumptions of the regulator and will be crucial for the later considerations. In a next step, we explain the counterparty risk modeling from an accounting perspective and we compute the impact of the hedge instruments (used to reduce the CVA risk charge) to the overall P&L volatility, assuming that the risk factor returns are normally distributed. Without the mismatch between the regulatory and the accounting regime, the hedge instruments would move anti-correlated to the corresponding accounting CVAs and the resulting common volatility would be small. Due to the mismatch, the CVA and the hedge instrument changes will not offset completely. For this reason we introduce a

[1]Due to the exclusion of DVA from the Basel III regulatory calculation, the mismatch potentially intensifies.

synthetic[2] total volatility $\sigma_{syn}$ consisting basically of the sum of the additional accounting P&L volatility $\sigma_{hed}$ caused by fair value changes of the hedge instruments (hedge P&L volatility) and the regulatory CVA volatility $\sigma_{CVA,reg}$ (i.e. basically the CVA risk charge)[3]:

$$\sigma_{syn}^2 = \sigma_{hed}^2 + \sigma_{CVA,reg}^2. \tag{1}$$

Hence, (1) defines a steering variable describing the common effects of CVA risk charge hedging and resulting P&L volatility. One should mention that formula (1) may suggest statistical independence of the two quantities. However, there exists a dependence in the following sense: both the regulatory CVA volatility and the hedge P&L volatility depend on the hedge amount. The more we hedge, the smaller the $\sigma_{CVA,reg}$. On the other hand, the more we hedge, the larger the $\sigma_{hed}$. The definition of the synthetic volatility as a sum of $\sigma_{hed}^2$ and $\sigma_{CVA,reg}^2$ can be motivated by the following consideration: the term $\sigma_{CVA,reg}^2$ is related to the regulatory capital demand for CVA risk. The other term, $\sigma_{hed}^2$, can be interpreted as capital demand for market risk of the hedge instruments. Although the hedge instruments are excluded from the regulatory capital demand computation for market risk, they potentially reduce the balance sheet equity and therefore may reduce the available regulatory capital. The sum in (1) is now motivated by the additivity of the total capital demand.

In the following we will consider $\sigma_{syn}$ as function of the hedge amount and search for its minimum. The hedge amount minimizing $\sigma_{syn}$ leads to the optimal allocation between CVA risk charge relief and P&L volatility. We will derive analytical solutions. The discussion of several special cases will provide an intuitive understanding of the optimal allocation. For technical reasons we exclude index hedges in the derivation of the optimal hedge strategy. However, it is easy to generalize the results to the case where index hedges are allowed.

## 2 Counterparty Risk from a Regulatory Perspective: The Standardized CVA Risk Charge

In this section we introduce the standardized CVA risk charge. A detailed explanation of all involved parameters is given in the Basel III document [2]. The formula for the standardized CVA risk charge is prescribed by the regulator and is used to determine the amount of regulatory capital which banks must hold in order to absorb possible losses caused by future deteriorations of the counterparties credit quality. We will see that the standardized CVA risk charge can be interpreted as volatility (i.e. standard deviation) of a normally distributed random variable. More precisely, we will show that the CVA risk charge can be interpreted as the 99 % quantile of a portfolio of

[2]We use the word synthetic since $\sigma_{syn}$ mixes a volatility measured in regulatory terms and a volatility measured in accounting terms.

[3]This connection will be explained later.

positions subject to normally distributed CVA changes (i.e. CVA P&L) only. This gives some insights into the regulators modeling assumptions for future CVA. It is worth to mention that the regulators modeling assumptions may hold or not hold. A detailed look at the regulators modeling assumptions can be found in [6].

In order to be prepared for later computations, we introduce in this section some notations and recall some facts about normally distributed random variables.

The standardized CVA risk charge $K$ is given by [2]:

$$K = \beta\sqrt{h}\Phi^{-1}(q) \tag{2}$$

with

- $h = 1$, the 1-year time horizon,
- $\Phi$ the cumulative distribution function of the standard normal distribution
- $q = 99\,\%$ the confidence level and
- $\beta$ defined by[4]

$$\beta^2 = \left(\sum_{i=1}^{n} 0.5 \cdot \omega_i \left(M_i EAD_i - M_i^{hed} B_i\right) - \omega_{ind} M_{ind} B_{ind}\right)^2 + \sum_{i=1}^{n} 0.75 \cdot \omega_i^2 \left(M_i EAD_i - M_i^{hed} B_i\right)^2 \tag{3}$$

with

- $\omega_i$ a weight depending on the rating of the counterparty $i$, $n$ is the number of counterparties
- $M_i$, $M_i^{hed}$, and $M_{ind}$ the effective maturities for the $i$th netting set (corresponding to counterparty $i$), the hedged instrument for counterparty $i$ and the index hedge
- $EAD_i$ the discounted regulatory exposure w.r.t. counterparty $i$
- $B_i$, $B_{ind}$ the discounted hedge notional amounts invested in the hedge instrument (CDS) for counterparty $i$ and the index hedge.

Formula (2) is determined by the regulator. In order to get a better understanding of this formula, we will derive a stochastic interpretation of it. Before that, we need to recall a fact about normal distributions: if the random vector $\vec{X}$ has a multivariate normal distribution, i.e. $\vec{X} \sim \mathcal{N}(0, \Sigma)$ with mean 0 and covariance matrix $\Sigma$, then, for a deterministic vector $\vec{a}$, the scalar product

$$\langle \vec{a}, \vec{X} \rangle := \sum_i a_i X_i \tag{4}$$

[4] For simplicity we consider only one index hedge. The results in this article can easily be generalized to more than one index hedge.

has a univariate normal distribution with mean 0 and variance

$$\sigma^2 = \langle \vec{a}, \Sigma\vec{a}\rangle. \tag{5}$$

Now we are able to derive the stochastic interpretation of the CVA risk charge, more precise the interpretation as volatility.

## 2.1 *Standardized CVA Risk Charge as Volatility*

In this section we will show that the regulators' modeling assumptions behind the standardized CVA risk charge are given by normally distributed CVA returns which are aggregated by using a one-factor Gaussian copula model.[5] We consider $n$ counterparties. By $R_i$, we denote the (one year) CVA P&L (i.e. those P&L effects caused by CVA changes) w.r.t. counterparty $i$.

**Lemma 1** *If one assumes $R_i \sim \mathcal{N}(0, \sigma_i^2)$ and further, if one assumes that the random vector*[6]

$$\vec{R} = (R_1, \ldots, R_n)^t$$

*is distributed according to a one-factor Gaussian copula model, i.e. $\vec{R} \sim \mathcal{N}(0, \Gamma)$ with $\Gamma_{ii} = \sigma_i^2$ and $\Gamma_{ij} = \rho\sigma_i\sigma_j$ with $\rho$ independent of $i$ and $j$ for $i \neq j$, then the 99 % quantile of the distribution of $\vec{R}$ is equal to the CVA risk charge (2).*

*Proof* Using (4) and (5), we find that the aggregated CVA return (common CVA P&L) $R_{CVA,reg} := \sum_{i=1}^n R_i = \langle \vec{1}, \vec{R}\rangle$[7] has the distribution $\mathcal{N}(0, \sigma_{CVA,reg}^2)$ with

$$\sigma_{CVA,reg}^2 = \langle \vec{1}, \Gamma\vec{1}\rangle = \sum_{i,j=1}^n \Gamma_{i,j} = \left(\sqrt{\rho}\sum_{i=1}^n \sigma_i\right)^2 + (1-\rho)\sum_{i=1}^n \sigma_i^2 \tag{6}$$

If we compare the above expression with (3), we see that this expression is equal to $\beta^2$ (with $B_{ind} = 0$, i.e. no index hedges) if we set $\rho = 0.25$ and $\sigma_i = \omega_i(M_i EAD_i - M_i^{hed} B_i)$. The quantile interpretation of the CVA risk charge (i.e. Formula (2)) follows from standard properties of the normal distribution.

The above lemma shows that the standardized CVA risk charge is basically the volatility of the sum $\sum_i R_i$ of $n$ normally distributed random variables. The normally distributed random variables are equicorrelated: $\rho(R_i, R_j) = 0.25$. Each CVA return $R_i$ has the volatility

$$\sigma_i = \omega_i(M_i EAD_i - M_i^{hed} B_i). \tag{7}$$

---

[5]This is a very strong assumption that might not be true in reality.

[6]By $\cdot^t$ we denote the transpose of a vector/matrix.

[7]By $\vec{1}$ we denote the vector $(1, \ldots, 1)^t$.

Hence, buying credit protection on counterparty $i$ reduces the corresponding CVA volatility. If we assume $M_i = M_i^{hed}$, the optimal hedge w.r.t. counterparty $i$ is given by a CDS with notional amount $B_i$ equals

$$B_i = EAD_i. \tag{8}$$

## 3 Counterparty Risk from an Accounting Perspective

As explained in the introduction, counterparty risk from an accounting perspective is quantified by a fair value adjustment called credit valuation adjustment (CVA). The CVA reduces the present value (PV) of a derivatives portfolio in order to incorporate counterparty risk:

$$PV = PV_{riskfree} - CVA,$$

whereby $PV_{riskfree}$ denotes the market value of the portfolio without counterparty risk and CVA is the adjustment to reflect counterparty risk. For the modeling of CVA, banks have some degrees of freedom. Typically, the accounting CVA is computed by means of the following formula (see e.g. [4]):

$$CVA = \int_0^T D(t)EE(t)dP(t) \tag{9}$$

with $T$ the effective maturity of the derivatives portfolio, $D(t)$ the risk-free discount curve, $EE(t) = E[\max\{0, PV(t)\}]$ the (risk-neutral) expected positive exposure at (future time point) $t$, and $dP(t)$ is the (risk-neutral) default probability of the counterparty in the infinitesimal interval $[t, t + dt]$. For the implementation of (9), a discretization of the integral is necessary. Many banks assume a constant $EE$ profile (i.e. $EE(t) = EE^*$ for all $t$). In that case, (9) simplifies to

$$CVA = EE^* \int_0^T D(t)dP(t). \tag{10}$$

Further, the (risk-neutral) default probabilities are typically modeled by a hazard rate model, i.e. one assumes that the default time is exponentially distributed with parameter $\lambda$. Using this assumption, we can write:

$$CVA = \lambda EE^* \int_0^T D(t)e^{-\lambda t}dt. \tag{11}$$

The approximation (11) will be helpful in the next section, where we describe the hedging of CVA from an accounting perspective

## 3.1 CVA Hedging from an Accounting Perspective

In previous sections we have seen that the regulatory CVA hedging (i.e. CVA risk charge hedging) can be achieved by buying credit protection. Effectively, (7) says that the regulatory exposure is reduced by the notional amount of the bought credit protection. At this place, we describe CVA hedging from an accounting perspective.

Let us consider a derivatives portfolio with a single counterparty. In order to hedge the corresponding counterparty risk, one can buy, for example, a single name CDS such that the CVA w.r.t. the counterparty together with the CDS is Delta neutral (i.e. up to first order, CVA movements are neutralized by the CDS movements). The condition for Delta neutrality is

$$\Delta CVA = \Delta CDS \tag{12}$$

whereby $\Delta$ describes the derivative of the CVA and CDS respectively (w.r.t. the credit spread of the counterparty). To be more precise, the default leg of the CDS should compensate the CVA movements. Using a standard valuation model for a CDS (see e.g. [4]) and computing the derivatives in (12), it is easy to see that (12) is equivalent to

$$B = EE^*, \tag{13}$$

i.e. the optimal hedge amount is given by $EE^*$. Typically, $EE^*$ is given by the average of the expected positive exposures $EE(t)$ at future time points $t$:

$$EE^* = \frac{1}{T}\int_0^T EE(t)dt. \tag{14}$$

If we compare (13) with (8) we see that the optimal hedge notional amount for hedging CVA risk from a regulatory perspective is the regulatory exposure $EAD$, while the optimal hedge notional amount for hedging accounting CVA risk is given by $EE^*$. In general it holds $EAD > EE^*$, due to conservative assumptions made by the regulator[8] (we refer to [6] for a detailed comparison of these two quantities). Thus, hedging CVA risk differs whether it is considered from an accounting or a regulatory perspective. This mismatch causes additional P&L volatility in the accounting framework, if the CVA risk is hedged from a regulatory perspective (i.e. if the CVA risk charge is hedged).

Finally we remark that we can write the CVA sensitivities $\Delta_{CVA} = \frac{d}{ds}CVA$ as

$$\Delta_{CVA} = EE^* \Delta_{CDS}, \tag{15}$$

whereby $\Delta_{CDS}$ is the sensitivity of (the default leg of) a CDS with notional amount $B = 1$.

[8]For example, the alpha multiplier in the IMM context overstates the EAD by a factor of 1.4. Further, the non-decreasing constraint to the exposure profile leads to an overstatement, see [6] for details.

# 4 Portfolio P&L

As explained above, the hedge instruments reduce the (regulatory) counterparty credit risk. But they may cause new market risk due to additional P&L volatility. However, although in accordance with Basel III eligible hedge instruments are excluded from market risk RWA calculations, the additional P&L volatility of the hedge instruments leads to fluctuations in reported equity. In order to describe the effects of hedging to the overall P&L, we introduce in the present section the corresponding framework. We divide the overall P&L in different parts: the P&L of the hedge instruments, the P&L of the remaining positions, and the CVA P&L. The framework will be helpful later on, when we want to quantify the impact of the CVA risk charge hedges to the accounting P&L.

## *4.1 Portfolio P&L Without CVA*

Let us assume that a bank holds derivatives with $n$ different counterparties for which single name CDS exists. The bank has to decide to which extent it hedges the counterparty risk w.r.t. these counterparties by either single name CDS or index hedges. By $\Sigma$ we denote the correlation matrix (of dimension $N \times N$, $N > n$) of all risk factors $r_i$, $i = 1, \dots, N$ the banks (trading) portfolio is exposed to. Without loss of generality, we assume that the correlations between the CDS of the considered $n$ counterparties are given by the first $n \times n$ components of $\Sigma$, i.e. $\Sigma_{i,j} = \rho(CDS_i, CDS_j)$, $i, j = 1, \dots, n$. Further, $\Sigma_{n+1,i}$ denotes the correlation between the index hedge and the CDS on counterparty $i \in \{1, \dots, n\}$. The whole portfolio $\Pi$ of the bank contains the hedge instruments (CDS and index hedge) as well as other instruments (e.g. bonds): $\Pi = \Pi_{hed} \cup \Pi_{rest}$. The sub-portfolio $\Pi_{hed}$ is driven by the credit spreads of the counterparties. Note that $\Pi_{rest}$ may depend on some of these credit spreads as well. In the following, we will assume the P&L of the portfolio $\Pi$ is given by:

$$P\&L = \sum_{i=1}^{n} (B_i \Delta_i + \Delta_{i,rest}) dr_i + B_{ind} \Delta_{ind} dr_{ind} + \sum_{j=n+2}^{N} \Delta_j dr_j, \tag{16}$$

whereby $\Delta_i$ denotes the sensitivity of $CDS_i$ w.r.t. the corresponding credit spread, $\Delta_{i,rest}$ denotes the sensitivity of the remaining positions which are sensitive w.r.t. the credit spread of counterparty $i$ as well,[9] $B_i$ (resp. $B_{ind}$) denotes the notional of $CDS_i$ (resp. the notional of the index hedge), and $dr_i$ describes the change of the risk factor $r_i$ (the first $n$ risk factors are the credit spreads) in the considered time period.

[9] For example, if $\Pi_{rest}$ contains a bond emitted by the counterparty $i$, then (ignoring the Bond-CDS Basis) $\Delta_{i,rest} = -\Delta_i$).

## 4.2 Impact with CVA

This section extends the above considerations to the case where we allow for a CVA component. We define the total P&L as the difference between the P&L given by (16) and the CVA P&L:

$$P\&L_{tot} = P\&L - P\&L_{CVA}, \tag{17}$$

whereby $P\&L_{CVA}$ is defined in a similar manner as in (16)[10]:

$$P\&L_{CVA} = \sum_{i=1}^{n+1} \Delta_{i,CVA} dr_i. \tag{18}$$

In (18), the risk factors $r_i$ are the same risk factors which appear in the first $n+1$ summands of (16). This is because the CVAs are driven by the same risk factors as the corresponding hedge instruments. Recall that in a setup where counterparty risk is completely hedged, the P&L of the hedge instruments is canceled out by the P&L of the CVAs. This is the case, if the corresponding sensitivity is equal. In Sect. 3.1 we have shown how one can achieve this (using the condition of Delta neutrality) by choosing the right hedge notional amounts.

## 4.3 Impact of CVA Risk Charge Hedging on the Accounting P&L Volatility

The additional P&L volatility caused by the hedge instruments is basically given by the residual volatility of the hedge instruments which is not canceled by the CVAs. In order to derive an expression for this volatility, we start with the derivation of the volatility of the total portfolio P&L. The residual volatility will consist of those parts of the total volatility which are sensitive w.r.t. the hedge instruments.

In order to proceed, we have to introduce the following notations: the vector $\vec{\Delta}_{CVA} \in \mathbb{R}^{n+1}$ contains the CVA sensitivities and the return vector $\vec{dr} \in \mathbb{R}^N$ describes the changes of the $N$ risk factors the trading book is exposed to. We further introduce the sensitivity vectors[11] $\vec{\Delta} = (\Delta_1, \ldots, \Delta_{ind}, \ldots, \Delta_N)^t \in \mathbb{R}^N$

[10] We consider only the credit spreads as risk factors. Exposure movements due to changes in market risk factors are not considered. This is unproblematic for the considerations in this article since we will end up with dynamic CVA hedging strategy (cf. Sect. 5) which incorporates the exposure changes.

[11] The first $n$ components of $\vec{\Delta}$ are the CDS sensitivities w.r.t. credit spread changes and the $n+1$th component is the sensitivity of the index hedge.

and[12] $\vec{\Delta}_{rest} = (\Delta_{1,rest}, \ldots, \Delta_{n,rest})^t \in \mathbb{R}^n$, the notional vector $\vec{B} = (B_1, \ldots, B_n, B_{ind})^t \in \mathbb{R}^{n+1}$ and the diagonal matrix $Q_\Delta = diag(\Delta_1, \ldots, \Delta_n, \Delta_{ind}) \in \mathbb{R}^{(n+1)\times(n+1)}$.

**Lemma 2** *If we assume that the portfolio P&L is given by (17) and if we further assume $\vec{dr} \sim \mathcal{N}(0, \Sigma)$ (for some correlation matrix $\Sigma$), then the squared volatility (i.e. the variance) of (17) is given by*[13]

$$
\begin{aligned}
\sigma^2_{P\&L_{tot}} &= \left\langle \begin{pmatrix} Q_\Delta \vec{B} \\ \vec{0} \end{pmatrix} \Sigma \begin{pmatrix} Q_\Delta \vec{B} \\ \vec{0} \end{pmatrix} \right\rangle + \left\langle \begin{pmatrix} \vec{\Delta}_{CVA} \\ \vec{0} \end{pmatrix} \Sigma \begin{pmatrix} \vec{\Delta}_{CVA} \\ \vec{0} \end{pmatrix} \right\rangle \\
&+ \left\langle \begin{pmatrix} \vec{\Delta}_{rest} \\ \vec{\Delta}_{N-n-1} \end{pmatrix} \Sigma \begin{pmatrix} \vec{\Delta}_{rest} \\ \vec{\Delta}_{N-n-1} \end{pmatrix} \right\rangle - 2 \left\langle \begin{pmatrix} Q_\Delta \vec{B} \\ \vec{0} \end{pmatrix} \Sigma \begin{pmatrix} \vec{\Delta}_{CVA} \\ \vec{0} \end{pmatrix} \right\rangle \\
&+ 2 \left\langle \begin{pmatrix} Q_\Delta \vec{B} \\ \vec{0} \end{pmatrix} \Sigma \begin{pmatrix} \vec{\Delta}_{rest} \\ \vec{\Delta}_{N-n-1} \end{pmatrix} \right\rangle - 2 \left\langle \begin{pmatrix} \vec{\Delta}_{rest} \\ \vec{\Delta}_{N-n-1} \end{pmatrix} \Sigma \begin{pmatrix} \vec{\Delta}_{CVA} \\ \vec{0} \end{pmatrix} \right\rangle . \qquad (19)
\end{aligned}
$$

*Proof* With the above defined vectors, we can write:

$$
\begin{aligned}
P\&L_{tot} &= \langle Q_\Delta \vec{B} - \vec{\Delta}_{CVA}, \vec{dr}_{n+1} \rangle + \langle \vec{\Delta}_{rest}, \vec{dr}_{n+1} \rangle + \langle \vec{\Delta}_{N-n-1}, \vec{dr}_{N-n-1} \rangle \\
&= \left\langle \begin{pmatrix} Q_\Delta \vec{B} \\ \vec{0}_{N-n-1} \end{pmatrix} - \begin{pmatrix} \vec{\Delta}_{CVA} \\ \vec{0}_{N-n-1} \end{pmatrix} + \begin{pmatrix} \vec{\Delta}_{rest} \\ \vec{\Delta}_{N-n-1} \end{pmatrix}, \vec{dr} \right\rangle \\
&= \langle \vec{a} - \vec{b} + \vec{c}, \vec{dr} \rangle \qquad (20)
\end{aligned}
$$

whereby $\vec{dr}_{n+1}$ denotes the $n+1$-dimensional vector consisting of the first $n+1$ components of $\vec{dr}$, $\vec{dr}_{N-n-1}$ consists of the remaining $N-n-1$ components of $\vec{dr}$, $\vec{\Delta}_{N-n-1}$ denotes the vector of the remaining $N-n-1$ sensitivities, and $\vec{0}_{N-n-1}$ is the $N-n-1$-dimensional vector whose components are all equal to 0.[14] Clearly, the vectors $\vec{a}$, $\vec{b}$ and $\vec{c}$ coincide with the respective summands of the left hand side of the scalar product in (20). If we use $\vec{dr} \sim \mathcal{N}(0, \Sigma)$, it follows from (4) to (5):

$$
\begin{aligned}
\sigma^2_{P\&L_{tot}} &= \langle \vec{a} - \vec{b} + \vec{c}, \Sigma(\vec{a} - \vec{b} + \vec{c}) \rangle \\
&= \langle \vec{a}, \Sigma\vec{a} \rangle + \langle \vec{b}, \Sigma\vec{b} \rangle + \langle \vec{c}, \Sigma\vec{c} \rangle - 2\langle \vec{a}, \Sigma\vec{b} \rangle + 2\langle \vec{a}, \Sigma\vec{c} \rangle - 2\langle \vec{c}, \Sigma\vec{b} \rangle . \qquad (21)
\end{aligned}
$$

If we plug in the expressions for $\vec{a}$, $\vec{b}$ and $\vec{c}$, we obtain (19). □

In order to be prepared for later computations, we will further simplify Expression (19). To this end, we introduce the following notations: by $\Sigma_{n+1}$ we denote the $(n+1) \times (n+1)$ matrix consisting of the first $n+1$ column and row entires of $\Sigma$ only, i.e. $\Sigma_{i,j}$, $i, j = 1, \ldots n+1$. The matrix $\Sigma_{N,n+1}$ is the $N \times (n+1)$ matrix

[12]The vector $\vec{\Delta}_{rest}$ contains the $n$ sensitivities w.r.t. credit spread changes of those trading book positions which are different from the CDSs used for hedging but are sensitive w.r.t. to the credit spreads of the hedge instruments as well.

[13]The vector $\vec{\Delta}_{N-n-1}$ is defined in the proof.

[14]In the following, we will omit the index $N-n-1$ and simply write $\vec{0}$.

obtained from $\Sigma$ by deleting the last $N-n-1$ columns and $\Sigma^t_{N,n+1}$ denotes its transpose matrix. With this notation and using that $\vec{0}$ cancels many components in (19), we can write:

$$\begin{aligned}\sigma^2_{P\&L_{tot}} &= \langle Q_\Delta \vec{B}, \Sigma_{n+1} Q_\Delta \vec{B}\rangle + \langle \vec{\Delta}_{CVA}\Sigma_{n+1}, \vec{\Delta}_{CVA}\rangle - 2\langle Q_\Delta \vec{B}, \Sigma_{n+1}\vec{\Delta}_{CVA}\rangle \\ &\quad + 2\left\langle \vec{B}, Q_\Delta \Sigma^t_{N,n+1}\begin{pmatrix}\vec{\Delta}_{rest}\\ \vec{\Delta}_{N-n-1}\end{pmatrix}\right\rangle - 2\left\langle \vec{\Delta}_{CVA}, \Sigma^t_{N,n+1}\begin{pmatrix}\vec{\Delta}_{rest}\\ \vec{\Delta}_{N-n-1}\end{pmatrix}\right\rangle \\ &\quad + \left\langle \begin{pmatrix}\vec{\Delta}_{rest}\\ \vec{\Delta}_{N-n-1}\end{pmatrix} \Sigma \begin{pmatrix}\vec{\Delta}_{rest}\\ \vec{\Delta}_{N-n-1}\end{pmatrix}\right\rangle.\end{aligned} \tag{22}$$

In (22), the first summand describes the volatility of the hedge instruments if they are considered as isolated from the remaining positions (i.e. those positions which are different from the hedge instruments). Analogously, the other quadratic terms (i.e. the second and the last summand in (22)) represent the volatility of the CVA and the remaining positions respectively. The cross terms (third, fourth, and fifth summand) describe the interactions between the volatility of the hedge instruments, the CVA and the remaining positions. For example, the third term describes the interaction between the CVA and the hedge instruments.

The P&L volatility $\sigma^2_{hed}$ caused by the hedge instruments is given by those terms of (22) which depend on the hedge instruments, i.e. those terms which depend on $\vec{B}$. These are the first, the third, and the fourth term of (22), i.e.

$$\sigma^2_{hed} = \langle Q_\Delta \vec{B}, \Sigma_{n+1} Q_\Delta \vec{B}\rangle - 2\langle Q_\Delta \vec{B}, \Sigma_{n+1}\vec{\Delta}_{CVA}\rangle + 2\left\langle \vec{B}, Q_\Delta \Sigma^t_{N,n+1}\begin{pmatrix}\vec{\Delta}_{rest}\\ \vec{\Delta}_{N-n-1}\end{pmatrix}\right\rangle. \tag{23}$$

The other terms of (22) describe the volatility caused by the remaining positions.

In order to simplify the notation, we write $\sigma^2_{hed}$ in the following way:

$$\sigma^2_{hed} = \langle A\vec{B}, \vec{B}\rangle + \langle \vec{B}, \vec{b}\rangle \tag{24}$$

with

$$A = Q_\Delta \Sigma_{n+1} Q_\Delta \tag{25}$$

and

$$\vec{b} = Q_\Delta \Sigma^t_{N,n+1}\begin{pmatrix}\vec{\Delta}_{rest}\\ \vec{\Delta}_{N-n-1}\end{pmatrix} - Q_\Delta \Sigma_{n+1}\vec{\Delta}_{CVA}. \tag{26}$$

Note that $\sigma^2_{hed}$ is not simply given by a quadratic form but also incorporates a linear part. The quadratic form describes the volatility of a portfolio consisting of the hedge instruments, while the linear part describes the correlations of the hedge instruments with the remaining positions and with the CVAs.

### 4.3.1 Definition of the Steering Variable

We now define a steering variable aiming to define a unified framework for CVA risk charge hedging and P&L volatility. The steering variable is given by a synthetic volatility consisting of the sum of the regulatory CVA volatility and the volatility of the accounting P&L caused by the hedge instruments:

$$\sigma_{syn}^2 = \sigma_{CVA,reg}^2 + \sigma_{hed}^2. \tag{27}$$

The synthetic volatility unifies both the regulatory and the accounting framework. It can be considered as a function of the hedge notional amounts. The minimum of $\sigma_{tot,syn}^2$ describes the optimal allocation between CVA risk charge reduction and P&L volatility. Note that $\sigma_{tot,syn}^2$ contains now the matrices $\Gamma$ and $\Sigma$, who describe the correlations between the same risk factors. This mismatch can be resolved, if the advanced CVA risk charge is used [2]. However, the use of different CVA sensitivities cannot be resolved. The most significant differences arise due to different exposure definitions: while the exposures $EAD_i$ contained in the regulatory CVA sensitivities are based on the effective EPE and multiplied by the alpha multiplier (for IMM banks), this is not the case for the exposures used to compute the accounting CVA sensitivities. In general, these mismatches will lead to smaller accounting CVA sensitivities. Thus, a complete hedging of the CVA risk charge leads to an overhedged accounting CVA. See [6] for a complete description of the sources of the mismatch. Another source of potential overhedging is the following: if accounting CVA is already hedged by instruments which are not eligible hedge instruments in the sense of Basel III, additional hedge instruments are necessary for the hedging of the CVA risk charge. These hedge instruments will cause additional P&L volatility, since their offsetting counterparts (i.e. the CVAs) are not present (since they are already hedged).

## 5 Determination of the Optimal Hedge Strategy

This section describes concretely how the mismatch between the regulatory regime and the accounting regime can be mitigated. The result will be a dynamic CVA hedging strategy based on an optimization principle of the steering variable introduced in the previous section. We will ignore index hedges but all results can easily be generalized to the case where index hedges are included.

As opposed to the previous sections, the vector $\vec{B}$ will not contain the component $B_{ind}$ in this section. As explained before, we want to minimize the synthetic volatility[15]

$$\sigma_{syn}^2(\vec{B}) = \sigma_{hed}^2(\vec{B}) + \sigma_{CVA}^2(\vec{B}) \tag{28}$$

[15]We ignore the index *tot*.

as a function of $\vec{B}$. The component $B_i^*$ of the minimum $\vec{B}^*$ describes the optimal notional amounts of $CDS_i$, used to hedge the counterparty risk w.r.t. counterparty $i$. We now determine $\vec{B}^*$ by computing the zeros of the first derivative of $\sigma_{syn}^2$.

**Theorem 1** *Under the same assumptions as in Lemma 2, the minimum $\vec{B}^*$ of (28) is given by*[16]

$$\vec{B}^* = H^{-1}\vec{f} \tag{29}$$

*with*

$$H := 2(A + Q_{M^{hed}} \Gamma Q_{M^{hed}}) \tag{30}$$

*and*

$$\vec{f} := 2Q_{M^{hed}} \Gamma Q_M \overrightarrow{EAD} - \vec{b}. \tag{31}$$

*Proof* In order to keep the display of the computations clear, we introduce the diagonal matrices $Q_M := diag(\omega_1 M_1, \ldots, \omega_n M_n)$ and $Q_{M^{hed}} := diag(\omega_1 M_1^{hed}, \ldots, \omega_n M_n^{hed})$ and the $n$-dimensional vector $\overrightarrow{EAD}$ whose components are given by the counterparty exposures. Using these definitions, we can write:

$$\sigma_{CVA}^2 = \langle Q_M \overrightarrow{EAD} - Q_{M^{hed}} \vec{B}, \Gamma(Q_M \overrightarrow{EAD} - Q_{M^{hed}} \vec{B}) \rangle. \tag{32}$$

whereby $\Gamma$ describes the constant correlation between the CVAs (all diagonal elements given by 1). Using (32) and (24), we can write:

$$\begin{aligned}
\frac{\partial \sigma_{syn}^2}{\partial \vec{B}} &= \frac{\partial}{\partial \vec{B}} (\langle A\vec{B}, \vec{B} \rangle + \langle \vec{b}, \vec{B} \rangle) \\
&\quad + \frac{\partial}{\partial \vec{B}} \langle Q_{M^{hed}} \vec{B}, \Gamma Q_{M^{hed}} \vec{B} \rangle \\
&\quad - 2\frac{\partial}{\partial \vec{B}} \langle Q_{M^{hed}} \vec{B}, \Gamma Q_M \overrightarrow{EAD} \rangle \\
&= 2A\vec{B} + \vec{b} + 2Q_{M^{hed}} \Gamma Q_{M^{hed}} \vec{B} - 2Q_{M^{hed}} \Gamma Q_M \overrightarrow{EAD} \\
&= H\vec{B} - \vec{f},
\end{aligned} \tag{33}$$

where we have used the notations (30) and (31). This shows (29). Further, we note that the matrix $H$ is derived from correlation matrices and therefore positive semi-definite. As a result, $H$ is indeed invertible. Moreover, it holds

$$\frac{\partial^2 \sigma_{syn}^2}{\partial^2 \vec{B}} = H.$$

Hence, the second derivative of $\sigma_{syn}^2$ is positive semi-definite and $B^*$ is indeed a minimum.

[16] All terms are introduced in the proof.

*Remark* The implementation of the optimal hedge strategy works as follows: one has to compute on a regular basis (e.g. daily, weekly, etc.) the optimal solution (29). To do this one needs the CVA sensitivities,[17] the trading book sensitivities, and the correlation matrix of the risk factors.[18] Afterwards, the CVA desk needs to buy credit protection described by the optimal solution. This reduces the capital demand for counterparty risk and (by construction) minimizes the accounting P&L of the bought credit protection.

The approach presented in this article is based on many simplifying assumptions and restricted to the standardized CVA risk charge. Obviously, one could relax these assumptions and apply a comparable optimization principle. In such a case, it would possibly be hard to derive an analytical solution. Instead, one would obtain a numerical solution.

## 5.1 Special Cases

For illustration purposes, we consider the case $n = 1$, i.e. the special case of a single netting set. In that case both $H$ and $\vec{f}$ are scalars:

$$H = 2\Delta^2 \Sigma_{1,1} + 2\omega^2 (M^{hed})^2$$

and

$$f = 2\omega^2 M M^{hed} EAD + 2\Delta \Delta_{CVA} \Sigma_{1,1} - \left( \Delta \Sigma_{1,1} \Delta_{rest} + \Delta \sum_{j=2}^{N} \Sigma_{1,j} \Delta_j \right), \tag{34}$$

whereby $\Delta$ describes the sensitivity of the hedge instrument of the considered counterparty, $\Delta_{rest}$ the sensitivity of the remaining positions (i.e. all positions without the CDS used for hedging purposes), $\Delta_{CVA}$ the sensitivity of accounting CVA and $\Delta_j$ are the sensitivities to the risk factors of the remaining positions. Thus, the optimal solution is

$$B^* = \frac{2\omega^2 M M^{hed} EAD + 2\sigma^2 \Delta \Delta_{CVA} - \left( \Delta \sigma^2 \Delta_{rest} + \Delta \sum_{j=2}^{N} \Sigma_{1,j} \Delta_j \right)}{2\Delta^2 \sigma^2 + 2\omega^2 (M^{hed})^2} \tag{35}$$

where we have used that $\Sigma_{1,1}$ is equal to the volatility $\sigma^2$ of the hedge instrument. First, in order to get a better understanding of $B^*$, let us assume that the risk factor (credit spread) of the hedge instrument is independent of the remaining positions, i.e.

[17] Banks which actively manage their CVA risk usually compute these sensitivities.

[18] Larger banks usually have these data available, e.g. for market risk management purposes.

$\Delta_{rest} = 0$ and $\Sigma_{1,j} = 0$, for $j = 2, \ldots, N$. In that case (35) (we assume additionally $M = M^{hed}$) becomes

$$B^* = \frac{2\omega^2 M^2 EAD + 2\Delta\Delta_{CVA}\sigma^2}{2\omega^2 M^2 + 2\Delta^2\sigma^2}. \tag{36}$$

We see already that $B^*$ is (at least from a certain volatility level) a decreasing function in $\sigma^2$, as we would expect it. Obviously, if we ignore the fact that the hedge instrument introduces further volatility (i.e. we assume $\sigma^2 = 0$), it holds

$$B^* = EAD.$$

It is easy to see that this is the optimal hedge amount if we minimize the CVA risk charge alone. As explained above, the most significant differences between the IFRS CVA and the regulatory CVA are the different exposure computation methodologies. In (36), these differences are reflected in $EAD$ and $\Delta_{CVA}$: while $EAD$ is based on the regulatory methodology, $\Delta_{CVA}$ is based on accounting CVA methodology.[19] For illustration purposes, let us assume that $\Delta_{CVA}$ is based on the same exposure methodology as the regulatory CVA sensitivities (and that the modeling assumptions Sect. 3 holds). This means, that cf. (15)

$$\Delta_{CVA} = EAD\Delta, \tag{37}$$

i.e. we use the regulatory exposure $EAD$ in (15) instead of the economical exposure $EE^*$. If we plug in (37) in (36), we obtain:

$$B^* = \frac{(2\omega^2 M^2 + 2\Delta^2\sigma^2)EAD}{2\omega^2 M^2 + 2\Delta^2\sigma^2} = EAD. \tag{38}$$

Thus, if we ignore the mismatch between the accounting and the regulatory CVA, the optimal hedge solution is given by the optimal hedge solution of the CVA risk charge only. If we include the mismatch, we can approximate the accounting CVA sensitivity by (cf. (15))

$$\Delta_{CVA} = EE^*\Delta. \tag{39}$$

As explained in Sect. 4.3.1, $EE^*$ is smaller than $EAD$. Using (36) and (39) yields:

$$B^* = \frac{2\omega^2 M^2 EAD + 2\Delta\sigma^2 EE^*}{2\omega^2 M^2 + 2\Delta^2\sigma^2} < \frac{2\omega^2 M^2 EAD + 2\Delta\sigma^2 EAD}{2\omega^2 M^2 + 2\Delta^2\sigma^2} = EAD. \tag{40}$$

Hence, the mismatch leads to a smaller optimal hedge amount than the current regulatory exposure.

---

[19]Note that $\Delta_{CVA}$ depends on the exposure as well (while $\Delta$ is based on a unit exposure, cf. (16)). But this exposure is computed based on accounting methodology. This is the main source of differences between the accounting and regulatory regimes.

We remark that it cannot be excluded that $B^*$ becomes negative. This is the case if the risk factors of the remaining positions are strongly correlated to the risk factor of the hedge instrument. In such a situation it seems to be reasonable to set $B^* = 0$.

**Acknowledgements** The KPMG Center of Excellence in Risk Management is acknowledged for organizing the conference "Challenges in Derivatives Markets - Fixed Income Modeling, Valuation Adjustments, Risk Management, and Regulation".

**Open Access** This chapter is distributed under the terms of the Creative Commons Attribution 4.0 International License (http://creativecommons.org/licenses/by/4.0/), which permits use, duplication, adaptation, distribution and reproduction in any medium or format, as long as you give appropriate credit to the original author(s) and the source, a link is provided to the Creative Commons license and any changes made are indicated.

The images or other third party material in this chapter are included in the work's Creative Commons license, unless indicated otherwise in the credit line; if such material is not included in the work's Creative Commons license and the respective action is not permitted by statutory regulation, users will need to obtain permission from the license holder to duplicate, adapt or reproduce the material.

## References

1. Basel Committee on Banking Supervision: International Convergence of Capital Measurement and Capital Standards (2006)
2. Basel Committee on Banking Supervision: A Global Regulatory Framework for More Resilient Banks and Banking Systems (2010)
3. Brigo, D., Morini, M., Pallavicini, A.: Counterparty Credit Risk Collateral and Funding. Wiley, Chichester (2013)
4. Gregory, J.: Counterparty Credit Risk. Wiley, Chichester (2012)
5. Kenyon, C., Stamm, R.: Discounting, LIBOR CVA and Funding. Palgrave Macmillan, Basingstoke (2012)
6. Pykhtin, M.: Model Foundations of the Basel III Standardized CVA Charge. Risk Magazine, London (2012)
7. Carver, L.: Capital or P&L? Deutsche Bank Losses Highlight CVA Trade-Off. Risk Magazine, London (2013)
8. Schubert, D.: How to Hedge CVA Without Being Hurt. Risk Magazine, London (2014)

# Capital Optimization Through an Innovative CVA Hedge

**Michael Hünseler and Dirk Schubert**

**Abstract** One of the lessons of the financial crisis as of late was the inherent credit risk attached to the value of derivatives. Since not all derivatives can be cleared by central counterparties, a significant amount of OTC derivatives will be subject to increased regulatory capital charges. These charges cover both current and future unexpected losses; the capital costs for derivatives transactions can become substantial if not prohibitive. At the same time, capital optimization through CDS hedging of counterparty risks will result in a hedge position beyond the economic risk ("overhedging") required to meet Basel II/III rules. In addition, IFRS accounting rules again differ from Basel, creating a mismatch when hedging CVA. Even worse, CVA hedging using CDS may introduce significant profit and loss volatility while satisfying the conditions for capital relief. An innovative approach to hedging CVA aims to solve these issues.

**Keywords** CVA · Hedging · CDS · Contingent financial guarantee · Risk charges · OTC derivatives

## 1 Preface

In the following the nexus between credit risk (counterparty risk), liquidity, and market risk is analyzed and a solution with respect to CVA hedging of OTC derivative contracts is proposed.

The starting point is the consideration of collateral and its respective recognition in different but "basic" financial instruments like repos and (partially un-) collateralized

M. Hünseler (✉)
Credit Portfolio Management, Assenagon Asset Management S.A., Zweigniederlassung München, Prannerstrae 8, 80333 Munich, Germany
e-mail: michael.huenseler@assenagon.com

D. Schubert
Financial Services KPMG AG Wirtschaftsprüfungsgesellschaft, The Squaire, Am Flughafen, 60549 Frankfurt am Main, Germany
e-mail: dschubert@kpmg.com

© The Author(s) 2016



K. Glau et al. (eds.), *Innovations in Derivatives Markets*, Springer Proceedings in Mathematics & Statistics 165, DOI 10.1007/978-3-319-33446-2_7

OTC derivative contracts as well as the comparison to corresponding uncollateralized financial instruments like money market loans or uncollateralized OTC derivative contracts. The role of collateral is analyzed with respect to its legal basis, its treatment in Financial Accounting (IFRS, refer to [4]) and regulatory reporting according to Basel II/III (cf. [1, 2]).

The analysis leads to a definition of the concept of liquidity and its relation to the use of collateral in financial markets. As will be shown, the concept of liquidity, inherent in the legal framework related to collateral of basic financial instruments, can be considered as a transformation of secured into unsecured financing and vice versa. Moreover, with respect to the associated valuation and risk the liquidity transformation exhibits similarities to the concept of wrong-way risk. The transformation of unsecured into secured financing can be used to derive new types of financial instruments, e.g. in the application to CVA hedging issues of OTC derivative contracts. In this case the hedging instrument also solves the issue of disentangling funding value adjustments (FVA) and counterparty value adjustments (CVA), which is intensively discussed by practitioners in context with the pricing of OTC derivatives.

## 2 The Role of Collateral in OTC Contracts and Its Legal Basis

In the following the main legal basis with respect to the role of collateral is outlined.

### *2.1 The Role of Legal Versus Economic Ownership*

There are two main properties which are of relevance in connection with the role of collateral, the transfer of legal ownership (i.e. the possibility of "re-hypothecation") in contrast to the economic ownership and the value of the collateral.

By entering into a repurchase agreement the legal title to the securities is transferred to the counterparty but economically the securities stay with the selling counterparty since the buying counterparty has the obligation to compensate the selling counterparty for income (manufactured payments) associated with the securities and to redeliver the securities. In case of an Event of Default, both obligations terminate. The treatment in an Event of Default provides that the residual claim is settled in cash and determined taking into account the cash side as well as the value of the collateral. In this case the obligation to redeliver securities transferred as collateral expires and the buying counterparty remains the legal owner. Thus the price risk of the collateral (uncertainty of value) is entirely borne by the legal owner.

In case of (only) economic ownership, e.g. a pledge, this is not necessarily the case, since the treatment in an Event of Default differs as e.g. this kind of "collateral" is part of the bankrupt/legal estate and therefore underlying the insolvency procedure.

Despite these legal differences, the regulatory rules according to Basel II/III and the accounting rules under IFRS also require different treatment of collateral. In general IFRS follows the economic ownership concept irrespective of the legal basis of the collateral while Basel II/III rather follows the legal ownership concept.

## 2.2 *Affected Market Participants*

Not all market participants are affected by the same accounting and regulatory rules. Banks have to follow IFRS and Basel II/III rules, while e.g. investment funds are not affected by Basel II/III rules but are governed by investment fund legislation, e.g. UCITS directive. These different legal frameworks for market participants impact the usage of collateral in OTC contracts, e.g. the assets of an investment fund under UCITS represent special assets and the use of repos and cash collateral is limited. In addition, these investment funds have no access to sources of liquidity other than the capital paid which limits the use of cash and the provision of cash collateral in context of derivatives exposure. For example, cash collateral received from OTC derivative contracts has to be kept in segregated accounts and cannot be used for any kind of (reverse) repo transaction. Alternatively, the use of a custodian for optimizing the provision of cash collateral can be considered.

## 2.3 *Financial Instruments Involving Collateral and Standard Legal Frameworks (Master Agreements)*

Analyzing the legal basis of collateral facilitates the definition of liquidity and liquidity transformation.

### 2.3.1 Derivatives Under ISDA Master Agreement

The type and use of collateral are governed in the CSA (credit support annex), which represents an integral part of the ISDA Master Agreement framework[1] and cannot be considered separately. The ISDA Master Agreement forms the legal framework and is applicable for the individual derivative contracts supplemented by the CSA. For example, default netting in the Event of Default (default of a counterparty) is governed by the ISDA Master Agreement including the netting of the collateral which in turn is defined in the CSA. The CSA defines the type(s) of collateral and the terms of margining/posting, while the transfer of the legal ownership is governed in the ISDA Master Agreement. In general ISDA Master Agreements contracted under English Law provide the legal transfer of ownership of the collateral while ISDA Master

[1] ISDA®, International Swaps and Derivatives Association, Inc., 2002 Master Agreement.

Agreements contracted under New York Law do not. In the latter re-hypothecation, i.e. the re-use of the received collateral for counterparties is prohibited.

In case of ISDA Master Agreements under English Law the derivative contracts are terminated in case of an Event of Default and the collateral is taken into account in order to determine the residual claim. The determination of the residual claim is performed independently from the estate of the insolvent party.

### 2.3.2 Repos Under GMRA

A repo or repurchase agreement under GMRA[2] can economically be seen as a collateralized loan and is typically motivated by the request for cash. In case of repurchase agreements, the legal title to the securities provided as collateral is transferred to the counterparty (buyer) in exchange of the desired cash (purchase price). The credit risk and liquidity of the underlying securities determine the haircut in the valuation of the collateral. Adverse changes in the inherent credit risk of the securities are offset by an increase in haircut and induce in terms of margining additional posting of collateral to the counterparty. At maturity the securities are legally transferred back to original owner (seller) in exchange for the agreed cash amount (repurchase price). In case of a counterparty's default the securities are not returned and the recovery risk of the securities is borne by their legal owner (the buyer).

### 2.3.3 Securities Lending Under GSLMA

In contrast to a repo, a securities lending under GSLMA[3] is motivated by the need for securities but is (commonly) also a secured financing transaction since the securities as well as the collateral are legally transferred to the respective counterparty. In the secured case the collateral can be cash or other securities.

## *2.4 Credit and Counterparty Risk Related to Collateral*

Consider the case that Bank 1 and Bank 2 enter into a repo transaction, where Bank 2 receives cash from Bank 1 in return for securities. There are two features of importance: Bank 1 needs cash funding, which requires an assumption with respect to the sources of funding, e.g. central bank, deposits. The corresponding assumption represents a component in determining the profitability of the repo. An additional feature is the inherent wrong-way risk within the repo transaction. In this case the

[2]Sifma, Securities Industry and Financial Markets Association and ICMA, International Capital Market Association, 2011 version Global Master Repurchase Agreement.

[3]ISLA, International Securities Lending Association, Global Master Securities Lending Agreement, Version: January 2010.

wrong-way risk for Bank 1 is defined as an adverse correlation (positive in the example above) between counterparty credit risk toward Bank 2 and market value of the collateral (securities). Assuming a long position in the underlying securities (collateral) for Bank 1, the wrong-way risk constitutes a decrease in value of the securities (collateral) and a simultaneous decrease in credit worthiness of Bank 2. In this case the risk for Bank 1 is the failure of Bank 2 in balancing the collateral posting. Since in a repo transaction the legal ownership is transferred to Bank 1, the net risk position comprises the price risk (in the Event of Default of Bank 2) associated with the collateral (securities) including the haircut and the cash claim (cash loan). A similar rationale holds in case of a short position in securities (collateral) since an event of default affects the ability to post as well as to return posted collateral. Similar considerations hold in case of a (partially) collateralized OTC derivative transaction, e.g. an interest rate swap.

## 3 Terms of Liquidity and Definition of Liquidity Transformation

Dealing with the concept of liquidity reveals that the term is not defined consistently or not uniformly in financial regulations. A natural way is to adopt legal definitions.

### *3.1 Terms of Liquidity*

There is a variety of definitions for the term liquidity, e.g. meeting payment obligations (liquidity of an entity), liquid marketable securities (ability to buy and sell financial instruments), etc. The analysis above reveals the interdependence of "liquidity" and counterparty credit risk, respectively credit risk. As such liquidity of an entity can be considered as the relatively measured ability for a bank to raise cash from a credit line or in return of collateral which in turn is dependent on the liquidity of financial instruments. The collateral itself is only accepted if the price of the collateral can be reliably determined, e.g. it is traded with sufficient frequency on an active market.

### *3.2 Comparison of Secured and Unsecured Financing*

The best way to illustrate the concept formation of liquidity respectively liquidity transformation is the comparison of unsecured and secured financing in case of a default event. Continuing the example above, the following comparison considers Bank 1 as cash provider.

1. Financial action

   Secured: Exchange of cash versus collateral
   Unsecured: Paying out cash of a loan granted

2. Prerequisite and term of liquidity

   Secured: "Liquid" collateral (price of collateral can be reliably determined)
   Unsecured: Credit line loan illiquid - not marketable

3. Net (relative) risk position in case of default

   Secured: Market value of collateral: Default Probability (issuer of the security received as collateral) × recovery rate of collateral × amount of collateral (proximate representation via haircut)
   Unsecured: Recovery rate of cash loan × exposure at default (EAD)

4. Relation to estate of insolvent party

   Secured: Only residual claim part of the estate of the insolvent party but amount of residual claim is determined independently of the estate of the insolvent party
   Unsecured: Entirely part of the estate of the insolvent party

5. Risk

   Secured: Credit risk of collateral issuer, correlation between counterparty risk and price of collateral (wrong-way risk in an adverse case)
   Unsecured: Credit risk with respect to the borrower

Note that in the comparison above the net (relative) risk position in both cases, for secured and unsecured financing, involves a recovery rate but the associated risk relates to different counterparties. In case of secured financing the default risk is coupled with the recovery risk (price risk) of the collateral and the risk position can be settled promptly in case of a default while in case of the unsecured financing the settlement of the recovery depends on the insolvency process.

This comparison in particular shows that the credit risk toward the counterparty in the unsecured financing transaction being rather illiquid is opposed to the market value risk of the received collateral which is assumed to be liquid in the secured case plus the correlation of this risk and the credit risk of the issuer of the securities taken as collateral. In the adverse case this risk correlation is also known as "wrong way risk".

## 3.3 Liquidity Transformation

Accordingly considering liquidity as an absolute quantity is not useful but as a relative quantity: a relation between secured financing and unsecured financing, which we term liquidity transformation. This transformation is not independent from credit respective counterparty risk, since each type of financing is associated with a different type of credit risk. The liquidity transformation is dependent on the type of entity and cannot be considered separately from its legal status. A bank has different access and a higher degree of freedom to assign liquidity irrespective of the purpose than, e.g. an investment fund.

## 4 New Approach to CVA Hedging

The new CVA hedging approach outlined below represents a response to current challenges in banking regulation and reveals the importance of liquidity transformation. The legal-based background described above can be used to explain current challenges of banking industry if in addition to prevailing market conditions the regulatory and financial accounting environments are taken into account. Recent environmental changes have immediate impact on banking business activities concerning counterparty risk and can be summarized as follows:

Regulatory and Accounting Aspects

- CCR (counterparty credit risk) is under scrutiny of regulators and financial accounting standard setters.
- Increased regulatory requirements on bilateral collateralization and clearing.
- Increased (regulatory) capital requirements for banks.
- Increased P/L volatility due to IFRS fair value accounting rules (e.g. recognition of CVA).

Business Impact

- Increased (regulatory) capital affects resp. limits banking business.
- Intensified application of credit risk mitigation by netting, collateralization and hedging.
- Increased demand for secured (collateralized) transactions
- Increased demand for (liquid / high quality) collateral.
- Increased demand for optimization of collateral.

### *4.1 Issue*

During the financial crises regulators and financial accounting setters notified the relevance of counterparty credit risk in OTC derivative contracts. In response to this relevance several regulatory (legislative) initiatives have been undertaken like central clearing, increased regulatory capital, etc. These impacted the business of banking industry in several ways: intensified use of credit risk mitigation techniques and increased demand for secured transactions (demand for collateral, cf. also [3]).

Despite the environmental changes credit risk mitigation is and remains essential to continue banking business. Considering equity as a scarce source, banks are forced to tighten their credit exposure in order to offset the increase in capital charges due to increased costs for CCR and other factors. The tightening of credit exposure limits banking business and increases the demand for credit risk mitigation techniques (including hedging).

The mentioned regulatory changes induce tremendous costs for the banking industry. Therefore, managing credit risk by commonly used CDS hedging strategies becomes expensive in presence of the banking regulation, so credit risk management will be rearranged, e.g. more offsetting positions, avoiding exposures (reducing limits) or transferred ("outsourced") outside the regulated banking sector, so e.g. investment funds are in a favorable position to manage a bank's risks. This also holds for counterparty credit risk following the idea to transfer counterparty credit risk to market participants outside the banking sector that are in the situation to manage this risk economically at lower cost than banks.

Additionally banking industry is faced with various different regulations. With respect to counterparty credit risk a bank is confronted with conflicting objectives resulting from regulatory requirements, i.e. Basel II/III, and financial accounting rules. Therefore, under current regulatory and accounting requirements banks cannot manage counterparty credit risk (CCR) of derivatives uniformly in respect of capital requirements and P/L volatility. This results from the fact that the hedging of counterparty credit risk exposure (in terms of Basel II/III requirements) requires the hedging of current and future changes of exposure, while IFRS only considers current exposure. So a bank is required to hedge more than the current exposure ("overhedging") in terms of Basel II/III. But since hedging is mainly carried out by derivatives as CDS, these CDS cause P/L volatility under IFRS, since derivatives are recognized at fair value through P/L.

As described above secured and unsecured financing is common practice in finance industry and can be observed in counterparty credit risk of OTC derivative contracts. As illustrated below in an uncollateralized OTC derivative trade between Bank A and counterparty B, the parties enter into an unsecured financing relationship. If the market value of the derivative trades of Bank A against counterparty B increases then Bank A is exposed to counterparty credit risk (CVA risk). Bank A implicitly provides counterparty B an illiquid credit line in the sense, that the positive exposure amount ("market value") is recognized as an asset which becomes a legal claim in the Event of Default. This exposure is not a tradable asset but needs to be funded thus it could be interpreted as an illiquid asset. In comparison to standard banking credit business, this credit line is unlimited and varies with the market value of the underlying derivative trades, which implies also unlimited funding. The current focus of discussions and research concentrates on measuring counterparty credit risk by exposure and default probability modeling (CVA risk) and the assignment of the appropriate discount rate for the OTC derivative trades reflecting the FVA. The discussed approaches share the following assumptions:

1. No market segmentation between collateralized and uncollateralized OTC derivative trades.
2. The application of the absence of arbitrage principle, which in particular assumes the unlimited use of liquidity by market participants.
3. Liquidity risk and credit risk cannot be decoupled.
4. The coincidence of counterparty credit risk and credit risk, which can be both hedged by the same type of hedging instruments (credit default swaps (CDS), contingent credit default swaps (CCDS)).
5. The absence of transaction costs, which are represented by regulatory costs (e.g. CVA risk charges according to Basel II/III) and reported earnings volatility under IFRS stemming from fair value accounting of counterparty fair value adjustments and derivative valuation.

These ideal assumptions are not necessarily met in reality, therefore alternative approaches have to be explored.

## *4.2 Solution*

Since banks with significant activities in derivatives markets can be affected quite heavily by the aforementioned issues, a workable solution should solve the build-in conflict of regulatory and accounting requirements. As a result, the solution contributes to an improved competitiveness of the bank in the context of derivative risk management, derivatives' pricing, and support the bank in conducting derivatives business which will ultimately benefit the economy as a whole. Consequently, a potential solution is about developing a financial instrument ("credit risk mitigating instrument") which reduces the Basel II/III CCR capital requirements and CVA risk charge without resulting in additional P/L volatility under IFRS. Such a financial instrument represents a solution to the issues described above since it creates:

- A market for counterparty credit risk exposure
  The positive exposure of an (un-) collateralized derivative portfolio can be considered as an illiquid asset in contrast, e.g. to a liquid issuance of a bank.
- A new asset type—make the derivative claim a tradable asset
  The idea is to make this exposure tradable in exchange for collateral by means of an instrument like Collateral Support Annex (CSA) which directly refers to the possibly varying positive exposure of a derivative portfolio.
- An active market involving banks and investment funds
  In order to increase liquidity and to avoid only a shift of capital charges from one institution to another due to hedging activities for the taken credit risk a transfer to a market participant outside the banking sector is considered.

The outline of a solution follows the liquidity transformation. The unsecured financing for OTC derivatives would be represented by uncollateralized OTC derivatives while secured financing requires corresponding posting of collateral. Pursuing the

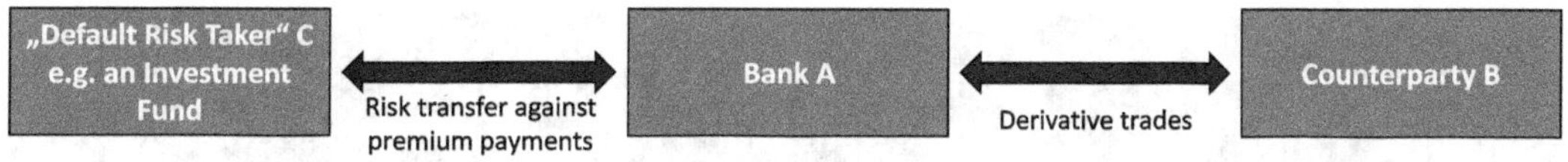


**Fig. 1** Secured OTC derivative transaction

aim of decoupling liquidity and counterparty risk, at least three parties are necessary to involve as demonstrated in the analysis on repos above. Therefore, the aim could not be achieved by cash collateralized bilateral OTC derivatives commonly used in the interbank market, since there is still a one-to-one correspondence between liquidity requirements (e.g. cash collateral postings) and counterparty risk. Additionally a bilateral CSA assumes that both counterparties have unlimited access to liquidity, which represents a difficulty if counterparty B is a corporate according to its limited access to collateral/cash. Therefore a secured financing transaction for CVA hedging has to be structured differently.

The secured financing transaction outlined in Fig. 1 involves a third party "Default Risk Taker" C, who is posting collateral to Bank A on behalf of counterparty B, i.e. whenever the value of the derivative trade is positive for Bank A. This transaction represents a tri-party CSA and works similar to a margining. The transaction between "Default Risk Taker" C and Bank A is an asymmetric contract, since if the value of the derivative trade is negative for Bank A, no collateral is provided to or by Bank A. In case of a default of counterparty B the posted collateral is not returned to "Default Risk Taker C". The structure described above represents the appropriate complement for a bilateral uncollateralized OTC derivative transaction.

The structure reveals the concept of liquidity transformation including a decoupling of liquidity and counterparty risk, since by using the contract the unsecured financing transaction is transformed into a secured financing transaction. Referring to the comparison of unsecured and secured financing described above (cf. Sect. 2.3), the proposed structure goes one step further by linking both market segments and transforming liquidity within one single transaction. By definition of the liquidity transformation, the transaction exchanges different types of credit risk.

### *4.3 Application*

The table in Fig. 2 shows the contemplation of the new CVA hedge structure (cash collateral with contingent financial guarantee, "CCCFG"; for more detail refer to [5]) to existing credit risk mitigation techniques applied in the banking industry. Its main features are summarized as follows:

- The proposed structure represents a credit risk mitigating instrument, which reduces the Basel II/III CCR capital requirements CVA risk charge, since the cash collateral provided by a third party is permitted under Basel II/III requirements and reduces the exposure according to Basel II/III.

| Aspects | Netting | Bilateral Collateralization | Credit Default Swap (CDS) based hedges | Contingent CDS |
|---|---|---|---|---|
| **Economics** | Reduction of the risk position by netting of exposures | Counterparty risk is reduced by posted (cash) collateral | Hedges of the counterparty default risk | Hedges of the counterparty default and exposure risk |
| **Operational** | ▪ Legally enforceable<br>▪ Default netting (ISDA standard) | ▪ Changes in OTC derivative contracts (CSA)<br>▪ Requires liquidity (an issue for corporates) | ▪ Delta Hedging required<br>▪ Liquid CDS | ▪ No Delta Hedging required<br>▪ Less liquid than CDS |
| **Financial Accounting** (IFRS) | IAS 32 requires simultaneous payment- and default netting | Posted collateral reduces fair value volatility | Fair value accounting through P&L | Fair value accounting through P&L |
| **Regulatory** (Basel II/III) | Basel differs from IFRS due to default netting | Reduces derivative exposure (credit risk mitigation) | Credit risk mitigation if requirements are met | Credit risk mitigation if requirements are met |

**Fig. 2** Current and new approaches for credit risk mitigation in banking industry

- Accordingly there is immediate regulatory capital relief, which results in an immediate saving respectively reduction of the cost of equity.
- The proposed structure simultaneously qualifies as a contingent financial guarantee such that there is no additional P/L volatility under IFRS. In particular the financial guarantee accounting under IFRS applies to the proposed structure by considering the case of default. In case of a default of OTC derivatives contracted under ISDA the final claim is determined. The financial guarantee under IFRS comes into effect only at default—not before—and "guarantees" the value of the final claim, which is recognized at amortized cost and physically transferred to counterparty C in return for cash to Bank A. The final claim takes into account the posted collateral until the Event of Default. For a more detailed description refer to [5].
- As becomes apparent from the table above the new CVA hedge structure is a separate financial instrument. This cash collateral with contingent financial guarantee ("CCCFG") differs from a "traditional" CDS/CCDS, since the collateral postings are directly related to the counterpartys exposure. In case of a CCDS the cash collateral refers to the CCDS contract itself reflecting its value and there is no direct legal link to the exposure subject to hedging by the CCDS. Additionally CCDS represents derivatives in terms of IFRS and not necessarily qualify as credit risk mitigation instrument under Basel II/III. If a CCDS qualifies as credit risk mitigation instrument it applies to the Basel II/III PD, while the CCCFG directly affects the exposure.
- Operationally the new CVA hedging instrument is more effective and less costly than CDS delta hedging approaches, since a constant adjustment of a hedging position using CDS induces transaction costs and depends also on the gamma of the risk position. Accordingly the hedge position is never "perfect".

- The approach is flexible with respect to counterparty risk profiles, since it applies to linear and nonlinear exposure profiles.
- The legal framework of the approach is based on ISDA, which ensures the operational effectiveness in terms of legal certainty and the recognition in front office IT systems in order to process the transaction.
- It has to be noticed that investment funds have to observe certain rules and regulations which come with the specific fund format and domicile. For example, funds fulfilling the highest standards are limited to invest in eligible assets which are characterized by sufficient liquidity in order to ensure that the fund is in a position to meet potential redemptions. Bilateral transactions that are illiquid by definition require a buy-and-hold investment strategy which may not be suitable for all investment funds.

## 4.4 Example

In the following for the sake of simplicity only a qualitative example is provided, since by comparing the induced costs the CVA hedge already indicates its profitability.

- Bank A holds a portfolio of uncollateralized derivatives (e.g. interest rate swaps (IRS)) with Counterparty B (e.g. a corporate) a netting set is considered.[4]
- Bank A enters into a CVA hedge transaction with Investment Fund C who is taking over credit (counterparty credit risk of B) and market risk and provides liquidity with reference to the uncollateralized derivative transaction(s) between Bank A and Counterparty B in terms of the cash collateral postings to Bank A. The transaction between Investment Fund C and Bank A is a unilateral (asymmetric) collateral contract in favour of Bank A (and on behalf of Counterparty B). The transaction chart follows Fig. 1.
- In the following table the impact for Bank A with and without CVA hedge is summarized:

With respect to the risk illustrated in the first line in the table above, the CVA hedge transaction mitigates entirely the risk of Bank A by transferring the risk to investment fund C. This results from the posted cash collateral of Investment Fund C to Bank A on behalf of counterparty C. Comparing the induced costs (second line in the table above) reveals that the (uncollateralized) derivative business is exposed to regulatory and cost of equity charges as well as funding costs. In case of the CVA hedge transaction all these costs are inapplicable, since the posted cash collateral by Investment Fund C to Bank A on behalf of counterparty B leads to entire regulatory capital and cost of capital relief and serves as funding to the derivative exposure between Bank A and counterparty B. On the other hand Bank A pays a fee to Investment Fund C for taking over the counterparty credit risk of B and also interest

[4]In order to keep legal and operational complexity in an event of default low one netting set is considered.

| Bank A | without CVA Hedge | with CVA Hedge |
|---|---|---|
| **Risk** | ▪ **Counterparty Credit Risk of B,**<br>▪ **Market Risk and**<br>▪ **Liquidity/Funding Provision** | **0** |
| **Induced Costs** | ▪ **Costs related to Counterparty Credit Risk B**<br>▪ **Cost of Equity on Regulatory Capital** (Basel II/III charges))<br>▪ **Costs associated with the Leverage Ratio (Basel III)**<br>▪ **Costs of Funding costs** (depending on Bank A's rating and funding model assumption) | ▪ **CVA hedge spread („fee payment")**<br>▪ **Interest on received cash collateral** |
| **Cash Flows** | ▪ **No Default:** derivative payments<br>▪ **Default:** residual claim times recovery rate | ▪ **No Default:** derivative payments, fee payment, receive cash collateral, pay interest on cash collateral, repayment of collateral at maturity (since exposure reduces to zero).<br>▪ **Default**: physical delivery of residual claim vs. keeping posted cash collateral and receiving difference payment up to the amount of residual claim |

**Fig. 3** Comparison derivatives exposure with and without CVA Hedge transaction from bank A's perspective

on the posted cash collateral. Describing the associated cash flow profiles the two situations, default and non-default of the counterparty, are distinguished (third line in the table above). While in case without CVA hedge structure the cash profiles are straightforward, with CVA hedge transaction in addition fee and interest payments on the collateral have to be considered in the non-default situation. In the event of default of counterparty B, the residual claim of the transaction is physically delivered to Investment Fund C in return for cash equal to the notional of the residual claim. This procedure follows standard ISDA rules (Fig. 3).

## 5 Conclusion

The new CVA hedging instrument is used in order to transfer counterparty credit risk to entities which are able to manage the risk on an economic basis at lower cost. Investment funds can act as "credit risk taker" and manage counterparty credit exposure at a lower cost than banks, since investment funds are not subject to regulatory capital requirements according to Basel II/III. It has to be noted though that an implementation of the solution described above requires an intense capability and knowledge of dealing with derivatives at the risk taking investment funds. On the other hand, since investment funds are not subject to the same regulations as those for banks described above they may become a natural partner for banks in this context.

The proposed structure bridges the difference between capital rules and financial accounting standards in order to optimize capital requirements and charges for CVA. This is achieved by its liquidity transformation property—the liquidity and credit risk transformation of the counterparty's exposure—and by meeting the Basel II/III and

IFRS requirements: simultaneous CCR capital and CVA risk charge relief as well as reduced P/L volatility in IFRS resulting from CVA accounting. While the objective outlined herein is predominantly to provide a suitable solution for CVA issues in context of derivatives transactions, it may also create interesting opportunities for investors of the risk taking investment funds.

This solution also contributes to valuation and the discussion on FVA and CVA, since it requires the pricing of the collateral between counterparties "at arm's length". This price determines the discount rate by applying the absence of arbitrage principle. As a consequence FVA is disentangled from CVA by using the proposed structure as a mean.

**Acknowledgements** The KPMG Center of Excellence in Risk Management is acknowledged for organizing the conference "Challenges in Derivatives Markets - Fixed Income Modeling, Valuation Adjustments, Risk Management, and Regulation".

**Open Access** This chapter is distributed under the terms of the Creative Commons Attribution 4.0 International License (http://creativecommons.org/licenses/by/4.0/), which permits use, duplication, adaptation, distribution and reproduction in any medium or format, as long as you give appropriate credit to the original author(s) and the source, a link is provided to the Creative Commons license and any changes made are indicated.

The images or other third party material in this book are included in the work's Creative Commons license, unless indicated otherwise in the credit line; if such material is not included in the work's Creative Commons license and the respective action is not permitted by statutory regulation, users will need to obtain permission from the license holder to duplicate, adapt or reproduce the material.

## References

1. Basel Committee on Banking Supervision: International Convergence of Capital Measurement and Capital Standards (2006)
2. Basel Committee on Banking Supervision: Basel III: A Global Regulatory Framework for More Resilient Banks and Banking Systems (2011)
3. Hünseler, M.: Credit Portfolio Management. Palgrave Macmillan, London (2013)
4. International Accounting Standards Board: International Financial Reporting Standards (IFRS) (2015)
5. Schubert, D.: How to hedge CVA without getting hurt, pp. 76–79. Risk Magazine, September Issue (2014)

# FVA and Electricity Bill Valuation Adjustment—Much of a Difference?

**Damiano Brigo, Christian P. Fries, John Hull, Matthias Scherer, Daniel Sommer and Ralf Werner**

**Abstract** Pricing counterparty credit risk, although being in the focus for almost a decade by now, is far from being resolved. It is highly controversial if any valuation adjustment besides the basic CVA should be taken into account, and if so, for what purpose. Even today, the handling of CVA, DVA, FVA, ... differs between the regulatory, the accounting, and the economic point of view. Eventually, if an agreement is reached that CVA has to be taken into account, it remains unclear if CVA can be modelled linearly, or if nonlinear models need to be resorted to. Finally, industry practice and implementation differ in several aspects. Hence, a unified theory and treatment of FVA and alike is not yet tangible. The conference *Challenges in Derivatives Markets*, held at Technische Universität München in March/April 2015, featured a panel discussion with panelists representing different points of view: John

D. Brigo (✉)
Department of Mathematics, Imperial College London, London, UK
e-mail: damiano.brigo@imperial.ac.uk

C.P. Fries
Department of Mathematics, LMU Munich, Theresienstrasse 39,
80333 Munich, Germany
e-mail: christian.fries@math.lmu.de

J. Hull
Joseph L. Rotman School of Management, University of Toronto, 105 St George St,
Toronto, ON M5S 3E6, Canada
e-mail: hull@rotman.utoronto.ca

M. Scherer
Lehrstuhl für Finanzmathematik, Technische Universität München, Parkring 11, 85748
Garching-Hochbrück, Germany
e-mail: scherer@tum.de

D. Sommer
KPMG Financial Risk Management, The Squaire am Flughafen, 60549
Frankfurt, Germany
e-mail: dsommer@kpmg.com

R. Werner
Professur für Wirtschaftsmathematik, Universität Augsburg,
Universitätsstraße 14, 86159 Augsburg, Germany
e-mail: ralf.werner@math.uni-augsburg.de

© The Author(s) 2016

K. Glau et al. (eds.), *Innovations in Derivatives Markets*, Springer Proceedings in Mathematics & Statistics 165, DOI 10.1007/978-3-319-33446-2_8

Hull, who argues that FVA might not exist at all; in contrast to Christian Fries, who sees the need of all relevant costs to be covered within valuation but not within adjustments. Damiano Brigo emphasises the nonlinearity of (most) valuation adjustments and is concerned about overlapping adjustments and double-counting. Finally, Daniel Sommer puts the exit price in the focus. The following (mildly edited) record of the panel discussion repeats the main arguments of the discussants—ultimately culminating in the awareness that if everybody charges an electricity bill valuation adjustment, it has to become part of any quoted price.

**Keywords** Counterparty credit risk · Credit valuation adjustment · Debit valuation adjustment · Wrong way risk

## 1 Welcome

*Matthias:* Welcome back from the coffee break. After the many interesting talks we already enjoyed today, we will now continue the conference with a panel discussion on current issues in counterparty credit risk. And we are very proud to present you such prestigious speakers on this topic—our anchorman Ralf Werner will introduce them to you in a minute (Fig. 1).

We hope that this discussion will provide you with insights on the current discussion about CVA, DVA, FVA, etc. that go beyond what you can read in scientific papers. In my personal view, these valuation adjustments are a special topic in financial mathematics, because they are not simply expressed by formulas some mathematicians invent and you implement in a spreadsheet. In contrast, these adjustments are chal-

**Fig. 1** View on the panel. From *left* to *right*: Matthias, Ralf, Daniel, Christian, Damiano, and John

lenges a whole bank has to work on as a team, because they can involve different departments, different asset classes, different trading desks, the IT-infrastructure, lots of data, etc. Hence, it is not something that is "done" after a scientific paper has been published. Moreover, there is no consensus—neither in academia nor in practice—on what adjustments should be used and how they must be computed. In this regard, I am very happy to see representatives from the financial industry as well as from academia gathering for this discussion.

I will now pass the microphone to Ralf Werner who will be our anchorman. Ralf is professor for "Wirtschaftsmathematik" at Augsburg University. Prior to this he was professor at the University of Applied Sciences in Munich, and prior to this he worked for several financial institutions—most of which have defaulted.

*Ralf:* Yes, indeed. Three in total.

*Matthias:* In any case, he gained quite some experience—practical and theoretical—with credit defaults that he is now sharing with you. Thank you very much Ralf!

*Ralf:* Thank you, Matthias, and a warm welcome to everybody from my side. I'm very honoured to chair this discussion. I don't think I will need to do much because we already had an excellent warm-up over lunchtime, and my experience is that these four experts in the panel won't need much input from my side to keep the discussions controversial, yet fruitful.

For the unlikely event that the discussion might get stuck, we have prepared a few additional questions. Further, any question or comment from the audience will be addressed immediately, i.e. we will interrupt whenever possible and whenever meaningful.

The idea is that each discussant has about ten minutes to address one or more topics he deems important. I'll try to dig a bit deeper and if you like you join in asking and eventually after 15 minutes we hand over to the next discussant. This means that in one hour we should be able to pretty much cover everything concerning DVA, FVA, CVA, multi-curve, whatsoever, within the scope of the conference.

Let me now introduce the participants in reverse alphabetical order. I would like to start with Daniel Sommer to my left. Daniel is not only representing one of the main sponsors of this conference, but he's further representing almost 20 years of experience in financial consulting. Daniel is a member of the financial risk management group at KPMG, and for more than ten years he's responsible partner for risk methodology. Daniel holds a PhD on interest-rate models from the University of Bonn, he has published several papers, he is working for all major banks in Germany, so in short he comes with a broad experience of what's going on in the market. I think this is an excellent opportunity for us to challenge his knowledge and his experience.

On the other end of the panel we have John Hull. I both asked John as well as Damiano during the lunch break, and we agreed that re-introducing both of them after we had such great and detailed introductions this morning prior to their talks is saying the same thing twice over. John will hopefully talk a bit about FVA, and I assume all of you have read his 2012 paper, see [7]. If not, my introduction may last another 60 s, so please at least run through the abstract of this great paper. It's an excellent work, starting heavy discussions in the community, I'd like to say—fruitful discussions, raising lots of interesting questions on FVA: *Is it really there? Should it be zero or not?* For me, somehow, the discussion is not yet over, so I am looking forward to what John has to say.

Besides John, between Daniel and Damiano, we have Christian Fries, our local panel member from the LMU. Christian was appointed professor for Financial Mathematics a few years ago. I should emphasise that besides his academic duties he is still mainly working at DZ BANK where he is responsible for model development, heading this department. Of course, I think you all know Christian from his open-source library and from his book, resp. on Monte Carlo methods in finance [5], and I'm sure we will gain a lot of insight from this mixed-role in practice and academia.

And, finally, we have Damiano Brigo with us, whom I would like to start right away without any further notice, so please, Damiano.

## 2 Damiano Brigo

*Damiano:* Okay, thank you. I made some of the points during the presentation, but I think it's worth summing up a little bit what's been happening from my point of view. I worked on what is now called CVA since, I think, 2002 or 2003 at the bank. At the time it was called counterparty risk pricing, not CVA, and nobody was really very interested because the spreads were small for most of the trades and so on, so the work was recycled a few years later, especially in 2007. But as we did that it was clear that this was only a small part of a much broader picture where we had to update the valuation paradigms used in investment banking and not only there (Fig. 2).

The big point that seems to come out, at least methodologically, from that big picture is nonlinearity, which shows up in a number of aspects that can or may be neglected in many cases but not always. So one of the aspects is the close-out, what

**Fig. 2** Damiano Brigo giving his presentation on "Nonlinear valuation under credit gap risk, collateral margins, funding costs, and multiple curves"

happens at default. What do you put in your simulation? Should you use a risk-free close-out, where at the first default you just stop and present-value the remaining cash flows without including any further credit, collateral, and funding liquidity effects? Or should you rather use a replacement closeout, where those effects are all included in the valuation at default?

This is a big question. If you go for the replacement, then the problem as we have seen becomes recursive, if you like, or nonlinear from a different point of view. And that's not because we mathematicians are trying to push BSDEs or semi-linear PDEs on you. It's simply because of the accounting assumptions. It's a basic fact, an accounting rule that says that you have to value your deal at default using a replacement value. This is a simple accounting rule, but it translates into a quite nightmarish nonlinear constraint in the valuation. Then when borrowing and lending rates are asymmetric in financing your hedge, if they are justified to be, then you have another source of nonlinearity because to price these costs of carry you need to know the future value of the hedge accounts and of the trade itself. And this induces another component of nonlinearity (see [4] and [3]).

If it's there or not depends on the funding model you adopt for your treasury. If the trading desk is always net borrowing and possible liquidity bases are symmetric, you don't have that, and you can more or less have a symmetric problem, but if it's not net borrowing then you do have an asymmetry in the funding rate: one is the credit risk of your bank, one is the credit risk of the external funder, plus liquidity bases. So, we all know that borrowing and lending don't happen at the same rates usually (well, we experience it personally, at least).

So, the nonlinearity is there. The big question is *Should we embrace it or keep it at arm's length?*, because it makes things too complicated in practice. The answer is the second one, and basically if there is any real nonlinearity in the picture, the required methods like BSDE's or semilinear PDE's are very hard to implement on large portfolios in an efficient way that ensures that you can value the book many times during trading activity very quickly—especially because nonlinearity means the price or the value is not obtained by adding up the values of the assets in the portfolio, so you need to price the portfolios at all the possible aggregation levels that you need, and if each component of such a run is slow, you can imagine what kind of operational nightmare you get into. So I don't think it's realistic or feasible at the moment that we embrace nonlinearity. We need to linearise, which means, in the two cases I mentioned, we assume that borrowing and lending rates are the same, which is true for some funding policies, and you also assume that you don't use a replacement closeout at default in the CVA calculation of the valuation adjustment for credit.

Then the other problem I would mention is keeping all the risks in separate boxes with a label on each box: *CVA: this is credit risk, FVA: this is funding cost, LVA: this is collateral cost* and so on. This is a little misleading because these risks interact in the way that I just described. Each cash flow involves the whole future value which depends on all the risks together. The classification in boxes is useful managerially because you want to assign responsibility in an organisation; you cannot have everyone responsible for everything unless you have a very illuminated kind of workplace, but if you don't, you want to assign responsibility for credit risk to the CVA desk, and maybe the funding costs to a different team in the CVA or XVA desk and so on. But if these aspects are so connected as I said, it's very hard to separate the risks in different boxes. Wrong-way risk is another aspect of the fact that the dependence makes the idea that you can have risk taken care of separately by the CVA desk for credit risk and by the traditional trading desk for the trade main market risk not very realistic. To some extent, you can do it, but it's not precise.

So, these are labels that we apply in order to be able to work operationally in a realistic setting, but they don't have the amount of rigour or precision that we would sometimes think they have in practice. So, should we, again, monitor and watch out for manifestations of nonlinearity like overlapping adjustments? We saw that in some set-ups DVA almost completely overlaps with the funding adjustment. And, so, should we be aware of these and avoid the double-counting, or should we forget it and just compute the different adjustments, add them up, and forget about all these overlaps and analyses?

I think it's important to have at least an initial understanding of these issues before throwing ourselves into very difficult calculations. There are many other things I could say. The nonlinearity makes the deal pricing very difficult—in funding costs especially. When you don't know the funding policy of the other institution, or maybe you don't agree with the funding policy of the other institution, but you're still asked to pay their funding prices, you might object and go to another bank, or you might in turn say, *I also have some funding costs, and I want to charge you.* And there is no transparency in the funding model of the treasury process. How can bilateral valuation be achieved in a transparent way? This is another problem.

So a number of authors conclude by saying the funding-adjusted value is a value; it's not a price. You can use it for profitability analysis internally, but you shouldn't charge it outright to a client because it's hard to justify this charge fully, as we have seen. On the other hand and this is the final point I want to raise, which is kind of a meta-topic, I would like to talk about the self-fulfilling aspect in financial methodology, that if two or three top banks start doing something, everybody else follows because this becomes the new standard. *Top bank A is doing this, top bank B is doing this, so we have to do this as well.* And then even if something is not justified based on financial principles, or it is not reasonable methodologically or even mathematically it doesn't matter because if you don't do it you place yourself out of the market.

This is very frustrating for a scientist, for someone who thinks there are underlying sound principles behind what's going on, but in the end you are forced to set the problem aside, because that's what the market is doing, and if you don't follow, you are automatically out.

I would like to conclude with that kind of provocative point, and I'm sure my colleagues will have more interesting points to make on it. Thank you.

*Ralf:* Thank you, Damiano. Is there anyone in the panel who wants to take up one of these points? Or in the audience?

*Christian:* I'd like to ask you, Damiano: you said *close-out* value. This is a very important discussion. So, from my point of view, is this an issue for the lawyers, or is this an issue for financial mathematics? What would you say?

*Damiano:* I think it's an issue for both in a sense, in that the lawyers should tell us if it makes sense to have this close-out there or not based on legal considerations. In the end, I don't think we can decide this with mathematics alone. With mathematics we can say, *If you adopt this close-out, the valuation problem is like this, and if you adopt this other, the valuation problem is like that*, but the decision must be taken based on accounting, financial, and legal principles, not based on mathematics.

I would say that the regulations should converge. We've had ISDA pushing a little towards the replacement close-out, but very mildly. ISDA wrote in 2009 that in determining a close-out amount, the determining party may consider any relevant information, including quotations (either firm or indicative) for replacement transactions supplied by one or more third parties (!) that may take into account the creditworthiness of the determining party at the time the quotation is provided (notice the use of *may*). In the end I think it's a decision for the regulators and the policy-makers. We discussed this earlier, but let me be more explicit. Are you thinking, with respect to your operational model, let's say, when the deal has defaulted do you think to actually replace it with a new one or simply to liquidate everything and close the position? This is the real question. If you think to replace it with another physical deal, and you intend to re-start the trade with another contracting party, then you should assume a replacement close-out. If you're thinking of liquidating the position, then it stops here, with a cash settlement, and you may use a risk-free closeout. However, from the point of view of continuity, mathematics seems to suggest that you should include the replacement because you value the trade, mark it to market every day, including credit and funding costs, and all of a sudden at the default event, you remove this. You create a discontinuity in valuation this way, which shows up as some funny effect, which I don't want to go into right now.

I think mathematics gives you some hint, but it's really a regulatory / accounting / legal discussion that we should have, and then use the maths to include the outcome properly into the valuation. That's my view.

*Ralf:* Let me exaggerate a bit, but will this lead into a situation where your line of reasoning is also applied to mortgages or government debt? Would Greece say, *I'll only pay 60 because I'm valued at 50 anyway, so this is the right replacement value?* Will this lead us into such kind of discussions?

*Damiano:* That is very hard to model because when you have such a large market effect, then the close-out itself could change the economy basically, so I don't think it's very realistic in that sense.

In fact, we found in the published paper [1] that there is no superior close-out. If you use the replacement close-out, you have some advantages in terms of continuity and consistency, but you'll have some problems when the correlation goes up towards the systemic risk scenario. In that case the risk-free close-out becomes more sensible economically. There is no clear-cut case, and you cannot make a regulation that depends on correlation or the level of perceived systemic risk switching from one close-out to the other. Can you imagine what happens when you are in the middle. I don't even want to go there (see [2]).

So I think we have to be very careful about the maths, and we have to clearly understand which level of aggregation, of size, we're talking about, and in the case of a country, I think that would be quite dangerous.

*Daniel:* I agree.

*Damiano:* At the global derivatives conference a couple of years ago, I was talking to some of the banking quants and I said, *Which close-out are you using?*, and they would say *We're using the risk-free close-out because that's the only thing we can implement on a large portfolio.*

*Ralf:* I agree. I've heard this is hidden in the recovery rate, anyway.

*Christian:* So maybe I'd like to comment or offer a question on this self-fulfilling prophecy because I do not understand it. I do understand that if there is some idiot in the market who's trading options at the wrong price, then I can use his incorrect pricing to have an implied volatility. Hence, I can imply his dumbness into my model and that's fine. But now you say that everybody is doing it, so we should do it. And I believe this does not apply to FVA. For me, FVA is a real cost and, for example, the market will now decree not to account for FVA, I still picture that I have lost, for example, if I issue a bond at LIBOR plus spread, and just put the money to the ECB for a zero interest rate, I have a loss, right? So, then I would say I would rather go out of the market instead of making the loss.

*Damiano:* Okay, so let me ask you another question. Suppose electricity bills become prohibitive and electricity skyrockets, will you start charging your client an electricity bill valuation adjustment because that's a real cost you're having? Or will this be embedded in the prices like in the old days.

*Christian:* It is.

*Damiano:* When you go and buy some bread from the baker, the baker doesn't charge you a running water and electricity bill valuation adjustment because he needs some water to run his bakery, you know ...

*Christian:* Yeah, but if you go to the bakery, he charges you such that he is covering all his costs.

*Damiano:* That's right.

*Christian:* It's just not transparent.

*Damiano:* That's right.

*Christian:* But the cost is inside the price.

*Damiano:* But then if you add these valuation adjustments one by one, one after the next, every year a new one, with the nonlinearity effects we see that they possibly overlap, you are overcharging sometimes, and this is not good, and that's what I feel is happening.

KVA. Think about it. KVA is a valuation adjustment on capital requirements, but the future CVA potential losses trigger capital requirements—so you have your valuation adjustment on a valuation adjustment. This is getting out of hand.

*Christian:* This point I understand, but that is regulatory …

*Damiano:* But going back to the *self-fulfilling prophecy*, the other thing I wanted to say: think about base correlation. For CDOs base correlation is a model. You use a Gaussian copula, flatten 7,750 correlations into one, apply different flat correlations to each different tranche on the same pool. To explain a panel of 15 CDOs you have 15 different and inconsistent models and then … I kid you not, once at an international conference I met one quant from a top bank who was lecturing about base correlation along the lines of *here's an example of calibration, this is a great model, you should use it, CDOs are great, invest in this.* And when I asked, after his talk, I have some questions for you about this model, he'd say, *Oh, I'm the marketing quant. I don't do models really.* And I said, *Take me to your leader!*, meaning the real quants then, and he said, *Oh, you cannot talk to them; they don't talk to the public. My function is to convince people, investors and the market that this is a great model, this is a great product, and everybody must come into this market.*

However what you are saying is partly true. If the market is kind of complete in a way, then by hedging your strategy according to the correct hedge you can prove that your price is right against an opponent, but if the market is largely incomplete, this is very hard to do. And this is what we look at when we look at funding costs. We don't know the hedging or the funding policy of another entity. It's not transparent. You don't know what they're doing, how they're financing, their short-term/long-term funding policy, their internal fund transfer pricing, their bases. You don't know many things.

*Christian:* This is exactly the point. The market is not complete here, and I cannot pass this risk to someone else. This is my example with the volatility: if someone is on the wrong volatility I can pass this risk to him, but with my funding it's still my risk and it's my cost to cover it. I believe it has to be in there. If you make it transparent, it's something different, maybe.

*Damiano:* Okay, but then you have to really watch out for the overlap as you add new risk. For example, in some formulations if you take into account the trading DVA and also the full funding benefit, you have the same thing twice. You have to be very careful there. So this practice of adding a new adjustment on top of the old ones every year is very dangerous because you may miss some of the overlaps. The banks are paying attention to it; it's not that bad. If it develops in the fact that in ten years we'll have 15 new valuation adjustment, this will be out of control.

*Audience member:* I have a question because I really like this bakery example, so let's say you have one bakery who sells bread for 1.80 and who doesn't have very high electricity costs, and you have another bakery which sells it for 2.00 because they have a lot higher electricity costs. So what is the market price, then? Is it 1.80?

*Damiano:* The price, if you look at a clean price versus an adjusted price, the price would be the clean price without costs. But then, of course, the price is adjusted into an operational price that takes into account the bill, but the bill is not quoted explicitly, it's embedded in the price, so that if you think this baker is too expensive, you'll go to the other one. Maybe the other one is out of town, so they have lower costs because of that.

But in the other industries, we always knew that the price of a good that you end up buying depends on many circumstances that are not in a theoretical price in a way. Somehow ironically, part of the finance industry arrived at this realisation quite late. But that's another matter. I took too much time and I don't want to monopolise this panel.

*John:* Don't forget that we have bid-offer spreads in this industry. Those bid-offer spreads are designed to cover overhead costs, so adding in costs for electricity and other things is not really the way to do it.

*Ralf:* Thank you, John. Let me hand over to Christian. Christian, maybe you want to tell us your opinion on what's going on in financial institutions at the moment. Maybe with some more focus on the practitioner's point of view.

## 3 Christian Fries

*Christian:* You've asked me to make a few statements and I take the role of the practitioner.

I have the same opinion as Damiano, but I'd like to make the point that I don't like the adjustments. And why? Maybe because the word "adjustment" already implies that you did something wrong. If I have to adjust something, it tells me that the original value is wrong. For example, in my car there is this small device that tells me how long it takes to get from Frankfurt to Munich, and what would I like to see there? With my car it takes five hours. I could also fly. It would take one hour if you take the plane, but you have to add four hours' adjustment. So I would prefer just to see the five because the five is correct. The one hour is no information for me.

Then, let me give you another example. Consider a swap which exchanges LIBOR against a fixed rate, and this swap is traded at a bank, usually at a swap desk, sometimes it's called flow trading. And then we have another swap that exchanges LIBOR capped and floored against the fixed rate; this swap is called a structured swap, and it's traded at a different desk. This desk is sometimes called nonlinear trading desk because these people are doing the nonlinear stuff, but except sometimes for information purposes, we do not express the price of the swap as the price of the linear product plus the nonlinear trading premium. So there is no such thing as an option-valuation adjustment, so we do not have an OVA or something like that.

*Daniel:* Going back a few years, people tried to calculate option-adjusted bond spreads.

*Christian:* Yes, I know, and I am sometimes reminded of it. And so there is one desk in the bank that is taking the responsibility for all this complex stuff. This desk is also making transactions through the swap desk because the desk needs to hedge its interest rate risk, so he's hedging out all linear stuff to the other guys, and he keeps all the nonlinear risks. Let me make a remark about FVA; I will come back to CVA. For me FVA has a strong analogy to cross-currency, to multi-currency models—at least if you have the same rate for borrowing and lending. Each issuer has its own currency. So what is his currency? His currency is the bond he's issuing. Everything has to be denominated in his own interest rate, his funding rate. There are even instruments on the market which profit from this arbitrage between two banks which have different funding. These are the total return swaps where one bank with poor funding goes to another bank with good funding and they exchange funding and they both profit from this deal. I mean, the market for total return swaps is currently dead because funding is for free, but these things existed. I have a little paper with my colleague Mark Lichtner on this (see [6]).

This currency analogy: we had this in multi-currencies for years. We know how to value instruments in different currencies, and we have the same phenomena in currencies. For example, the cross-currency swap exchanges a floating rate in one currency for a floating rate in another currency. From the theory, this should be zero: both are floaters which are at par, but cross-currency swaps trade at a premium. There is a cross-currency basis spread. The reason is that there is a preference in the market, that one likes to finance oneself in U.S. Dollars and not in Euros (or vice versa), so, for example, a Euro bank would prefer to go to Euro financing instead of U.S. Dollar financing. I believe that FVA is something very natural. Also in mathematical theory it has been there in this currency analogy since, and it should be recognised inside the valuation because we wouldn't value Euro derivatives using the U.S. Dollar curve, would we?

One more word to CVA. If I'm provocative, I would say, like Damiano already pointed out, counterparty risk isn't something new. We had a defaultable LIBOR market model years ago, and counterparty risk was used years ago maybe only for credit derivatives, but it's not so new, and what is actually new here is that we suddenly have to look at netting. So the big change for me in this valuation adjustment topic is that we are talking about portfolio effects. What Damiano said this morning: the sum of each individual product valuation doesn't give you the value of the portfolio. So you have portfolio effects, you have to value everything in a single huge valuation framework, but if you define all the products of a bank as a portfolio, as one single product—I believe that the theory to be able to do this is actually to some extent known—the big problem is how do you implement numerically what you do on the computational side. For me this is the main motivation for these valuation adjustments. It is because we have computational problems, and we like to decompose the valuations into valuations for which we can sum up the products.

Going back to FVA, I do not understand why many people still use the risk-free interest rate as the basis for this valuation, for your reference valuation—because, first of all, I don't believe there's such a thing as a risk-free interest rate; it's just a misnomer. And wouldn't it be better to keep the adjustments as small as possible such that the price which you calculate is already as close as possible to the true price? So, for example, my navigation system in the car tells me, from Frankfurt to Munich you need four hours and thirty minutes. Okay, when I drive you need five hours and thirty minutes, but it gives me a good proxy. The proxy is using the average information available.

So coming back to Damiano's talk, maybe we should simplify things. I like to have things simplified, and my question is how can you simplify things such that you can implement them in a bank. For example, we can simplify and say that treasury uses an average funding rate which is in the middle of the bid-offer, and we use that rate to calculate the funding costs so that we have symmetry there and so on.

Finally, I would like to have just one desk where nonlinear effects are managed. We could have this set-up, so the question is how can we have this set-up in a bank. We could have this set-up if we have internal transactions in the bank, and these transactions are fully collateralised. So we have these linear traders who trade collateralised transactions with this nonlinear trading desk, and the nonlinear trading desk has the residual.

My conclusion is that I would like to have one formula or one model which gives me the true price, and then we can set up internal transactions, but what is the good way to set up these internal transactions such that we can implement this in a bank? This is my concern.

*Audience member:* Talking about implementation in the bank: What can you implement? Where is banking nowadays? CVA, we have all the data for CVA, I assume. No clue on wrong-way risk on these correlations you need and you already think about FVA and adjustments on adjustments but still didn't manage to find a decent proxy for wrong-way risk? The question is, are we looking and are we solving the right problems? What is your impression?

*Christian:* The data is actually the critical thing here. We can include more and more effects in a nonlinear trading valuation framework by improving the model—for example like the approaches we have seen here including wrong-way risk, copulas, whatever, but the problem is that we actually do not have the data to calibrate the model.

For example, going back to John's talk this morning, I have a little comment here: you'll see the effect of this multi-curve switch from LIBOR to OIS, but in this calculation there is an assumption. The assumption is that the swap, which is LIBOR-collateralised, so we use LIBOR discounting, trades at the same swap rate as the swap rate that is OIS-collateralised, so we use OIS discounting, so if you have the same rates for the swap, you get different forward rates. That's what we saw this morning.

The problem is you do not observe the swap rate for a LIBOR-collateralised swap. So it could even be that the swap rates are different and the forwards are the same. If we value, for example, an uncollateralised product, we do not even know what the correct forward rate is because we would need the uncollateralised swap to calibrate this forward rate. Data already start at the very beginning. The problem is data.

*Ralf:* Do you agree, Damiano?

*Damiano:* I talked to one of the CVA traders at a top tier 1 bank. They told me they have what they call zero-order risks in mind more than cross-gamma hedging. What they don't have for many counterparties is a healthy default-probability curve because there's no liquidity in the relevant CDS, so maybe they have a product with the airport of Duckburg, and this airport hasn't issued a liquid bond and there is no CDS. Where do you obtain the default probability? From the rating? But that's a physical measure, not a risk-neutral measure. And then the wrong-way correlations: you should use market-implied correlations because you are pricing, but then, where do you get them? It's almost impossible to get them for many assets, and also, finally,

I would say that with CVA, you're right—we talk about KVA, but CVA is still very much a problem—and there is what I call payout risk, so depending on which close-out you use, and whether you include the first default check or not (some banks don't, because by avoiding it you avoid credit correlation, which is a bad beast in many cases), so depending on the type of CVA formula you implement—you have five, six different definitions of CVA—and that is payout risk. With old-style exotics, you had a very clear description of the payout, then you implemented the dynamics; you would get a price and hedge, and that would change with the model, and that would be model risk. Now with CVA we have payout risk. We don't even know which payout we are trading exactly, unless we have a very precise description of the CVA calculation.

But it's not like when you ask another bank, *What CVA charge are you applying to me?*, they tell you *It's a first-to-default inclusive, risk-free closeout* … They don't tell you that. … *And I'm using this kind of CDS curve.* Sometimes they don't tell you that, and you don't know.

*Ralf:* Daniel, do you have the same experience?

*Daniel:* Absolutely. I think even as many banks are talking about FVA these days, I think CVA is still an unresolved topic, and our observation is that even in a small market like the German market, there are a lot of different approaches taken by the banks to calculate CVA. The problem is becoming more difficult by the minute as the observable CDS prices, or tradable and liquid CDS prices get fewer and fewer. So this is an issue that gets more complicated by the minute.

And then another observation: we had a talk about wrong-way risk this morning, and we learned about the difficulties that this involves, and not surprisingly it's our observation that many banks are far from including wrong-way risk in their CVA calculations, so there's a long way to go before even CVA is settled.

*Ralf:* Okay, thank you very much, Daniel.

*John:* Maybe I should just respond to the point that Christian made about my presentation this morning. My swap rates were all fully collateralised swap rates, which would today reflect OIS discounting. I think Wolfgang [Rungaldier] called them the clean rates. As soon as you look at the uncollateralised market, any rates you see are contaminated by CVA and DVA.

You say, *Use LIBOR discounting.* I would say the correct thing to do even with uncollateralised transactions is still to use OIS discounting and calculate your CVA and DVA using spreads relative to the OIS curve. Forget about the LIBOR curve. The LIBOR curve is no longer appropriate for valuing derivatives. It could by chance be that LIBOR is the correct borrowing rate for the counterparty you're dealing with, but in most cases the borrowing rate of an uncollateralised end user is different from LIBOR, so LIBOR is not a relevant rate. I don't care whether we call the OIS rate the risk-free rate or not, but it is the best close-to-risk-free benchmark that we have.

*Ralf:* Thank you, John. It's now your turn, so please continue with your statement.

## 4 John Hull

*John:* Hard to know where to start because I have written quite a bit on FVA in the last few years. I've actually consciously decided to stop doing it because I realise I could spend the whole of the rest of my academic career writing about this, and I'd never convince most people.

Actually, my interest in FVA has got an interesting history. In the middle of 2012, I got a call from the editor of Risk magazine saying, *We're bringing out the 25th anniversary edition of Risk magazine. We'd like you to write an article for it.* I agreed to write the article. (No academic ever says no to writing an article.) I asked *What would you like me to write about?* He said, *We don't mind what you write about, so long as it's interesting to our readership. But, by the way, we need the article in three weeks.*

I went down the corridor to discuss this with my colleague Alan White. We had a number of interesting ideas for the article. After two and a half weeks we settled on FVA. The trouble was that we then had only three days to write the article. In retrospect, I wish we'd had longer. So what did that article say? That article said, you should not make an FVA adjustment. I'll explain why in a minute. The reaction to the article was interesting. Usually when you write these articles, nothing much happens. You get maybe a little bit of a response from a few other academics. But in this case we were absolutely inundated with emails from people about this article. Two-thirds of emails were saying *You're crazy. You don't know what you're talking about. Clearly there should be an FVA adjustment. We've been doing for a while now* ... and so on.

The other one-third were a little bit more positive, and some of them even went so far as to say, *We're glad someone's finally said this because we were a little uncomfortable with this FVA adjustment.* And, of course, Risk magazine realised that this was an exciting topic for them, so they started organising conferences on FVA.

Two people from Royal Bank of Scotland wrote a rejoinder to our article, which appeared in the next issue of Risk. And we were invited to write a rejoinder to the rejoinder, and so it went on. It was a really crazy time.

What I very quickly found out was that: Alan and I had a different perspective from most of the people we were corresponding with on this, and the reason was that we've been trained in finance. We've moved from finance into derivatives, and most of the people we were talking to had moved from physics or mathematics into derivatives. One important idea in corporate finance is that when you're valuing an investment, the discount rate should be determined by the riskiness of the investment. How you finance the investments is not important. Whether you finance it with debt or equity, it's the riskiness of the investment that matters. In other words, you should separate out the funding from the valuation of the investment (Fig. 3).

That was where we were coming from. In the case of derivatives a complication is that we can use risk-neutral valuation, so we've got a nice way of doing the valuation, but that does not alter the basic argument. Expected cash flows that are directly related

**Fig. 3** John Hull giving his presentation on "OIS discounting, interest rate derivatives, and the modeling of stochastic interest rate spreads"

to the investment should be taken into account. In the case of derivative transactions these expected cash flows include CVA and DVA.

So that's where we were coming from. We've modified our opinion a little bit recently. I think I'm more or less in the same camp as Damiano here, judging by his presentation. Let's suppose that you fund at OIS plus 200 basis points. If the whole of the 200 basis points is compensation for default risk, then you are actually getting a benefit from that 200 basis points, in that that 200 basis points is reflecting the losses to the lender (and benefits to you) of a possible default on your borrowings. That is what we call DVA 2, and what Damiano called DVA(F), and other people have called it FDA. This is not what we usually think of as DVA. What we usually think of as DVA is the fact that as a bank you might default on your derivatives, and that could be a gain to you. Here we are applying the same idea to the bank's debt.

DVA 2 cancels out FVA, and that was the main argument we made in that Risk magazine article. But if you say that the bank's borrowing rate is OIS plus 200 basis points where 120 basis points is for default risk, and 80 basis points is for other things—maybe liquidity—we can argue that 80 basis points is a dead-weight cost. It's part of the cost of doing business, you're not getting any benefit from that 80 basis points. You are getting benefit from the 120 basis points: a DVA-type benefit because you can default on your funding.

So I think I am in the same camp as Damiano. I think he called it LVA. This component of your funding cost which is not related to default risk, is arguably a genuine FVA. The problem is, of course, that it's very, very difficult to separate out the bit of your funding cost that's due to default risk and the bit of your funding cost that's due to other things.

And then another complication is, of course, that accountants assume—for example when calculating CVA—the whole of your credit spread reflects default risk.

I have lots and lots of discussions with people on this. You realise very quickly that you're never going to convince somebody who's in a different mindset from yourself on this. One important question, though, is what are we trying to do here? With these sorts of adjustments, are we trying to calculate a price we should charge a customer? (Obviously in this day and age, we would be talking about the price we should charge an end user because transactions with other banks are going to be fully collateralised.) Or are we concerned with internal accounting? Or is it financial accounting that is our objective? I've always taken the view that what we're really talking about here is what we record in our books as the value of this derivative. But if you take the view that what we're trying to do is to work out what we should charge an end user, a customer, then actually I have no problems doing whatever you like, even trying to convince a customer that the customer should pay an ECA, an electricity cost adjustment. We all know that what you're trying to do is get the best price you can and hopefully cover your costs.

What I found was when I was talking to people about FVA is you start talking about how derivatives should be accounted for and very quickly you slip into talking about how much the customer should be charged, which is a totally different issue. Obviously, there's all sorts of costs you've got to recover in terms of what you charge the customer.

Where are accountants coming from? As you all know, accountants want you to value derivatives at exit prices. The accounting bodies are quite clear, that the exit prices have nothing to do with your own costs. Exit prices should be related to what's going on in the marketplace. Therefore, your own funding costs can't possibly come into an exit price. If other dealers are using FVA in their pricing, their funding costs may be relevant, but your own funding costs are not relevant. An interesting question is how should we determine exit prices in a world where all dealers are incorporating FVA into their pricing. Should we build into our exit price an average of the funding costs of all dealers or the funding cost of the dealer that gives the most competitive price? You can argue about this, but it is difficult to argue that it is your own funding costs that should be used in accounting.

What we have found is there's a lot of confusion between DVA and FVA, and as I said there's really two distinct parts to DVA. There's the DVA associated with the fact that you may default on your derivatives. That's what we call DVA 1. It's the usual DVA. Your DVA 1 is your counterparty's CVA and vice versa. And then there's what we call DVA 2, which is the fact that you might default on your funding.

Banks have always been uncomfortable with DVA. Even though accounting bodies have approved DVA they dislike the idea of taking their own default risk into account. This has led some banks to replace DVA by FVA. In this context, FVA is sometimes divided into a funding benefit adjustment and a funding cost adjustment with the funding benefit adjustment being regarded as a substitute for DVA.

When you look at what's actually going on right now, banks are all over the place in terms of how they make funding value adjustments. I agree with Damiano that once JP Morgan announced that it is taking account of FVA, then everybody felt they had to do it as well. The correctness of FVA becomes a self-fulfilling prophecy. A bank's auditors are going to say, *Everybody else is doing this? Why aren't you doing it?* Whether or not you believe the models used by everyone else are correct, you have got to use those models to determine accounting values.

You can have research models for trading, but for accounting you've just got to do what everybody else does. When a critical mass of people move over to doing something, whether it's right or wrong, you've got to do it.

I notice from a recent article in Risk that the Basel committee is getting interested in funding value adjustments. And U.S. regulators are getting interested in funding value adjustments as well. In addition, I can tell you that a few months ago, Alan White and I were invited to FASB to talk to them about funding value adjustments. They have concerns about the use of FVA in accounting. They like derivatives accounting valuations to be based on market prices not on internal costs.

I think we are in a fairly fluid situation here. When JP Morgan has said, *We're doing it this way, and we're taking a one-and-half billion dollar hit* it is tempting to believe that everyone else will follow suit and that is the end of the story. I don't think it is the end of the story because we have not yet heard from accountants and regulators. Also, I think it is fair to say that the views of banks and the quants that work for them are evolving.

There's some good news. (Maybe it's not good news if you're a quant working for a bank.) The good news is that we're clearly moving to a world where all derivatives are fully collateralised. We're now in a situation where if you deal with another financial institution or another systemically important entity, you've got to be fully collateralised. Dealing with an end user, you don't have to be fully collateralised. But there's a lot of arguments (we talked about some of them at this conference) suggesting that end users will get a better deal if they are fully collateralised.

FVA is not going to be such a big issue going forward. Indeed, I think it's going to fade away as full collateralisation becomes the norm. But no doubt arguments about some other XVAs will continue.

*Ralf:* Thank you, John. I take away that for PhD students it is wise not to pursue too much research on FVA, then, it might not be worth the effort …

*Audience member:* Sorry, just if you'll allow me a little comment. Since the issue of the self-fulfilling prophecy was picked up also by John Hull, just a little comment from a mathematical point of view. If you do mathematics for the application, you need a model. Possibly a true model. So what is a true model? Now, if you do applications for the natural or physical sciences, possibly there is a true model. It is very complicated, and what you do, you choose a model that is a good compromise between representativity and tractability, right, so you can deal with this model and it's still relatively good.

Now we come to social / economic sciences. What is the true model? If, at some point, the majority sort of implicitly uses a sort of model, isn't that all of a sudden the true model that other people should follow, or am I wrong here?

*Damiano:* Like base correlation, for example?

*John:* Yes, I don't see it quite that way, though. I think opinions will fluctuate through time. Nearly all large global banks do make funding value adjustments now. There are two or three holdouts, but most of them do.

I think FVA is going to be more of a fad than a truth. I think that in five years' time we could be in the opposite position to today: everybody just decides they don't want to make these funding value adjustments. That's just my own personal opinion.

One thing I meant to say is that there are interactions between CVA and DVA. If one side defaults, you don't care about the other side defaulting later, and there are a number of other close-out issues. I agree with what Damiano says. Those create a lot of complications. And they are relevant because those are complications in assessing expected cash flows arising from the derivatives portfolio that you have with a counterparty. They're nothing to do with funding. They're to do with expected future cash flows, which are the relevant things to calculate a valuation. It does make the valuation more complicated, but to overlay that with funding adjustments I don't think is correct except insofar as some part of the funding value adjustment is the dead-weight cost I was talking about.

*Ralf:* Thank you, John. You mentioned valuation, so maybe this is the keyword to hand over to Daniel.

## 5 Daniel Sommer

*Daniel:* First, John, as you immediately addressed the accounting profession, I'm not an accountant but I work for a firm that does audit and accounting as some part of its business. Are our accountants just people who tell the banks to do what everybody else does? The story is slightly more complicated than that because what accountants are interested in, and I pick up this story about self-fulfilling prophecies, what they are interested in eventually is fair value. And, indeed, for financial instruments that's defined as the exit price. But then the big question is: How do you find out what the exit price actually is?

Because it's not like for all the instruments that we're talking about in this seminar here, it's not something that you can read on Bloomberg or any other data provider. It's nothing that people will tell you in the street immediately. It's rather a complicated exercise to find out what fair value actually is. What would be the exit price at which you could actually exit your position? It's at that point where that whole reasoning comes up with the notion of how other people are thinking about valuing a certain position. How are my counterparties, my potential counterparties in the market, thinking about it? And that gives a bit more sense to the statement *Do what everybody else does*. Because if everybody else is taking certain aspects of a financial instrument into consideration when valuing this asset, it's very likely that your exit price that you are offered will also take that into consideration. It's for that reason that accountants are interested in what everybody else is doing, and frankly speaking, yes, at KPMG, that was indeed the discussion we had with many banks over the last three/four years where we met the banks in London on various panels to discuss FVA with them. Those were quite open discussions. From one year to the other, we sort of made a roll call and asked who's going to do what next year and when do you think you will be moving to FVA, etc., just to get a feeling for where the market was going in order to have a better understanding of what the market thought fair value would be. In that sense, I think that gives a bit more meaning to accountants telling the banks to do what everybody else is doing.

Now, coming to the current situation, indeed, I think there is no major bank globally left who has not declared they were doing something on funding valuation adjustments, with a lot of banks having come up with that in their 2014 year-end accounts. So I think the pressure on those banks who have not yet done that is actually rising. That's something which I think is a matter of fact.

I'm happy to comment or give my personal opinion about FVA, and perhaps talk about it by going back to some anecdotal evidence which I came across during the financial crisis. Before that, let me just mention a few more things.

Indeed the regulators become interested in FVA, and I think that there are at least two big issues that will have real effects on the banks that will enter the regulatory discussion or should enter the regulatory discussion. One thing is, indeed, the overlap between FVA and DVA, where many banks are happy to scrap DVA to a certain extent and replace it with FVA because that will have an immediate effect on their available regulatory capital. Because as they do the calculations these days, they offset FVA benefits and FVA costs. Thus to reduce DVA, where they need to deduct DVA from core Tier 1 capital, has a real effect on the bank's balance sheets and profitability calculations regarding regulatory capital.

The other thing people mentioned and it is true: hedging FVA just as is the case with CVA is a complicated issue and involves also hedging the related market risk. And so the question that we have been debating for CVA for a long time already is whether you are allowed to include the market risk hedges in your internal model for market risk or not. We've seen some movements in this direction recently by the regulators, but I think that those are two questions that at least should be quite prominent in the regulatory debate coming up.

That's one thing. The other thing is related to accounting. People quite leisurely mentioned that, well, yes, we need to go from a single deal valuation to portfolio valuation. And indeed for CVA that's absolutely inevitable. If you do that, nevertheless, for an accountant that raises a few uncomfortable questions because it raises the question: What is actually the unit of account? Apparently it's not a single deal. It may be the netting set as far as CVA is concerned, but when you look at funding, the netting set may even be too small, so it may be some sort of funding set, so all the deals that you have in one currency or so. When you look at effects on the balance sheet, do you need to value your whole bank before you can actually value your derivatives correctly? That's a bit of an uncomfortable direction we're going into.

Those are a few comments on things that people have said up to now, but on FVA itself, let me give you a little anecdote that occurred to me during the financial crisis. During the financial crisis, the CFO and CEO of one of our top-ten German banks asked me: *Look, all the banks have to reduce the values of their ABS and CDO books. Actually, don't you think that if a book is match-funded, it should be worth more than if a book is not match-funded?* And this goes back to the real fundamental question of liquidity risk and whether liquidity should play a role in pricing. And everybody who's read Modigliani and Miller, would say, *By no means.* That would be the standard answer. Nevertheless, when you come to think about the situation that the banks were in during the financial crisis, actually having a match-funded book gave you at least the option to wait. And there's real value in that option, as the banks who were able to wait were able to realise this because much of the write-downs that happened during the financial crisis actually came back as defaults were not as heavy as would have been thought at the time and indicated through the quotes at the peak of the crisis. It wasn't even traded prices at the time; it was basically quotes that banks were valuing their books on.

One might think—a very personal view at this point—one might think that if banks go for match-funding their books, it's like buying a very, very deep out-of-the-money option that they can then exercise when things get really bad. So that's one comment I would like to make.

The other point is somewhat more disconcerting. What does being liquid mean in a world that has had the experience of the financial crisis? Is it sufficient to say that a bank is liquid if it can generate enough funds through the collateralised inter-bank money market? Or does a bank have to have access to sufficient central bank money to prove that it is liquid? At least the experience of the financial crisis showed the vulnerability of the inter-bank market and the importance of central bank money to keep the system afloat. In that case at least part of the liquidity costs of banks would be due to ensuring it has enough central bank money or assets that can swiftly be turned into the latter. But if that was so then this would change our whole valuation paradigm, which after all is based on the general equilibrium theory and the theory of value by Gérard Debreu and others. In this theory there is no need for a central bank to keep the system working. Therefore, acknowledging the existence of funding costs through the introduction of FVA may have far reaching consequences on the derivatives pricing theory compared to just the calculation of some odd valuation adjustment and quarreling about which funding curve to use to determine an exit price.

*Ralf:* Thank you, Daniel. John, do you want to comment on this? Is Miller and Modigliani still valid in such an environment?

*John:* Well, I think it is, but what Modigliani and Miller say is that if you cut the pie up, the sum of the pieces is worth the same as the whole. Now, the question is, who are the potential stakeholders you've got to look at when you cut the pie up.

I agree with pretty much everything that Daniel said. It makes a lot of sense.

*Ralf:* Christian?

*Christian:* I have a question maybe from the practitioner's side, also being a little bit of a quant with respect to the exit price, which keeps me puzzling. Just to make that clear, for me there are two prices at least. The exit price, I can realise it only once: by going out of business. There's only one opportunity to realise the exit price. There is, of course, the price which I use in calculating my risk sensitivities, my hedge, which I use in solving my optimal control problem, in my risk management problem.

So, for example, if the exit price would include a tax, there would be some kind of going-out-of-business tax, the exit price would clearly include this tax, but of course as long as I'd like to stay in business I would never charge that tax, and I would not include it in my hedging because it would never occur to me.

What is strange for me is that I believe that the good price for doing the optimal control problem, so how do you hedge and so on, is actually the price which is going to concern and not the exit price, but the balance sheet is using the exit price, and it appears to me as if management is always looking at the balance sheet. Isn't there some kind of contradictions? What is the price that should be used to find the optimal path for the company? To make the investment decisions and so on?

*Daniel:* First of all, it's very clear that what the accounting standards mean by exit price is by no means the price at which the bank would go out of business. It's a going concern still. Of course it's an artificial concept in the sense that you will never ... even if you were to sell just a portfolio of your trading book, you would probably not realise what accountants think of as the fair value because they explicitly rule out including portfolio effects on this fair value.

What this exit price actually means is, two people meet in the market and they agree on a certain price at which to exchange a position without changing the market equilibrium, it has to be small relative to the market.

*Christian:* For example, for my own bonds, the exit price is my bond value, which obviously includes my funding, and for uncollateralised derivatives it is the derivative valued with some average market funding, and if I take your example of fully matched funding, this is puzzling me because the bonds are on funding and the uncollateralised derivatives are not on funding.

*Ralf:* I think this goes in the same direction as my question to Damiano about the close-out value—what value to use. I think we probably will not solve this puzzle today. Looking at the time, I would like to thank all of you for your attention. Thank you very much to all panelists, and I suppose there's plenty of time for further discussions during the dinner tonight. Thank you!

## 5.1 *Acknowledgements, Credits, and Disclaimer*

All statements made in this panel discussion represent the personal views of the participants. Photographs of Damiano Brigo and John Hull by Astrid Eckert; photograph of the panel by Bettina Haas. The transcription of audio tape to text was made by Robin Black. For help with the manuscript we thank Florian Zyprian.

**Acknowledgements** The KPMG Center of Excellence in Risk Management is acknowledged for organizing the conference "Challenges in Derivatives Markets - Fixed Income Modeling, Valuation Adjustments, Risk Management, and Regulation".

**Open Access** This chapter is distributed under the terms of the Creative Commons Attribution 4.0 International License (http://creativecommons.org/licenses/by/4.0/), which permits use, duplication, adaptation, distribution and reproduction in any medium or format, as long as you give appropriate credit to the original author(s) and the source, a link is provided to the Creative Commons license and any changes made are indicated.

The images or other third party material in this book are included in the work's Creative Commons license, unless indicated otherwise in the credit line; if such material is not included in the work's Creative Commons license and the respective action is not permitted by statutory regulation, users will need to obtain permission from the license holder to duplicate, adapt or reproduce the material.

## References

1. Brigo, D., Morini, M.: Closeout convention tensions, Risk, pp. 86–90 (2011)
2. Brigo, D., Morini, M., Pallavicini, A.: Counterparty Credit Risk, Collateral and Funding: With Pricing Cases for all Asset Classes. Wiley, New York (2013). ISBN 978-0-470-74846-6
3. Brigo, D., Pallavicini, A.: Nonlinear consistent valuation of CCP cleared or CSA bilateral trades with initial margins under credit, funding and wrong-way risks. J. Financ. Eng. **1**(1), 1–60 (2014)
4. Pallavicini, A., Perini, D., Brigo, D.: Funding Valuation Adjustment: FVA consistent with CVA, DVA, WWR, Collateral, Netting and re-hyphotecation, working paper (2011)
5. Fries, C.: Mathematical Finance: Theory, Modeling, Implementation. Wiley, New York (2007)
6. Fries, C., Lichtner, M.: Collateralization and Funding Valuation Adjustments (FVA) for Total Return Swaps, working paper (2014)
7. Hull, J., White, A.: The FVA debate, Risk, 25th anniversary edn, pp. 83–85 (2012)

# Part II
# Fixed Income Modeling

# Multi-curve Modelling Using Trees

**John Hull and Alan White**

**Abstract** Since 2008 the valuation of derivatives has evolved so that OIS discounting rather than LIBOR discounting is used. Payoffs from interest rate derivatives usually depend on LIBOR. This means that the valuation of interest rate derivatives depends on the evolution of two different term structures. The spread between OIS and LIBOR rates is often assumed to be constant or deterministic. This paper explores how this assumption can be relaxed. It shows how well-established methods used to represent one-factor interest rate models in the form of a binomial or trinomial tree can be extended so that the OIS rate and a LIBOR rate are jointly modelled in a three-dimensional tree. The procedures are illustrated with the valuation of spread options and Bermudan swap options. The tree is constructed so that LIBOR swap rates are matched.

**Keywords** OIS · LIBOR · Interest rate trees · Multi-curve modelling

## 1 Introduction

Before the 2008 credit crisis, the spread between a LIBOR rate and the corresponding OIS (overnight indexed swap) rate was typically around 10 basis points. During the crisis this spread rose dramatically. This led practitioners to review their derivatives valuation procedures. A result of this review was a switch from LIBOR discounting to OIS discounting.

Finance theory argues that derivatives can be correctly valued by estimating expected cash flows in a risk-neutral world and discounting them at the risk-free rate. The OIS rate is a better proxy for the risk-free rate than LIBOR.[1] Another argument

[1] See for example Hull and White [15].

J. Hull (✉) · A. White
Joseph L. Rotman School of Management, University of Toronto, Toronto, ON, Canada
e-mail: hull@rotman.utoronto.ca

A. White
e-mail: awhite@rotman.utoronto.ca

© The Author(s) 2016

K. Glau et al. (eds.), *Innovations in Derivatives Markets*, Springer Proceedings in Mathematics & Statistics 165, DOI 10.1007/978-3-319-33446-2_9

(appealing to many practitioners) in favor of using the OIS rate for discounting is that the interest paid on cash collateral is usually the overnight interbank rate and OIS rates are longer term rates derived from these overnight rates. The use of OIS rates therefore reflects funding costs.

Many interest rate derivatives provide payoffs dependent on LIBOR. When LIBOR discounting was used, only one rate needed to be modelled to value these derivatives. Now that OIS discounting is used, more than one rate has to be considered. The spread between OIS and LIBOR rates is often assumed to be constant or deterministic. This paper provides a way of relaxing this assumption. It describes a way in which LIBOR with a particular tenor and OIS can be modelled using a three-dimensional tree.[2] It is an extension of ideas in the many papers that have been written on how one-factor interest rate models can be represented in the form of a two-dimensional tree. These papers include Ho and Lee [9], Black, Derman, and Toy [3], Black and Karasinski [4], Kalotay, Williams, and Fabozzi [18], Hainaut and MacGilchrist [8], and Hull and White [11, 13, 14, 16].

The balance of the paper is organized as follows. We first describe how LIBOR-OIS spreads have evolved through time. Second, we describe how a three-dimensional tree can be constructed to model both OIS rates and the LIBOR-OIS spread with a particular tenor. We then illustrate the tree-building process using a simple three-step tree. We investigate the convergence of the three-dimensional tree by using it to calculate the value of options on the LIBOR-OIS spread. We then value Bermudan swap options showing that in a low-interest-rate environment, the assumption that the spread is stochastic rather than deterministic can have a non-trivial effect on valuations.

## 2 The LIBOR-OIS Spread

LIBOR quotes for maturities of one-, three-, six-, and 12-months in a variety of currencies are produced every day by the British Bankers' Association based on submissions from a panel of contributing banks. These are estimates of the unsecured rates at which AA-rated banks can borrow from other banks. The $T$-month OIS rate is the fixed rate paid on a $T$-month overnight interest rate swap. In such a swap the payment at the end of $T$-months is the difference between the fixed rate and a rate which is the geometric mean of daily overnight rates. The calculation of the payment on the floating side is designed to replicate the aggregate interest that would be earned from rolling over a sequence of daily loans at the overnight rate. (In U.S. dollars, the overnight rate used is the effective federal funds rate.) The LIBOR-OIS spread is the LIBOR rate less the corresponding OIS rate.

[2] At the end of Hull and White [17] we described an attempt to do this using a two-dimensional tree. The current procedure is better. Our earlier procedure only provides an approximate answer because the correlation between spreads at adjacent tree nodes is not fully modelled.

LIBOR-OIS spreads were markedly different during the pre-crisis (December 2001–July 2007) and post-crisis (July 2009–April 2015) periods. This is illustrated in Fig. 1. In the pre-crisis period, the spread term structure was quite flat with the 12-month spread only about 4 basis points higher than the one-month spread on average. As shown in Fig. 1a, the 12-month spread was sometimes higher and sometimes lower than one-month spread. The average one-month spread was about 10 basis points during this period. Because the term structure of spreads was on average fairly flat and quite small, it was plausible for practitioners to assume the existence of a single LIBOR zero curve and use it as a proxy for the risk-free zero curve. During the post-crisis period there has been a marked term structure of spreads. As shown in Fig. 1b, it is almost always the case that the spread curve is upward sloping. The average one-month spread continues to be about 10 basis points, but the average 12-month spread is about 62 basis points.

There are two factors that explain the difference between LIBOR rates and OIS rates. The first of these may be institutional. If a regression model is used to extrapolate the spread curve for shorter maturities, we find the one-day spread in the post-crisis period is estimated to be about 5 basis points. This is consistent with the spread between one-day LIBOR and the effective fed funds rate. Since these are both rates that a bank would pay to borrow money for 24 h, they should be the same. The 5 basis point difference must be related to institutional practices that affect the two different markets.[3]

Given that institutional differences account for about 5 basis points of spread, the balance of the spread must be attributable to credit. OIS rates are based on a continually refreshed one-day rate whereas $\tau$-maturity LIBOR is a continually refreshed $\tau$-maturity rate.[4] The difference between $\tau$-maturity LIBOR and $\tau$-maturity OIS then reflects the degree to which the credit quality of the LIBOR borrower is expected to decline over $\tau$ years.[5] In the pre-crisis period the expected decline in the borrower credit quality implied by the spreads was small but during the post-crisis period it has been much larger.

The average hazard rate over the life of a LIBOR loan with maturity $\tau$ is approximately

$$\bar{\lambda} = \frac{L(\tau)}{1 - R}$$

where $L(\tau)$ is the spread of LIBOR over the risk-free rate and $R$ is the recovery rate in the event of default. Let $h$ be the hazard rate for overnight loans to high quality financial institutions (those that can borrow at the effective fed funds rate). This will also be the average hazard rate associated with OIS rates.

---

[3]For a more detailed discussion of these issues see Hull and White [15].

[4]A continually refreshed $\tau$-maturity rate is the rate realized when a loan is made to a party with a certain specified credit rating (usually assumed in this context to be AA) for time $\tau$. At the end of the period a new $\tau$-maturity loan is made to a possibly different party with the same specified credit rating. See Collin-Dufresne and Solnik [6].

[5]It is well established that for high quality borrowers the expected credit quality declines with the passage of time.

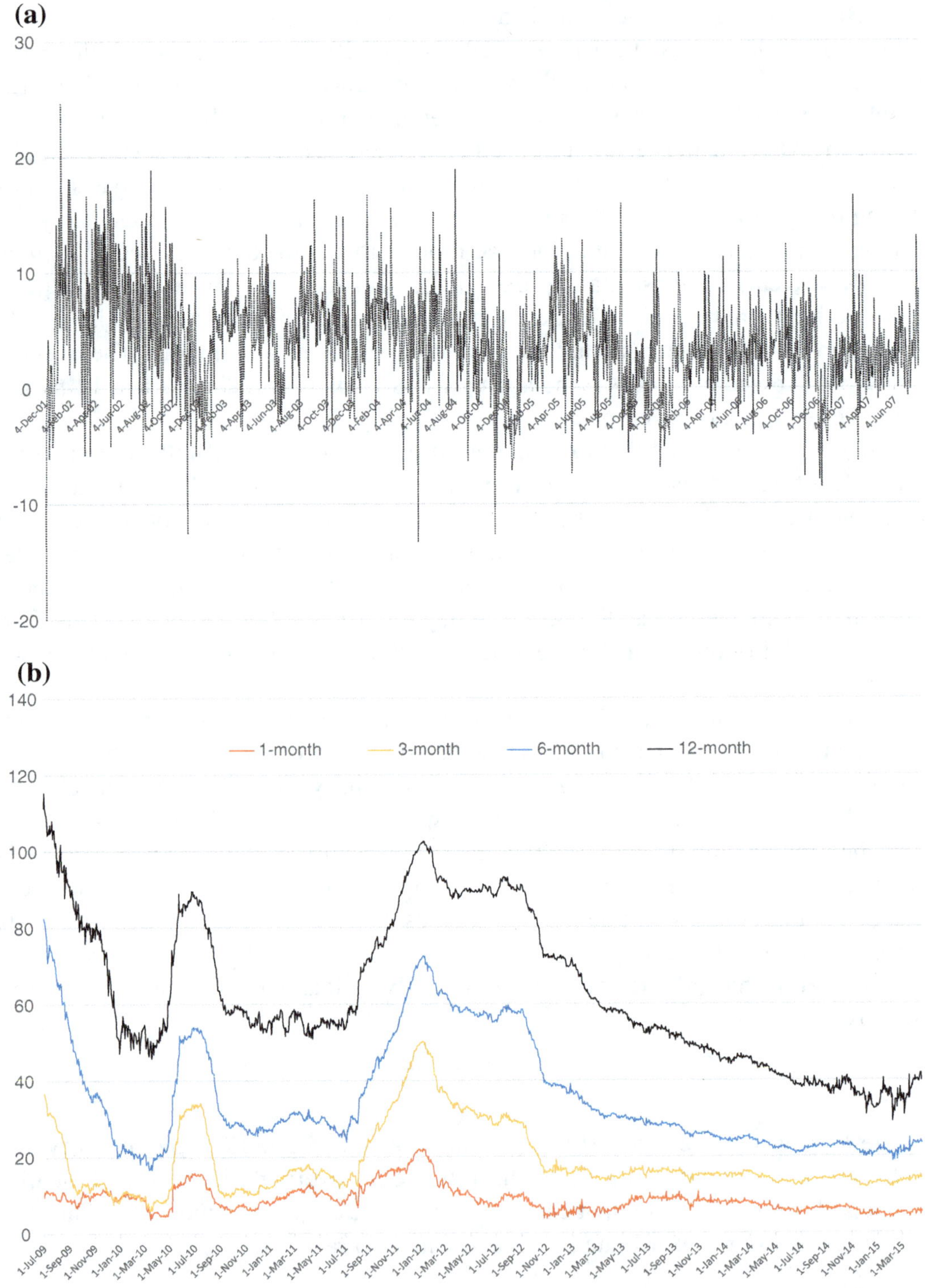


**Fig. 1** **a** Excess of 12-month LIBOR-OIS spread over one-month LIBOR-OIS spread December 4, 2001–July 31, 2007 period (basis points). Data Source: Bloomberg. **b** Post-crisis LIBOR-OIS spread for different tenors (basis points). Data Source: Bloomberg

Define $L^*(\tau)$ as the spread of LIBOR over OIS for a maturity of $\tau$ and $O(\tau)$ as the spread of OIS over the risk-free rate for this maturity. Because $L(\tau) = L^*(\tau) + O(\tau)$

$$\overline{\lambda} = \frac{L^*(\tau) + O(\tau)}{1 - R} = h + \frac{L^*(\tau)}{1 - R}$$

This shows that when we model OIS and LIBOR we are effectively modelling OIS and the difference between the LIBOR hazard rate and the OIS hazard rate.

One of the results of the post-crisis spread term structure is that a single LIBOR zero curve no longer exists. LIBOR zero curves can be constructed from swap rates, but there is a different LIBOR zero curve for each tenor. This paper shows how OIS rates and a LIBOR rate with a particular tenor can be modelled jointly using a three-dimensional tree.[6]

## 3 The Methodology

Suppose that we are interested in modelling OIS rates and the LIBOR rate with tenor of $\tau$. (Values of $\tau$ commonly used are one month, three months, six months and 12 months.) Define $r$ as the instantaneous OIS rate. We assume that some function of $r$, $x(r)$, follows the process

$$dx = [\theta(t) - a_r x]\,dt + \sigma_r\,dz_r \tag{1}$$

This is an Ornstein–Uhlenbeck process with a time-dependent reversion level. The function $\theta(t)$ is chosen to match the initial term structure of OIS rates; $a_r$ ($\geq$0) is the reversion rate of $x$; $\sigma_r$ (>0) is the volatility of $r$; and $dz_r$ is a Wiener process.[7]

Define $s$ as the spread between the LIBOR rate with tenor $\tau$ and the OIS rate with tenor $\tau$ (both rates being measured with a compounding frequency corresponding to the tenor). We assume that some function of $s$, $y(s)$, follows the process:

$$dy = [\phi(t) - a_s y]\,dt + \sigma_s\,dz_s \tag{2}$$

This is also an Ornstein–Uhlenbeck process with a time-dependent reversion level. The function $\phi(t)$ is chosen to ensure that all LIBOR FRAs and swaps that can be entered into today have a value of zero; $a_s$ ($\geq$0) is the reversion rate of $y$; $\sigma_s$ (>0) is

[6]Extending the approach so that more than one LIBOR rate is modelled is not likely to be feasible as it would involve using backward induction in conjunction with a four (or more)-dimensional tree. In practice, multiple LIBOR rates are most likely to be needed for portfolios when credit and other valuation adjustments are calculated. Monte Carlo simulation is usually used in these situations.

[7]This model does not allow interest rates to become negative. Negative interest have been observed in some currencies (particularly the euro and Swiss franc). If $-e$ is the assumed minimum interest rate, this model can be adjusted so that $x = \ln(r + e)$. The choice of $e$ is somewhat arbitrary, but changes the assumptions made about the behavior of interest rates in a non-trivial way.

the volatility of $s$; and $dz_s$ is a Wiener process. The correlation between $dz_r$ and $dz_s$ will be denoted by $\rho$.

We will use a three-dimensional tree to model $x$ and $y$. A tree is a discrete time, discrete space approximation of a continuous stochastic process for a variable. The tree is constructed so that the mean and standard deviation of the variable is matched over each time step. Results in Ames [1] show that in the limit the tree converges to the continuous time process. At each node of the tree, $r$ and $s$ can be calculated using the inverse of the functions $x$ and $y$.

We will first outline a step-by-step approach to constructing the three-dimensional tree and then provide more details in the context of a numerical example in Sect. 4.[8] The steps in the construction of the tree are as follows:

1. Model the instantaneous OIS rate using a tree. We assume that the process for $r$ is defined by Eq. (1) and that a trinomial tree is constructed as described in Hull and White [11, 13] or Hull [10]. However, the method we describe can be used in conjunction with other binomial and trinomial tree-building procedures such as those in Ho and Lee [9], Black, Derman and Toy [3], Black and Karasinski [4], Kalotay, Williams and Fabozzi [18] and Hull and White [14, 16]. Tree building procedures are also discussed in a number of texts.[9] If the tree has steps of length $\Delta t$, the interest rate at each node of the tree is an OIS rate with maturity $\Delta t$. We assume the tree can be constructed so that both the LIBOR tenor, $\tau$, and all potential payment times for the instrument being valued are multiples of $\Delta t$. If this is not possible, a tree with varying time steps can be constructed.[10]
2. Use backward induction to calculate at each node of the tree the price of an OIS zero-coupon bond with a life of $\tau$. For a node at time $t$ this involves valuing a bond that has a value of \$1 at time $t + \tau$. The value of the bond at nodes earlier than $t + \tau$ is found by discounting through the tree. For each node at time $t + \tau - \Delta t$ the price of the bond is $e^{-r\Delta t}$ where $r$ is the ($\Delta t$-maturity) OIS rate at the node. For each node at time $t + \tau - 2\Delta t$ the price is $e^{-r\Delta t}$ times a probability-weighted average of prices at the nodes at time $t + \tau - \Delta t$ which can be reached from that node, and so on. The calculations are illustrated in the next section. Based on the bond price calculated in this way, $P$, the $\tau$-maturity OIS rate, expressed with a compounding period of $\tau$, is[11]
$$\frac{1/P - 1}{\tau}$$
3. Construct a trinomial tree for the process for the spread function, $y$, in Eq. (2) when the function $\phi(t)$ is set equal to zero and the initial value of $y$ is set equal to

---

[8] Readers who have worked with interest rate trees will be able to follow our step-by-step approach. Other readers may prefer to follow the numerical example.

[9] See for example Brigo and Mercurio [5] or Hull [10].

[10] See for example Hull and White [14].

[11] The $r$-tree shows the evolution of the $\Delta t$-maturity OIS rate. Since we are interested in modelling the $\tau$-maturity LIBOR-OIS spread, it is necessary to determine the evolution of the $\tau$-maturity OIS rate.

zero.[12] We will refer to this as the "preliminary tree". When interest rate trees are built, the expected value of the short rate at each time step is chosen so that the initial term structure is matched. The adjustment to the expected rate at time $t$ is achieved by adding some constant, $\alpha_t$, to the value of $x$ at each node at that step.[13] The expected value of the spread at each step of the spread tree that is eventually constructed will similarly be chosen to match forward LIBOR rates. The current preliminary tree is a first step toward the construction of the final spread tree.

4. Create a three-dimensional tree from the OIS tree and the preliminary spread tree assuming zero correlation between the OIS rate and the spread. The probabilities on the branches of this three-dimensional tree are the product of the probabilities on the corresponding branches of the underlying two-dimensional trees.
5. Build in correlation between the OIS rate and the spread by adjusting the probabilities on the branches of the three-dimensional tree. The way of doing this is described in Hull and White [12] and will be explained in more detail later in this paper.
6. Using an iterative procedure, adjust the expected spread at each of the times considered by the tree. For the nodes at time $t$, we consider a receive-fixed forward rate agreement (FRA) applicable to the period between $t$ and $t + \tau$.[14] The fixed rate, $F$, equals the forward rate at time zero. The value of the FRA at a node, where the $\tau$-maturity OIS rate is $w$ and the $\tau$-maturity LIBOR-OIS spread is $s$, is[15]

$$\frac{F - (w + s)}{1 + w\tau}$$

The value of the FRA is calculated for all nodes at time $t$ and the values are discounted back through the three-dimensional tree to find the present value.[16] As discussed in step 3, the expected spread (i.e., the amount by which nodes are shifted from their positions in the preliminary tree) is chosen so that this present value is zero.

[12]As in the case of the tree for the interest rate function, $x$, the method can be generalized to accommodate a variety of two-dimensional and three-dimensional tree-building procedures.

[13]This is equivalent to determining the time varying drift parameter, $\theta(t)$, that is consistent with the current term structure.

[14]A forward rate agreement (FRA) is one leg of a fixed for floating interest rate swap. Typically, the forward rates underlying some FRAs can be observed in the market. Others can be bootstrapped from the fixed rates exchanged in interest rate swaps.

[15]$F$, $w$, and $s$ are expressed with a compounding period of $\tau$.

[16]Calculations are simplified by calculating Arrow–Debreu prices, first at all nodes of the two-dimensional OIS tree and then at all nodes of the three-dimensional tree. The latter can be calculated at the end of the fifth step as they do not depend on spread values. This is explained in more detail and illustrated numerically in Sect. 4.

## 4 A Simple Three-Step Example

We now present a simple example to illustrate the implementation of our procedure. We assume that the LIBOR maturity of interest is 12 months ($\tau = 1$). We assume that $x = \ln(r)$ with $x$ following the process in Eq. (1). Similarly we assume that $y = \ln(s)$ with $y$ following the process in Eq. (2). We assume that the initial OIS zero rates and 12 month LIBOR forward rates are those shown in Table 1. We will build a 1.5-year tree where the time step, $\Delta t$, equals 0.5 years. We assume that the reversion rate and volatility parameters are as shown in Table 2.

As explained in Hull and White [11, 13] we first build a tree for $x$ assuming that $\theta(t) = 0$. We set the spacing of the $x$ nodes, $\Delta x$, equal to $\sigma_r\sqrt{3\Delta t} = 0.3062$. Define node $(i, j)$ as the node at time $i\Delta t$ for which $x = j\Delta x$. (The middle node at each time has $j = 0$.) The normal branching process in the tree is from $(i, j)$ to one of $(i+1, j+1)$, $(i+1, j)$, and $(i+1, j-1)$. The transition probabilities to these three nodes are $p_u$, $p_m$, and $p_d$ and are chosen to match the mean and standard deviation

**Table 1** Percentage interest rates for the examples

| Maturity (years) | OIS zero rate | Forward 12-month LIBOR rate | Forward 12-month OIS rate | Forward Spread: 12-month LIBOR less 12-month OIS |
|---|---|---|---|---|
| 0 | 3.000 | 3.300 | 3.149 | 0.151 |
| 0.5 | 3.050 | 3.410 | 3.252 | 0.158 |
| 1.0 | 3.100 | 3.520 | 3.355 | 0.165 |
| 1.5 | 3.150 | 3.630 | 3.458 | 0.172 |
| 2.0 | 3.200 | 3.740 | 3.562 | 0.178 |
| 2.5 | 3.250 | 3.850 | 3.666 | 0.184 |
| 3.0 | 3.300 | 3.960 | 3.769 | 0.191 |
| 4.0 | 3.400 | 4.180 | 3.977 | 0.203 |
| 5.0 | 3.500 | 4.400 | 4.185 | 0.215 |
| 7.0 | 3.700 | | | |

The OIS zero rates are expressed with continuous compounding while all forward and forward spread rates are expressed with annual compounding. The OIS zero rates and LIBOR forward rates are exact. OIS zero rates and LIBOR forward rates for maturities other than those given are determined using linear interpolation. The rates in the final two columns are rounded values calculated from the given OIS zero rates and LIBOR forward rates

**Table 2** Reversion rates, volatilities, and correlation for the examples

| | |
|---|---|
| OIS reversion rate, $a_r$ | 0.22 |
| OIS volatility, $\sigma_r$ | 0.25 |
| Spread reversion rate, $a_s$ | 0.10 |
| Spread volatility, $\sigma_s$ | 0.20 |
| Correlation between OIS and spread, $\rho$ | 0.05 |

of changes in time $\Delta t$[17]

$$p_u = \frac{1}{6} + \frac{1}{2}(a_r^2 j^2 \Delta t^2 - a_r j \Delta t)$$
$$p_m = \frac{2}{3} - a_r^2 j^2 \Delta t^2$$
$$p_d = \frac{1}{6} + \frac{1}{2}(a_r^2 j^2 \Delta t^2 + a_r j \Delta t)$$

As soon as $j > 0.184/(a_r \Delta t)$, the branching process is changed so that $(i, j)$ leads to one of $(i+1, j)$, $(i+1, j-1)$, and $(i+1, j-2)$. The transition probabilities to these three nodes are

$$p_u = \frac{7}{6} + \frac{1}{2}(a_r^2 j^2 \Delta t^2 - 3a_r j \Delta t)$$
$$p_m = -\frac{1}{3} - a_r^2 j^2 \Delta t^2 + 2a_r j \Delta t$$
$$p_d = \frac{1}{6} + \frac{1}{2}(a_r^2 j^2 \Delta t^2 - a_r j \Delta t)$$

Similarly, as soon as $j < -0.184/(a_r \Delta t)$ the branching process is changed so that $(i, j)$ leads to one of $(i+1, j+2)$, $(i+1, j+1)$, and $(i+1, j)$. The transition probabilities to these three nodes are

$$p_u = \frac{1}{6} + \frac{1}{2}(a_r^2 j^2 \Delta t^2 + a_r j \Delta t)$$
$$p_m = -\frac{1}{3} - a_r^2 j^2 \Delta t^2 - 2a_r j \Delta t$$
$$p_d = \frac{7}{6} + \frac{1}{2}(a_r^2 j^2 \Delta t^2 + 3a_r j \Delta t)$$

We then use an iterative procedure to calculate in succession the amount that the $x$-nodes at each time step must be shifted, $\alpha_0, \alpha_{\Delta t}, \alpha_{2\Delta t}, \ldots$, so that the OIS term structure is matched. The first value, $\alpha_0$, is chosen so that the tree correctly prices a discount bond maturing $\Delta t$. The second value, $\alpha_{\Delta t}$, is chosen so that the tree correctly prices a discount bond maturing $2\Delta t$, and so on.

Arrow–Debreu prices facilitate the calculation. The Arrow–Debreu price for a node is the price of a security that pays off \$1 if the node is reached and zero otherwise. Define $A_{i,j}$ as the Arrow–Debreu price for node $(i, j)$ and define $r_{i,j}$ as the $\Delta t$-maturity interest rate at node $(i, j)$. The value of $\alpha_{i\Delta t}$ can be calculated using an iterative search procedure from the $A_{i,j}$ and the price at time zero, $P_{i+1}$, of a bond maturing at time $(i+1)\Delta t$ using

[17] See for example Hull ([10], p. 725).

$$P_{i+1} = \sum_j A_{i,j} \exp(-r_{i,j} \Delta t) \quad (3)$$

in conjunction with

$$r_{i,j} = \exp(\alpha_{i\Delta t} + j\Delta x) \quad (4)$$

where the summation in Eq. (3) is over all $j$ at time $i\Delta t$. The Arrow–Debreu prices can then be updated using

$$A_{i+1,k} = \sum_j A_{i,j} p_{j,k} \exp(-r_{i,j} \Delta t) \quad (5)$$

where $p(j, k)$ is the probability of branching from $(i, j)$ to $(i + 1, k)$, and the summation is over all $j$ at time $i\Delta t$. The Arrow–Debreu price at the base of the tree, $A_{0,0}$, is one. From this $\alpha_0$ can be calculated using Eqs. (3) and (4). The $A_{1,k}$ can then be calculated using Eqs. (4) and (5). After that $\alpha_{\Delta t}$ can be calculated using Eqs. (3) and (4), and so on.

It is then necessary to calculate the value of the 12-month OIS rate at each node (step 2 in the previous section). As the tree has six-month time steps, a two-period roll back is required in the case of our simple example. It is necessary to build a four-step tree. The value at the $j$th node at time $4\Delta t(= 2)$ of a discount bond that pays \$1 at time $5\Delta t(= 2.5)$ is $\exp(-r_{4,j}\Delta t)$.

Discounting these values back to time $3\Delta t(= 1.5)$ gives the price of a one-year discount bond at each node at $3\Delta t$ from which the bond's yield can be determined. This is repeated for a bond that pays \$1 at time $4\Delta t$ resulting in the one-year yields at time $2\Delta t$, and so on. The tree constructed so far and the values calculated are shown in Fig. 2.[18]

The next stage (step 3 in the previous section) is to construct a tree for the spread assuming that the expected future spread is zero (the preliminary tree). As in the case of the OIS tree, $\Delta t = 0.5$ and $\Delta y = \sigma_s\sqrt{3\Delta t} = 0.2449$. The branching process and probabilities are calculated as for the OIS tree (with $a_r$ replaced by $a_s$).

A three-dimensional tree is then created (step 4 in the previous section) by combining the spread tree and the OIS tree assuming zero correlation. We denote the node at time $i\Delta t$ where $x = j\Delta x$ and $y = k\Delta y$ by node $(i, j, k)$. Consider for example node $(2, -2, 2)$. This corresponds to node $(2, -2)$ in the OIS tree, node $I$ in Fig. 2, and node $(2, 2)$ in the spread tree. The probabilities for the OIS tree are $p_u = 0.0809$, $p_m = 0.0583$, $p_d = 0.8609$ and the branching process is to nodes where $j = 0$, $j = -1$, and $j = -2$. The probabilities for the spread tree are $p_u = 0.1217$, $p_m = 0.6567$, $p_d = 0.2217$ and the branching process is to nodes where $k = 1$, $k = 2$, and $k = 3$. Denote $p_{uu}$ as the probability of the highest move in the OIS tree being combined with the highest move in the spread tree; $p_{um}$ as the probability of the highest move in the OIS tree being combined with the middle move in the spread tree; and so on. The probability, $p_{uu}$ of moving from node $(2, -2, 2)$ to

[18]More details on the construction of the tree can be found in Hull [10].

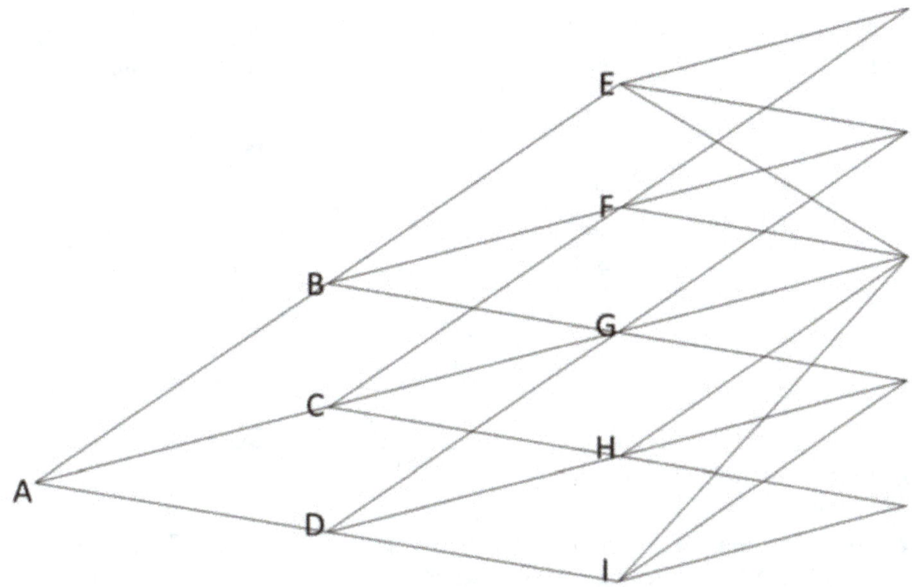


| Node | A | B | C | D | E | F | G | H | I |
|---|---|---|---|---|---|---|---|---|---|
| $x$-value | −3.490 | −3.167 | −3.473 | −3.779 | −2.841 | −3.147 | −3.454 | −3.760 | −4.066 |
| $r$-value | 3.050% | 4.213% | 3.102% | 2.284% | 5.835% | 4.296% | 3.163% | 2.329% | 1.715% |
| 12-month rate (ann. comp.) | 3.149% | 4.306% | 3.207% | 2.393% | 5.910% | 4.397% | 3.275% | 2.443% | 1.828% |
| $p_u$ | 0.1667 | 0.1177 | 0.1667 | 0.2277 | 0.8609 | 0.1177 | 0.1667 | 0.2277 | 0.0809 |
| $p_m$ | 0.6667 | 0.6546 | 0.6667 | 0.6546 | 0.0582 | 0.6546 | 0.6667 | 0.6546 | 0.0582 |
| $p_d$ | 0.1667 | 0.2277 | 0.1667 | 0.1177 | 0.0809 | 0.2277 | 0.1667 | 0.1177 | 0.8609 |
| Arrow-Debreu price | 1.0000 | 0.1641 | 0.6566 | 0.1641 | 0.0189 | 0.2129 | 0.5045 | 0.2140 | 0.0191 |

**Fig. 2** Tree for OIS rates in three-step example

node (3, 0, 3) is therefore $0.0809 \times 0.1217$ or 0.0098; the probability, $p_{um}$ of moving from node $(2, -2, 2)$ to node (3, 0, 2) is $0.0809 \times 0.6567$ or 0.0531 and so on. These (unadjusted) branching probabilities at node $(2, -2, 2)$ are shown in Table 4a.

The next stage (step 5 in the previous section) is to adjust the probabilities to build in correlation between the OIS rate and the spread (i.e., the correlation between $dz_r$ and $dz_s$). As explained in Hull and White [12], probabilities are changed as indicated in Table 3.[19] This leaves the marginal distributions unchanged. The resulting adjusted probabilities at node $(2, -2, 2)$ are shown in Table 4b. In the example we are currently considering the adjusted probabilities are never negative. In practice negative probabilities do occur, but disappear as $\Delta t$ tends zero. They tend to occur only on the edges of the tree where the non-standard branching process is used and do not interfere with convergence. Our approach when negative probabilities are encountered at a node is to change the correlation at that node to the greatest (positive or negative) correlation that is consistent with non-negative probabilities.

[19]The procedure described in Hull and White [12] applies to trinomial trees. For binomial trees the analogous procedure is to increase $p_{uu}$ and $p_{dd}$ by $\varepsilon$ while decreasing $p_{ud}$ and $p_{du}$ by $\varepsilon$ where $\varepsilon = \rho/4$.

**Table 3** Adjustments to probabilities to reflect correlation in a three-dimensional trinomial tree

| Probability | Change when $\rho > 0$ | Change when $\rho < 0$ |
|---|---|---|
| $p_{uu}$ | $+5e$ | $+e$ |
| $p_{um}$ | $-4e$ | $+4e$ |
| $p_{ud}$ | $-e$ | $-5e$ |
| $p_{mu}$ | $-4e$ | $+4e$ |
| $p_{mm}$ | $+8e$ | $-8e$ |
| $p_{md}$ | $-4e$ | $+4e$ |
| $p_{du}$ | $-e$ | $-5e$ |
| $p_{dm}$ | $-4e$ | $+4e$ |
| $p_{dd}$ | $+5e$ | $+e$ |

($e = \rho/36$ where $\rho$ is the correlation)

**Table 4** (a) The unadjusted branching probabilities at node $(2, -2, 2)$. The probabilities on the edge of the table are the branching probabilities at node $(2, -2)$ of the $r$-tree and $(2, 2)$ of the $s$-tree. (b) The adjusted branching probabilities at node $(2, -2, 2)$. The probabilities on the edge of the table are the branching probabilities at node $(2, -2)$ of the $r$-tree and $(2, 2)$ of the $s$-tree. The adjustment is based on a correlation of 0.05 so $e = 0.00139$

*a*

| | | | $r$-tree | | |
|---|---|---|---|---|---|
| | | | $p_u$ | $p_m$ | $p_d$ |
| | | | 0.0809 | 0.0583 | 0.8609 |
| $s$-tree | $p_u$ | 0.1217 | 0.0098 | 0.0071 | 0.1047 |
| | $p_m$ | 0.6567 | 0.0531 | 0.0383 | 0.5653 |
| | $p_d$ | 0.2217 | 0.0179 | 0.0129 | 0.1908 |

*b*

| | | | $r$-tree | | |
|---|---|---|---|---|---|
| | | | $p_u$ | $p_m$ | $p_d$ |
| | | | 0.0809 | 0.0583 | 0.8609 |
| $s$-tree | $p_u$ | 0.1217 | 0.0168 | 0.0015 | 0.1033 |
| | $p_m$ | 0.6567 | 0.0475 | 0.0494 | 0.5597 |
| | $p_d$ | 0.2217 | 0.0165 | 0.0074 | 0.1978 |

The tree constructed so far reflects actual OIS movements and artificial spread movements where the initial spread and expected future spread are zero. We are now in a position to calculate Arrow–Debreu prices for each node of the three-dimensional tree. These Arrow–Debreu prices remain the same when the positions of the spread nodes are changed because the Arrow–Debreu price for a node depends only on OIS rates and the probability of the node being reached. They are shown in Table 5.

The final stage involves shifting the position of the spread nodes so that the prices of all LIBOR FRAs with a fixed rate equal to the initial forward LIBOR rate are zero. An iterative procedure is used to calculate the adjustment to the values of $y$

**Table 5** Arrow–Debreu prices for simple three-step example

| $i = 1$ | $k = -1$ | $k = 0$ | $k = 1$ | | | | |
|---|---|---|---|---|---|---|---|
| $j = 1$ | 0.0260 | 0.1040 | 0.0342 | | | | |
| $j = 0$ | 0.1040 | 0.4487 | 0.1040 | | | | |
| $j = -1$ | 0.0342 | 0.1040 | 0.0260 | | | | |
| $i = 2$ | $k = -2$ | $k = -1$ | $k = 0$ | $k = 1$ | $k = 2$ | | |
| $j = 2$ | 0.0004 | 0.0037 | 0.0089 | 0.0051 | 0.0008 | | |
| $j = 1$ | 0.0045 | 0.0443 | 0.1064 | 0.0516 | 0.0061 | | |
| $j = 0$ | 0.0112 | 0.1100 | 0.2620 | 0.1100 | 0.0112 | | |
| $j = -1$ | 0.0061 | 0.0518 | 0.1070 | 0.0445 | 0.0046 | | |
| $j = -2$ | 0.0008 | 0.0052 | 0.0090 | 0.0037 | 0.0004 | | |
| $i = 3$ | $k = -3$ | $k = -2$ | $k = -1$ | $k = 0$ | $k = 1$ | $k = 2$ | $k = 3$ |
| $j = 2$ | 0.0001 | 0.0016 | 0.0085 | 0.0163 | 0.0109 | 0.0027 | 0.0002 |
| $j = 1$ | 0.0005 | 0.0094 | 0.0496 | 0.0932 | 0.0551 | 0.0116 | 0.0007 |
| $j = 0$ | 0.0012 | 0.0197 | 0.1016 | 0.1849 | 0.1016 | 0.0197 | 0.0012 |
| $j = -1$ | 0.0008 | 0.0117 | 0.0557 | 0.0941 | 0.0501 | 0.0095 | 0.0005 |
| $j = -2$ | 0.0002 | 0.0028 | 0.0111 | 0.0167 | 0.0087 | 0.0017 | 0.0001 |

at each node at each time step, $\beta_0, \beta_{\Delta t}, \beta_{2\Delta t}, \ldots$, so that the FRAs have a value of zero. Given that Arrow–Debreu prices have already been calculated this is a fairly straightforward search. When the $\alpha_{j\Delta t}$ are determined it is necessary to first consider $j = 0$, then $j = 1$, then $j = 2$, and so on because the $\alpha$-value at a particular time depends on the $\alpha$-values at earlier times. The $\beta$-values however are independent of each other and can be determined in any order, or as needed. In the case of our example, $\beta_0 = -6.493$, $\beta_{\Delta t} = -6.459$, $\beta_{2\Delta t} = -6.426$, $\beta_{3\Delta t} = -6.395$.

## 5 Valuation of a Spread Option

To illustrate convergence, we use the tree to calculate the value of a European call option that pays off 100 times $\max(s - 0.002, 0)$ at time $T$ where $s$ is the spread. First, we let $T = 1.5$ years and use the three-step tree developed in the previous section. At the third step of the tree we calculate the spread at each node. The spread at node $(3, j, k)$ is $\exp[\phi(3\Delta t) + k\Delta y]$. These values are shown in the second line of Table 6. Once the spread values have been determined the option payoffs, 100 times $\max(s - 0.002, 0)$, at each node are calculated. These values are shown in the rest of Table 6. The option value is found by multiplying each option payoff by the corresponding Arrow–Debreu price in Table 5 and summing the values. The resulting option value is 0.00670. Table 7 shows how, for a 1.5- and 5-year spread option, the value converges as the number of time steps per year is increased.

**Table 6** Spread and spread option payoff at time 1.5 years when spread option is evaluated using a three-step tree

| $i = 3$ | $k = -3$ | $k = -2$ | $k = -1$ | $k = 0$ | $k = 1$ | $k = 2$ | $k = 3$ |
|---|---|---|---|---|---|---|---|
| Spread | 0.0008 | 0.0010 | 0.0013 | 0.0017 | 0.0021 | 0.0027 | 0.0035 |
| $j = 2$ | 0.0000 | 0.0000 | 0.0000 | 0.0000 | 0.0133 | 0.0725 | 0.1482 |
| $j = 1$ | 0.0000 | 0.0000 | 0.0000 | 0.0000 | 0.0133 | 0.0725 | 0.1482 |
| $j = 0$ | 0.0000 | 0.0000 | 0.0000 | 0.0000 | 0.0133 | 0.0725 | 0.1482 |
| $j = -1$ | 0.0000 | 0.0000 | 0.0000 | 0.0000 | 0.0133 | 0.0725 | 0.1482 |
| $j = -2$ | 0.0000 | 0.0000 | 0.0000 | 0.0000 | 0.0133 | 0.0725 | 0.1482 |

**Table 7** Value of a European spread option paying off 100 times the greater of the spread less 0.002 and zero

| Time steps per year | 1.5-year option | 5-year option |
|---|---|---|
| 2 | 0.00670 | 0.0310 |
| 4 | 0.00564 | 0.0312 |
| 8 | 0.00621 | 0.0313 |
| 16 | 0.00592 | 0.0313 |
| 32 | 0.00596 | 0.0313 |

The market data used to build the tree is given in Tables 1 and 2

**Table 8** Value of a five-year European spread option paying off 100 times the greater of the spread less 0.002 and zero

| Spread volatility | Spread/OIS correlation | | | | | | |
|---|---|---|---|---|---|---|---|
| | –0.75 | –0.50 | –0.25 | 0 | 0.25 | 0.5 | 0.75 |
| 0.05 | 0.0141 | 0.0142 | 0.0142 | 0.0143 | 0.0143 | 0.0144 | 0.0144 |
| 0.10 | 0.0193 | 0.0194 | 0.0195 | 0.0195 | 0.0196 | 0.0196 | 0.0197 |
| 0.15 | 0.0250 | 0.0252 | 0.0253 | 0.0254 | 0.0254 | 0.0255 | 0.0256 |
| 0.20 | 0.0308 | 0.0309 | 0.0311 | 0.0313 | 0.0314 | 0.0316 | 0.0317 |
| 0.25 | 0.0367 | 0.0369 | 0.0371 | 0.0373 | 0.0374 | 0.0376 | 0.0377 |

The market data used to build the tree are given in Tables 1 and 2 except that the volatility of the spread and the correlation between the spread and the OIS rate are as given in this table. The number of time steps is 32 per year

Table 8 shows how the spread option price is affected by the assumed correlation and the volatility of the spread. All of the input parameters are as given in Tables 1 and 2 except that correlations between $-0.75$ and $0.75$, and spread volatilities between $0.05$ and $0.25$ are considered. As might be expected the spread option price is very sensitive to the spread volatility. However, it is not very sensitive to the correlation. The reason for this is that changing the correlation primarily affects the Arrow–Debreu prices and leaves the option payoffs almost unchanged. Increasing the correlation increases the Arrow–Debreu prices on one diagonal of the final nodes and decreases them on the other diagonal. For example, in the three-step tree used to evaluate the option, the Arrow–Debreu price for nodes (3, 2, 3) and (3, −2, −3) increase while those for nodes (3, −2, 3) and (3, 2, −3) decrease. Since the option payoffs at nodes (3, 2, 3) and (3, −2, 3) are the same, the changes on the Arrow–Debreu prices offset one another resulting in only a small correlation effect.

## 6 Bermudan Swap Option

We now consider how the valuation of a Bermudan swap option is affected by a stochastic spread in a low-interest-rate environment such as that experienced in the years following 2009. Bermudan swap options are popular instruments where the holder has the right to enter into a particular swap on a number of different swap payment dates.

The valuation procedure involves rolling back through the tree calculating both the swap price and (where appropriate) the option price. The swap's value is set equal to zero at the nodes on the swap's maturity date. The value at earlier nodes is calculated by rolling back adding in the present value of the next payment on each reset date. The option's value is set equal to $\max(S, 0)$ where $S$ is the swap value at the option's maturity. It is then set equal to $\max(S, V)$ for nodes on exercise dates where $S$ is the swap value and $V$ is the value of the option given by the roll back procedure.

We assume an OIS term structure that increases linearly from 15 basis points at time zero to 250 basis points at time 10 years. The OIS zero rate for maturity $t$ is therefore

$$0.0015 + \frac{0.0235t}{10}$$

The process followed by the instantaneous OIS rate was similar to that derived by Deguillaume, Rebonato and Pogodin [7], and Hull and White [16]. For short rates between 0 and 1.5 %, changes in the rate are assumed to be lognormal with a volatility of 100 %. Between 1.5 % and 6 % changes in the short rate are assumed to be normal with the standard deviation of rate moves in time $\Delta t$ being $0.015\sqrt{\Delta t}$. Above 6 % rate moves were assumed to be lognormal with volatility 25 %. This pattern of the short rate's variability is shown in Fig. 3.

The spread between the forward 12-month OIS and the forward 12-month LIBOR was assumed to be 50 basis points for all maturities. The process assumed for the 12-month LIBOR-OIS spread, $s$, is that used in the example in Sects. 4 and 5

$$\mathrm{d}\ln(s) = a_s[\phi(t) - \ln(s)] + \sigma_s\,\mathrm{d}z_s$$

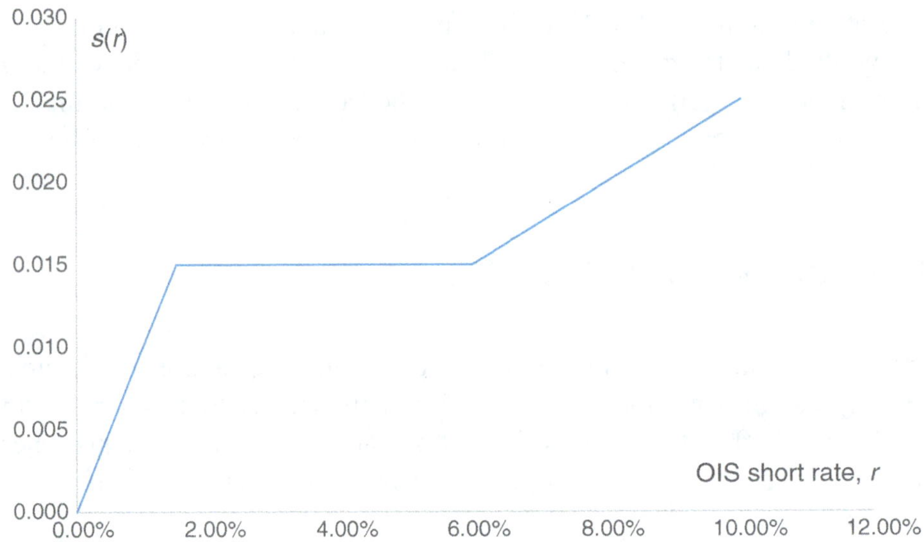


**Fig. 3** Variability assumed for short OIS rate, $r$, in Bermudan swap option valuation. The standard deviation of the short rate in time $\Delta t$ is $s(r)\sqrt{\Delta t}$

**Table 9** (a) Value in a low-interest rate environment, of a receive-fixed Bermudan swap option on a 5-year annual-pay swap where the notional principal is 100 and the option can be exercised at times 1, 2, and 3 years. The swap rate is 1.5 %. (b) Value in a low-interest-rate environment of a received-fixed Bermudan swap option on a 10-year annual-pay swap where the notional principal is 100 and the option can be exercised at times 1, 2, 3, 4, and 5 years. The swap rate is 3.0 %

| Spread volatility | Spread/OIS correlation | | | | | | |
|---|---|---|---|---|---|---|---|
| *a* | | | | | | | |
| | –0.5 | –0.25 | –0.1 | 0 | 0.1 | 0.25 | 0.5 |
| 0 | 0.398 | 0.398 | 0.398 | 0.398 | 0.398 | 0.398 | 0.398 |
| 0.3 | 0.333 | 0.371 | 0.393 | 0.407 | 0.421 | 0.441 | 0.473 |
| 0.5 | 0.310 | 0.373 | 0.407 | 0.429 | 0.449 | 0.480 | 0.527 |
| 0.7 | 0.309 | 0.389 | 0.432 | 0.459 | 0.485 | 0.522 | 0.580 |
| *b* | | | | | | | |
| | –0.5 | –0.25 | –0.1 | 0 | 0.1 | 0.25 | 0.5 |
| 0 | 2.217 | 2.218 | 2.218 | 2.218 | 2.218 | 2.218 | 2.218 |
| 0.3 | 2.100 | 2.164 | 2.201 | 2.225 | 2.248 | 2.283 | 2.339 |
| 0.5 | 2.031 | 2.141 | 2.203 | 2.242 | 2.280 | 2.335 | 2.421 |
| 0.7 | 1.980 | 2.134 | 2.218 | 2.271 | 2.321 | 2.392 | 2.503 |

A maximum likelihood analysis of data on the 12-month LIBOR-OIS spread over the 2012 to 2014 period indicates that the behavior of the spread can be approximately described by a high volatility in conjunction with a high reversion rate. We set $a_s$ equal to 0.4 and considered values of $\sigma_s$ equal to 0.30, 0.50, and 0.70. A number of alternative correlations between the spread process and the OIS process were also considered. We find that correlation of about $-0.1$ between one month OIS and the 12-month LIBOR OIS spread is indicated by the data.[20]

We consider two cases:

1. A $3 \times 5$ swap option. The underlying swap lasts 5 years and involves 12-month LIBOR being paid and a fixed rate of 1.5 % being received. The option to enter into the swap can be exercised at the end of years 1, 2, and 3.
2. A $5 \times 10$ swap option. The underlying swap lasts 10 years and involves 12-month LIBOR being paid and a fixed rate of 3.0 % being received. The option to enter into the swap can be exercised at the end of years 1, 2, 3, 4, and 5.

Table 9a shows results for the $3 \times 5$ swap option. In this case, even when the correlation between the spread rate and the OIS rate is relatively small, a stochastic spread is liable to change the price by 5–10 %. Table 9b shows results for the $5 \times 10$ swap option. In this case, the percentage impact of a stochastic spread is smaller. This is because the spread, as a proportion of the average of the relevant forward OIS rates, is lower. The results in both tables are based on 32 time steps per year. As the level of OIS rates increases the impact of a stochastic spread becomes smaller in both Table 9a, b.

Comparing Tables 8 and 9, we see that the correlation between the OIS rate and the spread has a much bigger effect on the valuation of a Bermudan swap option than on the valuation of a spread option. For a spread option we argued that option payoffs for high Arrow–Debreu prices tend to offset those for low Arrow–Debreu prices. This is not the case for a Bermudan swap option because the payoff depends on the LIBOR rate, which depends on the OIS rate as well as the spread.

## 7 Conclusions

For investment grade companies it is well known that the hazard rate is an increasing function of time. This means that the credit spread applicable to borrowing by AA-rated banks from other banks is an increasing function of maturity. Since 2008, markets have recognized this with the result that the LIBOR-OIS spread has been an increasing function of tenor.

Since 2008, practitioners have also switched from LIBOR discounting to OIS discounting. This means that two zero curves have to be modelled when most interest rate derivatives are valued. Many practitioners assume that the relevant LIBOR-OIS spread is either constant or deterministic. Our research shows that this is liable to lead to inaccurate pricing, particularly in the current low interest rate environment.

The tree approach we have presented provides an alternative to Monte Carlo simulation for simultaneously modelling spreads and OIS rates. It can be regarded as

[20]Because of the way LIBOR is calculated, daily LIBOR changes can be less volatile than the corresponding daily OIS changes (particularly if the Fed is not targeting a particular overnight rate). In some circumstances, it may be appropriate to consider changes over periods longer than one day when estimating the correlation.

an extension of the explicit finite difference method and is particularly useful when American-style derivatives are valued. It avoids the need to use techniques such as those suggested by Longstaff and Schwartz [19] and Andersen (2000) for handling early exercise within a Monte Carlo simulation.

Implying all the model parameters from market data is not likely to be feasible. One reasonable approach is to use historical data to determine the spread process and its correlation with the OIS process so that only the parameters driving the OIS process are implied from the market. The model can then be used in the same way that two-dimensional tree models for LIBOR were used pre-crisis.

**Acknowledgements** We are grateful to the Global Risk Institute in Financial Services for funding this research.

The KPMG Center of Excellence in Risk Management is acknowledged for organizing the conference "Challenges in Derivatives Markets - Fixed Income Modeling, Valuation Adjustments, Risk Management, and Regulation".

**Open Access** This chapter is distributed under the terms of the Creative Commons Attribution 4.0 International License (http://creativecommons.org/licenses/by/4.0/), which permits use, duplication, adaptation, distribution and reproduction in any medium or format, as long as you give appropriate credit to the original author(s) and the source, a link is provided to the Creative Commons license and any changes made are indicated.

The images or other third party material in this chapter are included in the work's Creative Commons license, unless indicated otherwise in the credit line; if such material is not included in the work's Creative Commons license and the respective action is not permitted by statutory regulation, users will need to obtain permission from the license holder to duplicate, adapt or reproduce the material.

## References

1. Ames, W.F.: Numerical Methods for Partial Differential Equations. Academic Press, New York (1977)
2. Anderson, L.: A simple approach to pricing Bermudan swap options in the multifactor LIBOR market model. J. Comput. Financ. **3**(2), 1–32 (2000)
3. Black, F., Derman, E., Toy, W.: A one-factor model of interest rates and its application to treasury bond prices. Financ. Anal. J. **46**(1), 1–32 (1990)
4. Black, F., Karasinski, P.: Bond and option pricing when short rates are lognormal. Financ. Anal. J. **47**(4), 52–59 (1991)
5. Brigo, D., Mercurio, F.: Interest Rate Models: Theory and Practice: With Smile Inflation and Credit, 2nd edn. Springer, Berlin (2007)
6. Collin-Dufresne, P., Solnik, B.: On the term structure of default premia in the swap and LIBOR market. J. Financ. **56**(3), 1095–1115 (2001)
7. DeGuillaume, N., Rebonato, R., Pogudin, A.: The nature of the dependence of the magnitude of rate moves on the level of rates: a universal relationship. Quant. Financ. **13**(3), 351–367 (2013)
8. Hainaut, D., MacGilchrist, R.: An interest rate tree driven by a Lévy process. J. Deriv. **18**(2), 33–45 (2010)
9. Ho, T.S.Y., Lee, S.-B.: Term structure movements and pricing interest rate contingent claims. J. Financ. **41**, 1011–1029 (1986)
10. Hull, J.: Options, Futures and Other Derivatives, 9th edn. Pearson, New York (2015)

11. Hull, J., White, A.: Numerical procedures for implementing term structure models I. J. Deriv. **2**(1), 7–16 (1994)
12. Hull, J., White, A.: Numerical procedures for implementing term structure models II. J. Deriv. **2**(2), 37–48 (1994)
13. Hull, J., White, A.: Using Hull-White interest rate trees. J. Deriv. **3**(3), 26–36 (1996)
14. Hull, J., White, A.: The general Hull-White model and super calibration. Financ. Anal. J. **57**(6), 34–43 (2001)
15. Hull, J., White, A.: LIBOR vs. OIS: The derivatives discounting dilemma. J. Invest. Manag. **11**(3), 14–27 (2013)
16. Hull, J., White, A.: A generalized procedure for building trees for the short rate and its application to determining market implied volatility functions. Quant. Financ. **15**(3), 443–454 (2015)
17. Hull, J., White, A.: OIS discounting, interest rate derivatives, and the modeling of stochastic interest rate spreads. J. Invest. Manag. **13**(1), 13–20 (2015)
18. Kalotay, A.J., Williams, G.O., Fabozzi, F.J.: A model for valuing bonds and embedded options. Financ. Anal. J. **49**(3), 35–46 (1993)
19. Longstaff, F.A., Schwartz, E.S.: Valuing American options by Monte Carlo simulation: a simple least squares approach. Rev. Financ. Stud. **14**(1), 113–147 (2001)

# Derivative Pricing for a Multi-curve Extension of the Gaussian, Exponentially Quadratic Short Rate Model

**Zorana Grbac, Laura Meneghello and Wolfgang J. Runggaldier**

**Abstract** The recent financial crisis has led to so-called multi-curve models for the term structure. Here we study a multi-curve extension of short rate models where, in addition to the short rate itself, we introduce short rate spreads. In particular, we consider a Gaussian factor model where the short rate and the spreads are second order polynomials of Gaussian factor processes. This leads to an exponentially quadratic model class that is less well known than the exponentially affine class. In the latter class the factors enter linearly and for positivity one considers square root factor processes. While the square root factors in the affine class have more involved distributions, in the quadratic class the factors remain Gaussian and this leads to various advantages, in particular for derivative pricing. After some preliminaries on martingale modeling in the multi-curve setup, we concentrate on pricing of linear and optional derivatives. For linear derivatives, we exhibit an adjustment factor that allows one to pass from pre-crisis single curve values to the corresponding post-crisis multi-curve values.

**Keywords** Multi-curve models · Short rate models · Short rate spreads · Gaussian exponentially quadratic models · Pricing of linear and optional interest rate derivatives · Riccati equations · Adjustment factors

---

L. Meneghello Present affiliation: Gruppo Banco Popolare *Disclaimer: The views, thoughts and opinions expressed in this paper are those of the authors in their individual capacity and should not be attributed to Gruppo Banco Popolare or to the authors as representatives or employees of Gruppo Banco Popolare.*

---

Z. Grbac (✉)
Laboratoire de Probabilités et Modèles Aléatoires, Université Paris Diderot - Paris 7, Case 7012, 75205 Paris Cedex 13, France
e-mail: grbac@math.univ-paris-diderot.fr

L. Meneghello · W.J. Runggaldier
Dipartimento di Matematica Pura ed Applicata, Università di Padova, Via Trieste 63, 35121 Padova, Italy
e-mail: meneghello.laura@yahoo.com

W.J. Runggaldier
e-mail: runggal@math.unipd.it

© The Author(s) 2016

K. Glau et al. (eds.), *Innovations in Derivatives Markets*, Springer Proceedings in Mathematics & Statistics 165, DOI 10.1007/978-3-319-33446-2_10

## 1 Introduction

The recent financial crisis has heavily impacted the financial market and the fixed income markets in particular. Key features put forward by the crisis are counterparty and liquidity/funding risk. In interest rate derivatives the underlying rates are typically Libor/Euribor. These are determined by a panel of banks and thus reflect various risks in the interbank market, in particular counterparty and liquidity risk. The standard no-arbitrage relations between Libor rates of different maturities have broken down and significant spreads have been observed between Libor rates of different tenors, as well as between Libor and OIS swap rates, where OIS stands for Overnight Indexed Swap. For more details on this issue see Eqs. (5)–(7) and the paragraph following them, as well as the paper by Bormetti et al. [1] and a corresponding version in this volume. This has led practitioners and academics alike to construct multi-curve models where future cash flows are generated through curves associated to the underlying rates (typically the Libor, one for each tenor structure), but are discounted by another curve.

For the pre-crisis single-curve setup various interest rate models have been proposed. Some of the standard model classes are: the short rate models; the instantaneous forward rate models in an Heath–Jarrow–Morton (HJM) setup; the market forward rate models (Libor market models). In this paper we consider a possible multi-curve extension of the short rate model class that, with respect to the other model classes, has in particular the advantage of leading more easily to a Markovian structure. Other multi-curve extensions of short rate models have appeared in the literature such as Kijima et al. [22], Kenyon [20], Filipović and Trolle [14], Morino and Runggaldier [27]. The present paper considers an exponentially quadratic model, whereas the models in the mentioned papers concern mainly the exponentially affine framework, except for [22] in which the exponentially quadratic models are mentioned. More details on the difference between the exponentially affine and exponentially quadratic short rate models will be provided below.

Inspired by a credit risk analogy, but also by a common practice of deriving multi-curve quantities by adding a spread over the corresponding single-curve risk-free quantities, we shall consider, next to the short rate itself, a short rate spread to be added to the short rate, one for each possible tenor structure. Notice that these spreads are added from the outset.

To discuss the basic ideas in an as simple as possible way, we consider just a two-curve model, namely with one curve for discounting and one for generating future cash flows; in other words, we shall consider a single tenor structure. We shall thus concentrate on the short rate $r_t$ and a single short rate spread $s_t$ and, for their dynamics, introduce a factor model. In the pre-crisis single-curve setting there are two basic factor model classes for the short rate: the exponentially affine and the exponentially quadratic model classes. Here we shall concentrate on the less common quadratic class with Gaussian factors. In the exponentially affine class where, to guarantee positivity of rates and spreads, one considers generally square root models for the factors, the distribution of the factors is $\chi^2$. In the exponentially quadratic class the factors have a more convenient Gaussian distribution.

The paper is structured as follows. In the preliminary Sect. 2 we mainly discuss issues related to martingale modeling. In Sect. 3 we introduce the multi-curve Gaussian, exponentially quadratic model class. In Sect. 4 we deal with pricing of linear interest rate derivatives and, finally, in Sect. 5 with nonlinear/optional interest rate derivatives.

## 2 Preliminaries

### 2.1 Discount Curve and Collateralization

In the presence of multiple curves, the choice of the curve for discounting the future cash flows, and a related choice of the numeraire for the standard martingale measure used for pricing, in other words, the question of absence of arbitrage, becomes non-trivial (see e.g. the discussion in Kijima and Muromachi [21]). To avoid issues of arbitrage, one should possibly have a common discount curve to be applied to all future cash flows independently of the tenor. A choice, which has been widely accepted and became practically standard, is given by the OIS-curve $T \mapsto p(t, T) = p^{OIS}(t, T)$ that can be stripped from OIS rates, namely the fair rates in an OIS. The arguments justifying this choice and which are typically evoked in practice, are the fact that the majority of the traded interest rate derivatives are nowadays being collateralized and the rate used for remuneration of the collateral is exactly the overnight rate, which is the rate the OIS are based on. Moreover, the overnight rate bears very little risk due to its short maturity and therefore can be considered relatively risk-free. In this context we also point out that prices, corresponding to fully collateralized transactions, are considered as clean prices (this terminology was first introduced by Crépey [6] and Crépey et al. [9]). Since collateralization is by now applied in the majority of cases, one may thus ignore counterparty and liquidity risk between individual parties when pricing interest rate derivatives, but cannot ignore the counterparty and liquidity risk in the interbank market as a whole. These risks are often jointly referred to as interbank risk and they are main drivers of the multi-curve phenomenon, as documented in the literature (see e.g. Crépey and Douady [7], Filipović and Trolle [14], and Gallitschke et al. [15]). We shall thus consider only *clean valuation* formulas, which take into account the multi-curve issue. Possible ways to account for counterparty risk and funding issues between individual counterparties in a contract are, among others, to follow a global valuation approach that leads to nonlinear derivative valuation (see Brigo et al. [3, 4] and other references therein, and in particular Pallavicini and Brigo [28] for a global valuation approach applied specifically to interest rate modeling), or to consider various valuation adjustments that are generally computed on top of the clean prices (see Crépey [6]). A fully nonlinear valuation is preferable, but is more difficult to achieve. On the other hand, valuation adjustments are more consolidated and also used in practice and this gives a further justification to still look for clean prices. Concerning the explicit role of collateral in the pricing of interest rate derivatives, we refer to the above-mentioned paper by Pallavicini and Brigo [28].

## 2.2 Martingale Measures

The fundamental theorem of asset pricing links the economic principle of absence of arbitrage with the notion of a martingale measure. As it is well known, this is a measure, under which the traded asset prices, expressed in units of a same numeraire, are local martingales. Models for interest rate markets are typically incomplete so that absence of arbitrage admits many martingale measures. A common approach in interest rate modeling is to perform martingale modeling, namely to model the quantities of interest directly under a generic martingale measure; one has then to perform a calibration in order to single out the specific martingale measure of interest. The modeling under a martingale measure now imposes some conditions on the model and, in interest rate theory, a typical such condition is the Heath–Jarrow–Morton (HJM) drift condition.

Starting from the OIS bonds, we shall first derive a suitable numeraire and then consider as martingale measure a measure $Q$ under which not only the OIS bonds, but also the FRA contracts seen as basic quantities in the bond market, are local martingales when expressed in units of the given numeraire. To this basic market one can then add various derivatives imposing that their prices, expressed in units of the numeraire, are local martingales under $Q$.

Having made the choice of the OIS curve $T \mapsto p(t, T)$ as the discount curve, consider the instantaneous forward rates $f(t, T) := -\frac{\partial}{\partial T} \log p(t, T)$ and let $r_t = f(t, t)$ be the corresponding short rate at the generic time $t$. Define the OIS bank account as

$$B_t = \exp\left(\int_0^t r_s ds\right) \tag{1}$$

and, as usual, the standard martingale measure $Q$ as the measure, equivalent to the physical measure $P$, that is associated to the bank account $B_t$ as numeraire. Hence the arbitrage-free prices of all assets, discounted by $B_t$, have to be local martingales with respect to $Q$. For derivative pricing, among them also FRA pricing, it is often more convenient to use, equivalently, the forward measure $Q^T$ associated to the OIS bond $p(t, T)$ as numeraire. The two measures $Q$ and $Q^T$ are related by their Radon–Nikodym density process

$$\left.\frac{dQ^T}{dQ}\right|_{\mathcal{F}_t} = \frac{p(t, T)}{B_t p(0, T)} \qquad 0 \leq t \leq T. \tag{2}$$

As already mentioned, we shall follow the traditional *martingale modeling*, whereby the model dynamics are assigned under the martingale measure $Q$. This leads to defining the OIS bond prices according to

$$p(t,T) = E^Q \left\{ \exp\left[ -\int_t^T r_u du \right] \mid \mathscr{F}_t \right\} \tag{3}$$

after having specified the $Q-$dynamics of $r$.

Coming now to the FRA contracts, recall that they concern a forward rate agreement, established at a time $t$ for a future interval $[T, T+\Delta]$, where at time $T+\Delta$ the interest corresponding to a floating rate is received in exchange for the interest corresponding to a fixed rate $R$. There exist various possible conventions concerning the timing of the payments. Here we choose payment in arrears, which in this case means at time $T+\Delta$. Typically, the floating rate is given by the Libor rate and, having assumed payments in arrears, we also assume that the rate is fixed at the beginning of the interval of interest, here at $T$. Recall that for expository simplicity we had reduced ourselves to a two-curve setup involving just a single Libor for a given tenor $\Delta$. The floating rate received at $T+\Delta$ is therefore the rate $L(T; T, T+\Delta)$, fixed at the inception time $T$. For a unitary notional, and using the $(T+\Delta)$-forward measure $Q^{T+\Delta}$ as the pricing measure, the arbitrage-free price at $t \le T$ of the FRA contract is then

$$P^{FRA}(t; T, T+\Delta, R) = \Delta p(t, T+\Delta) E^{T+\Delta} \left\{ L(T; T, T+\Delta) - R \mid \mathscr{F}_t \right\}, \tag{4}$$

where $E^{T+\Delta}$ denotes the expectation with respect to the measure $Q^{T+\Delta}$. From this expression it follows that the value of the fixed rate $R$ that makes the contract fair at time $t$ is given by

$$R_t = E^{T+\Delta} \left\{ L(T; T, T+\Delta) \mid \mathscr{F}_t \right\} := L(t; T, T+\Delta) \tag{5}$$

and we shall call $L(t; T, T+\Delta)$ the *forward Libor rate*. Note that $L(\cdot; T, T+\Delta)$ is a $Q^{T+\Delta}-$martingale by construction.

In view of developing a model for $L(T; T, T+\Delta)$, recall that, by absence of arbitrage arguments, the classical discrete compounding forward rate at time $t$ for the future time interval $[T, T+\Delta]$ is given by

$$F(t; T, T+\Delta) = \frac{1}{\Delta}\left( \frac{p(t,T)}{p(t, T+\Delta)} - 1 \right),$$

where $p(t,T)$ represents here the price of a risk-free zero coupon bond. This expression can be justified also by the fact that it represents the fair fixed rate in a forward rate agreement, where the floating rate received at $T+\Delta$ is

$$F(T; T, T+\Delta) = \frac{1}{\Delta}\left( \frac{1}{p(T, T+\Delta)} - 1 \right) \tag{6}$$

## 1 Introduction

The recent financial crisis has heavily impacted the financial market and the fixed income markets in particular. Key features put forward by the crisis are counterparty and liquidity/funding risk. In interest rate derivatives the underlying rates are typically Libor/Euribor. These are determined by a panel of banks and thus reflect various risks in the interbank market, in particular counterparty and liquidity risk. The standard no-arbitrage relations between Libor rates of different maturities have broken down and significant spreads have been observed between Libor rates of different tenors, as well as between Libor and OIS swap rates, where OIS stands for Overnight Indexed Swap. For more details on this issue see Eqs. (5)–(7) and the paragraph following them, as well as the paper by Bormetti et al. [1] and a corresponding version in this volume. This has led practitioners and academics alike to construct multi-curve models where future cash flows are generated through curves associated to the underlying rates (typically the Libor, one for each tenor structure), but are discounted by another curve.

For the pre-crisis single-curve setup various interest rate models have been proposed. Some of the standard model classes are: the short rate models; the instantaneous forward rate models in an Heath–Jarrow–Morton (HJM) setup; the market forward rate models (Libor market models). In this paper we consider a possible multi-curve extension of the short rate model class that, with respect to the other model classes, has in particular the advantage of leading more easily to a Markovian structure. Other multi-curve extensions of short rate models have appeared in the literature such as Kijima et al. [22], Kenyon [20], Filipović and Trolle [14], Morino and Runggaldier [27]. The present paper considers an exponentially quadratic model, whereas the models in the mentioned papers concern mainly the exponentially affine framework, except for [22] in which the exponentially quadratic models are mentioned. More details on the difference between the exponentially affine and exponentially quadratic short rate models will be provided below.

Inspired by a credit risk analogy, but also by a common practice of deriving multi-curve quantities by adding a spread over the corresponding single-curve risk-free quantities, we shall consider, next to the short rate itself, a short rate spread to be added to the short rate, one for each possible tenor structure. Notice that these spreads are added from the outset.

To discuss the basic ideas in an as simple as possible way, we consider just a two-curve model, namely with one curve for discounting and one for generating future cash flows; in other words, we shall consider a single tenor structure. We shall thus concentrate on the short rate $r_t$ and a single short rate spread $s_t$ and, for their dynamics, introduce a factor model. In the pre-crisis single-curve setting there are two basic factor model classes for the short rate: the exponentially affine and the exponentially quadratic model classes. Here we shall concentrate on the less common quadratic class with Gaussian factors. In the exponentially affine class where, to guarantee positivity of rates and spreads, one considers generally square root models for the factors, the distribution of the factors is $\chi^2$. In the exponentially quadratic class the factors have a more convenient Gaussian distribution.

The paper is structured as follows. In the preliminary Sect. 2 we mainly discuss issues related to martingale modeling. In Sect. 3 we introduce the multi-curve Gaussian, exponentially quadratic model class. In Sect. 4 we deal with pricing of linear interest rate derivatives and, finally, in Sect. 5 with nonlinear/optional interest rate derivatives.

# 2 Preliminaries

## *2.1 Discount Curve and Collateralization*

In the presence of multiple curves, the choice of the curve for discounting the future cash flows, and a related choice of the numeraire for the standard martingale measure used for pricing, in other words, the question of absence of arbitrage, becomes non-trivial (see e.g. the discussion in Kijima and Muromachi [21]). To avoid issues of arbitrage, one should possibly have a common discount curve to be applied to all future cash flows independently of the tenor. A choice, which has been widely accepted and became practically standard, is given by the OIS-curve $T \mapsto p(t, T) = p^{OIS}(t, T)$ that can be stripped from OIS rates, namely the fair rates in an OIS. The arguments justifying this choice and which are typically evoked in practice, are the fact that the majority of the traded interest rate derivatives are nowadays being collateralized and the rate used for remuneration of the collateral is exactly the overnight rate, which is the rate the OIS are based on. Moreover, the overnight rate bears very little risk due to its short maturity and therefore can be considered relatively risk-free. In this context we also point out that prices, corresponding to fully collateralized transactions, are considered as clean prices (this terminology was first introduced by Crépey [6] and Crépey et al. [9]). Since collateralization is by now applied in the majority of cases, one may thus ignore counterparty and liquidity risk between individual parties when pricing interest rate derivatives, but cannot ignore the counterparty and liquidity risk in the interbank market as a whole. These risks are often jointly referred to as interbank risk and they are main drivers of the multi-curve phenomenon, as documented in the literature (see e.g. Crépey and Douady [7], Filipović and Trolle [14], and Gallitschke et al. [15]). We shall thus consider only *clean valuation* formulas, which take into account the multi-curve issue. Possible ways to account for counterparty risk and funding issues between individual counterparties in a contract are, among others, to follow a global valuation approach that leads to nonlinear derivative valuation (see Brigo et al. [3, 4] and other references therein, and in particular Pallavicini and Brigo [28] for a global valuation approach applied specifically to interest rate modeling), or to consider various valuation adjustments that are generally computed on top of the clean prices (see Crépey [6]). A fully nonlinear valuation is preferable, but is more difficult to achieve. On the other hand,

and we have

$$F(t;T,T+\Delta) = E^{T+\Delta}\left\{F(T;T,T+\Delta) \mid \mathscr{F}_t\right\}. \quad (7)$$

This makes the forward rate coherent with the risk-free bond prices, where the latter represent the expectation of the market concerning the future value of money.

Before the financial crisis, $L(T;T,T+\Delta)$ was assumed to be equal to $F(T;T,T+\Delta)$, an assumption that allowed for various simplifications in the determination of derivative prices. After the crisis $L(T;T,T+\Delta)$ is no longer equal to $F(T;T,T+\Delta)$ and what one considers for $F(T;T,T+\Delta)$ is in fact the *OIS discretely compounded rate*, which is based on the OIS bonds, even though the OIS bonds are not necessarily equal to the risk-free bonds (see Sects. 1.3.1 and 1.3.2 of Grbac and Runggaldier [18] for more details on this issue). In particular, the Libor rate $L(T;T,T+\Delta)$ cannot be expressed by the right-hand side of (6). The fact that $L(T;T,T+\Delta) \neq F(T;T,T+\Delta)$ implies by (5) and (7) that also $L(t;T,T+\Delta) \neq F(t;T,T+\Delta)$ for all $t \le T$ and this leads to a *Libor-OIS spread* $L(t;T,T+\Delta) - F(t;T,T+\Delta)$.

Following some of the recent literature (see e.g. Kijima et al. [22], Crépey et al. [8], Filipović and Trolle [14]), one possibility is now to keep the classical relationship (6) also for $L(T;T,T+\Delta)$ thereby replacing however the bonds $p(t,T)$ by fictitious risky ones $\bar{p}(t,T)$ that are assumed to be affected by the same factors as the Libor rates. Such a bond can be seen as an average bond issued by a representative bank from the Libor group and it is therefore sometimes referred to in the literature as a *Libor bond*. This leads to

$$L(T;T,T+\Delta) = \frac{1}{\Delta}\left(\frac{1}{\bar{p}(T,T+\Delta)} - 1\right). \quad (8)$$

Recall that, for simplicity of exposition, we consider a single Libor for a single tenor $\Delta$ and so also a single fictitious bond. In general, one has one Libor and one fictitious bond for each tenor, i.e. $L^{\Delta}(T;T,T+\Delta)$ and $\bar{p}^{\Delta}(T,T+\Delta)$. Note that we shall model the bond prices $\bar{p}(t,T)$, for all $t$ and $T$ with $t \le T$, even though only the prices $\bar{p}(T,T+\Delta)$, for all $T$, are needed in relation (8). Moreover, keeping in mind that the bonds $\bar{p}(t,T)$ are fictitious, they do not have to satisfy the boundary condition $\bar{p}(T,T) = 1$, but we still assume this condition in order to simplify the modeling.

To derive a dynamic model for $L(t;T,T+\Delta)$, we may now derive a dynamic model for $\bar{p}(t,T+\Delta)$, where we have to keep in mind that the latter is not a traded quantity. Inspired by a credit-risk analogy, but also by a common practice of deriving multi-curve quantities by adding a spread over the corresponding single-curve (risk-free) quantities, which in this case is the short rate $r_t$, let us define then the Libor (risky) bond prices as

$$\bar{p}(t,T) = E^{Q}\left\{\exp\left[-\int_t^T (r_u + s_u)du\right] \mid \mathscr{F}_t\right\}, \quad (9)$$

with $s_t$ representing the short rate spread. In case of default risk alone, $s_t$ corresponds to the hazard rate/default intensity, but here it corresponds more generally to all the factors affecting the Libor rate, namely besides credit risk, also liquidity risk, etc. Notice also that the spread is introduced here from the outset. Having for simplicity considered a single tenor $\Delta$ and thus a single $\bar{p}(t, T)$, we shall also consider only a single spread $s_t$. In general, however, one has a spread $s_t^{\Delta}$ for each tenor $\Delta$.

We need now a dynamical model for both $r_t$ and $s_t$ and we shall define this model directly under the martingale measure $Q$ (*martingale modeling*).

## 3 Short Rate Model

### 3.1 The Model

As mentioned, we shall consider a dynamical model for $r_t$ and the single spread $s_t$ under the martingale measure $Q$ that, in practice, has to be calibrated to the market. For this purpose we shall consider a factor model with several factors driving $r_t$ and $s_t$.

The two basic factor model classes for the short rate in the pre-crisis single-curve setup, namely the exponentially affine and the exponentially quadratic model classes, both allow for flexibility and analytical tractability and this in turn allows for closed or semi-closed formulas for linear and optional interest rate derivatives. The former class is usually better known than the latter, but the latter has its own advantages. In fact, for the exponentially affine class one would consider $r_t$ and $s_t$ as given by a linear combination of the factors and so, in order to obtain positivity, one has to consider a square root model for the factors. On the other hand, in the Gaussian exponentially quadratic class, one considers mean reverting Gaussian factor models, but at least some of the factors in the linear combination for $r_t$ and $s_t$ appear as a square. In this way the distribution of the factors remains always Gaussian; in a square-root model it is a non-central $\chi^2$−distribution. Notice also that the exponentially quadratic models can be seen as dual to the square root exponentially affine models.

In the pre-crisis single-curve setting, the exponentially quadratic models have been considered, e.g. in El Karoui et al. [12], Pelsser [29], Gombani and Runggaldier [17], Leippold and Wu [24], Chen et al. [5], and Gaspar [16]. However, since the pre-crisis exponentially affine models are more common, there have also been more attempts to extend them to a post-crisis multi-curve setting (for an overview and details see e.g. Grbac and Runggaldier [18]). A first extension of exponentially quadratic models to a multi-curve setting can be found in Kijima et al. [22] and the present paper is devoted to a possibly full extension.

Let us now present the model for $r_t$ and $s_t$, where we consider not only the short rate $r_t$ itself, but also its spread $s_t$ to be given by a linear combination of the factors, where at least some of the factors appear as a square. To keep the presentation simple, we shall consider a small number of factors and, in order to model also a possible correlation between $r_t$ and $s_t$, the minimal number of factors is three. It also follows from some of the econometric literature that a small number of factors may suffice to adequately model most situations (see also Duffee [10] and Duffie and Gârleanu [11]).

Given three independent affine factor processes $\Psi_t^i$, $i = 1, 2, 3$, having under $Q$ the Gaussian dynamics

$$d\Psi_t^i = -b^i \Psi_t^i dt + \sigma^i dw_t^i, \quad i = 1, 2, 3, \tag{10}$$

with $b_i, \sigma_i > 0$ and $w_t^i$, $i = 1, 2, 3$, independent $Q-$Wiener processes, we let

$$\begin{cases} r_t = \Psi_t^1 + (\Psi_t^2)^2 \\ s_t = \kappa \Psi_t^1 + (\Psi_t^3)^2 \end{cases}, \tag{11}$$

where $\Psi_t^1$ is the common systematic factor allowing for instantaneous correlation between $r_t$ and $s_t$ with correlation intensity $\kappa$ and $\Psi_t^2$ and $\Psi_t^3$ are the idiosyncratic factors. Other factors may be added to drive $s_t$, but the minimal model containing common and idiosyncratic components requires three factors, as explained above. The common factor is particularly important because we want to take into account the realistic feature of non-zero correlation between $r_t$ and $s_t$ in the model.

*Remark 3.1* The zero mean-reversion level is here considered only for convenience of simpler formulas, but can be easily taken to be positive, so that short rates and spreads can become negative only with small probability (see Kijima and Muromachi [21] for an alternative representation of the spreads in terms of Gaussian factors that guarantee the spreads to remain nonnegative and still allows for correlation between $r_t$ and $s_t$). Note, however, that given the current market situation where the observed interest rates are very close to zero and sometimes also negative, even models with negative mean-reversion level have been considered, as well as models allowing for regime-switching in the mean reversion parameter.

*Remark 3.2* For the short rate itself one could also consider the model $r_t = \phi_t + \Psi_t^1 + (\Psi_t^2)^2$ where $\phi_t$ is a *deterministic shift extension* (see Brigo and Mercurio [2]) that allows for a good fit to the initial term structure in short rate models even with constant model parameters.

In the model (11) we have included a linear term $\Psi_t^1$ which may lead to negative values of rates and spreads, although only with small probability in the case of models of the type (10) with a positive mean reversion level. The advantage of including this linear term is more generality and flexibility in the model. Moreover, it allows to express $\bar{p}(t, T)$ in terms of $p(t, T)$ multiplied by a factor. This property will lead to an *adjustment factor* by which one can express post-crisis quantities in terms of corresponding pre-crisis quantities, see Morino and Runggaldier [27] in which this idea has been first proposed in the context of exponentially affine short rate models for multiple curves.

### 3.2 Bond Prices (OIS and Libor Bonds)

In this subsection we derive explicit pricing formulas for the OIS bonds $p(t,T)$ as defined in (3) and the fictitious Libor bonds $\bar{p}(t,T)$ as defined in (9). Thereby, $r_t$ and $s_t$ are supposed to be given by (11) with the factor processes $\Psi_t^i$ evolving under the standard martingale measure $Q$ according to (10). Defining the matrices

$$F = \begin{bmatrix} -b^1 & 0 & 0 \\ 0 & -b^2 & 0 \\ 0 & 0 & -b^3 \end{bmatrix}, \; D = \begin{bmatrix} \sigma^1 & 0 & 0 \\ 0 & \sigma^2 & 0 \\ 0 & 0 & \sigma^3 \end{bmatrix} \tag{12}$$

and considering the vector factor process $\Psi_t := [\Psi_t^1, \Psi_t^2, \Psi_t^3]'$ as well as the multivariate Wiener process $W_t := [w_t^1, w_t^2, w_t^3]'$, where $'$ denotes transposition, the dynamics (10) can be rewritten in synthetic form as

$$d\Psi_t = F\Psi_t dt + DdW_t. \tag{13}$$

Using results on exponential quadratic term structures (see Gombani and Runggaldier [17], Filipović [13]), we have

$$\begin{aligned} p(t,T) &= E^Q\left\{e^{-\int_t^T r_u du}\Big|\mathscr{F}_t\right\} = E^Q\left\{e^{-\int_t^T (\Psi_u^1 + (\Psi_u^2)^2)du}\Big|\mathscr{F}_t\right\} \\ &= \exp\Big[-A(t,T) - B'(t,T)\Psi_t - \Psi_t' C(t,T)\Psi_t\Big] \end{aligned} \tag{14}$$

and, setting $R_t := r_t + s_t$,

$$\begin{aligned} \bar{p}(t,T) &= E^Q\left\{e^{-\int_t^T R_u du}\Big|\mathscr{F}_t\right\} = E^Q\left\{e^{-\int_t^T ((1+\kappa)\Psi_u^1 + (\Psi_u^2)^2 + (\Psi_u^3)^2)du}\Big|\mathscr{F}_t\right\} \\ &= \exp\Big[-\bar{A}(t,T) - \bar{B}'(t,T)\Psi_t - \Psi_t' \bar{C}(t,T)\Psi_t\Big], \end{aligned} \tag{15}$$

where $A(t,T)$, $\bar{A}(t,T)$, $B(t,T)$, $\bar{B}(t,T)$, $C(t,T)$ and $\bar{C}(t,T)$ are scalar, vector, and matrix-valued deterministic functions to be determined.

For this purpose we recall the Heath–Jarrow–Morton (HJM) approach for the case when $p(t,T)$ in (14) represents the price of a risk-free zero coupon bond. The HJM approach leads to the so-called HJM drift conditions that impose conditions on the coefficients in (14) so that the resulting prices $p(t,T)$ do not imply arbitrage possibilities. Since the risk-free bonds are traded, the no-arbitrage condition is expressed by requiring $\frac{p(t,T)}{B_t}$ to be a $Q$−martingale for $B_t$ defined as in (1) and it is exactly this martingality property to yield the drift condition. In our case, $p(t,T)$ is the price of an OIS bond that is not necessarily traded and in general does not coincide with the price of a risk-free bond. However, whether the OIS bond is traded or not, $\frac{p(t,T)}{B_t}$ is a $Q$−martingale by the very definition of $p(t,T)$ in (14) (see the first equality in (14)) and so we can follow the same HJM approach to obtain conditions on the coefficients in (14) also in our case.

For what concerns, on the other hand, the coefficients in (15), recall that $\bar{p}(t,T)$ is a fictitious asset that is not traded and thus is not subject to any no-arbitrage condition. Notice, however, that by analogy to $p(t,T)$ in (14), by its very definition given in the first equality in (15), $\frac{\bar{p}(t,T)}{\bar{B}_t}$ is a $Q$−martingale for $\bar{B}_t$ given by $\bar{B}_t := \exp \int_0^t R_u du$. The two cases $p(t,T)$ and $\bar{p}(t,T)$ can thus be treated in complete analogy provided that we use for $\bar{p}(t,T)$ the numeraire $\bar{B}_t$.

We shall next derive from the $Q$−martingality of $\frac{p(t,T)}{B_t}$ and $\frac{\bar{p}(t,T)}{\bar{B}_t}$ conditions on the coefficients in (14) and (15) that correspond to the classical HJM drift condition and lead thus to ODEs for these coefficients. For this purpose we shall proceed by analogy to Sect. 2 in [17], in particular to the proof of Proposition 2.1 therein, to which we also refer for more detail.

Introducing the "instantaneous forward rates" $f(t,T) := -\frac{\partial}{\partial T}\log p(t,T)$ and $\bar{f}(t,T) := -\frac{\partial}{\partial T}\log \bar{p}(t,T)$, and setting

$$a(t,T) := \frac{\partial}{\partial T}A(t,T), \quad b(t,T) := \frac{\partial}{\partial T}B(t,T), \quad c(t,T) := \frac{\partial}{\partial T}C(t,T) \tag{16}$$

and analogously for $\bar{a}(t,T), \bar{b}(t,T), \bar{c}(t,T)$, from (14) and (15) we obtain

$$f(t,T) = a(t,T) + b'(t,T)\Psi_t + \Psi_t' c(t,T)\Psi_t, \tag{17}$$

$$\bar{f}(t,T) = \bar{a}(t,T) + \bar{b}'(t,T)\Psi_t + \Psi_t' \bar{c}(t,T)\Psi_t. \tag{18}$$

Recalling that $r_t = f(t,t)$ and $R_t = \bar{f}(t,t)$, this implies, with $a(t) := a(t,t)$, $b(t) := b(t,t)$, $c(t) := c(t,t)$ and analogously for the corresponding quantities with a bar, that

$$r_t = a(t) + b'(t)\Psi_t + \Psi_t' c(t)\Psi_t \tag{19}$$

and

$$R_t = r_t + s_t = \bar{a}(t) + \bar{b}'(t)\Psi_t + \Psi_t' \bar{c}(t)\Psi_t. \tag{20}$$

Comparing (19) and (20) with (11), we obtain the following conditions where $i,j = 1,2,3$, namely

$$\begin{cases} a(t) = 0 \\ b^i(t) = \mathbf{1}_{\{i=1\}} \\ c^{ij}(t) = \mathbf{1}_{\{i=j=2\}} \end{cases} \qquad \begin{cases} \bar{a}(t) = 0 \\ \bar{b}^i(t) = (1+\kappa)\mathbf{1}_{\{i=1\}} \\ \bar{c}^{ij}(t) = \mathbf{1}_{\{i=j=2\}\cup\{i=j=3\}}. \end{cases}$$

Using next the fact that

$$p(t,T) = \exp\left[-\int_t^T f(t,s)ds\right], \quad \bar{p}(t,T) = \exp\left[-\int_t^T \bar{f}(t,s)ds\right],$$

and imposing $\frac{p(t,T)}{B_t}$ and $\frac{\bar{p}(t,T)}{\bar{B}_t}$ to be $Q-$martingales, one obtains ordinary differential equations to be satisfied by $c(t,T)$, $b(t,T)$, $a(t,T)$ and analogously for the quantities with a bar. Integrating these ODEs with respect to the second variable and recalling (16) one obtains (for the details see the proof of Proposition 2.1 in [17])

$$\begin{cases} C_t(t,T) + 2FC(t,T) - 2C(t,T)DDC(t,T) + c(t) = 0, & C(T,T) = 0 \\ \bar{C}_t(t,T) + 2F\bar{C}(t,T) - 2\bar{C}(t,T)DD\bar{C}(t,T) + \bar{c}(t) = 0, & \bar{C}(T,T) = 0 \end{cases} \tag{21}$$

with

$$c(t) = \begin{bmatrix} 0 & 0 & 0 \\ 0 & 1 & 0 \\ 0 & 0 & 0 \end{bmatrix} \quad \bar{c}(t) = \begin{bmatrix} 0 & 0 & 0 \\ 0 & 1 & 0 \\ 0 & 0 & 1 \end{bmatrix}. \tag{22}$$

The special forms of $F, D, c(t)$ and $\bar{c}(t)$ together with boundary conditions $C(T,T) = 0$ and $\bar{C}(T,T) = 0$ imply that only $C^{22}$, $\bar{C}^{22}$, $\bar{C}^{33}$ are non-zero and satisfy

$$\begin{cases} C_t^{22}(t,T) - 2b^2C^{22}(t,T) - 2(\sigma^2)^2(C^{22}(t,T))^2 + 1 = 0, & C^{22}(T,T) = 0 \\ \bar{C}_t^{22}(t,T) - 2b^2\bar{C}^{22}(t,T) - 2(\sigma^2)^2(\bar{C}^{22}(t,T))^2 + 1 = 0, & \bar{C}^{22}(T,T) = 0 \\ \bar{C}_t^{33}(t,T) - 2b^3\bar{C}^{33}(t,T) - 2(\sigma^3)^2(\bar{C}^{33}(t,T))^2 + 1 = 0, & \bar{C}^{33}(T,T) = 0 \end{cases} \tag{23}$$

that can be shown to have as solution

$$\begin{cases} C^{22}(t,T) = \bar{C}^{22}(t,T) = \frac{2(e^{(T-t)h^2}-1)}{2h^2+(2b^2+h^2)(e^{(T-t)h^2}-1)} \\ \bar{C}^{33}(t,T) = \frac{2(e^{(T-t)h^3}-1)}{2h^3+(2b^3+h^3)(e^{(T-t)h^3}-1)} \end{cases} \tag{24}$$

with $h^i = \sqrt{4(b^i)^2 + 8(\sigma^i)^2} > 0$, $i = 2, 3$.

Next, always by analogy to the proof of Proposition 2.1 in [17], the vectors of coefficients $B(t,T)$ and $\bar{B}(t,T)$ of the first order terms can be seen to satisfy the following system

$$\begin{cases} B_t(t,T) + B(t,T)F - 2B(t,T)DDC(t,T) + b(t) = 0, & B(T,T) = 0 \\ \bar{B}_t(t,T) + \bar{B}(t,T)F - 2\bar{B}(t,T)DD\bar{C}(t,T) + \bar{b}(t) = 0, & \bar{B}(T,T) = 0 \end{cases} \tag{25}$$

with

$$b(t) = [1,0,0] \quad \bar{b}(t) = [(1+\kappa),0,0].$$

Noticing similarly as above that only $B^1(t,T)$, $\bar{B}^1(t,T)$ are non-zero, system (25) becomes

$$\begin{cases} B_t^1(t,T) - b^1B^1(t,T) + 1 = 0 & B^1(T,T) = 0 \\ \bar{B}_t^1(t,T) - b^1\bar{B}^1(t,T) + (1+\kappa) = 0 & \bar{B}^1(T,T) = 0 \end{cases} \tag{26}$$

leading to the explicit solution

$$\begin{cases} B^1(t,T) = \frac{1}{b^1}\left(1 - e^{-b^1(T-t)}\right) \\ \bar{B}^1(t,T) = \frac{1+\kappa}{b^1}\left(1 - e^{-b^1(T-t)}\right) = (1+\kappa)B^1(t,T). \end{cases} \tag{27}$$

Finally, $A(t,T)$ and $\bar{A}(t,T)$ have to satisfy

$$\begin{cases} A_t(t,T) + (\sigma^2)^2 C^{22}(t,T) - \frac{1}{2}(\sigma^1)^2 (B^1(t,T))^2 = 0, \\ \bar{A}_t(t,T) + (\sigma^2)^2 \bar{C}^{22}(t,T) + (\sigma^3)^2 \bar{C}^{33}(t,T) - \frac{1}{2}(\sigma^1)^2 (\bar{B}^1(t,T))^2 = 0 \end{cases} \tag{28}$$

with boundary conditions $A(T,T) = 0, \bar{A}(T,T) = 0$. The explicit expressions can be obtained simply by integrating the above equations.

Summarizing, we have proved the following:

**Proposition 3.1** *Assume that the OIS short rate $r$ and the spread $s$ are given by (11) with the factor processes $\Psi_t^i$, $i = 1, 2, 3$, evolving according to (10) under the standard martingale measure $Q$. The time-$t$ price of the OIS bond $p(t,T)$, as defined in (3), is given by*

$$p(t,T) = \exp[-A(t,T) - B^1(t,T)\Psi_t^1 - C^{22}(t,T)(\Psi_t^2)^2], \tag{29}$$

*and the time-$t$ price of the fictitious Libor bond $\bar{p}(t,T)$, as defined in (9), by*

$$\begin{aligned} \bar{p}(t,T) &= \exp[-\bar{A}(t,T) - (\kappa+1)B^1(t,T)\Psi_t^1 - C^{22}(t,T)(\Psi_t^2)^2 - \bar{C}^{33}(t,T)(\Psi_t^3)^2] \\ &= p(t,T)\exp[-\tilde{A}(t,T) - \kappa B^1(t,T)\Psi_t^1 - \bar{C}^{33}(t,T)(\Psi_t^3)^2], \end{aligned} \tag{30}$$

*where $\tilde{A}(t,T) := \bar{A}(t,T) - A(t,T)$ with $A(t,T)$ and $\bar{A}(t,T)$ given by (28), $B^1(t,T)$ given by (27) and $C^{22}(t,T)$ and $C^{33}(t,T)$ given by (24).*

In particular, expression (30) gives $\bar{p}(t,T)$ in terms of $p(t,T)$. Based on this we shall derive in the following section the announced *adjustment factor* allowing to pass from pre-crisis quantities to the corresponding post-crisis quantities.

### 3.3 Forward Measure

The underlying factor model was defined in (10) under the standard martingale measure $Q$. For derivative prices, which we shall determine in the following two sections, it will be convenient to work under forward measures, for which, given the single tenor $\Delta$, we shall consider a generic $(T+\Delta)$-forward measure. The density process to change the measure from $Q$ to $Q^{T+\Delta}$ is

$$\mathcal{L}_t := \frac{dQ^{T+\Delta}}{dQ}\Big|_{\mathcal{F}_t} = \frac{p(t, T+\Delta)}{p(0, T+\Delta)} \frac{1}{B_t} \tag{31}$$

from which it follows by (29) and the martingale property of $\left(\frac{p(t,T+\Delta)}{B_t}\right)_{t \leq T+\Delta}$ that

$$d\mathcal{L}_t = \mathcal{L}_t \left(-B^1(t, T+\Delta)\sigma^1 dw_t^1 - 2C^{22}(t, T+\Delta)\Psi_t^2 \sigma^2 dw_t^2\right).$$

This implies by Girsanov's theorem that

$$\begin{cases} dw_t^{1,T+\Delta} = dw_t^1 + \sigma^1 B^1(t, T+\Delta)dt \\ dw_t^{2,T+\Delta} = dw_t^2 + 2C^{22}(t, T+\Delta)\Psi_t^2 \sigma^2 dt \\ dw_t^{3,T+\Delta} = dw_t^3 \end{cases} \tag{32}$$

are $Q^{T+\Delta}$–Wiener processes. From the $Q$–dynamics (10) we then obtain the following $Q^{T+\Delta}$–dynamics for the factors

$$\begin{aligned} d\Psi_t^1 &= -\left[b^1\Psi_t^1 + (\sigma^1)^2 B^1(t, T+\Delta)\right] dt + \sigma^1 dw_t^{1,T+\Delta} \\ d\Psi_t^2 &= -\left[b^2\Psi_t^2 + 2(\sigma^2)^2 C^{22}(t, T+\Delta)\Psi_t^2\right] dt + \sigma^2 dw_t^{2,T+\Delta} \\ d\Psi_t^3 &= -b^3\Psi_t^3 dt + \sigma^3 dw_t^{3,T+\Delta}. \end{aligned} \tag{33}$$

*Remark 3.3* While in the dynamics (10) for $\Psi_t^i$, $(i = 1, 2, 3)$ under $Q$ we had for simplicity assumed a zero mean-reversion level, under the $(T+\Delta)$-forward measure the mean-reversion level is for $\Psi_t^1$ now different from zero due to the measure transformation.

**Lemma 3.1** *Analogously to the case when $p(t, T)$ represents the price of a risk-free zero coupon bond, also for $p(t, T)$ viewed as OIS bond we have that $\frac{p(t,T)}{p(t,T+\Delta)}$ is a $Q^{T+\Delta}$–martingale.*

*Proof* We have seen that also for OIS bonds as defined in (3) we have that, with $B_t$ as in (1), the ratio $\frac{p(t,T)}{B_t}$ is a $Q$–martingale. From Bayes' formula we then have

$$\begin{aligned} E^{T+\Delta}\left\{\frac{p(T,T)}{p(T,T+\Delta)} \mid \mathcal{F}_t\right\} &= \frac{E^Q\left\{\frac{1}{p(0,T+\Delta)}\frac{1}{B_{T+\Delta}}\frac{p(T,T)}{p(T,T+\Delta)} \mid \mathcal{F}_t\right\}}{E^Q\left\{\frac{1}{p(0,T+\Delta)}\frac{1}{B_{T+\Delta}} \mid \mathcal{F}_t\right\}} \\ &= \frac{E^Q\left\{\frac{p(T,T)}{p(T,T+\Delta)} E^Q\left\{\frac{1}{B_{T+\Delta}} \mid \mathcal{F}_T\right\} \mid \mathcal{F}_t\right\}}{\frac{p(t,T+\Delta)}{B_t}} = \frac{B_t E^Q\left\{\frac{p(T,T)}{p(T,T+\Delta)}\frac{p(T,T+\Delta)}{B_T} \mid \mathcal{F}_t\right\}}{p(t,T+\Delta)} \\ &= \frac{B_t E^Q\left\{\frac{p(T,T)}{B_T} \mid \mathcal{F}_t\right\}}{p(t,T+\Delta)} = \frac{p(t,T)}{p(t,T+\Delta)}, \end{aligned}$$

thus proving the statement of the lemma. □

We recall that we denote the expectation with respect to the measure $Q^{T+\Delta}$ by $E^{T+\Delta}\{\cdot\}$. The dynamics in (33) lead to Gaussian distributions for $\Psi_t^i,\ i=1,2,3$ that, given $B^1(\cdot)$ and $C^{22}(\cdot)$, have mean and variance

$$E^{T+\Delta}\{\Psi_t^i\} = \bar{\alpha}_t^i = \bar{\alpha}_t^i(b^i,\sigma^i) \quad , \quad Var^{T+\Delta}\{\Psi_t^i\} = \bar{\beta}_t^i = \bar{\beta}_t^i(b^i,\sigma^i),$$

which can be explicitly computed. More precisely, we have

$$\begin{cases} \bar{\alpha}_t^1 &= e^{-b^1 t}\Big[\Psi_0^1 - \frac{(\sigma^1)^2}{2(b^1)^2}e^{-b^1(T+\Delta)}(1-e^{2b^1 t}) - \frac{(\sigma^1)^2}{(b^1)^2}(1-e^{b^1 t})\Big] \\ \bar{\beta}_t^1 &= e^{-2b^1 t}(e^{2b^1 t}-1)\frac{(\sigma^1)^2}{2(b^1)} \\ \bar{\alpha}_t^2 &= e^{-(b^2 t + 2(\sigma^2)^2\tilde{C}^{22}(t,T+\Delta))}\Psi_0^2 \\ \bar{\beta}_t^2 &= e^{-(2b^2 t + 4(\sigma^2)^2\tilde{C}^{22}(t,T+\Delta))}\int_0^t e^{2b^2 s + 4(\sigma^2)^2\tilde{C}^{22}(s,T+\Delta)}(\sigma^2)^2 ds \\ \bar{\alpha}_t^3 &= e^{-b^3 t}\Psi_0^3 \\ \bar{\beta}_t^3 &= e^{-2b^3 t}\frac{(\sigma^3)^2}{2b^3}(e^{2b^3 t}-1), \end{cases} \tag{34}$$

with

$$\begin{aligned}\tilde{C}^{22}(t,T+\Delta) = &\frac{2(2\log(2b^2(e^{(T+\Delta-t)h^2}-1)+h^2(e^{(T+\Delta-t)h^2}+1))+t(2b^2+h^2))}{(2b^2+h^2)(2b^2-h^2)} \\ &- \frac{2(2\log(2b^2(e^{(T+\Delta)h^2}-1)+h^2(e^{(T+\Delta)h^2}+1))}{(2b^2+h^2)(2b^2-h^2)}\end{aligned} \tag{35}$$

and $h^2 = \sqrt{(2b^2)^2 + 8(\sigma^2)^2}$, and where we have assumed deterministic initial values $\Psi_0^1$, $\Psi_0^2$ and $\Psi_0^3$. For details of the above computation see the proof of Corollary 4.1.3. in Meneghello [25].

## 4 Pricing of Linear Interest Rate Derivatives

We have discussed in Sect. 3.2 the pricing of OIS and Libor bonds in the Gaussian, exponentially quadratic short rate model introduced in Sect. 3.1. In the remaining part of the paper we shall be concerned with the pricing of interest rate derivatives, namely with derivatives having the Libor rate as underlying rate. In the present section we shall deal with the basic linear derivatives, namely FRAs and interest rate swaps, while nonlinear derivatives will then be dealt with in the following Sect. 5. For the FRA rates discussed in the next Sect. 4.1 we shall in Sect. 4.1.1 exhibit an *adjustment factor* allowing to pass from the single-curve FRA rate to the multi-curve FRA rate.

## 4.1 FRAs

We start by recalling the definition of a standard forward rate agreement. We emphasize that we use a text-book definition which differs slightly from a market definition, see Mercurio [26].

**Definition 4.1** Given the time points $0 \leq t \leq T < T + \Delta$, a *forward rate agreement* (FRA) is an OTC derivative that allows the holder to lock in at the generic date $t \leq T$ the interest rate between the inception date $T$ and the maturity $T + \Delta$ at a fixed value $R$. At maturity $T + \Delta$ a payment based on the interest rate $R$, applied to a notional amount of $N$, is made and the one based on the relevant floating rate *(generally the spot Libor rate $L(T; T, T + \Delta)$)* is received.

Recalling that for the Libor rate we had postulated the relation (8) to hold at the inception time $T$, namely

$$L(T; T, T + \Delta) = \frac{1}{\Delta}\left(\frac{1}{\bar{p}(T, T + \Delta)} - 1\right),$$

the price, at $t \leq T$, of the FRA with fixed rate $R$ and notional $N$ can be computed under the $(T + \Delta)$-forward measure as

$$\begin{aligned} P^{FRA}&(t; T, T + \Delta, R, N) \\ &= N\Delta p(t, T + \Delta)E^{T+\Delta}\{L(T; T, T + \Delta) - R \mid \mathscr{F}_t\} \\ &= Np(t, T + \Delta)E^{T+\Delta}\left\{\frac{1}{\bar{p}(T, T + \Delta)} - (1 + \Delta R) \mid \mathscr{F}_t\right\}, \end{aligned} \tag{36}$$

Defining

$$\bar{\nu}_{t,T} := E^{T+\Delta}\left\{\frac{1}{\bar{p}(T, T + \Delta)} \mid \mathscr{F}_t\right\}, \tag{37}$$

it is easily seen from (36) that the *fair rate of the FRA, namely the FRA rate*, is given by

$$\bar{R}_t = \frac{1}{\Delta}\left(\bar{\nu}_{t,T} - 1\right). \tag{38}$$

In the *single-curve case* we have instead

$$R_t = \frac{1}{\Delta}\left(\nu_{t,T} - 1\right), \tag{39}$$

where, given that $\frac{p(\cdot,T)}{p(\cdot,T+\Delta)}$ is a $Q^{T+\Delta}-$martingale (see Lemma 3.1),

$$\nu_{t,T} := E^{T+\Delta}\left\{\frac{1}{p(T, T + \Delta)} \mid \mathscr{F}_t\right\} = \frac{p(t, T)}{p(t, T + \Delta)}, \tag{40}$$

which is the classical expression for the FRA rate in the single-curve case. Notice that, contrary to (37), the expression in (40) can be explicitly computed on the basis of bond price data without requiring an interest rate model.

#### 4.1.1 Adjustment Factor

We shall show here the following:

**Proposition 4.1** *We have the relationship*

$$\bar{\nu}_{t,T} = \nu_{t,T} \cdot Ad_t^{T,\Delta} \cdot Res_t^{T,\Delta} \tag{41}$$

*with*

$$\begin{aligned} Ad_t^{T,\Delta} := E^Q\left\{\frac{p(T,T+\Delta)}{\bar{p}(T,T+\Delta)} \mid \mathscr{F}_t\right\} = E^Q\Big\{\exp\Big[\tilde{A}(T,T+\Delta) \\ + \kappa B^1(T,T+\Delta)\Psi_T^1 + \bar{C}^{33}(T,T+\Delta)(\Psi_T^3)^2\Big] \mid \mathscr{F}_t\Big\} \end{aligned} \tag{42}$$

*and*

$$Res_t^{T,\Delta} = \exp\Big[-\kappa\frac{(\sigma^1)^2}{2(b^1)^3}\left(1-e^{-b^1\Delta}\right)\left(1-e^{-b^1(T-t)}\right)^2\Big], \tag{43}$$

*where* $\tilde{A}(t,T)$ *is defined after* (30), $B^1(t,T)$ *in* (27) *and* $\bar{C}^{33}(t,T)$ *in* (24).

*Proof* Firstly, from (30) we obtain

$$\frac{p(T,T+\Delta)}{\bar{p}(T,T+\Delta)} = e^{\tilde{A}(T,T+\Delta)+\kappa B^1(T,T+\Delta)\Psi_T^1+\bar{C}^{33}(T,T+\Delta)(\Psi_T^3)^2}. \tag{44}$$

In (37) we now change back from the $(T+\Delta)$-forward measure to the standard martingale measure using the density process $\mathscr{L}_t$ given in (31). Using furthermore the above expression for the ratio of the OIS and the Libor bond prices and taking into account the definition of the short rate $r_t$ in terms of the factor processes, we obtain

$$\begin{aligned} \bar{\nu}_{t,T} &= E^{T+\Delta}\left\{\frac{1}{\bar{p}(T,T+\Delta)}\Big|\mathscr{F}_t\right\} = \mathscr{L}_t^{-1}E^Q\left\{\frac{\mathscr{L}_T}{\bar{p}(T,T+\Delta)}\Big|\mathscr{F}_t\right\} \\ &= \frac{1}{p(t,T+\Delta)}E^Q\left\{\exp\Big(-\int_t^T r_u du\Big)\frac{p(T,T+\Delta)}{\bar{p}(T,T+\Delta)}\Big|\mathscr{F}_t\right\} \\ &= \frac{1}{p(t,T+\Delta)}\exp[\tilde{A}(T,T+\Delta)]E^Q\left\{e^{\bar{C}^{33}(T,T+\Delta)(\Psi_T^3)^2}\Big|\mathscr{F}_t\right\} \end{aligned}$$

$$
\begin{aligned}
&\cdot E^Q\left\{e^{-\int_t^T(\Psi_u^1+(\Psi_u^2)^2)du}e^{\kappa B^1(T,T+\Delta)\Psi_T^1}\Big|\mathcal{F}_t\right\}\\
&=\frac{1}{p(t,T+\Delta)}\exp[\tilde{A}(T,T+\Delta)]E^Q\left\{e^{\tilde{C}^{33}(T,T+\Delta)(\Psi_T^3)^2}\Big|\mathcal{F}_t\right\}\\
&\cdot E^Q\left\{e^{-\int_t^T\Psi_u^1du}e^{\kappa B^1(T,T+\Delta)\Psi_T^1}\Big|\mathcal{F}_t\right\}E^Q\left\{e^{-\int_t^T(\Psi_u^2)^2du}\Big|\mathcal{F}_t\right\}, \qquad (45)
\end{aligned}
$$

where we have used the independence of the factors $\Psi^i$, $i = 1, 2, 3$ under $Q$.

Recall now from the theory of affine processes (see e.g. Lemma 2.1 in Grbac and Runggaldier [18]) that, for a process $\Psi_t^1$ satisfying (10), we have for all $\delta, K \in \mathbb{R}$

$$
E^Q\left\{\exp\left[-\int_t^T\delta\Psi_u^1du-K\Psi_T^1\right]\mid\mathcal{F}_t\right\}=\exp[\alpha^1(t,T)-\beta^1(t,T)\Psi_t^1], \qquad (46)
$$

where

$$
\begin{cases}
\beta^1(t,T)=Ke^{-b^1(T-t)}-\frac{\delta}{b^1}\left(e^{-b^1(T-t)}-1\right)\\
\alpha^1(t,T)=\frac{(\sigma^1)^2}{2}\int_t^T(\beta^1(u,T))^2du.
\end{cases}
$$

Setting $K = -\kappa B^1(T, T+\Delta)$ and $\delta = 1$, and recalling from (27) that $B^1(t,T) = \frac{1}{b^1}\left(1-e^{-b^1(T-t)}\right)$, this leads to

$$
\begin{aligned}
&E^Q\left\{e^{-\int_t^T\Psi_u^1du}e^{\kappa B^1(T,T+\Delta)\Psi_T^1}\Big|\mathcal{F}_t\right\}\\
&=\exp\left[\frac{(\sigma^1)^2}{2}(\kappa B^1(T,T+\Delta))^2\int_t^Te^{-2b^1(T-u)}du\right.\\
&-\kappa B^1(T,T+\Delta)(\sigma^1)^2\int_t^TB^1(u,T)e^{-b^1(T-u)}du+\frac{(\sigma^1)^2}{2}\int_t^T(B^1(u,T))^2du\\
&\left.+\left(\kappa B^1(T,T+\Delta)e^{-b^1(T-t)}-B^1(t,T)\right)\Psi_t^1\right]. \qquad (47)
\end{aligned}
$$

On the other hand, from the results of Sect. 3.2 we also have that, for a process $\Psi_t^2$ satisfying (10),

$$
E^Q\left\{\exp\left[-\int_t^T(\Psi_u^2)^2du\right]\mid\mathcal{F}_t\right\}=\exp\left[-\alpha^2(t,T)-C^{22}(t,T)(\Psi_t^2)^2\right],
$$

where $C^{22}(t,T)$ corresponds to (24) and (see (28))

$$
\alpha^2(t,T)=(\sigma^2)^2\int_t^TC^{22}(u,T)du.
$$

This implies that

$$\begin{aligned} & E^Q\left\{\exp\left[-\int_t^T (\Psi_u^2)^2 du\right] \mid \mathscr{F}_t\right\} \\ & = \exp\left[-(\sigma^2)^2 \int_t^T C^{22}(u,T)du - C^{22}(t,T)\left(\Psi_t^2\right)^2\right]. \end{aligned} \tag{48}$$

Replacing (47) and (48) into (45), and recalling the expression for $p(t,T)$ in (29) with $A(\cdot)$, $B^1(\cdot)$, $C^{22}(\cdot)$ according to (28), (27) and (24) respectively, we obtain

$$\begin{aligned} \bar{\nu}_{t,T} = & \frac{p(t,T)}{p(t,T+\Delta)} e^{\tilde{A}(T,T+\Delta)} E^Q\left[e^{\tilde{C}^{33}(T,T+\Delta)(\Psi_T^3)^2} | \mathscr{F}_t\right] \\ & \cdot \exp\left[\frac{(\sigma^1)^2}{2}(\kappa B^1(T,T+\Delta))^2 \int_t^T e^{-2b^1(T-u)} du + \kappa B^1(T,T+\Delta) e^{-b^1(T-t)} \Psi_t^1\right] \\ & \cdot \exp\left[-\kappa B^1(T,T+\Delta)(\sigma^1)^2 \int_t^T B^1(u,T) e^{-b^1(T-u)} du\right]. \end{aligned} \tag{49}$$

We recall the expression (44) for $\frac{p(T,T+\Delta)}{\bar{p}(T,T+\Delta)}$ and the fact that, according to (46), we have

$$\begin{aligned} & E^Q\left\{e^{\kappa B^1(T,T+\Delta)\Psi_T^1} | \mathscr{F}_t\right\} \\ & = \exp\left[\frac{(\sigma^1)^2}{2}(\kappa B^1(T,T+\Delta))^2 \int_t^T e^{-2b^1(T-u)} du + \kappa B^1(T,T+\Delta) e^{-b^1(T-t)} \Psi_t^1\right]. \end{aligned}$$

Inserting these expressions into (49) we obtain the result, namely

$$\begin{aligned} \bar{\nu}_{t,T} = & \frac{p(t,T)}{p(t,T+\Delta)} E^Q\left\{\frac{p(T,T+\Delta)}{\bar{p}(T,T+\Delta)} | \mathscr{F}_t\right\} \\ & \cdot \exp\left[-\kappa B^1(T,T+\Delta)(\sigma^1)^2 \int_t^T B^1(u,T) e^{-b^1(T-u)} du\right] \\ = & \frac{p(t,T)}{p(t,T+\Delta)} E^Q\left\{\frac{p(T,T+\Delta)}{\bar{p}(T,T+\Delta)} | \mathscr{F}_t\right\} \\ & \cdot \exp\left[-\frac{\kappa}{b^1}(e^{-b^1\Delta}-1)(\sigma^1)^2\left(\frac{1}{2(b^1)^2}(1-e^{-2b^1(T-t)}) - \frac{1}{(b^1)^2}(1-e^{-b^1(T-t)})\right)\right], \end{aligned} \tag{50}$$

where we have also used the fact that

$$\begin{aligned} \int_t^T B^1(u,T) e^{-b^1(T-u)} du & = \int_t^T \frac{1}{b^1}\left(1 - e^{-b^1(T-u)}\right) e^{-b^1(T-u)} du \\ & = -\frac{1}{2(b^1)^2}\left(1 - e^{-2b^1(T-t)}\right) + \frac{1}{(b^1)^2}\left(1 - e^{-b^1(T-t)}\right). \end{aligned}$$

□

*Remark 4.1* The adjustment factor $Ad_t^{T,\Delta}$ allows for some intuitive interpretations. Here we mention only the easiest one for the case when $\kappa = 0$ (independence of $r_t$ and $s_t$). In this case we have $r_t + s_t > r_t$ implying that $\bar{p}(T, T+\Delta) < p(T, T+\Delta)$ so that $Ad_t^{T,\Delta} \geq 1$. Furthermore, always for $\kappa = 0$, the residual factor has value $Res_t^{T,\Delta} = 1$. All this in turn implies $\bar{\nu}_{t,T} \geq \nu_{t,T}$ and with it $\bar{R}_t \geq R_t$, which is what one would expect to be the case.

*Remark 4.2* (*Calibration to the initial term structure*). The parameters in the model (10) for the factors $\Psi_t^i$ and thus also in the model (11) for the short rate $r_t$ and the spread $s_t$ are the coefficients $b^i$ and $\sigma^i$ for $i = 1, 2, 3$. From (14) notice that, for $i = 1, 2$, these coefficients enter the expressions for the OIS bond prices $p(t, T)$ that can be assumed to be observable since they can be bootstrapped from the market quotes for the OIS swap rates. We may thus assume that these coefficients, i.e. $b^i$ and $\sigma^i$ for $i = 1, 2$, can be calibrated as in the pre-crisis single-curve short rate models. It remains to calibrate $b^3$, $\sigma^3$ and, possibly the correlation coefficient $\kappa$. Via (15) they affect the prices of the fictitious Libor bonds $\bar{p}(t, T)$ that are, however, not observable. One may observe though the FRA rates $R_t$ and $\bar{R}_t$ and thus also $\nu_{t,T}$, as well as $\bar{\nu}_{t,T}$. Via (41) this would then allow one to calibrate also the remaining parameters. This task would turn out to be even simpler if one would have access to the value of $\kappa$ by other means.

We emphasize that in order to ensure a good fit to the initial bond term structure, a deterministic shift extension of the model or time-dependent coefficients $b^i$ could be considered. We recall also that we have assumed the mean-reversion level equal to zero for simplicity; in practice it would be one more coefficient to be calibrated for each factor $\Psi_t^i$.

## 4.2 Interest Rate Swaps

We first recall the notion of a *(payer) interest rate swap*. Given a collection of dates $0 \leq T_0 < T_1 < \cdots < T_n$ with $\gamma \equiv \gamma_k := T_k - T_{k-1}$ $(k = 1, \cdots, n)$, as well as a notional amount $N$, a payer swap is a financial contract, where a stream of interest payments on the notional $N$ is made at a fixed rate $R$ in exchange for receiving an analogous stream corresponding to the Libor rate. Among the various possible conventions concerning the fixing for the Libor and the payment dates, we choose here the one where, for each interval $[T_{k-1}, T_k]$, the Libor rates are fixed in advance and the payments are made in arrears. The swap is thus initiated at $T_0$ and the first payment is made at $T_1$. A *receiver swap* is completely symmetric with the interest at the fixed rate being received; here we concentrate on payer swaps.

The arbitrage-free price of the swap, evaluated at $t \leq T_0$, is given by the following expression where, analogously to $E^{T+\Delta}\{\cdot\}$, we denote by $E^{T_k}\{\cdot\}$ the expectation with respect to the forward measure $Q^{T_k}$ $(k = 1, \cdots, n)$

$$
\begin{aligned}
P^{Sw}(t; T_0, T_n, R) &= \gamma \sum_{k=1}^{n} p(t, T_k) E^{T_k} \{L(T_{k-1}; T_{k-1}, T_k) - R | \mathscr{F}_t\} \\
&= \gamma \sum_{k=1}^{n} p(t, T_k) \left(L(t; T_{k-1}, T_k) - R\right). \qquad (51)
\end{aligned}
$$

For easier notation we have assumed the notional to be 1, i.e. $N = 1$.

We shall next obtain an explicit expression for $P^{Sw}(t; T_0, T_n, R)$ starting from the first equality in (51). To this effect, recalling from (24) that $C^{22}(t, T) = \bar{C}^{22}(t, T)$, introduce again some shorthand notation, namely

$$
\begin{aligned}
A_k &:= \bar{A}(T_{k-1}, T_k),\ B_k^1 := B^1(T_{k-1}, T_k), \\
C_k^{22} &:= C^{22}(T_{k-1}, T_k) = \bar{C}^{22}(T_{k-1}, T_k),\ \bar{C}_k^{33} := \bar{C}^{33}(T_{k-1}, T_k).
\end{aligned} \qquad (52)
$$

The crucial quantity to be computed in (51) is the following one

$$
\begin{aligned}
E^{T_k}\{\gamma L(T_{k-1}; T_{k-1}, T_k) | \mathscr{F}_t\} &= E^{T_k}\left\{\frac{1}{\bar{p}(T_{k-1}, T_k)} | \mathscr{F}_t\right\} - 1 \\
= e^{A_k} E^{T_k}\{\exp((\kappa + 1) B_k^1 \Psi_{T_{k-1}}^1 &+ C_k^{22}(\Psi_{T_{k-1}}^2)^2 + \bar{C}_k^{33}(\Psi_{T_{k-1}}^3)^2) | \mathscr{F}_t\} - 1, \qquad (53)
\end{aligned}
$$

where we have used the first relation on the right in (30). The expectations in (53) have to be computed under the measures $Q^{T_k}$, under which, by analogy to (33), the factors have the dynamics

$$
\begin{aligned}
d\Psi_t^1 &= -\left[b^1 \Psi_t^1 + (\sigma^1)^2 B^1(t, T_k)\right] dt + \sigma^1 dw_t^{1,k} \\
d\Psi_t^2 &= -\left[b^2 \Psi_t^2 + 2(\sigma^2)^2 C^{22}(t, T_k) \Psi_t^2\right] dt + \sigma^2 dw_t^{2,k} \\
d\Psi_t^3 &= -b^3 \Psi_t^3 dt + \sigma^3 dw_t^{3,k}.
\end{aligned} \qquad (54)
$$

where $w^{i,k}$, $i = 1, 2, 3$, are independent Wiener processes with respect to $Q^{T_k}$. A straightforward generalization of (46) to the case where the factor process $\Psi_t^1$ satisfies the following affine Hull–White model

$$
d\Psi_t^1 = (a^1(t) - b^1 \Psi_t^1) dt + \sigma^1 dw_t
$$

can be obtained as follows

$$
E^Q\left\{\exp\left[-\int_t^T \delta \Psi_u^1 du - K \Psi_T^1\right] | \mathscr{F}_t\right\} = \exp[\alpha^1(t, T) - \beta^1(t, T) \Psi_t^1], \qquad (55)
$$

with

$$
\begin{cases}
\beta^1(t, T) = K e^{-b^1(T-t)} - \frac{\delta}{b^1}\left(e^{-b^1(T-t)} - 1\right) \\
\alpha^1(t, T) = \frac{(\sigma^1)^2}{2} \int_t^T (\beta^1(u, T))^2 du - \int_t^T a^1(u) \beta^1(u, T) du.
\end{cases} \qquad (56)
$$

We apply this result to our situation where under $Q^{T_k}$ the process $\Psi_t^1$ satisfies the first SDE in (54) and thus corresponds to the above dynamics with $a^1(t) = -(\sigma^1)^2 B^1(t, T_k)$. Furthermore, setting $K = -(\kappa + 1) B_k^1$ and $\delta = 0$, we obtain for the first expectation in the second line of (53)

$$E^{T_k}\{\exp((\kappa + 1)B_k^1 \Psi_{T_{k-1}}^1 | \mathcal{F}_t\} = \exp[\Gamma^1(t, T_k) - \rho^1(t, T_k)\, \Psi_t^1], \tag{57}$$

with

$$\begin{cases} \rho^1(t, T_k) &= -(\kappa + 1)B_k^1 e^{-b^1(T_k - t)} \\ \Gamma^1(t, T_k) &= \frac{(\sigma^1)^2}{2} \displaystyle\int_t^{T_k} \left(\rho^1(u, T_k)\right)^2 du + (\sigma^1)^2 \int_t^{T_k} B^1(u, T_k)\rho^1(u, T_k) du. \end{cases} \tag{58}$$

For the remaining two expectations in the second line of (53) we shall use the following:

**Lemma 4.1** *Let a generic process $\Psi_t$ satisfy the dynamics*

$$d\Psi_t = b(t)\Psi_t dt + \sigma\, dw_t \tag{59}$$

*with $w_t$ a Wiener process. Then, for all $C \in \mathbb{R}$ such that $E^Q\left\{\exp\left[C\,(\Psi_T)^2\right]\right\} < \infty$, we have*

$$E^Q\left\{\exp\left[C\,(\Psi_T)^2\right] \mid \mathcal{F}_t\right\} = \exp\left[\Gamma(t, T) - \rho(t, T)\,(\Psi_t)^2\right] \tag{60}$$

*with $\rho(t, T)$ and $\Gamma(t, T)$ satisfying*

$$\begin{cases} \rho_t(t, T) + 2b(t)\rho(t, T) - 2(\sigma)^2\,(\rho(t, T))^2 = 0\,; \quad \rho(T, T) = -C \\ \Gamma_t(t, T) = (\sigma)^2 \rho(t, T). \end{cases} \tag{61}$$

*Proof* An application of Itô's formula yields that the nonnegative process $\Phi_t := (\Psi_t)^2$ satisfies the following SDE

$$d\Phi_t = \left((\sigma)^2 + 2b(t)\,\Phi_t\right) dt + 2\sigma\sqrt{\Phi_t}\, dw_t.$$

We recall that a process $\Phi_t$ given in general form by

$$d\Phi_t = (a + \lambda(t)\Phi_t)dt + \eta\sqrt{\Phi_t}\, dw_t,$$

with $a, \eta > 0$ and $\lambda(t)$ a deterministic function, is a CIR process. Thus, $(\Psi_t)^2$ is equivalent in distribution to a CIR process with coefficients given by

$$\lambda(t) = 2b(t) \quad , \quad \eta = 2\sigma \quad , \quad a = (\sigma)^2.$$

From the theory of affine term structure models (see e.g. Lamberton and Lapeyre [23], or Lemma 2.2 in Grbac and Runggaldier [18]) it now follows that

$$E^Q\left\{\exp\left[C\,(\Psi_T)^2\right] \mid \mathscr{F}_t\right\} = E^Q\left\{\exp\left[C\,\Phi_T\right] \mid \mathscr{F}_t\right\} = \exp\left[\Gamma(t,T) - \rho(t,T)\,\Phi_t\right]$$
$$= \exp\left[\Gamma(t,T) - \rho(t,T)\,(\Psi_t)^2\right]$$

with $\rho(t,T)$ and $\Gamma(t,T)$ satisfying (61).

**Corollary 4.1** *When $b(t)$ is constant with respect to time, i.e. $b(t) \equiv b$, so that also $\lambda(t) \equiv \lambda$, then the equations for $\rho(t,T)$ and $\Gamma(t,T)$ in (61) admit an explicit solution given by*

$$\begin{cases} \rho(t,T) = \frac{4bhe^{2b(T-t)}}{4(\sigma)^2 he^{2b(T-t)}-1} \quad \text{with} \quad h := \frac{C}{4(\sigma)^2 C + 4b} \\ \Gamma(t,T) = -(\sigma)^2 \int_t^T \rho(u,T)du. \end{cases} \tag{62}$$

Coming now to the second expectation in the second line of (53) and using the second equation in (54), we set

$$b(t) := -\left[b^2 + 2(\sigma^2)^2 C^{22}(t,T_k)\right],\ \sigma := \sigma^2,\ C = C_k^{22}$$

and apply Lemma 4.1, provided that the parameters $b^2$ and $\sigma^2$ of the process $\Psi^2$ are such that $C = C_k^{22}$ satisfies the assumption from the lemma. We thus obtain

$$E^{T_k}\{\exp(C_k^{22}(\Psi_{T_{k-1}}^2)^2)|\mathscr{F}_t\} = \exp[\Gamma^2(t,T_k) - \rho^2(t,T_k)(\Psi_t^2)^2], \tag{63}$$

with $\rho^2(t,T)$, $\Gamma^2(t,T)$ satisfying

$$\begin{cases} \rho_t^2(t,T) - 2\left[b^2 + 2(\sigma^2)^2 C^{22}(t,T_k)\right]\rho^2(t,T) - 2(\sigma^2)^2(\rho^2(t,T))^2 = 0 \\ \rho^2(T_k,T_k) = -C_k^{22} \\ \Gamma^2(t,T) = -(\sigma^2)^2 \int_t^T \rho^2(u,T)du. \end{cases} \tag{64}$$

Finally, for the third expectation in the second line of (53), we may take advantage of the fact that the dynamics of $\Psi_t^3$ do not change when passing from the measure $Q$ to the forward measure $Q^{T_k}$. We can then apply Lemma 4.1, this time with (see the third equation in (54))

$$b(t) := -b^3,\ \sigma := \sigma^3,\ C = \bar{C}_k^{33}$$

and ensuring that the parameters $b^3$ and $\sigma^3$ of the process $\Psi^3$ are such that $C = \bar{C}_k^{33}$ satisfies the assumption from the lemma. Since $b(t)$ is constant with respect to time, also Corollary 4.1 applies and we obtain

$$E^{T_k}\{\exp(\bar{C}_k^{33}(\Psi_{T_{k-1}}^3)^2)|\mathscr{F}_t\} = \exp[\Gamma^3(t,T_k) - \rho^3(t,T_k)(\Psi_t^3)^2],$$

where

$$\begin{cases} \rho^3(t,T_k) &= \frac{-4b^3 h_k^3 e^{-2b^3(T_k-t)}}{4(\sigma^3)^2 h_k^3 e^{-2b^3(T_k-t)}-1} \quad \text{with} \quad h_k^3 = \frac{\bar{C}_k^{33}}{4(\sigma^3)^2\bar{C}_k^{33}-4b^3} \\ \Gamma^3(t,T_k) &= -(\sigma^3)^2 \int_t^{T_k} \rho^3(u,T_k)du. \end{cases} \tag{65}$$

With the use of the explicit expressions for the expectations in (53), and taking also into account the expression for $p(t,T)$ in (29), it follows immediately that the arbitrage-free swap price in (51) can be expressed according to the following

**Proposition 4.2** *The price of a payer interest rate swap at $t \leq T_0$ is given by*

$$\begin{aligned} P^{Sw}(t;T_0,T_n,R) &= \gamma \sum_{k=1}^{n} p(t,T_k) E^{T_k}\left\{L(T_{k-1};T_{k-1},T_k) - R|\mathcal{F}_t\right\} \\ &= \sum_{k=1}^{n} p(t,T_k)\Big(D_{t,k} e^{-\rho^1(t,T_k)\Psi_t^1 - \rho^2(t,T_k)(\Psi_t^2)^2 - \rho^3(t,T_k)(\Psi_t^3)^2} - (R\gamma+1)\Big) \\ &= \sum_{k=1}^{n}\Big(D_{t,k} e^{-A_{t,k}} e^{-\tilde{B}^1_{t,k}\Psi_t^1 - \tilde{C}^{22}_{t,k}(\Psi_t^2)^2 - \tilde{C}^{33}_{t,k}(\Psi_t^3)^2} \\ &\qquad - (R\gamma+1)e^{-A_{t,k}} e^{-B^1_{t,k}\Psi_t^1 - C^{22}_{t,k}(\Psi_t^2)^2}\Big), \end{aligned} \tag{66}$$

*where*

$$\begin{array}{l} A_{t,k} := A(t,T_k),\ B^1_{t,k} := B^1(t,T_k),\ C^{22}_{t,k} := C^{22}(t,T_k) \\ \tilde{B}^1_{t,k} := B^1_{t,k} + \rho^1(t,T_k),\ \tilde{C}^{22}_{t,k} := C^{22}_{t,k} + \rho^2(t,T_k),\ \tilde{C}^{33}_{t,k} := \rho^3(t,T_k) \\ D_{t,k} := e^{A_k}\exp[\Gamma^1(t,T_k) + \Gamma^2(t,T_k) + \Gamma^3(t,T_k)], \end{array} \tag{67}$$

*with $\rho^i(t,T_k)$, $\Gamma^i(t,T_k)$ $(i = 1,2,3)$ determined according to (58), (64), and (65) respectively and with $A_k$ as in (52).*

## 5 Nonlinear/optional Interest Rate Derivatives

In this section we consider the main nonlinear interest rate derivatives with the Libor rate as underlying. They are also called *optional derivatives* since they have the form of an option. In Sect. 5.1 we shall consider the case of caps and, symmetrically, that of floors. In the subsequent Sect. 5.2 we shall then concentrate on swaptions as options on a payer swap of the type discussed in Sect. 4.2.

### 5.1 Caps and Floors

Since floors can be treated in a completely symmetric way to the caps simply by interchanging the roles of the fixed rate and the Libor rate, we shall concentrate here on caps. Furthermore, to keep the presentation simple, we consider here just a single caplet for the time interval $[T, T+\Delta]$ and for a fixed rate $R$ (recall also that we consider just one tenor $\Delta$). The payoff of the caplet at time $T+\Delta$ is thus $\Delta(L(T;T,T+\Delta)-R)^+$, assuming the notional $N=1$, and its time-$t$ price $P^{Cpl}(t;T+\Delta,R)$ is given by the following risk-neutral pricing formula under the forward measure $Q^{T+\Delta}$

$$P^{Cpl}(t;T+\Delta,R) = \Delta p(t,T+\Delta)E^{T+\Delta}\left\{(L(T;T,T+\Delta)-R)^+ \mid \mathscr{F}_t\right\}.$$

In view of deriving pricing formulas, recall from Sect. 3.3 that, under the $(T+\Delta)-$forward measure, at time $T$ the factors $\Psi_T^i$ have independent Gaussian distributions (see (34)) with mean and variance given, for $i=1,2,3$, by

$$E^{T+\Delta}\{\Psi_t^i\} = \bar{\alpha}_t^i = \bar{\alpha}_t^i(b^i,\sigma^i), \qquad Var^{T+\Delta}\{\Psi_t^i\} = \bar{\beta}_t^i = \bar{\beta}_t^i(b^i,\sigma^i).$$

In the formulas below we shall consider the joint probability density function of $(\Psi_T^1,\Psi_T^2,\Psi_T^3)$ under the $T+\Delta$ forward measure, namely, using the independence of the processes $\Psi_t^i$, $(i=1,2,3)$,

$$f_{(\Psi_T^1,\Psi_T^2,\Psi_T^3)}(x_1,x_2,x_3) = \prod_{i=1}^{3} f_{\Psi_T^i}(x_i) = \prod_{i=1}^{3} \mathscr{N}(x_i,\bar{\alpha}_T^i,\bar{\beta}_T^i), \tag{68}$$

and use the shorthand notation $f_i(\cdot)$ for $f_{\Psi_T^i}(\cdot)$ in the sequel. We shall also write $\bar{A}, B^1, C^{22}, \bar{C}^{33}$ for the corresponding functions evaluated at $(T, T+\Delta)$ and given in (28), (27) and (24) respectively.

Setting $\tilde{R} := 1+\Delta R$, and recalling the first equality in (30), the time-0 price of the caplet can be expressed as

$$\begin{aligned} P^{Cpl}(0;T+\Delta,R) &= \Delta p(0,T+\Delta)E^{T+\Delta}\left\{(L(T;T,T+\Delta)-R)^+\right\} \\ &= p(0,T+\Delta)E^{T+\Delta}\left\{\left(\frac{1}{\bar{p}(T,T+\Delta)}-\tilde{R}\right)^+\right\} \\ &= p(0,T+\Delta)E^{T+\Delta}\left\{\left(e^{\bar{A}+(\kappa+1)B^1\Psi_T^1+C^{22}(\Psi_T^2)^2+\bar{C}^{33}(\Psi_T^3)^2}-\tilde{R}\right)^+\right\} \\ &= p(0,T+\Delta)\int_{\mathbb{R}^3}\left(e^{\bar{A}+(\kappa+1)B^1x+C^{22}y^2+\bar{C}^{33}z^2}-\tilde{R}\right)^+ \\ &\qquad \cdot f_{(\Psi_T^1,\Psi_T^2,\Psi_T^3)}(x,y,z)d(x,y,z). \end{aligned} \tag{69}$$

To proceed, we extend to the multi-curve context an idea suggested in Jamshidian [19] (where it is applied to the pricing of coupon bonds) by considering the function

$$g(x,y,z) := \exp[\bar{A}+(\kappa+1)B^1x+C^{22}y^2+\bar{C}^{33}z^2]. \tag{70}$$

Noticing that $\bar{C}^{33}(T, T+\Delta) > 0$ (see (24) together with the fact that $h^3 > 0$ and $2b^3 + h^3 > 0$), for fixed $x, y$ the function $g(x, y, z)$ can be seen to be continuous and increasing for $z \geq 0$ and decreasing for $z < 0$ with $\lim_{z\to\pm\infty} g(x, y, z) = +\infty$. It will now be convenient to introduce some objects according to the following:

**Definition 5.1** Let a set $M \subset \mathbb{R}^2$ be given by

$$M := \{(x, y) \in \mathbb{R}^2 \mid g(x, y, 0) \leq \tilde{R}\} \tag{71}$$

and let $M^c$ be its complement. Furthermore, for $(x, y) \in M$ let

$$\bar{z}^1 = \bar{z}^1(x, y)\,, \quad \bar{z}^2 = \bar{z}^2(x, y)$$

be the solutions of $g(x, y, z) = \tilde{R}$. They satisfy $\bar{z}^1 \leq 0 \leq \bar{z}^2$.

Notice that, for $z \leq \bar{z}^1 \leq 0$ and $z \geq \bar{z}^2 \geq 0$, we have $g(x, y, z) \geq g(x, y, \bar{z}^k) = \tilde{R}$, and for $z \in (\bar{z}^1, \bar{z}^2)$, we have $g(x, y, z) < \tilde{R}$. In $M^c$ we have $g(x, y, z) \geq g(x, y, 0) > \tilde{R}$ and thus no solution of the equation $g(x, y, z) = \tilde{R}$.

In view of the main result of this subsection, given in Proposition 5.1 below, we prove as a preliminary the following:

**Lemma 5.1** *Assuming that the (nonnegative) coefficients $b^3, \sigma^3$ in the dynamics (10) of the factor $\Psi_t^3$ satisfy the condition*

$$b^3 \geq \frac{\sigma^3}{\sqrt{2}}, \tag{72}$$

*we have that $1 - 2\bar{\beta}_T^3 \bar{C}^{33} > 0$, where $\bar{C}^{33} = \bar{C}^{33}(T, T+\Delta)$ is given by (24) and where $\bar{\beta}_T^3 = \frac{(\sigma^3)^2}{2b^3}(1 - e^{-2b^3 T})$ according to (34).*

*Proof* From the definitions of $\bar{\beta}_T^3$ and $\bar{C}^{33}$ we may write

$$1 - 2\bar{\beta}_T^3 \bar{C}^{33} = 1 - \left(1 - e^{-2b^3 T}\right) \frac{2\left(e^{\Delta h^3} - 1\right)}{2\frac{b^3 h^3}{(\sigma^3)^2} + \frac{b^3}{(\sigma^3)^2}(2b^3 + h^3)\left(e^{\Delta h^3} - 1\right)}. \tag{73}$$

Notice next that $b^3 > 0$ implies that $1 - e^{-2b^3 T} \in (0, 1)$ and that $\frac{b^3 h^3}{(\sigma^3)^2} \geq 0$. From (73) it then follows that a sufficient condition for $1 - 2\bar{\beta}_T^3 \bar{C}^{33} > 0$ to hold is that

$$2 \leq \frac{b^3}{(\sigma^3)^2}(2b^3 + h^3). \tag{74}$$

Given that, see definition after (24), $h^3 = 2\sqrt{(b^3)^2 + 2(\sigma^3)^2} \geq 2b^3$, the condition (74) is satisfied under our assumption (72). □

**Proposition 5.1** *Under assumption (72) we have that the time-0 price of the caplet for the time interval $[T, T+\Delta]$ and with fixed rate $R$ is given by*

$$
\begin{aligned}
P^{Cpl}(0; T+\Delta, R) = p(0, T+\Delta)\Bigg[\int_M & e^{\bar{A}+(\kappa+1)B^1 x + C^{22}(y)^2} \\
& \cdot \Big[\gamma(\bar{\alpha}_T^3, \bar{\beta}_T^3, \bar{C}^{33})\Big(\Phi(d^1(x,y)) + \Phi(-d^2(x,y))\Big) \\
& - e^{\bar{C}^{33}(\bar{z}^1(x,y))^2}\Phi(d^3(x,y)) + e^{\bar{C}^{33}(\bar{z}^2(x,y))^2}\Phi(-d^4(x,y))\Big] \\
& \times f_1(x) f_2(y) dx dy + \gamma(\bar{\alpha}_T^3, \bar{\beta}_T^3, \bar{C}^{33})\int_{M^c} e^{\bar{A}+(\kappa+1)B^1 x + C^{22}(y)^2} \\
& \times f_1(x) f_2(y) dx dy - \tilde{R}\, Q^{T+\Delta}\Big\{(\Psi_T^1, \Psi_T^2) \in M^c\Big\}\Bigg],
\end{aligned}
\tag{75}
$$

*where $\Phi(\cdot)$ is the cumulative standard Gaussian distribution function, $M$ and $M^c$ are as in Definition 5.1,*

$$
\begin{cases}
d^1(x,y) := \dfrac{\sqrt{1-2\bar{\beta}_T^3\bar{C}^{33}}\,\bar{z}^1(x,y) - (\bar{\alpha}_T^3 - \theta\bar{\beta}_T^3)}{\sqrt{\bar{\beta}_T^3}} \\
d^2(x,y) := \dfrac{\sqrt{1-2\bar{\beta}_T^3\bar{C}^{33}}\,\bar{z}^2(x,y) - (\bar{\alpha}_T^3 - \theta\bar{\beta}_T^3)}{\sqrt{\bar{\beta}_T^3}} \\
d^3(x,y) := \dfrac{\bar{z}^1(x,y) - \bar{\alpha}_T^3}{\sqrt{\bar{\beta}_T^3}} \\
d^4(x,y) := \dfrac{\bar{z}^2(x,y) - \bar{\alpha}_T^3}{\sqrt{\bar{\beta}_T^3}}
\end{cases}
\tag{76}
$$

*with* $\theta := \frac{\bar{\alpha}_T^3\left(1-1/\sqrt{1-2\bar{\beta}_T^3\bar{C}^{33}}\right)}{\bar{\beta}_T^3}$, *which by Lemma 5.1 is well defined under the given assumption (72), and with* $\gamma(\bar{\alpha}_T^3, \bar{\beta}_T^3, \bar{C}^{33}) := \frac{e^{\left(\frac{1}{2}(\theta)^2\bar{\beta}_T^3 - \bar{\alpha}_T^3\theta\right)}}{\sqrt{1-2\bar{\beta}_T^3\bar{C}^{33}}}$.

*Remark 5.1* Notice that, once the set $M$ and its complement $M^c$ from Definition 5.1 are made explicit, the integrals, as well as the probability in (75), can be computed explicitly.

*Proof* On the basis of the sets $M$ and $M^c$ we can continue (69) as

$$
\begin{aligned}
P^{Cpl}(0; T+\Delta, R) &= p(0, T+\Delta)\int_{\mathbb{R}^3}\left(e^{\bar{A}+(\kappa+1)B^1 x + C^{22}y^2 + \bar{C}^{33}z^2} - \tilde{R}\right)^+ \\
&\quad \cdot f_{(\Psi_T^1, \Psi_T^2, \Psi_T^3)}(x,y,z) d(x,y,z) \\
&= p(0, T+\Delta)\int_{M\times\mathbb{R}}\left(e^{\bar{A}+(\kappa+1)B^1 x + C^{22}y^2 + \bar{C}^{33}z^2} - \tilde{R}\right)^+ \\
&\quad \cdot f_{(\Psi_T^1, \Psi_T^2, \Psi_T^3)}(x,y,z) d(x,y,z)
\end{aligned}
$$

$$+p(0,T+\Delta)\int_{M^c\times\mathbb{R}}\left(e^{\bar{A}+(\kappa+1)B^1x+C^{22}y^2+\bar{C}^{33}z^2}-\tilde{R}\right)^+$$
$$\cdot f_{(\Psi_T^1,\Psi_T^2,\Psi_T^3)}(x,y,z)d(x,y,z)$$
$$=: P^1(0;T+\Delta)+P^2(0;T+\Delta). \tag{77}$$

We shall next compute separately the two terms in the last equality in (77) distinguishing between two cases according to whether $(x, y) \in M$ or $(x, y) \in M^c$.

*Case (i):* For $(x, y) \in M$ we have from Definition 5.1 that there exist $\bar{z}^1(x, y) \leq 0$ and $\bar{z}^2(x, y) \geq 0$ so that for $z \in [\bar{z}^1, \bar{z}^2]$ we have $g(x, y, z) \leq g(x, y, \bar{z}^k) = \tilde{R}$. For $P^1(0; T + \Delta)$ we now obtain

$$\begin{aligned}P^1(0;T+\Delta) &= p(0,T+\Delta)\\
&\cdot\int_M e^{\bar{A}+(\kappa+1)B^1x+C^{22}y^2}\Big(\int_{-\infty}^{\bar{z}^1(x,y)}(e^{\bar{C}^{33}z^2}-e^{\bar{C}^{33}(\bar{z}^1)^2})f_3(z)dz\\
&+\int_{\bar{z}^2(x,y)}^{+\infty}(e^{\bar{C}^{33}z^2}-e^{\bar{C}^{33}(\bar{z}^2)^2})f_3(z)dz\Big)f_2(y)f_1(x)dydx.\end{aligned} \tag{78}$$

Next, using the results of Sect. 3.3 concerning the Gaussian distribution $f_3(\cdot) = f_{\Psi_T^3}(\cdot)$, we obtain the calculations in (79) below, where, recalling Lemma 5.1, we make successively the following changes of variables: $\zeta := \sqrt{1-2\bar{\beta}_T^3\bar{C}^{33}}z$, $\theta := \frac{\bar{\alpha}_T^3(1-1/\sqrt{1-2\bar{\beta}_T^3\bar{C}^{33}})}{\bar{\beta}_T^3}$, $s := \frac{\zeta-(\bar{\alpha}_T^3-\theta\bar{\beta}_T^3)}{\sqrt{\bar{\beta}_T^3}}$ and where $d^i(x, y)$, $i = 1, \cdots, 4$ are as defined in (76)

$$\begin{aligned}
\int_{-\infty}^{\bar{z}^1(x,y)} e^{\bar{C}^{33}z^2}f_3(z)dz &= \int_{-\infty}^{\bar{z}^1(x,y)} e^{\bar{C}^{33}z^2}\frac{1}{\sqrt{2\pi\bar{\beta}_T^3}}e^{-\frac{1}{2}\frac{(z-\bar{\alpha}_T^3)^2}{\bar{\beta}_T^3}}dz\\
&= \int_{-\infty}^{\bar{z}^1(x,y)}\frac{1}{\sqrt{2\pi\bar{\beta}_T^3}}e^{-\frac{1}{2}\frac{(\sqrt{1-2\bar{\beta}_T^3\bar{C}^{33}}z-\bar{\alpha}_T^3)^2}{\bar{\beta}_T^3}}e^{-\frac{\bar{\alpha}_T^3(\sqrt{1-2\bar{\beta}_T^3\bar{C}^{33}}-1)}{\bar{\beta}_T^3}z}dz\\
&= \int_{-\infty}^{\sqrt{1-2\bar{\beta}_T^3\bar{C}^{33}}\bar{z}^1(x,y)}\frac{1}{\sqrt{2\pi\bar{\beta}_T^3}}e^{-\frac{1}{2}\frac{(\zeta-\bar{\alpha}_T^3)^2}{\bar{\beta}_T^3}}e^{-\frac{\bar{\alpha}_T^3(1-1/\sqrt{1-2\bar{\beta}_T^3\bar{C}^{33}})}{\bar{\beta}_T^3}\zeta}\frac{1}{\sqrt{1-2\bar{\beta}_T^3\bar{C}^{33}}}d\zeta\\
&= \frac{1}{\sqrt{1-2\bar{\beta}_T^3\bar{C}^{33}}}\int_{-\infty}^{\sqrt{1-2\bar{\beta}_T^3\bar{C}^{33}}\bar{z}^1(x,y)}\frac{1}{\sqrt{2\pi\bar{\beta}_T^3}}e^{-\frac{1}{2}\frac{(\zeta-\bar{\alpha}_T^3)^2}{\bar{\beta}_T^3}}e^{-\theta\zeta}d\zeta\\
&= \frac{e^{(\frac{1}{2}(\theta)^2\bar{\beta}_T^3-\bar{\alpha}_T^3\theta)}}{\sqrt{1-2\bar{\beta}_T^3\bar{C}^{33}}}\int_{-\infty}^{d^1(x,y)}\frac{1}{\sqrt{2\pi}}e^{-\frac{s^2}{2}}ds = \frac{e^{(\frac{1}{2}(\theta)^2\bar{\beta}_T^3-\bar{\alpha}_T^3\theta)}}{\sqrt{1-2\bar{\beta}_T^3\bar{C}^{33}}}\Phi(d^1(x,y)).
\end{aligned} \tag{79}$$

On the other hand, always using the results of Sect. 3.3 concerning the Gaussian distribution $f_3(\cdot) = f_{\Psi_T^3}(\cdot)$ and making this time the change of variables $\zeta := \frac{(z-\bar{\alpha}_T^3)}{\sqrt{\bar{\beta}_T^3}}$, we obtain

$$\int_{-\infty}^{\bar{z}^1(x,y)} e^{\bar{C}^{33}(\bar{z}^1)^2} f_3(z)dz = e^{\bar{C}^{33}(\bar{z}^1)^2} \int_{-\infty}^{\bar{z}^1(x,y)} \frac{1}{\sqrt{2\pi\bar{\beta}_T^3}} e^{-\frac{1}{2}\frac{(z-\bar{\alpha}_T^3)^2}{\bar{\beta}_T^3}} dz$$

$$= e^{\bar{C}^{33}(\bar{z}^1)^2} \int_{-\infty}^{d^3(x,y)} \frac{1}{\sqrt{2\pi}} e^{-\frac{1}{2}\zeta^2} d\zeta = e^{\bar{C}^{33}(\bar{z}^1)^2} \Phi(d^3(x,y)). \tag{80}$$

Similarly, we have

$$\int_{\bar{z}^2(x,y)}^{+\infty} e^{\bar{C}^{33}z^2} f_3(z)dz = \frac{1}{\sqrt{1-2\bar{\beta}_T^3\bar{C}^{33}}} e^{(\frac{1}{2}(\theta)^2\bar{\beta}_T^3 - \bar{\alpha}_T^3\theta)} \Phi(-d^2(x,y))$$

$$\int_{\bar{z}^2(x,y)}^{+\infty} e^{\bar{C}^{33}(\bar{z}^1)^2} f_3(z)dz = e^{\bar{C}^{33}(\bar{z}^2)^2} \Phi(-d^4(x,y)). \tag{81}$$

*Case (ii):* We come next to the case $(x, y) \in M^c$, for which $g(x, y, z) \geq g(x, y, 0) > \tilde{R}$. For $P^2(0; T+\Delta)$ we obtain

$$\begin{aligned}
P^2(0;T+\Delta) &= p(0,T+\Delta)\int_{M^c\times\mathbb{R}} \left(e^{\bar{A}+(\kappa+1)B^1x+C^{22}y^2+\bar{C}^{33}z^2} - \tilde{R}\right) \\
&\quad \cdot f_3(z)f_2(y)f_1(x)dzdydx \\
&= p(0,T+\Delta)\Big(e^{\bar{A}}\int_{M^c} e^{(\kappa+1)B^1x+C^{22}y^2} f_1(x)f_2(y)dxdy \int_{\mathbb{R}} e^{\bar{C}^{33}z^2} f_3(z)dz \\
&\quad - \tilde{R}Q^{T+\Delta}[(\Psi_T^1,\Psi_T^2)\in M^c]\Big) \\
&= p(0,T+\Delta)\Big(e^{\bar{A}}\Big[\int_{M^c} e^{(\kappa+1)B^1x+C^{22}y^2} f_1(x)f_2(y)dxdy\Big] \frac{e^{(\frac{1}{2}(\theta^3)^2\bar{\beta}_T^3 - \bar{\alpha}_T^3\theta^3)}}{\sqrt{1-2\bar{\beta}_T^3\bar{C}^{33}}} \\
&\quad - \tilde{R}Q^{T+\Delta}[(\Psi_T^1,\Psi_T^2)\in M^c]\Big),
\end{aligned} \tag{82}$$

where we computed the integral over $\mathbb{R}$ analogously to (79).

Adding the two expressions derived for Cases (i) and (ii), we obtain the statement of the proposition. □

## 5.2 Swaptions

We start by recalling some of the most relevant aspects of a (payer) swaption. Considering a swap (see Sect. 4.2) for a given collection of dates $0 \leq T_0 < T_1 < \cdots < T_n$, a swaption is an option to enter the swap at a pre-specified initiation date $T \le T_0$, which is thus also the maturity of the swaption and that, for simplicity of notation, we assume to coincide with $T_0$, i.e. $T = T_0$. The arbitrage-free swaption price at $t \le T_0$ can be computed as

$$P^{Swn}(t; T_0, T_n, R) = p(t, T_0)E^{T_0}\left\{\left(P^{Sw}(T_0; T_n, R)\right)^+ | \mathscr{F}_t\right\}, \tag{83}$$

where we have used the shorthand notation $P^{Sw}(T_0; T_n, R) = P^{Sw}(T_0; T_0, T_n, R)$.

We first state the next Lemma, that follows immediately from the expression for $\rho^3(t, T_k)$ and the corresponding expression for $h_k^3$ in (65).

**Lemma 5.2** *We have the equivalence*

$$\rho^3(t, T_k) > 0 \Leftrightarrow h_k^3 \in \left(0, \frac{1}{4(\sigma^3)^2 e^{-2b^3(T_k-t)}}\right). \tag{84}$$

This lemma prompts us to split the swaption pricing problem into two cases:

$$\begin{aligned} &\textbf{Case(1)}: \quad h_k^3 < 0 \text{ or } h_k^3 > \frac{1}{4(\sigma^3)^2 e^{-2b^3(T_k-t)}} \\ &\textbf{Case(2)}: \quad 0 < h_k^3 < \frac{1}{4(\sigma^3)^2 e^{-2b^3(T_k-t)}}. \end{aligned} \tag{85}$$

Note from the definition of $\rho^3(t, T_k)$ that $h_k^3 \neq \frac{1}{4(\sigma^3)^2 e^{-2b^3(T_k-t)}}$ and that $h_k^3 = 0$ would imply $\bar{C}_k^{33} = 0$ which corresponds to a trivial case in which the factor $\Psi^3$ is not present in the dynamics of the spread $s$, hence the inequalities in Case (1) and Case (2) above are indeed strict.

To proceed, we shall introduce some more notation. In particular, instead of only one function $g(x, y, z)$ as in (70), we shall consider also a function $h(x, y)$, more precisely, we shall define here the continuous functions

$$g(x, y, z) := \sum_{k=1}^{n} D_{0,k} e^{-A_{0,k}} e^{-\tilde{B}_{0,k}^1 x - \tilde{C}_{0,k}^{22} y^2 - \tilde{C}_{0,k}^{33} z^2} \tag{86}$$

$$h(x, y) := \sum_{k=1}^{n} (R\gamma + 1) e^{-A_{0,k}} e^{-B_{0,k}^1 x - C_{0,k}^{22} y^2}, \tag{87}$$

with the coefficients given by (67) for $t = T_0$. Note that by a slight abuse of notation we write $D_{0,k}$ for $D_{T_0,k}$ and similarly for other coefficients above, always meaning $t = T_0$ in (67). We distinguish the two cases specified in (85):

For *Case (1)* we have (see (67) and Lemma 5.2) that $\tilde{C}^{33}_{0,k} = \rho^3(T_0, T_k) < 0$ for all $k = 1, \cdots, n$, and so the function $g(x, y, z)$ in (86) is, for given $(x, y)$, monotonically increasing for $z \geq 0$ and decreasing for $z < 0$ with

$$\lim_{z \to \pm\infty} g(x, y, z) = +\infty.$$

For *Case (2)* we have instead that $\tilde{C}^{33}_{0,k} = \rho^3(T_0, T_k) > 0$ for all $k = 1, \cdots, n$ and so the nonnegative function $g(x, y, z)$ in (86) is, for given $(x, y)$, monotonically decreasing for $z \geq 0$ and increasing for $z < 0$ with

$$\lim_{z \to \pm\infty} g(x, y, z) = 0.$$

Analogously to Definition 5.1 we next introduce the following objects:

**Definition 5.2** Let a set $\bar{M} \subset \mathbb{R}^2$ be given by

$$\bar{M} := \{(x, y) \in \mathbb{R}^2 \mid g(x, y, 0) \leq h(x, y)\}. \tag{88}$$

Since $g(x, y, z)$ and $h(x, y)$ are continuous, $\bar{M}$ is closed, measurable and connected. Let $\bar{M}^c$ be its complement. Furthermore, we define two functions $\bar{z}^1(x, y)$ and $\bar{z}^2(x, y)$ distinguishing between the two Cases (1) and (2) as specified in (85).

Case (1) If $(x, y) \in \bar{M}$, we have $g(x, y, 0) \leq h(x, y)$ and so there exist $\bar{z}^1(x, y) \leq 0$ and $\bar{z}^2(x, y) \geq 0$ for which, for $i = 1, 2$,

$$\begin{aligned} g(x, y, \bar{z}^i) &= \sum_{k=1}^{n} D_{0,k} e^{-A_{0,k}} e^{-\tilde{B}^1_{0,k} x - \tilde{C}^{22}_{0,k} y^2 - \tilde{C}^{33}_{0,k} (\bar{z}^i)^2} \\ &= \sum_{k=1}^{n} (R\gamma + 1) e^{-A_{0,k}} e^{-B^1_{0,k} x - C^{22}_{0,k} y^2} = h(x, y) \end{aligned} \tag{89}$$

and, for $z \notin [\bar{z}^1, \bar{z}^2]$, one has $g(x, y, z) \geq g(x, y, \bar{z}^i)$.
If $(x, y) \in \bar{M}^c$, we have $g(x, y, 0) > h(x, y)$ so that $g(x, y, z) \geq g(x, y, 0) > h(x, y)$ for all $z$ and we have no points corresponding to $\bar{z}^1(x, y)$ and $\bar{z}^2(x, y)$ above.

Case (2) If $(x, y) \in \bar{M}$, we have, as for Case (1), $g(x, y, 0) \leq h(x, y)$ and so there exist $\bar{z}^1(x, y) \leq 0$ and $\bar{z}^2(x, y) \geq 0$ for which, for $i = 1, 2$, (89) holds. However, this time it is for $z \in [\bar{z}^1, \bar{z}^2]$ that one has $g(x, y, z) \geq g(x, y, \bar{z}^i)$.
If $(x, y) \in M^c$, then we are in the same situation as for Case (1).

Starting from (83) combined with (66) and taking into account the set $\bar{M}$ according to Definition 5.2, we can obtain the following expression for the swaption price at $t = 0$. As for the caps, here too we consider the joint Gaussian distribution $f_{(\Psi^1_{T_0}, \Psi^2_{T_0}, \Psi^3_{T_0})}(x, y, z)$ of the factors under the $T_0$−forward measure $Q^{T_0}$ and we have

$$
\begin{aligned}
P^{Swn}(0;T_0,T_n,R) &= p(0,T_0)E^{T_0}\left\{\left(P^{Sw}(T_0;T_n,R)\right)^+ | \mathscr{F}_0\right\} \\
&= p(0,T_0)\int_{\mathbb{R}^3}\Big[\sum_{k=1}^{n} D_{0,k}e^{-A_{0,k}}\exp(-\tilde{B}^1_{0,k}x-\tilde{C}^{22}_{0,k}y^2-\tilde{C}^{33}_{0,k}z^2) \\
&\quad -\sum_{k=1}^{n}(R\gamma+1)e^{-A_{0,k}}\exp(-B^1_{0,k}x-C^{22}_{0,k}y^2)\Big]^+ f_{(\Psi^1_{T_0},\Psi^2_{T_0},\Psi^3_{T_0})}(x,y,z)dxdydz \\
&= p(0,T_0)\int_{\bar{M}\times\mathbb{R}}\Big[\sum_{k=1}^{n} D_{0,k}e^{-A_{0,k}}\exp(-\tilde{B}^1_{0,k}x-\tilde{C}^{22}_{0,k}y^2-\tilde{C}^{33}_{0,k}z^2) \\
&\quad -\sum_{k=1}^{n}(R\gamma+1)e^{-A_{0,k}}\exp(-B^1_{0,k}x-C^{22}_{0,k}y^2)\Big]^+ f_{(\Psi^1_{T_0},\Psi^2_{T_0},\Psi^3_{T_0})}(x,y,z)dxdydz \\
&\quad +p(0,T_0)\int_{\bar{M}^c\times\mathbb{R}}\Big[\sum_{k=1}^{n} D_{0,k}e^{-A_{0,k}}\exp(-\tilde{B}^1_{0,k}x-\tilde{C}^{22}_{0,k}y^2-\tilde{C}^{33}_{0,k}z^2) \\
&\quad -\sum_{k=1}^{n}(R\gamma+1)e^{-A_{0,k}}\exp(-B^1_{0,k}x-C^{22}_{0,k}y^2)\Big]^+ f_{(\Psi^1_{T_0},\Psi^2_{T_0},\Psi^3_{T_0})}(x,y,z)dxdydz \\
&=: P^1(0;T_0,T_n,R)+P^2(0;T_0,T_n,R).
\end{aligned}
\tag{90}
$$

We can now state and prove the main result of this subsection consisting in a pricing formula for swaptions for the Gaussian exponentially quadratic model of this paper. We have

**Proposition 5.2** *Assume that the parameters in the model are such that, if $h^3_k$ belongs to Case (1) in (85) and $h^3_k > 0$, then $h^3_k > \frac{1}{4(\sigma^3)^2e^{-2b^3T_k}}$. The arbitrage-free price at $t=0$ of the swaption with payment dates $T_1<\cdots<T_n$ such that $\gamma=\gamma_k := T_k-T_{k-1}$ $(k=1,\cdots,n)$, with a given fixed rate $R$ and a notional $N=1$, can be computed as follows where we distinguish between the Cases (1) and (2) specified in Definition 5.2.*

**Case (1)** *We have*

$$
\begin{aligned}
P^{Swn}(0;T_0,T_n,R) = p(0,T_0)\Bigg\{\sum_{k=1}^{n} e^{-A_{0,k}}\Bigg[\int_{\bar{M}} & D_{0,k}\exp(-\tilde{B}^1_{0,k}x-\tilde{C}^{22}_{0,k}y^2) \\
&\cdot\Bigg(\frac{e^{(\frac{1}{2}(\theta_k)^2\bar{\beta}^3_{T_0}-\bar{\alpha}^3_{T_0}\theta_k)}}{\sqrt{1+2\bar{\beta}^3_{T_0}\tilde{C}^{33}_{0,k}}}\Phi(d^1_k(x,y)) - e^{-\tilde{C}^{33}_{0,k}(\bar{z}^1)^2}\Phi(d^2_k(x,y)) \\
&+\frac{e^{(\frac{1}{2}(\theta_k)^2\bar{\beta}^3_{T_0}-\bar{\alpha}^3_{T_0}\theta_k)}}{\sqrt{1+2\bar{\beta}^3_{T_0}\tilde{C}^{33}_{0,k}}}\Phi(-d^3_k(x,y)) - e^{-\tilde{C}^{33}_{0,k}(\bar{z}^2)^2}\Phi(-d^4_k(x,y))\Bigg)
\end{aligned}
$$

$$\times f_2(y) f_1(x) dy dx + \int_{\bar{M}^c} \Big( D_{0,k} e^{-\tilde{B}^1_{0,k} x - \tilde{C}^{22}_{0,k} y^2} \frac{e^{(\frac{1}{2}(\theta_k)^2 \bar{\beta}^3_{T_0} - \bar{\alpha}^3_{T_0} \theta_k)}}{\sqrt{1 + 2\bar{\beta}^3_{T_0} \tilde{C}^{33}_{0,k}}}$$
$$- (R\gamma + 1) e^{-B^1_{0,k} x - C^{22}_{0,k} y^2} \Big) f_2(y) f_1(x) dy dx \Big] \Big\}. \tag{91}$$

**Case (2)** *We have*

$$P^{Swn}(0; T_0, T_n, R) = p(0, T_0) \Big\{ \sum_{k=1}^{n} e^{-A_{0,k}}$$
$$\Big[ \int_{\bar{M}} D_{0,k} \exp(-\tilde{B}^1_{0,k} x - \tilde{C}^{22}_{0,k} y^2) \Big( \frac{e^{(\frac{1}{2}(\theta_k)^2 \bar{\beta}^3_{T_0} - \bar{\alpha}^3_{T_0} \theta_k)}}{\sqrt{1 + 2\bar{\beta}^3_{T_0} \tilde{C}^{33}_{0,k}}}$$
$$\times \Big[ \Phi(d^3_k(x,y)) - \Phi(d^1_k(x,y)) \Big] - e^{-\tilde{C}^{33}_{0,k} (\bar{z}^1)^2} \Big[ \Phi(d^4_k(x,y))$$
$$- \Phi(d^2_k(x,y)) \Big] \Big) f_2(y) f_1(x) dy dx$$
$$+ \int_{\bar{M}^c} \Big( D_{0,k} e^{-\tilde{B}^1_{0,k} x - \tilde{C}^{22}_{0,k} y^2} \frac{e^{(\frac{1}{2}(\theta_k)^2 \bar{\beta}^3_{T_0} - \bar{\alpha}^3_{T_0} \theta_k)}}{\sqrt{1 + 2\bar{\beta}^3_{T_0} \tilde{C}^{33}_{0,k}}}$$
$$- (R\gamma + 1) e^{-B^1_{0,k} x - C^{22}_{0,k} y^2} \Big) f_2(y) f_1(x) dy dx \Big] \Big\}. \tag{92}$$

*The coefficients in these formulas are as specified in (67) for $t = T_0$, $f_1(x)$, $f_2(x)$ are the Gaussian densities corresponding to (68) for $T = T_0$ and the functions $d^i_k(x, y)$, for $i = 1, \ldots, 4$ and $k = 1, \ldots, n$, are given by*

$$\begin{cases} d^1_k(x,y) := \frac{\sqrt{1+2\bar{\beta}^3_{T_0} \tilde{C}^{33}_{0,k}}\, \bar{z}^1(x,y) - (\bar{\alpha}^3_{T_0} - \theta_k \bar{\beta}^3_{T_0})}{\sqrt{\bar{\beta}^3_{T_0}}} \\ d^2_k(x,y) := \frac{\bar{z}^1(x,y) - \bar{\alpha}^3_{T_0}}{\sqrt{\bar{\beta}^3_{T_0}}} \\ d^3_k(x,y) := \frac{\sqrt{1+2\bar{\beta}^3_{T_0} \tilde{C}^{33}_{0,k}}\, \bar{z}^2(x,y) - (\bar{\alpha}^3_{T_0} - \theta_k \bar{\beta}^3_{T_0})}{\sqrt{\bar{\beta}^3_{T_0}}} \\ d^4_k(x,y) := \frac{\bar{z}^2(x,y) - \bar{\alpha}^3_{T_0}}{\sqrt{\bar{\beta}^3_{T_0}}} \end{cases} \tag{93}$$

*with* $\theta_k := \frac{\bar{\alpha}^3_{T_0}\left(1 - 1/\sqrt{1+2\bar{\beta}^3_{T_0} \tilde{C}^{33}_{0,k}}\right)}{\bar{\beta}^3_{T_0}}$, *for* $k = 1, \ldots, n$, *and where* $\bar{z}^1 = \bar{z}^1(x, y)$, $\bar{z}^2 = \bar{z}^2(x, y)$ *are solutions in* $z$ *of the equation* $g(x, y, z) = h(x, y)$.

*In addition, the mean and variance values for the Gaussian factors* $(\Psi^1_{T_0}, \Psi^2_{T_0}, \Psi^3_{T_0})$ *are here given by*

$$\begin{cases} \bar{\alpha}^1_{T_0} = e^{-b^1 T_0}\Psi^1_0 - \frac{(\sigma^1)^2}{2(b^1)^2}e^{-b^1 T_0}(1-e^{2b^1 T_0}) - \frac{(\sigma^1)^2}{(b^1)^2}(1-e^{b^1 T_0})\Big] \\ \bar{\beta}^1_{T_0} = e^{-2b^1 T_0}(e^{2b^1 T_0}-1)\frac{(\sigma^1)^2}{2(b^1)} \\ \bar{\alpha}^2_{T_0} = e^{-b^2 T_0}\Psi^2_0 \\ \bar{\beta}^2_{T_0} = e^{-2b^2 T_0}\int_0^{T_0} e^{2b^2 u + 4(\sigma^2)^2 \bar{C}^{22}(u,T_0)}(\sigma^2)^2 du \\ \bar{\alpha}^3_{T_0} = e^{-b^3 T_0}\Psi^3_0 \\ \bar{\beta}^3_{T_0} = e^{-2b^3 T_0}\frac{(\sigma^3)^2}{2b^3}(e^{2b^3 T_0}-1). \end{cases} \tag{94}$$

*Remark 5.2* A remark analogous to Remark 5.1 applies here too concerning the sets $\bar{M}$ and $\bar{M}^c$.

*Proof* First of all notice that, when $h^3_k < 0$ or $h^3_k > \frac{1}{4(\sigma^3)^2 e^{-2b^3 T_k}}$ in Case (1), this implies $1 + 2\bar{\beta}^3_{T_0}\tilde{C}^{33}_{0,k} \geq 0$ (in Case (2) we always have $1 + 2\bar{\beta}^3_{T_0}\tilde{C}^{33}_{0,k} \geq 0$). Hence, the square-root of the latter expression in the various formulas of the statement of the proposition is well-defined. This can be checked, similarly as in the proof of Lemma 5.1, by direct computation taking into account the definitions of $\bar{\beta}^3_{T_0}$ in (94) and of $\tilde{C}^{33}_{0,k}$ in (67) and (65) for $t = T_0$.

We come now to the statement for:

**Case 1.** We distinguish between whether $(x, y) \in \bar{M}$ or $(x, y) \in \bar{M}^c$ and compute separately the two terms in the last equality in (90).

**(i)** For $(x, y) \in \bar{M}$ we have from Definition 5.2 that there exist $\bar{z}^1(x, y) \leq 0$ and $\bar{z}^2(x, y) \geq 0$ so that, for $z \notin [\bar{z}^1, \bar{z}^2]$, one has $g(x, y, z) \geq g(x, y, \bar{z}^i)$. Taking into account that, under $Q^{T_0}$, the random variables $\Psi^1_{T_0}, \Psi^2_{T_0}, \Psi^3_{T_0}$ are independent, so that we shall write $f_{(\Psi^1_{T_0},\Psi^2_{T_0},\Psi^3_{T_0})}(x, y, z) = f_1(x)f_2(y)f_3(z)$ (see also (68) and the line following it), we obtain

$$\begin{aligned} P^1(0; T_0, T_n, R) = p(0, T_0)\Big[\sum_{k=1}^{n} D_{0,k}e^{-A_{0,k}} \int_M \exp(-\tilde{B}^1_{0,k}x - \tilde{C}^{22}_{0,k}y^2) \\ \cdot \Big(\int_{-\infty}^{\bar{z}^1(x,y)} \exp(-\tilde{C}^{33}_{0,k}z^2)f_3(z)dz \\ - \int_{-\infty}^{\bar{z}^1(x,y)} \exp(-\tilde{C}^{33}_{0,k}(\bar{z}^1)^2)f_3(z)dz \\ + \int_{\bar{z}^2(x,y)}^{+\infty} \exp(-\tilde{C}^{33}_{0,k}z^2)f_3(z)dz \\ - \int_{\bar{z}^2(x,y)}^{+\infty} \exp(-\tilde{C}^{33}_{0,k}(\bar{z}^2)^2)f_3(z)dz\Big)f_2(y)f_1(x)dydx\Big]. \end{aligned} \tag{95}$$

By means of calculations that are completely analogous to those in the proof of Proposition 5.1, we obtain, corresponding to (79)–(81) respectively and with the same meaning of the symbols, the following explicit expressions for the integrals in the last four lines of (95), namely

$$\int_{-\infty}^{\bar{z}^1(x,y)} e^{-\tilde{C}_{0,k}^{33} z^2} f_3(z)dz = \frac{e^{\left(\frac{1}{2}(\theta_k)^2 \bar{\beta}_{T_0}^3 - \bar{\alpha}_{T_0}^3 \theta_k\right)}}{\sqrt{1 + 2\bar{\beta}_{T_0}^3 \tilde{C}_{0,k}^{33}}} \Phi(d_k^1(x, y)), \tag{96}$$

$$\int_{-\infty}^{\bar{z}^1(x,y)} e^{-\tilde{C}_{0,k}^{33} (\bar{z}^1)^2} f_3(z)dz = e^{-\tilde{C}_{0,k}^{33} (\bar{z}^1)^2} \Phi(d_k^2(x, y)), \tag{97}$$

and, similarly,

$$\begin{aligned}
&\int_{\bar{z}^2(x,y)}^{+\infty} e^{-\tilde{C}_{0,k}^{33} z^2} f_3(z)dz = \frac{e^{\left(\frac{1}{2}(\theta_k)^2 \bar{\beta}_{T_0}^3 - \bar{\alpha}_{T_0}^3 \theta_k\right)}}{\sqrt{1 + 2\bar{\beta}_{T_0}^3 \tilde{C}_{0,k}^{33}}} \Phi(-d_k^3(x, y)), \\
&\int_{\bar{z}^2(x,y)}^{+\infty} e^{-\tilde{C}_{0,k}^{33} (\bar{z}^2)^2} f_3(z)dz = e^{-\tilde{C}_{0,k}^{33} (\bar{z}^2)^2} \Phi(-d_k^4(x, y)),
\end{aligned} \tag{98}$$

where the $d_k^i(x, y)$, for $i = 1, \ldots, 4$ and $k = 1, \ldots, n$, are as specified in (93).

**(ii)** If $(x, y) \in \bar{M}^c$ then, according to Definition 5.2 we have $g(x, y, z) \geq g(x, y, 0) > h(x, y)$ for all $z$. Noticing that, analogously to (96),

$$\int_{\mathbb{R}} e^{-\tilde{C}_{0,k}^{33} \zeta^2} f_3(\zeta)d\zeta = \frac{e^{\left(\frac{1}{2}(\theta_k)^2 \bar{\beta}_{T_0}^3 - \bar{\alpha}_{T_0}^3 \theta_k\right)}}{\sqrt{1 + 2\bar{\beta}_{T_0}^3 \tilde{C}_{0,k}^{33}}}$$

we obtain the following expression

$$\begin{aligned}
P^2(0; T_0, T_n, R) &= p(0, T_0) \sum_{k=1}^{n} e^{-A_{0,k}} \Big[ \int_{\bar{M}^c \times \mathbb{R}} \Big( D_{0,k} e^{-\tilde{B}_{0,k}^1 x - \tilde{C}_{0,k}^{22} y^2 - \tilde{C}_{0,k}^{33} z^2} \\
&\quad - (R\gamma + 1) e^{-B_{0,k}^1 x - C_{0,k}^{22} y^2} \Big) f_3(z) f_2(y) f_1(x) dz dy dx \Big] \\
&= p(0, T_0) \sum_{k=1}^{n} e^{-A_{0,k}} \Big[ D_{0,k} \Big( \int_{M^c} e^{-\tilde{B}_{0,k}^1 x - \tilde{C}_{0,k}^{22} y^2} f_2(y) f_1(x) dy dx \Big) \\
&\qquad \times \frac{e^{\left(\frac{1}{2}(\theta_k)^2 \bar{\beta}_{T_0}^3 - \bar{\alpha}_{T_0}^3 \theta_k\right)}}{\sqrt{1 + 2\bar{\beta}_{T_0}^3 \tilde{C}_{0,k}^{33}}} - (R\gamma + 1) \Big( \int_{\bar{M}^c} e^{-B_{0,k}^1 x - C_{0,k}^{22} y^2} f_2(y) f_1(x) dy dx \Big) \Big].
\end{aligned} \tag{99}$$

Adding the two expressions in (i) and (ii) we obtain the statement for Case 1.

**Case (2).** Also for this case we distinguish between whether $(x, y) \in \bar{M}$ or $(x, y) \in \bar{M}^c$ and, again, compute separately the two terms in the last equality in (90).

**(i)** For $(x, y) \in \bar{M}$ we have that there exist $\bar{z}^1(x, y) \leq 0$ and $\bar{z}^2(x, y) \geq 0$ so that, contrary to Case 1), one has $g(x, y, z) \geq g(x, y, \bar{z}^i)$ when $z \in [\bar{z}^1, \bar{z}^2]$. It follows that

$$\begin{aligned} P^1(0; T_0, T_n, R) &= p(0, T_0)\Bigg[\sum_{k=1}^{n} D_{0,k} e^{-A_{0,k}} \int_{\bar{M}} \exp(-\tilde{B}^1_{0,k}x - \tilde{C}^{22}_{0,k}y^2) \\ &\quad \cdot \Bigg(\int_{\bar{z}^1(x,y)}^{\bar{z}^2(x,y)} \exp(-\tilde{C}^{33}_{0,k}z^2) f_3(z)dz \\ &\quad - \int_{\bar{z}^1(x,y)}^{\bar{z}^2(x,y)} \exp(-\tilde{C}^{33}_{0,k}(\bar{z}^1)^2) f_3(z)dz\Bigg) f_2(y) f_1(x) dy dx\Bigg] \\ &= p(0, T_0)\Bigg[\sum_{k=1}^{n} D_{0,k} e^{-A_{0,k}} \int_{\bar{M}} \exp(-\tilde{B}^1_{0,k}x - \tilde{C}^{22}_{0,k}y^2) \\ &\quad \cdot \Bigg(\frac{e^{\left(\frac{1}{2}(\theta_k)^2 \bar{\beta}^3_{T_0} - \bar{\alpha}^3_{T_0}\theta_k\right)}}{\sqrt{1 + 2\bar{\beta}^3_{T_0}\tilde{C}^{33}_{0,k}}} \left(\Phi(d^3_k(x, y)) - \Phi(d^1_k(x, y))\right) \\ &\quad - e^{-\tilde{C}^{33}_{0,k}(\bar{z}^1)^2} \left(\Phi(d^4_k(x, y)) - \Phi(d^2_k(x, y))\right)\Bigg) f_2(y) f_1(x) dy dx\Bigg], \end{aligned} \tag{100}$$

where we have made use of (96) and (97), (98).

**(ii)** For $(x, y) \in \bar{M}^c$ we can conclude exactly as we did it for Case (1) and, by adding the two expressions in (i) and (ii), we obtain the statement also for Case (2).

**Acknowledgements** The KPMG Center of Excellence in Risk Management is acknowledged for organizing the conference "Challenges in Derivatives Markets - Fixed Income Modeling, Valuation Adjustments, Risk Management, and Regulation".

**Open Access** This chapter is distributed under the terms of the Creative Commons Attribution 4.0 International License (http://creativecommons.org/licenses/by/4.0/), which permits use, duplication, adaptation, distribution and reproduction in any medium or format, as long as you give appropriate credit to the original author(s) and the source, a link is provided to the Creative Commons license and any changes made are indicated.

The images or other third party material in this chapter are included in the work's Creative Commons license, unless indicated otherwise in the credit line; if such material is not included in the work's Creative Commons license and the respective action is not permitted by statutory regulation, users will need to obtain permission from the license holder to duplicate, adapt or reproduce the material.

## References

1. Bormetti, G., Brigo, D., Francischello, M., Pallavicini, A.: Impact of multiple curve dynamics in credit valuation adjustments under collateralization. Preprint, arXiv:1507.08779 (2015)
2. Brigo, D., Mercurio, F.: Interest Rate Models – Theory and Practice, 2nd edn. Springer, Berlin (2006)

3. Brigo, D., Pallavicini, A., Perini, D.: Funding, collateral and hedging: uncovering the mechanics and the subtleties of funding valuation adjustments. Preprint, arXiv:1210.3811, 2012
4. Brigo, D., Morini, M., Pallavicini, A.: Counterparty Credit Risk, Collateral and Funding: With Pricing Cases for All Asset Classes. Wiley, New Jersey (2013)
5. Chen, L., Filipović, D., Poor, H.V.: Quadratic term structure models for risk-free and defaultable rates. Math. Financ. **14**, 515–536 (2004)
6. Crépey, S.: Bilateral counterparty risk under funding constraints - Part II: CVA. Math. Financ. **25**(1), 23–50 (2015)
7. Crépey, S., Douady, R.: LOIS: credit and liquidity. Risk Mag. pp. 82–86 (2013)
8. Crépey, S., Grbac, Z., Nguyen, H.N.: A multiple-curve HJM model of interbank risk. Math. Financ. Econ. **6**(3), 155–190 (2012)
9. Crépey, S., Bielecki, T.R., Brigo, D.: Counterparty Risk and Funding–A Tale of Two Puzzles. Financial Mathematics Series. Chapman & Hall/CRC, Boca Raton (2014)
10. Duffee, G.: Estimating the price of default risk. Rev. Financ. Stud. **12**, 197–226 (1999)
11. Duffie, D., Gârleanu, N.: Risk and valuation of collateralized debt obligations. Financ. Anal. J. **57**, 41–59 (2001)
12. El Karoui, N., Myneni, R., Viswanathan, R.: Arbitrage pricing and hedging of interest rate claims with state variables, theory and applications. Working Paper (1992)
13. Filipović, D.: Separable term structures and the maximal degree problem. Math. Financ. **12**, 341–349 (2002)
14. Filipović, D., Trolle, A.B.: The term structure of interbank risk. J. Financ. Econ. **109**(3), 707–733 (2013)
15. Gallitschke, J., Müller, S., Seifried, F.T.: Post-crisis interest rates: XIBOR mechanics and basis spreads. Preprint, SSRN/2448657 (2014)
16. Gaspar, R.M.: General quadratic term structures for bond, futures and forward prices. SSE/EFI Working paper Series in Economics and Finance, p. 559 (2004)
17. Gombani, A., Runggaldier, W.J.: A filtering approach to pricing in multifactor term structure models. Int. J. Theor. Appl. Financ. **4**, 303–320 (2001)
18. Grbac, Z., Runggaldier, W.J.: Interest Rate Modeling: Post-Crisis Challenges and Approaches. Springer Briefs in Quantitative Finance. Springer International Publishing (2015)
19. Jamshidian, F.: An exact bond option pricing formula. J. Financ. **44**, 205–209 (1989)
20. Kenyon, C.: Short-rate pricing after the liquidity and credit shocks: including the basis. Risk Mag. pp. 83–87 (2010)
21. Kijima, M., Muromachi, Y.: Reformulation of the arbitrage-free pricing method under the multi-curve environment. Preprint (2015)
22. Kijima, M., Tanaka, K., Wong, T.: A multi-quality model of interest rates. Quant. Financ. **9**(2), 133–145 (2009)
23. Lamberton, D., Lapeyre, B.: Introduction to Stochastic Calculus Applied to Finance. Chapman and Hall/CRC, Boca Raton (2007)
24. Leippold, M., Wu, L.: Asset pricing under the quadratic class. J. Financ. Quant. Anal. **37**(2), 271–291 (2002)
25. Meneghello, L.: Interest rate derivatives pricing in multicurve factor models. Master Thesis, University of Padova (2014)
26. Mercurio, F.: LIBOR market models with stochastic basis. Preprint, SSRN/1563685 (2010)
27. Morino, L., Runggaldier, W.J.: On multicurve models for the term structure. In: Dieci, R., He, X.Z., Hommes, C. (eds.) Nonlinear Economic Dynamics and Financial Modelling, pp. 275–290. Springer, Berlin (2014)
28. Pallavicini, A., Brigo, D.: Interest-rate modelling in collateralized markets: multiple curves, credit-liquidity effects, CCPs. Preprint, arXiv:1304.1397 (2013)
29. Pelsser, A.: A tractable yield-curve model that guarantees positive interest rates. Rev. Deriv. Res. **1**, 269–284 (1997)

# Multi-curve Construction

## Definition, Calibration, Implementation and Application of Rate Curves

**Christian P. Fries**

**Abstract** In this chapter we discuss the definition, construction, interpolation and application of *curves*. We will discuss discount curves, a tool for the valuation of deterministic cash-flows and forward curves, a tool for the valuation of linear cash-flows of an index. A curve is mainly a tool to interpolate certain basic financial products (zero coupon bonds, FRAs) with respect to maturity date and fixing date, such that it can be used to value products, which can be represented as linear functions of possibly interpolated values of a discount or forward curve. For this, the chosen interpolation method and interpolation entity plays an important role. Distinguishing forward curves from discount curves (representing the collateralization of the forward) motivates an alternative interpolation method, namely interpolation of the forward value (the product of the forward and the discount factor). In addition, treating forward curves as native curves (instead of representing them by pseudo-discount curves) will avoid other problems, like that of overlapping instruments. Besides the interpolation, we discuss the calibration of the curves for which we give a generic object-oriented implementation in Fries (Curve calibration. Object-oriented reference implementation, 2010–2015, [11]). We give some numerical results, which have been obtained using this implementation and conclude with a remark on how to define term-structure models (analog to a LIBOR market model) based on the definition of the performance index of an accrual account associated with a discount curve.

**Keywords** Multi-curve construction · Interest rate curves · Interest rate curve interpolation · Cross-currency curves · Term structure models

---

C.P. Fries (✉)
DZ BANK AG, Frankfurt, Germany
e-mail: email@christian-fries.de

C.P. Fries
Department of Mathematics, LMU Munich, Munich, Germany

© The Author(s) 2016

K. Glau et al. (eds.), *Innovations in Derivatives Markets*, Springer Proceedings in Mathematics & Statistics 165, DOI 10.1007/978-3-319-33446-2_11

## 1 Introduction

Dynamic multi-curve term structure models, as the one discussed in this book, often use given interest rate curves as initial data. The classical (single curve) example is the HJM oder LMM model, where

$$\mathrm{d}f(t,T) = \mu(t,T)\mathrm{d}t + \Sigma(t,T)\mathrm{d}W(t), \qquad f(t_0,T) = f_0(T).$$

While research on multi-curve interest rates models was and is very active, see, e.g., [5, 6, 15, 20–22], references therein and the other chapters of in this book, the construction of the initial interest rate curve, here $f_0(T)$, naturally does not get a similar strong attention. However, a good curve construction is of high importance for practitioners, since it has a strong impact on the delta-hedge (that is, the first-order interest rate risk).

The market standard of (forward) curve construction is to calibrate an interpolated curve to given market instruments, often via an iterative procedure (bootstrapping). With respect to the interpolation of (interest rate) forward curves, a common approach is to represent a forward curve in terms of (pseudo-)discount factors (aka. synthetic discount factors) and apply an interpolation scheme on these discount factors. While this approach is in general not backed by an economic concept, it also introduces several (self-made) problems, e.g., the interpolation of (so-called) overlapping instruments, see Sect. 5.3.

In this paper we focus on the curve construction, provide an open source implementation and suggest appealing alternative interpolation schemes motivated from the multi-curve setup: direct interpolation of the forward curve or direct interpolation of the forward value curve, where the forward value is the product of a forward and the associated discount factor. While linear interpolation of the forward is a common scheme,[1] the interpolation of the forward value appears to be a new approach.

Nevertheless, the paper puts both methods on a solid foundation by deriving the schemes from the multi-curve definition of forward curves. Both interpolation schemes ease some of the complications associated with synthetic discount factors.

Once the curves and interpolations are defined, we are considering the problem of calibrating a set of curves to given market quotes. The value of an instrument is in general determined by a whole collection of curves, e.g., one or two discount curves and zero or more forward curves. To simplify the implementation, we define a generalized swap, which allows to represent most calibration instruments (FRAs, swaps, tenor basis swaps, cross-currency swaps, etc.) by a single class.

[1] Some trading systems, like Murex, do offer it as an option.

## 2 Foundations, Assumptions, Notation

Under well-known assumptions the valuation of a future cash flow can be written as an expectation,[2] that is the time $t_0$-value $V(t_0)$ is

$$V(t_0) \;=\; N(t_0) \cdot \mathrm{E}^{\mathbb{Q}^N}\left(\frac{V(T)}{N(T)} \mid \mathscr{F}_{t_0}\right) \quad \text{for } t_0 \leq T, \tag{1}$$

where $V(T)$ is the time $T$ cash-flow, $N$ is the value process of a traded asset (or collateral account) which can serve as a *numéraire* and $\mathbb{Q}^N$ is the equivalent martingale measure associated with $N$. Equation (1) is the starting point for *curve construction* in the following sense: If the above valuation formula holds, then the value of a linear function of future cash-flows is the linear function of the values of the single cash flows. In other words: we can represent the valuation of so-called linear products by a *basis* consisting of the values of elementary products. This basis of elementary products is the set of curves, where "the curve" is formed by the parameter $T$.

Note that here and in the following, we consider the valuation for a fixed $t_0$. We are not concerned with the description of a dynamic model (describing $t \mapsto V(t)$ as a stochastic process).

**Definition 1** Let $I$ denote an index, that is, $I(T)$ is an $\mathscr{F}_T$-measurable random variable and $d > 0$ is some payment offset, then we define the (time $t_0$-)valuation curve with respect to $T$ as the map

$$T \mapsto C(T) \;:=\; N(t_0) \cdot \mathrm{E}^{\mathbb{Q}^N}\left(\frac{I(T)}{N(T+d)} \mid \mathscr{F}_{t_0}\right). \tag{2}$$

For $I \equiv 1$ and $d = 0$ the curve in (2) represents the curve of (synthetical) zero-coupon bond prices $T \mapsto P(T; t_0)$, also known as *discount curve*.[3] For arbitrary indices $I$ (with fixed payment offset $d$[4]), the curve $T \mapsto C(T)/P(T; t_0)$ is known as the *forward curve*. Obviously both curves depend on $N$ and $t_0$.

Note that the specific stochastic behavior of $I$ and $N$ does not play a role when looking at $t_0$ only in the sense that we are only interested in the time $t_0$-expectation. That is, we could define $t \mapsto N(t)$ and $t \mapsto I(t)$ to be $\mathscr{F}_{t_0}$-measurable for all times $t$ and still generate any given discount curve and forward curve, respectively. There

---

[2]Since we are only considering the linearity of the valuation at a fixed time $t_0$, we just require that some fundamental theorem of asset pricing holds, for example, assuming that the price processes are locally bounded semi-martingales and the *no free lunch with vanishing risk* condition holds, [7].

[3]We will use the notation $P(T; t)$ (instead of the more common $P(t, T)$) for a the time-$t$ value of zero-coupon bond maturing in $T$, since we consider $t = t_0$ as fixed. Sometimes we even drop the argument and just write $P(T)$. Similar for forward curves. The curves considered here are parametrized by $T$ for a fixed time $t$.

[4]In practice the payment offset may depend on $t_0$ and $T$ due to business day adjustments. Our implementation handles this, but to ease notation we drop the dependence here.

is no arbitrage constraint with respect to $t$ yet, since for different $t$ the index $I(t)$ represents different assets (underlyings).

Thus, with respect to the processes $1/N$ and $I/N$ we just require that they fulfill regularity assumptions such that (2) exists.[5]

On the other hand, the interpretation of the curve as a curve of valuations in the sense of (2) does play a role, when we consider the construction of the curve via interpolation of observed market prices. Here, the linearity of the expectation operator E allows to link market prices to different points of the curve.

Curves, like discount curves and forward curves solve, among others, two important problems:

- Valuation of linear instruments. This is performed by decomposing instruments into the value of single cash flows (zero coupon bonds and FRAs), which then allows to synthesize the valuation of linear functions of the individual cash flows (e.g., swaps).
- Valuation of a time $T$ cash-flow as interpolation of valuations of cash flows at discrete times $\{T_i\}_{i=0}^{n}$ (where $T_i \geq t_0$ for all $i$), e.g., swaps referencing cash flows on illiquid maturities.

Thus, curves are simply a methodology to interpolate on the cash flows with respect to their payment time.[6] Apart from this, the curves also represent the initial data for advanced term structure models (like the LIBOR market model). Hence, careful construction of curves is also key to (interest rate) derivatives valuation, when interpolated curves are the initial values of a dynamic model.

For details on the evolution of multi-curve construction see the recent book by Henrard, [18] (citing a preprint of the present paper). A very detailed description of multi-curve bootstrapping, which also details market conventions and convexity adjustments of the calibration instruments, can be found in [2]. For market conventions also see [17]. Here, we do not consider a possible convexity adjustment due to different market conventions (they should be part of the valuation formulas) and rather focus on the curves and their interpolation schemes. Also, we do not need to consider a bootstrapping, since we set up the calibration as a system of equations passed to a multi-dimensional optimization algorithm.

Usually (and here), the curves are used to interpolate at the fixed time $t_0$ only. If a curve interpolation should also be used for times $t > t_0$ within a dynamic multi-curve model, then this may impose additional constraints on the admissible interpolations schemes. For example, (2) implies that linear interpolation of time-$t$ zero-coupon bond prices for $t > t_0$ implies linear interpolation of the time-$t$ zero-coupon bond prices, which in turn implies a special interpolation of forward rates in a LIBOR market model, see Sect. 19.5 in [10]. In this case the linear interpolation of the discount curve and forward value curve would not introduce an arbitrage violation, given that

[5]For example, let $1/N$ and $I/N$ be Itô stochastic processes with integrable drift and bounded quadratic variation.

[6]This also applies to forward curve, see below, although in these cases there is also an associated fixing time of an index and it is maybe more consistent to parametrize the curve w.r.t. the fixing of the index.

the interpolation points are the same for all times. In practice term-structure models are often constructed with their own curve interpolations, such that the interpolation used for the initial data differs from the interpolation used for the simulated curves (while the model is still calibrated and arbitrage-free given that the drift is specified accordingly). In the following we focus on the interpolation of the initial data—that is, the time-$t_0$ curves, which is of greater importance for the deltas of interpolated products, where only the linear part matters.

In the above valuation formula (1) it is assumed that $V$ and $N$ are expressed in the same currency. If the two are in different currency, one of them has to be converted by an exchange rate, which we will denote by $FX$. Let $V$ be in currency $U_2$ and the numéraire $N$ in currency $U_1$, then the valuation formula is given by

$$V(t_0) = FX^{\frac{U_2}{U_1}}(t_0) \cdot N(t_0) \cdot \mathrm{E}^{\mathbb{Q}^N}\left( \frac{V(T)}{FX^{\frac{U_2}{U_1}}(T) \cdot N(T)} \mid \mathcal{F}_{t_0} \right),$$

where $FX^{\frac{U_2}{U_1}}(t)$ denotes the time $t$ exchange rate for one unit of currency $U_1$ into one unit of currency $U_2$. Furthermore, $FX^{\frac{U_1}{U_2}} = \left(FX^{\frac{U_2}{U_1}}\right)^{-1}$.

As discussed in [12], the valuation of a collateralized claim can be written as an expectation with respect to a specific numéraire, namely the collateral account $N = N^{\mathsf{C}}$.[7] We denote the currency of the collateral numéraire by $[\mathsf{C}]$. Let $U$ denote the currency of the cash flow $V(T)$. Assume that the cash flow $V(T)$ is collateralized by units of $N^{\mathsf{C}}$. In this case the Eq. (1) holds with the numéraire $N = N^{\mathsf{C}}$, $U_2 = U$, $U_1 = [C]$ (given that $V(t)$ is the collateral amount in the account $N^{\mathsf{C}}$).

*Remark 1* From the above we see that collateralization in a different currency can be interpreted twofold:

1. We may consider a payment converted to collateral currency and valued with respect to the collateral numéraire $N^{\mathsf{C}}$, or, alternatively,
2. we may consider a payment in the currency $U$ collateralized with respect to the collateral account $N^{U,\mathsf{C}} := FX^{\frac{U}{[\mathsf{C}]}} \cdot N^{\mathsf{C}}$.

We will adopt the latter interpretation, which will also make the valuation look more consistent[8]

$$V(t_0) = N^{U,\mathsf{C}}(t_0) \cdot \mathrm{E}^{\mathbb{Q}^{U,N^{\mathsf{C}}}}\left( \frac{V(T)}{N^{U,\mathsf{C}}(T)} \mid \mathcal{F}_{t_0} \right). \tag{3}$$

Note that this interpretation will then give rise to a new discount curve: the discount curve associated with $N^{U,\mathsf{C}}$, being the discount curve of a foreign currency ($U$) cash flow collateralized by a $C$.

---

[7] See also [8, 14].

[8] As has been noted in [12], the measures agree, i.e., $\mathbb{Q}^{U,N^{\mathsf{C}}} = \mathbb{Q}^{N^{\mathsf{C}}}$.

*Remark 2* For an uncollateralized product the role of the collateral account is taken by the funding account and the corresponding numéraire is the funding account. Since the valuation formulas are identical to the case of a "special" collateral account (agreeing with the funding account), we will consider an uncollateralized product as a product with a different collateralization.

In the following we use the notation $U$ for the currency unit of a cash flow, i.e., we may consider $U = 1€$ or $U = 1\$$. We will need this notation only when we consider cross-currency basis swaps. The symbols $V$ and $N$ (as well as $P$ defined below) will denote value processes including the corresponding currency unit, e.g., $V(t_0) = 0.25€$. The symbol $V$ refers to the value of the product under consideration, while $N$ denotes the numéraire, e.g., the OIS accrued collateral account. The symbol $X$ denotes a real number while $I$ denotes a real valued stochastic process, both can be considered as rates, i.e., unit-less indices, e.g., $X = 2.5\,\%$. For example $X$ will denote the fix rate in a swap, $I$ will denote the floating rate index in a swap, $U$ denotes the currency unit of the two legs, $N$ will be used to define the discount factor and the value of the swap. The value of the swap is then denoted by $V$.

## 3 Discount Curves

Consider a fixed constant cash flow $X$, paid in currency $U$ in time $T$, collateralized by an account $\mathsf{C}$. Since $X$ is a constant and the expectation operator is linear, we can express the time-$t_0$ value $V(t_0)$ of this cash flow as

$$V(t_0) \;=\; X \cdot P^{U,\mathsf{C}}(T;\, t_0), \tag{4}$$

where

$$P^{U,\mathsf{C}}(T;\, t_0) \;:=\; N^{U,\mathsf{C}}(t_0) \cdot \mathrm{E}^{\mathbb{Q}^{N^{U,\mathsf{C}}}}\left(\frac{1 \cdot U}{N^{U,\mathsf{C}}(T)} \mid \mathscr{F}_{t_0}\right) \tag{5}$$

defines the value of a theoretical zero coupon bond. Note that Eq. (4) can be used in two ways. First, for given market prices we may determine $P^{U,\mathsf{C}}(T;\, t_0)$—that is we calibrate the curve $T \mapsto P^{U,\mathsf{C}}(T;\, t_0)$. Second, for given $P^{U,\mathsf{C}}(T;\, t_0)$ we may value a constant cash flow.

This defines the discount curve:

**Definition 2** Let $P^{U,\mathsf{C}}(T;\, t_0)$ denote the time $t_0$ value expressed in currency unit $U$ of a unit cash-flow of 1 unit of the currency $U$ in $T$, collateralized by a collateral account $\mathsf{C}$. In this case we call $T \mapsto P^{U,\mathsf{C}}(T;\, t_0)$ given by (5) the *discount curve* for cash flows in currency $U$ collateralized by the account $C$.

*Remark 3* By assumption (of a frictionless no-arbitrage market, (1)) the value of a fixed constant future cash-flow $X$ is a linear function of its amount. Hence, we have that the time $t_0$ value of a cash flow $X$ in $T$ and currency $U$, collateralized with an account $C$ is

$$X \cdot P^{U,\mathsf{C}}(T; t_0).$$

In other words, the discount curve allows us to valuate all fixed (deterministic) cash flows in a given currency, collateralized by a given account.

The discount factor $P^{U,\mathsf{C}}(T; t_0)$ represents the price of an (idealized) zero-coupon bond. Although a zero-coupon bond is usually not a market-traded asset, we may represent market-traded coupon bonds as a linear combination of zero-coupon bonds, and vice versa. If $\mathsf{C}$ denotes some cash-collateral account, there is no such thing as a collateralized bond, but in that case $P^{U,\mathsf{C}}(T; t_0)$ has the natural interpretation of representing the time-$t$ value of a collateralized unit currency time-$T$ cash flow. In any case, $P^{U,\mathsf{C}}(T; t_0)$ can be considered a linear function of traded asset (within its collateralization scheme).

## 4 Forward Curves

The same approach can now be applied to a payoff of a cash flow $X \cdot I(T_1)$, paid in currency $U$ in time $T_2$ ($T_1 \leq T_2$), collateralized by account $\mathsf{C}$, where $X$ is a constant and $I$ is an adapted process representing index.[9] Its value is

$$V(t_0) = N^{U,\mathsf{C}}(t_0) \cdot \mathrm{E}^{\mathbb{Q}^{N^{U,\mathsf{C}}}} \left( \frac{X \cdot I(T_1) \cdot U}{N^{U,\mathsf{C}}(T_2)} \mid \mathcal{F}_{t_0} \right).$$

We can express the value as $V(t_0) = X \cdot F_I^{U,\mathsf{C}}(T_1, T_2; t_0) \cdot P^{U,\mathsf{C}}(T_2; t_0)$, where

$$F_I^{U,\mathsf{C}}(T_1, T_2; t_0) = N^{U,\mathsf{C}}(t_0) \cdot \mathrm{E}^{\mathbb{Q}^{N^{U,\mathsf{C}}}} \left( \frac{I(T_1) \cdot U}{N^{U,\mathsf{C}}(T_2)} \mid \mathcal{F}_{t_0} \right) / P^{U,\mathsf{C}}(T_2; t_0). \quad (6)$$

This definition allows us to derive $F_I^{U,\mathsf{C}}(T_1, T_2; t_0)$ from given market prices. Conversely, given $P^{U,\mathsf{C}}(T_2; t_0)$ and $F_I^{U,\mathsf{C}}(T_1, T_2; t_0)$ we may value all linear payoff functions of $I(T_1)$ paid in $T_2$.

In (6) the forward depends on the fixing time $T_1$ and the payment time $T_2$. However, the offset of the payment time from the fixing time $d = T_2 - T_1$ can be viewed as a property of the index (a constant) and hence, the forward represents a curve $T \mapsto F_I^{U,\mathsf{C}}(T, T + d; t_0)$.

**Definition 3** Let $t \mapsto I(t)$ denote an index, that is $I$ is an adapted stochastic real valued process. Let

$$V_I^{U,\mathsf{C}}(T, T + d; t_0) := N^{U,\mathsf{C}}(t_0) \cdot \mathrm{E}^{\mathbb{Q}^{N^{U,\mathsf{C}}}} \left( \frac{I(T) \cdot U}{N^{U,\mathsf{C}}(T + d)} \mid \mathcal{F}_{t_0} \right)$$

[9] Examples for $I$ are LIBOR rates or the performance of an EONIA accrual account.

denote the time $t_0$-value of a payment of $I(T)$ paid in $T+d$ in currency $U$, collateralized by an account $\mathsf{C}$ (where $d \geq 0$). We assume that $I$ and $N$ is such that the expectation exists for all $T$. Then we define the *forward of a payment of $I(T)$ paid in $T+d$ in currency $U$, collateralized by an account $C$* as

$$F_I^{U,\mathsf{C}}(T;t_0) \;:=\; \frac{V_I^{U,\mathsf{C}}(T,T+d;t_0)}{P^{U,\mathsf{C}}(T+d;t_0)}.$$

*Remark 4* The forward curve allows us to value a future payment of the index $I$ by

$$V_I^{U,\mathsf{C}}(T,T+d;t_0) \;=\; F_I^{U,\mathsf{C}}(T;t_0)\cdot P^{U,\mathsf{C}}(T+d;t_0)$$

and by assumption (of a frictionless no-arbitrage market, (1)), the forward curve allows us to evaluate all linear cash flows $X \cdot I$ (in currency $U$, collateralized by an account $\mathsf{C}$) by $X \cdot F_I^{U,\mathsf{C}}(T;t_0)\cdot P^{U,\mathsf{C}}(T+d;t_0)$.

Note that $F_I^{U,\mathsf{C}}$ is not a classical single curve forward rate, related to some discount curve. Due to our definition of the forward curve, the curve includes all valuation effects related to the index, in particular a possible convexity adjustment. For example: if we would consider an in-arrears index and an in-advance index we would obtain two different forward curves which differ by the in-arrears convexity adjustment!

## 4.1 Performance Index of a Discount Curve (or "Self-Discounting")

The OIS swap pays the performance of an account, accruing with the overnight rate, that is:

**Definition 4** (*Overnight Index Swap*) Let $N^{\mathsf{C}}(t)$ denote the account accruing at the overnight rate $r(t)$, $N^{\mathsf{C}}(t_0) = 1U$, i.e. on a given time discretization (accrual periods) $\{t_i\}_{i=0}^n$

$$N^{\mathsf{C}}(t_k) \;:=\; \prod_{i=0}^{k}(1+r(t_i)\Delta t_i) \;\approx\; \exp\left(\int_{t_0}^{t_k} r(s)\mathrm{d}s\right).$$

The overnight index swap pays a fix coupon and receives the performance $I_i^{\mathsf{C}}$ of the accrual account, that is

$$I_i^{\mathsf{C}}(T_i,T_{i+1}) \;:=\; \frac{N^{\mathsf{C}}(T_{i+1})}{N^{\mathsf{C}}(T_i)} - 1.$$

in $T_{i+1}$ with a quarterly tenor $T_0, T_1, \ldots$.

The time-$t_0$ linear forward of the index above is $\frac{P^{U,\mathsf{C}}(T_i;t_0)-P^{U,\mathsf{C}}(T_{i+1};t_0)}{P^{U,\mathsf{C}}(T_{i+1};t_0)}$ (and dividing by $T_{i+1} - T_i$ this gives the linear forward rate). Hence, this is the same situation as for single curve interest rate theory swaps.

The OIS swap is collateralized with respect to the account $N^{\mathsf{C}}$. Due to this, it is sometimes called "self-discounted". However, we may give an appealing alternative view, defining the forward curve from the discount curve (and not the other way around):

Let us consider a discount factor curve $P^{U,\mathsf{C}}(T;t)$ as seen in time $t$. The curve allows the definition of a special index, namely the performance rate of the collateral account $\mathsf{C}$ in currency $U$ over a period of period length $d$:
Let $I^{\mathsf{C}}(T_i) := \frac{1-P^{U,\mathsf{C}}(T_i+d;T_i)}{P^{U,\mathsf{C}}(T_i+d;T_i)}$, where $P^{U,\mathsf{C}}(T_i+d;T_i)$ is the discount factor for the maturity $T_i+d$ as seen in time $T_i$. The index $I^{\mathsf{C}}(T_i)$ is the payment we have to receive in $T_i+d$ collateralized with respect to the collateral account $\mathsf{C}$, such that $1+I^{\mathsf{C}}(T_i)$ in $T_{i+1}$ has the same value as 1 in $T_i$. This index has a special property, namely that its forward can be expressed in terms of the discount factor curve $P^{U,\mathsf{C}}$ too: The time $t_0$ forward of $I^{\mathsf{C}}(T_i)$ is $F^{U,\mathsf{C}}(T_i;t_0)$ where

$$\begin{aligned} F^{U,\mathsf{C}}(T_i;t_0) \cdot P^{U,\mathsf{C}}(T_i+d;t_0) &= N^{U,\mathsf{C}}(t_0) \cdot \mathrm{E}^{\mathbb{Q}^{N^{U,\mathsf{C}}}}\left( \frac{I^{\mathsf{C}}(T_i) \cdot U}{N^{U,\mathsf{C}}(T_i+d)} \mid \mathscr{F}_{t_0} \right) \\ &= P^{U,\mathsf{C}}(T_i;t_0) - P^{U,\mathsf{C}}(T_i+d;t_0). \end{aligned}$$

Consequently this index has the special property that its forward can be expressed by the associated discount factors evaluated at different maturities.

**Definition 5** (*Forward associated with a Discount Curve*) Let $P^{U,\mathsf{C}}(T_i+d;t_0)$ denote a discount curve. For a given period length $d$ we define the forward $F^{d,U,\mathsf{C}}(T_i;t_0)$ as

$$F^{d,U,\mathsf{C}}(T_i;t_0) := \frac{P^{U,\mathsf{C}}(T_i;t_0) - P^{U,\mathsf{C}}(T_i+d;t_0)}{P^{U,\mathsf{C}}(T_i+d;t_0) \cdot d}. \tag{7}$$

$F^{d,U,\mathsf{C}}(T_i;t_0)$ is the forward associated with the performance index of $P^{U,\mathsf{C}}$ over a period of length $d$.

*Remark 5* The above definition relates a forward curve and discount factor curve. Note however, that we define a forward from a discount factor curve and that this definition is backed by a clear interpretation of the underlying index. Conversely, we may define a discount curve from a forward curve "implicitly" such that the relation (7) holds. Note however, that a generalization of this relation should be considered with care, since the associated product may not exist.

The definition above is an idealization in the sense that we assume that interval points over which the performance is measured correspond to the payment dates. In practice (EONIA is an example) there might be some small deviations from this assumption (e.g. payment offsets of a few days). In this case (7) does not hold (but may be still considered an approximation).

Products like the OIS swaps are sometimes called "self-discounting" since the discounting is performed on a curve corresponding to the index they fix. From the above, we find an alternative (and maybe more natural) interpretation, namely that the swap pays the performance index of its collateral account, i.e., it pays the index associated with the discount curve.

## 5 Interpolation of Curves

In this section we consider a discount curve $P^{U,\mathrm{C}}$ and an associated forward curve $F^{U,\mathrm{C}}$. To simplify notation we set $D(T) := P^{U,\mathrm{C}}(T; t_0)$ and $F(T) := F^{U,\mathrm{C}}(T; t_0)$.

Forwards and discount factors are linked together by Definition 3, which says that the time-$t_0$ value of a forward contract $V(t_0, T)$ with fixing in $T$ is the product of the forward $F(T)$ and the associated discount factor $D(T + d)$, i.e., $V(t_0, T) = F(T) \cdot D(T + d)$. Note that $T \mapsto V(t_0, T)$ and $T \mapsto D(T)$ are *value curves*, i.e., for a fixed $T$ the quantities $V(t_0, T)$ and $D(T)$ are values of financial products. However, $F(T)$ is a derived quantity, the forward.

Since $V$ and $D$ represent values of financial products, there is a natural interpretation for a linear interpolation of different values $V(T_i)$ and of different values of $D(T_i)$, since this would correspond to a portfolio of such products. Note that defining an interpolation method for $V$ and $D$ implies a (possible more complex) interpolation method of $F$.

On the other hand, it is common practice to define an interpolation method for a rate curve (both forward curve and discount factor curve) via zero rates, sometimes even regardless of the nature of the curve, which then implies the interpolation of the value curves $D$ and $V$. Some of these interpolations will result in natural interpolations on the value process $V$, others not. Other examples for interpolations of $F$ and $D$ are:

- log-linear interpolation of the forward, log-linear interpolation of the discount factor: the case is equivalent to log-linear interpolation of the value.
- linear interpolation of the forward, log-linear interpolation of the discount factor: the case is equivalent with a linear interpolation of the value, with an interpolation weight being a function of the discount factor ratio.

In [16] interpolations on the discount factors, on the logarithm of discount factors, on the yield and directly on the forwards were discussed. Highlighting some disadvantages of cubic splines, they introduced two new interpolation methods (monotone convex spline and minimal cubic spline) which overcome most of the shortfalls of the other interpolations. In [19] some issues of these methods were pointed out, favoring a harmonic spline interpolation. In [1] a modified Bessel spline on the logarithm of the discount factors was proposed.

Based on the formal setup presented in the present paper, the stability of cumulated error of a dynamic hedge was considered as a criterion for the interpolation methods and compared for a large collection of methods in [13].

At this point, we would like to stress the importance of the *interpolation entity*, that is, whether we interpolate on a forward or on a synthetic discount factor (in the sense of Definition 5). While the interpolation method (e.g., *linear* compared to *spline*) is often in the focus (discussing locality versus smoothness, [16]), the choice of the interpolation entity has a strong impact on the delta hedge, see Table 1.

Depending on the application, it is popular to represent a curve by a parametric curve. This is done especially for discount curves. Examples are the Nelson–Siegel (NS) and the Nelson–Siegel–Svensson (NSS) parametrization. Our benchmark implementation in [11] allows to use NS or NSS in the calibration.[10]

## 5.1 Implementing the Interpolation of a Curve: Interpolation Method and Interpolation Entities

In this paper we focus on interpolation schemes based on given interpolation points. Implementing the interpolation of a curve that way, it is convenient to distinguish the *interpolation method*, e.g., linear interpolation of interpolation points $\{(T_i, x_i)\}$, and the *interpolation entity*, that is, a (bijective) transformation from $(T, x)$ to the actual curve. For example, for discount curves one might consider a linear interpolation of the zero rate. In this case the interpolation method is *linear interpolation* and the interpolation entity is $(T, x(T)) = (T, \frac{\log(D(T))}{T})$ for $T > 0$, where $D$ denotes the discount curve. Given $0 < T_i \leq T \leq T_{i+1}$ and discount factors $D(T_j)$, a linear interpolation of the zero rates would then imply the interpolation

$$D(T) := \exp\left(\left(\frac{T - T_i}{T_{i+1} - T_i}\frac{\log(D(T_{i+1}))}{T_{i+1}} + \frac{T_{i+1} - T}{T_{i+1} - T_i}\frac{\log(D(T_i))}{T_i}\right) \cdot T\right).$$

In our benchmark implementation [11], this functionality is provided for a large number of interpolation methods (constant, linear, Akima, spline, etc.) and interpolation entities (value, log-value, log-value-per-time) by the class `net.finmath.marketdata.model.curves.Curve`.[11] For forward curves we provide two additional interpolation entities: forward and synthetic discount factor (see below).

## 5.2 Interpolation Time

For both, parametric curves (like NSS) and non-parametric interpolation schemes, it is important to specify the convention used to transform product maturities (dates) to real numbers (time $T$). For example, we might use a daycount convention (like

[10] See http://finmath.net/finmath-lib/apidocs/net/finmath/marketdata/model/curves/DiscountCurveNelsonSiegelSvensson.html.

[11] See http://finmath.net/finmath-lib/apidocs/net/finmath/marketdata/model/curves/Curve.html.

ACT/365) and measure $T$ as a daycount fraction between evaluation date and maturity date, that is $T := \text{dcf}(\text{evaluation date, maturity date})$. Clearly, a change in the time parametrization will change the interpretation of the curve parameters (for a parametric curve). Also, some daycount convention actually introduces non-linear time transformations.

## 5.3 Interpolation of Forward Curves

### 5.3.1 The Classical Approach

For forward curves, a common approach is to consider an interpolation of the forward as an independent entity (like for the discount curve). For interest rate forwards, a popular interpolation scheme (coming from the single curve interpretation of interest rates forwards) is to represent the forward in terms of synthetic discount factors. That is, if $d$ denotes a period length associated with the forward and if $F(T_i)$ is given for $T_i = i \cdot d$, then one might consider interpolation of (pseudo-)discount factor $D^F(T_i) := \prod_{k=0}^{i-1}(1 + F(T_k) \cdot d)^{-1}$, possibly considering another transformation on $D^F(T)$ to define the actual interpolation entity. See [3] for a corresponding multi-curves bootstrap algorithm.

It is obvious that this definition of the interpolation entity for forward curve is complex, results in problems for non-equidistant interpolation points and is—without further assumptions—not backed by a meaningful interpretation. First, in a multi-curve setup this approach lacks an economic justification. Second, it may introduce problems:

- The common approach of a linear interpolation of the logarithm of the synthetic discount factor representing the forward curve results in an almost piecewise constant interpolation of the forward, see [13]. This may result into "jumps" when products are aging.
- The use of synthetic discount factors defines a forward with fixing time $T$ in terms of (interpolated) discount factors at times $T$ and $T + d$ (where $d$ is the period length). The method is a common practice (also considered in [1]). However, considering forwards for overlapping periods, this may introduce oscillations and result in implausible delta-hedges (see Table 1).

### 5.3.2 Alternative Interpolation Schemes for Forward Curves

The definition of the forward curve in the multi-curve setup suggests an appealing alternative for the creation of an interpolated forward: Like a discount factor curve, the curve $V(T) = F(T) \cdot D(T + d)$ represents the value of a financial product. Hence, we may consider the interpolation of $V$ like we did for the curve $D$. For example, if we consider linear interpolation of the value curve $V$, we interpolate the forward curve $F$ by considering the interpolation entity $F(T) \cdot D(T + d)$ with a given discount curve $D$, i.e., we have

$$F(T) := \frac{1}{D(T+d)} \left( \frac{T - T_i}{T_{i+1} - T_i} F(T_{i+1}) D(T_{i+1} + d) + \frac{T_{i+1} - T}{T_{i+1} - T_i} F(T_i) D(T_i + d) \right)$$

for $T_i \leq T \leq T_{i+1}$ and given points $F(T_j)$.

Given that log-linear interpolation is a popular interpolation scheme for discount curves one may consider log-linear interpolation of $V$. This interpolation scheme has the restriction that the forward is required to be positive. Since negative interest rates are possible, this interpolation scheme is not appropriate for interest rate curves.

### 5.4 *Assessment of the Interpolation Method*

The assessment of the quality of performance of an interpolation method is difficult. Some basic criteria (like continuity, locality, etc.) have been reviewed in [16]. Locality, i.e., how does a local change in input data affect the curve, is a desired property from a hedging perspective. In [13] a long-term dynamic hedging is used to asses the performance of an interpolation scheme. The results in [13] suggest that among the local methods, linear interpolation of the forward curve and log-linear interpolation of the discount curve were the best performing schemes when using the cumulated dynamic hedge error as a primary criterion.

## 6 Implementation of the Calibration of Curves

A curve (discount curve or forward curve) is used to encode values of market instruments. A forward curve together with its associated discount curve, allows to value all linear products (linear payoffs) in the corresponding currency under the corresponding collateralization.

The standard way to calibrate a curve is, hence, to obtain given market values of (linear) instruments (e.g., swaps). For each market value a single "point" in a single curve is calibrated. Hence the total number of calibrated curve interpolation points (aggregated across all curves) equals the number of market instruments.

By "sorting" and combining the calibration instruments, the corresponding equations can be brought into the form of a system of equations with a triangular structure, i.e., the value of the $n$th calibration instrument only depends on the first $n$ curve points. This allows for an iterative construction of the curve.

However, here (and in the associated reference implementation [11]) we propose the calibration of the curves using a multi-variate optimization algorithm, like the Levenberg–Marquardt algorithm or a Differential Evolution algorithm. This approach brings several advantages, e.g., the freedom to specify the calibration instruments and the ability to extend the approach to over-determined systems of equations.

In addition, we can handle the case of curve-interdependence, for example to calibrate certain discount curves from cross-currency swaps. This comes at the cost of slower performance in terms of required calculation time.

What remains is to specify the valuation equations for the calibration instruments. To simplify implementation, we may generalize the definition of a "swap" comprising plain swaps, tenor basis swaps and cross-currency swaps.

## 6.1 Generalized Definition of a Swap

Many of the following calibration instruments (from OIS swaps to cross-currency basis-swaps) fit under a generalized definition of a swap. The swap consists of two legs. Each leg consists of several periods $[T_i, T_{i+1}]$. To ease notation, we do not distinguish between period start time, period end time, fixing time of the index and payment time. We assume that for the period $[T_i, T_{i+1}]$ index fixing is in $T_i$ and payment is in $T_{i+1}$. This is done purely to ease notation, the generalization to distinguished times is straightforward.

**Definition 6** (*Swap Leg*) A swap leg pays a multiple $\alpha$ of the index $I$ fixed in $T_i$ plus some fixed payment $X$, both in currency unit $U$ collateralized by the collateral account $\mathsf{C}$ and paid in time $T_{i+1}$. Here $\alpha$ and $X$ are constants (possibly zero). The value of the swap leg can be expressed in terms of forwards and discount factors as

$$V^{U,\mathsf{C}}_{SwapLeg}(\alpha I, X, \{T_i\}_{i=0}^{n}) = \sum_{i=0}^{n-1} \left(\alpha F^{U,\mathsf{C}}(T_i) + X\right) \cdot P^{U,\mathsf{C}}(T_{i+1}),$$

where $F^{U,\mathsf{C}}$ denotes the forward curve of the index $I$ paid in currency $U$ collateralized with respect to $\mathsf{C}$ and $P^{U,\mathsf{C}}$ denotes the corresponding discount curve.

A swap leg with notional exchange has the payments as in Definition 6 together with an additional payment of $-1$ in $T_i$ and $+1$ in $T_{i+1}$. The value of the swap leg with notional exchange can be expressed in terms of forwards and discount factors as

$$V^{U,\mathsf{C}}_{SwapLeg}(\alpha I, X, \{T_i\}_{i=0}^{n}) = \sum_{i=0}^{n-1} \Big(\left(\alpha F^{U,\mathsf{C}}(T_i) + X\right) \cdot P^{U,\mathsf{C}}(T_{i+1}) \\ + P^{U,\mathsf{C}}(T_{i+1}) - P^{U,\mathsf{C}}(T_i)\Big),$$

where $F^{U,\mathsf{C}}$ denotes the forward curve of the index $I$ paid in currency $U$ collateralized with respect to $\mathsf{C}$ and $P^{U,\mathsf{C}}$ denotes the corresponding discount curve.

**Definition 7** (*Swap*) A swap exchanges the payments of two swap legs, the receiver leg and the payer leg. We allow that the legs have different indices, different fixed payments, different payment times, different currency units, but are collateralized with respect to the same account $\mathsf{C}$. The swaps receive a swap leg with value $V^{U_1,\mathsf{C}}_{SwapLeg}(\alpha_1 I_1, X_1, \{T^1_i\}^{n_1}_{i=0})$ and pay a leg with value $V^{U_2,\mathsf{C}}_{SwapLeg}(\alpha_2 I_2, X_2, \{T^2_i\})$. Since the currency unit of the two legs may be different, the value of the swap in currency $U_1$ is

$$V_{Swap} = V^{U_1,\mathsf{C}}_{SwapLeg}(\alpha_1 I_1, X_1, \{T^1_i\}^{n_1}_{i=0}) - V^{U_2,\mathsf{C}}_{SwapLeg}(\alpha_2 I_2, X_2, \{T^2_i\}^{n_2}_{i=0}) \cdot FX^{\frac{U_1}{U_2}}$$

Many instruments can be represented (and hence valued) in this form. We will now list a few of them.

## 6.2 Calibration of Discount Curve to Swap Paying the Collateral Rate (aka. Self-Discounted Swaps)

Discount curves can be calibrated to swaps paying the performance index of their collateral account. For example, a swap as in Definition 7 where both legs pay in the same currency $U = U_1 = U_2$. In a receiver swap the receiver leg pays a fixed rate $C$, and the payer leg pays an index $I$. Thus the value of the swap can be expressed in terms of the discount factors $P^{U,\mathsf{C}}(T_{i+1}; t)$ only, which allows to calibrate this curve using these swaps. Overnight index swaps are an example.

For the swap paying the performance of the collateral account we have

$$\begin{aligned} X_1 &= C = \text{const.} = \text{given}, \; X_2 = 0, \\ F^{U_1,\mathsf{C}}_1(T^1_i; t_0) &= 0, \qquad F^{U_2,\mathsf{C}}_2(T^2_i; t_0) = \frac{P^{U,\mathsf{C}}(T^2_i; t_0) - P^{U,\mathsf{C}}(T^2_{i+1}; t_0)}{P^{U,\mathsf{C}}(T^2_{i+1}; t_0)(T^2_{i+1} - T^2_i)}, \\ P^{U_1,\mathsf{C}}_1 &= P^{U,\mathsf{C}} = \text{calibrated}, \; P^{U_2,\mathsf{C}}_2 = P^{U,\mathsf{C}} = \text{calibrated}. \end{aligned}$$

In a situation where the number of interpolation points matches the number of swaps (e.g., a bootstrapping), we calibrate the time $T$ discount factor $P^{U,\mathsf{C}}(T; t_0)$ with $T = \max(T^1_n, T^2_n)$ being the last payment time from a given swap.

## 6.3 Calibration of Forward Curves

Given a calibrated discount curve $P^{U,\mathsf{C}}$ we consider a swap with payments in currency $U$ collateralized with respect to the account $\mathsf{C}$, paying some index $I$ and receiving some fixed cash flow $C$. An example is swaps paying the 3M LIBOR rate. For such a swap we have

$$\begin{aligned}
X_1 &= C = \text{const.} = \text{given}, & X_2 &= 0, \\
F_1^{U_1,\mathsf{C}}(T_i^1) &= 0, & F_2^{U_2,\mathsf{C}}(T_i^2) &= F^{U,\mathsf{C}}(T_i^2) = \text{calibrated}, \\
P_1^{U_1,\mathsf{C}} &= P^{U,\mathsf{C}} = \text{given}, & P_2^{U_2,\mathsf{C}} &= P^{U,\mathsf{C}} = \text{given}.
\end{aligned}$$

From one such swap we calibrate the time $T$ forward $F^{U,\mathsf{C}}(T)$ of $I(T)$ with $T = T_{n-1}^2$ (the last fixing time).

Given a calibrated discount curve $P^{U,\mathsf{C}}$ and a calibrate forward curve $F_1^{U,\mathsf{C}}$ belonging to the index $I_1$, both in currency $U$ and collateralized with respect to the account $\mathsf{C}$, we consider a swap collateralized with respect to the account $\mathsf{C}$, paying some index $I_2 = I$ in currency $U$, receiving the index $I_1$ in currency $U$. An example is tenor basis swaps paying the 6M LIBOR rate, receiving the 3M LIBOR rate. For such a swap we have

$$\begin{aligned}
X_1 &= C_1 = \text{const.} = \text{given}, & X_2 &= C_2 = \text{const.} = \text{given}, \\
F_1^{U_1,\mathsf{C}}(T_i^1) &= F_1^{U,\mathsf{C}}(T_i^1) = \text{given}, & F_2^{U_2,\mathsf{C}}(T_i^2) &= F_2^{U,\mathsf{C}}(T_i^2) = \text{calibrated}, \\
P_1^{U_1,\mathsf{C}} &= P^{U,\mathsf{C}} = \text{given}, & P_2^{U_2,\mathsf{C}} &= P^{U,\mathsf{C}} = \text{given}.
\end{aligned}$$

From one such swap we calibrate the time $T$ forward $F_2^{U,\mathsf{C}}(T)$ of $I(T)$ with $T = T_{n-1}^2$ (the last fixing time of index $I_2$).

## 6.4 *Calibration of Discount Curves When Payment and Collateral Currency Differ*

### 6.4.1 Fixed Payment in Other Currency

Given a calibrated discount curve $P^{U_1,\mathsf{C}}$ we consider a swap collateralized with respect to the account $\mathsf{C}$, paying some index $I_1$ in currency $U_1$, and receiving some fixed cash flow $C_2$ in currency $U_2$. An example for such a swap is a cross-currency swap paying floating index $I$ in collateral currency and receiving fixed $C_2$ in a different currency.[12] For such a swap we have

$$\begin{aligned}
X_1 &= C_1 = \text{const.} = \text{given}, & X_2 &= C_2 = \text{const.} = \text{given}, \\
F_1^{U_1,\mathsf{C}}(T_i^1) &= F_1^{U_1,\mathsf{C}}(T_i^1) = \text{given}, & F_2^{U_2,\mathsf{C}}(T_i^2) &= 0, \\
P_1^{U_1,\mathsf{C}} &= P^{U_1,\mathsf{C}} = \text{given}, & P_2^{U_2,\mathsf{C}} &= P^{U_2,\mathsf{C}} = \text{calibrated}.
\end{aligned}$$

We calibrate the discount factor $P^{U_2,\mathsf{C}}(T; t_0)$ with $T = T_n^2$ (last payment time in currency $U_2$).

[12] Usually cross-currency swaps exchange two floating indices, we will consider this case below.

### 6.4.2 Float Payment in Other Currency

If instead of a fixed payment we have that an index $I_2$ is paid in an other currency $U_2$ we may encounter the problem that the swap has two unknowns, namely the discount curve $P^{U_2,\mathsf{C}}$ for payments in currency $U_2$ collateralized with respect to $\mathsf{C}$ and the forward curve $F_2^{U_2,\mathsf{C}}$ of the index $I_2$ paid in currency $U_2$ collateralized with respect to $\mathsf{C}$. The two curves can be obtained jointly from two different swaps: first a fix-versus-float swaps in currency $U_2$ collateralized by $\mathsf{C}$, and second, a cross-currency swap exchanging the index $I_2$ with an index $I_1$ in currency $U_1$ for which the forward $F_1^{U_1,\mathsf{C}}$ is known. For the first instrument we denote the fixed payment by $C_1$, $C_2$. For the second instrument we denote the fixed payment by $s_1$, $s_2$ (usually a spread). For the first instrument we have

$$\begin{aligned} X_1 &= C_1 = \text{const.} = \text{given}, & X_2 &= C_2 = \text{const.} = \text{given}, \\ F_1^{U_1,\mathsf{C}}(T_i^1) &= 0, & F_2^{U_2,\mathsf{C}}(T_i^2) &= F_2^{U_2,\mathsf{C}}(T_i^2) = \text{calibrated}, \\ P_1^{U_1,\mathsf{C}} &= P_2^{U_2,\mathsf{C}} = \text{calibrated}, & P_2^{U_2,\mathsf{C}} &= \text{calibrated}. \end{aligned}$$

For the second swap we have

$$\begin{aligned} X_1 &= s_1 = \text{const.} = \text{given}, & X_2 &= s_2 = \text{const.} = \text{given}, \\ F_1^{U_1,\mathsf{C}}(T_i^1) &= F_1^{U_1,\mathsf{C}}(T_i^1) = \text{given}, & F_2^{U_2,\mathsf{C}}(T_i^2) &= F_2^{U_2,\mathsf{C}}(T_i^2) = \text{calibrated}, \\ P_1^{U_1,\mathsf{C}} &= \text{given}, & P_2^{U_2,\mathsf{C}} &= \text{calibrated}. \end{aligned}$$

We calibrate the discount factor $P^{U_2,\mathsf{C}}(T;t_0)$ with $T = T_n^2$ and the forward $F_2^{U_2,\mathsf{C}}(\mathrm{T})$ with $T = T_{n-1}^2$.

Often market data are not available to calibrate the forward $F_2^{U_2,\mathsf{C}}$, but the forward $F_2^{U_2,\mathsf{C}_2}$ collateralized with respect to a different account $\mathsf{C}_2$ is available. The two forwards differ by a possible convexity adjustment. One possible approximation (which would follow from the assumption that forwards are independent of their collateralization) is to use $F_2^{U_2,\mathsf{C}} \approx F_2^{U_2,\mathsf{C}_2}$.

The joint calibration of the two curves can be decomposed into two independent calibration steps, which would then allow to re-use a traditional bootstrap algorithm, see, e.g., [4].

***Calibration of Discount Curves as Spread Curves***

We consider a swap leg with notional exchange and tenor $\{T_i\}_{i=0}^n$, paying an index $I$ plus some constant $X = s(T_n) = const.$ Here $s(T_n)$ has the interpretation of a maturity-dependent spread. If this leg is in currency $U$ and with respect to a collateral account (here funding account) $\mathsf{D}$, then its value is

$$\begin{aligned} V_{SwapLeg}^{U,\mathsf{D}}(\alpha I, X, \{T_i\}_{i=0}^n) = \sum_{i=0}^{n-1} \Big( \big(\alpha F^{U,\mathsf{D}}(T_i) + X\big) \cdot P^{U,\mathsf{D}}(T_{i+1}) \\ + P^{U,\mathsf{D}}(T_{i+1}) - P^{U,\mathsf{D}}(T_i) \Big) . \end{aligned}$$

An example of such an instrument is an (uncollateralized) floating rate bond, paying a 3M rate plus some spread. If we assume that the forward $F^{U,\mathsf{D}}(T_i)$ is known, this instrument can be used to calibrate the discount curve $P^{U,\mathsf{D}}$. In fact $I+X$ represents the performance of the funding account associated with $P^{U,\mathsf{D}}$.

If the forward $F^{U,\mathsf{D}}(T_i)$ is not known, we encounter the same problem as for cross-currency swaps, namely that the forward curve $F^{U,\mathsf{D}}(T_i)$ and the discount curve $P^{U,\mathsf{D}}$ need to be calibrated jointly to two instruments. The first one is a swap which is collateralized with respect to the funding account $\mathsf{D}$, i.e., it is an uncollateralized swap. The second is the funding floater.

For the first instrument, the uncollateralized swap, we have

$$\begin{aligned} X_1 &= C_1 = \text{const.} = \text{given}, & X_2 &= C_2 = \text{const.} = \text{given}, \\ F_1^{U,\mathsf{D}}(T_i^1) &= 0 = \text{given}, & F_2^{U,\mathsf{D}}(T_i^2) &= F^{U,\mathsf{D}}(T_i^2) = \text{calibrated}, \\ P_1^{U,\mathsf{D}} &= P^{U,\mathsf{D}} = \text{calibrated}, & P_2^{U,\mathsf{D}} &= P^{U,\mathsf{D}}. \end{aligned}$$

For the second instrument, the funding floating rate bond (uncollateralized swap leg with notional exchange) we have

$$\begin{aligned} X_1 &= S = \text{const.} = \text{given}, \\ F_1^{U,\mathsf{D}}(T_i^1) &= F^{U,\mathsf{D}}(T_i^1) = \text{calibrated}, \\ P_1^{U,\mathsf{D}} &= P^{U,\mathsf{D}} = \text{calibrated}. \end{aligned}$$

*Remark 6* The calibration of the funding curve $P^{U,\mathsf{D}}$ is analog to the calibration of the cross-currency discount curve $P^{U_2,\mathsf{C}}$.

In the above, we consider the *funding floater* as a floating rate bond. Note however, that bonds (in contrast to swaps) do not permit negative coupons, hence they have an implicit floor. There are ways to solve this problem: either one has to incorporate an option premium in the calibration procedure (which does require a model for the volatility) or one considers only market data of fixed bonds together with uncollateralized swaps (which likely requires some assumption since usually this calibration instrument is not observed). See the following section.

## 6.5 *Lack of Calibration Instruments (for Difference in Collateralization)*

The calibration of cross-currency curves (forward curve and discount curves for currency $U_2$ with collateralization in currency $U_1$, see Sect. 6.4) and the calibration of un-collateralized curves (forward curves and discount curves for uncollateralized products, see section "Calibration of Discount Curves as Spread Curves") may require market data which are not available, e.g., the forward of an index $I$ paid in currency $U_2$ collateralized in a different currency or by a different account. This issue has been pointed out by [14].

In this case the curve can be obtained by adding additional assumptions. Two simple examples are:

- the market rates are assumed to be independent of the type of collateralization, or
- the forward rates are assumed to be independent of the type of collateralization.

The two assumptions lead to different results, since they imply different correlations which will lead to different (convexity) adjustments. For details on the example see [11], where a sample calculation with assuming identical market rates for 3M swaps collateralized in USD-OIS or EUR-OIS results in a difference of around 1 or 2 basis points (0.01 %) for the forward curves.

### *6.6 Implementation*

The definition of the various calibration instruments indicated that an iterative bootstrapping algorithm (there the curve is built in a step-by-step process solving only one dimensional problems in one variable) is no longer straightforward. This is due to the interdependence of discount and forward curves. While this problem may be solved in some cases via a pre-processing (see [4]), we suggest a different route: we propose to solve the calibration problem via a single optimization run on the full multi-dimensional problem. This also allows to calibrate curve in the sense of a best fit in cases where we use more calibration instruments than curve points, resulting in an overdetermined system.

We provide an object-oriented implementation at [11] implementing the Java classes for `Curves`, `DiscountCurves`, `ForwardCurves`, `Solver`, `SwapLeg` and `Swap`.

A detailed discussion of the implementation can be found in the associated JavaDocs and is left out here to shorten the presentation.

## 7 Redefining Forward Rate Market Models

Having discussed the setup of curves, we would like to conclude with a remark on how the curves are integrated into term-structure models, specifically, how the multi-curve setup harmonizes with a classical single curve standard LIBOR market model, which can then be extended to a fully multi-curve model.

If $N^{\mathsf{C}}$ denotes an accrual account, i.e., $N^{\mathsf{C}}$ is a process with $N^{\mathsf{C}}(t_0) = 1U$ (e.g., a collateral account), then $N^{\mathsf{C}}$ defines a discount curve, namely the discount curve $T \mapsto P^{U,\mathsf{C}}(T;t_0) =: P^{\mathsf{C}}(T;t_0)$ of fixed payments made in $T$, valued in $t$ and collateralized by units of $N^{\mathsf{C}}$.

Now let $\{T_i\}$ denote a given tenor discretization. As shown in Sect. 4.1 the period-$[T_i, T_{i+1}]$ performance index $I^{\mathsf{C}}(T_i, T_{i+1})$ of the an accrual account, i.e., $I^{\mathsf{C}}(T_i, T_{i+1}; T_i) := \frac{N^{\mathsf{C}}(T_{i+1})}{N^{\mathsf{C}}(T_i)} - 1$ has the property that its time *t forward* (of a payment of $I^{\mathrm{C}}(T_i, T_{i+1})$ made in $T_{i+1}$, collateralized in units of $N^{\mathrm{C}}$) (following the definition of a forward from Definition 3) is given as $F^{U,\mathrm{C}}(T_i, T_{i+1}; t) := \frac{P^{\mathrm{C}}(T_i;t) - P^{\mathrm{C}}(T_{i+1};t)}{P^{\mathrm{C}}(T_{i+1};t_0)}$.

This relation allows us to create a term-structure model for the curve $P^{\mathrm{C}}$ which has the same structural properties as a standard single curve (LIBOR) market model. This model is given by a joint modeling of the processes $L_i(t) := \frac{F^{U,\mathrm{C}}(T_i,T_{i+1};t)}{T_{i+1}-T_i}$, e.g., as log-normal processes under the measure $\mathbb{Q}^{N^{\mathrm{C}}}$ and the additional assumption that the process $P^{\mathrm{C}}(T_i; t)$ is deterministic on its short period $t \in (T_{i-1}, T_i]$.

From these two assumptions it follows that the processes $L_i$ have the structure of a standard LIBOR market model and $\mathbb{Q}^{N^{\mathrm{C}}}$ corresponds to the spot measure. Indeed we have $\prod_{j=0}^{i-1} 1 + L_j(T_j) \cdot (T_{j+1} - T_j) = N^{\mathrm{C}}(T_i)$.

What we have described is how to use the standard LIBOR market model as a term structure model for the collateral account $N^{\mathrm{C}}$ (e.g., the OIS curve). Now, modeling all other rates (including LIBOR) can be performed by modeling (possibly stochastic) spreads over this curve. This is analog to a defaultable market model.

An alternative is to start with a stochastic model for the forward rates, where now the forward curve defines the initial value of the model SDEs, and then define the discount curve (numéraire) via deterministic or stochastic spreads. This approach has a practical advantage, since for LIBOR rates implied volatilities are more liquid than for OIS rates. See, e.g., [20] and references therein. An implementation of the standard LMM with a deterministic adjustment for the discount curve is provided by the author at [9].

## 8 Some Numerical Results

### 8.1 *Impact of the Interpolation Entity of a Forward Curve on the Delta Hedge*

Using our reference implementation [11], we investigate the interpolation of forward curves using different interpolation methods and interpolation entities. While interpolation of (synthetic) discount factors is—motivated from its single curve origin—a very popular interpolation method, it may result in very implausible deltas, if the curve is constructed from overlapping instruments. Table 1 shows the delta of an 8x11 FRA calculated on a curve constructed from 0x3, 1x4, 2x5, 3x6, 4x7, 5x8, 6x9, 7x10, 9x12 FRA (note that the 8x11 is missing in the curve construction). The plausible hedge would be to use the adjacent 7x10 and 9x12 FRAs. Using the interpolation entity `DISCOUNTFACTOR` we find non-zero deltas for instruments prior to the 7x10 FRA, summing up to zero. This effect stems from the error propagation inherent in the definition of the interpolation entity. The interpolation entity `FORWARD` does not show this effect.

**Table 1** The delta of an 7Mx10M FRA with respect to different calibration instruments, where the 7Mx10M FRA is not part of the calibration instruments, hence interpolates

| Risk Factor | Delta of an 7Mx10M FRA using the interpolation entity | |
|---|---|---|
| | `DISCOUNTFACTOR` (%) | `FORWARD` (%) |
| 0Dx3M | 44.5 | 0.0 |
| 1Mx4M | −95.9 | 0.0 |
| 2Mx5M | 52.4 | 0.0 |
| 3Mx6M | 44.0 | 0.0 |
| 4Mx7M | −97.0 | 0.0 |
| 5Mx8M | 52.4 | 0.0 |
| 6Mx9M | 47.6 | 48.4 |
| 7Mx10M | 0.0 | 0.0 |
| 8Mx11M | 51.9 | 51.6 |
| 9Mx12M | 0.0 | 0.0 |

Different interpolation entities result in very different delta hedges. The popular interpolation entity of a synthetic discount factor results in counterintuitive hedges. The interpolation method is `LINEAR` in both cases. It is the choice of the interpolation entity which introduces the effect

## 8.2 *Impact of the Lack of Calibration Instruments for the Case of a Foreign Swap Collateralized in Domestic Currency*

Based on the curve framework and the calibration instruments defined in this paper and implemented at [11] we have investigated the impact of the assumptions, which had to be made due to the lack of calibration instruments for foreign currency swaps. Since a foreign currency swap collateralized in domestic currency is (currently) not a liquid instrument, the *foreign forward with respect to domestic collateralization* cannot be calibrated. Hence, a model assumption is required. Two possible assumptions are: (1) the forward rate is independent from its collateralization—that is, use the foreign forward curve derived from instruments collateralized in *foreign* currency, or, (2) the market (swap) rates are independent from its collateralization—that is, use the foreign market (par-)swap rates form foreign currency swaps collateralized in foreign currency together with a domestic currency discount curve to calibrate a foreign currency forward rate curve with respect to domestic collateralization. Both approaches result in different forward curves. The impact can be assessed using the spreadsheet available at [11]. For 2012 market data the difference for an USD forward curve collateralized in EUR can be found to be around two basis points. While the first assumption (re-using the forward curve) is likely the more natural one, and maybe a market standard, the calculation shows that the assumption has a considerable impact on the resulting curve, see Fig. 1.

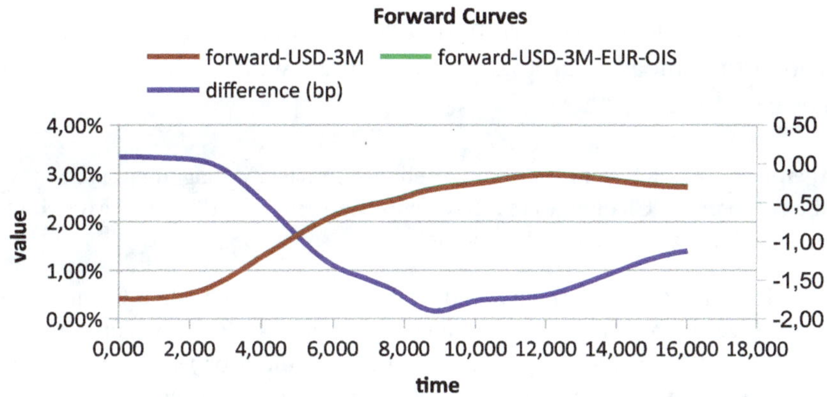


**Fig. 1** Forward curve (USD-3M) calibrated from swaps with different collateralization (USD-OIS and EUR-OIS) assuming independence of the market rates of from the type of collateralization

### *8.3 Impact of the Interpolation Scheme on the Hedge Efficiency*

Also based on the framework presented here, the impact of the different interpolation schemes has been investigated in [13], where indication was found that among the local interpolation schemes, it is indeed better to use a different interpolation scheme for forward curves than for discount curves. For details we refer to [13].

## 9 Conclusion

We have presented the re-definition of discount curves and forward curves, which clearly distinguishes the two as different objects (with some relation for the special case of OIS curves). This re-definition results in curves, representing values with well-defined economic interpretations. We then discussed some interpolation schemes for these curves, where our re-definition suggests to apply different interpolation schemes for discount and forward curves. This stands in contrast to the classical approach where a forward curve had been represented via synthetic discount factors, using the same interpolation schemes for both types of curves.

We have presented the calibration, defining the calibration instruments. Based on this, we provide an open source, object-oriented implementation at [11].[13]

Based on this benchmark implementation it was possible to assess the impact of assumptions, which had to be made due to the lack of calibration instruments, e.g., for the case of cross-currency swaps, and the impact of the different interpolation schemes. Indication was found that it is better to use a different interpolation scheme for forward curves than for discount curves. With respect to delta hedges one should

[13] A complete description of the implementation is given at http://www.finmath.net/finmath-lib, including source code and numerical examples. They are left out in this paper.

favor forward interpolation over synthetic discount factor interpolation. Among forward interpolation, linear interpolation performed well with respect to the hedge performance.

**Acknowledgements** The KPMG Center of Excellence in Risk Management is acknowledged for organizing the conference "Challenges in Derivatives Markets - Fixed Income Modeling, Valuation Adjustments, Risk Management, and Regulation".

**Open Access** This chapter is distributed under the terms of the Creative Commons Attribution 4.0 International License (http://creativecommons.org/licenses/by/4.0/), which permits use, duplication, adaptation, distribution and reproduction in any medium or format, as long as you give appropriate credit to the original author(s) and the source, a link is provided to the Creative Commons license and any changes made are indicated.

The images or other third party material in this chapter are included in the work's Creative Commons license, unless indicated otherwise in the credit line; if such material is not included in the work's Creative Commons license and the respective action is not permitted by statutory regulation, users will need to obtain permission from the license holder to duplicate, adapt or reproduce the material.

## References

1. Ametrano, F.M., Bianchetti, M.: Bootstrapping the illiquidity: multiple yield curves construction for market coherent forward rates estimation. Ohio State University (2000)
2. Ametrano, F.M., Bianchetti, M.: Everything you always wanted to know about multiple interest rate curve bootstrapping but were afraid to ask. Preprint (2013)
3. Chibane, M., Selvaraj, J.P., Sheldon, G.: Building curves on a good basis. Social Scientific Research Network (2009). http://ssrn.com/abstract=1394267
4. Clark, J.: Constructing a non-USD swap discounting curve with USD collateral. http://www.edurisk.ie
5. Crépey, S., Grbac, Z., Nguyen, H., Skovmand, D.: A Lévy HJM multiple-curve model with application to CVA computation. Quant. Financ. **15**(3), 401–419 (2015)
6. Cuchiero, C., Fontana, C., Gnoatto, A.: A general HJM framework for multiple yield curve modeling. Financ. Stoch. **6**, 397 (2016)
7. Delbaen, F., Schachermayer, W.: A general version of the fundamental theorem of asset pricing. Math. Annalen **300**, 463–520 (1994)
8. Fillipovic, D., Trolle, A.B.: The term structure of interbank risk. J. Financ. Econ. **109**(3), 707–733 (2012)
9. Fries, C.P.: Libor market model. Object oriented reference implementation 2004–2015. http://www.finmath.net/topics/libormarketmodel
10. Fries, C.P.: Mathematical Finance. Theory, Modeling, Implementation. Wiley, Hoboken (2007). http://www.christian-fries.de/finmath/book
11. Fries, C.P.: Curve calibration. Object oriented reference implementation 2010–2015. http://www.finmath.net/topics/curvecalibration
12. Fries, C.P.: Funded replication: fund exchange process and the valuation with different funding-accounts (cross-currency analogy to funding revisited). Wilmott **63**, 36–41 (2013). http://papers.ssrn.com/abstract=2115839
13. Fries, C.P., Plum, C.: Interest rate curve interpolations and their assessment via hedge simulations. Preprint (2015). http://ssrn.com/abstract=2635903
14. Fujii, M., Shimadaz, Y., Takahashi, A.: A note on construction of multiple swap curves with and without collateral (2010)

15. Grbac, Z., Papapantoleon, A., Schoenmakers, J., Skovmand, D.: Affine LIBOR models with multiple curves: theory, examples and calibration. SIAM. J. Financ. Math. **6**(1), 984–1025 (2015)
16. Hagan, P.S., West, G.: Interpolation methods for curve construction. Appl. Math. Financ. **13**(2), 89–129 (2006)
17. Henrard, M.: Interest rate instruments and market conventions guide. OpenGamma (2013)
18. Henrard, M.: Interest Rate Modelling in the Multi-Curve Framework: Foundations, Evolution and Implementation. Palgrave Macmillan, Basingstoke (2014)
19. Le Floc'h, F.: Stable interpolation for the yield curve. Social Scientific Research Network (2013)
20. Mercurio, F.: LIBOR market models with stochastic basis. Bloomberg Education and Quantitative Research Paper, (2010-05-FRONTIERS) (2010)
21. Mercurio, F.: Modern LIBOR market models: using different curves for projecting rates and discounting. Bloomberg Education and Quantitative Research Paper, 13(1), 113–137 (2010)
22. Moreni, M., Pallavicini, A.: Parsimonious HJM modelling for multiple yield-curve dynamics. Quant. Financ. **14**(2), 199–210 (2014)

# Impact of Multiple-Curve Dynamics in Credit Valuation Adjustments

**Giacomo Bormetti, Damiano Brigo, Marco Francischello and Andrea Pallavicini**

**Abstract** We present a detailed analysis of interest rate derivatives valuation under credit risk and collateral modeling. We show how the credit and collateral extended valuation framework in Pallavicini et al. (2011) can be helpful in defining the key market rates underlying the multiple interest rate curves that characterize current interest rate markets. We introduce the collateralized valuation measures and formulate a consistent realistic dynamics for the rates emerging from our analysis. We point out limitations of multiple curve models with deterministic basis considering valuation of particularly sensitive products such as basis swaps.

**Keywords** Multiple curves · Evaluation adjustments · Basis swaps · Collateral · HJM model

## 1 Introduction

After the onset of the crisis in 2007, all market instruments are quoted by taking into account, more or less implicitly, credit- and collateral-related adjustments. As a consequence, when approaching modeling problems one has to carefully check standard theoretical assumptions which often ignore credit and liquidity issues. One has to go back to market processes and fundamental instruments by limiting oneself to use models based on products and quantities that are available on the market.

G. Bormetti (✉)
University of Bologna, Piazza di Porta San Donato 5, 40126 Bologna, Italy
e-mail: giacomo.bormetti@unibo.it

D. Brigo · M. Francischello
Imperial College London, London SW7 2AZ, UK
e-mail: damiano.brigo@imperial.ac.uk

M. Francischello
e-mail: m.francischello14@imperial.ac.uk

A. Pallavicini
Imperial College London and Banca IMI, Largo Mattioli, 3, 20121 Milan, Italy
e-mail: a.pallavicini@imperial.ac.uk

© The Author(s) 2016

K. Glau et al. (eds.), *Innovations in Derivatives Markets*, Springer Proceedings in Mathematics & Statistics 165, DOI 10.1007/978-3-319-33446-2_12

Referring to market observables and processes is the only means we have to validate our theoretical assumptions, so as to drop them if in contrast with observations. This general recipe is what is guiding us in this paper, where we try to adapt interest rate models for valuation to the current landscape.

A detailed analysis of the updated valuation problem one faces when including credit risk and collateral modeling (and further funding costs) has been presented elsewhere in this volume, see for example [6, 7]. We refer to those papers and references therein for a detailed discussion. Here we focus our updated valuation framework to consider the following key points: (i) focus on interest rate derivatives; (ii) understand how the updated valuation framework can be helpful in defining the key market rates underlying the multiple interest rate curves that characterize current interest rate markets; (iii) define collateralized valuation measures; (iv) formulate a consistent realistic dynamics for the rates emerging from the above analysis; (v) show how the framework can be applied to valuation of particularly sensitive products such as basis swaps under credit risk and collateral posting;(vi) point out limitations in some current market practices such as explaining the multiple curves through deterministic fudge factors or shifts where the option embedded in the credit valuation adjustment (CVA) calculation would be priced without any volatility. For an extended version of this paper we remand to [3]. This paper is an extended and refined version of ideas originally appeared in [24].

## 2 Valuation Equation with Credit and Collateral

Classical interest-rate models were formulated to satisfy no-arbitrage relationships by construction, which allowed one to price and hedge forward-rate agreements in terms of risk-free zero-coupon bonds. Starting from summer 2007, with the spreading of the credit crunch, market quotes of forward rates and zero-coupon bonds began to violate usual no-arbitrage relationships. The main driver of such behavior was the liquidity crisis reducing the credit lines along with the fear of an imminent systemic break-down. As a result the impact of counterparty risk on market prices could not be considered negligible any more.

This is the first of many examples of relationships that broke down with the crisis. Assumptions and approximations stemming from valuation theory should be replaced by strategies implemented with market instruments. For instance, inclusion of CVA for interest-rate instruments, such as those analyzed in [8], breaks the relationship between risk-free zero-coupon bonds and LIBOR forward rates. Also, funding in domestic currency on different time horizons must include counterparty risk adjustments and liquidity issues, see [15], breaking again this relationship. We thus have, against the earlier standard theory,

$$L(T_0, T_1) \neq \frac{1}{T_1 - T_0}\left(\frac{1}{P_{T_0}(T_1)} - 1\right), \quad F_t(T_0, T_1) \neq \frac{1}{T_1 - T_0}\left(\frac{P_t(T_0)}{P_t(T_1)} - 1\right), \tag{1}$$

where $P_t(T)$ is a zero-coupon bond price at time $t$ for maturity $T$, $L$ is the LIBOR rate and $F$ is the related LIBOR forward rate. A direct consequence is the impossibility to describe all LIBOR rates in terms of a unique zero-coupon yield curve. Indeed, since 2009 and even earlier, we had evidence that the money market for the Euro area was moving to a multi-curve setting. See [1, 19, 20, 27].

## 2.1 Valuation Framework

In order to value a financial product (for example a derivative contract), we have to discount all the cash flows occurring after the trading position is entered. We follow the approach of [25, 26] and we specialize it to the case of interest-rate derivatives, where collateralization usually happens on a daily basis, and where gap risk is not large. Hence we prefer to present such results when cash flows are modeled as happening in a continuous time-grid, since this simplifies notation and calculations. We refer to the two names involved in the financial contract and subject to default risk as investor (also called name "I") and counterparty (also called name "C"). We denote by $\tau_I$, and $\tau_C$, respectively, the default times of the investor and counterparty. We fix the portfolio time horizon $T > 0$, and fix the risk-neutral valuation model $(\Omega, \mathscr{G}, \mathbb{Q})$, with a filtration $(\mathscr{G}_t)_{t\in[0,T]}$ such that $\tau_C$, $\tau_I$ are $(\mathscr{G}_t)_{t\in[0,T]}$-stopping times. We denote by $\mathbb{E}_t[\,\cdot\,]$ the conditional expectation under $\mathbb{Q}$ given $\mathscr{G}_t$, and by $\mathbb{E}_{\tau_i}[\,\cdot\,]$ the conditional expectation under $\mathbb{Q}$ given the stopped filtration $\mathscr{G}_{\tau_i}$. We exclude the possibility of simultaneous defaults, and define the first default event between the two parties as the stopping time $\tau := \tau_C \wedge \tau_I$.

We will also consider the market sub-filtration $(\mathscr{F}_t)_{t\geq 0}$ that one obtains implicitly by assuming a separable structure for the complete market filtration $(\mathscr{G}_t)_{t\geq 0}$. $\mathscr{G}_t$ is then generated by the pure default-free market filtration $\mathscr{F}_t$ and by the filtration generated by all the relevant default times monitored up to $t$ (see for example [2]).

We introduce a risk-free rate $r$ associated with the risk-neutral measure. We therefore need to define the related stochastic discount factor $D(t, u, r)$ that in general will denote the risk-neutral default-free discount factor, given by the ratio

$$D(t, u, r) = B_t/B_u\ , \quad dB_t = r_t B_t dt,$$

where $B$ is the bank account numeraire, driven by the risk-free instantaneous interest rate $r_t$ and associated to the risk-neutral measure $\mathbb{Q}$. This rate $r_t$ is assumed to be $(\mathscr{F}_t)_{t\in[0,T]}$ adapted and is the key variable in all pre-crisis term structure modeling.

We now want to price a collateralized derivative contract, and in particular we assume that collateral re-hypothecation is allowed, as done in practice (see [4] for a discussion on re-hypothecation). We thus write directly the adjustment payout terms as carry costs cash flows, each accruing at the relevant rate, namely the price $V_t$ of a derivative contract, inclusive of collateralized credit and debit risk, margining costs, can be derived by following [25, 26], and is given by:

$$V_t = \mathbb{E}\left[\int_t^T D(t,u;r)\left(1_{\{u<\tau\}}d\pi_u + 1_{\{\tau\in du\}}\theta_u + (r_u - c_u)C_u du\right) \mid \mathscr{G}_t\right] \tag{2}$$

where

- $\pi_u$ is the coupon process of the product, without credit or debit risk and without collateral cash flows;
- $C_u$ is the collateral process, and we use the convention that $C_u > 0$ while $I$ is the collateral receiver and $C_u < 0$ when $I$ is the collateral poster. $(r_u - c_u)C_u$ are the collateral margining costs and the collateral rate is defined as $c_t := c_t^+ 1_{\{C_t>0\}} + c_t^- 1_{\{C_t<0\}}$ with $c^\pm$ defined in the CSA contract. In general we may assume the processes $c^+, c^-$ to be adapted to the default-free filtration $\mathscr{F}_t$.
- $\theta_u = \theta_u(C, \varepsilon)$ is the on-default cash flow process that depends on the collateral process $C_u$ and the close-out value $\varepsilon_u$.[1] It is primarily this term that originates the credit and debit valuation adjustments (CVA/DVA) terms, that may also embed collateral and gap risk due to the jump at default of the value of the considered deal (e.g. in a credit derivative), see for example [5].

Notice that the above valuation equation (2) is not suited for explicit numerical evaluations, since the right-hand side is still depending on the derivative price via the indicators within the collateral rates and possibly via the close-out term, leading to recursive/nonlinear features. We could resort to numerical solutions, as in [11], but, since our goal is valuing interest-rate derivatives, we prefer to further specialize the valuation equation for such deals.

## 2.2 The Master Equation Under Change of Filtration

In this first work we develop our analysis without considering a dependence between the default times if not through their spreads, or more precisely by assuming that the default times are $\mathscr{F}$-conditionally independent. Moreover, we assume that the collateral account and the close-out processes are $\mathscr{F}$-adapted. Thus, we can simplify the valuation equation given by (2) by switching to the default-free market filtration. By following the filtration switching formula in [2], we introduce for any $\mathscr{G}_t$-adapted process $X_t$ a unique $\mathscr{F}_t$-adapted process $\widetilde{X}_t$, defined such that $1_{\{\tau>t\}}X_t = 1_{\{\tau>t\}}\widetilde{X}_t$. Hence, we can write the pre-default price process as given by $1_{\{\tau>t\}}\widetilde{V}_t = V_t$ where the right-hand side is given in Eq. (2) and where $\tilde{V}_t$ is $\mathscr{F}_t$-adapted. Before changing filtration, we have to specify the form of the close-out payoff:

$$\theta_\tau = \varepsilon_\tau(\tau,T) - 1_{\{\tau_C<\tau_I\}} LGD_C(\varepsilon_\tau(\tau,T) - C_\tau)^+ - 1_{\{\tau_I<\tau_C\}} LGD_I(\varepsilon_\tau(\tau,T) - C_\tau)^-$$

[1] The closeout value is the residual value of the contract at default time and the CSA specifies the way it should be computed.

where $LGD \leq 1$ is the loss given default, $(x)^+$ indicates the positive part of $x$ and $(x)^- = -(-x)^+$. For an extended discussion of the term $\theta_\tau$ we refer to [3]. Moreover, to derive an explicit valuation formula we assume that gap risk is not present, namely $\tilde{V}_{\tau-} = \tilde{V}_\tau$, and we consider a particular form for collateral and close-out prices, namely we model the close-out value as

$$\varepsilon_s(t,T) = \mathbb{E}\left[\int_t^T D(t,u,r)d\pi_u \mid \mathscr{G}_s\right], \quad C_t \doteq \alpha_t \varepsilon_t(t,T)$$

with $0 \leq \alpha_t \leq 1$ and where $\alpha_t$ is $\mathscr{F}_t$-adapted. This means that the close-out is the risk-free mark to market at first default time and the collateral is a fraction $\alpha_t$ of the close-out value. An alternative approximation that does not impose a proportionality between the account value processes can be found in [9]. We obtain, by switching to the default-free market filtration $\mathscr{F}$ the following.[2]

**Proposition 1** (Master equation under $\mathscr{F}$-conditionally independent default times, no gap risk and $\mathscr{F}_t$ measurable payout $\pi_t$) *Under the above assumption, Valuation Equation (2) is further specified as* $V_t = 1_{\{\tau>t\}}\widetilde{V}_t$

$$\begin{aligned}
\widetilde{V}_t =& \varepsilon_t(t,T) + \mathbb{E}\left[\int_t^T D(t,u;r+\lambda)(r_u - c_u)\alpha_u\varepsilon_u(u,T)du \mid \mathscr{F}_t\right] \\
&- \mathbb{E}\left[\int_t^T D(t,u;r+\lambda)\lambda_u^C(1-\alpha_u)LGD_C(\varepsilon_u(u,T))^+du \mid \mathscr{F}_t\right] \\
&- \mathbb{E}\left[\int_t^T D(t,u;r+\lambda)\lambda_u^I(1-\alpha_u)LGD_I(\varepsilon_u(u,T))^-du \mid \mathscr{F}_t\right]
\end{aligned}$$

*where we introduced the pre-default intensity $\lambda_t^I$ of the investor and the pre-default intensity $\lambda_t^C$ of the counterparty as*

$$1_{\{\tau_I>t\}}\lambda_t^I\,dt := \mathbb{Q}\{\tau_I \in dt \mid \tau_I > t, \mathscr{F}_t\}, \; 1_{\{\tau_C>t\}}\lambda_t^C\,dt := \mathbb{Q}\{\tau_C \in dt \mid \tau_C > t, \mathscr{F}_t\}$$

*along with their sum $\lambda_t$ and the discount factor for any rate $x_u$, namely* $D(t,T,x) := \exp\{-\int_t^T x_u du\}$.

## 3 Valuing Collateralized Interest-Rate Derivatives

As we mentioned in the introduction, we will base our analysis on real market processes. All liquid market quotes on the money market (MM) correspond to instruments with daily collateralization at overnight rate $(e_t)$, both for the investor and the counterparty, namely $c_t \doteq e_t$.

[2] We refer to [3] and [6] for a precise derivation of the proposition.

Notice that the collateral accrual rate is symmetric, so that we no longer have a dependency of the accrual rates on the collateral price, as opposed to the general master equation case. Moreover, we further assume $r_t \doteq e_t$ .

This makes sense because $e_t$ being an overnight rate, it embeds a low counterparty risk and can be considered a good proxy for the risk-free rate $r_t$. We will describe some of these MM instruments, such as OIS and Interest Rate Swaps (IRS), along with their underlying market rates, in the following sections. For the remaining of this section we adopt the perfect collateralization approximation of Eq. (1) to derive the valuation equations for OIS and IRS products, hence assuming no gap-risk, while in the numeric experiments of Sect. 4 we will consider also uncollateralized deals. Furthermore, we assume that daily collateralization can be considered as a continuous-dividend perfect collateralization. See [4] for a discussion on the impact of discrete-time collateralization on interest-rate derivatives.

## 3.1 Overnight Rates and OIS

Among other instruments, the MM usually quotes the prices of overnight indexed swaps (OIS). Such contracts exchange a fix-payment leg with a floating leg paying a discretely compounded rate based on the same overnight rate used for their collateralization. Since we are going to price OIS under the assumption of perfect collateralization, namely we are assuming that daily collateralization may be viewed as done on a continuous basis, we approximate also daily compounding in OIS floating leg with continuous compounding, which is reasonable when there is no gap risk. Hence the discounted payoff of a one-period OIS with tenor $x$ and maturity $T$ is given by

$$D(t, T, e)\left(1 + xK - \exp\left\{\int_{T-x}^{T} e_u du\right\}\right)$$

where $K$ is the fixed rate payed by the OIS. Furthermore, we can introduce the (par) fix rates $K = E_t(T, x; e)$ that make the one-period OIS contract fair, namely priced 0 at time $t$. They are implicitly defined via

$$\widetilde{V}_t^{\text{OIS}}(K) := \mathbb{E}\left[\left(1 + xK - \exp\left\{\int_{T-x}^{T} e_u du\right\}\right) D(t, T; e) \mid \mathscr{F}_t\right]$$

with $\widetilde{V}_t^{\text{OIS}}(E_t(T, x; e)) = 0$ leading to

$$E_t(T, x; e) := \frac{1}{x}\left(\frac{P_t(T - x; e)}{P_t(T; e)} - 1\right) \tag{3}$$

where we define collateralized zero-coupon bonds[3] as

$$P_t(T; e) := \mathbb{E}\left[ D(t, T; e) \mid \mathscr{F}_t \right]. \tag{4}$$

One-period OIS rates $E_t(T, x; e)$, along with multi-period ones, are actively traded on the market. Notice that we can bootstrap collateralized zero-coupon bond prices from OIS quotes.

## 3.2 LIBOR Rates, IRS and Basis Swaps

LIBOR rates ($L_t(T)$) used to be linked to the term structure of default-free interlink interest rates in a fundamental way. In the classical term structure theory, LIBOR rates would satisfy fundamental no-arbitrage conditions with respect to zero-coupon bonds that we no longer consider to hold, as we pointed out earlier in (1). We now deal with a new definition of forward LIBOR rates that may take into account collateralization. LIBOR rates are still the indices used as reference rate for many collateralized interest-rate derivatives (IRS, basis swaps, ...). IRS contracts swap a fix-payment leg with a floating leg paying simply compounded LIBOR rates. IRS contracts are collateralized at overnight rate $e_t$. Thus, a discounted one-period IRS payoff with maturity $T$ and tenor $x$ is given by

$$D(t, T, e)x(K - L_{T-x}(T))$$

where $K$ is the fix rate payed by the IRS. Furthermore, we can introduce the (par) fix rates $K = F_t(T, x; e)$ that render the one-period IRS contract fair, i.e. priced at zero. They are implicitly defined via

$$\widetilde{V}_t^{\mathrm{IRS}}(K) := \mathbb{E}\left[ (xK - xL_{T-x}(T))\, D(t, T; e) \mid \mathscr{F}_t \right]$$

with $\widetilde{V}_t^{\mathrm{IRS}}(F_t(T, x; e)) = 0$, leading to the following definition of forward LIBOR rate

$$F_t(T, x; e) := \frac{\mathbb{E}\left[ L_{T-x}(T) D(t, T; e) \mid \mathscr{F}_t \right]}{\mathbb{E}\left[ D(t, T; e) \mid \mathscr{F}_t \right]} = \frac{\mathbb{E}\left[ L_{T-x}(T) D(t, T; e) \mid \mathscr{F}_t \right]}{P_t(T; e)}$$

The above definition may be simplified by a suitable choice of the measure under which we take the expectation. In particular, we can consider the following Radon–Nikodym derivative, defining the collateralized $T$-forward measure $\mathbb{Q}^{T;e}$,

[3]Notice that we are only defining a price process for hypothetical collateralized zero-coupon bond. We are not assuming that collateralized bonds are assets traded on the market.

$$Z_t(T;e) := \left.\frac{d\mathbb{Q}^{T;e}}{d\mathbb{Q}}\right|_{\mathscr{F}_t} := \frac{\mathbb{E}\left[D(0,T;e) \mid \mathscr{F}_t\right]}{P_0(T;e)} = \frac{D(0,t;e)P_t(T;e)}{P_0(T;e)}$$

which is a positive $\mathbb{Q}$-martingale, normalized so that $Z_0(T;e) = 1$.

Thus, for any payoff $\phi_T$, perfectly collateralized at overnight rate $e_t$, we can express prices as expectations under the collateralized $T$-forward measure and in particular, we can write LIBOR forward rates as

$$F_t(T,x;e) := \frac{\mathbb{E}\left[L_{T-x}(T)D(t,T;e) \mid \mathscr{F}_t\right]}{\mathbb{E}\left[D(t,T;e) \mid \mathscr{F}_t\right]} = \mathbb{E}^{T;e}\left[L_{T-x}(T) \mid \mathscr{F}_t\right]. \quad (5)$$

One-period forward rates $F_t(T,x;e)$, along with multi-period ones (swap rates), are actively traded on the market. Once collateralized zero-coupon bonds are derived, we can bootstrap forward rate curves from such quotes. See, for instance, [1] or [27] for a discussion on bootstrapping algorithms.

Basis swaps are an interesting product that became more popular after the market switched to a multi-curve structure. In fact, in a basis swap there are two floating legs, one pays a LIBOR rate with a certain tenor and the other pays the LIBOR rate with a shorter tenor plus a spread that makes the contract fair at inception. More precisely, the payoff of a basis swap whose legs pay respectively a LIBOR rate with tenors $x < y$ with maturity $T = nx = my$ is given by

$$\sum_{i=1}^{n} D(t, T-(n-i)x, e)x(L_{T-(n-i-1)x}(T-(n-i)x) + K)$$
$$- \sum_{j=1}^{m} D(t, T-(m-j)y, e)yL_{T-(m-j-1)y}(T-(m-j)y).$$

It is clear that apart from being traded per se, this instrument is naturally present in the banks portfolios as result of the netting of opposite swap positions with different tenors.

### 3.3 Modeling Constraints

Our aim is to set up a multiple-curve dynamical model starting from collateralized zero-coupon bonds $P_t(T;e)$, and LIBOR forward rates $F_t(T,x;e)$. As we have seen we can bootstrap the initial curves for such quantities from directly observed quotes in the market. Now, we wish to propose a dynamics that preserves the martingale properties satisfied by such quantities. Thus, without loss of generality, we can define collateralized zero-coupon bonds under the $\mathbb{Q}$ measure as

$$dP_t(T;e) = P_t(T;e)\left(e_t\,dt - \sigma_t^P(T;e)^*\,dW_t^e\right)$$

and LIBOR forward rates under the $\mathbb{Q}^{T;e}$ measure as

$$dF_t(T,x;e) = \sigma_t^F(T,x;e)^* \, dZ_t^{T;e}$$

where $W^e$ and $Z^{T;e}$ are correlated standard (column) vector[4] Brownian motions with correlation matrix $\rho$, and the volatility vector processes $\sigma^P$ and $\sigma^F$ may depend on bonds and forward LIBOR rates themselves.

The following definition of $f_t(T,e)$ is not strictly necessary, and we could keep working with bonds $P_t(T;e)$, using their dynamics. However, as it is customary in interest rate theory to model rates rather than bonds, we may try to formulate quantities that are closer to the standard HJM framework. In this sense we can define instantaneous forward rates $f_t(T;e)$, by starting from (collateralized) zero-coupon bonds, as given by

$$f_t(T;e) := -\partial_T \log P_t(T;e)$$

We can derive instantaneous forward-rate dynamics by Itô lemma, and we obtain the following dynamics under the $\mathbb{Q}^{T;e}$ measure

$$df_t(T;e) = \sigma_t(T;e)\, dW_t^{T;e}\ , \quad \sigma_t(T;e) := \partial_T \, \sigma_t^P(T;e)$$

where the $W^{T;e}$s are Brownian motions and partial differentiation is meant to be applied component-wise.

Hence, we can summarize our modeling assumptions in the following way. Since linear products (OIS, IRS, basis swaps…) can be expressed in terms of simpler quantities, namely collateralized zero-coupon bonds $P_t(T;e)$ and LIBOR forward rates $F_t(T,x;e)$, we focus on their modeling. The initial term structures for collateralized products may be bootstrapped from market data, and for volatility and dynamics, we can write rates dynamics by enforcing suitable no-arbitrage martingale properties, namely

$$df_t(T;e) = \sigma_t(T;e) \cdot dW_t^{T;e}, \quad dF_t(T,x;e) = \sigma_t^F(T,x;e) \cdot dZ_t^{T;e}. \tag{6}$$

As we explained in the introduction, this is where the multiple curve picture finally shows up: we have a curve with LIBOR-based forward rates $F_t(T,x;e)$, that are collateral adjusted expectation of LIBOR market rates $L_{T-x}(T)$ we take as primitive rates from the market, and we have instantaneous forward rates $f_t(T;e)$ that are OIS-based rates. OIS rates $f_t(T;e)$ are driven by collateral fees, whereas LIBOR forward rates $F_t(T,x;e)$ are driven both by collateral rates and by the primitive LIBOR market rates.

[4]In the following we will consider $N$-dimensional vectors as $N \times 1$ matrices. Moreover, given a matrix $A$, we will indicate $A^*$ its transpose, and if $B$ is another conformable matrix we indicate $AB$ the usual matrix product.

# 4 Interest-Rate Modeling

We can now specialize our modeling assumptions to define a model for interest-rate derivatives which is on one hand flexible enough to calibrate the quotes of the MM, and on the other hand robust. Our aim is to use an HJM framework using a single family of Markov processes to describe all the term structures and interest rate curves we are interested in.

In the literature many authors proposed generalizations of the HJM framework to include multiple yield curves. In particular, we cite the works of [12–14, 16, 20–23]. A survey of the literature can be found in [17].

In such works the problem is faced in a pragmatic way by considering each forward rate as a single asset without investigating the microscopical dynamics implied by liquidity and credit risks. However, the hypothesis of introducing different underlying assets may lead to over-parametrization issues that affect the calibration procedure. Indeed, the presence of swap and basis-swap quotes on many different yield curves is not sufficient, as the market quotes swaption premia only on few yield curves. For instance, even if the Euro market quotes one-, three-, six- and twelve-month swap contracts, liquidly traded swaptions are only those indexed to the three-month (maturity one-year) and the six-month (maturities from two to thirty years) Euribor rates. Swaptions referring to other Euribor tenors or to overnight rates are not actively quoted.

In order to solve such problem [23] introduces a parsimonious model to describe a multi-curve setting by starting from a limited number of (Markov) processes, so as to extend the logic of the HJM framework to describe with a unique family of Markov processes all the curves we are interested in.

## 4.1 *Multiple-Curve Collateralized HJM Framework*

We follow [22, 23] by reformulating their theory under the $\mathbb{Q}^{T;e}$ measure. We model only observed rates as in market model approaches and we consider a common family of processes for all the yield curves of a given currency, so that we are able to build parsimonious yet flexible models. Hence let us summarize the basic requirements the model must fulfill:

(i) existence of OIS rates, which we can describe in terms of instantaneous forward rates $f_t(T; e)$;

(ii) existence of LIBOR rates assigned by the market, typical underlyings of traded derivatives, with associated forwards $F_t(T, x; e)$;

(iii) no arbitrage dynamics of the $f_t(T; e)$ and the $F_t(T, x; e)$ (both being $(T, e)$-forward measure martingales);

(iv) possibility of writing both $f_t(T; e)$ and $F_t(T, x; e)$ as functions of a common family of Markov processes, so that we are able to build parsimonious yet flexible models.

While the first two points are related to the set of financial quantities we are about to model, the last two are conditions we impose on their dynamics, and will be granted by the right choice of model volatilities. Hence, we choose under $\mathbb{Q}^{T;e}$ measure, the following dynamics:

$$
\begin{aligned}
df_t(T;e) &= \sigma_t(T)^* dW_t^{T;e} \\
dF_t(T,x;e) &= (k(T,x) + F_t(T,x;e))\, \Sigma_t(T,x)^* dW_t^{T;e}
\end{aligned}
\tag{7}
$$

where we introduce the families of (stochastic $N$-dimensional) volatility processes $\sigma_t(T)$ and $\Sigma_t(T,x)$, the vector of $N$ independent $\mathbb{Q}^{T;e}$-Brownian motions $W_t^{T;e}$, and the set of deterministic shifts $k(T,x)$, such that $\lim_{x\to 0} xk(T,x) = 1$. This limit condition ensures that the model approaches a standard default- and liquidity-free HJM model when the tenor goes to zero. We bootstrap $f_0(T;e)$ and $F_0(T,x;e)$ from market quotes.

In order to get a model with a reduced number of common driving factors in the spirit of HJM approaches, it is sufficient to conveniently tie together the volatility processes $\sigma_t(T)$ and $\Sigma_t(T,x)$ through a third volatility process $\sigma_t(u,T,x)$.

$$
\sigma_t(T) := \sigma_t(T;T,0)\ , \quad \Sigma_t(T,x) := \int_{T-x}^{T} \sigma_t(u;T,x)\, du. \tag{8}
$$

Under this parametrization the OIS curve dynamics is the very same as the risk-free curve in an ordinary HJM framework. Indeed, we have for linearly compounding forward rates

$$
dE_t(T,x;e) = (1/x + E_t(T,x;e)) \int_{T-x}^{T} \sigma_t(u)^* du\; dW_t^{T;e}.
$$

In the generalized version of the HJM framework proposed by [23] we have an explicit expression for both the collateralized zero-coupon bonds $P_t(T;e)$ and the LIBOR forward rates $F_t(T,x;e)$. The first result is a direct consequence of modeling the OIS curve as the risk-free curve in a standard HJM framework, while the second result can be achieved only if a particular form of the volatilities is selected. We obtain this if we generalize the approach of [28] by introducing the following separability constraint

$$
\begin{aligned}
\sigma_t(u,T,x) &:= h(t)q(u,T,x)g(t,u), \\
g(t,u) &:= \exp\left\{-\int_t^u a(s)ds\right\}\ , \quad q(u;u,0) := Id,
\end{aligned}
\tag{9}
$$

where $h_t$ is an $N \times N$ matrix process, $q(u,T,x)$ is a deterministic $N \times N$ diagonal matrix function, and $a(s)$ is a deterministic $N$-dimensional vector function. The condition on $q(u;T,x)$ being the identity matrix, when $T = u$ ensures that a standard HJM framework holds for collateralized zero-coupon bonds.

We can work out an explicit expression for the LIBOR forward rates, by plugging the expression of the volatilities into Eq. (7). We obtain

$$\log\left(\frac{k(T,x)+F_t(T,x;e)}{k(T,x)+F_0(T,x;e)}\right) \\ = G(t,T-x,T;T,x)^*\left(X_t+Y_t\left(G_0(t,t,T)-\frac{1}{2}G(t,T-x,T;T,x)\right)\right), \tag{10}$$

where the stochastic vector process $X_t$ and the auxiliary matrix process $Y_t$ are defined under the $\mathbb{Q}$ measure as in the ordinary HJM framework

$$X_t^i = \sum_{k=1}^{N}\int_0^t g_i(s,t)\left(h_{ik,s}dW_{k,s}+(h_s^*h_s)_{ik}\int_s^t dy g_k(s,y)\,ds\right) \quad ,i=1\ldots N$$

$$Y_t^{ik} = \int_0^t g_i(s,t)(h_s^*h_s)_{ik}g_k(s,t)ds \quad i,k=1\ldots N$$

and

$$G_0(t,T_0,T_1)=\int_{T_0}^{T_1} g(t,s)ds, \quad G(t,T_0,T_1,T,x)=\int_{T_0}^{T_1} q(s,T,x)g(t,s)ds.$$

It is worth noting that the integral representation of forward LIBOR volatilities given by Eq. (8), together with the common separability constraint given in Eq. (9) are sufficient conditions to ensure the existence of a reconstruction formula for all OIS and LIBOR forward rates based on the very same family of Markov processes (see [3]).

We are interested in some specification of this model, in particular a variant of the Hull and White model (HW), a variant of the Cheyette model (Ch) and the Moreni and Pallavicini model (MP). The HW model [18] is the simplest one, and is obtained choosing

$$h(t)\doteq R\ , \quad q(u,T,x)\doteq Id\ , \quad a(s)\doteq a\ , \quad \kappa(T,x)\doteq\frac{1}{x} \tag{11}$$

where $a$ is a constant vector, and $R$ is the Cholesky decomposition of the correlation matrix that we want our $X_t$ vector to have. In this case we obtain $\sigma_t(u;T,x) = R\cdot e^{-a(u-t)}$, where the exponential is intended to be component-wise. Then we note that $X_t$ is a mean reverting Gaussian process while the $Y_t$ process is deterministic.

In order to model implied volatility smiles, we can add a stochastic volatility process to our model, as shown in [22]. In particular we can obtain a variant of the Ch model ([10]), considering a common square-root process for all the entries of $h$, as in [29]. More precisely we replace $h(t)$ in (11) with $h(t)\doteq\sqrt{v_t}R$. With $a$ and $R$ as before and $v_t$ being a process with the following dynamic:

$$dv_t = \eta\,(1 - v_t)\,dt + \nu_0\left(1 + (\nu_1 - 1)e^{-\nu_2 t}\right)\sqrt{v_t}\,dZ_t\,, \quad v_0 = \bar{v} \tag{12}$$

where $Z_t$ is a Brownian motion correlated to $W_t$. Obtaining as a volatility process $\sigma_t(u; T, x) = \sqrt{v_t}R \cdot e^{-a(u-t)}$.

As the last specification of the framework we consider the MP model which uses a different shift $k(T, x)$, and introduces a dependence on the tenor in the volatility process.

$$h(t) \doteq \sqrt{v_t}R\,, \quad q(u, T, x)^{i,i} \doteq e^{x\eta^i}\,, \quad a(s) \doteq a\,, \quad \kappa(T, x) \doteq \frac{e^{-\gamma x}}{x} \tag{13}$$

With $a$ and $R$ as before and $v_t$ being defined by (12). Here we have for the volatility $\sigma_t(u; T, x) = \sqrt{v_t}R \cdot e^{\eta x - a(u-t)}$.

To better appreciate the difference between the Ch model and the MP model one could compute the quantity

$$\beta_t(x_1, x_2; e) := \frac{1}{x_2}\log\left(\frac{\frac{1}{x_2} + E_t(t + x_2, x_2; e)}{\frac{1}{x_2} + F_t(t + x_2, x_2; e)}\right) - \frac{1}{x_1}\log\left(\frac{\frac{1}{x_1} + E_t(t + x_1, x_1; e)}{\frac{1}{x_1} + F_t(t + x_1, x_1; e)}\right)$$

which represents the time-normalized difference between two forward rates with different tenors and thus can be used as a proxy for the value of a basis swap. We have that in the HW and in the Ch models $\beta_t(x_1, x_2; e)$ is deterministic while in the MP model is a stochastic quantity. This suggests that the MP model should be able to better capture the dynamics of the basis between two rates with different tenors. We refer the reader to [3] for a more detailed analysis of the issue, and to [23] for calibration and valuation examples for the swaptions and cap/floor market.

## 4.2 Numerical Results

We apply our framework to simple but relevant products: an IRS and a basis swap. We analyze the impact of the choice of an interest rate model on the portfolio valuation, in particular we measure the dependency of the price on the correlations between interest-rates and credit spreads, the so-called wrong-way risk. We model the market risks by simulating the following processes in a multiple-curve HJM model under the pricing measure $\mathbb{Q}$. The overnight rate $e_t$ and the LIBOR forward rates $F_t(T; e)$ are simulated according to the dynamics given in Sect. 4.1. Maintaining the same notation of the aforementioned section, we choose $N = 2$, and for our numerical experiments we use a HW model, a Ch model and an MP model, all calibrated to swaption at-the-money volatilities listed on the European market.

As we have already noted, the Ch model introduces a stochastic volatility and hence has an increased number of parameters with respect to the HW model. The MP model aims at better modeling the basis between rates with different tenors, while keeping the model parsimonious in terms of extra parameters with respect to the Ch model. In particular the HW model is able to reproduce the ATM quotes but is not able to correctly reproduce the volatility smile. On the other hand, the introduction of a stochastic volatility process helps in recovering the market data smile and thus the Ch and the MP models have similar results in properly fitting the smile. The detailed results of the calibration are available in [3].

For what concerns the credit part, the default intensities of the investor and the counterparty are given by two CIR++ processes $\lambda^i_t = y^i_t + \psi^i(t)$ under the $\mathbb{Q}^{T;e}$ measure, i.e. they follow

$$dy^i_t = \gamma^i(\mu^i - y^i_t)\,dt + \zeta^i\sqrt{y^i_t}\,dZ^i_t\,, \quad i \in \{I, C\}$$

where the two $Z^i$s are Brownian motions correlated with the $W^{T;e}$s, and they are calibrated to the market data shown in [4]. In particular, two different market settings are used in the numerical examples: the medium risk and the high risk settings. The correlations among the risky factors are induced by correlating the Brownian motions as in [8].

We now analyze the impact of wrong-way risk on the bilateral adjustment, namely CVA plus DVA, of IRS and basis swaps when collateralization is switched off, namely we want to evaluate Eq. (1) when $\alpha_t \doteq 0$. For an extended analysis see [3]. Wrong-way risk is expressed with respect to the correlation between the default intensities and a proxy of market risk, namely the short rate $e_t$.

In Fig. 1 we show the variation of the bilateral adjustment for a ten years IRS receiving a fix rate yearly and paying 6 m Libor twice a year and for a ten years basis swap receiving 3 m Libor plus spread and paying 6 m Libor. It is clear that for a product like the IRS, not subject to the basis dynamic, we have that the big difference among the models is the presence of a stochastic volatility. In fact we can see that the Ch model and the MP model are almost indistinguishable while the results of the HW model are different from the stochastic volatility ones. Moreover we can

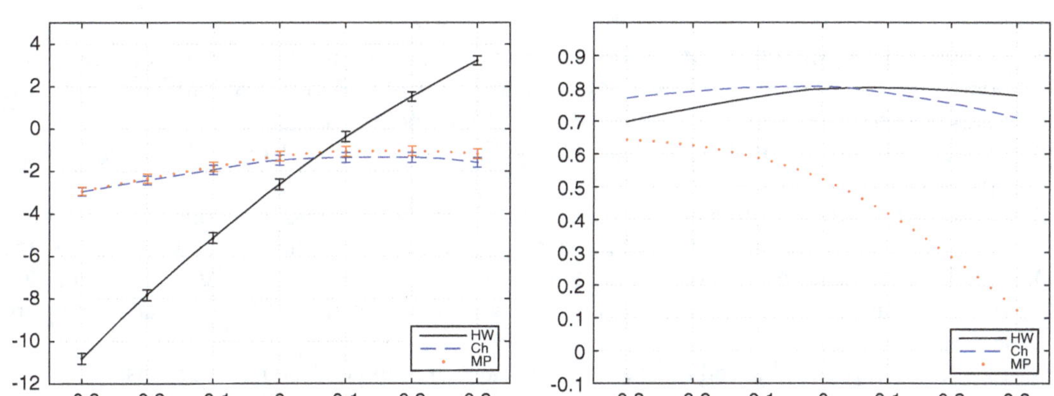


**Fig. 1** Wrong-way risk for different models. On the horizontal axis correlation among credit and market risks; on the vertical axis the bilateral adjustment, namely CVA + DVA, in basis points. *Left panel* a 10y IRS receiving a fix rate and paying 6 m Libor. *Right panel* a 10y basis swap receiving 3 m Libor plus spread and paying 6 m Libor. Montecarlo error is displayed where significant

observe that all the models have the same trend, i.e. the bilateral adjustment grows as correlation increase. In fact this can be explained by the fact that a higher correlation means that the deal will be more profitable when it will be more risky (since we are receiving the fixed rate and paying the floating one), hence the bilateral adjustment will be bigger.

In the case of a basis swap instead, we see that, as said before, the HW model and the Ch model do not have a basis dynamic and hence the curve represented is almost flat. On the other hand the MP model is able to capture the dynamics of the basis and hence we can see that the more the overnight rate is correlated with the credit risk the smaller the bilateral adjustment becomes.

We conclude by pointing out that our analysis will be extended to partially collateralized deals in future work. In such a context funding costs enter the picture in a more comprehensive way. Some initial suggestions in this respect were given in [24].

**Acknowledgements** The KPMG Center of Excellence in Risk Management is acknowledged for organizing the conference "Challenges in Derivatives Markets - Fixed Income Modeling, Valuation Adjustments, Risk Management, and Regulation".

**Open Access** This chapter is distributed under the terms of the Creative Commons Attribution 4.0 International License (http://creativecommons.org/licenses/by/4.0/), which permits use, duplication, adaptation, distribution and reproduction in any medium or format, as long as you give appropriate credit to the original author(s) and the source, a link is provided to the Creative Commons license and any changes made are indicated.

The images or other third party material in this chapter are included in the work's Creative Commons license, unless indicated otherwise in the credit line; if such material is not included in the work's Creative Commons license and the respective action is not permitted by statutory regulation, users will need to obtain permission from the license holder to duplicate, adapt or reproduce the material.

## References

1. Ametrano, F.M., Bianchetti, M.: Bootstrapping the illiquidity: multiple yield curves construction for market coherent forward rates estimation. In: Mercurio, F. (ed.) Modeling Interest Rates: Latest Advances for Derivatives Pricing. Risk Books, London (2009)
2. Bielecki, T., Rutkowski, M.: Credit Risk: Modeling, Valuation and Hedging. Springer Finance. Springer, Berlin (2002)
3. Bormetti, G., Brigo, D., Francischello, M., Pallavicini, A.: Impact of multiple curve dynamics in credit valuation adjustments under collateralization. arXiv preprint arXiv:1507.08779 (2015)
4. Brigo, D., Capponi, A., Pallavicini, A., Papatheodorou, V.: Collateral margining in arbitrage-free counterparty valuation adjustment including re-hypothecation and netting. arXiv preprint arXiv:1101.3926 (2011)
5. Brigo, D., Capponi, A., Pallavicini, A.: Arbitrage-free bilateral counterparty risk valuation under collateralization and application to credit default swaps. Math. Financ. **24**(1), 125–146 (2014)
6. Brigo, D., Francischello, M., Pallavicini, A.: Invariance, existence and uniqueness of solutions of nonlinear valuation PDEs and FBSDEs inclusive of credit risk, collateral and funding costs. arXiv preprint arXiv:1506.00686 (2015). A refined version of this report by the same authors is being published in this same volume

7. Brigo, D., Liu, Q., Pallavicini, A., Sloth, D.: Nonlinear valuation under collateral, credit risk and funding costs: a numerical case study extending Black-Scholes. arXiv preprint arXiv:1404.7314 (2014). A refined version of this report by the same authors is being published in this same volume
8. Brigo, D., Pallavicini, A.: Counterparty risk under correlation between default and interest rates. In: Miller, J., Edelman, D., Appleby, J. (eds.) Numerical Methods for Finance. Chapman Hall, Atlanta (2007)
9. Brigo, D., Pallavicini, A.: Nonlinear consistent valuation of CCP cleared or CSA bilateral trades with initial margins under credit, funding and wrong-way risks. J. Financ. Eng. **1**(1), 1–61 (2014)
10. Cheyette, O.: Markov representation of the Heath–Jarrow–Morton model. Available at SSRN 6073 (1992)
11. Crépey, S., Gerboud, R., Grbac, Z., Ngor, N.: Counterparty risk and funding: the four wings of theTVA. Int. J. Theor. Appl. Financ. **16**(2), 1350006-1–1350006-31 (2013)
12. Crépey, S., Grbac, Z., Nguyen, H.: A multiple-curve HJM model of interbank risk. Math. Financ. Econ. **6**(3), 155–190 (2012)
13. Crépey, S., Grbac, Z., Ngor, N., Skovmand, D.: A Lévy HJM multiple-curve model with application to CVA computation. Quant. Financ. **15**(3), 401–419 (2015)
14. Cuchiero, C., Fontana, C., Gnoatto, A.: A general HJM framework for multiple yield curve modeling. Financ. Stoch. **20**(2), 267–320 (2016)
15. Filipović, D., Trolle, A.B.: The term structure of interbank risk. J. Financ. Eng. **109**(3), 707–733 (2013)
16. Fujii, M., Takahashi, A.: Derivative pricing under asymmetric and imperfect collateralization and CVA. Quant. Financ. **13**(5), 749–768 (2013)
17. Henrard, M.: Interest Rate Modelling in the Multi-Curve Framework: Foundations, Evolution and Implementation. Palgrave Macmillan, Basingstoke (2014)
18. Hull, J., White, A.: Pricing interest-rate-derivative securities. Rev. Financ. Stud. **3**(4), 573–592 (1990)
19. Mercurio, F.: Interest rates and the credit crunch: New formulas and market models. Bloomberg Portfolio Research Paper (2009)
20. Mercurio, F.: LIBOR market models with stochastic basis. Risk Mag. **23**(12), 84–89 (2010)
21. Mercurio, F., Xie, Z.: The basis goes stochastic. Risk Mag. **23**(12), 78–83 (2012)
22. Moreni, N., Pallavicini, A.: Parsimonious multi-curve HJM modelling with stochastic volatility. In: Bianchetti, M., Morini, M. (eds.) Interest Rate Modelling After the Financial Crisis. Risk Books, London (2013)
23. Moreni, N., Pallavicini, A.: Parsimonious HJM modelling for multiple yield curve dynamics. Quant. Financ. **14**(2), 199–210 (2014)
24. Pallavicini, A., Brigo, D.: Interest-rate modelling in collateralized markets: multiple curves, credit-liquidity effects, CCPs. arXiv preprint arXiv:1304.1397 (2013)
25. Pallavicini, A., Perini, D., Brigo, D.: Funding valuation adjustment: FVA consistent with CVA, DVA, WWR, collateral, netting and re-hyphotecation. arXiv preprint arXiv:1112.1521 (2011)
26. Pallavicini, A., Perini, D., Brigo, D.: Funding, collateral and hedging: uncovering the mechanics and the subtleties of funding valuation adjustments. arXiv preprint arXiv:1210.3811 (2012)
27. Pallavicini, A., Tarenghi, M.: Interest-rate modelling with multiple yield curves. Available at SSRN 1629688 (2010)
28. Ritchken, P., Sankarasubramanian, L.: Volatility structures of forward rates and the dynamics of the term structure. Math. Financ. **7**, 157–176 (1995)
29. Trolle, A., Schwartz, E.: A general stochastic volatility model for the pricing of interest rate derivatives. Rev. Financ. Stud. **22**(5), 2007–2057 (2009)

# A Generalized Intensity-Based Framework for Single-Name Credit Risk

**Frank Gehmlich and Thorsten Schmidt**

**Abstract** The intensity of a default time is obtained by assuming that the default indicator process has an absolutely continuous compensator. Here we drop the assumption of absolute continuity with respect to the Lebesgue measure and only assume that the compensator is absolutely continuous with respect to a general $\sigma$-finite measure. This allows for example to incorporate the Merton-model in the generalized intensity-based framework. We propose a class of generalized Merton models and study absence of arbitrage by a suitable modification of the forward rate approach of Heath–Jarrow–Morton (1992). Finally, we study affine term structure models which fit in this class. They exhibit stochastic discontinuities in contrast to the affine models previously studied in the literature.

**Keywords** Credit risk · HJM · Forward-rate · Structural approach · Reduced-form approach · Stochastic discontinuities

## 1 Introduction

The two most common approaches to credit risk modeling are the *structural* approach, pioneered in the seminal work of Merton [23], and the *reduced-form* approach which can be traced back to early works of Jarrow, Lando, and Turnbull [18, 22] and to [1].

Default of a company happens when the company is not able to meet its obligations. In many cases the debt structure of a company is known to the public, such that default happens with positive probability at times which are known a priori. This, however, is excluded in the intensity-based framework and it is the purpose of this article to put forward a generalization which allows to incorporate such effects. Examples in the literature are, e.g., structural models like [13, 14, 23]. The recently

---

F. Gehmlich (✉) · T. Schmidt
Department of Mathematics, University of Freiburg, Eckerstr 1, 79106 Freiburg, Germany
e-mail: gehmlichfrank@gmail.com

T. Schmidt
e-mail: thorsten.schmidt@stochastik.uni-freiburg.de

© The Author(s) 2016

K. Glau et al. (eds.), *Innovations in Derivatives Markets*, Springer Proceedings in Mathematics & Statistics 165, DOI 10.1007/978-3-319-33446-2_13

missed coupon payment by Argentina is an example for such a credit event as well as the default of Greece on the 1st of July 2015.[1]

It is a remarkable observation of [2] that it is possible to extend the reduced-form approach beyond the class of intensity-based models. The authors study a class of first-passage time models under a filtration generated by a Brownian motion and show its use for pricing and modeling credit risky bonds. Our goal is to start with even weaker assumptions on the default time and to allow for jumps in the compensator of the default time at deterministic times. From this general viewpoint it turns out, surprisingly, that previously used HJM approaches lead to arbitrage: the whole term structure is absolutely continuous and cannot compensate for points in time bearing a positive default probability. We propose a suitable extension with an additional term allowing for discontinuities in the term structure at certain random times and derive precise drift conditions for an appropriate no-arbitrage condition. The related article [12] only allows for the special case of finitely many risky times, an assumption which is dropped in this article.

The structure of this article is as follows: in Sect. 2, we introduce the general setting and study drift conditions in an extended HJM-framework which guarantee absence of arbitrage in the bond market. In Sect. 3 we study a class of affine models which are stochastically discontinuous. Section 4 concludes.

## 2 A General Account on Credit Risky Bond Markets

Consider a filtered probability space $(\Omega, \mathscr{A}, \mathbb{G}, P)$ with a filtration $\mathbb{G} = (\mathscr{G}_t)_{t\geq 0}$ (the *general* filtration) satisfying the usual conditions, i.e. it is right-continuous and $\mathscr{G}_0$ contains the $P$-null sets $N_0$ of $\mathscr{A}$. Throughout, the probability measure $P$ denotes the objective measure. As we use tools from stochastic analysis, all appearing filtrations shall satisfy the usual conditions. We follow the notation from [17] and refer to this work for details on stochastic processes which are not laid out here.

The filtration $\mathbb{G}$ contains all available information in the market. The default of a company is public information and we therefore assume that the default time $\tau$ is a $\mathbb{G}$-stopping time. We denote the *default indicator process* $H$ by

$$H_t = 1_{\{t\geq\tau\}}, \quad t \geq 0,$$

such that $H_t = 1_{[\![\tau,\infty[\![}(t)$ is a right-continuous, increasing process. We will also make use of the *survival process* $1 - H = 1_{[\![0,\tau[\![}$. The following remark recalls the essentials of the well-known intensity-based approach.

[1] Argentina's missed coupon payment on \$29 billion debt was voted a credit event by the International Swaps and Derivatives Association, see the announcements in [16, 24]. Regarding the failure of 1.5 Billion EUR of Greece on a scheduled debt repayment to the International Monetary fund, see e.g. [9].

*Remark 1* (*The intensity-based approach*) The intensity-based approach consists of two steps: first, denote by $\mathbb{H} = (\mathscr{H}_t)_{t\geq 0}$ the filtration generated by the default indicator, $\mathscr{H}_t = \sigma(H_s : 0 \leq s \leq t) \vee N_0$, and assume that there exists a sub-filtration $\mathbb{F}$ of $\mathbb{G}$, i.e. $\mathscr{F}_t \subset \mathscr{G}_t$ holds for all $t \geq 0$ such that

$$\mathscr{G}_t = \mathscr{F}_t \vee \mathscr{H}_t, \quad t \geq 0. \tag{1}$$

Viewed from this perspective, $\mathbb{G}$ is obtained from the default information $\mathbb{H}$ by a *progressive enlargement*[2] with the filtration $\mathbb{F}$. This assumption opens the area for the largely developed field of enlargements of filtration with a lot of powerful and quite general results.

Second, the following key assumption specifies the default intensity: assume that there is an $\mathbb{F}$-progressive process $\lambda$, such that

$$P(\tau > t|\mathscr{F}_t) = \exp\Big(-\int_0^t \lambda_s ds\Big), \quad t \geq 0. \tag{2}$$

It is immediate that the inclusion $\mathscr{F}_t \subset \mathscr{G}_t$ is strict under existence of an intensity, i.e. $\tau$ is not an $\mathbb{F}$-stopping time. Arbitrage-free pricing can be achieved via the following result: Let $Y$ be a non-negative random variable. Then, for all $t \geq 0$,

$$E[1_{\{\tau>t\}}Y|\mathscr{G}_t] = 1_{\{\tau>t\}}e^{\int_0^t \lambda_s ds}E[1_{\{\tau>t\}}Y|\mathscr{F}_t].$$

Of course, this result holds also when a pricing measure $Q$ is used instead of $P$. For further literature and details we refer for example to [11], Chap. 12, and to [3].

## 2.1 The Generalized Intensity-Based Framework

The default indicator process $H$ is a bounded, cádlág, and increasing process, hence a submartingale of class (D), that is, the family $(X_T)$ over all stopping times $T$ is uniformly integrable. By the Doob–Meyer decomposition,[3] the process

$$M_t = H_t - \Lambda_t, \quad t \geq 0 \tag{3}$$

is a true martingale where $\Lambda$ denotes the dual $\mathbb{F}$-predictable projection, also called compensator, of $H$. As 1 is an absorbing state, $\Lambda_t = \Lambda_{t\wedge\tau}$. To keep the arising technical difficulties at a minimum, we assume that there is an increasing process $A$ such that

[2]Note that here $\mathbb{G}$ is right-continuous and $P$-complete by assumption which is a priori not guaranteed by (1). One can, however, use the right-continuous extension and we refer to [15] for a precise treatment and for a guide to the related literature.

[3]See [20], Theorem 1.4.10.

$$\Lambda_t = \int_0^{t \wedge \tau} \lambda_s dA(s), \quad t \geq 0, \tag{4}$$

with a non-negative and predictable process $\lambda$. The process $\lambda$ is called *generalized intensity* and we refer to Chap. VIII.4 of [5] for a more detailed treatment of generalized intensities (or, equivalently, dual predictable projections) in the context of point processes.

Note that with $\Delta M \leq 1$ we have that $\Delta\Lambda = \lambda_s \Delta A(s) \leq 1$. Whenever $\lambda_s \Delta A(s) > 0$, there is a positive probability that the company defaults at time $s$. We call such times *risky times*, i.e. predictable times having a positive probability of a default occurring right at that time. Note that under our assumption (4), all risky times are deterministic. The relationship between $\Delta\Lambda(s)$ and the default probability at time $s$ will be clarified in Example 3.

## 2.2 An Extension of the HJM Approach

A credit risky bond with maturity $T$ is a contingent claim promising to pay one unit of currency at $T$. The price of the bond with maturity $T$ at time $t \leq T$ is denoted by $P(t, T)$. If no default occurred prior to or at $T$ we have that $P(T, T) = 1$. We will consider zero recovery, i.e. the bond loses its total value at default, such that $P(t, T) = 0$ on $\{t \geq \tau\}$. The family of stochastic processes $\{(P(t, T)_{0 \leq t \leq T}), T \geq 0\}$ describes the evolution of the *term structure* $T \mapsto P(., T)$ over time.

Besides the bonds there is a *numéraire* $X^0$, which is a strictly positive, adapted process. We make the weak assumption that $\log X^0$ is absolutely continuous, i.e. $X_t^0 = \exp(\int_0^t r_s ds)$ with a progressively measurable process $r$, called the short rate. For practical applications one would use the overnight index swap (OIS) rate for constructing such a numéraire.

The aim of the following is to extend the HJM approach in an appropriate way to the generalized intensity-based framework in order to obtain arbitrage-free bond prices. First approaches in this direction were [7, 25] and a rich source of literature is again [3]. Absence of arbitrage in such an infinite dimensional market can be described in terms of no asymptotic free lunch (NAFL) or the more economically meaningful no asymptotic free lunch with vanishing risk, see [6, 21].

Consider a pricing measure $Q^* \sim P$. Our intention is to find conditions which render $Q^*$ an equivalent local martingale measure. In the following, only occasionally the measure $P$ will be used, such that from now on, all appearing terms (like martingales, almost sure properties, etc.) are to be considered with respect to $Q^*$.

To ensure that the subsequent analysis is meaningful, we make the following technical assumption.

**Assumption 2.1** The generalized default intensity $\lambda$ is non-negative, predictable, and $A$-integrable on $[0, T^*]$:

$$\int_0^{T^*} \lambda_s dA(s) < \infty, \quad Q^*\text{-a.s.}$$

Moreover, $A$ has vanishing singular part, i.e.

$$A(t) = t + \sum_{0<s\le t} \Delta A(s). \tag{5}$$

The representation (5) of $A$ is without loss of generality: indeed, if the continuous part $A^c$ is absolutely continuous, i.e. $A^c(t) = \int_0^t a(s)ds$, replacing $\lambda_s$ by $\lambda_s a(s)$ gives the compensator of $H$ with respect to $\tilde{A}$ whose continuous part is $t$.

Next, we aim at building an arbitrage-free framework for bond prices. In the generalized intensity-based framework, the (HJM) approach does allow for arbitrage opportunities at risky times. We therefore consider the following generalization: consider a $\sigma$-finite (deterministic) measure $\nu$. We could be general on $\nu$, allowing for an absolutely continuous, a singular continuous, and a pure-jump part. However, for simplicity, we leave the singular continuous part aside and assume that

$$\nu = \nu^{ac} + \nu^d$$

where $\nu^{ac}(ds) = ds$ and $\nu^d$ distributes mass only to points, i.e. $\nu^d(A) = \sum_{i\ge1} w_i\, \delta_{u_i}(A)$, for $0 < u_1 < u_2 < \cdots$ and positive weights $w_i > 0$, $i \ge 1$; here $\delta_u$ denotes the Dirac measure at $u$. Moreover, we assume that defaultable bond prices are given by

$$\begin{aligned} P(t,T) &= \mathbb{1}_{\{\tau>t\}} \exp\left( - \int_t^T f(t,u)\nu(du) \right) \\ &= \mathbb{1}_{\{\tau>t\}} \exp\left( - \int_t^T f(t,u)du - \sum_{i\ge1} \mathbb{1}_{\{u_i\in(t,T]\}} w_i f(t,u_i) \right), \quad 0 \le t \le T \le T^*. \end{aligned} \tag{6}$$

The sum in the last line gives the extension over the (HJM) approach which allows us to deal with risky times in an arbitrage-free way.

The family of processes $(f(t,T))_{0\le t\le T}$ for $T \in [0,T^*]$ are assumed to be Itô processes satisfying

$$f(t,T) = f(0,T) + \int_0^t a(s,T)ds + \int_0^t b(s,T)\cdot dW_s \tag{7}$$

with an $n$-dimensional $Q^*$-Brownian motion $W$.

Denote by $\mathscr{B}$ the Borel $\sigma$-field over $\mathbb{R}$.

missed coupon payment by Argentina is an example for such a credit event as well as the default of Greece on the 1st of July 2015.[1]

It is a remarkable observation of [2] that it is possible to extend the reduced-form approach beyond the class of intensity-based models. The authors study a class of first-passage time models under a filtration generated by a Brownian motion and show its use for pricing and modeling credit risky bonds. Our goal is to start with even weaker assumptions on the default time and to allow for jumps in the compensator of the default time at deterministic times. From this general viewpoint it turns out, surprisingly, that previously used HJM approaches lead to arbitrage: the whole term structure is absolutely continuous and cannot compensate for points in time bearing a positive default probability. We propose a suitable extension with an additional term allowing for discontinuities in the term structure at certain random times and derive precise drift conditions for an appropriate no-arbitrage condition. The related article [12] only allows for the special case of finitely many risky times, an assumption which is dropped in this article.

The structure of this article is as follows: in Sect. 2, we introduce the general setting and study drift conditions in an extended HJM-framework which guarantee absence of arbitrage in the bond market. In Sect. 3 we study a class of affine models which are stochastically discontinuous. Section 4 concludes.

## 2 A General Account on Credit Risky Bond Markets

Consider a filtered probability space $(\Omega, \mathscr{A}, \mathbb{G}, P)$ with a filtration $\mathbb{G} = (\mathscr{G}_t)_{t \geq 0}$ (the *general* filtration) satisfying the usual conditions, i.e. it is right-continuous and $\mathscr{G}_0$ contains the $P$-null sets $N_0$ of $\mathscr{A}$. Throughout, the probability measure $P$ denotes the objective measure. As we use tools from stochastic analysis, all appearing filtrations shall satisfy the usual conditions. We follow the notation from [17] and refer to this work for details on stochastic processes which are not laid out here.

The filtration $\mathbb{G}$ contains all available information in the market. The default of a company is public information and we therefore assume that the default time $\tau$ is a $\mathbb{G}$-stopping time. We denote the *default indicator process* $H$ by

$$H_t = 1_{\{t \geq \tau\}}, \quad t \geq 0,$$

such that $H_t = 1_{[\![\tau,\infty[\![}(t)$ is a right-continuous, increasing process. We will also make use of the *survival process* $1 - H = 1_{[\![0,\tau[\![}$. The following remark recalls the essentials of the well-known intensity-based approach.

[1] Argentina's missed coupon payment on \$29 billion debt was voted a credit event by the International Swaps and Derivatives Association, see the announcements in [16, 24]. Regarding the failure of 1.5 Billion EUR of Greece on a scheduled debt repayment to the International Monetary fund, see e.g. [9].

*Remark 1* (*The intensity-based approach*) The intensity-based approach consists of two steps: first, denote by $\mathbb{H} = (\mathcal{H}_t)_{t\geq 0}$ the filtration generated by the default indicator, $\mathcal{H}_t = \sigma(H_s : 0 \leq s \leq t) \vee N_0$, and assume that there exists a sub-filtration $\mathbb{F}$ of $\mathbb{G}$, i.e. $\mathcal{F}_t \subset \mathcal{G}_t$ holds for all $t \geq 0$ such that

$$\mathcal{G}_t = \mathcal{F}_t \vee \mathcal{H}_t, \quad t \geq 0. \tag{1}$$

Viewed from this perspective, $\mathbb{G}$ is obtained from the default information $\mathbb{H}$ by a *progressive enlargement*[2] with the filtration $\mathbb{F}$. This assumption opens the area for the largely developed field of enlargements of filtration with a lot of powerful and quite general results.

Second, the following key assumption specifies the default intensity: assume that there is an $\mathbb{F}$-progressive process $\lambda$, such that

$$P(\tau > t|\mathcal{F}_t) = \exp\Big(-\int_0^t \lambda_s ds\Big), \quad t \geq 0. \tag{2}$$

It is immediate that the inclusion $\mathcal{F}_t \subset \mathcal{G}_t$ is strict under existence of an intensity, i.e. $\tau$ is not an $\mathbb{F}$-stopping time. Arbitrage-free pricing can be achieved via the following result: Let $Y$ be a non-negative random variable. Then, for all $t \geq 0$,

$$E[1_{\{\tau>t\}}Y|\mathcal{G}_t] = 1_{\{\tau>t\}}e^{\int_0^t \lambda_s ds}E[1_{\{\tau>t\}}Y|\mathcal{F}_t].$$

Of course, this result holds also when a pricing measure $Q$ is used instead of $P$. For further literature and details we refer for example to [11], Chap. 12, and to [3].

## 2.1 The Generalized Intensity-Based Framework

The default indicator process $H$ is a bounded, cádlág, and increasing process, hence a submartingale of class (D), that is, the family $(X_T)$ over all stopping times $T$ is uniformly integrable. By the Doob–Meyer decomposition,[3] the process

$$M_t = H_t - \Lambda_t, \quad t \geq 0 \tag{3}$$

is a true martingale where $\Lambda$ denotes the dual $\mathbb{F}$-predictable projection, also called compensator, of $H$. As 1 is an absorbing state, $\Lambda_t = \Lambda_{t\wedge\tau}$. To keep the arising technical difficulties at a minimum, we assume that there is an increasing process $A$ such that

[2]Note that here $\mathbb{G}$ is right-continuous and $P$-complete by assumption which is a priori not guaranteed by (1). One can, however, use the right-continuous extension and we refer to [15] for a precise treatment and for a guide to the related literature.

[3]See [20], Theorem 1.4.10.

**Assumption 2.2** We require the following technical assumptions:

(i) the initial forward curve is measurable, and integrable on $[0, T^*]$:

$$\int_0^{T^*} |f(0,u)| < \infty, \quad Q^*\text{-a.s.},$$

(ii) the *drift parameter* $a(\omega, s, t)$ is $\mathbb{R}$-valued $\mathscr{O} \otimes \mathscr{B}$-measurable and integrable on $[0, T^*]$:

$$\int_0^{T^*} \int_0^{T^*} |a(s,u)| ds\, \nu(du) < \infty, \quad Q^*\text{-a.s.},$$

(iii) the *volatility parameter* $b(\omega, s, t)$ is $\mathbb{R}^n$-valued, $\mathscr{O} \otimes \mathscr{B}$-measurable, and

$$\sup_{s,t \le T^*} \| b(s,t) \| < \infty, \quad Q^*\text{-a.s.}$$

(iv) it holds that

$$0 \le \lambda(u_i) \Delta A(u_i) < w_i, \quad i \ge 1.$$

Set

$$\begin{aligned} \bar{a}(t,T) &= \int_t^T a(t,u)\nu(du), \\ \bar{b}(t,T) &= \int_t^T b(t,u)\nu(du), \\ H'(t) &= \int_0^t \lambda_s ds - \sum_{u_i \le t} \log\left(\frac{w_i - \lambda_{u_i} \Delta A(u_i)}{w_i}\right). \end{aligned} \tag{8}$$

The following proposition gives the desired drift condition in the generalized Merton models.

**Theorem 1** *Assume that Assumptions 2.1 and 2.2 hold. Then $Q^*$ is an ELMM if and only if the following conditions hold: $\{s : \Delta A(s) \neq 0\} \subset \{u_1, u_2, \ldots\}$, and*

$$\int_0^t f(s,s)\nu(ds) = \int_0^t r_s ds + H'(t), \tag{9}$$

$$\bar{a}(t,T) = \frac{1}{2} \| \bar{b}(t,T) \|^2, \tag{10}$$

*for $0 \le t \le T \le T^*$ $dQ^* \otimes dt$-almost surely on $\{t < \tau\}$.*

The first condition, (9), can be split in the continuous and pure-jump part, such that (9) is equivalent to

$$f(t,t) = r_s + \lambda_s$$
$$f(t,u_i) = \log \frac{w_i}{w_i - \lambda(u_i)\Delta A(u_i)} \geq 0.$$

The second relation states explicitly the connection of the forward rate at a risky time $u_i$ to the probability $Q^*(\tau = u_i|\mathscr{F}_{u_i-})$, given that $\tau \geq u_i$, of course. It simplifies moreover, if $\Delta A(u_i) = w_i$ to

$$f(t,u_i) = -\log(1 - \lambda(u_i)). \tag{11}$$

For the proof we first provide the canonical decomposition of

$$J(t,T) := \int_t^T f(t,u)\nu(du), \quad 0 \leq t \leq T.$$

**Lemma 1** *Assume that Assumption 2.2 holds. Then, for each* $T \in [0, T^*]$ *the process* $(J(t,T))_{0\leq t\leq T}$ *is a special semimartingale and*

$$J(t,T) = \int_0^T f(0,u)\nu(du) + \int_0^t \bar{a}(u,T)du + \int_0^t \bar{b}(u,T)dW_u - \int_0^t f(u,u)\nu(du).$$

*Proof* Using the stochastic Fubini Theorem (as in [26]), we obtain

$$\begin{aligned}
J(t,T) &= \int_t^T \left( f(0,u) + \int_0^t a(s,u)ds + \int_0^t b(s,u)dW_s \right)\nu(du) \\
&= \int_0^T f(0,u)\nu(du) + \int_0^t \int_s^T a(s,u)\nu(du)ds + \int_0^t \int_s^T b(s,u)\nu(du)dW_s \\
&\quad - \int_0^t f(0,u)\nu(du) - \int_0^t \int_s^t a(s,u)\nu(du)ds - \int_0^t \int_s^t b(s,u)\nu(du)dW_s \\
&= \int_0^T f(0,u)\nu(du) + \int_0^t \bar{a}(s,T)ds + \int_0^t \bar{b}(s,T)dW_s \\
&\quad - \int_0^t \left( f(0,u) - \int_0^u a(s,u)ds - \int_0^u b(s,u)dW_s \right)\nu(du),
\end{aligned}$$

and the claim follows.

*Proof* (*Proof of Theorem 1*) Set, $E(t) = 1_{\{\tau>t\}}$, and $F(t,T) = \exp\Big(-\int_t^T f(t,u)$ $\nu(du)\Big)$, such that $P(t,T) = E(t)F(t,T)$. Integration by parts yields that

$$dP(t,T) = F(t-,T)dE(t) + E(t-)dF(t,T) + d[E, F(.,T)]_t =: (1') + (2') + (3'). \tag{12}$$

In view of (1′), we obtain from (4), that

$$E(t) + \int_0^{t\wedge\tau} \lambda_s dA(s) =: M_t^1 \tag{13}$$

is a martingale. Regarding (2′), note that from Lemma 1 we obtain by Itô's formula that

$$\begin{aligned} \frac{dF(t,T)}{F(t-,T)} &= \left( f(t,t) - \bar{a}(t,T) + \frac{1}{2} \parallel \bar{b}(t,T) \parallel^2 \right) dt \\ &\quad + \sum_{i\geq 0} \left(e^{f(t,t)} - 1\right) w_i \delta_{u_i}(dt) + dM_t^2, \end{aligned} \tag{14}$$

with a local martingale $M^2$. For the remaining term (3′), note that

$$\begin{aligned} \sum_{0<s\leq t} \Delta E(s) \Delta F(s,T) &= \int_0^t F(s-,T)(e^{f(s,s)} - 1)\nu(\{s\}) dE(s) \\ &= \int_0^t F(s-,T)(e^{f(s,s)} - 1)\nu(\{s\}) dM_s^1 \\ &\quad - \int_0^{t\wedge\tau} F(s-,T)(e^{f(s,s)} - 1)\nu(\{s\})\lambda_s dA(s). \end{aligned} \tag{15}$$

Inserting (14) and (15) into (12) we obtain

$$\begin{aligned} \frac{dP(t,T)}{P(t-,T)} &= -\lambda_t dA(t) \\ &\quad + \left( f(t,t) - \bar{a}(t,T) + \frac{1}{2} \parallel \bar{b}(t,T) \parallel^2 \right) dt \\ &\quad + \sum_{i\geq 0} \left(e^{f(t,t)} - 1\right) w_i \delta_{u_i}(dt) \\ &\quad - \int_{\mathbb{R}} \nu(\{t\})(e^{f(t,t)} - 1)\lambda_t dA(t) + dM_t^3 \end{aligned}$$

with a local martingale $M^3$. We obtain a $Q^*$-local martingale if and only if the drift vanishes. Next, we can separate between absolutely continuous and discrete part. The absolutely continuous part yields (10) and $f(t,t) = r_t + \lambda_t \; dQ^* \otimes dt$-almost surely. It remains to compute the discontinuous part, which is given by

$$\sum_{i:u_i\leq t} P(u_i-,T)(e^{f(u_i,u_i)} - 1)w_i - \sum_{0<s\leq t} P(s-,T)e^{f(s,s)}\lambda_s \Delta A(s),$$

for $0 \le t \le T \le T^*$. This yields $\{s : \Delta A(s) \ne 0\} \subset \{u_1, u_2, \dots\}$. The discontinuous part vanishes if and only if

$$1_{\{u_i \le T^* \wedge T\}} e^{-f(u_i, u_i)} w_i = 1_{\{u_i \le T^* \wedge T\}} \Big( w_i - \lambda_{u_i} \Delta A(u_i) \Big), \quad i \ge 1,$$

which is equivalent to

$$1_{\{u_i \le T^* \wedge T\}} f(u_i, u_i) = -\, 1_{\{u_i \le T^* \wedge T\}} \log \frac{w_i - \lambda_{u_i} \Delta A(u_i)}{w_i}, \quad i \ge 1.$$

We obtain (9) and the claim follows.

*Example 1* (*The Merton model*) The paper [23] considers a simple capital structure of a firm, consisting only of equity and a zero-coupon bond with maturity $U > 0$. The firm defaults at $U$ if the total market value of its assets is not sufficient to cover the liabilities.

We are interested in setting up an arbitrage-free market for credit derivatives and consider a market of defaultable bonds $P(t, T), 0 \le t \le T \le T^*$ with $0 < U \le T^*$ as basis for more complex derivatives. In a stylized form the Merton model can be represented by a Brownian motion $W$ denoting the normalized logarithm of the firm's assets, a constant $K > 0$ and the default time

$$\tau = \begin{cases} U & \text{if } W_U \le K \\ \infty & \text{otherwise.} \end{cases}$$

Assume for simplicity a constant interest rate $r$ and let $\mathbb{F}$ be the filtration generated by $W$. Then $P(t, T) = e^{-r(T-t)}$ whenever $T < U$ because these bonds do not carry default risk. On the other hand, for $t < U \le T$,

$$P(t, T) = e^{-r(T-t)} E^*[1_{\{\tau > T\}} | \mathscr{F}_t] = e^{-r(T-t)} E^*[1_{\{\tau = \infty\}} | \mathscr{F}_t] = e^{-r(T-t)} \Phi\left( \frac{W_t - K}{\sqrt{U - t}} \right),$$

where $\Phi$ denotes the cumulative distribution function of a standard normal random variable and $E^*$ denotes the expectation with respect to $Q^*$. For $t \to U$ we recover $P(U, U) = 1_{\{\tau = \infty\}}$. The derivation of representation (6) with $\nu(du) := du + \delta_U(du)$ is straightforward. A simple calculation with

$$P(t, T) = 1_{\{\tau > t\}} \exp\left( - \int_t^T f(t, u) du - f(t, U) 1_{\{t < U \le T\}} \right) \tag{16}$$

yields $f(t, T) = r$ for $T \ne U$ and

$$f(t, U) = -\log \Phi\left( \frac{W_t - K}{\sqrt{U - t}} \right).$$

By Itô's formula we obtain

$$b(t,U) = -\frac{\varphi\left(\frac{W_t-K}{\sqrt{U-t}}\right)}{\Phi\left(\frac{W_t-K}{\sqrt{U-t}}\right)}(U-t)^{-1/2},$$

and indeed, $a(t,U) = \frac{1}{2}b^2(t,U)$. Note that the conditions for Proposition 1 hold and, the market consisting of the bonds $P(t,T)$ satisfies NAFL, as expected. More flexible models of arbitrage-free bond prices can be obtained if the market filtration $\mathbb{F}$ is allowed to be more general, as we show in Sect. 3 on affine generalized Merton models.

*Example 2* (*An extension of the Black–Cox model*) The model suggested in [4] uses a first-passage time approach to model credit risk. Default happens at the first time, when the firm value falls below a pre-specified boundary, the default boundary. We consider a stylized version of this approach and continue the Example 1. Extending the original approach, we include a zero-coupon bond with maturity $U$. The reduction of the firm value at $U$ is equivalent to considering a default boundary with an upward jump at that time. Hence, we consider a Brownian motion $W$ and the default boundary

$$D(t) = D(0) + K1_{\{U \geq t\}}, \quad t \geq 0,$$

with $D(0) < 0$, and let default be the first time when $W$ hits $D$, i.e.

$$\tau = \inf\{t \geq 0 : W_t \leq D(t)\}$$

with the usual convention that $\inf \emptyset = \infty$. The following lemma computes the default probability in this setting and the forward rates are directly obtained from this result together with (16). The filtration $\mathbb{G} = \mathbb{F}$ is given by the natural filtration of the Brownian motion $W$ after completion. Denote the random sets

$$\Delta_1 := \left\{(x,y) \in \mathbb{R}^2 : x\sqrt{T-U} \leq D(U) - \left(y\sqrt{U-t} + W_t\right), y\sqrt{U-t} + W_t > D(0)\right\}$$

$$\Delta_2 := \left\{(x,y) \in \mathbb{R}^2 : x\sqrt{T-U} \leq D(U) - \left(y\sqrt{U-t} + 2D(0) - W_t\right), \right.$$
$$\left. y\sqrt{U-t} + D(0) - W_t > 0\right\}.$$

**Lemma 2** *Let $D(0) < 0$, $U > 0$ and $D(U) \geq D(0)$. For $0 \leq t < U$, it holds on $\{\tau > t\}$, that*

$$P(\tau > T|\mathscr{F}_t) = 1 - 2\Phi\left(\frac{D(0) - W_t}{\sqrt{T-t}}\right) - 1_{\{T \geq U\}}2(\Phi_2(\Delta_1) - \Phi_2(\Delta_2)), \quad (17)$$

*where $\Phi_2$ is the distribution of a two-dimensional standard normal distribution and the sets $\Delta_t = \Delta_t(D)$, $t \geq U$ are given by*

$$\Delta_t = \Big\{(x, y) \in \mathbb{R}^2 : x\sqrt{T-U} + y\sqrt{U} \le -D(U), \Big\}.$$

*For* $t \ge U$ *it holds on* $\{\tau > t\}$, *that*

$$P(\tau > T|\mathscr{F}_t) = 1 - 2\Phi\Big(\frac{D(U) - W_t}{\sqrt{T-t}}\Big).$$

*Proof* The first part of (17) where $T < U$ follows directly from the reflection principle and the property that $W$ has independent and stationary increments. Next, consider $0 \le t < U \le T$. Then, on $\{W_U > D(U)\}$,

$$P(\inf_{[U,T]} W > D(U)|\mathscr{F}_U) = 1 - 2\Phi\Big(\frac{D(U) - W_U}{\sqrt{T-U}}\Big). \tag{18}$$

Moreover, on $\{W_t > D(0)\}$ it holds for $x > D(0)$ that

$$\begin{aligned}
P(\inf_{[0,U]} W > D(0), W_U > x|\mathscr{F}_t) &= P(W_U > x|\mathscr{F}_t) - P(W_U < x, \inf_{[0,U]} W \le D(0)|\mathscr{F}_t) \\
&= \Phi\Big(\frac{W_t - x}{\sqrt{U-t}}\Big) - \Phi\Big(\frac{2D(0) - x - W_t}{\sqrt{U-t}}\Big).
\end{aligned}$$

Hence, $E[g(W_U)1_{\{\inf_{[0,U]} W > D(0)\}}|\mathscr{F}_t] = 1_{\{\inf_{[0,t]} W > D(0)\}} \int_{D(0)}^{\infty} g(x) f_t(x)dx$ with density

$$f_t(x) = 1_{\{x > D(0)\}} \frac{1}{\sqrt{U-t}} \Big[\phi\Big(\frac{W_t - x}{\sqrt{U-t}}\Big) - \phi\Big(\frac{2D(0) - x - W_t}{\sqrt{U-t}}\Big)\Big].$$

Together with (18) this yields on $\{\inf_{[0,t]} W > D(0)\}$

$$\begin{aligned}
P(\inf_{[0,T]} (W - D) > 0|\mathscr{F}_t) &= \int_{D(0)}^{\infty} \Big[1 - 2\Phi\Big(\frac{D(U) - x}{\sqrt{T-U}}\Big)\Big] f_t(x)dx \\
&= P(\inf_{[t,T]} W > D(0)|\mathscr{F}_t) - 2\int_{D(0)}^{\infty} \Phi\Big(\frac{D(U) - x}{\sqrt{T-U}}\Big) f_t(x)dx.
\end{aligned}$$

It remains to compute the integral. Regarding the first part, letting $\xi$ and $\eta$ be independent and standard normal, we obtain that

$$\begin{aligned}
&\int_{D(0)}^{\infty} \Phi\Big(\frac{D(U) - x}{\sqrt{T-U}}\Big) \frac{1}{\sqrt{U-t}} \phi\Big(\frac{x - W_t}{\sqrt{U-t}}\Big) dx \\
&= P_t\Big(\sqrt{T-U}\xi \le D(U) - (\sqrt{U-t}\eta + W_t), \sqrt{U-t}\eta + W_t > D(0)\Big) \\
&= \Phi_2(\Delta_1),
\end{aligned}$$

where we abbreviate $P_t(\cdot) = P(\cdot|\mathscr{F}_t)$. In a similar way,

$$\int_{D(0)}^{\infty} \Phi\Big(\frac{D(U)-x}{\sqrt{T-U}}\Big)\frac{1}{\sqrt{U-t}}\phi\Big(\frac{x-(2D(0)-W_t)}{\sqrt{U-t}}\Big)dx$$
$$= P_t\Big(\sqrt{T-U}\xi \le D(U) - (\sqrt{U-t}\eta + 2D(0) - W_t), \sqrt{U-t}\eta + D(0) - W_t > 0\Big)$$
$$= \Phi_2(\Delta_2)$$

and we conclude.

## 3 Affine Models in the Generalized Intensity-Based Framework

Affine processes are a well-known tool in the financial literature and one reason for this is their analytical tractability. In this section we closely follow [12] and shortly state the appropriate affine models which fit the generalized intensity framework. For proofs, we refer the reader to this paper.

The main point is that affine processes in the literature are assumed to be *stochastically continuous* (see [8, 10]). Due to the discontinuities introduced in the generalized intensity-based framework, we propose to consider *piecewise continuous affine processes*.

*Example 3* Consider a non-negative integrable function $\lambda$, a constant $\lambda' \ge 0$ and a deterministic time $u > 0$. Set

$$K(t) = \int_0^t \lambda(s)ds + 1_{\{t\ge u\}}\kappa, \quad t \ge 0.$$

Let the default time $\tau$ be given by $\tau = \inf\{t \ge 0 : K_t \ge \zeta\}$ with a standard exponential-random variable $\zeta$. Then $P(\tau = u) = 1 - e^{-\kappa} =: \lambda'$. Considering $\nu(ds) = ds + \delta_u(ds)$ with $u_1 = u$ and $w_1 = 1$, we are in the setup of the previous section. The drift condition (9) holds, if

$$f(u,u) = -\log(1-\lambda') = \kappa.$$

Note, however, that $K$ is not the compensator of $H$. Indeed, the compensator of $H$ equals $\Lambda_t = \int_0^{t\wedge\tau} \lambda(s)ds + 1_{\{t\ge u\}}\lambda'$, see [19] for general results in this direction.

The purpose of this section is to give a suitable extension of the above example involving affine processes. Recall that we consider a $\sigma$-finite measure

$$\nu(du) = du + \sum_{i\ge 1} w_i \delta_{u_i}(du),$$

as well as $A(u) = u + \sum_{i \geq 1} 1_{\{u \geq u_i\}}$. The idea is to consider an affine process $X$ and study arbitrage-free doubly stochastic term structure models where the compensator $\Lambda$ of the default indicator process $H = 1_{\{\cdot \leq \tau\}}$ is given by

$$\Lambda_t = \int_0^t \left(\phi_0(s) + \psi_0(s)^\top \cdot X_s\right) ds + \sum_{i \geq 1} 1_{\{t \geq u_i\}} \left(1 - e^{-\phi_i - \psi_i^\top \cdot X_{u_i}}\right). \tag{19}$$

Note that by continuity of $X$, $\Lambda_t(\omega) < \infty$ for almost all $\omega$. To ensure that $\Lambda$ is non-decreasing we will require that $\phi_0(s) + \psi_0(s)^\top \cdot X_s \geq 0$ for all $s \geq 0$ and $\phi_i + \psi_i^\top \cdot X_{u_i} \geq 0$ for all $i \geq 1$.

Consider a state space in canonical form $\mathscr{X} = \mathbb{R}^m_{\geq 0} \times \mathbb{R}^n$ for integers $m, n \geq 0$ with $m + n = d$ and a $d$-dimensional Brownian motion $W$. Let $\mu$ and $\sigma$ be defined on $\mathscr{X}$ by

$$\mu(x) = \mu_0 + \sum_{i=1}^d x_i \mu_i, \tag{20}$$

$$\frac{1}{2}\sigma(x)^\top \sigma(x) = \sigma_0 + \sum_{i=1}^d x_i \sigma_i, \tag{21}$$

where $\mu_0, \mu_i \in \mathbb{R}^d$, $\sigma_0, \sigma_i \in \mathbb{R}^{d \times d}$, for all $i \in \{1, \ldots, d\}$. We assume that the parameters $\mu^i$, $\sigma^i$, $i = 0, \ldots, d$ are admissible in the sense of Theorem 10.2 in [11]. Then the continuous, unique strong solution of the stochastic differential equation

$$dX_t = \mu(X_t)dt + \sigma(X_t)dW_t, \quad X_0 = x, \tag{22}$$

is an *affine* process $X$ on the state space $\mathscr{X}$, see Chap. 10 in [11] for a detailed exposition.

We call a bond-price model *affine* if there exist functions $A : \mathbb{R}_{\geq 0} \times \mathbb{R}_{\geq 0} \to \mathbb{R}$, $B : \mathbb{R}_{\geq 0} \times \mathbb{R}_{\geq 0} \to \mathbb{R}^d$ such that

$$P(t, T) = 1_{\{\tau > t\}} e^{-A(t,T) - B(t,T)^\top \cdot X_t}, \tag{23}$$

for $0 \leq t \leq T \leq T^*$. We assume that $A(., T)$ and $B(., T)$ are right-continuous. Moreover, we assume that $t \mapsto A(t, .)$ and $t \mapsto B(t, .)$ are differentiable from the right and denote by $\partial_t^+$ the right derivative. For the convenience of the reader we state the following proposition giving sufficient conditions for absence of arbitrage in an affine generalized intensity-based setting. It extends [12] where only finitely many risky times were treated.

**Proposition 1** *Assume that* $\phi_0 : \mathbb{R}_{\geq 0} \to \mathbb{R}$, $\psi_0 : \mathbb{R}_{\geq 0} \to \mathbb{R}^d$ *are continuous,* $\psi_0(s) + \psi_0(s)^\top \cdot x \geq 0$ *for all* $s \geq 0$ *and* $x \in \mathscr{X}$ *and the constants* $\phi_i \in \mathbb{R}$ *and* $\psi_i \in \mathbb{R}^d$, $i \geq 1$ *satisfy* $\phi_i + \psi_i^\top \cdot x \geq 0$ *for all* $1 \leq i \leq n$ *and* $x \in \mathscr{X}$ *as well as* $\sum_{i \geq 1} |w_i|(|\phi_i| + |\psi_{i,1}| + \cdots + |\psi_{i,d}|) < \infty$. *Moreover, let the functions* $A : \mathbb{R}_{\geq 0} \times \mathbb{R}_{\geq 0} \to \mathbb{R}$ *and*

*$B : \mathbb{R}_{\geq 0} \times \mathbb{R}_{\geq 0} \to \mathbb{R}^d$ be the unique solutions of*

$$\begin{aligned} A(T,T) &= 0 \\ A(u_i,T) &= A(u_i-,T) - \phi_i w_i \\ -\partial_t^+ A(t,T) &= \phi_0(t) + \mu_0^\top \cdot B(t,T) - B(t,T)^\top \cdot \sigma_0 \cdot B(t,T), \end{aligned} \tag{24}$$

*and*

$$\begin{aligned} B(T,T) &= 0 \\ B_k(u_i,T) &= B_k(u_i-,T) - \psi_{i,k} w_i \\ -\partial_t^+ B_k(t,T) &= \psi_{0,k}(t) + \mu_k^\top \cdot B(t,T) - B(t,T)^\top \cdot \sigma_k \cdot B(t,T), \end{aligned} \tag{25}$$

*for $0 \leq t \leq T$. Then, the doubly-stochastic affine model given by (19) and (23) satisfies NAFL.*

*Proof* By construction,

$$\begin{aligned} A(t,T) &= \int_t^T a'(t,u)du + \sum_{i:u_i \in (t,T]} \phi_i w_i \\ B(t,T) &= \int_t^T b'(t,u)du + \sum_{i:u_i \in (t,T]} \psi_i w_i \end{aligned}$$

with suitable functions $a'$ and $b'$ and $a'(t,t) = \phi_0(t)$ as well as $b'(t,t) = \psi_0(t)$. A comparison of (23) with (6) yields the following: on the one hand, for $T = u_i \in \mathscr{U}$, we obtain $f(t,u_i) = \phi_i + \psi_i^\top \cdot X_t$. Hence, the coefficients $a(t,T)$ and $b(t,T)$ in (7) for $T = u_i \in \mathscr{U}$ compute to $a(t,u_i) = \psi_i^\top \cdot \mu(X_t)$ and $b(t,u_i) = \psi_i^\top \cdot \sigma(X_t)$.

On the other hand, for $T \notin \mathscr{U}$ we obtain that $f(t,T) = a'(t,T) + b'(t,T)^\top \cdot X_t$. Then, the coefficients $a(t,T)$ and $b(t,T)$ can be computed as follows: applying Itô's formula to $f(t,T)$ and comparing with (7) yields that

$$\begin{aligned} a(t,T) &= \partial_t a'(t,T) + \partial_t b'(t,T)^\top \cdot X_t + b'(t,T)^\top \cdot \mu(X_t) \\ b(t,T) &= b'(t,T)^\top \cdot \sigma(X_t). \end{aligned} \tag{26}$$

Set $\bar{a}'(t,T) = \int_t^T a'(t,u)du$ and $\bar{b}'(t,T) = \int_t^T b'(t,u)du$ and note that,

$$\int_t^T \partial_t a'(t,u)du = \partial_t \bar{a}'(t,T) + a'(t,t).$$

As $\partial_t^+ A(t,T) = \partial_t \bar{a}'(t,T)$, and $\partial_t^+ B(t,T) = \partial_t \bar{b}'(t,T)$, we obtain from (26) that

$$
\begin{aligned}
\bar{a}(t,T) &= \int_t^T a(t,u)\nu(du) = \int_t^T a(t,u)du + \sum_{u_i\in(t,T]} w_i\psi_i^\top\cdot\mu(X_t)\\
&= \partial_t^+ A(t,T) + a'(t,t) + \left(\partial_t^+ B(t,T) + b'(t,t)\right)^\top\cdot X_t + B(t,T)^\top\cdot\mu(X_t),\\
\bar{b}(t,T) &= \int_t^T b(t,u)\nu(du) = \int_t^T b(t,u)du + \sum_{u_i\in(t,T]} w_i\psi_i^\top\cdot\sigma(X_t)\\
&= B(t,T)^\top\cdot\sigma(X_t)
\end{aligned}
$$

for $0\le t\le T\le T^*$. We now show that under our assumptions, the drift conditions (9) and (10) hold: Observe that, by Eqs. (24), (25), and the affine specification (20), and (21), the drift condition (10) holds. Moreover, from (11),

$$
\Delta H'(u_i) = \phi_i + \psi_i^\top\cdot X_{u_i}
$$

and $\lambda_s = \phi_0(s) + \psi_0(s)^\top\cdot X_s$ by (19). We recover $\Delta\Lambda_{u_i} = 1-\exp(-\phi_i-\psi_i^\top\cdot X_{u_i})$ taking values in [0, 1) by assumption. Hence, (9) holds and the claim follows.

*Example 4* In the one-dimensional case we consider $X$, given as solution of

$$
dX_t = (\mu_0+\mu_1 X_t)dt + \sigma\sqrt{X_t}dW_t,\quad t\ge 0.
$$

Consider only one risky time $u_1=1$ and let $\phi_0=\phi_1=0$, $\psi_0=1$, such that

$$
\Lambda = \int_0^t X_s ds + 1_{\{u\ge 1\}}(1-e^{-\psi_1 X_1}).
$$

Hence the probability of having no default at time 1 just prior to 1 is given by $e^{-\psi_1 X_1}$, compare Example 3.

An arbitrage-free model can be obtained by choosing $A$ and $B$ according to Proposition 1 which can be immediately achieved using Lemma 10.12 from [11] (see in particular Sect. 10.3.2.2 on the CIR short-rate model): denote $\theta=\sqrt{\mu_1^2+2\sigma^2}$ and

$$
\begin{aligned}
L_1(t) &= 2(e^{\theta t}-1),\\
L_2(t) &= \theta(e^{\theta t}+1)+\mu_1(e^{\theta t}-1),\\
L_3(t) &= \theta(e^{\theta t}+1)-\mu_1(e^{\theta t}-1),\\
L_4(t) &= \sigma^2(e^{\theta t}-1).
\end{aligned}
$$

Then

$$
A_0(s) = \frac{2\mu_0}{\sigma^2}\log\left(\frac{2\theta e^{\frac{(\sigma-\mu_1)t}{2}}}{L_3(t)}\right),\quad B_0(s) = -\frac{L_1(t)}{L_3(t)}
$$

are the unique solutions of the Riccati equations $B_0' = \sigma^2 B_0^2 - \mu_1 B_0$ with boundary condition $B_0(0) = 0$ and $A_0' = -\mu_0 B_0$ with boundary condition $A_0(0) = 0$. Note that with $A(t, T) = A_0(T - t)$ and $B(t, T) = B_0(T - t)$ for $0 \le t \le T < 1$, the conditions of Proposition 1 hold. Similarly, for $1 \le t \le T$, choosing $A(t, T) = A_0(T - t)$ and $B(t, T) = B_0(T - t)$ implies again the validity of (24) and (25). On the other hand, for $0 \le t < 1$ and $T \ge 1$ we set $u(T) = B(1, T) + \psi_1 = B_0(T - 1) + \psi_1$, according to (25), and let

$$A(t, T) = \frac{2\mu_0}{\sigma^2} \log\left( \frac{2\theta e^{\frac{(\sigma-\mu_1)(1-t)}{2}}}{L_3(1-t) - L_4(1-t)u(T)} \right)$$

$$B(t, T) = -\frac{L_1(1-t) - L_2(1-t)u(T)}{L_3(1-t) - L_4(1-t)u(T)}.$$

It is easy to see that (24) and (25) are also satisfied in this case, in particular $\Delta A(1, T) = -\phi_1 = 0$ and $\Delta B(1, T) = -\psi_1$. Note that, while $X$ is continuous, the bond prices are not even stochastically continuous because they jump almost surely at $u_1 = 1$. We conclude by Proposition 1 that this affine model is arbitrage-free. ◇

## 4 Conclusion

In this article we studied a new class of dynamic term structure models with credit risk where the compensator of the default time may jump at predictable times. This framework was called generalized intensity-based framework. It extends existing theory and allows to include Merton's model, in a reduced-form model for pricing credit derivatives. Finally, we studied a class of highly tractable affine models which are only piecewise stochastically continuous.

**Acknowledgements** The KPMG Center of Excellence in Risk Management is acknowledged for organizing the conference "Challenges in Derivatives Markets - Fixed Income Modeling, Valuation Adjustments, Risk Management, and Regulation".

**Open Access** This chapter is distributed under the terms of the Creative Commons Attribution 4.0 International License (http://creativecommons.org/licenses/by/4.0/), which permits use, duplication, adaptation, distribution and reproduction in any medium or format, as long as you give appropriate credit to the original author(s) and the source, a link is provided to the Creative Commons license and any changes made are indicated.

The images or other third party material in this chapter are included in the work's Creative Commons license, unless indicated otherwise in the credit line; if such material is not included in the work's Creative Commons license and the respective action is not permitted by statutory regulation, users will need to obtain permission from the license holder to duplicate, adapt or reproduce the material.

## References


1. Artzner, P., Delbaen, F.: Default risk insurance and incomplete markets. Math. Financ. **5**(3), 187–195 (1995)
2. Bélanger, A., Shreve, S.E., Wong, D.: A general framework for pricing credit risk. Math. Financ. **14**(3), 317–350 (2004)
3. Bielecki, T., Rutkowski, M.: Credit Risk: Modeling, Valuation and Hedging. Springer, Berlin (2002)
4. Black, F., Cox, J.C.: Valuing corporate securities: some effects of bond indenture provisions. J. Financ. **31**, 351–367 (1976)
5. Brémaud, P.: Point Processes and Queues. Springer, Berlin (1981)
6. Cuchiero, C., Klein, I., Teichmann, J.: A new perspective on the fundamental theorem of asset pricing for large financial markets. arXiv:1412.7562v2 (2014)
7. Duffie, D., Singleton, K.: Modeling term structures of defaultable bonds. Rev. Financ. Stud. **12**, 687–720 (1999)
8. Duffie, D., Filipović, D., Schachermayer, W.: Affine processes and applications in finance. Ann. Appl. Probab. **13**, 984–1053 (2003)
9. Eavis, P.: Greece is placed in arrears, as the I.M.F. spells default. http://www.nytimes.com/2015/07/01/business/international/greece-is-placed-in-arrears-as-the-imf-spells-default.html (2015)
10. Filipović, D.: Time-inhomogeneous affine processes. Stoch. Process. Appl. **115**(4), 639–659 (2005)
11. Filipović, D.: Term Structure Models: A Graduate Course. Springer, Berlin (2009)
12. Gehmlich, F., Schmidt, T.: Dynamic defaultable term structure modelling beyond the intensity paradigm. arXiv:1411.4851v3 (2015)
13. Geske, R.: The valuation of corporate liabilities as compound options. J. Financ. Quant. Anal. **12**, 541–552 (1977)
14. Geske, R., Johnson, H.E.: The valuation of corporate liabilities as compound options: a correction. J. Financ. Quant. Anal. **19**(2), 231–232 (1984)
15. Guo, X., Zeng, Y.: Intensity process and compensator: a new filtration expansion approach and the Jeulin-Yor theorem. Ann. Appl. Probab. **18**(1), 120–142 (2008)
16. ISDA: ISDA Americas credit derivatives determinations committee: Argentine republic failure to pay credit event. http://www2.isda.org/news/isda-americas-credit-derivatives-determinations-committee-argentine-republic-failure-to-pay-credit-event (2014)
17. Jacod, J., Shiryaev, A.: Limit Theorems for Stochastic Processes, 2nd edn. Springer, Berlin (2003)
18. Jarrow, R., Turnbull, S.: Pricing options on financial securities subject to default risk. J. Financ. **5**, 53–86 (1995)
19. Jeanblanc, M., Rutkowski, M.: Modeling default risk: an overview. In: Mathematical Finance: Theory and Practice Fudan University. Modern Mathematics Series, pp. 171–269. High Education Press, Beijing (2000)
20. Karatzas, I., Shreve, S.E.: Brownian Motion and Stochastic Calculus. Springer, Berlin (1988)
21. Klein, I., Schmidt, T., Teichmann, J.: When roll-overs do not qualify as numéraire: bond markets beyond short rate paradigms. arXiv:1310.0032 (2015)
22. Lando, D.: Three essays on contingent claim pricing. Ph.D. thesis, Cornell University (1994)
23. Merton, R.: On the pricing of corporate debt: the risk structure of interest rates. J. Financ. **29**, 449–470 (1974)
24. Reuters: Argentina debt talks must continue after default: U.S. judge. http://www.reuters.com/article/2014/08/01/us-argentina-debt-idUSKBN0G13Z720140801 (2014)
25. Schönbucher, P.: Pricing credit risk derivatives. *Working paper* (1998)
26. Veraar, M.: The stochastic Fubini theorem revisited. Stochastics **84**(4), 543–551 (2012)

# Option Pricing and Sensitivity Analysis in the Lévy Forward Process Model

**Ernst Eberlein, M'hamed Eddahbi and Sidi Mohamed Lalaoui Ben Cherif**

**Abstract** The purpose of this article is to give a closed Fourier-based valuation formula for a caplet in the framework of the Lévy forward process model which was introduced in Eberlein and Özkan, Financ. Stochast. 9:327-348, 2005, [5]. Afterwards, we compute Greeks by two approaches which come from totally different mathematical fields. The first is based on the integration-by-parts formula, which lies at the core of the application of the Malliavin calculus to finance. The second consists in using Fourier-based methods for pricing derivatives as exposed in Eberlein, Quantitative Energy Finance, 2014, [3]. We illustrate the results in the case where the jump part of the underlying model is driven by a time-inhomogeneous Gamma process and alternatively by a Variance Gamma process.

**Keywords** Option valuation · Lévy forward process model · Fourier transform · Time-inhomogeneous Lévy processes · Malliavin calculus · Greeks and sensitivity analysis

---

We acknowledge financial support from the Federal Foreign Office of Germany which has been granted within a program of the German Academic Exchange Service (DAAD).

---

E. Eberlein (✉)
Department of Mathematical Stochastics, University of Freiburg, Eckerstr. 1, 79104 Freiburg im Breisgau, Germany
e-mail: eberlein@stochastik.uni-freiburg.de

M. Eddahbi
Faculty of Sciences and Techniques, Department of Mathematics, Cadi Ayyad University, B.P. 549, Marrakech, Morocco
e-mail: m.eddahbi@uca.ma

S.M. Lalaoui Ben Cherif
Faculty of Sciences Semlalia, Department of Mathematics, Cadi Ayyad University, B.P. 2390, Marrakech, Morocco
e-mail: mohamed.lalaoui@ced.uca.ac.ma

© The Author(s) 2016 
K. Glau et al. (eds.), *Innovations in Derivatives Markets*, Springer Proceedings in Mathematics & Statistics 165, DOI 10.1007/978-3-319-33446-2_14

## 1 Introduction

To compute expectations which arise as prices of derivative products is a key issue in quantitative finance. The effort which is necessary to get these values depends to a high degree on the sophistication of the model approach which is used. Simple models such as the classical geometric Brownian motion lead to easy-to-evaluate formulas for expectations but entail at the same time a high model risk. As has been shown in numerous studies, the empirical return distributions which one can observe are far from normality. This is true for all categories of financial markets: equity, fixed income, foreign exchange as well as credit markets (see e.g. Eberlein and Keller (1995) [4] for the analysis of stock price data and Eberlein and Kluge (2007) [7] for data from fixed income markets). A first step to reduce model risk and to improve the performance of the model consists in introducing volatility as a stochastic quantity. Some of the stochastic volatility models became quite popular. Nevertheless one must be aware that the distributions which diffusion processes with non-deterministic coefficients generate on a given time horizon are not known. They can only be determined approximately on the basis of simulations of process paths. In order to get more realistic distributions, an excellent choice is to replace the driving Brownian motion in classical models by a suitably chosen Lévy process. This can also be interpreted in the sense that instead of making volatility stochastic one can go over to a stochastic clock. The reason is that many Lévy processes can be obtained as time-changed Brownian motions. For example, the Variance Gamma process results when one replaces linear time by a Gamma process as subordinator. Of course, one can also consider both: a more powerful driver and stochastic volatility.

Lévy processes are in a one-to-one correspondence to the rich class of infinitely divisible distributions and at the same time analytically well tractable. Due to the higher number of available parameters, this class of distributions is flexible enough to allow a much better fit to empirical return distributions. The systematic error which results from the assumption of normality is avoided. The generating distribution of a Lévy process shows up as the distribution of increments of length one. Consequently, any distribution which one gets by fitting a parametrized subclass to empirical return data can be implemented not only approximately but exactly into Lévy-driven models. Suitably parametrized model classes which have been used successfully so far are driven by generalized hyperbolic, normal inverse Gaussian (NIG), or Variance Gamma (VG) processes, just to mention a few.

As noted above, advanced models with superior statistical properties require more demanding numerical methods. Efficient and accurate algorithms are crucial in this context, in particular for calibration purposes. For pricing of derivatives the historical distribution, which can be derived from price data of the underlying and which is used for risk management, is of less interest. Calibration usually means to estimate the risk-neutral distribution parameters. In other words, one exploits price data of derivatives. In most cases this is given in terms of volatilities. Whereas years ago calibration was usually done overnight, many trading desks recalibrate nowadays on an intraday basis. During a calibration procedure in each iteration step a large number of model prices have to be computed and compared to market prices. A method which almost always works to get the corresponding expectations is Monte Carlo simulation. Its disadvantage is that it is computationally intensive and therefore too slow for many purposes. Another classical approach is to represent prices as solutions of partial differential equations (PDEs) which in the case of Lévy processes with jumps become partial integro–differential equations (PIDEs). This approach, which is based on the Feynman–Kac formula, applies to a wide range of valuation problems, in particular it allows to compute prices of American options as well. Nevertheless, the numerical solution of PIDEs rests on sophisticated discretization methods and corresponding programs. In this paper we concentrate on the third, namely the Fourier-based approach.

To manage portfolios of derivatives, traders have to understand how sensitive prices of derivative products are with respect to changes in the underlying parameters. For this purpose they need to know the Greeks which are given by the partial derivatives of the pricing functional with respect to those parameters. Usually Greeks are estimated by means of a finite difference approximation. Two kinds of errors are produced this way: the first one comes from the approximation of the derivative by a finite difference and the second one results from the numerical computation of the expectation. To eliminate one of the sources of error, Fournié et al. (1999) [9] adopted a new approach which consists in shifting the differential operator from the pricing functional to the diffusion kernel. This procedure results in an expectation operator applied to the payoff multiplied by a random weight function.

In the following we focus on a discrete tenor interest rate model which has been introduced in Eberlein and Özkan (2005) [5]. This so-called Lévy forward process model is driven by a time-inhomogeneous Lévy process and is developed on the basis of a backward induction that is necessary to get the LIBOR rates in a convenient homogeneous form. A major advantage of the forward process approach is that it is invariant under the measure change in the sense that the driving process remains a time-inhomogeneous Lévy process. Moreover, the measure changes do not only have the invariance property but in addition they are analytically and consequently also numerically much simpler compared to the corresponding measure changes in the so-called LIBOR model. The reason is that in each induction step the forward process itself represents up to a norming constant the density process on which the measure change is based. As a consequence, any approximation such as the 'frozen drift' approximation or more sophisticated versions of it are completely avoided. This means that the approximation error with which one has to struggle in the LIBOR approach does not show up in the forward process approach.

Another important aspect is that in the latter model the increments of the driving process translate directly into increments of the LIBOR rates. This is not the case for the LIBOR model where the increments of the LIBOR rates are proportional to the corresponding increments of the driving process scaled with the current value of the LIBOR rate. Expressed in terms of the terminology which will be developed in Sects. 2 and 3 this means that in the Lévy LIBOR model

$$L(t+\Delta t, T_k) - L(t, T_k) \sim L(t, T_k)\left(L_{t+\Delta t}^{T_{k+1}} - L_t^{T_{k+1}}\right), \tag{1}$$

whereas in the Lévy forward process model

$$L(t+\Delta t, T_k) - L(t, T_k) \sim \delta_k^{-1}\left(L_{t+\Delta t}^{T_{k+1}} - L_t^{T_{k+1}}\right). \tag{2}$$

The fact that the increments of the LIBOR rate process do not depend on current LIBOR values, translates into increased flexibility and a superior model performance of the forward process approach.

In addition to the differences in mathematical properties there is a fundamental economic difference. The forward process approach allows for negative interest rates as well as for negative starting values. This is of crucial importance in particular in the current economic environment where negative rates are common. Models where by construction interest rates stay strictly positive are not able to produce realistic valuations for a large collection of interest rate derivatives in a deflationary or near-deflationary environment.

As far as the calculation of Greeks in this setting is concerned, we refer to Glasserman and Zhao (1999) [12], Glasserman (2004) [11], and Fries (2007) [10] where some treatment of this issue is given. The classical diffusion-based LIBOR market model offers a high degree of analytical tractability. However, this model cannot reproduce the phenomenon of changing volatility smiles along the maturity axis. In order to gain more flexibility in a first step one can replace the driving Brownian motion by a (time-homogeneous) Lévy process. However, one observes that the shape of the volatility surface produced by cap and floor prices is too sophisticated in order to be matched with sufficient accuracy by a model which is driven by a time-homogeneous process. To achieve a more accurate calibration of the model across different strikes and maturities one has to use the more flexible class of time-inhomogeneous Lévy processes (see e.g. Eberlein and Özkan (2005) [5] and Eberlein and Kluge (2006) [6]). Graphs in the latter paper show in particular that interest rate models driven by time-inhomogeneous Lévy processes are able to reproduce implied volatility curves (smiles) observed in the market across all maturities with high accuracy. If one restricts the approach to (time-homogeneous) Lévy processes as drivers, the smiles flatten out too fast at longer maturities. Consequently, we have analytical—the invariance under measure changes—as well as statistical reasons to choose time-inhomogeneous Lévy processes as drivers. In implementations of the model already a rather mild form of time-inhomogeneity turns out to be sufficient. Typically one has to glue together three pieces of (time-homogeneous) Lévy processes in order to cover the full range of maturities with sufficient accuracy. In terms of parameters this means that instead of three or four one uses nine or twelve parameters.

The first goal of this paper is to give a closed Fourier-based valuation formula for a caplet in the framework of the Lévy forward process model. The second aim is to study sensitivities. We discuss two approaches for this purpose. The first is based on the integration-by-parts formula, which lies at the core of the application of the Malliavin calculus to finance as developed in Fournié et al. (1999) [9], León et al.

(2002) [14], Petrou (2008) [17], Yablonski (2008) [19]. This approach is appropriate if the driving process has a diffusion component. The second approach which covers purely discontinuous drivers as well relies on Fourier-based methods for pricing derivatives. For a survey of Fourier-based methods see Eberlein (2014) [3]. We illustrate the result by applying the formula to the pricing of a caplet where the jump-part of the underlying model is driven by a time-inhomogeneous Gamma process and alternatively by a Variance Gamma process.

## 2 The Lévy Forward Process Model

Let $0 = T_0 < T_1 < \cdots < T_{n-1} < T_n = T^*$ denote a discrete tenor structure and set $\delta_k = T_{k+1} - T_k$ for all $k \in \{0, \ldots, n-1\}$. Because we proceed by backward induction, let us use the notation $T_i^* := T_{n-i}$ and $\delta_i^* = \delta_{n-i}$ for $i \in \{1, \ldots, n\}$. For zero-coupon bond prices $B(t, T_i^*)$ and $B(t, T_{i-1}^*)$, the forward process is defined by

$$F(t, T_i^*, T_{i-1}^*) = \frac{B(t, T_i^*)}{B(t, T_{i-1}^*)}. \tag{3}$$

Hence, modeling forward processes means specifying the dynamics of ratios of successive bond prices. Let $(\Omega; \mathscr{F}=\mathscr{F}_{T^*}; \mathbb{F}; \mathbb{P}_{T^*})$ be a complete stochastic basis where $\mathbb{P}_{T^*}$ should be regarded as the forward martingale measure for the settlement date $T^* > 0$ and the filtration $\mathbb{F} = (\mathscr{F}_t)_{t\in[0,T^*]}$ satisfies the usual conditions. Consider a time-inhomogeneous Lévy process $L^{T^*}$ defined on $(\Omega; \mathscr{F} = \mathscr{F}_{T^*}; \mathbb{F}; \mathbb{P}_{T^*})$ starting at 0 with local characteristics $(b^{T^*}, c, F^{T^*})$ such that the drift term $b_s^{T^*} \in \mathbb{R}$, the volatility coefficient $c_s$ and the Lévy measure $F_s^{T^*}$ satisfy the following conditions

$$\exists\, \sigma > 0, \quad \forall\, s \in [0, T^*]: \quad c_s > \sigma, \quad F_s^{T^*}(\{0\}) = 0 \tag{4}$$

and

$$\int_0^{T^*} \left( |b_s^{T^*}| + |c_s| + \int_{\mathbb{R}} \left(|x|^2 \wedge 1\right) F_s^{T^*}(dx) \right) ds < \infty. \tag{5}$$

We impose as usual a further integrability condition. Note that the processes which we will define later, are by construction martingales and therefore every single random variable has to be integrable.

**Assumption 2.1** ($\mathbb{EM}$) There exists a constant $M > 1$ such that

$$\int_0^{T^*} \int_{\{|x|>1\}} \exp(ux) F_s^{T^*}(dx) ds < \infty, \quad \forall\, u \in [-M, M]. \tag{6}$$

Under ($\mathbb{EM}$) the random variable $L_t^{T^*}$ has a finite expectation and its law is given by the characteristic function

$$\mathbb{E}\left[e^{iuL_t^{T^*}}\right] = \exp\left(\int_0^t \left(iub_s^{T^*} - \frac{1}{2}u^2 c_s + \int_{\mathbb{R}} \left(e^{iux} - 1 - iux\right) F_s^{T^*}(dx)\right) ds\right). \quad (7)$$

Furthermore, the process $L^{T^*}$ is a special semimartingale, and thus its canonical representation has the simple form

$$L_t^{T^*} = \int_0^t b_s^{T^*} ds + \int_0^t \sqrt{c_s} dW_s^{T^*} + \int_0^t \int_{\mathbb{R}} x \widetilde{\mu}^{L^{T^*}}(ds, dx), \quad (8)$$

where $(W_t^{T^*})_{t \geq 0}$ is a $\mathbb{P}_{T^*}$-standard Brownian motion and $\widetilde{\mu}^{L^{T^*}} := \mu^{L^{T^*}} - \nu^{T^*}$ is the $\mathbb{P}_{T^*}$-compensated random measure of jumps of $L^{T^*}$. As usual, $\mu^{L^{T^*}}$ denotes the random measure of jumps of $L^{T^*}$ and $\nu^{T^*}(ds, dx) := F_s^{T^*}(dx)ds$ the $\mathbb{P}_{T^*}$-compensator of $\mu^{L^{T^*}}$. We denote by $\theta_s$ the cumulant function associated with the process $L^{T^*}$ as given in (8) with local characteristics $(b^{T^*}, c, F^{T^*})$, that is, for appropriate $z \in \mathbb{C}$

$$\theta_s(z) = zb_s^{T^*} + \frac{z^2}{2} c_s + \int_{\mathbb{R}} \left(e^{zx} - 1 - zx\right) F_s^{T^*}(dx), \quad (9)$$

where $c$ and $F^{T^*}$ are free parameters, whereas the drift characteristic $b^{T^*}$ will later be chosen to guarantee that the forward process is a martingale. The following ingredients are needed.

**Assumption 2.2** ($\mathbb{LR}$.1) For any maturity $T_i^*$ there is a bounded, deterministic function $\lambda(\cdot, T_i^*) : [0, T^*] \longmapsto \mathbb{R}$ which represents the volatility of the forward process $F(\cdot, T_i^*, T_{i-1}^*)$. These functions satisfy

$\lambda(s, T_i^*) > 0$, $\forall s \in [0, T_i^*]$ and $\lambda(s, T_i^*) = 0$ for $s > T_i^*$ for any maturity $T_i^*$,
$\sum_{i=1}^{n-1} \lambda(s, T_i^*) \leq M, \quad \forall s \in [0, T^*]$ where $M$ is the constant from Assumption ($\mathbb{EM}$).

**Assumption 2.3** ($\mathbb{LR}$.2) The initial term structure of zero-coupon bond prices $B(0, T_i^*)$ is strictly positive for all $i \in \{1, \ldots, n\}$.

We begin to construct the forward process with the most distant maturity and postulate

$$F(t, T_1^*, T^*) = F(0, T_1^*, T^*) \exp\left(\int_0^t \lambda(s, T_1^*) dL_s^{T^*}\right). \quad (10)$$

One forces this process to become a $\mathbb{P}_{T^*}$-martingale by choosing $b^{T^*}$ such that

$$\int_0^t \lambda(s, T_1^*) b_s^{T^*} ds = -\frac{1}{2} \int_0^t c_s \lambda^2(s, T_1^*) ds - \int_0^t \int_{\mathbb{R}} \left( e^{x\lambda(s,T_1^*)} - 1 - x\lambda(s, T_1^*) \right) \nu^{T^*}(ds, dx). \quad (11)$$

Then the forward process $F(\cdot, T_1^*, T^*)$ can be given as a stochastic exponential

$$F(t, T_1^*, T^*) = F(0, T_1^*, T^*) \mathscr{E}_t \left( Z(\cdot, T_1^*) \right) \quad (12)$$

with

$$Z(t, T_1^*) = \int_0^t \sqrt{c_s} \lambda(s, T_1^*) dW_s^{T^*} + \int_0^t \int_{\mathbb{R}} (e^{x\lambda(s,T_1^*)} - 1) \widetilde{\mu}^{L^{T^*}}(ds, dx). \quad (13)$$

Since the forward process $F(\cdot, T_1^*, T^*)$ is a $\mathbb{P}_{T^*}$-martingale, we can use it as a density process and define the forward martingale measure $\mathbb{P}_{T_1^*}$ by setting

$$\frac{d\mathbb{P}_{T_1^*}}{d\mathbb{P}_{T^*}} = \frac{F(T_1^*, T_1^*, T^*)}{F(0, T_1^*, T^*)} = \mathscr{E}_{T_1^*} \left( Z(\cdot, T_1^*) \right). \quad (14)$$

By the semimartingale version of Girsanov's theorem (see Jacod and Shiryaev (1987) [13])

$$W_t^{T_1^*} := W_t^{T^*} - \int_0^t \sqrt{c_s} \lambda(s, T_1^*) ds \quad (15)$$

is a $\mathbb{P}_{T_1^*}$-standard Brownian motion and

$$\nu^{T_1^*}(dt, dx) := e^{x\lambda(s,T_1^*)} \nu^{T^*}(dt, dx) = e^{x\lambda(s,T_1^*)} F_s^{T^*}(dx) ds \quad (16)$$

is the $\mathbb{P}_{T_1^*}$-compensator of $\mu^{L^{T^*}}$.

Continuing this way one gets the forward processes $F(\cdot, T_i^*, T_{i-1}^*)$ such that for all $i \in \{1, \ldots, n\}$

$$F(t, T_i^*, T_{i-1}^*) = F(0, T_i^*, T_{i-1}^*) \exp \left( \int_0^t \lambda(s, T_i^*) dL_s^{T_{i-1}^*} \right). \quad (17)$$

The drift term $b^{T_{i-1}^*}$ is chosen in such a way that the forward process $F(\cdot, T_i^*, T_{i-1}^*)$ becomes a martingale under the forward measure $\mathbb{P}_{T_{i-1}^*}$, that is

$$\int_0^t \lambda(s, T_i^*) b_s^{T_{i-1}^*} ds = -\frac{1}{2} \int_0^t c_s \lambda^2(s, T_i^*) ds - \int_0^t \int_{\mathbb{R}} \left( e^{x\lambda(s,T_i^*)} - 1 - x\lambda(s, T_i^*) \right) \nu^{T_{i-1}^*}(ds, dx). \quad (18)$$

We propose the following choice for the functions $b^{T^*_{i-1}}$ for all $i \in \{1, \ldots, n\}$

$$\begin{cases} b_s^{T^*_{i-1}} = -\frac{c_s}{2}\lambda(s, T_i^*) - \int_{\mathbb{R}} \left( \frac{e^{x\lambda(s,T_i^*)} - 1}{\lambda(s, T_i^*)} - x \right) F_s^{T^*_{i-1}}(dx), \; 0 \leq s < T_i^* \\ b_s^{T^*_{i-1}} = 0, \qquad s \geq T_i^*. \end{cases} \tag{19}$$

The driving process $L^{T^*_{i-1}}$ becomes therefore

$$\begin{aligned} L_t^{T^*_{i-1}} &= -\int_0^t \left( \frac{c_s}{2}\lambda(s, T_i^*) + \int_{\mathbb{R}} \left( \frac{e^{x\lambda(s,T_i^*)} - 1}{\lambda(s, T_i^*)} - x \right) F_s^{T^*_{i-1}}(dx) \right) ds \\ &\quad + \int_0^t \sqrt{c_s} dW_s^{T^*_{i-1}} + \int_0^t \int_{\mathbb{R}} x(\mu^{T^*} - \nu^{T^*_{i-1}})(ds, dx) \end{aligned} \tag{20}$$

under the successive forward measures $\mathbb{P}_{T_i^*}$ which are given by the recursive relation

$$\begin{cases} \frac{d\mathbb{P}_{T_i^*}}{d\mathbb{P}_{T^*_{i-1}}} = \frac{F(T_i^*, T_i^*, T^*_{i-1})}{F(0, T_i^*, T^*_{i-1})} = \mathscr{E}_{T_i^*}\left(Z(\cdot, T_i^*)\right), \quad i \in \{1, \ldots, n\} \\ \mathbb{P}_{T_0^*} = \mathbb{P}_{T^*} \end{cases} \tag{21}$$

with

$$Z(t, T_i^*) = \int_0^t \sqrt{c_s}\lambda(s, T_i^*) dW_s^{T^*_{i-1}} + \int_0^t \int_{\mathbb{R}} (e^{x\lambda(s,T_i^*)} - 1)\widetilde{\mu}^{L^{T^*_{i-1}}}(ds, dx), \tag{22}$$

where $(W_t^{T^*_{i-1}})_{t\geq 0}$ is a $\mathbb{P}_{T^*_{i-1}}$-standard Brownian motion such that

$$\begin{cases} W_t^{T_i^*} = W_t^{T^*_{i-1}} - \int_0^t \sqrt{c_s}\lambda(s, T_i^*) ds, \quad i \in \{1, \ldots, n\} \\ W_t^{T_0^*} = W_t^{T^*}. \end{cases} \tag{23}$$

$\widetilde{\mu}^{L^{T^*}}_{i-1} := \mu^{L^{T^*}} - \nu^{T^*_{i-1}}$ is the $\mathbb{P}_{T^*_{i-1}}$-compensated random measure of jumps of $L^{T^*}$ and $\nu^{T^*_{i-1}}(ds, dx) = F_s^{T^*_{i-1}}(dx)ds$ is the $\mathbb{P}_{T^*_{i-1}}$-compensator of $\mu^{L^{T^*}}$ such that

$$\begin{cases} F_s^{T_i^*}(dx) = e^{x\lambda(s,T_i^*)} F_s^{T^*_{i-1}}(dx), \quad i \in \{1, \ldots, n\} \\ F_s^{T_0^*}(dx) = F_s^{T^*}(dx). \end{cases} \tag{24}$$

Setting $\Lambda^i(s) := \sum_{j=1}^i \lambda(s, T_j^*)$, we conclude that for all $i \in \{1, \ldots, n\}$

$$W_t^{T_i^*} = W_t^{T^*} - \int_0^t \sqrt{c_s}\Lambda^i(s)ds \tag{25}$$

and

$$F_s^{T_i^*}(dx) = \exp\left(x\Lambda^i(s)\right) F_s^{T^*}(dx). \tag{26}$$

Note that the coefficients $\sqrt{c_s}\Lambda^i(s)$ and $\exp(x\Lambda^i(s))$, which appear in this measure change, are deterministic functions and therefore the measure change is structure preserving, i.e. the driving process is still a time-inhomogeneous Lévy process after the measure change.

Since the forward process $F(\cdot, T_i^*, T_{i-1}^*)$ is by construction a $\mathbb{P}_{T_{i-1}^*}$-martingale, the process $\frac{F(\cdot, T_i^*, T_{i-1}^*)}{F(0, T_i^*, T_{i-1}^*)}$, which is the density process

$$\left.\frac{d\mathbb{P}_{T_i^*}}{d\mathbb{P}_{T_{i-1}^*}}\right|_{\mathscr{F}_t} = \frac{F(t, T_i^*, T_{i-1}^*)}{F(0, T_i^*, T_{i-1}^*)} \tag{27}$$

is a $\mathbb{P}_{T_{i-1}^*}$-martingale as well. By iterating the relation (21) we get on $\mathscr{F}_{T_{i-1}^*}$

$$\begin{aligned} \frac{d\mathbb{P}_{T_{i-1}^*}}{d\mathbb{P}_{T^*}} &= \frac{B(0, T^*)}{B(0, T_{i-1}^*)} \prod_{j=1}^{i-1} F(T_{i-1}^*, T_j^*, T_{j-1}^*) \\ &= \exp\left(\sum_{j=1}^{i-1} \int_0^{T_{i-1}^*} \lambda(s, T_j^*) dL_s^{T_{j-1}^*}\right). \end{aligned} \tag{28}$$

Applying Proposition III.3.8 of Jacod and Shiryaev (1987) [13], we see that its restriction to $\mathscr{F}_t$ for $t \in [0, T_i^*]$

$$\left.\frac{d\mathbb{P}_{T_i^*}}{d\mathbb{P}_{T^*}}\right|_{\mathscr{F}_t} = \frac{B(0, T^*)}{B(0, T_i^*)} \prod_{j=1}^{i} F(t, T_j^*, T_{j-1}^*) \tag{29}$$

is a $\mathbb{P}_{T^*}$-martingale.

## 3 Fourier-Based Methods for Option Pricing

We will derive an explicit valuation formula for standard interest rate derivatives such as caps and floors in the Lévy forward process model. Since floor prices can be derived from the corresponding put-call-parity relation we concentrate on caps. Recall that a cap is a sequence of call options on subsequent LIBOR rates. Each single option is called a caplet. The payoff of a caplet with strike rate $K$ and maturity $T_i^*$ is

$$\delta_i^* \left(L(T_i^*, T_i^*) - K\right)^+, \tag{30}$$

where the payment is made at time point $T_{i-1}^*$. The forward LIBOR rates $L(T_i^*, T_i^*)$ are the discretely compounded, annualized interest rates which can be earned from investment during a future interval starting at $T_i^*$ and ending at $T_{i-1}^*$ considered at the time point $T_i^*$. These rates can be expressed in terms of the forward prices as follows

$$L(T_i^*, T_i^*) = \frac{1}{\delta_i^*}\left(F(T_i^*, T_i^*, T_{i-1}^*) - 1\right). \tag{31}$$

Its time-0-price, denoted by $Cplt_0(T_i^*, K)$, is given by

$$Cplt_0(T_i^*, K) = B(0, T_{i-1}^*)\delta_i^* \mathbb{E}_{\mathbb{P}_{T_{i-1}^*}}\left[\left(L(T_i^*, T_i^*) - K\right)^+\right]. \tag{32}$$

Instead of basing the pricing on the Lévy LIBOR model one can use the Lévy forward process approach (see Eberlein and Özkan (2005) [5]). It is then more natural to write the pricing formula (32) in the form

$$Cplt_0(T_i^*, K) = B(0, T_{i-1}^*)\mathbb{E}_{\mathbb{P}_{T_{i-1}^*}}\left[\left(F(T_i^*, T_i^*, T_{i-1}^*) - \widetilde{K}_i\right)^+\right], \tag{33}$$

where $\widetilde{K}_i := 1 + \delta_i^* K$. From (17), the forward process $F(\cdot, T_i^*, T_{i-1}^*)$ is given by

$$\begin{aligned} F(T_i^*, T_i^*, T_{i-1}^*) = F(0, T_i^*, T_{i-1}^*) &\exp\left(\int_0^{T_i^*} b_s^{T_{i-1}^*}\lambda(s, T_i^*)ds\right) \\ &\times \exp\left(\int_0^{T_i^*} \sqrt{c_s}\lambda(s, T_i^*)dW_s^{T_{i-1}^*}\right) \\ &\times \exp\left(\int_0^{T_i^*}\int_{\mathbb{R}} x\lambda(s, T_i^*)\widetilde{\mu}_{i-1}^{L^{T^*}}(ds, dx)\right). \end{aligned} \tag{34}$$

Using the relations (25) and (26) we obtain for $t \in [0, T_i^*]$

$$F(t, T_i^*, T_{i-1}^*) = F(0, T_i^*, T_{i-1}^*)\exp\left(\int_0^t \lambda(s, T_i^*)dL_s^{T^*} + d(t, T_i^*)\right), \tag{35}$$

where

$$d(t,T_i^*) = \int_0^t \lambda(s,T_i^*)\left[b_s^{T_{i-1}^*} - b_s^{T^*} - \Lambda^{i-1}(s)c_s\right]ds \\ - \int_0^t \lambda(s,T_i^*)\int_{\mathbb{R}} x\left(e^{x\Lambda^{i-1}(s)} - 1\right)F_s^{T^*}(dx)ds. \tag{36}$$

Remember that on $\mathscr{F}_{T_{i-1}^*}$

$$\frac{d\mathbb{P}_{T_{i-1}^*}}{d\mathbb{P}_{T^*}} = \exp\left(\sum_{j=1}^{i-1}\int_0^{T_{i-1}^*}\lambda(s,T_j^*)dL_s^{T^*} + \sum_{j=1}^{i-1} d(T_{i-1}^*,T_j^*)\right). \tag{37}$$

Keeping in mind Assumption 2.2 ($\mathbb{LR}$.1), we find

$$\exp\left(-\sum_{j=1}^{i-1} d(T_{i-1}^*,T_j^*)\right) = \mathbb{E}_{\mathbb{P}_{T^*}}\left[\exp\left(\int_0^{T_{i-1}^*}\Lambda^{i-1}(s)dL_s^{T^*}\right)\right]. \tag{38}$$

Using Proposition 8 in Eberlein and Kluge (2006) [6], we find

$$\exp\left(-\sum_{j=1}^{i-1} d(T_{i-1}^*,T_j^*)\right) = \exp\left(\int_0^{T_{i-1}^*}\theta_s\left(\Lambda^{i-1}(s)\right)ds\right). \tag{39}$$

Consequently,

$$\frac{d\mathbb{P}_{T_{i-1}^*}}{d\mathbb{P}_{T^*}} = \exp\left(\int_0^{T_{i-1}^*}\Lambda^{i-1}(s)dL_s^{T^*} - \int_0^{T_{i-1}^*}\theta_s\left(\Lambda^{i-1}(s)\right)ds\right). \tag{40}$$

Knowing that the process $\left(\frac{F(\cdot,T_i^*,T_{i-1}^*)}{F(0,T_i^*,T_{i-1}^*)}\right)$ is a $\mathbb{P}_{T_{i-1}^*}$-martingale, we reach

$$\exp(-d(T_i^*,T_i^*)) = \mathbb{E}_{\mathbb{P}_{T_{i-1}^*}}\left[\exp\left(\int_0^{T_i^*}\lambda(s,T_i^*)dL_s^{T^*}\right)\right]. \tag{41}$$

Hence,

$$\begin{aligned} &\exp(-d(T_i^*,T_i^*)) \\ &= \exp\left(-\int_0^{T_i^*}\theta_s\left(\Lambda^{i-1}(s)\right)ds\right)\mathbb{E}_{\mathbb{P}_{T^*}}\left[\exp\left(\int_0^{T_i^*}\Lambda^i(s)dL_s^{T^*}\right)\right] \\ &= \exp\left(\int_0^{T_i^*}\left[\theta_s\left(\Lambda^i(s)\right) - \theta_s\left(\Lambda^{i-1}(s)\right)\right]ds\right). \end{aligned} \tag{42}$$

Thus,

$$d(T_i^*, T_i^*) = \int_0^{T_i^*} \left[-\theta_s\left(\Lambda^i(s)\right) + \theta_s\left(\Lambda^{i-1}(s)\right)\right] ds. \tag{43}$$

Define the random variable $X_{T_i^*}$ as the logarithm of $F(T_i^*, T_i^*, T_{i-1}^*)$. Therefore,

$$X_{T_i^*} = \ln\left(F(0, T_i^*, T_{i-1}^*)\right) + \int_0^{T_i^*} \lambda(s, T_i^*) dL_s^{T^*} + d(T_i^*, T_i^*). \tag{44}$$

**Proposition 3.1** *Suppose there is a real number $R \in (1, 1+\varepsilon)$ such that the moment-generating function of $X_{T_i^*}$ with respect to $\mathbb{P}_{T_{i-1}^*}$ is finite at R, i.e. $M_{X_{T_i^*}}(R) < \infty$, then*

$$\begin{aligned}
\mathrm{Cplt}_0(T_i^*, K) = {} & \frac{\widetilde{K}_i B(0, T_{i-1}^*)}{2\pi} \int_{\mathbb{R}} \left\{ \left( \frac{F(0, T_i^*, T_{i-1}^*)}{\widetilde{K}_i} \right)^{R+\mathrm{i}u} \right. \\
& \times \exp\left( \int_0^{T_i^*} \int_{\mathbb{R}} e^{x\Lambda^{i-1}(s)} \left[ \left( e^{(R+\mathrm{i}u)x\lambda(s,T_i^*)} - 1 \right) - (R+\mathrm{i}u)\left( e^{x\lambda(s,T_i^*)} - 1 \right) \right] F_s^{T^*}(dx) ds \right) \\
& \left. \times \exp\left( \int_0^{T_i^*} \frac{c_s}{2} (R+\mathrm{i}u)(R+\mathrm{i}u-1)\lambda^2(s, T_i^*) ds \right) \right\} \frac{du}{(R+\mathrm{i}u)(R+\mathrm{i}u-1)}.
\end{aligned} \tag{45}$$

*Proof* The time-0-price of the caplet with strike rate $K$ and maturity $T_i^*$ has the form

$$\begin{aligned}
Cplt_0(T_i^*, K) &= B(0, T_{i-1}^*) \mathbb{E}_{\mathbb{P}_{T_{i-1}^*}} \left[ \left( e^{X_{T_i^*}} - \widetilde{K}_i \right)^+ \right] \\
&= B(0, T_{i-1}^*) \mathbb{E}_{\mathbb{P}_{T_{i-1}^*}} \left[ f\left(X_{T_i^*}\right) \right],
\end{aligned} \tag{46}$$

where the function $f : \mathbb{R} \to \mathbb{R}^+$ is defined by $f(x) = (e^x - \widetilde{K}_i)^+$.

Applying Theorem 2.2 in Eberlein et al. (2010) [8] (by the definition of $X_{T_i^*}$ we have $s = 0$ here), we get

$$Cplt_0(T_i^*, K) = \frac{B(0, T_{i-1}^*)}{2\pi} \int_{\mathbb{R}} M_{X_{T_i^*}}(R + \mathrm{i}u) \hat{f}(-u + \mathrm{i}R) du, \tag{47}$$

where the Fourier transform $\hat{f}$ is given by

$$\hat{f}(-u + \mathrm{i}R) = \frac{\widetilde{K}_i^{1-R-\mathrm{i}u}}{(R + \mathrm{i}u)(R + \mathrm{i}u - 1)} \tag{48}$$

and the moment-generating function $M_{X_{T_i^*}}$ is given by

$$\begin{aligned} M_{X_{T_i^*}}(R+\mathrm{i}u) &= \mathbb{E}_{\mathbb{P}_{T_{i-1}^*}}\left[\exp\left((R+\mathrm{i}u)X_{T_i^*}\right)\right] \\ &= \left(F(0,T_i^*,T_{i-1}^*)\right)^{R+\mathrm{i}u}\exp\left((R+\mathrm{i}u)d(T_i^*,T_i^*)\right) \\ &\times\mathbb{E}_{\mathbb{P}_{T_{i-1}^*}}\left[\exp\left(\int_0^{T_i^*}(R+\mathrm{i}u)\lambda(s,T_i^*)dL_s^{T^*}\right)\right]. \end{aligned} \tag{49}$$

Making a change of measure, we find

$$\begin{aligned} M_{X_{T_i^*}}(R+\mathrm{i}u) &= \left(F(0,T_i^*,T_{i-1}^*)\right)^{R+\mathrm{i}u}\exp\left((R+\mathrm{i}u)d(T_i^*,T_i^*)\right) \\ &\times\frac{\mathbb{E}_{\mathbb{P}_{T^*}}\left[\exp\left(\int_0^{T_i^*}\left((R+\mathrm{i}u)\lambda(s,T_i^*)+\Lambda^{i-1}(s)\right)dL_s^{T^*}\right)\right]}{\mathbb{E}_{\mathbb{P}_{T^*}}\left[\exp\left(\int_0^{T_i^*}\Lambda^{i-1}(s)dL_s^{T^*}\right)\right]}. \end{aligned} \tag{50}$$

Using Proposition 8 in Eberlein and Kluge (2006) [6], we can prove easily that

$$\begin{aligned} M_{X_{T_i^*}}(R+\mathrm{i}u) &= \left(F(0,T_i^*,T_{i-1}^*)\right)^{R+\mathrm{i}u} \\ &\times\exp\left((R+\mathrm{i}u)\int_0^{T_i^*}\left[-\theta_s\left(\Lambda^i(s)\right)+\theta_s\left(\Lambda^{i-1}(s)\right)\right]ds\right) \\ &\times\frac{\exp\left(\int_0^{T_i^*}\theta_s\left((R+\mathrm{i}u)\lambda(s,T_i^*)+\Lambda^{i-1}(s)\right)ds\right)}{\exp\left(\int_0^{T_i^*}\theta_s\left(\Lambda^{i-1}(s)\right)ds\right)} \\ &= \left(F(0,T_i^*,T_{i-1}^*)\right)^{R+\mathrm{i}u}\exp\left(\int_0^{T_i^*}\theta_s\left((R+\mathrm{i}u)\lambda(s,T_i^*)+\Lambda^{i-1}(s)\right)ds\right) \\ &\times\exp\left(\int_0^{T_i^*}\left[(-R-\mathrm{i}u)\theta_s\left(\Lambda^i(s)\right)-(1-R-\mathrm{i}u)\theta_s\left(\Lambda^{i-1}(s)\right)\right]ds\right). \end{aligned} \tag{51}$$

Taking into account the choice of the drift coefficient in (19), the cumulant function $\theta_s$ (see (9)) and the moment-generating function $M_{X_{T_i^*}}$, respectively, become

$$\begin{aligned} \theta_s(R+\mathrm{i}u) &= (R+\mathrm{i}u)\int_{\mathbb{R}}\left(\frac{e^{x(R+\mathrm{i}u)}-1}{R+\mathrm{i}u}-\frac{(e^{x\lambda(s,T_1^*)}-1)}{\lambda(s,T_1^*)}\right)F_s^{T^*}(dx) \\ &+\frac{c_s}{2}(R+\mathrm{i}u)\left(R+\mathrm{i}u-\lambda(s,T_1^*)\right) \end{aligned} \tag{52}$$

and

$$M_{X_{T_i^*}}(R+\mathrm{i}u) = \left(F(0,T_i^*,T_{i-1}^*)\right)^{R+\mathrm{i}u}\exp\left(\int_0^{T_i^*}\frac{c_s}{2}(R+\mathrm{i}u)(R+\mathrm{i}u-1)\lambda^2(s,T_i^*)ds\right)$$

$$\times \exp\left(\int_0^{T_i^*}\int_{\mathbb{R}} e^{x\Lambda^{i-1}(s)}\left(e^{(R+\mathrm{i}u)x\lambda(s,T_i^*)}-1\right)F_s^{T^*}(dx)ds\right)$$
$$\times \exp\left(-(R+\mathrm{i}u)\int_0^{T_i^*}\int_{\mathbb{R}} e^{x\Lambda^{i-1}(s)}\left(e^{x\lambda(s,T_i^*)}-1\right)F_s^{T^*}(dx)ds\right). \quad (53)$$

Finally, from (48) and (53) we conclude that

$$Cplt_0(T_i^*,K) = \frac{\widetilde{K}_i B(0,T_{i-1}^*)}{2\pi}\int_{\mathbb{R}}\left\{\left(\frac{F(0,T_i^*,T_{i-1}^*)}{\widetilde{K}_i}\right)^{R+iu}\right.$$
$$\times \exp\left(\int_0^{T_i^*}\int_{\mathbb{R}} e^{x\Lambda^{i-1}(s)}\left[\left(e^{(R+\mathrm{i}u)x\lambda(s,T_i^*)}-1\right)-(R+\mathrm{i}u)\left(e^{x\lambda(s,T_i^*)}-1\right)\right]F_s^{T^*}(dx)ds\right)$$
$$\left.\times \exp\left(\int_0^{T_i^*}\frac{c_s}{2}(R+\mathrm{i}u)(R+\mathrm{i}u-1)\lambda^2(s,T_i^*)ds\right)\right\}\frac{du}{(R+\mathrm{i}u)(R+\mathrm{i}u-1)}. \quad (54)$$

# 4 Sensitivity Analysis

## 4.1 Greeks Computed by the Malliavin Approach

In this section we present an application of the Malliavin calculus to the computation of Greeks within the Lévy forward process model. We refer to the literature, for example Di Nunno et al. (2008) [2] as well as Nualart (2006) [15] for details on the theoretical aspects of Malliavin calculus. Another important reference is Yablonski (2008) [19]. See also the Appendix for a short presentation of definitions and results used in the sequel. The forward process $F(t,T_i^*,T_{i-1}^*)$ under the forward measures $\mathbb{P}_{T_{i-1}^*}$ can be written as stochastic exponential

$$F(t,T_i^*,T_{i-1}^*) = F(0,T_i^*,T_{i-1}^*)\mathscr{E}_t\left(Z(\cdot,T_i^*)\right) \quad (55)$$

with

$$Z(t,T_i^*) = \int_0^t \sqrt{c_s}\lambda(s,T_i^*)dW_s^{T_{i-1}^*} + \int_0^t\int_{\mathbb{R}}(e^{x\lambda(s,T_i^*)}-1)\widetilde{\mu}^{L^{T_{i-1}^*}}(ds,dx). \quad (56)$$

Expressed in a differential form we get the $\mathbb{P}_{T_{i-1}^*}$-dynamics

$$\frac{dF(t,T_i^*,T_{i-1}^*)}{F(t-,T_i^*,T_{i-1}^*)} = \sqrt{c_t}\lambda(t,T_i^*)dW_t^{T_{i-1}^*} + \int_{\mathbb{R}}(e^{x\lambda(t,T_i^*)}-1)\widetilde{\mu}^{L^{T_{i-1}^*}}(dt,dx), \quad (57)$$

where $F(t-,T_i^*,T_{i-1}^*)$ is the pathwise left limit of $F(\cdot,T_i^*,T_{i-1}^*)$ at the point $t$.

As in the classical Malliavin calculus we are able to associate the solution of (57) with the process $Y(t, T_i^*, T_{i-1}^*) := \frac{\partial F(t,T_i^*,T_{i-1}^*)}{\partial F(0,T_i^*,T_{i-1}^*)}$; called the first variation process of $F(t, T_i^*, T_{i-1}^*)$. The following proposition provides a simpler expression for the Malliavin derivative operator $D_{r,0}$ when applied to the forward process rates $F(t, T_i^*, T_{i-1}^*)$ (see Di Nunno et al. (2008) [2], Theorem 17.4 and Yablonski (2008) [19], Definition 17. for details). We will denote the domain of the operator $D_{r,0}$ in $L^2(\Omega)$ by $\mathbb{D}^{1,2}$, meaning that $\mathbb{D}^{1,2}$ is the closure of the class of smooth random variables $\mathscr{S}$ (see (100) in the Appendix).

**Proposition 4.1** *Let $F(t, T_i^*, T_{i-1}^*)_{t\in[0,T^*]}$ be the solution of (57). Then $F(t, T_i^*, T_{i-1}^*) \in \mathbb{D}^{1,2}$ and the Malliavin derivative is given by*

$$\begin{aligned} &D_{r,0}F(t, T_i^*, T_{i-1}^*) \\ &\quad = Y(t, T_i^*, T_{i-1}^*)Y(r-, T_i^*, T_{i-1}^*)^{-1}F(r-, T_i^*, T_{i-1}^*)\lambda(r, T_i^*)\sqrt{c_r}\mathbf{1}_{\{r\leq t\}}. \end{aligned} \tag{58}$$

### 4.1.1 Variation in the Initial Forward Price

In this section, we provide an expression for the *Delta*, the partial derivative of the expectation $Cplt_0(T_i^*, K)$ with respect to the initial condition $F(0, T_i^*, T_{i-1}^*)$ which is given by

$$\Delta(F(0, T_i^*, T_{i-1}^*)) = \frac{\partial Cplt_0(T_i^*, K)}{\partial F(0, T_i^*, T_{i-1}^*)}. \tag{59}$$

The derivative with respect to the initial LIBOR rate is then an easy consequence.

$$\begin{aligned} \Delta(L(0, T_i^*)) &= \frac{\partial Cplt_0(T_i^*, K)}{\partial L(0, T_i^*)} \\ &= \Delta(F(0, T_i^*, T_{i-1}^*))\frac{\partial F(0, T_i^*, T_{i-1}^*)}{\partial L(0, T_i^*)} \\ &= \delta_i^* \Delta(F(0, T_i^*, T_{i-1}^*)), \end{aligned} \tag{60}$$

since

$$L(0, T_i^*) = \frac{1}{\delta_i^*}\left(F(0, T_i^*, T_{i-1}^*) - 1\right). \tag{61}$$

Let us define the set

$$\widetilde{T}_i = \left\{h_i \in L^2([0, T_i^*]) : \int_0^{T_i^*} h_i(u)du = 1\right\}. \tag{62}$$

**Proposition 4.2** *For all functions $h_i \in \widetilde{T}_i$, we have*

$$\Delta(F(0, T_i^*, T_{i-1}^*)) = \frac{B(0, T_{i-1}^*)}{F(0, T_i^*, T_{i-1}^*)} \mathbb{E}_{\mathbb{P}_{T^*}}\Bigg[ \left(F(T_i^*, T_i^*, T_{i-1}^*) - \widetilde{K}_i\right)^+ \\ \times \exp\left(\int_0^{T_i^*} \Lambda^{i-1}(s) dL_s^{T^*} - \int_0^{T_i^*} \theta_s\left(\Lambda^{i-1}(s)\right) ds\right) \\ \times \left(\int_0^{T_i^*} \frac{h_i(u) dW_u^{T^*}}{\lambda(u, T_i^*)\sqrt{c_u}} - \int_0^{T_i^*} \frac{h_i(u)\Lambda^{i-1}(u) du}{\lambda(u, T_i^*)}\right)\Bigg]. \tag{63}$$

*Proof* We consider a more general payoff of the form $H(F(T_i^*, T_i^*, T_{i-1}^*))$ such that $H : \mathbb{R} \longrightarrow \mathbb{R}$ is a locally integrable function satisfying

$$\mathbb{E}_{\mathbb{P}_{T_{i-1}^*}}\left[H(F(T_i^*, T_i^*, T_{i-1}^*))^2\right] < \infty\cdot \tag{64}$$

First, assume that $H$ is a continuously differentiable function with compact support. Then we can differentiate inside the expectation and get

$$\begin{aligned} \Delta_H(F(0, T_i^*, T_{i-1}^*)) &:= \frac{\partial \mathbb{E}_{\mathbb{P}_{T_{i-1}^*}}\left[H(F(T_i^*, T_i^*, T_{i-1}^*))\right]}{\partial F(0, T_i^*, T_{i-1}^*)} \\ &= \mathbb{E}_{\mathbb{P}_{T_{i-1}^*}}\left[H'(F(T_i^*, T_i^*, T_{i-1}^*)) \frac{\partial F(T_i^*, T_i^*, T_{i-1}^*)}{\partial F(0, T_i^*, T_{i-1}^*)}\right] \\ &= \mathbb{E}_{\mathbb{P}_{T_{i-1}^*}}\left[H'(F(T_i^*, T_i^*, T_{i-1}^*)) Y(T_i^*, T_i^*, T_{i-1}^*)\right]. \end{aligned} \tag{65}$$

Using Proposition 4.1 we find for any $h_i \in \widetilde{T}_i$

$$Y(T_i^*, T_i^*, T_{i-1}^*) = \int_0^{T_i^*} D_{u,0} F(T_i^*, T_i^*, T_{i-1}^*) \frac{h_i(u) Y(u-, T_i^*, T_{i-1}^*) du}{F(u-, T_i^*, T_{i-1}^*)\lambda(u, T_i^*)\sqrt{c_u}}. \tag{66}$$

From the chain rule (see Yablonski (2008) [19], Proposition 4.8) we find

$$\begin{aligned} \Delta_H(F(0, T_i^*, T_{i-1}^*)) &= \mathbb{E}_{\mathbb{P}_{T_{i-1}^*}}\Bigg[\int_0^{T_i^*} H'(F(T_i^*, T_i^*, T_{i-1}^*)) D_{u,0} F(T_i^*, T_i^*, T_{i-1}^*) \\ &\qquad \times \frac{h_i(u) Y(u-, T_i^*, T_{i-1}^*) du}{F(u-, T_i^*, T_{i-1}^*)\lambda(u, T_i^*)\sqrt{c_u}}\Bigg] \\ &= \mathbb{E}_{\mathbb{P}_{T_{i-1}^*}}\Bigg[\int_0^{T_i^*} D_{u,0} H(F(T_i^*, T_i^*, T_{i-1}^*)) \\ &\qquad \times \frac{h_i(u) Y(u-, T_i^*, T_{i-1}^*) du}{F(u-, T_i^*, T_{i-1}^*)\lambda(u, T_i^*)\sqrt{c_u}}\Bigg] \end{aligned}$$

$$= \mathbb{E}_{\mathbb{P}_{T^*_{i-1}}}\left[\int_0^{T_i^*}\int_{\mathbb{R}} D_{u,x} H(F(T_i^*, T_i^*, T_{i-1}^*)) \times \frac{h_i(u)Y(u-, T_i^*, T_{i-1}^*)du\delta_0(dx)}{F(u-, T_i^*, T_{i-1}^*)\lambda(u, T_i^*)\sqrt{c_u}}\right], \tag{67}$$

where $\delta_0(dx)$ is the Dirac measure at 0.

By the definition of the Skorohod integral $\delta(\cdot)$ (see Yablonski (2008) [19], Sect. 5), we reach

$$\begin{aligned}&\Delta_H(F(0, T_i^*, T_{i-1}^*)) \\ &= \mathbb{E}_{\mathbb{P}_{T^*_{i-1}}}\left[H(F(T_i^*, T_i^*, T_{i-1}^*))\delta\left(\frac{h_i(\cdot)Y(\cdot-, T_i^*, T_{i-1}^*)\delta_0(\cdot)}{F(\cdot-, T_i^*, T_{i-1}^*)\lambda(\cdot, T_i^*)\sqrt{c_\cdot}}\right)\right].\end{aligned} \tag{68}$$

However, the stochastic process

$$\left(\frac{h_i(u)Y(u-, T_i^*, T_{i-1}^*)}{F(u-, T_i^*, T_{i-1}^*)\lambda(u, T_i^*)\sqrt{c_u}}\right)_{0\le u\le T_i^*} \tag{69}$$

is a predictable process, thus the Skorohod integral coincides with the Itô stochastic integral and we get

$$\begin{aligned}&\Delta_H(F(0, T_i^*, T_{i-1}^*)) \\ &= \mathbb{E}_{\mathbb{P}_{T^*_{i-1}}}\left[H(F(T_i^*, T_i^*, T_{i-1}^*))\int_0^{T_i^*}\frac{h_i(u)Y(u-, T_i^*, T_{i-1}^*)dW_u^{T^*_{i-1}}}{F(u-, T_i^*, T_{i-1}^*)\lambda(u, T_i^*)\sqrt{c_u}}\right].\end{aligned} \tag{70}$$

By Lemma 12.28. p. 208 in Di Nunno et al. (2008) [2] the result (70) holds for any locally integrable function $H$ such that

$$\mathbb{E}_{\mathbb{P}_{T^*_{i-1}}}\left[H(F(T_i^*, T_i^*, T_{i-1}^*))^2\right] < \infty. \tag{71}$$

In particular, if one takes

$$H(F(T_i^*, T_i^*, T_{i-1}^*)) = B(0, T_{i-1}^*)\left(F(T_i^*, T_i^*, T_{i-1}^*) - \widetilde{K}_i\right)^+, \tag{72}$$

we can express the derivatives of the expectation $Cplt_0(T_i^*, K, \delta_i^*)$ with respect to the initial condition $F(0, T_i^*, T_{i-1}^*)$ in the form of a weighted expectation as follows

$$\begin{aligned}\Delta(F(0, T_i^*, T_{i-1}^*)) = B(0, T_{i-1}^*)\mathbb{E}_{\mathbb{P}_{T^*_{i-1}}}\Bigg[&\left(F(T_i^*, T_i^*, T_{i-1}^*) - \widetilde{K}_i\right)^+ \\ &\times\int_0^{T_i^*}\frac{h_i(u)Y(u-, T_i^*, T_{i-1}^*)dW_u^{T^*_{i-1}}}{\lambda(u, T_i^*)\sqrt{c_u}F(u-, T_i^*, T_{i-1}^*)}\Bigg].\end{aligned} \tag{73}$$

We show easily that

$$Y(u-, T_i^*, T_{i-1}^*) = \frac{F(u-, T_i^*, T_{i-1}^*)}{F(0, T_i^*, T_{i-1}^*)}, \tag{74}$$

hence

$$\begin{aligned} &\Delta(F(0, T_i^*, T_{i-1}^*)) \\ &= \frac{B(0, T_{i-1}^*)}{F(0, T_i^*, T_{i-1}^*)} \mathbb{E}_{\mathbb{P}_{T_{i-1}^*}} \left[ \left(F(T_i^*, T_i^*, T_{i-1}^*) - \widetilde{K}_i\right)^+ \int_0^{T_i^*} \frac{h_i(u) dW_u^{T_{i-1}^*}}{\lambda(u, T_i^*)\sqrt{c_u}} \right]. \end{aligned} \tag{75}$$

In accordance with (25) we can write

$$W_t^{T_{i-1}^*} = W_t^{T^*} - \int_0^t \Lambda^{i-1}(s)\sqrt{c_s} ds. \tag{76}$$

By making a measure change using the fact (see (40)) that

$$\left.\frac{d\mathbb{P}_{T_{i-1}^*}}{d\mathbb{P}_{T^*}}\right|_{\mathscr{F}_{T_i^*}} = \exp\left(\int_0^{T_i^*} \Lambda^{i-1}(s) dL_s^{T^*} - \int_0^{T_i^*} \theta_s\left(\Lambda^{i-1}(s)\right) ds\right), \tag{77}$$

we end up with

$$\begin{aligned} \Delta(F(0, T_i^*, T_{i-1}^*)) = &\frac{B(0, T_{i-1}^*)}{F(0, T_i^*, T_{i-1}^*)} \mathbb{E}_{\mathbb{P}_{T^*}} \Bigg[ \left(F(T_i^*, T_i^*, T_{i-1}^*) - \widetilde{K}_i\right)^+ \\ &\times \exp\left(\int_0^{T_i^*} \Lambda^{i-1}(s) dL_s^{T^*} - \int_0^{T_i^*} \theta_s\left(\Lambda^{i-1}(s)\right) ds\right) \\ &\times \left(\int_0^{T_i^*} \frac{h_i(u) dW_u^{T^*}}{\lambda(u, T_i^*)\sqrt{c_u}} - \int_0^{T_i^*} \frac{h_i(u)\Lambda^{i-1}(u)}{\lambda(u, T_i^*)} du\right)\Bigg]. \end{aligned} \tag{78}$$

## 4.2 *Greeks Computed by the Fourier-Based Valuation Method*

Thanks to the Fourier-based valuation formula obtained in (45) and the structure of the forward process model as an exponential semimartingale, we can calculate readily the Greeks. We focus on the variation to the initial condition, i.e. Delta.

**Proposition 4.3** *Suppose there is a real number $R \in (1, 1+\varepsilon)$ such that the moment-generating function of $X_{T_i^*}$ with respect to $\mathbb{P}_{T_{i-1}^*}$ is finite at R, i.e. $M_{X_{T_i^*}}(R) < \infty$, then*

$$
\begin{aligned}
\Delta(F(0, T_i^*, T_{i-1}^*)) = \frac{B(0, T_{i-1}^*)}{2\pi} \int_{\mathbb{R}} \Bigg\{ \left( \frac{F(0, T_i^*, T_{i-1}^*)}{\widetilde{K}_i} \right)^{R+\mathrm{i}u-1} \\
\times \exp\left( \int_0^{T_i^*} \int_{\mathbb{R}} e^{x\Lambda^{i-1}(s)} \left( e^{(R+\mathrm{i}u)x\lambda(s,T_i^*)} - 1 \right) F_s^{T^*}(dx)ds \right) \\
\times \exp\left( - \int_0^{T_i^*} \int_{\mathbb{R}} e^{x\Lambda^{i-1}(s)} (R+\mathrm{i}u) \left( e^{x\lambda(s,T_i^*)} - 1 \right) F_s^{T^*}(dx)ds \right) \\
\times \exp\left( \int_0^{T_i^*} \frac{c_s}{2} (R+\mathrm{i}u)(R+\mathrm{i}u-1)\lambda^2(s, T_i^*)ds \right) \Bigg\} \frac{du}{R+\mathrm{i}u-1}. \quad (79)
\end{aligned}
$$

*Proof* Based on the Sect. 4 in Eberlein et al. (2010) [8], this proposition can be shown easily.

## 4.3 Examples

### 4.3.1 Variance Gamma Process (VG)

We suppose that the jump component of the driving process $L^{T^*}$ (see (8)) is described by a Variance Gamma process with the Lévy density $\nu$ given by

$$
\nu(dx) = F_{VG}(x)dx \quad (80)
$$

such that

$$
F_{VG}(x) := \frac{1}{\eta|x|} \exp\left( \frac{\theta}{\sigma^2}x - \frac{1}{\sigma}\sqrt{\frac{2}{\eta} + \frac{\theta^2}{\sigma^2}}|x| \right), \quad (81)
$$

where $(\theta, \sigma, \eta)$ are the parameters such that $\theta \in \mathbb{R}$, $\sigma > 0$ and $\eta > 0$.

Let us put $B = \frac{\theta}{\sigma^2}$ and $C = \frac{1}{\sigma}\sqrt{\frac{2}{\eta} + \frac{\theta^2}{\sigma^2}}$ and get

$$
F_{VG}(x) = \frac{\exp(Bx - C|x|)}{\eta|x|}. \quad (82)
$$

In this case, the moment-generating function $M_{X_{T_i^*}}$ is given by

$$
M_{X_{T_i^*}}(z) = \left(F(0, T_i^*, T_{i-1}^*)\right)^z \exp\left( \int_0^{T_i^*} \left( \frac{c_s z}{2}(z-1)\lambda^2(s, T_i^*) + I^{VG}(s, z) \right) ds \right), \quad (83)
$$

where the generalized integral $I^{VG}(s, z)$ is given by

$$\begin{aligned} I^{VG}(s,z) := &\int_{\mathbb{R}} \left(e^{x\left(z\lambda(s,T_i^*)+\Lambda^{i-1}(s)\right)} - e^{x\Lambda^{i-1}(s)}\right) F_{VG}(x)dx \\ &- \int_{\mathbb{R}} z\left(e^{x\Lambda^{i}(s)} - e^{x\Lambda^{i-1}(s)}\right) F_{VG}(x)dx. \end{aligned} \tag{84}$$

Now substituting $F_{VG}(x)$ by its explicit expression we get

$$\begin{aligned} I^{VG}(s,z) = &\int_{\mathbb{R}} \left(e^{x\left(z\lambda(s,T_i^*)+\Lambda^{i-1}(s)\right)} - e^{x\Lambda^{i-1}(s)}\right) \exp\left(Bx - C|x|\right) \frac{dx}{\eta|x|} \\ &- \int_{\mathbb{R}} z\left(e^{x\Lambda^{i}(s)} - e^{x\Lambda^{i-1}(s)}\right) \exp\left(Bx - C|x|\right) \frac{dx}{\eta|x|} \\ = &\int_0^{+\infty} \left(e^{x\left(z\lambda(s,T_i^*)+\Lambda^{i-1}(s)\right)} - e^{x\Lambda^{i-1}(s)}\right) \exp\left(Bx - Cx\right) \frac{dx}{\eta x} \\ &- \int_0^{+\infty} z\left(e^{x\Lambda^{i}(s)} - e^{x\Lambda^{i-1}(s)}\right) \exp\left(Bx - Cx\right) \frac{dx}{\eta x} \\ &- \int_{-\infty}^{0} \left(e^{x\left(z\lambda(s,T_i^*)+\Lambda^{i-1}(s)\right)} - e^{x\Lambda^{i-1}(s)}\right) \exp\left(Bx + Cx\right) \frac{dx}{\eta x} \\ &+ \int_{-\infty}^{0} z\left(e^{x\Lambda^{i}(s)} - e^{x\Lambda^{i-1}(s)}\right) \exp\left(Bx + Cx\right) \frac{dx}{\eta x}, \end{aligned}$$

or

$$\begin{aligned} I^{VG}(s,z) = &\int_0^{+\infty} \left[\frac{e^{\left(z\lambda(s,T_i^*)+\Lambda^{i-1}(s)+B-C\right)x} - e^{\left(\Lambda^{i-1}(s)+B-C\right)x}}{\eta x}\right] dx \\ &- \int_0^{+\infty} \left[z\frac{e^{\left(\Lambda^{i}(s)+B-C\right)x} - e^{\left(\Lambda^{i-1}(s)+B-C\right)x}}{\eta x}\right] dx \\ &- \int_{-\infty}^{0} \left[\frac{e^{\left(z\lambda(s,T_i^*)+\Lambda^{i-1}(s)+B+C\right)x} - e^{\left(\Lambda^{i-1}(s)+B+C\right)x}}{\eta x}\right] dx \\ &+ \int_{-\infty}^{0} \left[z\frac{e^{\left(\Lambda^{i}(s)+B+C\right)x} - e^{\left(\Lambda^{i-1}(s)+B+C\right)x}}{\eta x}\right] dx \\ = &\int_0^{+\infty} \left[\frac{e^{\left(z\lambda(s,T_i^*)+\Lambda^{i-1}(s)+B-C\right)x} - e^{\left(\Lambda^{i-1}(s)+B-C\right)x}}{\eta x}\right] dx \\ &- \int_0^{+\infty} \left[z\frac{e^{\left(\Lambda^{i}(s)+B-C\right)x} - e^{\left(\Lambda^{i-1}(s)+B-C\right)x}}{\eta x}\right] dx \\ &+ \int_0^{+\infty} \left[\frac{e^{-\left(z\lambda(s,T_i^*)+\Lambda^{i-1}(s)+B+C\right)x} - e^{-\left(\Lambda^{i-1}(s)+B+C\right)x}}{\eta x}\right] dx \\ &- \int_0^{+\infty} \left[z\frac{e^{-\left(\Lambda^{i}(s)+B+C\right)x} - e^{-\left(\Lambda^{i-1}(s)+B+C\right)x}}{\eta x}\right] dx. \end{aligned}$$

Using the notations

$$\alpha_i(s,z) = -\left(z\lambda(s,T_i^*) + \Lambda^{i-1}(s) + B - C\right), \tag{85}$$

$$\beta_i(s) = -\left(\Lambda^{i-1}(s) + B - C\right), \tag{86}$$

$$\gamma_i(s) = -\left(\Lambda^{i}(s) + B - C\right), \tag{87}$$

we end up with

$$\begin{aligned} I^{VG}(s,z) &= \int_0^{+\infty}\left[\frac{e^{-\alpha_i(s,z)x} - e^{-\beta_i(s)x}}{x} - z\frac{e^{-\gamma_i(s)x} - e^{-\beta_i(s)x}}{x}\right]dx \\ &+ \int_0^{+\infty}\left[\frac{e^{-(2C-\alpha_i(s,z))x} - e^{-(2C-\beta_i(s))x}}{x} - z\frac{e^{-(2C-\gamma_i(s))x} - e^{-(2C-\beta_i(s))x}}{x}\right]dx. \end{aligned}$$

Using Frullani's integral (see for details Ostrowski (1949) [16]), we can show that, if $\alpha \in \mathbb{C}$ and $\beta \in \mathbb{C}$ such that $\mathscr{Re}(\alpha) > 0$, $\mathscr{Re}(\beta) > 0$ and $\frac{\beta}{\alpha} \in \mathbb{C} \setminus \mathbb{R}^-$ where $\mathbb{R}^- = ]-\infty;0]$,

$$I_{(\alpha,\beta)} := \int_0^{+\infty} \frac{e^{-\alpha x} - e^{-\beta x}}{x}dx = Log\left(\frac{\beta}{\alpha}\right), \tag{88}$$

where $Log$ is the principal value of the logarithm. Consequently

$$\begin{aligned} I^{VG}(s,z) &= Log\left(\frac{\beta_i(s)}{\alpha_i(s,z)}\right) - zLog\left(\frac{\beta_i(s)}{\gamma_i(s)}\right) \\ &+ Log\left(\frac{2C-\beta_i(s)}{2C-\alpha_i(s,z)}\right) - zLog\left(\frac{2C-\beta_i(s)}{2C-\gamma_i(s)}\right) \\ &= Log\left(\frac{\beta_i(s)}{\alpha_i(s,z)}\right) + Log\left(\frac{2C-\beta_i(s)}{2C-\alpha_i(s,z)}\right) \\ &- z\left(Log\left(\frac{\beta_i(s)}{\gamma_i(s)}\right) + Log\left(\frac{2C-\beta_i(s)}{2C-\gamma_i(s)}\right)\right) \\ &= Log\left(\frac{\beta_i(s)\,(2C-\beta_i(s))}{\alpha_i(s,z)\,(2C-\alpha_i(s,z))}\right) - zLog\left(\frac{\beta_i(s)\,(2C-\beta_i(s))}{\gamma_i(s)\,(2C-\gamma_i(s))}\right). \end{aligned}$$

The moment-generating function $M_{X_{T_i^*}}$ becomes

$$\begin{aligned} M_{X_{T_i^*}}(z) &= \left(F(0,T_i^*,T_{i-1}^*)\right)^z \exp\left(\int_0^{T_i^*} \frac{c_s z}{2}(z-1)\lambda^2(s,T_i^*)ds\right) \\ &\times \exp\left(\int_0^{T_i^*} Log\left(\frac{\beta_i(s)\,(2C-\beta_i(s))}{\alpha_i(s,z)\,(2C-\alpha_i(s,z))}\right)ds\right) \\ &\times \exp\left(-\int_0^{T_i^*} zLog\left(\frac{\beta_i(s)\,(2C-\beta_i(s))}{\gamma_i(s)\,(2C-\gamma_i(s))}\right)ds\right) \end{aligned}$$

or

$$
\begin{aligned}
M_{X_{T_i^*}}(R+\mathrm{i}u) = {} & \left(F(0,T_i^*,T_{i-1}^*)\right)^{R+\mathrm{i}u} \\
& \times \exp\left(\int_0^{T_i^*} \frac{c_s}{2}(R+\mathrm{i}u)(R+\mathrm{i}u-1)\lambda^2(s,T_i^*)ds\right) \\
& \times \exp\left(\int_0^{T_i^*} Log\left(\frac{\beta_i(s)\,(2C-\beta_i(s))}{\alpha_i(s,R+\mathrm{i}u)\,(2C-\alpha_i(s,R+\mathrm{i}u))}\right)ds\right) \\
& \times \exp\left(-\int_0^{T_i^*} (R+\mathrm{i}u) Log\left(\frac{\beta_i(s)\,(2C-\beta_i(s))}{\gamma_i(s)\,(2C-\gamma_i(s))}\right)ds\right).
\end{aligned}
$$

The valuation formula becomes

$$
\begin{aligned}
Cplt_0(T_i^*,K) = {} & \frac{B(0,T_{i-1}^*)}{2\pi}\int_{\mathbb{R}} \frac{\widetilde{K}_i^{1-R-\mathrm{i}u} M_{X_{T_i^*}}(R+\mathrm{i}u)}{(R+\mathrm{i}u)(R+\mathrm{i}u-1)}du \\
= {} & \frac{\widetilde{K}_i B(0,T_{i-1}^*)}{2\pi}\int_{\mathbb{R}} \left\{ \left(\frac{F(0,T_i^*,T_{i-1}^*)}{\widetilde{K}_i}\right)^{R+\mathrm{i}u} \right. \\
& \times \exp\left(\int_0^{T_i^*} \frac{c_s}{2}(R+\mathrm{i}u)(R+\mathrm{i}u-1)\lambda^2(s,T_i^*)ds\right) \\
& \times \exp\left(\int_0^{T_i^*} Log\left(\frac{\beta_i(s)\,(2C-\beta_i(s))}{\alpha_i(s,R+\mathrm{i}u)\,(2C-\alpha_i(s,R+\mathrm{i}u))}\right)ds\right) \\
& \left. \times \exp\left(-\int_0^{T_i^*} (R+\mathrm{i}u) Log\left(\frac{\beta_i(s)\,(2C-\beta_i(s))}{\gamma_i(s)\,(2C-\gamma_i(s))}\right)ds\right)\right\} \frac{du}{(R+\mathrm{i}u)(R+\mathrm{i}u-1)}. \qquad (89)
\end{aligned}
$$

The *Delta* is given by

$$
\begin{aligned}
\Delta(F(0,T_i^*,T_{i-1}^*)) = {} & \frac{B(0,T_{i-1}^*)}{2\pi}\int_{\mathbb{R}} \left\{ \left(\frac{F(0,T_i^*,T_{i-1}^*)}{\widetilde{K}_i}\right)^{R+\mathrm{i}u-1} \right. \\
& \times \exp\left(\int_0^{T_i^*} \frac{c_s}{2}(R+\mathrm{i}u)(R+\mathrm{i}u-1)\lambda^2(s,T_i^*)ds\right) \\
& \times \exp\left(\int_0^{T_i^*} Log\left(\frac{\beta_i(s)\,(2C-\beta_i(s))}{\alpha_i(s,R+\mathrm{i}u)\,(2C-\alpha_i(s,R+\mathrm{i}u))}\right)ds\right) \\
& \left. \times \exp\left(-\int_0^{T_i^*} (R+\mathrm{i}u) Log\left(\frac{\beta_i(s)\,(2C-\beta_i(s))}{\gamma_i(s)\,(2C-\gamma_i(s))}\right)ds\right)\right\} \frac{du}{R+\mathrm{i}u-1}. \qquad (90)
\end{aligned}
$$

### 4.3.2 Inhomogeneous Gamma Process (IGP)

We suppose that the jump component of the driving process $L^{T^*}$, is described by an inhomogeneous Gamma process (IGP), which has been introduced by Berman (1981) [1] as follows

**Definition 4.4** Let $A(t)$ be a nondecreasing function from $\mathbb{R}^+ \longrightarrow \mathbb{R}^+$ and $B > 0$. A Gamma process with shape function $A$ and scale parameter $B$ is a stochastic process $(L_t)_{t\geq 0}$ on $\mathbb{R}^+$ such that:

1. $L_0 = 0$;
2. Independent increments: for every increasing sequence of time points $t_0, \dots, t_n$, the random variables $L_{t_0}, L_{t_1} - L_{t_0}, \dots, L_{t_n} - L_{t_{n-1}}$ are independent;
3. for $0 \leq s < t$, the distribution of the random variable $L_t - L_s$ is given by the Gamma distribution $\Gamma(A(t) - A(s); B)$.

We suppose that the shape function $A$ is differentiable, hence we can write

$$A(t) = A(0) + \int_0^t \dot{A}(s)ds \tag{91}$$

for all $t \in \mathbb{R}^+$ where $\dot{A}$ denotes the derivative of $A$. In this case, the Lévy density of the Gamma process $L$ is given by

$$F_s^G(x) = \dot{A}(s)\frac{e^{-Bx}}{x}\mathbf{1}_{\{x>0\}}. \tag{92}$$

The moment-generating function (53) has the form

$$\begin{aligned}
M_{X_{T_i^*}}(z) &= \left(F(0, T_i^*, T_{i-1}^*)\right)^z \exp\left(\int_0^{T_i^*} \frac{c_s z}{2}(z-1)\lambda^2(s, T_i^*)ds\right) \\
&\quad \times \exp\left(\int_0^{T_i^*}\int_{\mathbb{R}} e^{x\Lambda^{i-1}(s)}\left[\left(e^{zx\lambda(s,T_i^*)} - 1\right) - z\left(e^{x\lambda(s,T_i^*)} - 1\right)\right] F_s^G(x)dxds\right) \\
&= \left(F(0, T_i^*, T_{i-1}^*)\right)^z \exp\left(\int_0^{T_i^*} \frac{c_s z}{2}(z-1)\lambda^2(s, T_i^*)ds\right) \\
&\quad \times \exp\left(\int_0^{T_i^*} \dot{A}(s)\int_{\mathbb{R}} e^{x\Lambda^{i-1}(s)}\left(e^{zx\lambda(s,T_i^*)} - 1\right)\frac{e^{-Bx}}{x}\mathbf{1}_{\{x>0\}}dxds\right) \\
&\quad \times \exp\left(-z\int_0^{T_i^*} \dot{A}(s)\int_{\mathbb{R}} e^{x\Lambda^{i-1}(s)}\left(e^{x\lambda(s,T_i^*)} - 1\right)\frac{e^{-Bx}}{x}\mathbf{1}_{\{x>0\}}dxds\right) \\
&= \left(F(0, T_i^*, T_{i-1}^*)\right)^z \exp\left(\int_0^{T_i^*}\left(\frac{c_s z}{2}(z-1)\lambda^2(s, T_i^*) + \dot{A}(s)I^G(s, z)\right)ds\right),
\end{aligned}$$

where

$$\begin{aligned}
I^G(s, z) &= \int_0^{+\infty} \frac{e^{\left(z\lambda(s,T_i^*) + \Lambda^{i-1}(s) - B\right)x} - e^{\left(\Lambda^{i-1}(s) - B\right)x}}{x}dx \\
&\quad - \int_0^{+\infty} z\frac{e^{\left(\Lambda^i(s) - B\right)x} - e^{\left(\Lambda^{i-1}(s) - B\right)x}}{x}dx.
\end{aligned}$$

Setting

$$\alpha_i(s,z) = -\left(z\lambda(s,T_i^*) + \Lambda^{i-1}(s) - B\right), \tag{93}$$

$$\beta_i(s) = -\left(\Lambda^{i-1}(s) - B\right), \tag{94}$$

$$\gamma_i(s) = -\left(\Lambda^{i}(s) - B\right) \tag{95}$$

and using Frullani's integral, we find that

$$\begin{aligned} I^G(s,z) &= \int_0^{+\infty} \left[ \frac{e^{-\alpha_i(s,z)x} - e^{-\beta_i(s)x}}{x} - z\frac{e^{-\gamma_i(s)x} - e^{-\beta_i(s)x}}{x} \right] dx \\ &= Log\left(\frac{\beta_i(s)}{\alpha_i(s,z)}\right) - zLog\left(\frac{\beta_i(s)}{\gamma_i(s)}\right) \\ &= Log\left(\frac{\Lambda^{i-1}(s) - B}{z\lambda(s,T_i^*) + \Lambda^{i-1}(s) - B}\right) - zLog\left(\frac{\Lambda^{i-1}(s) - B}{\Lambda^{i}(s) - B}\right). \end{aligned}$$

Therefore, we get the form

$$\begin{aligned} M_{X_{T_i^*}}(z) &= \left(F(0,T_i^*,T_{i-1}^*)\right)^z \exp\left(\int_0^{T_i^*} \frac{c_s z}{2}(z-1)\lambda^2(s,T_i^*)ds\right) \\ &\times \exp\left(\int_0^{T_i^*} \dot{A}(s) Log\left(\frac{\Lambda^{i-1}(s) - B}{z\lambda(s,T_i^*) + \Lambda^{i-1}(s) - B}\right) ds\right) \\ &\times \exp\left(-z\int_0^{T_i^*} \dot{A}(s) Log\left(\frac{\Lambda^{i-1}(s) - B}{\Lambda^{i}(s) - B}\right) ds\right) \end{aligned}$$

or

$$\begin{aligned} M_{X_{T_i^*}}(R+iu) &= \left(F(0,T_i^*,T_{i-1}^*)\right)^{R+iu} \\ &\times \exp\left(\int_0^{T_i^*} \frac{c_s}{2}(R+iu)(R+iu-1)\lambda^2(s,T_i^*)ds\right) \\ &\times \exp\left(\int_0^{T_i^*} \dot{A}(s) Log\left(\frac{\Lambda^{i-1}(s) - B}{(R+iu)\lambda(s,T_i^*) + \Lambda^{i-1}(s) - B}\right) ds\right) \\ &\times \exp\left(-(R+iu)\int_0^{T_i^*} \dot{A}(s) Log\left(\frac{\Lambda^{i-1}(s) - B}{\Lambda^{i}(s) - B}\right) ds\right). \end{aligned}$$

The valuation formula becomes

$$\begin{aligned} Cplt_0(T_i^*,K) &= \frac{B(0,T_{i-1}^*)}{2\pi}\int_{\mathbb{R}} \frac{\widetilde{K}_i^{1-R-iu} M_{X_{T_i^*}}(R+iu)}{(R+iu)(R+iu-1)} du \\ &= \frac{\widetilde{K}_i B(0,T_{i-1}^*)}{2\pi}\int_{\mathbb{R}} \frac{du}{(R+iu)(R+iu-1)} \left\{ \left(\frac{F(0,T_i^*,T_{i-1}^*)}{\widetilde{K}_i}\right)^{R+iu} \right. \end{aligned}$$

$$\times \exp\left(\int_0^{T_i^*} \frac{c_s}{2}(R+iu)(R+iu-1)\lambda^2(s,T_i^*)ds\right)$$
$$\times \exp\left(\int_0^{T_i^*} \dot{A}(s) Log\left(\frac{\Lambda^{i-1}(s)-B}{(R+iu)\lambda(s,T_i^*)+\Lambda^{i-1}(s)-B}\right)ds\right)$$
$$\times \exp\left(-\int_0^{T_i^*} (R+iu)\dot{A}(s) Log\left(\frac{\Lambda^{i-1}(s)-B}{\Lambda^{i}(s)-B}\right)ds\right)\Bigg\}. \tag{96}$$

The Greek *Delta* is given by

$$\Delta(F(0,T_i^*,T_{i-1}^*)) = \frac{B(0,T_{i-1}^*)}{2\pi}\int_{\mathbb{R}}\Bigg\{\left(\frac{F(0,T_i^*,T_{i-1}^*)}{\widetilde{K}_i}\right)^{R+iu-1}$$
$$\times \exp\left(\int_0^{T_i^*} \frac{c_s}{2}(R+iu)(R+iu-1)\lambda^2(s,T_i^*)ds\right)$$
$$\times \exp\left(\int_0^{T_i^*} \dot{A}(s) Log\left(\frac{\Lambda^{i-1}(s)-B}{(R+iu)\lambda(s,T_i^*)+\Lambda^{i-1}(s)-B}\right)ds\right)$$
$$\times \exp\left(-\int_0^{T_i^*} (R+iu)\dot{A}(s) Log\left(\frac{\Lambda^{i-1}(s)-B}{\Lambda^{i}(s)-B}\right)ds\right)\Bigg\}\frac{du}{R+iu-1}. \tag{97}$$

**Acknowledgments** The KPMG Center of Excellence in Risk Management is acknowledged for organizing the conference "Challenges in Derivatives Markets - Fixed Income Modeling, Valuation Adjustments, Risk Management, and Regulation".

# A Appendix

## *A.1 Isonormal Lévy Process (ILP)*

Let $\mu$ and $\nu$ be $\sigma$-finite measures without atoms on the measurable spaces $(\mathrm{T}, \mathscr{A})$ and $(\mathrm{T}\times \mathrm{X}_0, \mathscr{B})$, respectively. Define a new measure

$$\pi(dt,dz) := \mu(dt)\delta_{\Theta}(dz) + \nu(dt,dz) \tag{98}$$

on a measurable space $(\mathrm{T}\times\mathrm{X}, \mathscr{G})$, where $\mathrm{X} = \mathrm{X}_0 \cup \{\Theta\}$, $\mathscr{G} = \sigma(\mathscr{A}\times\{\Theta\}, \mathscr{B})$ and $\delta_{\Theta}(dz)$ is the measure which gives mass one to the point $\Theta$. We assume that the Hilbert space $\mathrm{H} := \mathrm{L}^2(\mathrm{T}\times\mathrm{X}, \mathscr{G}, \pi)$ is separable.

**Definition A.1** We say that a stochastic process $\mathrm{L} = \{\mathrm{L}(h), h \in \mathrm{H}\}$ defined on a complete probability space $(\Omega, \mathscr{F}, P)$ is an isonormal Lévy process (or Lévy process on $H$) if the following conditions are satisfied:

1. The mapping $h \longrightarrow L(h)$ is linear;

2. $\mathrm{E}[e^{ixL(h)}] = \exp(\Psi(x,h))$, where $\Psi(x,h)$ is equal to

$$\int_{\mathrm{T}\times\mathrm{X}} \left( (e^{\mathrm{i}xh(t,z)} - 1 - \mathrm{i}xh(t,z))\mathbf{1}_{\mathrm{X}_0}(z) - \frac{1}{2}x^2h^2(t,z)\mathbf{1}_{\Theta}(z) \right) \pi(dt,dz). \quad (99)$$

## A.2 The Derivative Operator

Let $\mathscr{S}$ denote the class of smooth random variables, that is the class of random variables $\xi$ of the form

$$\xi = f(L(h_1), \ldots, L(h_n)), \quad (100)$$

where $f$ belongs to $C_b^\infty(\mathbb{R}^n)$, $h_1, \ldots, h_n$ are in $H$, and $n \geq 1$. The set $\mathscr{S}$ is dense in $L^p(\Omega)$ for any $p \geq 1$.

**Definition A.2** The stochastic derivative of a smooth random variable of the form (100) is the $H$-valued random variable $D\xi = \{D_{t,x}\xi, (t,x) \in T \times X\}$ given by

$$\begin{aligned} D_{t,x}\xi = & \sum_{k=1}^{n} \frac{\partial f}{\partial y_k}(L(h_1), \ldots, L(h_n))h_k(t,x)\mathbf{1}_{\Theta}(x) \\ & + (f(L(h_1) + h_1(t,x), \ldots, L(h_n) + h_n(t,x)) \\ & - f(L(h_1), \ldots, L(h_n)))\, \mathbf{1}_{X_0}(x). \end{aligned} \quad (101)$$

We will consider $D\xi$ as an element of $L^2(T \times X \times \Omega) \cong L^2(\Omega; H)$; namely $D\xi$ is a random process indexed by the parameter space $T \times X$.

1. If the measure $\nu$ is zero or $h_k(t,x) = 0$, $k = 1, \ldots, n$ when $x \neq \Theta$ then $D\xi$ coincides with the Malliavin derivative (see, e.g. Nualart (2006) [15] Definition 1.2.1 p.38).
2. If the measure $\mu$ is zero or $h_k(t,x) = 0$, $k = 1, \ldots, n$ when $x = \Theta$ then $D\xi$ coincides with the difference operator (see, e.g. Picard (1996) [18]).

## A.3 Integration by Parts Formula

**Theorem A.3** *Suppose that $\xi$ and $\eta$ are smooth random variables and $h \in H$. Then*

*1.*

$$\mathrm{E}[\xi L(h)] = \mathrm{E}[\langle D\xi; h\rangle_H]; \quad (102)$$

2.

$$\mathrm{E}[\xi\eta L(h)] = \mathrm{E}[\eta\,\langle D\xi; h\rangle_H] + \mathrm{E}[\xi\,\langle D\eta; h\rangle_H] + \mathrm{E}[\langle D\eta; h\mathbf{1}_{X_0} D\xi\rangle_H]. \quad (103)$$

As a consequence of the above theorem we obtain the following result:

The expression of the derivative $D\xi$ given in (101) does not depend on the particular representation of $\xi$ in (100).
The operator $D$ is closable as an operator from $L^2(\Omega)$ to $L^2(\Omega; H)$.

We will denote the closure of $D$ again by $D$ and its domain in $L^2(\Omega)$ by $\mathbb{D}^{1,2}$.

### A.4 The Chain Rule

**Proposition A.4** (see Yablonski (2008), Proposition 4.8) *Suppose $F = (F_1, F_2, \ldots, F_n)$ is a random vector whose components belong to the space $\mathbb{D}^{1,2}$. Let $\phi \in \mathscr{C}^1(\mathbb{R}^n)$ be a function with bounded partial derivatives such that $\phi(F) \in \mathrm{L}^2(\Omega)$. Then $\phi(F) \in \mathbb{D}^{1,2}$ and*

$$D_{t,x}\phi(F) = \begin{cases} \sum_{i=1}^{n} \frac{\partial\phi}{\partial x_i}(F) D_{t,\Theta} F_i; & x = \Theta \\ \phi(F_1 + D_{t,x}F_1, \ldots, F_n + D_{t,x}F_n) - \phi(F_1, \ldots, F_n); & x \neq \Theta. \end{cases} \quad (104)$$

### A.5 Regularity of Solutions of SDEs Driven by Time-Inhomogeneous Lévy Processes

We focus on a class of models in which the price of the underlying asset is given by the following stochastic differential equation (see Di Nunno et al. [2] and Petrou [17] for details)

$$\begin{aligned} dS_t &= b(t, S_{t-})dt + \sigma(t, S_{t-})dW_t \\ &\quad + \int_{\mathbb{R}_0} \varphi(t, S_{t-}, z)\tilde{N}(dt, dz), \\ S_0 &= x, \end{aligned} \quad (105)$$

where $\mathbb{R}_0 := \mathbb{R}^d \setminus \{0_{\mathbb{R}^d}\}$, $x \in \mathbb{R}^d$, $\{W_t, 0 \le t \le T\}$ is an $m$-dimensional standard Brownian motion, $\tilde{N}$ is a compensated Poisson random measure on $[0, T] \times \mathbb{R}_0$ with compensator $\nu_t(dz)dt$. The coefficients $b : \mathbb{R}^+ \times \mathbb{R}^d \longrightarrow \mathbb{R}^d$, $\sigma : \mathbb{R}^+ \times \mathbb{R}^d \longrightarrow \mathbb{R}^d \times \mathbb{R}^m$ and $\varphi : \mathbb{R}^+ \times \mathbb{R}^d \times \mathbb{R} \longrightarrow \mathbb{R}^d \times \mathbb{R}$, are continuously differentiable with bounded derivatives and the family of positive measures $(\nu_t)_{t\in[0,T]}$ satisfies $\int_0^T (\int_{\mathbb{R}_0} (\|z\|^2 \wedge 1)\nu_t(dz))dt < \infty$ and $\nu_t(\{0\}) = 0$. The coefficients are assumed to satisfy the following linear growth condition

$$\|b(t,x)\|^2 + \|\sigma(t,x)\|^2 + \int_{\mathbb{R}_0} \|\varphi(t,x,z)\|^2 \nu_t(dz) \leq C(1+\|x\|^2), \tag{106}$$

for all $t \in [0,T]$, $x \in \mathbb{R}^d$, where $C$ is a positive constant. Furthermore, we suppose that there exists a function $\rho : \mathbb{R} \longrightarrow \mathbb{R}$ with

$$\sup_{0\leq t\leq T} \int_{\mathbb{R}_0} |\rho(z)|^2 \nu_t(dz) < \infty, \tag{107}$$

and a positive constant $K$ such that

$$\|\varphi(t,x,z) - \varphi(t,y,z)\| \leq K|\rho(z)|\|x-y\|, \tag{108}$$

for all $t \in [0,T]$, $x, y \in \mathbb{R}^d$ and $z \in \mathbb{R}_0$.

In the sequel we provide a theorem which proves that under specific conditions the solution of a stochastic differential equation belongs to the domain $\mathbb{D}^{1,2}$.

**Theorem A.5** *Let $(S_t)_{t\in[0,T]}$ be the solution of (105). Then $S_t \in \mathbb{D}^{1,2}$ for all $t \in [0,T]$ and the derivative $D_{r,0}S_t$ satisfies the following linear equation*

$$\begin{aligned} D_{r,0}S_t &= \int_r^t \frac{\partial b}{\partial x}(u, S_{u-}) D_{r,0}S_{u-}du + \sigma(r, S_{r-}) \\ &+ \int_r^t \frac{\partial \sigma}{\partial x}(u, S_{u-}) D_{r,0}S_{u-}dW_u \\ &+ \int_r^t \int_{\mathbb{R}_0} \frac{\partial \varphi}{\partial x}(u, S_{u-}, y) D_{r,0}S_{u-}\tilde{N}(du,dy) \end{aligned} \tag{109}$$

*for $0 \leq r \leq t$ a.e. and $D_{r,0}S_t = 0$ a.e. otherwise.*

As in the classical Malliavin calculus we are able to associate the solution of (105) to the first variation process $Y_t := \nabla_x S_t$. Then, we will also provide a specific expression for $D_{r,0}S_t$, the Wiener directional derivative of the $S_t$.

**Proposition A.6** *Let $(S_t)_{t\in[0,T]}$ be the solution of (105). Then the derivative satisfies the following equation*

$$D_{r,0}S_t = Y_t Y_{r-}^{-1} \sigma(r, S_{r-}) \mathbf{1}_{\{r\leq t\}} \quad a.e. \tag{110}$$

*where $(Y_t)_{t\in[0,T]}$ is the first variation process of $(S_t)_{t\in[0,T]}$.*

**Open Access** This chapter is distributed under the terms of the Creative Commons Attribution 4.0 International License (http://creativecommons.org/licenses/by/4.0/), which permits use, duplication, adaptation, distribution and reproduction in any medium or format, as long as you give appropriate credit to the original author(s) and the source, a link is provided to the Creative Commons license and any changes made are indicated.

The images or other third party material in this chapter are included in the work's Creative Commons license, unless indicated otherwise in the credit line; if such material is not included in the work's Creative Commons license and the respective action is not permitted by statutory regulation, users will need to obtain permission from the license holder to duplicate, adapt or reproduce the material.

## References


1. Berman, M.: Inhomogeneous and modulated gamma processes. Biometrika **68**, 143–152 (1981)
2. Di Nunno, G., Øksendal, B., Proske, F.: Malliavin Calculus for Lévy Processes with Applications to Finance. Springer, Berlin (2008)
3. Eberlein, E.: Fourier-based valuation methods in mathematical finance. In: Benth, F.E., Kholodnyi, V.A., Laurence, P. (eds.) Quantitative Energy Finance, pp. 85–114. Springer, New York (2014)
4. Eberlein, E., Keller, U.: Hyperbolic distributions in finance. Bernoulli **1**(3), 281–299 (1995)
5. Eberlein, E., Özkan, F.: The Lévy LIBOR model. Financ. Stochast. **9**, 327–348 (2005)
6. Eberlein, E., Kluge, W.: Exact pricing formulae for caps and swaptions in a Lévy term structure model. J. Comput. Financ. **9**(2), 99–125 (2006)
7. Eberlein, E., Kluge, W.: Calibration of Lévy term structure models. In: Fu, M., Jarrow, R., Yen, J.-Y., Elliott, R. (eds.) Advances in Mathematical Finance, Applied and Numerical Harmonic Analysis, pp. 147–172. Birkhäuser, Boston (2007)
8. Eberlein, E., Glau, K., Papapantoleon, A.: Analysis of Fourier transform valuation formulas and applications. Appl. Math. Financ. **17**, 211–240 (2010)
9. Fournié, E., Lasry, J.-M., Lebuchoux, J., Lions, P.-L., Touzi, N.: Applications of Malliavin calculus to Monte Carlo methods in finance. Financ. Stochast. **3**(4), 391–412 (1999)
10. Fries, C.: Mathematical Finance: Theory, Modeling, Implementation. Wiley, Chichester (2007)
11. Glasserman, P.: Monte Carlo Methods in Financial Engineering. Springer, New York (2004)
12. Glasserman, P., Zhao, X.: Fast Greeks by simulation in forward LIBOR models. J. Comput. Financ. **3**(1), 5–39 (1999)
13. Jacod, J., Shiryaev, A.N.: Limit Theorems for Stochastic Processes. Springer, Berlin (1987)
14. León, J.A., Solé, J.L., Utzet, F., Vives, J.: On Lévy processes, Malliavin calculus and market models with jumps. Financ. Stochast. **6**, 197–225 (2002)
15. Nualart, D.: The Malliavin Calculus and Related Topics, 2nd edn. Springer, Berlin (2006)
16. Ostrowski, A.M.: On some generalizations of the Cauchy-Frullani integral. Proc. Natl. Acad. Sci. **35**, 612–615 (1949)
17. Petrou, E.: Malliavin calculus in Lévy spaces and applications to finance. Electron. J. Probab. **13**(27), 852–879 (2008)
18. Picard, J.: On the existence of smooth densities for jump processes. Probab. Theory Related Fields **105**(4), 481–511 (1996)
19. Yablonski, A.: The calculus of variations for processes with independent increments. Rocky Mt. J. Math. **38**(2), 669–701 (2008)

# Inside the EMs Risky Spreads and CDS-Sovereign Bonds Basis

**Vilimir Yordanov**

**Abstract** The paper considers a no-arbitrage setting for pricing and relative value analysis of risky sovereign bonds. The typical case of an emerging market country (EM) that has bonds outstanding both in foreign hard currency (Eurobonds) and local soft currency (treasuries) is inspected. The resulting two yield curves give rise to a credit and currency spread that need further elaboration. We discuss their proper measurement and also derive and analyze the necessary no-arbitrage conditions that must hold. Then we turn attention to the CDS-Bond basis in this multi-curve environment. For EM countries the concept shows certain specifics both in theoretical background and empirical performance. The paper further focuses on analyzing these peculiarities. If the proper measurement of the basis in the standard case of only hard currency debt being issued is still problematic, the situation is much more complicated in a multi-curve setting when a further contingent claim on the sovereign risk in the face of local currency debt curve appears. We investigate the issue and provide relevant theoretical and empirical input.

**Keywords** HJM · Foreign debt · Domestic debt · Z-Spread · CDS-Bond basis

## 1 Introduction

Local currency debt of EM sovereigns became a hot topic both for practitioners and academics in the recent years. Major investment banks and asset managers consider it a separate asset class and publish regularly special local currency investment reports. A joint working group of IMF, WB, EBRD, and OECD demonstrated recently an official interest in a thorough investigation of this market segment and support for its development, thus forming a strict policy agenda. It was recognized that not only do the local bonds complete the market and thus bring market efficiency, but also

V. Yordanov (✉)
Vienna Graduate School of Finance, Vienna, Austria
e-mail: research@vjord.com

V. Yordanov
Karlsruhe Institute of Technology, Karlsruhe, Germany

© The Author(s) 2016

K. Glau et al. (eds.), *Innovations in Derivatives Markets*, Springer Proceedings in Mathematics & Statistics 165, DOI 10.1007/978-3-319-33446-2_15

they could act as a shock absorber to the volatile capital inflows. Furthermore, they provide flexibility to the governments in financing their budget deficit. However, these instruments are not well understood from a no-arbitrage point of view and a formal setting is lacking. Such a setting would provide not only a better picture for their inherent risk-return characteristics, but would also be an indispensable tool for market research and strategy. The aim of this paper is exactly to focus attention on the large set of open questions the local currency debt gives rise to and lay the ground for a formal relative value analysis with a special emphasis on the CDS-Bond basis.

The paper begins with our general modeling no-arbitrage approach under an HJM reduced credit risk setting. It serves as a basis and gives a financial engineering intuition about the nature of the problem. The default of the sovereign is represented as the first jump of a counting process. For the dynamics of the interest rates and the exchange rate we use jump diffusions controlling the jumps and correlations in a suitable way, so that we have high precision in capturing the structural macrofinancial effects. We derive the no-arbitrage conditions that must hold in that multi-curve environment and then analyze their informational content. Then we turn to an application related to correctly extracting the credit and currency spreads and measuring the CDS-Bond basis on a broader scope. This provides basic building blocks for relative value trades under presence of the local currency yield curve which could serve as an additional pillar.

The literature on integrating the foreign and domestic debt of a risky sovereign in a consistent way is at a nascent stage both from an academic and practitioners' point of view. Related technically but different in essence is the work of Ehlers and Schönbucher [9] who give a reduced form model for CDS of an obligor denominated in different currencies which accounts for dependence between the exchange rate and the credit spread. Eberlain and Koval [8] give a high generalization of the cross-currency term structure models, but similarly they deal only with hard currencies. Regarding the CDS-Bond basis, Berd et al. [2] provide a thorough analysis of the shortcomings of the Z-spread as a risky spread metric.[1] Alizalde et al. [10] further discuss the issue and provide extensive simulations. Interesting new measures for the basis are given in Bernhard and Mai [3] which need further elaboration and development. However, all these references deal with the single-curve case with an extension to the multi-curve case pending.

## 2 Local Currency Bonds No-Arbitrage HJM Setting

In this section we first lay the foundations in brief for pricing of risky debt in a general reduced form setting. Then we add the local currency debt into the picture and discuss the risky spreads. We conclude by derivation and analysis of the no-arbitrage conditions.

[1] The Z-spread represents a simple shift of the discounting risk-free curve so that the price of the risky bond is attained.

## 2.1 Risky Bonds Under Marked Point Process

The first task is to model default in a suitable way. We start with the most general formulation and then modify it appropriately. We consider a filtered probability space $(\Omega, (G_t)_{t\geq 0}, P)$ which supports an $n$-dimensional Brownian motion $W^P = (W_1, W_2, \ldots, W_n)$ under the objective probability measure $P$ and a marked point process $\mu : (\Omega, B(R^+), \varepsilon) \to R^+$ with markers $(\tau_i, X_i)$ representing the jump times and their sizes in a measurable space $(E, \varepsilon)$, where $E = [0, 1]$ and by $\varepsilon$ we denote the Borel subsets of $E$. We assume that $\mu(\omega; dt, dx)$ has a separable compensator of the form:

$$\upsilon : (\Omega, B(R^+), \varepsilon) \to R^+ \quad \text{and} \quad \upsilon(\omega; dt, dx) = h(\omega; t)F_t(\omega; dx)dt,$$

where $h(\omega; t) = \int_{R^+} \upsilon(\omega; t, dx)$ is a $G_t$ measurable intensity and the marks have a conditional distribution of the jumps of $F_t(\omega; dx)$. Thus, we have the identity $\int_E F_t(\omega; dx) = 1$. Furthermore, we can define the total loss function $L(\omega; t) = \int_0^t \int_E l(\omega; s, x)\mu(\omega; ds, dx)$ and the recovery $R(\omega; t) = 1 - \int_0^t \int_E l(\omega; s, x)\mu(\omega; ds, dx)$. The function $l(\omega; t, x)$ scales the marks in a suitable way, and having control over it, we can define it such that our model is tractable enough. We define also the sum of the jumps by $S(\omega; t) = \int_0^t \int_E x\mu(\omega; ds, dx)$ and their number by $N(\omega; t) = \int_0^t \int_E \mu(\omega; ds, dx)$.

Effectively, the marked point process as a sequence of random jumps $(\tau_i, X_i)$ is characterized by the probability measure $\mu(\omega; dt, dx)$, which gives the number of jumps with size $dx$ in a small time interval of $dt$. The compensator $\upsilon(\omega; t, dx)$ provides a full probability characterization of the process. It incorporates in itself two effects. On one hand, we have the intensity $h(\omega; t)dt$, which gives the conditional probability of jump of the process in a small time interval of $dt$ incorporating the whole market information up to $t$. On the other hand, we have the conditional distribution $F_t(\omega; dx)$ of the markers $X$ in case of a jump realization.

We can look at the jumps of the marked point process as sequential defaults of an obligor at random times $\tau_i$ that lead to losses $X_i$ at each of them. They can also be considered a set of restructuring events leading to losses for the creditors. Under this general setting, the prices of the riskless and risky bonds are given by:

- **Riskless bond**:

$$P(t, T) = E^Q\left(\exp\left(-\int_t^T r(s)ds\right)|G_t\right) = \exp\left(-\int_t^T f(t, s)ds\right) \quad (1)$$

- **Risky bond**:

$$P^*(t,T) = E^Q\left(\exp\left(-\int_t^T r(s)ds\right) R(\omega;T)|G_t\right)$$
$$= R(t)\exp\left(-\int_t^T f^*(t,s)ds\right), \tag{2}$$

where $r(t)$, $f(t,T)$, and $f^*(t,T)$ are the riskless spot, riskless forward, and risky forward rates respectively.

Depending on how we specify the convention of recovery, we can get further simplification of the formulas. However, this should be well motivated and come either from the legal definitions of the debt contracts or their economic grounding.

Under a recovery of market value (RMV) setting, default is a percentage mark down, $q$, from the previous recovery. So we have $R(\omega;\tau_i) = (1 - q(\omega;\tau_i, X_i))$ $R(\omega;\tau_i-)$ and $l(\omega;\tau_i)$ has the form $l(\omega;\tau_i) = -q(\omega;\tau_i, X_i) \times R(\omega;\tau_i-)$. This definition allows us to write:

$$\mu(\omega, dt, dx) = \sum_{s>0} 1_{\{\Delta N(\omega,s)\neq 0\}}\delta_{(s,\Delta N(\omega,s))}(dt, dx)$$
$$dR(\omega;t) = -R(\omega;t)\int_E q(\omega;t,x)\,\mu(\omega;dt,dx);\ R(\omega;0) = 1$$

and if we assume no jumps of the intensity and the risk-free rate at default times (contagion effects), we have no change for the risk-free bond pricing formula and for the risky one and as in [13] we get:

$$P^{*RMV}(t,T) = E^Q\left(\exp\left(-\int_t^T r(s)ds\right)R(\omega;T)|G_t\right)$$
$$= R(t)E^Q\left(\exp\left(-\int_t^T (r(s) + h(s)\int_E q(\omega;s,x)\,F_s(dx))ds\right)|G_t\right)$$
$$= R(t)\exp\left(-\int_t^T f^{*RMV}(t,s)ds\right) \tag{3}$$

Note that within this setting there is no "last default". The intensity is defined for the whole marked point process and not just for a concrete single default time, so it does not go to zero after default realizations. This combined with the fact that intensity is continuous makes the market filtration $G_t$ behave like a background filtration in the pricing formulas. So we can avoid using the generalized Duffie, Schroder, and Skiadas [7] formula. Furthermore, we can denote $q_e(t) = \int_E q(\omega;t,x)\,F_t(dx)$ to be the expected loss. So we have that the pricing formula is dependent on the generalized intensity $h(t)q_e(t)$. Due to the multiplicative nature of the last expression, only from market information, as discussed in Schönbucher (2003), we cannot distinguish between the pure intensity effect $h(t)$ and the recovery induced one $q_e(t)$.

Under a recovery of par (RP) setting, in case of default, the recovery is a separate fixed or random quantity independent of the default indicator and the risk-free rate. So we have $E = \{0, 1 - R(\omega)\}$ and $\upsilon(\omega; dt, dx) = h(\omega; t)(1 - R_e)dt$ with $R_e = E^Q(R(\omega) \mid G_t)$. Since we have just one jump, we can write:

$$\mu(\omega, dt, dx) = 1_{\{\Delta N(\omega,t)\neq 0\}}\delta_{(t,\Delta N(\omega,t))}(dt, dx)$$

The bond price is:

$$\begin{aligned} P^{*RP}(t, T) &= E^Q\left(\exp\left(-\int_t^T r(s)ds\right)\left(R(\omega)\, 1_{\{\tau\leq T\}} + 1_{\{\tau>T\}}\right) |G_t\right) \\ &= 1_{\{\tau>t\}} \exp\left(-\int_t^T f^{*RP}(t, s)ds\right) \end{aligned} \quad (4)$$

In contrast to RMV, here, as discussed in Schönbucher (2003), he can distinguish between the pure intensity and recovery induced effects.

## 2.2 *Model Formulation*

In this section we develop our HJM model for pricing of local and foreign currency bonds of a risky country. However, before this being done formally, it is essential to elaborate on the nature of the problem. Although we do not put here explicitly macrofinancial structure, but just proxy it by jumps and correlations, it, by all means, stays in the background and must be conceptually considered.

### 2.2.1 General Notes

A risky emerging market country can have bonds denominated both in local and foreign currency that give rise to two risky yield curves and risky spreads—credit and currency. Generally, the latter arise due to the possibility of the respective credit events to occur and their severity. To investigate them, formal assumptions are needed both on their characteristics and interdependence.

We will consider that the two types of debt have different priorities. The country is first engaged to meeting the foreign debt obligation from its limited international reserves. The impossibility of this being done leads to default or restructuring. In both cases, we have a credit event according to the ISDA classification. The foreign debt has a senior status. The spread that arises reflects the credit risk of the country. It is a function of: (1) the probability of the credit event to occur; (2) the expected loss given default; (3) the risk aversion of the market participants to the credit event.

The domestic debt economically stands differently. It reflects the priority of the payments in hard currency and it incurs instantly the losses in case of default of the country. So this debt is the first to be affected by a default and is subordinated. Technically, the credit event can be avoided under a flexible exchange rate regime because the country can always make a debt monetization and pay the amounts due in local currency taking advantage of the fact that there is no resource constraint on it. However, the price for this is inflation pick-up and exchange rate depreciation. This leads to real devaluation of the domestic debt. It is exactly the seigniorage and the dilution effect that cause the loss in the value.[2] This resembles the case of a firm issuing more equity to avoid default. The spread of the domestic debt over the foreign one forms the currency spread. Its nature is very broad, and it is not only due to the currency mismatch. Namely, it is a function of: (1) the probability of the credit event to occur and the need for monetization; (2) the negative side effect of the credit event on the exchange rate by a sudden depreciation of the latter; (3) the volatility of the exchange rate; (4) the expected depreciation of the exchange rate without taking into consideration the monetization; (5) the risk aversion of market participants to the credit event and the need for monetization, the sudden exchange rate depreciation and its size; (6) the risk aversion of the market participants to the volatility of the exchange rate. All these effects are captured by our model.

### 2.2.2 Multi-currency Risky Bonds Model

We use the setting of Sect. 2.1 modified to a multi-currency debt. Firstly, we consider the case of no monetization and then analyze the case with monetization. Secondly, to avoid using an additional marked point process, and thus a second intensity, the default on the foreign debt is modeled indirectly. Namely, we assume that default on domestic debt leads to default on foreign debt, but due to the different priority of the two, we have just different losses incurred, respectively recoveries. This means that by controlling recoveries we control default and the inherent subordination without imposing too much structure. If the default on the domestic debt is so strong that it leads to a default on the foreign debt as well, we incur zero recovery on the domestic debt and some positive one on the foreign debt. If the insolvency is mild, we have a loss only on the domestic debt, so we incur some positive recovery on the domestic debt and a full recovery on the foreign debt. Thirdly, for notational purposes, we take as a benchmark Germany and EUR as the base hard currency. Lastly, we employ the recovery of market value assumption. The reason for this is twofold. On one hand, in that way, we are consistent with the HJM methodology of Schönbucher [12] for a single risky curve under RMV and produce parsimonious no-arbitrage conditions for the extension to a multi-curve environment. On the other

[2]This pattern can be observed historically for almost all EM countries resorting to a galloping inflation to avoid a nominal domestic debt default. The Russian default of 1998 somehow seems to be a partial notable exception where there was along with the inflation surge an actual default on certain ruble ($RUR$) bonds—GKOs and OFZs.

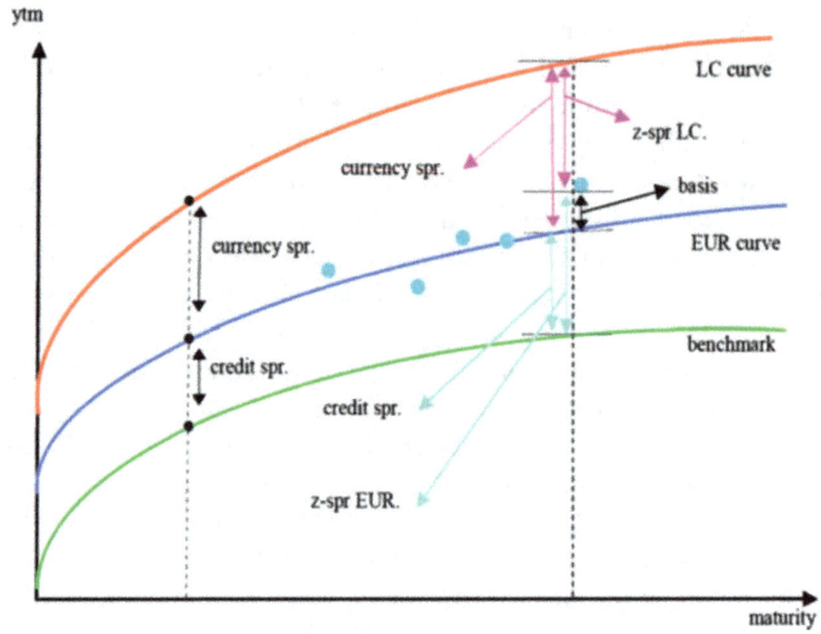


**Fig. 1** Risky spreads

hand, as pointed out in Bonnaud et al. [5], for bonds denominated in a different currency than the numerator employed in discounting, the RMV assumption should be the working engine. Their argument is exactly as ours above, in case of default, the sovereign would rather dilute by depreciating the exchange rate and thus the remaining cash flows of the bond produce in essence the RMV structure. Moreover, rather than using EUR denominated bonds, we could take advantage of the CDS quotes and produce synthetic bonds having an RMV recovery structure. Using them is actually preferable for empirical work since major academic studies argue that it is the CDS market that first captures the market information about the credit risk stance of the risky sovereign. Furthermore, with a few exceptions, if the EM sovereigns have in most cases both well developed local currency treasury markets and are subject to CDS quotation, they do have only few Eurobonds outstanding. Figure 1 represents the typical situation the risky sovereign faces.

*Mathematical formulation* We continue with the model setup. Firstly, we give the suitable notation and assumptions. Then we move to the derivation of the no-arbitrage conditions and the pricing.

- **Notation**
  $f_{EUR}(t, T)$—nominal forward rate, EUR, Ger.
  $f^*_{EUR}(t, T)$—nominal forward rate, EUR, EM
  $f^*_{LC}(t, T)$—nominal forward rate in LC, EM
  $r_{EUR}(t)$—nominal short rate, EUR, Ger.
  $r^*_{EUR}(t)$—nominal short rate, EUR, EM
  $r^*_{LC}(t)$—nominal short rate in LC, EM
  $h^*_{EUR}(t, T) = f^*_{EUR}(t, T) - f_{EUR}(t, T)$—credit spr., EM

$h^*_{LC,EUR}(t,T) = f^*_{LC}(t,T) - f^*_{EUR}(t,T)$—currency spr., EM
$h^*_{LC}(t,T) = f^*_{LC}(t,T) - f_{EUR}(t,T)$—general currency spr., EM
$P_{EUR}(t,T) = \exp(-\int_t^T f_{EUR}(t,s)ds)$—bond, EUR, Ger.
$P^*_{f,EUR}(t,T) = R_{f,EUR}(t)\exp(-\int_t^T f^*_{EUR}(t,s)ds)$—for. bond price., EUR, EM
$P^*_{d,LC}(t,T) = R_{d,LC}(t)\exp(-\int_t^T f^*_{LC}(t,s)ds)$—dom. bond price., LC, EM
$B_{EUR}(t) = \exp(\int_0^t r_{EUR}(s)ds)$—bank account, EUR, Ger.
$B^*_{f,EUR}(t) = R_{f,EUR}(t)\exp(\int_0^t r^*_{EUR}(s)ds)$—for. bank account, EUR, EM
$B^*_{d,LC}(t) = R_{d,LC}(t)\exp(\int_0^t r^*_{LC}(s)ds)$—dom. bank account, LC, EM
$X(t)$—exchange rate, EUR for 1 LC, $\widetilde{X}(t)$—exchange rate, LC for 1 EUR
$R_{f,EUR}(t)$—bond recovery, EUR, EM, $R_{d,LC}(t)$—bond recovery, LC, EM

We use the asterisk to denote risk, the first letter ($d$ or $f$) to denote domestic or foreign debt, and finally the currency of denomination is shown as $EUR$ or LC.[3]

- **Currency denominations**
$P^*_{d,EUR}(t,T) = X(t)P^*_{d,LC}(t,T)$—dom. bond, EUR
$P^*_{f,LC}(t,T) = \widetilde{X}(t)P^*_{f,EUR}(t,T)$—for. bond, LC
$B^*_{d,EUR}(t) = X(t)B^*_{d,LC}(t)$—dom. bank account, EUR
$B^*_{f,LC}(t) = \widetilde{X}(t)B^*_{f,EUR}(t)$—for. bank account, LC
- **Intensities**

Foreign debt, EUR:

| | |
|---|---|
| Intensity: | $h_{EUR}(t) = h(t)$ |
| Compensator: | $h_{EUR}(t)q_{e,EUR}(t) = h(t)\int_E q_{f,EUR}(\omega;t,x)\,F_t(dx)$ |

Domestic debt, LC:

| | |
|---|---|
| Intensity: | $h_{LC}(t) = h(t)$ |
| Compensator: | $h_{LC}(t)q_{e,LC}(t) = h(t)\int_E q_{d,LC}(\omega;t,x)\,F_t(dx)$ |

The compensator (generalized intensity) characterizes default. Controlling in a suitable way the recovery, we can control the compensator and thus the default event. We turn attention now to the dynamics of the instruments under consideration.

- **Forward rates**
$df_{EUR}(t,T) = \alpha_{EUR}(t,T)dt + \sum_{i=1}^n \sigma_{EUR,i}(t,T)dW_i^P(t)$
$df^*_{EUR}(t,T) = \alpha^*_{EUR}(t,T)dt + \sum_{i=1}^n \sigma^*_{EUR,i}(t,T)dW_i^P(t)$
$+\int_E \delta^*_{EUR}(x,t,T)\mu(dx,dt)$

[3]It must be further noted that we actually used standard definitions for the risky forward rates as in Schönbucher [12]. Namely, $f^*_{EUR/LC}(t,T) = -\frac{\partial}{\partial T}\log P^*_{f,EUR/d,LC}(t,T)$ with terminal conditions $P^*_{f,EUR/d,LC}(T,T) = R_{f,EUR/d,LC}(T)$. The risky bank accounts economically just represent a unit of currency invested at the respective short rates and continuously rolled over accounting for any default losses. However, since the forward rates, resp. the bonds, are our basic modeling object, it would be more precise to consider the bank accounts derived quantities from them similar to Björk et al. [4] without going here deeper into the modified technical details.

$df^*_{LC}(t,T) = \alpha^*_{LC}(t,T)dt + \sum_{i=1}^{n} \sigma^*_{LC,i}(t,T)dW_i^P(t)$
$+\int_E \delta^*_{LC}(x,t,T)\mu(dx,dt)$

We assume that in case of default there is a market turmoil leading to a jump in both curves. At maturity $T$, the $EUR$ curve jumps by a size of $\int_E \delta^*_{EUR}(x,t,T)\mu(dx,dt)$, and that of the local currency by $\int_E \delta^*_{LC}(x,t,T)\mu(dx,dt)$. The terms $\delta^*_{EUR}(x,t,T)$ and $\delta^*_{LC}(x,t,T)$ show the jump sizes of the respective curves for every maturity. As indicated at the beginning of the section, everywhere we will work under the market filtration $G_t$ so both the Brownian motions and the point process are adapted to it.

- **Recoveries**

$\frac{dR_{f,EUR}(t)}{R_{f,EUR}(t)} = -\int_E q_{f,EUR}(x,t)\mu(dx,dt)$

$\frac{dR_{d,LC}(t)}{R_{d,LC}(t)} = -\int_E q_{d,LC}(x,t)\mu(dx,dt)$

After each default we have a devaluation of the respective bond by an expected value of $\int_E q_{f/d}(x,t)\mu(dx,dt)$. The stochasticity of the loss is captured by the random jump size $q(.,.)$ as elaborated in Sect. 2.1.

- **Bank accounts**

$\frac{dB_{EUR}(t)}{B_{EUR}(t)} = r_{EUR}(t)dt$

$\frac{dB^*_{f,EUR}(t)}{B^*_{f,EUR}(t)} = r^*_{EUR}(t)dt - \int_E q_{f,EUR}(x,t)\mu(dx,dt)$

$\frac{dB^*_{d,LC}(t)}{B^*_{d,LC}(t)} = r^*_{LC}(t)dt - \int_E q_{d,LC}(x,t)\mu(dx,dt)$

- **Exchange rate**

$\frac{dX(t)}{X(t)} = \alpha_X(t)dt + \sum_{i=1}^{n} \sigma_{X,i}(t)dW_i^P(t) - \int_E \delta_X(x,t)\mu(dx,dt)$

We assume that in case of default the market turmoil causes an exchange rate devaluation by $\int_E \delta_X(x,t)\mu(dx,dt)$.

- **Bond prices**

$P_{EUR}(t,T) = \exp(-\int_t^T f_{EUR}(t,s)ds) = E^{Q^f}(\exp(-\int_t^T r_{EUR}(s)ds)|G_t)$

$P^*_{f,EUR}(t,T) = R_{f,EUR}(t)\exp(-\int_t^T f^*_{EUR}(t,s)ds)$

$= E^{Q^f}(\exp(-\int_t^T r_{EUR}(s)ds)R_{f,EUR}(T)|G_t)$

$P^*_{d,EUR}(t,T) = P^*_{d,LC}(t,T)X(t) = R_{d,LC}(t)X(t)\exp(-\int_t^T f^*_{LC}(t,s)ds)$

$= E^{Q^f}(\exp(-\int_t^T r_{EUR}(s)ds)R_{d,LC}(T)X(T)|G_t)$

It must be emphasized that the effects of exchange rate, recovery, and the expected devaluation sizes are incorporated in the respective forward rates of the bonds. Furthermore, the expectations are taken under $Q^f$, the foreign risk-neutral measure.

- **Arbitrage**

  Under standard regularity conditions, for the system to be free of arbitrage, all traded assets denominated in euro must have a rate of return $r_{EUR}$ under $Q^f$. This means that the processes:

$$\frac{P_{EUR}(t,T)}{B_{EUR}(t)}, \frac{B^*_{f,EUR}(t)}{B_{EUR}(t)}, \frac{P^*_{f,EUR}(t,T)}{B_{EUR}(t)}, \frac{B^*_{d,LC}(t)X(t)}{B_{EUR}(t)}, \frac{P^*_{d,LC}(t,T)X(t)}{B_{EUR}(t)}$$

  must be local martingales under $Q^f$. For our purposes being martingales would be enough.
  Taking the stochastic differentials of the upper expressions, omitting the technicalities to the appendix, we can get the respective no-arbitrage conditions.

- Spreads:

$$r^*_{EUR}(t) - r_{EUR}(t) = h(t)\varphi_{q_{f,EUR}}(t) \tag{5.1}$$

$$\begin{aligned} r^*_{LC}(t) - r^*_{EUR}(t) &= -\alpha_X(t) - \phi(t)\sigma_X(t) \\ &+h(t)(\varphi_{\delta_X}(t) - \varphi_{q_{d,LC},\delta_X}(t) + \varphi_{q_{d,LC}}(t) - \varphi_{q_{f,EUR}}(t)) \end{aligned} \tag{5.2}$$

- Drifts:

  $\alpha_{EUR}(t,T) = \sigma_{EUR}(t,T)\int_t^T \sigma_{EUR}(t,v)dv - \sigma_{EUR}(t,T)\phi(t)$

  $\alpha^*_{EUR}(t,T) = \sigma^*_{EUR}(t,T)\int_t^T \sigma^*_{EUR}(t,v)dv - \sigma^*_{EUR}(t,T)\phi(t)$
  $+h_{EUR}(t)\varphi^{q_{f,EUR},\delta_X}_{\theta^*_{EUR}}(t)$

  $\alpha^*_{LC}(t,T) = \sigma^*_{LC}(t,T)\int_t^T \sigma^*_{LC}(t,v)dv - \sigma^*_{LC}(t,T)\phi(t) - \sigma^*_{LC}(t,T)\sigma_X(t,T)$
  $+h_{LC}(t)\varphi^{q_{d,LC},\delta_X}_{\theta^*_{LC}}(t)$,

  where we have used the notation:

  $\theta^*_{EUR} = \exp(-\int_t^T \delta^*_{EUR}(x,t,s)ds)$ , $\theta^*_{LC} = \exp(-\int_t^T \delta^*_{LC}(x,t,s)ds)$
  $\varphi^{x,y,\ldots}_{a.b,\ldots}(t) = \int_E (ab\ldots)((1-x)(1-y)\ldots)\Phi(t,x)F_t(dx)$

  and used vector notation and scalar products where necessary for simplicity.

  By $\Phi(t,x)$ and $\phi(t)$ we denoted the Girsanov's kernels of the counting process and the Brownian motion respectively when changing the probability measure from $P$ to $Q^f$. The term $\varphi(t)$ represents the scaled expected jump sizes of the counting process. We can give the interpretation that $\phi(t)$ is the market price of diffusion risk and $\varphi(t)$ is the market price of jump risk. Parametrizing the volatilities and the market prices of risk, as well as imposing suitable dynamics for $h(t)$, we give a full characterization of our system. Furthermore, the intensity could be a function of the underlying processes of the rates, so we could get correlation between the intensity, the interest rates, and the exchange rate.

*Spreads diagnostics from a reduced form point of view* It is important to give a deeper interpretation of the no-arbitrage conditions and see which factors drive the credit and currency spreads. Despite the heavy notation, the analysis actually goes fluently. The drift equations give the modified HJM drift restrictions. The slight change from the classical riskless case is due to the jumps that arise. Equation (5.1) shows that the credit risk is proportional to the intensity of default and the scaled expected LGD by the coefficient controlling the risk aversion. The higher they are, the higher the spread is. Equation (5.2) gives the currency spread. It arises due to two main reasons. Firstly, the intensity of default and the difference between the two *LGDs* in local currency and euro, scaled by the coefficient for the risk aversion, act as in the previous case. They also make explicit the subordination. Secondly, the expected local currency depreciation, its volatility, and the risk aversion to diffusion risk act similarly to the standard uncovered interest parity (UIP) relationship. The higher they are, the higher the spread is. It is both important and interesting to note that inflation does not appear directly and it influences the spreads, as the next section shows, only through a secondary channel.

*Monetization* The analysis so far considered a loss of $1 - R_{d,LC}(T)$ on default of the domestic debt. However, if a full monetization is applied, then we would have $R_{d,LC}(T) = 1$ and thus $\varphi_{q_{d,LC}}(t) = 0$ and $\varphi_{q_{d,LC},\delta_X}(t) = 0$. If such a monetary injection is neutral to nominal values, it is certainly not to real ones. Devaluation arises due to the negative market sentiment following the default and the higher amount of money in circulation. Its effect can be measured differently based on what we take as a base—the price index or the exchange rate. Most naturally, we can expect both of them to depreciate due to the structural macrolinks that exist between these variables. For quantifying the amount we would need a macromodel which is beyond the scope of the reduced form model presented. The latter only shows what characteristics the market prices in general without imposing concrete macrolinks among them. Depending on what the base is, we would have a direct estimation of certain type of indicators and an indirect one of the rest up to their structural influence on the former. If the inflation is taken as a base, then we would have the comparison of inflation indexed bonds to the non-indexed ones. The spread between them would give an estimate for the expected inflation. Unfortunately, such an analysis is unrealistic due to the fact that such bonds are issued very rarely by emerging market countries. If the exchange rate is taken as a base, then we would have the comparison of domestic debt bonds to foreign debt bonds. The spread between them would give an estimate for the currency risk and the devaluation effect. The estimate for the inflation would be indirect and based on hypothetical structural links.

Whether the country would monetize or declare a formal default is based on strategic considerations. It is a matter of structural analysis which option it would take. By all means, its decision is priced. In case of default, the pricing formula is Eq. (5.2). In case of monetization, we would have a jump in the exchange rate. Let us denote its size by $\widehat{\delta_X}$. It will be different from the no-monetization one, $\delta_X$, due to the different regimes that are followed, and we would thus get:

$$r^*_{LC}(t) - r^*_{EUR}(t) = h(t)(\varphi_{\widehat{\delta}_X}(t) - \varphi_{q_{f,EUR}}(t)) - \alpha_X(t) - \phi(t)\sigma_X(t) \quad (6)$$

There is no a priori no-arbitrage argument that $\varphi_{\widehat{\delta}_X}(t) = \varphi_{\delta_X}(t) - \varphi_{q_{d,LC},\delta_X}(t) + \varphi_{q_{d,LC}}(t)$ must hold so that the two scenarios are equivalent.[4] The only information we get from the market is an estimate for the generalized intensity being $h(t)\varphi_{\widehat{\delta}_X}(t)$ or $h(t)(\varphi_{\delta_X}(t) - \varphi_{q_{d,LC},\delta_X}(t) + \varphi_{q_{d,LC}}(t))$ but not knowing which possible scenario will be realized.

## 3 CDS-Bond Basis

### 3.1 General Notes

The setting we built gives us an alternative for evaluating the CDS-Bond basis. This is represented in Fig. 1. There the LC zero-coupon yield curve is built by employing local currency treasuries and an appropriate smoothing method. The EUR zero-coupon yield curve is built by employing CDS quotes with the maths represented in the sequel. Along with the curves, there are few Eurobonds represented in light blue colored dots. Both credit and currency spreads can be computed for them employing a standard Z-spread methodology. Despite its various shortcomings, as discussed in Berd et al. [2] and Elizalde et al. [10], it allows us to have a certain measure for the spreads and it is widely accepted by practitioners. Subtracting from the yield curves' implied credit and currency spreads the bond implied spreads, we get two alternative specifications for the CDS-Bonds basis. Several things need a comment.

Firstly, the two basis measures are not equal by default. The one representing the credit spread is subject to Z-spread measurement based on a parallel shift of the benchmark curve. So it depends on the whole benchmark curve and has nothing to do with the LC one. Vice versa, the basis implied by the LC curve is subject to Z-spread measurement based on a parallel shift of the LC curve. So it depends on the whole *LC* curve, but has nothing to do with the benchmark one. This provides intuition how the introduction of the LC curve brings additional information in the picture and provides more market completeness that must be utilized in relative value trades.

Secondly, as mentioned above, the EUR curve is built by utilizing CDS quotes. As shown below, in the procedure employed, an assumption is needed for the recovery scheme. What it should be depends on our purposes. On one hand, if we would like to just extract the credit and currency spreads from the yield curves and calibrate a reduced form model,[5] it would be convenient to employ the setting from Sect. 2. So

---

[4]This is a delicate issue. As indicated, a further structural analysis is needed for a complete answer. The crucial point is that the two scenarios affect in a different way the monetary base. It will have a neutral effect on the macro variables in general and the risky spreads in particular only in case the economy is at the macro potential. Exactly when that is not the case, we can expect that the two scenarios will not be equivalent. A further elaboration on these issues from a structural point of view could be found in Yordanov [15, 16].

[5]We postpone the factors to build realization of the model from Sect. 2 so that it becomes operative for calibration and consequent further analysis to the forthcoming follow-up paper of Yordanov [17].

an RMV assumption for the EUR curve is the most appropriate one since the same assumption is imposed also for the LC curve and when subtracting the corresponding zero yields, we subtract apples from apples. On the other hand, if we like to extract the basis, we must be careful since the Eurobonds are priced under a firmly established RP assumption. So for a standard calculation via a Z-spread based on the benchmark curve we need an RP built EUR curve to be consistent. With the many problems of the Z-spread, it would be definitely bad to add further ones coming from a recovery assumption inconsistency which would only further contribute to an imprecise basis measurement. For a calculation via a Z-spread based on the LC curve, we should not use the RMV LC curve but a modified one. From the RMV LC curve we need to build an RP one and then compute the Z-spread and the basis to be consistent.

## 3.2 Technical Notes

Here we provide the technical notes regarding the above discussion.

- **EUR curve**
  Using OIS differential discounting as in Doctor and Goulden [6], we could modify[6] the standard CDS bootstrap procedure of ISDA and extract at time $t$ the $T-$maturity default probabilities $p^R_{EUR}(t,T)$ under a recovery assumption of $R$. Then we would get in a straightforward way the $EUR$ zero coupon yields $(ytm)$ and credit spreads $(spr)$ under RMV and RP:
  - **RMV**:
    $\mathrm{spr}^{RMV,R}_{EUR}(t,T) = -\frac{(1-R)\log(1-p^R_{EUR}(t,T))}{T-t}$
    $\mathrm{ytm}^{RMV,R}_{EUR}(t,T) = \mathrm{spr}^{RMV,R}_{EUR}(t,T) + \exp(-y_{EUR}(t,T)(T-t))$
  - **RP**:
    $\mathrm{spr}^{RP,R}_{EUR}(t,T) = -\frac{\log(Rp^R_{EUR}(t,T)+1-p^R_{EUR}(t,T))}{T-t}$
    $\mathrm{ytm}^{RP,R}_{EUR}(t,T) = \mathrm{spr}^{RP,R}_{EUR}(t,T) + \exp(-y_{EUR}(t,T)(T-t))$,
    where $y_{EUR}(t,T)$ is the $T-$maturity zero yield of the riskless benchmark curve (e.g. German bunds).
- **LC curve**
  - **RMV**:
    $\mathrm{ytm}^{RMV,R}_{LC}(t,T)$–observed from the market

[6]The OIS discounting should be given a special comment since there is still no consensus on how to bootstrap OIS swaps to form the discount factors for the CDS swap bootstrap. The problem comes from the presence of gaps for certain maturities. A possible specification is given in West [14].

$$\mathrm{spr}_{LC,EUR}^{RMV,R}(t,T) = \mathrm{ytm}_{LC}^{RMV,R}(t,T) - \mathrm{ytm}_{EUR}^{RMV,R}(t,T)$$

$$p_{LC}^{R}(t,T) = 1 - \exp\left(-\frac{\mathrm{spr}_{LC,EUR}^{RMV,R}(t,T)}{1-R}(T-t)\right)$$

- **RP**:

$$\mathrm{spr}_{LC,EUR}^{RP,R}(t,T) = -\frac{\log(Rp_{LC}^{R}(t,T)+1-p_{LC}^{R}(t,T))}{T-t}$$

$$\mathrm{ytm}_{LC}^{RP,R}(t,T) = \mathrm{spr}_{LC,EUR}^{RP,R}(t,T) + \mathrm{ytm}_{EUR}^{RP,R}(t,T)$$

Note that similarly to the EUR curve procedure, the LC curve one relies on the premise that both the RMV and RP cases must share the same $p_{LC}^{R}(t,T)$, which stands for the probability of default on the LC debt. However, according to the analysis we had in Sect. 2 on the no-arbitrage conditions, due to the monetization, such probability actually does not formally exist. Here it is only a derived quantity since although we assume the same point process as a driver of default on both the LC and EUR debt, we can control the compensator by changing the recoveries. However, we could just take the formulas above for the RP spread as definitions. Taking the limit case of zero EUR debt, they would be entirely consistent to the RP in case of EUR debt, thus providing a justification for our method.

### *3.3 CDS-Bond Basis Empirics*

For illustration we provide visualization of the Z-spread measured basis according to the two alternative ways for a set of European EM countries. They are chosen so that they have both Eurobonds outstanding in EUR and a liquid LC curve. The data sources are: Bloomberg, Datastream, and CBonds. We build the LC curves by employing the Bloomberg BFV curves. Since they are par curves, see Lee [11], we transform them to zero-coupon yield ones. For spreads extraction we use both EUR and USD denominated CDS. We give preference to the former, but in case of missing quotes we use USD quotes instead by making a quanto adjustment using cross currency basis swaps. The countries under focus are: Bulgaria (BGN), Czech Rep. (CZK), Hungary (HUF), Lithuania (LTL), Poland (PLN), Romania (RON), and Slovakia (SKK).

Since there are plenty of bonds outstanding, aggregate measures are presented based on duration weighting. The events: 1—GM turmoil of May 09, 2005, 2—Liquidity crisis of August 09, 2007, 3—Bear Sterns default of March 14, 2008, 4—Lehman default of September 15, 2008, 5—Greek turmoil of April 23, 2010, 6—August 5, 2011—the US rating downgrade, 7—06 May, 2012—ECB refi-rate woes are marked by the vertical dashed lines.

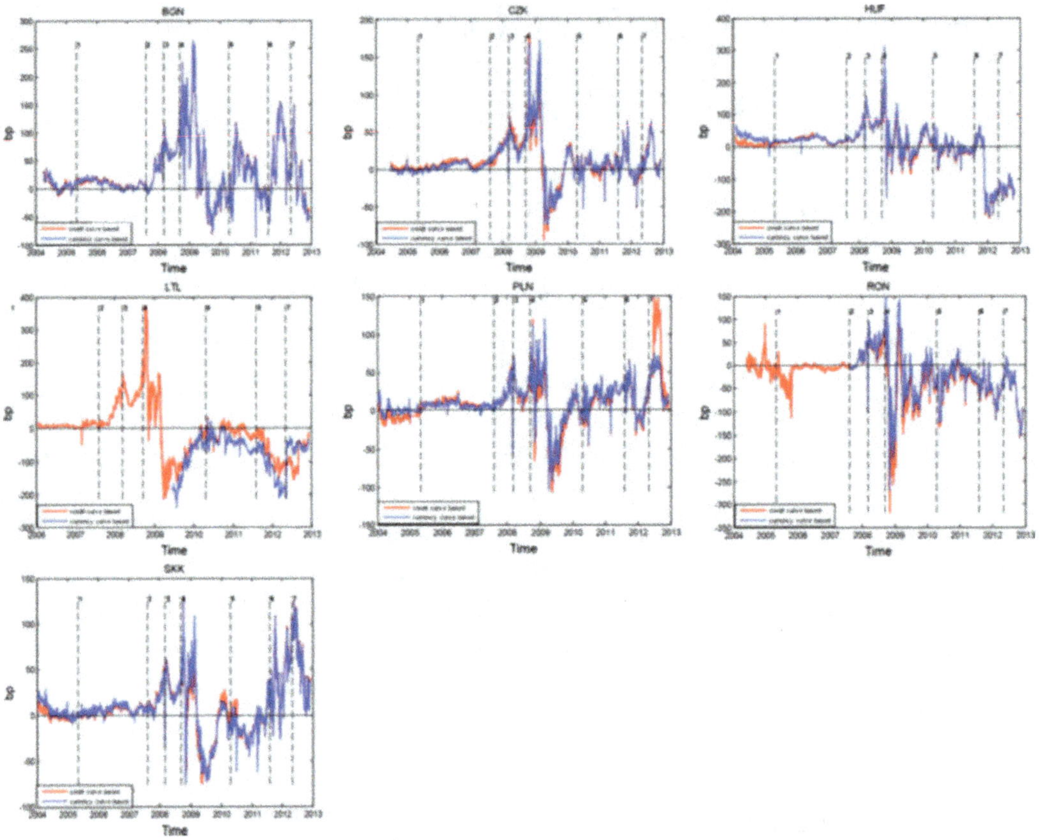


**Fig. 2** CDS-Bond basis across countries

The short conclusion from the patterns in Fig. 2 is that the bonds provide important input for extracting the credit and currency spreads. The two alternative basis formulations preserve general shape similarity, but still give different results that should not be underestimated. This is not surprising since the outcome is driven by the difference in shapes between the benchmark and the LC curves. Market strategists and arbitrage traders have a large scope for interpretations and trades design.

## 4 Conclusion

The paper considers the credit and currency spreads of a risky EM country. The necessary no-arbitrage conditions are derived and their informational content is analyzed. An application of the setting is made to proper building of the foreign and local currency yield curves of a sovereign as well as to providing ideas for relative value diagnostics in a multi-currency framework. In that direction, an alternative measure for the CDS-Bond basis is discussed when the local currency curve is employed as a pillar. The aim of the paper is both to point out the rich opportunities the setting gives for market-related research that could be of use to strategists and policy officers and to make the first several steps toward investigating such opportunities.

**Acknowledgements** The KPMG Center of Excellence in Risk Management is acknowledged for organizing the conference "Challenges in Derivatives Markets - Fixed Income Modeling, Valuation Adjustments, Risk Management, and Regulation".

## Appendix

Here we briefly elaborate on the derivation of Eqs. (5.1) and (5.2). Applying the Girsanov's theorem and the Ito's Lemma for jump diffusions to Eq. (2), we get the dynamics:

$$\begin{aligned}\frac{dP^*_{f,EUR}(t,T)}{P^*_{f,EUR}(t,T)} &= \left(-\int_t^T \alpha^*_{EUR}(t,s)ds + r^*_{EUR}(t) + \frac{1}{2}||\int_t^T \sigma^*_{EUR}(t,s)ds||^2\right)dt \\ &-\left(\int_t^T \sigma^*_{EUR}(t,s)ds\right)dW^P(t) \\ &+\int_E (1-q_{f,EUR}(x,t))\left(\exp\left(-\int_t^T \delta^*_{EUR}(x,t,s)ds\right)-1\right)\mu(dx,dt) \\ &-\int_E q_{f,EUR}(x,t)\mu(dx,dt)\end{aligned}$$

$$\begin{aligned}\frac{dP^*_{d,LC}(t,T)}{P^*_{d,LC}(t,T)} &= \left(-\int_t^T \alpha^*_{LC}(t,s)ds + r^*_{LC}(t) + \frac{1}{2}||\int_t^T \sigma^*_{LC}(t,s)ds||^2\right)dt \\ &-\left(\int_t^T \sigma^*_{LC}(t,s)ds\right)dW^P(t) \\ &+\int_E (1-q_{d,LC}(x,t))\left(\exp\left(-\int_t^T \delta^*_{LC}(x,t,s)ds\right)-1\right)\mu(dx,dt) \\ &-\int_E q_{d,LC}(x,t)\mu(dx,dt)\end{aligned}$$

Furthermore, we have the dynamics of the exchange rate:

$$\frac{dX(t)}{X(t)} = \alpha_X(t)dt + \sum_{i=1}^{n} \sigma_{X,i}(t)dW_i^P(t) - \int_E \delta_X(x,t)\mu(dx,dt)$$

So using the no-arbitrage conditions and equating the expected local drifts to the risk-free rate, we get the results shown.

**Open Access** This chapter is distributed under the terms of the Creative Commons Attribution 4.0 International License (http://creativecommons.org/licenses/by/4.0/), which permits use, duplication, adaptation, distribution and reproduction in any medium or format, as long as you give appropriate credit to the original author(s) and the source, a link is provided to the Creative Commons license and any changes made are indicated.

The images or other third party material in this chapter are included in the work's Creative Commons license, unless indicated otherwise in the credit line; if such material is not included in the work's Creative Commons license and the respective action is not permitted by statutory regulation, users will need to obtain permission from the license holder to duplicate, adapt or reproduce the material.

## References

1. Bai, J., Collin-Dufresne, P.: The CDS-Bond Basis During the Financial Crisis of 2007–2009. WP SSRN.2024531 (2011)
2. Berd, A., Mashal, R., Wang, P.: Definig. Estimating and Using Credit Term Structures, Lehman Brothers Research (2004)
3. Bernhart, G., Mai, J.: Negative Basis Measurement: Finding the Holy Scale. XAIA Investment Research (2012)
4. Björk, T., Di Masi, G., Kabanov, Y., Runggaldier, W.: Towards a general theory of bond markets. Financ. Stoch. **1**, 141–174 (1997)
5. Bonnaud, J., Carlier, L., Laurent, J., Vila, J.: Sovereign recovery schemes: discounting and risk management issues. In: 29th International Conference of the French Finance Association (AFFI) (2012)
6. Doctor, S., Goulden, J.: Differential Discounting for CDS. JPMorgan Europe Credit Research (2012)
7. Duffie, D., Schroder, M., Skiadas, C.: Recursive Valuation of Defaultable Securities and the Timing of Resolution Uncertainty. WP 195, Kellog Graduate School of Management, Department of Finance, Northwestern University (1994)
8. Eberlein, E., Koval, N.: A cross-currency Lévy market model. Quant. Financ. **6**, 465–480 (2006)
9. Ehlers, P., Schönbucher, P.: The Influence of FX Risk on Credit Spreads. WP, ETH Zurich (2006)
10. Elizalde, A., Doctor, S., Saltuk, Y.: Bond-CDS Basis Handbook. JPMorgan Research (2009)
11. Lee, M.: Bloomberg fair value market curves. In: International Bond Conference, Taipei (2007)
12. Schönbucher, P.: Term structure of defaultable bonds. Rev. Deriv. Stud. Special Issue: Credit Risk **2**(2/3), 161–192 (1998)
13. Schönbucher, P.: Credit Derivatives Pricing Models: Models. Wiley, Pricing and Implementation (2003)
14. West, G., Post-crisis methods for bootstrapping the yield curve. WP, Financial Modelling Agency (2011). http://finmod.co.za/OIS%20Curve.pdf
15. Yordanov, V.: Risky Sovereign Capital Structure: Fundamentals. WP SSRN.2349370 (2015)
16. Yordanov, V.: Risky Sovereign Capital Structure: Macrofinancial Diagnostics. WP SSRN.2600238 (2015)
17. Yordanov, V.: Multi-currency Risky Sovereign Bonds Arbitrage. WP SSRN.2349324 (2015)

# Part III
# Financial Engineering

# Basket Option Pricing and Implied Correlation in a One-Factor Lévy Model

**Daniël Linders and Wim Schoutens**

**Abstract** In this paper we employ a one-factor Lévy model to determine basket option prices. More precisely, basket option prices are determined by replacing the distribution of the real basket with an appropriate approximation. For the approximate basket we determine the underlying characteristic function and hence we can derive the related basket option prices by using the Carr–Madan formula. We consider a three-moments-matching method. Numerical examples illustrate the accuracy of our approximations; several Lévy models are calibrated to market data and basket option prices are determined. In the last part we show how our newly designed basket option pricing formula can be used to define implied Lévy correlation by matching model and market prices for basket options. Our main finding is that the implied Lévy correlation smile is flatter than its Gaussian counterpart. Furthermore, if (near) at-the-money option prices are used, the corresponding implied Gaussian correlation estimate is a good proxy for the implied Lévy correlation.

**Keywords** Basket option · Implied correlation · One-factor Lévy model · Variance-Gamma

## 1 Introduction

Nowadays, an increased volume of multi-asset derivatives is traded. An example of such a derivative is a *basket option*. The basic version of such a multivariate product has the same characteristics as a vanilla option, but now the underlying is a basket of stocks instead of a single stock. The pricing of these derivatives is not a trivial task because it requires a model that jointly describes the stock prices involved.

D. Linders (✉)
Faculty of Business and Economics, KU Leuven, Naamsestraat 69,
3000 Leuven, Belgium
e-mail: daniel.linders@kuleuven.be

W. Schoutens
Faculty of Science, KU Leuven, Celestijnenlaan 200, 3001 Heverlee, Belgium
e-mail: Wim@Schoutens.be

© The Author(s) 2016

K. Glau et al. (eds.), *Innovations in Derivatives Markets*, Springer Proceedings in Mathematics & Statistics 165, DOI 10.1007/978-3-319-33446-2_16

Stock price models based on the lognormal model proposed in Black and Scholes [6] are popular choices from a computational point of view; however, they are not capable of capturing the skewness and kurtosis observed for log returns of stocks and indices. The class of Lévy processes provides a much better fit for the observed log returns and, consequently, the pricing of options and other derivatives in a Lévy setting is much more reliable. In this paper we consider the problem of pricing multi-asset derivatives in a multivariate Lévy model.

The most straightforward extension of the univariate Black and Scholes model is based on the *Gaussian copula model*, also called the multivariate Black and Scholes model. In this framework, the stocks composing the basket at a given point in time are assumed to be lognormally distributed and a Gaussian copula is connecting these marginals. Even in this simple setting, the price of a basket option is not given in a closed form and has to be approximated; see e.g. Hull and White [23], Brooks et al. [8], Milevsky and Posner [39], Rubinstein [42], Deelstra et al. [18], Carmona and Durrleman [12] and Linders [29], among others. However, the normality assumption for the marginals used in this pricing framework is too restrictive. Indeed, in Linders and Schoutens [30] it is shown that calibrating the Gaussian copula model to market data can lead to non-meaningful parameter values. This dysfunctioning of the Gaussian copula model is typically observed in distressed periods. In this paper we extend the classical Gaussian pricing framework in order to overcome this problem.

Several extensions of the Gaussian copula model are proposed in the literature. For example, Luciano and Schoutens [32] introduce a multivariate Variance Gamma model where dependence is modeled through a common jump component. This model was generalized in Semeraro [44], Luciano and Semeraro [33], and Guillaume [21]. A stochastic correlation model was considered in Fonseca et al. [19]. A framework for modeling dependence in finance using copulas was described in Cherubini et al. [14]. The pricing of basket options in these advanced multivariate stock price models is not a straightforward task. There are several attempts to derive closed form approximations for the price of a basket option in a non-Gaussian world. In Linders and Stassen [31], approximate basket option prices in a multivariate Variance Gamma model are derived, whereas Xu and Zheng [48, 49] consider a local volatility jump diffusion model. McWilliams [38] derives approximations for the basket option price in a stochastic delay model. Upper and lower bounds for basket option prices in a general class of stock price models with known joint characteristic function of the logreturns are derived in Caldana et al. [10].

In this paper we start from the one-factor Lévy model introduced in Albrecher et al. [1] to build a multivariate stock price model with correlated Lévy marginals. Stock prices are assumed to be driven by an idiosyncratic and a systematic factor. The idea of using a common market factor is not new in the literature and goes back to Vasicek [47]. Conditional on the common (or market) factor, the stock prices are independent. We show that our model generalizes the Gaussian model (with single correlation). Indeed, the idiosyncratic and systematic components are constructed from a Lévy process. Employing a Brownian motion in that construction delivers the Gaussian copula model, but other Lévy models arise by employing different Lévy processes like VG, NIG, Meixner, etc. As a result, this new *one-factor Lévy model* is more flexible and can capture other types of dependence.

The correlation is by construction always positive and, moreover, we assume a single correlation. Stocks can, in reality, be negatively correlated and correlations between different stocks will differ. From a tractability point of view, however, reporting a single correlation number is often preferred over $n(n-1)/2$ pairwise correlations. The single correlation can be interpreted as a mean level of correlation and provides information about the general dependence among the stocks composing the basket. Such a single correlation appears, for example, in the construction of a correlation swap. Therefore, our framework may have applications in the pricing of such correlation products. Furthermore, calibrating a full correlation matrix may require an unrealistically large amount of data if the index consists of many stocks.

In the first part of this paper, we consider the problem of finding accurate approximations for the price of a basket option in the one-factor Lévy model. In order to value a basket option, the distribution of this basket has to be determined. However, the basket is a weighted sum of dependent stock prices and its distribution function is in general unknown or too complex to work with. Our valuation formula for the basket option is based on a moment-matching approximation. To be more precise, the (unknown) basket distribution is replaced by a shifted random variable having the same first three moments than the original basket. This idea was first proposed in Brigo et al. [7], where the Gaussian copula model was considered. Numerical examples illustrating the accuracy and the sensitivity of the approximation are provided.

In the second part of the paper we show how the well-established notions of implied volatility and implied correlation can be generalized in our multivariate Lévy model. We assume that a finite number of options, written on the basket and the components, are traded. The prices of these derivatives are observable and will be used to calibrate the parameters of our stock price model. An advantage of our modeling framework is that each stock is described by a volatility parameter and that the marginal parameters can be calibrated separately from the correlation parameter. We give numerical examples to show how to use the vanilla option curves to determine an implied Lévy volatility for each stock based on a Normal, VG, NIG, and Meixner process and determine basket option prices for different choices of the correlation parameter.

An *implied Lévy correlation* estimate arises when we tune the single correlation parameter such that the model price exactly hits the market price of a basket option for a given strike. We determine implied correlation levels for the stocks composing the Dow Jones Industrial Average in a Gaussian and a Variance Gamma setting. We observe that implied correlation depends on the strike and in the VG model, this implied Lévy correlation *smile* is flatter than in the Gaussian copula model. The standard technique to price non-traded basket options (or other multi-asset derivatives) is by interpolating on the implied correlation curve. It is shown in Linders and Schoutens [30] that in the Gaussian copula model, this technique can sometimes lead to non-meaningful correlation values. We show that the Lévy version of the implied correlation solves this problem (at least to some extent). Several papers consider the problem of measuring implied correlation between stock prices;

see e.g. Fonseca et al. [19], Tavin [46], Ballotta et al. [4], and Austing [2]. Our approach is different in that we determine implied correlation estimates in the one-factor Lévy model using multi-asset derivatives consisting of many assets (30 assets for the Dow Jones). When considering multi-asset derivatives with a low dimension, determining the model prices of these multi-asset derivatives becomes much more tractable. A related paper is Linders and Stassen [31], where the authors also use high-dimensional multi-asset derivative prices for calibrating a multivariate stock price model. However, whereas the current paper models the stock returns using correlated Lévy distributions, the cited paper uses time-changed Brownian motions with a common time change.

## 2 The One-Factor Lévy Model

We consider a market where $n$ stocks are traded. The price level of stock $j$ at some future time $t$, $0 \leq t \leq T$ is denoted by $S_j(t)$. Dividends are assumed to be paid continuously and the dividend yield of stock $j$ is constant and deterministic over time. We denote this dividend yield by $q_j$. The current time is $t = 0$. We fix a future time $T$ and we always consider the random variables $S_j(T)$ denoting the time-$T$ prices of the different stocks involved. The price level of a basket of stocks at time $T$ is denoted by $S(T)$ and given by

$$S(T) = \sum_{j=1}^{n} w_j S_j(T),$$

where $w_j > 0$ are weights which are fixed upfront. In case the basket represents the price of the Dow Jones, the weights are all equal. If this single weight is denoted by $w$, then $1/w$ is referred to as the Dow Jones Divisor.[1] The pay-off of a basket option with strike $K$ and maturity $T$ is given by $(S(T) - K)_+$, where $(x)_+ = \max(x, 0)$. The price of this basket option is denoted by $C[K, T]$. We assume that the market is arbitrage-free and that there exists a risk-neutral pricing measure $\mathbb{Q}$ such that the basket option price $C[K, T]$ can be expressed as the discounted risk-neutral expected value. In this pricing formula, discounting is performed using the risk-free interest rate $r$, which is, for simplicity, assumed to be deterministic and constant over time. Throughout the paper, we always assume that all expectations we encounter are well-defined and finite.

[1]More information and the current value of the Dow Jones Divisor can be found here: http://www.djindexes.com.

## 2.1 The Model

The most straightforward way to model dependent stock prices is to use a Black and Scholes model for the marginals and connect them with a Gaussian copula. A crucial (and simplifying) assumption in this approach is the normality assumption. It is well-known that log returns do not pass the test for normality. Indeed, log returns exhibit a skewed and leptokurtic distribution which cannot be captured by a normal distribution; see e.g. Schoutens [43].

We generalize the Gaussian copula approach by allowing the risk factors to be distributed according to any infinitely divisible distribution with known characteristic function. This larger class of distributions increases the flexibility to find a more realistic distribution for the log returns. In Albrecher et al. [1] a similar framework was considered for pricing CDO tranches; see also Baxter [5]. The Variance Gamma case was considered in Moosbrucker [40, 41], whereas Guillaume et al. [22] consider the pricing of CDO-squared tranches in this one-factor Lévy model. A unified approach for these CIID models (conditionally independent and identically distributed) is given in Mai et al. [36].

Consider an infinitely divisible distribution for which the characteristic function is denoted by $\phi$. A stochastic process $X$ can be built using this distribution. Such a process is called a Lévy process with mother distribution having the characteristic function $\phi$. The Lévy process $X = \{X(t) | t \geq 0\}$ based on this infinitely divisible distribution starts at zero and has independent and stationary increments. Furthermore, for $s, t \geq 0$ the characteristic function of the increment $X(t+s) - X(t)$ is $\phi^s$.

Assume that the random variable $L$ has an infinitely divisible distribution and denote its characteristic function by $\phi_L$. Consider the Lévy process $X = \{X(t) | t \in [0, 1]\}$ based on the distribution $L$. We assume that the process is standardized, i.e. $\mathbb{E}[X(1)] = 0$ and $\mathrm{Var}[X(1)] = 1$. One can then show that $\mathrm{Var}[X(t)] = t$, for $t \geq 0$. Define also a series of independent and standardized processes $X_j = \{X_j(t) | t \in [0, 1]\}$, for $j = 1, 2, \ldots, n$. The process $X_j$ is based on an infinitely divisible distribution $L_j$ with characteristic function $\phi_{L_j}$. Furthermore, the processes $X_1, X_2, \ldots, X_n$ are independent from $X$. Take $\rho \in [0, 1]$. The r.v. $A_j$ is defined by

$$A_j = X(\rho) + X_j(1-\rho), \quad j = 1, 2, \ldots n. \tag{1}$$

In this construction, $X(\rho)$ and $X_j(1-\rho)$ are random variables having the characteristic function $\phi_L^\rho$ and $\phi_{L_j}^{1-\rho}$, respectively. Denote the characteristic function of $A_j$ by $\phi_{A_j}$. Because the processes $X$ and $X_j$ are independent and standardized, we immediately find that

$$\mathbb{E}[A_j] = 0, \quad \mathrm{Var}[A_j] = 1 \quad \text{and} \quad \phi_{A_j}(t) = \phi_L^\rho(t)\phi_{L_j}^{1-\rho}(t), \quad \text{for } j = 1, 2, \ldots, n. \tag{2}$$

Note that if $X$ and $X_j$ are both Lévy processes based on the same mother distribution $L$, we obtain the equality $A_j \stackrel{\mathrm{d}}{=} L$.

The parameter $\rho$ describes the correlation between $A_i$ and $A_j$, if $i \neq j$. Indeed, it was proven in Albrecher et al. [1] that in case $A_j, j = 1, 2, \ldots, n$ is defined by (1), we have that

$$\text{Corr}\left[A_i, A_j\right] = \rho. \tag{3}$$

We model the stock price levels $S_j(T)$ at time $T$ for $j = 1, 2, \ldots, n$ as follows

$$S_j(T) = S_j(0)e^{\mu_j T + \sigma_j \sqrt{T} A_j}, \quad j = 1, 2, \ldots, n, \tag{4}$$

where $\mu_j \in \mathbb{R}$ and $\sigma_j > 0$. Note that in this setting, each time-$T$ stock price is modeled as the exponential of a Lévy process. Furthermore, a drift $\mu_j$ and a volatility parameter $\sigma_j$ are added to match the characteristics of stock $j$. Our model, which we will call the *one-factor Lévy model*, can be considered as a generalization of the Gaussian model. Indeed, instead of a normal distribution, we allow for a Lévy distribution, while the Gaussian copula is generalized to a Lévy-based copula.[2] This model can also, at least to some extent, be considered as a generalization to the multidimensional case of the model proposed in Corcuera et al. [17] and the parameter $\sigma_j$ in (4) can then be interpreted as the Lévy space (implied) volatility of stock $j$. The idea of building a multivariate asset model by taking a linear combination of a systematic and an idiosyncratic process can also be found in Kawai [26] and Ballotta and Bonfiglioli [3].

## 2.2 *The Risk-Neutral Stock Price Processes*

If we take

$$\mu_j = (r - q_j) - \frac{1}{T} \log \phi_L\left(-\mathrm{i}\sigma_j\sqrt{T}\right), \tag{5}$$

we find that

$$\mathbb{E}[S_j(T)] = e^{(r-q_j)T} S_j(0), \quad j = 1, 2, \ldots, n.$$

From expression (5) we conclude that the risk-neutral dynamics of the stocks in the one-factor Lévy model are given by

$$S_j(T) = S_j(0)e^{(r-q_j-\omega_j)T + \sigma_j \sqrt{T} A_j}, \quad j = 1, 2, \ldots, n, \tag{6}$$

where $\omega_j = \log \phi_L\left(-\mathrm{i}\sigma_j\sqrt{T}\right)/T$. We always assume $\omega_j$ to be finite. The first three moments of $S_j(T)$ can be expressed in terms of the characteristic function $\phi_{A_j}$. By

[2]The Lévy-based copula refers to the copula between the r.v.'s $A_1, A_2, \ldots, A_n$ and is different from the Lévy copula introduced in Kallsen and Tankov [25].

the martingale property, we have that $\mathbb{E}\left[S_j(T)\right] = S_j(0)\mathrm{e}^{(r-q_j)T}$. The risk-neutral variance $\mathrm{Var}\left[S_j(T)\right]$ can be written as follows

$$\mathrm{Var}\left[S_j(T)\right] = S_j(0)^2\mathrm{e}^{2(r-q_j)T}\left(\mathrm{e}^{-2\omega_j T}\phi_{A_j}\left(-\mathrm{i}2\sigma_j\sqrt{T}\right) - 1\right).$$

The second and third moment of $S_j(T)$ are given by:

$$\mathbb{E}\left[S_j(T)^2\right] = \mathbb{E}[S_j(T)]^2 \frac{\phi_{A_j}\left(-\mathrm{i}2\sigma_j\sqrt{T}\right)}{\phi_{A_j}\left(-\mathrm{i}\sigma_j\sqrt{T}\right)^2},$$

$$\mathbb{E}\left[S_j(T)^3\right] = \mathbb{E}[S_j(T)]^3 \frac{\phi_{A_j}\left(-\mathrm{i}3\sigma_j\sqrt{T}\right)}{\phi_{A_j}\left(-\mathrm{i}\sigma_j\sqrt{T}\right)^3}.$$

We always assume that these quantities are finite. If the process $X_j$ has mother distribution $L$, we can replace $\phi_{A_j}$ by $\phi_L$ in expression (5) and in the formulas for $\mathbb{E}\left[S_j(T)^2\right]$ and $\mathbb{E}\left[S_j(T)^3\right]$. From here on, we always assume that all Lévy processes are built on the same mother distribution. However, all results remain to hold in the more general case.

## 3 A Three-Moments-Matching Approximation

In order to price a basket option, one has to know the distribution of the random sum $S(T)$, which is a weighted sum of dependent random variables. This distribution is in most situations unknown or too cumbersome to work with. Therefore, we search for a new random variable which is sufficiently 'close' to the original random variable, but which is more attractive to work with. More concretely, we introduce in this section a new approach for approximating $C[K, T]$ by replacing the sum $S(T)$ with an appropriate random variable $\widetilde{S}(T)$ which has a simpler structure, but for which the first three moments coincide with the first three moments of the original basket $S(T)$. This moment-matching approach was also considered in Brigo et al. [7] for the multivariate Black and Scholes model.

Consider the Lévy process $Y = \{Y(t) \mid 0 \leq t \leq 1\}$ with infinitely divisible distribution $L$. Furthermore, we define the random variable $A$ as

$$A = Y(1).$$

In this case, the characteristic function of $A$ is given by $\phi_L$. The sum $S(T)$ is a weighted sum of dependent random variables and its cdf is unknown. We approximate the sum $S(T)$ by $\widetilde{S}(T)$, defined by

$$\widetilde{S}(T) = \bar{S}(T) + \lambda, \tag{7}$$

where $\lambda \in \mathbb{R}$ and

$$\bar{S}(T) = S(0) \exp\left\{(\bar{\mu} - \bar{\omega})T + \bar{\sigma}\sqrt{T}A\right\}. \tag{8}$$

The parameter $\bar{\mu} \in \mathbb{R}$ determines the drift and $\bar{\sigma} > 0$ is the volatility parameter. These parameters, as well as the shifting parameter $\lambda$, are determined such that the first three moments of $\widetilde{S}(T)$ coincide with the corresponding moments of the real basket $S(T)$. The parameter $\bar{\omega}$, defined as follows

$$\bar{\omega} = \frac{1}{T} \log \phi_L\left(-\mathrm{i}\bar{\sigma}\sqrt{T}\right),$$

is assumed to be finite.

## 3.1 Matching the First Three Moments

The first three moments of the basket $S(T)$ are denoted by $m_1$, $m_2$, and $m_3$ respectively. In the following lemma, we express the moments $m_1, m_2$, and $m_3$ in terms of the characteristic function $\phi_L$ and the marginal parameters. A proof of this lemma is provided in the appendix.

**Lemma 1** *Consider the one-factor Lévy model* (6) *with infinitely divisible mother distribution L. The first two moments $m_1$ and $m_2$ of the basket $S(T)$ can be expressed as follows*

$$m_1 = \sum_{j=1}^{n} w_j \mathbb{E}\left[S_j(T)\right], \tag{9}$$

$$m_2 = \sum_{j=1}^{n}\sum_{k=1}^{n} w_j w_k \mathbb{E}\left[S_j(T)\right]\mathbb{E}\left[S_k(T)\right]\left(\frac{\phi_L\left(-i(\sigma_j+\sigma_k)\sqrt{T}\right)}{\phi_L\left(-i\sigma_j\sqrt{T}\right)\phi_L\left(-i\sigma_k\sqrt{T}\right)}\right)^{\rho_{j,k}} \tag{10}$$

*where*

$$\rho_{j,k} = \begin{cases} \rho, & \text{if } j \neq k; \\ 1, & \text{if } j = k. \end{cases}$$

*The third moment $m_3$ of the basket $S(T)$ is given by*

$$m_3 = \sum_{j=1}^{n}\sum_{k=1}^{n}\sum_{l=1}^{n} w_j w_k w_l \mathbb{E}\left[S_j(T)\right]\mathbb{E}\left[S_k(T)\right]\mathbb{E}\left[S_l(T)\right]$$
$$\times \frac{\phi_L\left(-i\left(\sigma_j+\sigma_k+\sigma_l\right)\sqrt{T}\right)^{\rho}}{\phi_L\left(-i\sigma_j\sqrt{T}\right)\phi_L\left(-i\sigma_k\sqrt{T}\right)\phi_L\left(-i\sigma_l\sqrt{T}\right)}A_{j,k,l}, \tag{11}$$

*where*

$$A_{j,k,l} = \begin{cases} \left(\phi_L\left(-i\sigma_j\sqrt{T}\right)\phi_L\left(-i\sigma_k\sqrt{T}\right)\phi_L\left(-i\sigma_l\sqrt{T}\right)\right)^{1-\rho}, & \text{if } j \neq k,\ k \neq l \text{ and } j \neq l; \\ \left(\phi_L\left(-i(\sigma_j+\sigma_k)\sqrt{T}\right)\phi_L\left(-i\sigma_l\sqrt{T}\right)\right)^{1-\rho}, & \text{if } j = k,\ k \neq l; \\ \left(\phi_L\left(-i(\sigma_k+\sigma_l)\sqrt{T}\right)\phi_L\left(-i\sigma_j\sqrt{T}\right)\right)^{1-\rho}, & \text{if } j \neq k,\ k = l; \\ \left(\phi_L\left(-i(\sigma_j+\sigma_l)\sqrt{T}\right)\phi_L\left(-i\sigma_k\sqrt{T}\right)\right)^{1-\rho}, & \text{if } j = l,\ k \neq l; \\ \phi_L\left(-i\left(\sigma_j+\sigma_k+\sigma_l\right)\sqrt{T}\right)^{1-\rho}, & \text{if } j = k = l. \end{cases}$$

In Sect. 2.2 we derived the first three moments for each stock $j, j = 1, 2, \ldots, n$. Taking into account the similarity between the price $S_j(T)$ defined in (6) and the approximate r.v. $\bar{S}(T)$, defined in (8), we can determine the first three moments of $\bar{S}(T)$:

$$\mathbb{E}\left[\bar{S}(T)\right] = S(0)e^{\bar{\mu}T} =: \xi,$$
$$\mathbb{E}\left[\bar{S}(T)^2\right] = \mathbb{E}\left[\bar{S}(T)\right]^2 \frac{\phi_L\left(-i2\bar{\sigma}\sqrt{T}\right)}{\phi_L\left(-i\bar{\sigma}\sqrt{T}\right)^2} =: \xi^2\alpha,$$
$$\mathbb{E}\left[\bar{S}(T)^3\right] = \mathbb{E}\left[\bar{S}(T)\right]^3 \frac{\phi_L\left(-i3\bar{\sigma}\sqrt{T}\right)}{\phi_L\left(-i\bar{\sigma}\sqrt{T}\right)^3} =: \xi^3\beta.$$

These expressions can now be used to determine the first three moments of the approximate r.v. $\widetilde{S}(T)$:

$$\mathbb{E}\left[\widetilde{S}(T)\right] = \mathbb{E}\left[\bar{S}(T)\right] + \lambda,$$
$$\mathbb{E}\left[\widetilde{S}(T)^2\right] = \mathbb{E}\left[\bar{S}(T)^2\right] + \lambda^2 + 2\lambda\mathbb{E}\left[\bar{S}(T)\right],$$
$$\mathbb{E}\left[\widetilde{S}(T)^3\right] = \mathbb{E}\left[\bar{S}(T)^3\right] + \lambda^3 + 3\lambda^2\mathbb{E}\left[\bar{S}(T)\right] + 3\lambda\mathbb{E}\left[\bar{S}(T)^2\right].$$

Determining the parameters $\bar{\mu}$, $\bar{\sigma}$ and the shifting parameter $\lambda$ by matching the first three moments, results in the following set of equations

$$m_1 = \xi + \lambda,$$
$$m_2 = \xi^2\alpha + \lambda^2 + 2\lambda\xi,$$
$$m_3 = \xi^3\beta + \lambda^3 + 3\lambda^2\xi + 3\lambda\xi^2\alpha.$$

These equations can be recast in the following set of equations

$$\lambda = m_1 - \xi,$$
$$\xi^2 = \frac{m_2 - m_1^2}{\alpha - 1},$$
$$0 = \left(\frac{m_2 - m_1^2}{\alpha - 1}\right)^{3/2} (\beta + 2 - 3\alpha) + 3m_1m_2 - 2m_1^3 - m_3.$$

Remember that $\alpha$ and $\beta$ are defined by

$$\alpha = \frac{\phi_L\left(-\mathrm{i}2\bar{\sigma}\sqrt{T}\right)}{\phi_L\left(-\mathrm{i}\bar{\sigma}\sqrt{T}\right)^2} \quad \text{and} \quad \beta = \frac{\phi_L\left(-\mathrm{i}3\bar{\sigma}\sqrt{T}\right)}{\phi_L\left(-\mathrm{i}\bar{\sigma}\sqrt{T}\right)^3}.$$

Solving the third equation results in the parameter $\bar{\sigma}$. Note that this equation does not always have a solution. This issue was also discussed in Brigo et al. [7] for the Gaussian copula case. However, in our numerical studies we did not encounter any numerical problems. If we know $\bar{\sigma}$, we can also determine $\xi$ and $\lambda$ from the first two equations. Next, the drift $\bar{\mu}$ can be determined from

$$\bar{\mu} = \frac{1}{T} \log \frac{\xi}{S(0)}.$$

## 3.2 *Approximate Basket Option Pricing*

The price of a basket option with strike $K$ and maturity $T$ is denoted by $C[K, T]$. This unknown price is approximated in this section by $C^{MM}[K, T]$, which is defined as

$$C^{MM}[K, T] = \mathrm{e}^{-rT}\mathbb{E}\left[\left(\widetilde{S}(T) - K\right)_+\right].$$

Using expression (7) for $\widetilde{S}(T)$, the price $C^{MM}[K, T]$ can be expressed as

$$C^{MM}[K, T] = \mathrm{e}^{-rT}\mathbb{E}\left[\left(\bar{S}(T) - (K - \lambda)\right)_+\right].$$

Note that the distribution of $\bar{S}(T)$ is also depending on the choice of $\lambda$. In order to determine the price $C^{MM}[K, T]$, we should be able to price an option written on $\bar{S}(T)$, with a shifted strike $K - \lambda$. Determining the approximation $C^{MM}[K, T]$ using the Carr–Madan formula requires knowledge about the characteristic function $\phi_{\log \bar{S}(T)}$ of $\log \bar{S}(T)$:

$$\phi_{\log \bar{S}(T)}(u) = \mathbb{E}\left[\mathrm{e}^{\mathrm{i}u \log \bar{S}(T)}\right].$$

Using expression (8) we find that

$$\phi_{\log \bar{S}(T)}(u) = \mathbb{E}\left[\exp\left\{\mathrm{i}u\left(\log S(0) + (\bar{\mu} - \bar{\omega})T + \bar{\sigma}\sqrt{T}A\right)\right\}\right].$$

The characteristic function of $A$ is $\phi_L$, from which we find that

$$\phi_{\log \bar{S}(T)}(u) = \exp\left\{\mathrm{i}u\left(\log S(0) + (\bar{\mu} - \bar{\omega})T\right)\right\}\phi_L\left(u\bar{\sigma}\sqrt{T}\right).$$

Note that nowhere in this section we used the assumption that the basket weights $w_j$ are strictly positive. Therefore, the three-moments-matching approach proposed in this section can also be used to price, e.g. spread options. However, for pricing spread options, alternative methods exist; see e.g. Carmona and Durrleman [11], Hurd and Zhou [24] and Caldana and Fusai [9].

### 3.3 The FFT Method and Basket Option Pricing

Consider the random variable $X$. In this section we show that if the characteristic function $\phi_{\log X}$ of this r.v. $X$ is known, one can approximate the discounted stop-loss premium

$$\mathrm{e}^{-rT}\mathbb{E}\left[(X-K)_+\right],$$

for any $K > 0$.

Let $\alpha > 0$ and assume that $\mathbb{E}\left[X^{\alpha+1}\right]$ exists and is finite. It was proven in Carr and Madan [13] that the price $\mathrm{e}^{-rT}\mathbb{E}\left[(X-K)_+\right]$ can be expressed as follows

$$\mathrm{e}^{-rT}\mathbb{E}\left[(X-K)_+\right] = \frac{\mathrm{e}^{-\alpha\log(K)}}{\pi}\int_0^{+\infty}\exp\left\{-\mathrm{i}v\log(K)\right\}g(v)\mathrm{d}v, \tag{12}$$

where

$$g(v) = \frac{\mathrm{e}^{-rT}\phi_{\log X}\left(v - (\alpha+1)\mathrm{i}\right)}{\alpha^2 + \alpha - v^2 + \mathrm{i}(2\alpha+1)v}. \tag{13}$$

The approximation $C^{MM}[K, T]$ was introduced in Sect. 3 and the random variable $X$ now denotes the moment-matching approximation $\widetilde{S}(T) = \bar{S}(T) + \lambda$. The approximation $C^{MM}[K, T]$ can then be determined as the option price written on $\bar{S}(T)$ and with shifted strike price $K - \lambda$.

**Table 1** Overview of infinitely divisible distributions

| | Gaussian | Variance Gamma |
|---|---|---|
| Parameters | $\mu \in \mathbb{R}, \sigma > 0$ | $\mu, \theta \in \mathbb{R}, \sigma, \nu > 0$ |
| Notation | $\mathcal{N}(\mu, \sigma^2)_\sigma$ | $VG(\sigma, \nu, \theta, \mu)$ |
| $\phi(u)$ | $\mathrm{e}^{\mathrm{i}u\mu+\frac{1}{2}\sigma^2 u_\sigma}$ | $\mathrm{e}^{\mathrm{i}u\mu}\left(1-\mathrm{i}u\theta\nu+u^2\sigma^2\nu/2\right)^{-1/\nu}$ |
| Mean | $\mu$ | $\mu+\theta$ |
| Variance | $\sigma^2$ | $\sigma^2{}_\sigma+\nu\theta^2$ |
| Standardized version | $\mathcal{N}(0, 1)$ | $VG(\kappa\sigma, \nu, \kappa\theta, -\kappa\theta)$ where $\kappa = \frac{1}{\sqrt{\sigma^2+\theta^2{}_\sigma \nu}}$ |
| | **Normal Inverse Gaussian** | **Meixner** |
| Parameters | $\alpha, \delta > 0, \beta \in (-\alpha, \alpha), \mu \in \mathbb{R}$ | $\alpha, \delta > 0, \beta \in (-\pi, \pi), \mu \in \mathbb{R}$ |
| Notation | $NIG(\alpha, \beta, \delta, \mu)$ | $MX(\alpha, \beta, \delta, \mu)$ |
| $\phi(u)$ | $\mathrm{e}^{\mathrm{i}u\mu-\delta\left(\sqrt{\alpha^2-(\beta+\mathrm{i}u)^2}-\sqrt{\alpha^2-\beta^2{}_\sigma}\right)}$ | $\mathrm{e}^{\mathrm{i}u\mu}\left(\frac{\cos(\beta/2)}{\cosh((\alpha u-\mathrm{i}\beta)/2)}\right)^{2\delta}$ |
| Mean | $\mu+\frac{\delta\beta}{\sqrt{\alpha^2-\beta^2{}_\sigma}}$ | $\mu+\alpha\delta\tan(\beta/2)$ |
| Variance | $\alpha^2\delta\left(\alpha^2-\beta^2\right)^{-3/2}$ | $\cos^{-2}(\beta/2)\alpha^2{}_\sigma\delta/2$ |
| Standardized version | $NIG\left(\alpha, \beta, (\alpha^2-\beta^2)^{3/2}, \frac{-(\alpha^2-\beta^2)\beta}{\alpha^2}\right)$ | $MX\left(\alpha, \beta, \frac{2\cos^2(\frac{\beta}{2})}{\alpha^2{}_\sigma}, \frac{-\sin(\beta)}{\alpha}\right)$ |

## 4 Examples and Numerical Illustrations

The Gaussian copula model with equicorrelation is a member of our class of one-factor Lévy models. In this section we discuss how to build the Gaussian, Variance Gamma, Normal Inverse Gaussian, and Meixner models. However, the reader is invited to construct one-factor Lévy models based on other Lévy-based distributions; e.g. CGMY, Generalized hyperbolic, etc. distributions.

Table 1 summarizes the Gaussian, Variance Gamma, Normal Inverse Gaussian, and the Meixner distributions, which are all infinitely divisible. In the last row, it is shown how to construct a standardized version for each of these distributions. We assume that $L$ is distributed according to one of these standardized distributions. Hence, $L$ has zero mean and unit variance. Furthermore, the characteristic function $\phi_L$ of $L$ is given in closed form. We can then define the Lévy processes $X$ and $X_j$, $j = 1, 2, \ldots, n$ based on the mother distribution $L$. The random variables $A_j$, $j = 1, 2, \ldots, n$, are modeled using expression (1).

**Table 2** Basket option prices in the one-factor VG model with $S_1(0) = 40,\ S_2(0) = 50,\ S_3(0) = 60,\ S_4(0) = 70$, and $\rho = 0$

| $K$ | $C^{mc}[K, T]$ | $C^{MM}[K, T]$ | Length CI |
|---|---|---|---|
| $\sigma_1 = 0.2; \sigma_2 = 0.2; \sigma_3 = 0.2; \sigma_4 = 0.2$ | | | |
| 50 | 6.5748 | 6.5676 | 4.27E-03 |
| 55 | 2.4363 | 2.4781 | 3.05E-03 |
| 60 | 0.2651 | 0.2280 | 9.29E-04 |
| $\sigma_1 = 0.5; \sigma_2 = 0.5; \sigma_3 = 0.5; \sigma_4 = 0.5$ | | | |
| 55 | 4.1046 | 4.2089 | 6.31E-03 |
| 60 | 1.7774 | 1.7976 | 4.13E-03 |
| 65 | 0.5474 | 0.4637 | 2.16E-03 |
| $\sigma_1 = 0.8; \sigma_2 = 0.8; \sigma_3 = 0.8; \sigma_4 = 0.8$ | | | |
| 60 | 3.2417 | 3.3371 | 7.16E-03 |
| 65 | 1.6806 | 1.6429 | 5.08E-03 |
| 70 | 0.7581 | 0.6375 | 3.30E-03 |
| $\sigma_1 = 0.6; \sigma_2 = 1.2; \sigma_3 = 0.3; \sigma_4 = 0.9$ | | | |
| 55 | 5.5067 | 5.6719 | 9.44E-03 |
| 60 | 3.2266 | 3.3305 | 7.31E-03 |
| 65 | 1.6972 | 1.6750 | 5.26E-03 |
| 70 | 0.7889 | 0.6830 | 3.52E-03 |

## 4.1 *Variance Gamma*

Although pricing basket option under a normality assumption is tractable from a computational point of view, it introduces a high degree of model risk; see e.g. Leoni and Schoutens [28]. The Variance Gamma distribution has already been proposed as a more flexible alternative to the Brownian setting; see e.g. Madan and Seneta [34] and Madan et al. [35].

We consider two numerical examples where $L$ has a Variance Gamma distribution with parameters $\sigma = 0.5695, \nu = 0.75, \theta = -0.9492, \mu = 0.9492$. Table 2 contains the numerical values for the first illustration, where a four-basket option paying $\left(\frac{1}{4}\sum_{j=1}^{4} S_j(T) - K\right)_+$ at time $T$ is considered. We use the following parameter values: $r = 6\,\%, T = 0.5, \rho = 0$ and $S_1(0) = 40,\ S_2(0) = 50,\ S_3(0) = 60,\ S_4(0) = 70$. These parameter values are also used in Sect. 5 of Korn and Zeytun [27]. We denote by $C^{mc}[K, T]$ the corresponding Monte Carlo estimate for the price $C[K, T]$. Here, $10^7$ number of simulations are used. The approximation of the basket option price $C[K, T]$ using the moment-matching approach outlined in Sect. 3 is denoted by $C^{MM}[K, T]$. A comparison between the empirical density and the approximate density is provided in Fig. 1.

In the second example, we consider the basket $S(T) = w_1 X_1(T) + w_2 X_2(T)$, written on two non-dividend paying stocks. We use as parameter values the ones also used in Sect. 7 of Deelstra et al. [18], hence $r = 5\,\%$, $X_1(0) = X_2(0) = 100$, and $w_1 = w_2 = 0.5$. Table 3 gives numerical values for these basket options. Note that strike prices are expressed in terms of forward moneyness. A basket strike price $K$ has forward moneyness equal to $K/\mathbb{E}[S]$. We can conclude that the three-moments-matching approximation gives acceptable results. For far out-of-the-money call options, the approximation is not always able to closely approximate the real basket option price.

We also investigate the sensitivity with respect to the Variance Gamma parameters $\sigma$, $\nu$, and $\theta$ and to the correlation parameter $\rho$. We consider a basket option consisting of 3 stocks, i.e. $n = 3$. From Tables 2 and 3, we observe that the error is the biggest in case we consider different marginal volatilities and the option under consideration is an out-of-the-money basket call. Therefore, we put $\sigma_1 = 0.2$, $\sigma_2 = 0.4$, $\sigma_3 = 0.6$ and we determine the prices $C^{mc}[K,T]$ and $C^{MM}[K,T]$ for $K = 105.13$. The other parameter values are: $r = 0.05$, $\rho = 0.5$, $w_1 = w_2 = w_3 = 1/3$ and $T = 1$. The first panel of Fig. 2 shows the relative error for varying $\sigma$. The second panel of Fig. 2 shows the relative error in function of $\nu$. The sensitivity with respect to $\theta$ is shown in the third panel of Fig. 2. Finally, the fourth panel of Fig. 2 shows the relative error in function of $\rho$.

The numerical results show that the approximations do not always manage to closely approximate the true basket option price. Especially when some of the volatilities deviate substantially from the other ones, the accuracy of the approximation deteriorates. The dysfunctioning of the moment-matching approximation in the Gaussian copula model was already reported in Brigo et al. [7]. However, in order to calibrate the Lévy copula model to available option data, the availability of a basket option pricing formula which can be evaluated in a fast way, is of crucial importance. Table 4 shows the CPU times[3] for the one-factor VG model for different basket dimensions. The calculation time of approximate basket option prices when 100 stocks are involved is less than one second. Therefore, the moment-matching approximation is a good candidate for calibrating the one-factor Lévy model.

## 4.2 Pricing Basket Options

In this subsection we explain how to determine the price of a basket option in a realistic situation where option prices of the components of the basket are available and used to calibrate the marginal parameters. In our example, the basket under consideration consists of 2 major stock market indices ($n = 2$), the S&P500 and the Nasdaq:

$$\text{Basket} = w_1 \text{S\&P 500} + w_2 \text{Nasdaq}.$$

The pricing date is February 19, 2009 and we determine prices for the Normal, VG, NIG, and Meixner case. The details of the basket are listed in Table 5. The weights

[3]The numerical illustrations are performed on an Intel Core i7, 2.70 GHz.

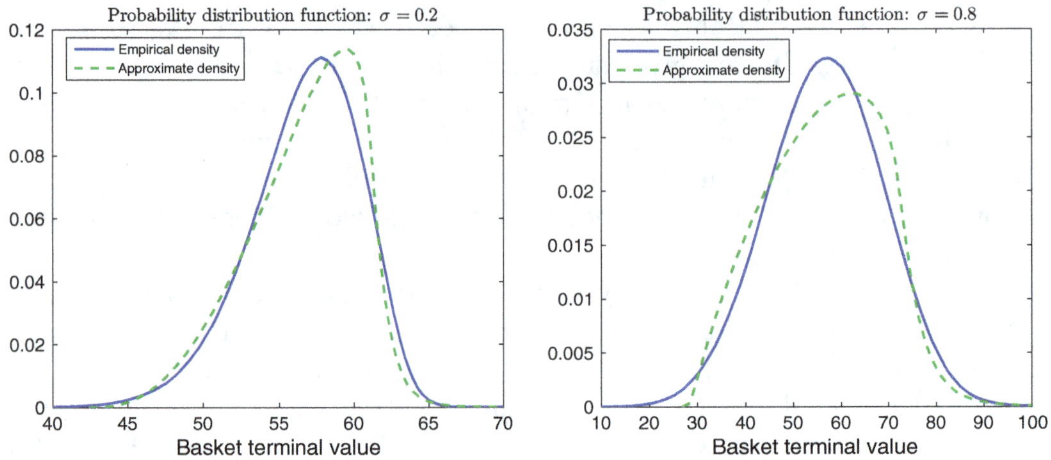


**Fig. 1** Probability density function of the real basket (*solid line*) and the approximate basket (*dashed line*). The basket option consists of 4 stocks and $r = 0.06$, $\rho = 0$, $T = 1/2$, $w_1 = w_2 = w_3 = w_4 = \frac{1}{4}$. All volatility parameters are equal to $\sigma$

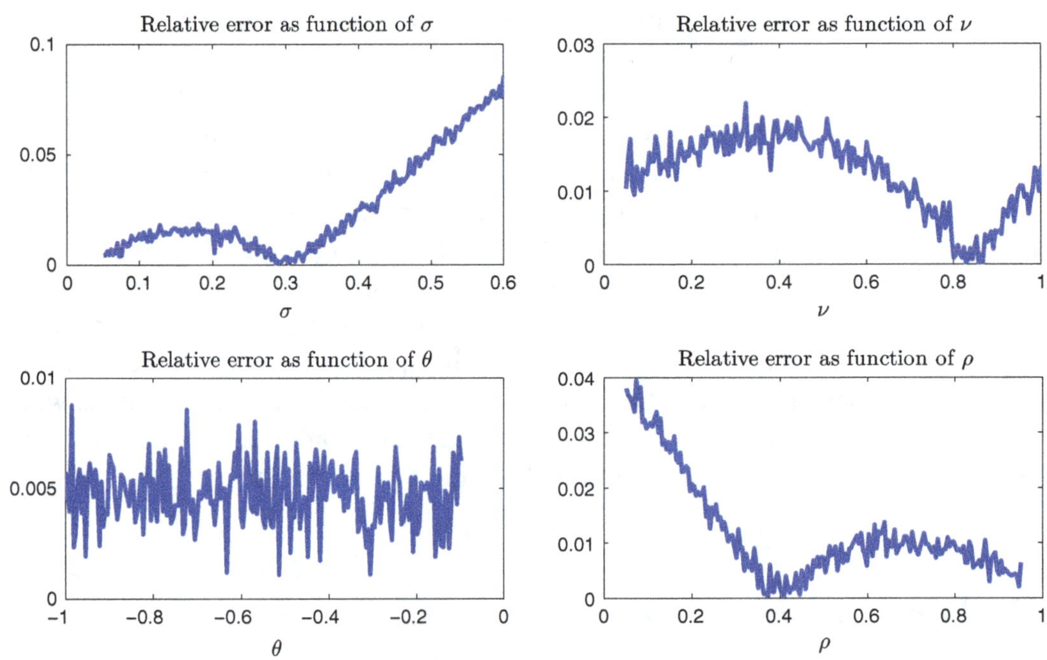


**Fig. 2** Relative error in the one-factor VG model for the three-moments-matching approximation. The basket option consists of 3 stocks and $r = 0.05$, $\rho = 0.5$, $T = 1$, $\sigma_1 = 0.2$, $\sigma_2 = 0.4$, $\sigma_3 = 0.6$, $w_1 = w_2 = w_3 = \frac{1}{3}$. The strike price is $K = 105.13$. In the benchmark model, the VG parameters are $\sigma = 0.57$, $\nu = 0.75$, $\theta = -0.95$, $\mu = 0.95$

$w_1$ and $w_2$ are chosen such that the initial price $S(0)$ of the basket is equal to 100. The maturity of the basket option is equal to 30 days.

The S&P 500 and Nasdaq option curves are denoted by $C_1$ and $C_2$, respectively. These option curves are only partially known. The traded strikes for curve $C_j$ are denoted by $K_{i,j}$, $i = 1, 2, \ldots, N_j$, where $N_j > 1$. If the volatilities $\sigma_1$ and $\sigma_2$

**Table 3** Basket option prices in the one-factor VG model with $r = 0.05$, $w_1 = w_2 = 0.5$, $X_1(0) = X_2(0) = 100$ and $\sigma_1 = \sigma_2$

| | $T$ | $\rho$ | $\sigma_1$ | $C^{mc}[K, T]$ | $C^{MM}[K, T]$ | Length CI |
|---|---|---|---|---|---|---|
| $K = 115.64$ | 1 | 0.3 | 0.2 | 1.3995 | 1.3113 | 4.08E-03 |
| | | | 0.4 | 5.5724 | 5.6267 | 1.26E-02 |
| | | 0.7 | 0.2 | 1.8963 | 1.8706 | 4.96E-03 |
| | | | 0.4 | 6.9451 | 7.0095 | 1.47E-02 |
| $K = 127.80$ | 3 | 0.3 | 0.2 | 4.4427 | 4.4565 | 1.14E-02 |
| | | | 0.4 | 11.3138 | 11.5920 | 2.77E-02 |
| | | 0.7 | 0.2 | 5.6002 | 5.6368 | 1.34E-02 |
| | | | 0.4 | 13.7444 | 13.9336 | 3.23E-02 |
| $K = 105.13$ | 1 | 0.3 | 0.2 | 5.5312 | 5.5965 | 8.78E-03 |
| | | | 0.4 | 10.1471 | 10.3515 | 1.73E-02 |
| | | 0.7 | 0.2 | 6.327 | 6.3731 | 9.74E-03 |
| | | | 0.4 | 11.7163 | 11.8379 | 1.95E-02 |
| $K = 116.18$ | 3 | 0.3 | 0.2 | 8.9833 | 9.1489 | 1.66E-02 |
| | | | 0.4 | 15.8784 | 16.2498 | 3.27E-02 |
| | | 0.7 | 0.2 | 10.3513 | 10.4528 | 1.86E-02 |
| | | | 0.4 | 18.4042 | 18.6214 | 3.73E-02 |
| $K = 94.61$ | 1 | 0.3 | 0.2 | 12.3514 | 12.4371 | 1.29E-02 |
| | | | 0.4 | 16.213 | 16.4493 | 2.17E-02 |
| | | 0.7 | 0.2 | 13.0696 | 13.1269 | 1.40E-02 |
| | | | 0.4 | 17.7431 | 17.8690 | 2.40E-02 |
| $K = 104.57$ | 3 | 0.3 | 0.2 | 15.1888 | 15.3869 | 2.15E-02 |
| | | | 0.4 | 21.3994 | 21.7592 | 3.76E-02 |
| | | 0.7 | 0.2 | 16.5069 | 16.6232 | 2.36E-02 |
| | | | 0.4 | 23.8489 | 24.0507 | 4.23E-02 |

and the characteristic function $\phi_L$ of the mother distribution $L$ are known, we can determine the model price of an option on asset $j$ with strike $K$ and maturity $T$. This price is denoted by $C_j^{model}[K, T; \Theta, \sigma_j]$, where $\Theta$ denotes the vector containing the model parameters of $L$. Given the systematic component, the stocks are independent. Therefore, we can use the observed option curves $C_1$ and $C_2$ to calibrate the model parameters as follows:

**Algorithm 1** (*Determining the parameters $\Theta$ and $\sigma_j$ of the one-factor Lévy model*)

Step 1: Choose a parameter vector $\Theta$.
Step 2: For each stock $j = 1, 2, \ldots, n$, determine the volatility $\sigma_j$ as follows:

$$\sigma_j = \arg\min_{\sigma} \frac{1}{N_j} \sum_{i=1}^{N_j} \frac{\left| C_j^{model}[K_{i,j}, T; \Theta, \sigma] - C_j[K_{i,j}] \right|}{C_j[K_{i,j}]},$$

**Table 4** The CPU time (in seconds) for the one-factor VG model for increasing basket dimension $n$

| $n$ | CPU TIMES |
|---|---|
| | Moment Matching |
| 5 | 0.1991 |
| 10 | 0.1994 |
| 20 | 0.1922 |
| 30 | 0.2043 |
| 40 | 0.2335 |
| 50 | 0.2888 |
| 60 | 0.3705 |
| 70 | 0.4789 |
| 80 | 0.5909 |
| 90 | 0.6862 |
| 100 | 0.8680 |

The following parameters are used: $r = 0.05$, $T = 1$, $\rho = 0.5$, $w_j = \frac{1}{n}$, $\sigma_j = 0.4$, $q_j = 0$, $S_j(0) = 100$, for $j = 1, 2, \ldots, n$. The basket strike is $K = 105.13$

**Table 5** Input data for the basket option

| Date | Feb 19, 2009 | |
|---|---|---|
| Maturity | March 21, 2009 | |
| | S&P 500 | Nasdaq |
| Forward | 777.76 | 1116.72 |
| Weights | 0.06419 | 0.0428 |

Step 3: Determine the total error:

$$\text{error} = \sum_{j=1}^{n} \frac{1}{N_j} \sum_{i=1}^{N_j} \frac{\left| C_j^{model}[K_{i,j}, T; \Theta, \sigma_j] - C_j[K_{i,j}] \right|}{C_j[K_{i,j}]}.$$

Repeat these three steps until the parameter vector $\Theta$ is found for which the total error is minimal. The corresponding volatilities $\sigma_1, \sigma_2, \ldots, \sigma_n$ are called the implied Lévy volatilities.

Only a limited number of option quotes is required to calibrate the one-factor Lévy model. Indeed, the parameter vector $\Theta$ can be determined using all available option quotes. Additional, one volatility parameter has to be determined for each stock. However, other methodologies for determining $\Theta$ exist. For example, one can fix the parameter $\Theta$ upfront, as is shown in Sect. 5.2. In such a situation, only one implied Lévy volatility has to be calibrated for each stock.

The calibrated parameters together with the calibration error are listed in Table 6. Note that the relative error in the VG, Meixner, and NIG case is significantly smaller

**Table 6** One-factor Lévy models: Calibrated model parameters

| Model | Calibration error (%) | Model Parameters | | | Volatilities | |
|---|---|---|---|---|---|---|
| Normal | 10.89 | $\mu_{normal}$ | $\sigma_{normal}$ | | $\sigma_1$ | $\sigma_2$ |
| | | 0 | 1 | | 0.2821 | 0.2734 |
| VG | 2.83 | $\sigma_{VG}$ | $\nu_{VG}$ | $\theta_{VG}$ | | |
| | | 0.3477 | 0.49322 | −0.3919 | 0.3716 | 0.3628 |
| Meixner | 2.81 | $\alpha_{Meixner}$ | $\beta_{Meixner}$ | | | |
| | | 1.1689 | −1.6761 | | 0.3799 | 0.3709 |
| NIG | 2.89 | $\alpha_{NIG}$ | $\beta_{NIG}$ | | | |
| | | 2.2768 | −1.4951 | | 0.3863 | 0.3772 |

**Table 7** Basket option prices for the basket given in Table 5

| $\rho$ | $K$ | $C^{BLS}[K,T]$ | $C^{VG}[K,T]$ | $C^{Meixner}[K,T]$ | $C^{NIG}[K,T]$ |
|---|---|---|---|---|---|
| 0.1 | 90 | 10.1783 | 10.7380 | 10.7893 | 10.8087 |
| | 95 | 5.9457 | 6.7092 | 6.7482 | 6.7418 |
| | 100 | 2.8401 | 3.4755 | 3.4843 | 3.4642 |
| | 105 | 1.0724 | 1.3375 | 1.3381 | 1.3374 |
| | 110 | 0.3158 | 0.3613 | 0.3690 | 0.3766 |
| | 120 | 0.0133 | 0.0198 | 0.0204 | 0.0197 |
| 0.5 | 90 | 10.3557 | 11.1445 | 11.2037 | 11.2169 |
| | 95 | 6.3160 | 7.2359 | 7.2754 | 7.2605 |
| | 100 | 3.3139 | 4.0376 | 4.0436 | 4.0154 |
| | 105 | 1.4699 | 1.7870 | 1.7798 | 1.7706 |
| | 110 | 0.5480 | 0.5857 | 0.5907 | 0.5980 |
| | 120 | 0.0461 | 0.0419 | 0.0421 | 0.0415 |
| 0.8 | 90 | 10.5000 | 11.4203 | 11.4837 | 11.4932 |
| | 95 | 6.5745 | 7.5877 | 7.6280 | 7.6091 |
| | 100 | 3.6292 | 4.4229 | 4.4287 | 4.3970 |
| | 105 | 1.7462 | 2.1247 | 2.1149 | 2.1010 |
| | 110 | 0.7301 | 0.7923 | 0.7954 | 0.8015 |
| | 120 | 0.0852 | 0.0726 | 0.0726 | 0.0723 |

The time to maturity is 30 days

than in the normal case. Using the calibrated parameters for the mother distribution $L$ together with the volatility parameters $\sigma_1$ and $\sigma_2$, we can determine basket option prices in the different model settings. Note that here and in the sequel of the paper, we always use the three-moments-matching approximation for determining basket option prices. We put $T = 30$ days and consider the cases where the correlation parameter $\rho$ is given by 0.1, 0.5, and 0.8. The corresponding basket option prices are listed in Table 7. One can observe from the table that each model generates a different basket option price, i.e. there is model risk. However, the difference between the

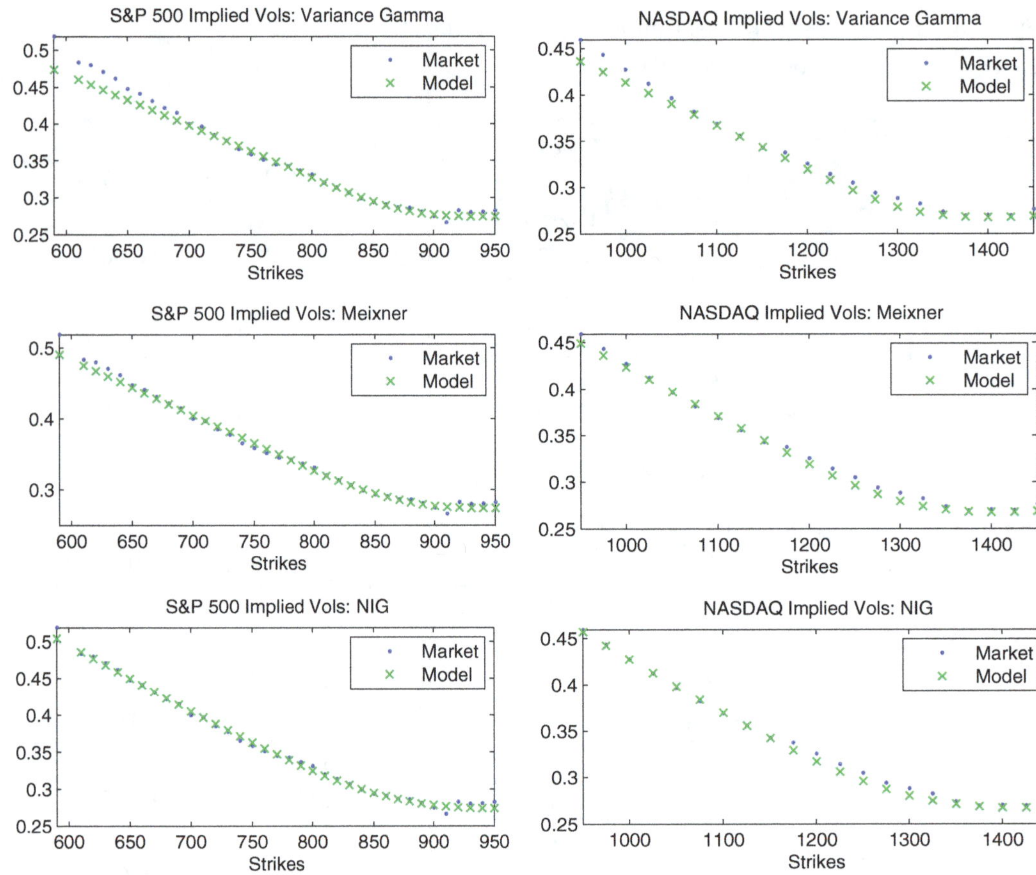


**Fig. 3** Implied market and model volatilities for February 19, 2009 for the S&P 500 (*left*) and the Nasdaq (*right*), with time to maturity 30 days

Gaussian and the non-Gaussian models is much more pronounced than the difference within the non-Gaussian models. We also find that using normally distributed log returns, one underestimates the basket option prices. Indeed, the basket option prices $C^{VG}[K,T]$, $C^{Meixner}[K,T]$ and $C^{NIG}[K,T]$ are larger than $C^{BLS}[K,T]$. In the next section, however, we encounter situations where the Gaussian basket option price is larger than the corresponding VG price for out-of-the-money options. The reason for this behavior is that marginal log returns in the non-Gaussian situations are negatively skewed, whereas these distributions are symmetric in the Gaussian case. This skewness results in a lower probability of ending in the money for options with a sufficiently large strike (Fig. 3).

## 5 Implied Lévy Correlation

In Sect. 4.2 we showed how the basket option formulas can be used to obtain basket option prices in the Lévy copula model. The parameter vector $\Theta$ describing the mother distribution $L$ and the implied Lévy volatility parameters $\sigma_j$ can be calibrated using the observed vanilla option curves $C_j[K, T]$ of the stocks composing the basket $S(T)$; see Algorithm 1. In this section we show how an implied Lévy correlation estimate $\rho$ can be obtained if in addition to the vanilla options, market prices for a basket option are also available.

We assume that $S(T)$ represents the time-$T$ price of a stock market index. Examples of such stock market indices are the Dow Jones, S&P 500, EUROSTOXX 50, and so on. Furthermore, options on $S(T)$ are traded and their prices are observable for a finite number of strikes. In this situation, pricing these index options is not a real issue; we denote the market price of an index option with maturity $T$ and strike $K$ by $C[K, T]$. Assume now that the stocks composing the index can be described by the one-factor Lévy model (6). If the parameter vector $\Theta$ and the marginal volatility vector $\underline{\sigma} = (\sigma_1, \sigma_2, \ldots, \sigma_n)$ are determined using Algorithm 1, the model price $C^{model}[K, T; \underline{\sigma}, \Theta, \rho]$ for the basket option only depends on the choice of the correlation $\rho$. An *implied correlation* estimate for $\rho$ arises when we match the model price with the observed index option price.

**Definition 1** (*Implied Lévy correlation*) Consider the one-factor Lévy model defined in (6). The *implied Lévy correlation* of the index $S(T)$ with moneyness $\pi = S(T)/S(0)$, denoted by $\rho\,[\pi]$, is defined by the following equation:

$$C^{model}\left[K, T; \underline{\sigma}, \Theta, \rho\,[\pi]\right] = C[K, T], \tag{14}$$

where $\underline{\sigma}$ contains the marginal implied volatilities and $\Theta$ is the parameter vector of $L$.

Determining an implied correlation estimate $\rho\,[K/S(0)]$ requires an inversion of the pricing formula $\rho \to C^{model}[K, T; \underline{\sigma}, \Theta, \rho]$. However, the basket option price is not given in a closed form and determining this price using Monte Carlo simulation would result in a slow procedure. If we determine $C^{model}[K, T; \underline{\sigma}, \Theta, \rho]$ using the three-moments-matching approach, implied correlations can be determined in a fast and efficient way. The idea of determining implied correlation estimates based on an approximate basket option pricing formula was already proposed in Chicago Board Options Exchange [15], Cont and Deguest [16], Linders and Schoutens [30], and Linders and Stassen [31].

Note that in case we take $L$ to be the standard normal distribution, $\rho[\pi]$ is an implied Gaussian correlation; see e.g. Chicago Board Options Exchange [15] and Skintzi and Refenes [45]. Equation (14) can be considered as a generalization of the implied Gaussian correlation. Indeed, instead of determining the single correlation parameter in a multivariate model with normal log returns and a Gaussian copula, we can now extend the model to the situation where the log returns follow a Lévy distribution. A similar idea was proposed in Garcia et al. [20] and further studied in Masol and Schoutens [37]. In these papers, Lévy base correlation is defined using CDS and CDO prices.

The proposed methodology for determining implied correlation estimates can also be applied to other multi-asset derivatives. For example, implied correlation estimates can be extracted from traded spread options [46], best-of basket options [19], and quanto options [4]. Implied correlation estimates based on various multi-asset products are discussed in Austing [2].

## 5.1 Variance Gamma

In order to illustrate the proposed methodology for determining implied Lévy correlation estimates, we use the Dow Jones Industrial Average (DJ). The DJ is composed of 30 underlying stocks and for each underlying we have a finite number of option prices to which we can calibrate the parameter vector $\Theta$ and the Lévy volatility parameters $\sigma_j$. Using the available vanilla option data for June 20, 2008, we will work out the Gaussian and the Variance Gamma case.[4] Note that options on components of the Dow Jones are of American type. In the sequel, we assume that the American option price is a good proxy for the corresponding European option price. This assumption is justified because we use short term and out-of-the-money options.

The single volatility parameter $\sigma_j$ is determined for stock $j$ by minimizing the relative error between the model and the market vanilla option prices; see Algorithm 1. Assuming a normal distribution for $L$, this volatility parameter is denoted by $\sigma_j^{BLS}$, whereas the notation $\sigma_j^{VG}$, $j = 1, 2, \ldots, n$ is used for the VG model. For June 20, 2008, the parameter vector $\Theta$ for the VG copula model is given in Table 9 and the implied volatilities are listed in Table 8. Figure 4 shows the model (Gaussian and VG) and market prices for General Electric and IBM, both members of the Dow Jones, based on the implied volatility parameters listed in Table 8. We observe that the Variance Gamma copula model is more suitable in capturing the dynamics of the components of the Dow Jones than the Gaussian copula model.

Given the volatility parameters for the Variance Gamma case and the normal case, listed in Table 8, the implied correlation defined by Eq. (14) can be determined based on the available Dow Jones index options on June 20, 2008. For a given index strike $K$, the moneyness $\pi$ is defined as $\pi = K/S(0)$. The implied Gaussian correlation (also called Black and Scholes correlation) is denoted by $\rho^{BLS}[\pi]$ and the corresponding implied Lévy correlation, based on a VG distribution, is denoted by $\rho^{VG}[\pi]$. In order to match the vanilla option curves more closely, we take into account the implied volatility smile and use a volatility parameter with moneyness $\pi$ for each stock $j$, which we denote by $\sigma_j[\pi]$. For a detailed and step-by-step plan for the calculation of these volatility parameters, we refer to Linders and Schoutens [30].

Figure 5 shows that both the implied Black and Scholes and implied Lévy correlation depend on the moneyness $\pi$. However, for low strikes, we observe that $\rho^{VG}[\pi] < \rho^{BLS}[\pi]$, whereas the opposite inequality holds for large strikes, making the implied Lévy correlation curve less steep than its Black and Scholes counterpart. In Linders and Schoutens [30], the authors discuss the shortcomings of the implied Black and Scholes correlation and show that implied Black and Scholes correlations

[4] All data used for calibration are extracted from an internal database of the KU Leuven.

**Table 8** Implied Variance Gamma volatilities $\sigma_j^{VG}$ and implied Black and Scholes volatilities $\sigma_j^{BLS}$ for June 20, 2008

| Stock | $\sigma_j^{VG}$ | $\sigma_j^{BLS}$ |
|---|---|---|
| Alcoa Incorporated | 0.6509 | 0.5743 |
| American Express Company | 0.4923 | 0.4477 |
| American International Group | 0.5488 | 0.4849 |
| Bank of America | 0.6003 | 0.5482 |
| Boeing Corporation | 0.3259 | 0.2927 |
| Caterpillar | 0.3009 | 0.2671 |
| JP Morgan | 0.5023 | 0.4448 |
| Chevron | 0.3252 | 0.3062 |
| Citigroup | 0.6429 | 0.5684 |
| Coca Cola Company | 0.2559 | 0.2343 |
| Walt Disney Company | 0.3157 | 0.2810 |
| DuPont | 0.2739 | 0.2438 |
| Exxon Mobile | 0.2938 | 0.2609 |
| General Electric | 0.3698 | 0.3300 |
| General Motors | 0.9148 | 0.8092 |
| Hewlet–Packard | 0.3035 | 0.2704 |
| Home Depot | 0.3604 | 0.3255 |
| Intel | 0.4281 | 0.3839 |
| IBM | 0.2874 | 0.2509 |
| Johnson & Johnson | 0.1741 | 0.1592 |
| McDonald's | 0.2508 | 0.2235 |
| Merck & Company | 0.3181 | 0.2896 |
| Microsoft | 0.3453 | 0.3068 |
| 3M | 0.2435 | 0.2202 |
| Pfizer | 0.2779 | 0.2572 |
| Procter & Gamble | 0.1870 | 0.1671 |
| AT&T | 0.3013 | 0.2688 |
| United Technologies | 0.2721 | 0.2434 |
| Verizon | 0.3116 | 0.2847 |
| Wal-Mart Stores | 0.2701 | 0.2397 |

can become larger than one for low strike prices. Our more general approach and using the implied Lévy correlation solves this problem at least to some extent. Indeed, the region where the implied correlation stays below 1 is much larger for the flatter implied Lévy correlation curve than for its Black and Scholes counterpart. We also observe that near the at-the-money strikes, VG and Black and Scholes correlation estimates are comparable, which may be a sign that in this region, the use of implied Black and Scholes correlation (as defined in Linders and Schoutens [30]) is justi-

**Table 9** Calibrated VG parameters for different trading days

| | | | VG Parameters | | |
|---|---|---|---|---|---|
| | $S(0)$ | $T$ (days) | $\sigma$ | $\nu$ | $\theta$ |
| March 25, 2008 | 125.33 | 25 | 0.2981 | 0.5741 | −0.1827 |
| April 18, 2008 | 128.49 | 29 | 0.3606 | 0.5247 | −0.2102 |
| June 20, 2008 | 118.43 | 29 | 0.3587 | 0.4683 | −0.1879 |
| July 18, 2008 | 114.97 | 29 | 0.2639 | 0.5222 | −0.1641 |
| August 20, 2008 | 114.17 | 31 | 0.2467 | 0.3770 | −0.1887 |

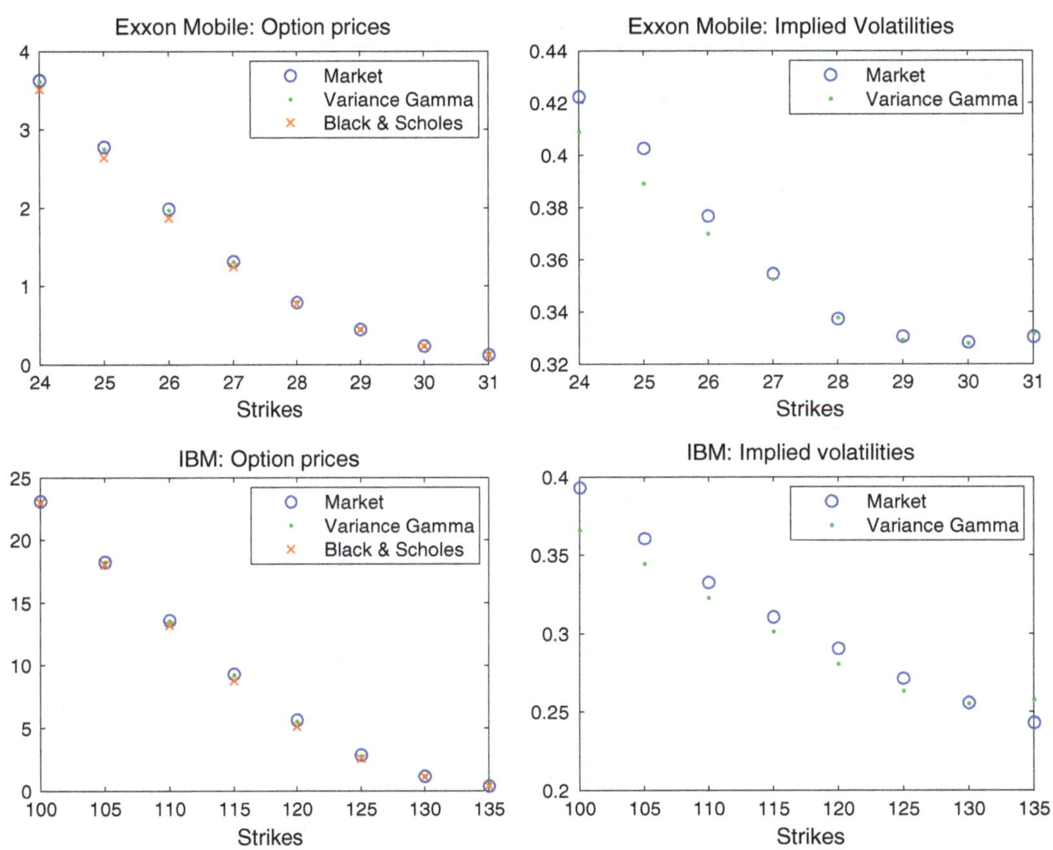


**Fig. 4** Option prices and implied volatilities (model and market) for Exxon Mobile and IBM on June 20, 2008 based on the parameters listed in Table 8. The time to maturity is 30 days

fied. Figure 7 shows implied correlation curves for March, April, July and August, 2008. In all these situations, the time to maturity is close to 30 days. The calibrated parameters for each trading day are listed in Table 9.

We determine the implied correlation $\rho^{VG}[\pi]$ such that model and market quote for an index option with moneyness $\pi = K/S(0)$ coincide. However, the model price is determined using the three-moments-matching approximation and

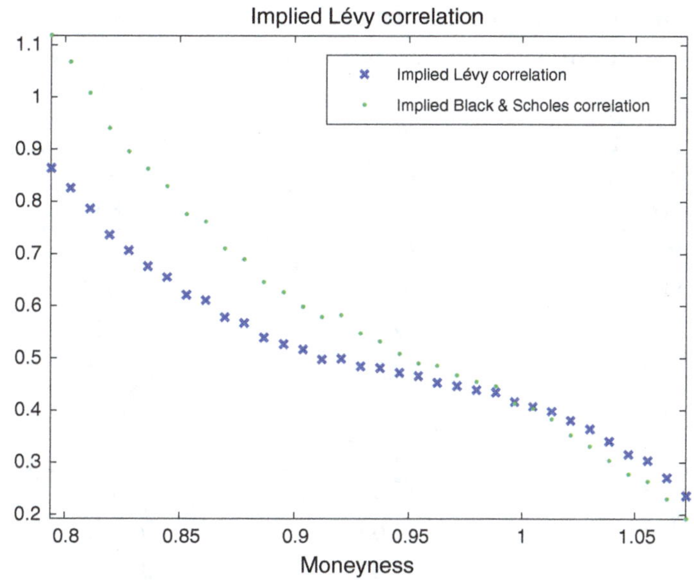


**Fig. 5** Implied correlation smile for the Dow Jones, based on a Gaussian (*dots*) and a one-factor Variance Gamma model (*crosses*) for June 20, 2008

may deviate from the real model price. Indeed, we determine $\rho^{VG}[\pi]$ such that $C^{MM}\left[K, T; \underline{\sigma}, \Theta, \rho\left[\pi\right]\right] = C[K, T]$. In order to test if the implied correlation estimate obtained is accurate, we determine the model price $C^{mc}\left[K, T; \underline{\sigma}, \Theta, \rho\left[\pi\right]\right]$ using Monte Carlo simulation, where we plug in the volatility parameters and the implied correlation parameters. The results are listed in Table 10 and shown in Fig. 6. We observe that model and market prices are not exactly equal, but the error is still acceptable.

## *5.2 Double Exponential*

In the previous subsection, we showed that the Lévy copula model allows for determining robust implied correlation estimates. However, calibrating this model can be a computational challenging task. Indeed, in case we deal with the Dow Jones Industrial Average, there are 30 underlying stocks and each stock has approximately 5 traded option prices. Calibrating the parameter vector $\Theta$ and the volatility parameters $\sigma_j$ has to be done simultaneously. This contrasts sharply with the Gaussian copula model, where the calibration can be done stock per stock.

In this subsection we consider a model with the computational attractive calibration property of the Gaussian copula model, but without imposing any normality assumption on the marginal log returns. To be more precise, given the convincing arguments exposed in Fig. 7 we would like to keep $L$ a $VG(\sigma, \nu, \theta, \mu)$ distribution. However, we do not calibrate the parameter vector $\Theta = (\sigma, \nu, \theta, \mu)$ to the vanilla option curves, but we fix these parameters upfront as follows

$$\mu = 0, \quad \theta = 0, \quad \nu = 1 \quad \text{and} \quad \sigma = 1.$$

**Table 10** Market quotes for Dow Jones Index options for different basket strikes on June 20, 2008

| Basket strikes | Market call prices | Implied VG correlation | VG call prices |
|---|---|---|---|
| 94 | 24.45 | 0.8633 | 24.4608 |
| 95 | 23.45 | 0.8253 | 23.4794 |
| 96 | 22.475 | 0.786 | 22.4899 |
| 97 | 21.475 | 0.7358 | 21.4887 |
| 98 | 20.5 | 0.7062 | 20.5303 |
| 99 | 19.5 | 0.6757 | 19.5308 |
| 100 | 18.525 | 0.6546 | 18.5551 |
| 101 | 17.55 | 0.6203 | 17.5705 |
| 102 | 16.575 | 0.6101 | 16.6062 |
| 103 | 15.6 | 0.5778 | 15.6313 |
| 104 | 14.65 | 0.5668 | 14.6954 |
| 105 | 13.675 | 0.5386 | 13.7209 |
| 106 | 12.725 | 0.5266 | 12.7672 |
| 107 | 11.8 | 0.5164 | 11.8280 |
| 108 | 10.85 | 0.4973 | 10.8922 |
| 109 | 9.95 | 0.4989 | 9.9961 |
| 110 | 9.05 | 0.484 | 9.0813 |
| 111 | 8.2 | 0.4809 | 8.2202 |
| 112 | 7.35 | 0.4719 | 7.3519 |
| 113 | 6.525 | 0.4656 | 6.5193 |
| 114 | 5.7 | 0.4527 | 5.6755 |
| 115 | 4.95 | 0.4467 | 4.8908 |
| 116 | 4.225 | 0.4389 | 4.1554 |
| 117 | 3.575 | 0.4344 | 3.4788 |
| 118 | 2.935 | 0.4162 | 2.8118 |
| 119 | 2.375 | 0.4068 | 2.2337 |
| 120 | 1.88 | 0.3976 | 1.7227 |
| 121 | 1.435 | 0.3798 | 1.2977 |
| 122 | 1.065 | 0.3636 | 0.9549 |
| 123 | 0.765 | 0.3399 | 0.6906 |
| 124 | 0.52 | 0.3147 | 0.4793 |
| 125 | 0.36 | 0.3029 | 0.3517 |
| 126 | 0.22 | 0.2702 | 0.2321 |
| 127 | 0.125 | 0.2357 | 0.1479 |

For each price we find the corresponding implied correlation and the model price using a one-factor Variance Gamma model with parameters listed in Table 9

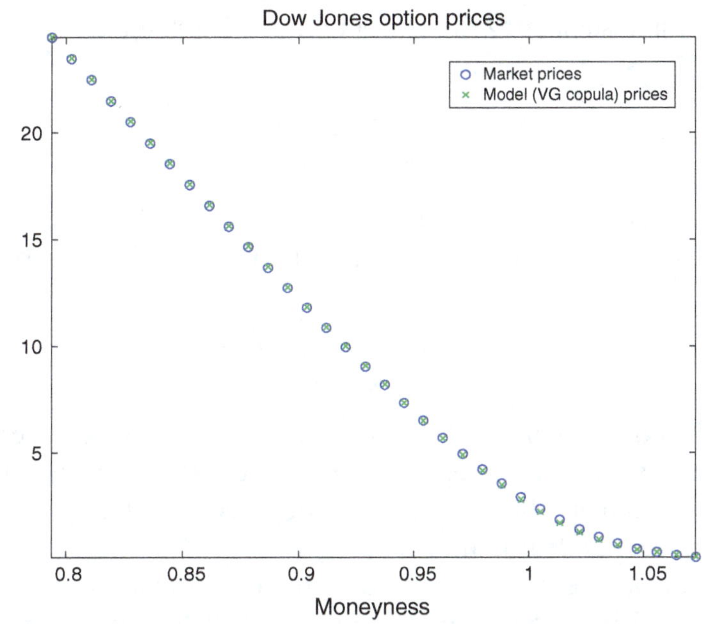


**Fig. 6** Dow Jones option prices: Market prices (*circles*) and the model prices using a one-factor Variance Gamma model and the implied VG correlation smile (*crosses*) for June 20, 2008

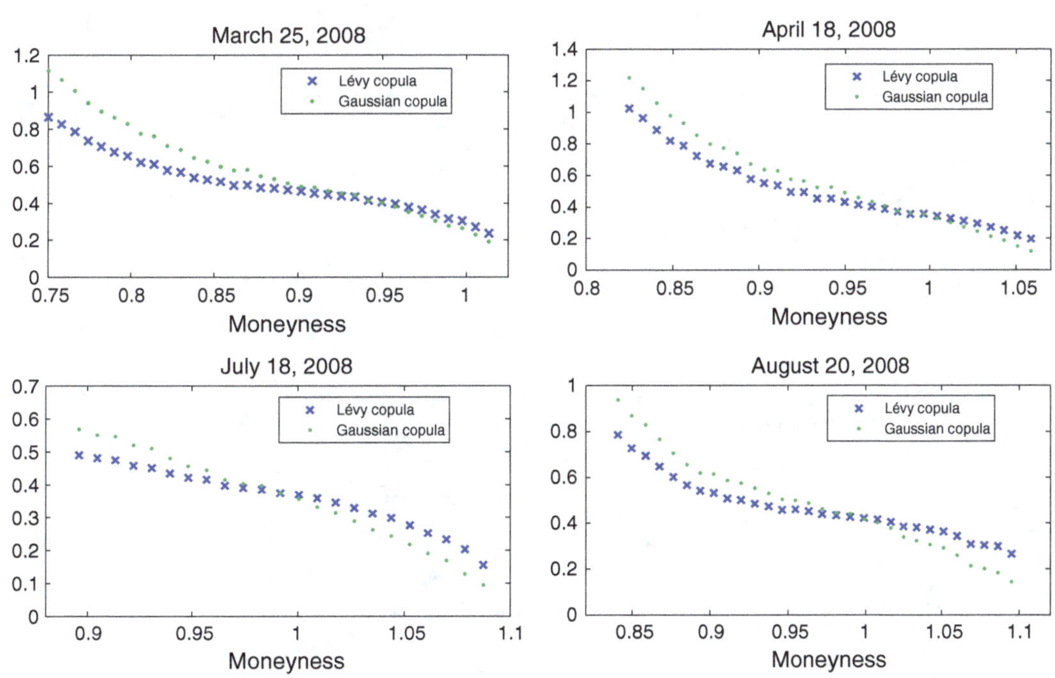


**Fig. 7** Implied correlation smile for the Dow Jones, based on a Gaussian (*dots*) and a one-factor Variance Gamma model (*crosses*) for different trading days

In this setting, $L$ is a standardized distribution and its characteristic function $\phi_L$ is given by

$$\phi_L(u) = \frac{1}{1 + \frac{u^2}{2}}, \quad u \in \mathbb{R}.$$

From its characteristic function, we see that $L$ has a *Standard Double Exponential distribution*, also called Laplace distribution, and its pdf $f_L$ is given by

$$f_L(u) = \frac{\sqrt{2}}{2} \mathrm{e}^{-\frac{|u|}{\sqrt{2}}}$$

The Standard Double Exponential distribution is symmetric and centered around zero, while it has variance 1. Note, however, that it is straightforward to generalize this distribution such that it has center $\mu$ and variance $\sigma^2$. Moreover, the kurtosis of this Double Exponential distribution is 6.

By using the Double Exponential distribution instead of the more general Variance Gamma distribution, some flexibility is lost for modeling the marginals. However, the Double Exponential distribution is still a much better distribution for modeling the stock returns than the normal distribution. Moreover, in this simplified setting, the only parameters to be calibrated are the marginal volatility parameters,

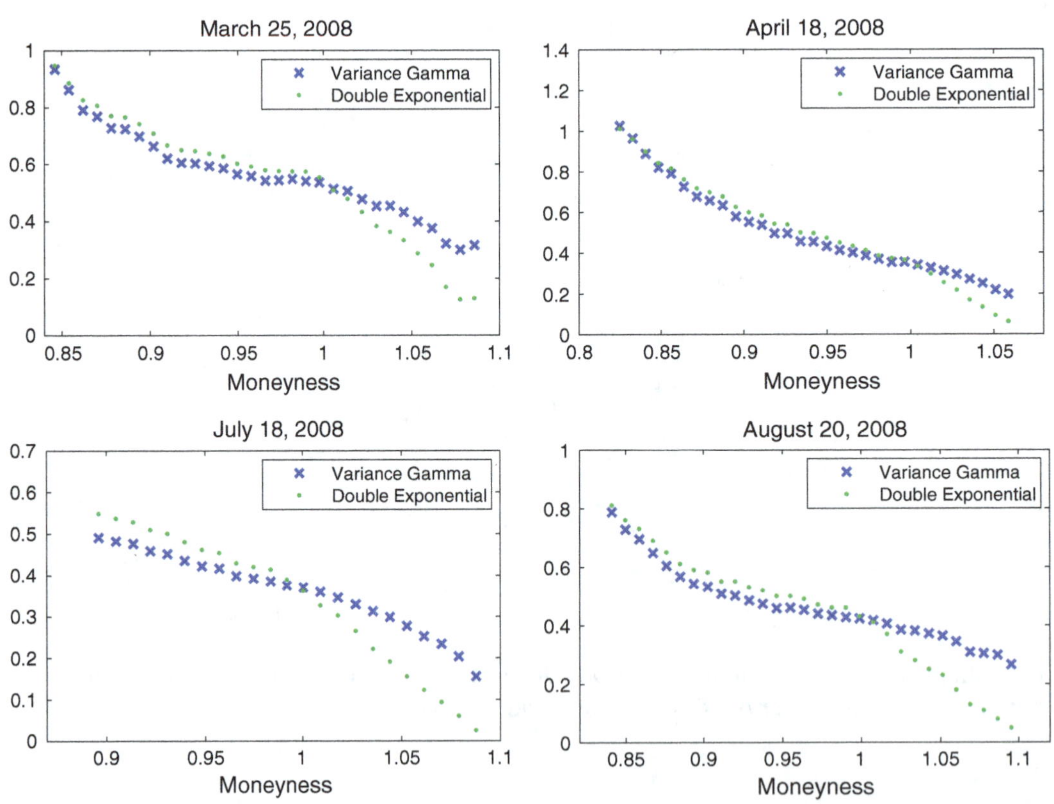


**Fig. 8** Implied correlation smiles in the one-factor Variance Gamma and the Double Exponential model

which we denote by $\sigma_j^{DE}$, and the correlation parameter $\rho^{DE}$. Similar to the Gaussian copula model, calibrating the volatility parameter $\sigma_j^{DE}$ only requires the option curve of stock $j$. As a result, the time to calibrate the Double Exponential copula model is comparable to its Gaussian counterpart and much shorter than the general Variance Gamma copula model.

Consider the DJ on March 25, 2008. The time to maturity is 25 days. We determine the implied marginal volatility parameter for each stock in a one-factor Variance Gamma model and a Double Exponential framework. Given this information, we can determine the prices $C^{VG}[K,T]$ and $C^{DE}[K,T]$ for a basket option in a Variance-Gamma and a Double Exponential model, respectively. Figure 8 shows the implied Variance Gamma and the Double Exponential correlations. We observe that the implied correlation based on a one-factor VG model is larger than its Double Exponential counterpart for a moneyness bigger than one, whereas both implied correlation estimates are relatively close to each other in the other situation.

## 6 Conclusion

In this paper we introduced a one-factor Lévy model and we proposed a three-moments-matching approximation for pricing basket options. Well-known distributions like the Normal, Variance Gamma, NIG, Meixner, etc., can be used in this one-factor Lévy model. We calibrate these different models to market data and determine basket option prices for the different model settings. Our newly designed (approximate) basket option pricing formula can be used to define implied Lévy correlation. The one-factor Lévy model provides a flexible framework for deriving implied correlation estimates in different model settings. Indeed, by employing a Brownian motion and a Variance Gamma process in our model, we can determine Gaussian and VG-implied correlation estimates, respectively. We observe that the VG implied correlation is an improvement of the Gaussian-implied correlation.

**Acknowledgements** The authors acknowledge the financial support of the Onderzoeksfonds KU Leuven (GOA/13/002: Management of Financial and Actuarial Risks: Modeling, Regulation, Disclosure and Market Effects). Daniël Linders also acknowledges the support of the AXA Research Fund (Measuring and managing herd behavior risk in stock markets). The authors also thank Prof. Jan Dhaene, Prof. Alexander Kukush, the anonymous referees and the editors for helpful comments.

The KPMG Center of Excellence in Risk Management is acknowledged for organizing the conference "Challenges in Derivatives Markets - Fixed Income Modeling, Valuation Adjustments, Risk Management, and Regulation".

## Appendix: Proof of Lemma 1

The proof for expression (9) is straightforward.

Starting from the multinomial theorem, we can write the second moment $m_2$ as follows

$$\begin{aligned}m_2 &= \mathbb{E}\left[(w_1S_1(T)+w_2S_2(T)+\dots w_nS_n(T))^2\right]\\ &= \mathbb{E}\left[\sum_{i_1+i_2+\dots+i_n=2}\frac{2}{i_1!i_2!\dots i_n!}\prod_{j=1}^{n}\left(w_jS_j(T)\right)^{i_j}\right].\end{aligned}$$

Considering the cases $(i_n=0)$, $(i_n=1)$ and $(i_n=2)$ separately, we find

$$m_2 = \mathbb{E}\left[\left(\sum_{j=1}^{n-1}w_jS_j(T)\right)^2 + 2w_nS_n(T)\sum_{j=1}^{n-1}w_jS_j(T) + w_j^2S_n^2(T)\right].$$

Continuing recursively gives

$$m_2 = \sum_{j=1}^{n}\sum_{k=1}^{n}w_jw_k\mathbb{E}\left[S_j(T)S_k(T)\right]. \tag{15}$$

We then find that

$$\begin{aligned}m_2 &= \sum_{j=1}^{n}\sum_{k=1}^{n}w_jw_kS_j(0)S_k(0)\\ &\quad\times\mathbb{E}\left[\exp\left\{(2r-q_j-q_k-\omega_j-\omega_k)T+(\sigma_jA_j+\sigma_kA_k)\sqrt{T}\right\}\right]\\ &= \sum_{j=1}^{n}\sum_{k=1}^{n}w_jw_k\frac{\mathbb{E}\left[S_j(T)\right]\mathbb{E}\left[S_k(T)\right]}{\phi_L\left(-\mathrm{i}\sigma_j\sqrt{T}\right)\phi_L\left(-\mathrm{i}\sigma_k\sqrt{T}\right)}\mathbb{E}\left[\exp\left\{(\sigma_jA_j+\sigma_kA_k)\sqrt{T}\right\}\right].\end{aligned}$$

In the last step, we used the Expression $\omega_j = \log\phi_L\left(\mathrm{i}\sigma_j\sqrt{T}\right)/T$. If we use expression (1) to decompose $A_j$ and $A_k$ in the common component $X(\rho)$ and the independent components $X_j(1-\rho)$ and $X_k(1-\rho)$, we find the following expression for $m_2$

$$m_2 = \sum_{j=1}^{n}\sum_{k=1}^{n}w_jw_k\frac{\mathbb{E}\left[S_j(T)\right]\mathbb{E}\left[S_k(T)\right]}{\phi_L\left(-\mathrm{i}\sigma_j\sqrt{T}\right)\phi_L\left(-\mathrm{i}\sigma_k\sqrt{T}\right)}\mathbb{E}\left[e^{(\sigma_j+\sigma_k)X(\rho)}e^{\sigma_j\sqrt{T}X_j(1-\rho)}e^{\sigma_k\sqrt{T}X_k(1-\rho)}\right].$$

The r.v. $X(\rho)$ is independent from $X_j(1-\rho)$ and $X_k(1-\rho)$. Furthermore, the characteristic function of $X(\rho)$ is $\phi_L^{\rho}$, which results in

$$m_2 = \sum_{j=1}^{n}\sum_{k=1}^{n} w_j w_k \frac{\mathbb{E}\left[S_j(T)\right]\mathbb{E}\left[S_k(T)\right]}{\phi_L\left(-\mathrm{i}\sigma_j\sqrt{T}\right)\phi_L\left(-\mathrm{i}\sigma_k\sqrt{T}\right)}\phi_L\left(-\mathrm{i}(\sigma_j+\sigma_k)\sqrt{T}\right)^{\rho}$$
$$\times\,\mathbb{E}\left[\mathrm{e}^{\sigma_j\sqrt{T}X_j(1-\rho)}\mathrm{e}^{\sigma_k\sqrt{T}X_k(1-\rho)}\right].$$

If $j \neq k$, $X_j(1-\rho)$ and $X_k(1-\rho)$ are i.i.d. with characteristic function $\phi_L^{1-\rho}$, which gives the following expression for $m_2$:

$$m_2 = \sum_{j=1}^{n}\sum_{k=1}^{n} w_j w_k \mathbb{E}\left[S_j(T)\right]\mathbb{E}\left[S_k(T)\right]\left(\frac{\phi_L\left(-\mathrm{i}(\sigma_j+\sigma_k)\sqrt{T}\right)}{\phi_L\left(-\mathrm{i}\sigma_j\sqrt{T}\right)\phi_L\left(-\mathrm{i}\sigma_k\sqrt{T}\right)}\right)^{\rho}.$$

If $j = k$, we find that

$$\mathbb{E}\left[\mathrm{e}^{\sigma_j\sqrt{T}X_j(1-\rho)}\mathrm{e}^{\sigma_k\sqrt{T}X_k(1-\rho)}\right] = \phi_L\left(-\mathrm{i}\left(\sigma_j+\sigma_k\right)\sqrt{T}\right),$$

which gives

$$m_2 = \sum_{j=1}^{n}\sum_{k=1}^{n} w_j w_k \mathbb{E}\left[S_j(T)\right]\mathbb{E}\left[S_k(T)\right]\frac{\phi_L\left(-\mathrm{i}(\sigma_j+\sigma_k)\sqrt{T}\right)}{\phi_L\left(-\mathrm{i}\sigma_j\sqrt{T}\right)\phi_L\left(-\mathrm{i}\sigma_k\sqrt{T}\right)}.$$

This proves expression (10) for $m_2$.

We can write $m_3$ as follows

$$\begin{aligned} m_3 &= \mathbb{E}\left[\left(\sum_{j=1}^{n} w_j S_j(T)\right)^3\right] \\ &= \mathbb{E}\left[\left(\sum_{j=1}^{n} w_j S_j(T)\right)^2 \sum_{l=1}^{n} w_l S_l(T)\right]. \end{aligned}$$

Using expression (15), we find the following Expression for $m_3$:

$$\begin{aligned} m_3 &= \mathbb{E}\left[\left(\sum_{j=1}^{n}\sum_{k=1}^{n} w_j w_k S_j(T) S_k(t)\right)\sum_{l=1}^{n} w_l S_l(T)\right] \\ &= \sum_{j=1}^{n}\sum_{k=1}^{n}\sum_{l=1}^{n} w_j w_k w_l \mathbb{E}\left[S_j(T)S_k(T)S_l(T)\right]. \end{aligned}$$

Similar calculations as for $m_2$ result in

$$m_3 = \sum_{j=1}^{n} \sum_{k=1}^{n} \sum_{l=1}^{n} w_j w_k w_l \mathbb{E}\left[S_j(T)\right] \mathbb{E}\left[S_k(T)\right] \mathbb{E}\left[S_l(T)\right]$$

$$\times \frac{\phi_L\left(-\mathrm{i}(\sigma_j + \sigma_k + \sigma_l)\sqrt{T}\right)^{\rho}}{\phi_L\left(-\mathrm{i}\sigma_j\sqrt{T}\right)\phi_L\left(-\mathrm{i}\sigma_k\sqrt{T}\right)\phi_L\left(-\mathrm{i}\sigma_l\sqrt{T}\right)} A_{j,k,l},$$

where

$$A_{j,k,l} = \mathbb{E}\left[\mathrm{e}^{\sigma_j\sqrt{T}X_j(1-\rho)}\mathrm{e}^{\sigma_k\sqrt{T}X_k(1-\rho)}\mathrm{e}^{\sigma_l\sqrt{T}X_l(1-\rho)}\right].$$

Differentiating between the situations $(j = k = l)$, $(j = k, k \neq l)$, $(j \neq k, k = l)$, $(j \neq k, k \neq l, j = l)$ and $(j \neq k \neq l, j \neq l)$, we find expression (11).

**Open Access** This chapter is distributed under the terms of the Creative Commons Attribution 4.0 International License (http://creativecommons.org/licenses/by/4.0/), which permits use, duplication, adaptation, distribution and reproduction in any medium or format, as long as you give appropriate credit to the original author(s) and the source, a link is provided to the Creative Commons license and any changes made are indicated.

The images or other third party material in this chapter are included in the work's Creative Commons license, unless indicated otherwise in the credit line; if such material is not included in the work's Creative Commons license and the respective action is not permitted by statutory regulation, users will need to obtain permission from the license holder to duplicate, adapt or reproduce the material.

## References

1. Albrecher, H., Ladoucette, S., Schoutens, W.: A generic one-factor Lévy model for pricing synthetic CDOs. In: Fu, M., Jarrow, R., Yen, J.-Y., Elliott, R. (eds.) Advances in Mathematical Finance, pp. 259–277. Applied and Numerical Harmonic Analysis, Birkhäuser Boston (2007)
2. Austing, P.: Smile Pricing Explained. Financial Engineering Explained. Palgrave Macmillan (2014)
3. Ballotta, L., Bonfiglioli, E.: Multivariate asset models using Lévy processes and applications. Eur. J. Financ. http://dx.doi.org/10.1080/1351847X.2013.870917 (2014)
4. Ballotta, L., Deelstra, G., Rayée, G.: Extracting the implied correlation from quanto derivatives, Technical report. working paper (2014)
5. Baxter, M.: Lévy simple structural models. Int. J. Theor. Appl. Financ. (IJTAF) **10**(04), 593–606 (2007)
6. Black, F., Scholes, M.: The pricing of options and corporate liabilities. J. Polit. Econ. **81**(3), 637–654 (1973)
7. Brigo, D., Mercurio, F., Rapisarda, F., Scotti, R.: Approximated moment-matching dynamics for basket-options pricing. Quant. Financ. **4**(1), 1–16 (2004)
8. Brooks, R., Corson, J., Wales, J.D.: The pricing of index options when the underlying assets all follow a lognormal diffusion. Adv. Futures Options Res. **7** (1994)

9. Caldana, R., Fusai, G.: A general closed-form spread option pricing formula. J. Bank. Financ. **37**(12), 4893–4906 (2013)
10. Caldana, R., Fusai, G., Gnoatto, A., Graselli, M.: General close-form basket option pricing bounds. Quant. Financ. http://dx.doi.org/10.2139/ssrn.2376134 (2014)
11. Carmona, R., Durrleman, V.: Pricing and hedging spread options. SIAM Rev. **45**(4), 627–685 (2003)
12. Carmona, R., Durrleman, V.: Generalizing the Black–Scholes formula to multivariate contingent claims. J. Comput. Financ. **9**, 43–67 (2006)
13. Carr, P., Madan, D.B.: Option valuation using the Fast Fourier Transform. J. Comput. Financ. **2**, 61–73 (1999)
14. Cherubini, U., Luciano, E., Vecchiato, W.: Copula Methods in Finance. The Wiley Finance Series. Wiley (2004)
15. Chicago Board Options Exchange: CBOE S&P 500 implied correlation index. Working Paper (2009)
16. Cont, R., Deguest, R.: Equity correlations implied by index options: estimation and model uncertainty analysis. Math. Financ. **23**(3), 496–530 (2013)
17. Corcuera, J.M., Guillaume, F., Leoni, P., Schoutens, W.: Implied Lévy volatility. Quant. Financ. **9**(4), 383–393 (2009)
18. Deelstra, G., Liinev, J., Vanmaele, M.: Pricing of arithmetic basket options by conditioning. Insur. Math. Econ. **34**(1), 55–77 (2004)
19. Fonseca, J., Grasselli, M., Tebaldi, C.: Option pricing when correlations are stochastic: an analytical framework. Rev. Deriv. Res. **10**(2), 151–180 (2007)
20. Garcia, J., Goossens, S., Masol, V., Schoutens, W.: Lévy base correlation. Wilmott J. **1**, 95–100 (2009)
21. Guillaume, F.: The $\alpha$VG model for multivariate asset pricing: calibration and extension. Rev. Deriv. Res. **16**(1), 25–52 (2013)
22. Guillaume, F., Jacobs, P., Schoutens, W.: Pricing and hedging of CDO-squared tranches by using a one factor Lévy model. Int. J. Theor. Appl. Financ. **12**(05), 663–685 (2009)
23. Hull, J., White, S.: Efficient procedures for valuing European and American path-dependent options. J. Deriv. **1**(1), 21–31 (1993)
24. Hurd, T.R., Zhou, Z.: A Fourier transform method for spread option pricing. SIAM J. Fin. Math. **1**(1), 142–157 (2010)
25. Kallsen, J., Tankov, P.: Characterization of dependence of multidimensional Lévy processes using Lévy copulas. J. Multivar. Anal. **97**(7), 1551–1572 (2006)
26. Kawai, R.: A multivariate Lévy process model with linear correlation. Quant. Financ. **9**(5), 597–606 (2009)
27. Korn, R., Zeytun, S.: Efficient basket Monte Carlo option pricing via a simple analytical approximation. J. Comput. Appl. Math. **243**(1), 48–59 (2013)
28. Leoni, P., Schoutens, W.: Multivariate smiling. Wilmott Magazin. 82–91 (2008)
29. Linders, D.: Pricing index options in a multivariate Black & Scholes model, Research report AFI-1383 FEB. KU Leuven—Faculty of Business and Economics, Leuven (2013)
30. Linders, D., Schoutens, W.: A framework for robust measurement of implied correlation. J. Comput. Appl. Math. **271**, 39–52 (2014)
31. Linders, D., Stassen, B.: The multivariate Variance Gamma model: basket option pricing and calibration. Quant. Financ. http://dx.doi.org/10.1080/14697688.2015.1043934 (2015)
32. Luciano, E., Schoutens, W.: A multivariate jump-driven financial asset model. Quant. Financ. **6**(5), 385–402 (2006)
33. Luciano, E., Semeraro, P.: Multivariate time changes for Lévy asset models: characterization and calibration. J. Comput. Appl. Math. **233**, 1937–1953 (2010)
34. Madan, D.B., Seneta, E.: The Variance Gamma (V.G.) model for share market returns. J. Bus. **63**(4), 511–524 (1990)
35. Madan, D.B., Carr, P., Chang, E.C.: The Variance Gamma process and option pricing. Eur. Financ. Rev. **2**, 79–105 (1998)

36. Mai, J.-F., Scherer, M., Zagst, R.: CIID frailty models and implied copulas. In: Proceedings of the workshop Copulae in Mathematical and Quantitative Finance, Cracow, 10-11 July 2012, Springer, pp. 201–230 (2012)
37. Masol, V., Schoutens, W.: Comparing alternative Lévy base correlation models for pricing and hedging CDO tranches. Quant. Financ. **11**(5), 763–773 (2011)
38. McWilliams, N.: Option pricing techniques understochastic delay models. Ph.D. thesis, University of Edinburgh (2011)
39. Milevsky, M., Posner, S.: A closed-form approximation for valuing basket options. J. Deriv. **5**(4), 54–61 (1998)
40. Moosbrucker, T.: Explaining the correlation smile using Variance Gamma distributions. J. Fixed Income **16**(1), 71–87 (2006)
41. Moosbrucker, T.: Pricing CDOs with correlated variance gamma distributions, Technical report, Centre for Financial Research, Univ. of Cologne. colloquium paper (2006)
42. Rubinstein, M.: Implied binomial trees. J. Financ. **49**(3), 771–818 (1994)
43. Schoutens, W.: Lévy Processes in Finance: Pricing Financial Derivatives. Wiley (2003)
44. Semeraro, P.: A multivariate Variance Gamma model for financial applications. Int. J. Theor. Appl. Financ. (IJTAF) **11**(01), 1–18 (2008)
45. Skintzi, V.D., Refenes, A.N.: Implied correlation index: a new measure of diversification. J. Futures Mark. **25**, 171–197 (2005). doi:10.1002/fut.20137
46. Tavin, B.: Hedging dependence risk with spread options via the power frank and power student t copulas, Technical report, Université Paris I Panthéon-Sorbonne. Available at SSRN: http://ssrn.com/abstract=2192430 (2013)
47. Vasicek, O.: Probability of loss on a loan portfolio. KMV Working Paper (1987)
48. Xu, G., Zheng, H.: Basket options valuation for a local volatility jump diffusion model with the asymptotic expansion method. Insur. Math. Econ. **47**(3), 415–422 (2010)
49. Xu, G., Zheng, H.: Lower bound approximation to basket option values for local volatility jump-diffusion models. Int. J. Theor. Appl. Financ. **17**(01), 1450007 (2014)

# Pricing Shared-Loss Hedge Fund Fee Structures

**Ben Djerroud, David Saunders, Luis Seco and Mohammad Shakourifar**

**Abstract** The asset management business is driven by fee structures. In the context of hedge funds, fees have usually been a hybrid combination of two different types, which has coined a well-known business term of "2 and 20". As an attempt to provide better alignment with their investors, in a new context of low interest rates and lukewarm performance, a new type of fund fees has been introduced in the last few years that offers a more symmetric payment structure, which we will refer to as *shared loss*. In this framework, in return for receiving performance fees, the fund manager provides some downside protection against losses to the investors. We show that the position values of the investor and the hedge fund manager can be formulated as portfolios of options, and discuss issues regarding pricing and fairness of the fee rates, and incentives for both investors and hedge fund managers. In particular, we will be able to show that, from a present value perspective, these fee structures can be set up as being favorable either to the hedge fund manager or to the investor. The paper is based on an arbitrage-free pricing framework. However, if one is to take

This research was supported in part by the Natural Sciences and Engineering Research Council of Canada.

B. Djerroud · M. Shakourifar (✉)
Sigma Analysis & Management, Toronto, ON, Canada
e-mail: mohammad@sigmanalysis.com

B. Djerroud
e-mail: ben_d@sigmanalysis.com

D. Saunders
Department of Statistics and Actuarial Science, University of Waterloo, Waterloo, Canada
e-mail: dsaunders@uwaterloo.ca

L. Seco
Department of Mathematics, University of Toronto, Toronto, Canada
e-mail: seco@math.utoronto.ca

© The Author(s) 2016

K. Glau et al. (eds.), *Innovations in Derivatives Markets*, Springer Proceedings in Mathematics & Statistics 165, DOI 10.1007/978-3-319-33446-2_17

into account the value to the business that investor capital brings to a fund, which is not part of our framework, it is possible to create a situation where both investors as well as asset managers win.

**Keywords** Hedge funds · Fee structures · First-loss · Shared-loss · Black-Scholes option pricing

## 1 Introduction

Hedge Funds are pooled investment vehicles overseen by a management company. They generally aim at absolute return portfolios and their success is usually linked to market inefficiencies, such as instrument mispricing, misguided market consensus or, in general terms, the manager's intelligence to anticipate market moves. The nature of these investments is that they exploit investment opportunities that are rare. This is a characteristic that they share with private equity investments, but they share with the mutual fund industry the fact that they often trade in liquid, marketable securities. Fund sizes are more in line with private equity investing than with the mammoth mutual fund industry. Their compensation structure, because of their limited access to opportunity, is also more in line with the private equity universe, and usually consists in a fixed, asset-based fee, and a variable, performance fee base. Because of market conditions that have been in place over the last several years, in particular the low interest rate environment, coupled with the lukewarm performance of the hedge fund sector in the recent years, investors have become increasingly more sensitive to fee structures. The traditional 2&20 fee structure, consisting of a flat fee of 2 % of assets under management together with a performance fee of 20 % of net profits is considered unfair on the basis of the asymmetry: the management company will always earn a fee, whereas the investor is only guaranteed to pay that fee. The advent of the 40-ACT funds[1] has, in particular, dispensed with the performance fee base in favor of a fixed management fee, which is more in line with the mutual fund industry than with the hedge fund industry. This compensation model essentially rewards funds for becoming asset gatherers instead of the alpha-seeking business the hedge fund was set out to be. In this paper we will examine, from a quantitative perspective, a suite of symmetric performance fee structures which are gaining traction with more sophisticated investors, known as first-loss (or shared-loss) fee structures. In this new framework, in return for receiving performance fees, the fund manager provides some downside protection against losses to the investors.

The issue of the incentives created by hedge fund fees bears much similarity to issues surrounding the structure of executive compensation. At first glance, the optionality inherent in both would seem to incentivize greater risk taking. However, the reality is more subtle. Carpenter [2] studies the case of executive compensation,

[1] Pooled investment vehicles, enforced and regulated by the Securities and Exchange Commission, that are packaged and sold to retail and institutional investors in the public markets.

when the manager cannot hedge options provided as compensation by trading the underlying. In certain conditions, a utility-maximizing manager may choose to reduce rather than increase the volatility of the underlying firm. Ross [9] gives necessary and sufficient conditions for a fee schedule to make a utility-maximizing manager more or less risk-averse. Hodder and Jackwerth [6] consider the effects of hedge fund fee incentives on a risk manager with power utility, and also in the presence of a liquidation barrier. They find that over a one-year horizon, risk-taking varies dramatically with fund value, but that this effect is moderated over longer time horizons. Kouwenberg and Ziemba [7] consider loss-averse hedge fund managers and find that higher incentive fees lead to riskier fund management strategies. However, this effect is reduced if a significant portion of the manager's own money is invested in the fund. They further provide empirical evidence showing that hedge funds with incentive fees have significantly lower mean returns (net of fees), and find a positive correlation between fee levels and downside risk. They find that risk is increasing with respect to the performance fee if the manager's objective function is based on cumulative prospect theory, rather than utility, and provide empirical evidence. Recent work on the analysis of hedge fund fee structures includes that of Goetzmann et al. [3], who value a fee structure with a highwater mark provision, using a PDE approach with a fixed investment portfolio, Panageas and Westerfield [8], who consider the portfolio selection decision of maximizing the present value of fees for a risk-neutral manager over an infinite horizon, and Guasoni and Obłój [4], who extend this work to managers with risk-averse power utility. Closest to the current work is He and Kou [5], who analyze shared-loss fee structures for hedge funds by looking at the portfolio selection decision of a hedge fund manager whose preferences are modeled using cumulative prospect theory. The problem is considered in the presence of a manager investing in the fund, and with a predetermined liquidation barrier. Analytical solutions of the portfolio selection problem are provided, and the result (cumulative prospect theory) for both the investor and the manager is examined. It is found that depending on the parameter values, either a traditional fee structure or a first-loss fee structure may result in a riskier investment strategy. While for some parameter values, the first-loss structure improves the utility of both the investor and the hedge fund manager, they find that for typical values, the manager is better off, while the investor is worse off. In this paper, we investigate the shared-loss fee structures from the perspective of risk-neutral valuation, with no further assumptions about investor preferences, while He and Kou [5] solve the stochastic control problem (under the real-world measure) corresponding to the manager maximizing the utility function from cumulative prospect theory, and also evaluate the investor's payoff using the same type of criterion.

The paper is organized as follows. First, we will review the traditional fee structures in some detail. Next, we will introduce the notion and mechanics of the first-loss structures, and a framework for a fee pricing based on the theory of option price valuation. After that, we will introduce the concept of net fee, a number that will allow us to determine whether the investor or the management company is the net winner in a given fee agreement. Finally, we will present a set of computational examples that will display the net fee as a function of the agreement and market variables.

## 2 Hedge Fund Fees

The hedge fund manager charges two types of fees to the fund investors:

- A fixed management fee, usually ranging from 1 % to 2 % of net asset values.
- A performance fee, most commonly equal to 20 % of net profits obtained by the fund.

In this paper we assume a single investor and a single share issued by the fund. The extension to the case of multiple investors and multiple shares is straightforward. Although fees are paid according to a determined schedule (usually monthly or quarterly for management fees and annual for performance fees), we will assume a single payment at the end of a fixed term $T$.

The fund value evolution and fee payment mechanics are denoted as follows: the initial fund supplied by the investor is $X_0$. The hedge fund manager then invests fund assets to create future gross values $X_t$, for $t > 0$. The gross fund value $X_t$ is split between the investor's worth $I_t$ (the net asset value) and the manager's fee $M_t$:

$$X_t = I_t + M_t.$$

At time 0, $X_0 = I_0$ and $M_0 = 0$.

There are countless variations to this basic framework, including hurdles, clawbacks, etc. (for more details on first-loss arrangements see Banzaca [1]). We will ignore those and assume the commonly used version of a management fee equal to $m \cdot X_0$ ($m$ represents a fixed percentage of the initial investment by the investor), and a performance fee of

$$\alpha \cdot (X_T - (1+m)X_0))_+ ,$$

payable only when it is positive, and equal to zero when it is negative. Hence,

$$M_T = m \cdot X_0 + \alpha \cdot (X_T - (1+m)X_0)_+) \tag{1}$$

In other words, while the management fee is a fixed future liability to the investor, the performance fee is a contingent claim on the part of the manager. As a consequence, we will be pricing the management fee simply as a fixed guaranteed fee with a predetermined future cash value, and we will be valuing the performance fee as the value of a certain call option. In our setting, we will assume normally distributed log-returns for the invested assets $X_t$, which allows us to value the performance fee in the Black–Scholes framework. It is worth mentioning that hedge funds managers can speculate on volatility, credit risks, etc. and in contrast to the traditional money managers, they can go long and short. The diversity in investment styles and the different levels of gross and net exposure that they can employ could result in leptokurtic (non-normal) properties in their returns, which is revealed through frequent large negative returns to the left of the return distribution. Generalization of the current framework to models that account for non-normality of the hedge fund returns, for example by employing generalized autoregressive conditional heteroskedasticity (GARCH) models, could be a subject for future research.

## 3 The First-Loss Model

Calpers announced in 2014 that they were exiting hedge fund investments WSJ [10]. While not the main stated reason for their decision, one they mentioned was high fees payable to their hedge fund managers, something that has caught the attention of investors worldwide in the contemporary context of a widely accepted notion that hedge fund fees nowadays are too high. Certain hedge funds are reacting to this shifting balance of power between the sell-side and the buy-side of the investment business with the creation of innovative fee structures which still reward the intellectual capital of the hedge fund manager and allow for business growth but at the same time offer the investor a more symmetric compensation structure.

An example of a first-loss structure is the following:

- The investor provides an investment of \$100M to a fund.
- The fund manager will absorb the first-loss up to 10 % of the initial investment.
- The investor pays a management fee of 1 % to the manager, and performance fee of 50 %.

In our paper we will present a quantitative comparison of the fees payable to the manager and the risk-neutral valuation of the guarantee offered to the investor. We want to note, for the sake of completeness, that there are many other qualitative considerations which are relevant when analyzing both the fee structure as well as the business value offered to a management company by the investor, which are not the objective of this paper. In fact, hedge fund start-ups have become more difficult in recent times, increasing value to any investor action that allows a hedge fund business to succeed. That value is linked to a wide variety of fund characteristics, including the size of assets under management (AUM), the track record, or historical performance, and the reputation of its investor base, among others.

In addition to the initial investment $X_0$, the management fee $m$ and the performance fee $\alpha$, payable at a fixed time horizon $T$, we will now also consider a deposit amount $c$, as a percentage of the initial investment $X_0$, which the manager will provide as a guarantee for losses. Our objective is to analyze the relationship between all four variables to determine whether the investor, or the manager, is the net winner of value-add from a risk-neutral valuation perspective.

## 4 An Option Pricing Framework

The fund value $X_t$ is split between the investors $I_t$ and the manager $M_t$, where, $X_t = I_t + M_t$. In the following sub-sections we derive the payoff function of each player separately, and then price the positions accordingly.

### 4.1 Payoff to the Investor

The payoff to the investor at the terminal time $T$ is:

$$I_T = \begin{cases} X_T - mX_0 - \alpha(X_T - mX_0 - X_0) & \text{when } X_T - mX_0 \geq X_0 \\ X_0 & \text{when } (1-c)X_0 \leq X_T - mX_0 \leq X_0 \\ X_T + (c-m)X_0 & \text{when } X_T - mX_0 \leq (1-c)X_0 \end{cases}$$

or, writing the payoff in a more compact form:

$$\begin{aligned} I_T = \quad & X_T - mX_0 && \text{(pays a management fee)} \\ & -\alpha(X_T - mX_0 - X_0)_+ && \text{(pays a performance fee)} \\ & +(X_0 - X_T + mX_0)_+ - ((1-c)X_0 - X_T + mX_0)_+ && \text{(receives a guarantee)} \end{aligned}$$

Thus, we see that the position of the investor is equivalent to the following portfolio:

- A position in the hedge fund assets, with initial investment $X_0$, less management fee, that is, $X_0 - mX_0$.
- A short position in $\alpha$ call options on the hedge fund assets, with strike price $X_0 + mX_0$ (the performance fee, or performance call option, given to the hedge fund manager).
- A long position in a put option on the fund assets, with the strike price $X_0 + mX_0$ (the insurance put option).
- A short position in a put option on the fund assets, with strike price $(1-c)X_0 + mX_0$ (yielding a cap on the insurance payment).

### 4.2 Payoff to the Manager

The payoff to the manager is $M_T = X_T - I_T$. In other words, the payoff to the hedge fund manager results from the manager having the opposite position in all of the options of the investor. More explicitly,

$$
\begin{aligned}
M_T = \quad & mX_0 && \text{(receives a management fee)} \\
& +\alpha(X_T - mX_0 - X_0)+ && \text{(receives a performance fee)} \\
& -(X_0 - X_T + mX_0)+ + ((1-c)X_0 - X_T + mX_0)+ && \text{(provides a guarantee)}
\end{aligned}
$$

which implies that the hedge fund manager has a portfolio of options consisting of:

- A constant position in the fixed management fee of $mX_0$.
- A long position in $\alpha$ call options on the hedge fund assets, with strike price $X_0 + mX_0$.
- A short position in a put option on the fund assets, with the strike price $X_0 + mX_0$.
- A long position in a put option on the fund assets, with strike price $(1-c)X_0 + mX_0$.

Note that net income to the management company is now no longer guaranteed to be positive. In addition, since the options trades constitute a zero-sum game (the positions of the manager and the investor are opposite each other), the sum of the investor payoff and the manager payoff is equal to $X_T$.

## 4.3 *Valuation: Pricing Fees as Derivatives*

In this section, we will value the positions of the investor and the hedge fund manager using a simple Black–Scholes model for the underlying fund value process. In particular, we employ risk-neutral valuation, and assume that under the risk-neutral probabilities, the fund value process satisfies the stochastic differential equation:

$$dX_t = rX_t\,dt \;+\; \sigma\, X_t\, dW_t, \tag{2}$$

with solution:

$$X_t = X_0 \exp\left((r - \tfrac{\sigma^2}{2})t + \sigma W_t\right) \tag{3}$$

where $W_t$ is a standard Brownian motion, and $r$ and $\sigma$ are positive constants, giving the continuously compounded risk-free interest rate and the volatility of the hedge fund assets respectively. It should be noted that the Black–Scholes framework is applicable to our context as the underlying, that is the fund value, can be dynamically traded. Moreover, in a managed account context, even the liquidity of the fund can be made to match the liquidity of the underlying traded securities.

The Black–Scholes formula can be used to derive the price of the investor's position under the Black–Scholes model:

$$
\begin{aligned}
V_I(0) = X_0 - e^{-rT} mX_0 - \alpha C(X_0, T, X_0 + mX_0, r, \sigma) \\
+P(X_0, T, X_0 + mX_0, r, \sigma) - P(X_0, T, (1-c)X_0 + mX_0, r, \sigma)
\end{aligned} \tag{4}
$$

where $C(X, T, K, r, \sigma)$ is the Black–Scholes price of a call option on a non-dividend paying asset with current value of the underlying $X$, time to expiration $T$, strike price

$K$, risk-free interest rate $r$ and volatility $\sigma$, and $P(X, T, K, r, \sigma)$ is the Black–Scholes put option price with the same parameters as arguments.

# 5 Consequences of the Derivative Pricing Framework

## 5.1 Graphical Analysis

To compare and contrast the traditional and shared-loss fee structures, in our base case we take the investment horizon to be one month, that is $T = 1/12$, the performance fee $\alpha = 50\,\%$, the manager deposit $c = 10\,\%$, the risk-free interest rate $r = 2\,\%$, the volatility $\sigma = 15\,\%$, and the initial investment $X_0 = \$1$. For simplicity and without loss of generality we assume a *zero management fee* for our base case.

With our base case parameters, the total value of the investor's payoff is 1.0073, and the value of the manager's payoff is −0.0073. Notice that the value of the investor's payoff is greater than the initial investment of 1. In contrast, the price of the traditional investor payoff (without the insurance part of the payoff—i.e. removing both put options) is 0.9909, and the value of the manager's payoff in this instance is 0.0091.

### 5.1.1 Payoff Functions of the Investor and the Manager

The payoff functions of the investor under the shared-loss and the traditional fee structures are given in Fig. 1. The payoff to the hedge fund manager using the aforementioned benchmark values and under the shared-loss fee structure is also depicted in Fig. 2 along with the traditional payoff structure with only the performance fee $\alpha(X_T - X_0)_+$. Observe that since the options trades constitute a zero-sum game (the positions of the manager and the investor are opposite each other), the sum of the investor payoff and the manager payoff is equal to $X_T$.

Figure 3 illustrates the 'fair performance fee', where investor gets a payoff with present value equal to his initial cash injection, $X_0$, given volatility and manager's deposit levels, i.e. we set $V_I(0) = X_0$. The fair performance fee can be easily obtained from Eq. (4) as,

$$\alpha_{\text{fair}} = \frac{-e^{-rT} mX_0 + P(X_0, T, X_0 + mX_0, r, \sigma) - P(X_0, T, (1-c)X_0 + mX_0, r, \sigma)}{C(X_0, T, X_0 + mX_0, r, \sigma)}$$

Interested reader can derive explicit, well-known expressions for the sensitivities of the $\alpha_{\text{fair}}$ relative to different parameters in terms of the Greeks and Vega of the involving options. As can be seen from the figure, for small values of volatility, the fair performance fee is indifferent to the levels of manager's deposit; however, as volatility increases, a higher level of deposit by the manager translates into a higher

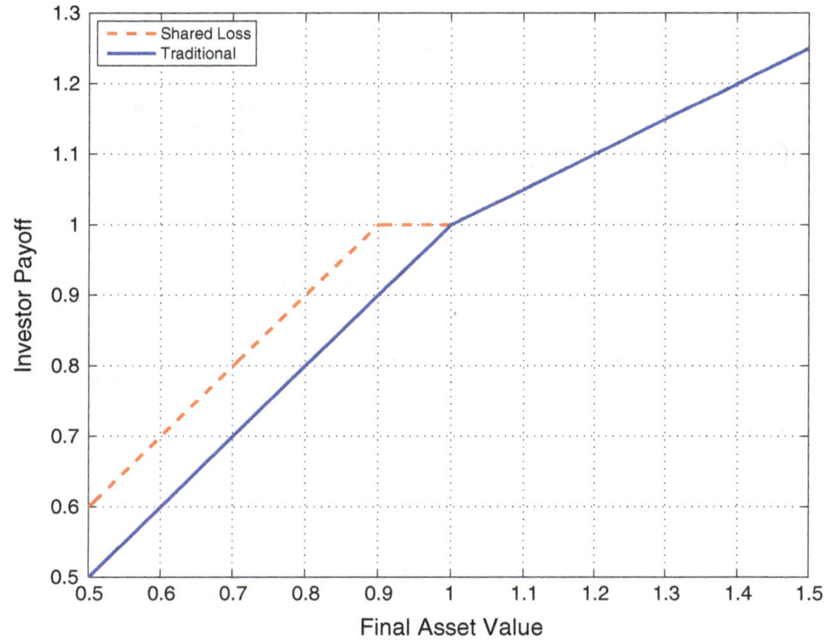


**Fig. 1** Payoff for the hedge fund investor

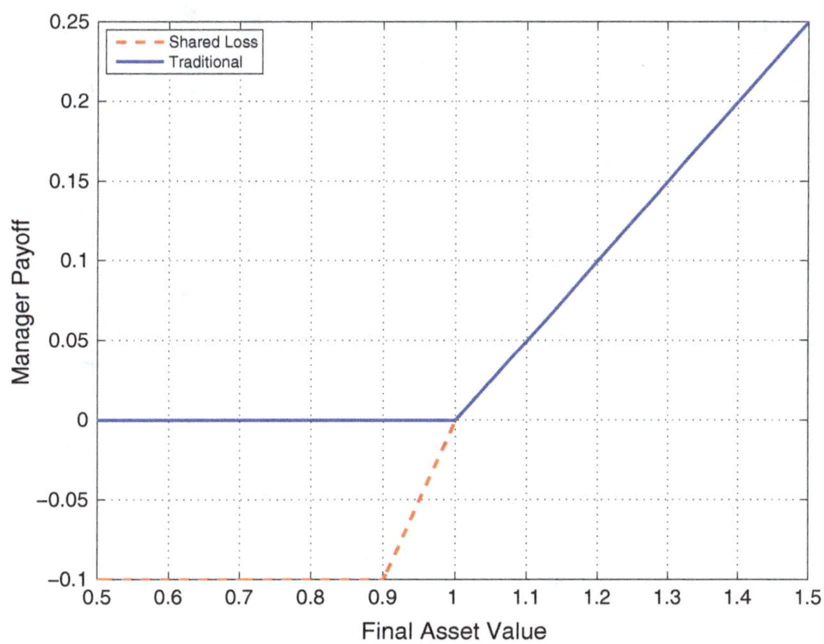


**Fig. 2** Payoff for the hedge fund manager

performance fee paid by the investor to make the deal a fair one. In Fig. 4, we normalize the volatility on the horizontal axis by the manager's deposit defined *as a percentage of the initial investment* $X_0$. For a given level of deposit, the higher the volatility of the underlying investment, the higher the probability that the loss incurred by the manager exceeds the deposit. In other words, the probability that the manager

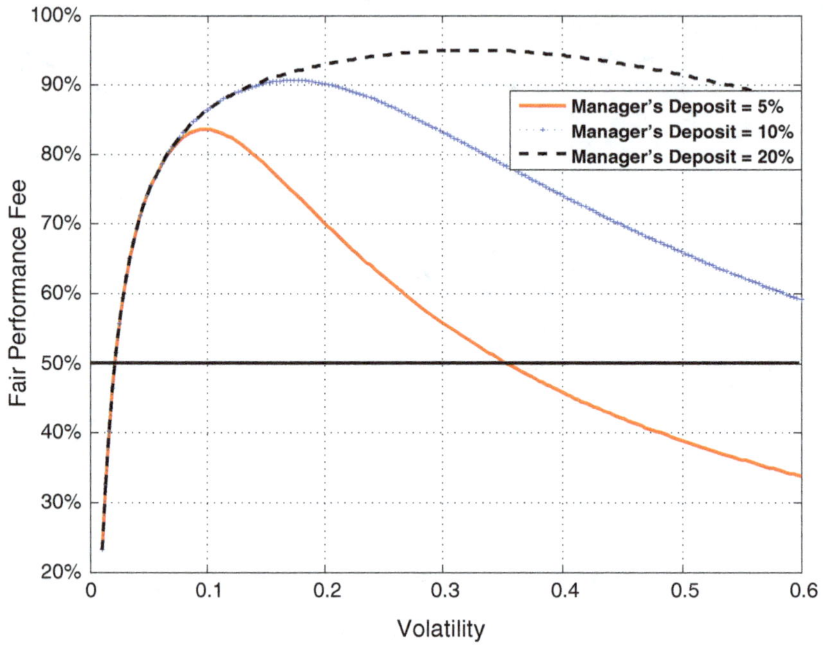


**Fig. 3** Fair performance fee versus volatility

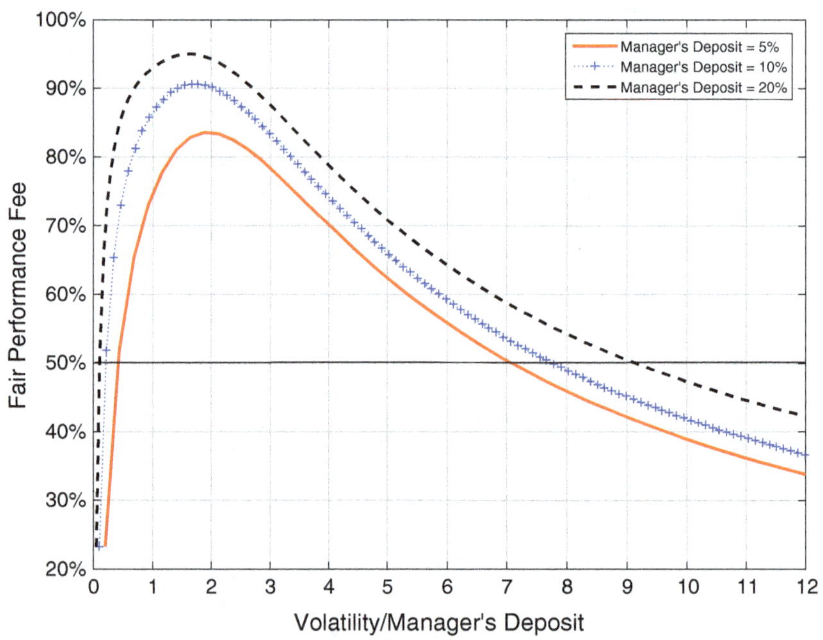


**Fig. 4** Fair performance fee versus normalized (by deposit) volatility

exercises the put option offered by the investor increases, which results in a reversal in the fair performance fee for higher levels of volatility. This is clearly illustrated in Fig. 4 where volatility and deposit are combined in a single scaling variable, that is, volatility/deposit, *where the deposit is expressed as a percentage of the initial investment* $X_0$. The corresponding maximum value for the fair performance fee increases with the size of the deposit; that's because for higher deposits, the manager will have to lose more and more before the investor starts bearing the residual loss, therefore his compensation should be higher accordingly. Note that the x-axis in Figs. 3 and 4 is incorporating the annual volatility of the fund assets; however, the performance fee is crystallized on a monthly basis which suggests a comparison between the deposit level and *monthly* volatility, as opposed to annual volatility. Since returns are assumed to follow a normal distribution in our Black–Scholes framework, one can explicitly calculate the probability of the returns falling into a certain interval, in particular, with about 68 % probability, the return falls within 1 standard deviation of the mean. This explains why the curves for various deposits reach a maximum roughly around the same level of (annual) volatility/deposit ratio, in the [1, 2] interval.

## 5.2 *Sensitivity Analysis*

In this section, we perform a sensitivity analysis of the prices of the investor's and manager's payouts, as a function of the different model parameters.

### 5.2.1 Volatility ($\sigma$)

Figure 5 shows the value of the investor's position as a function of the volatility parameter $\sigma$, as $\sigma$ ranges from 5 % to 60 %.

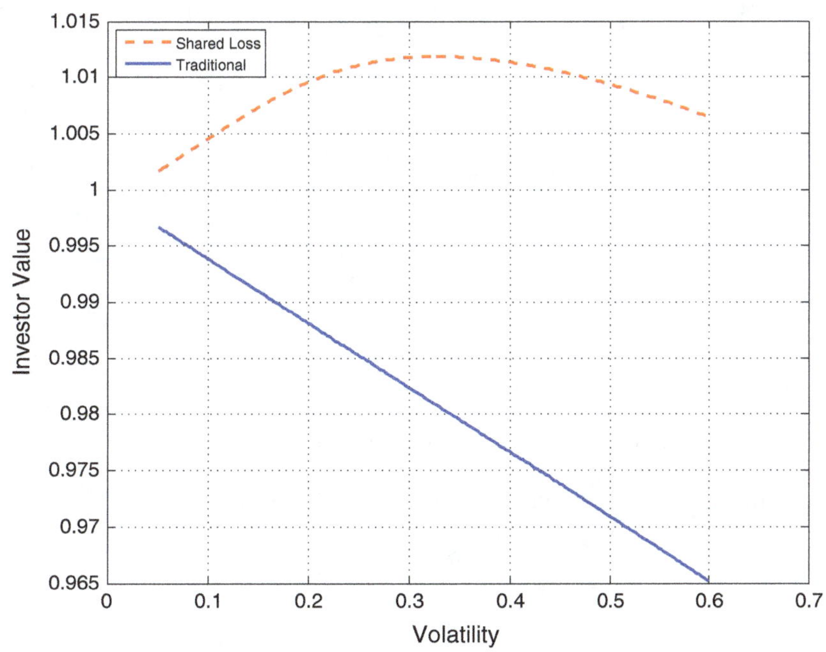


**Fig. 5** Value of the investor's position versus volatility $\sigma$

We see that the position is initially an increasing function of the volatility, owing to the increasing value of the investor's put option as a function of $\sigma$. However, as the volatility becomes very large, the value of the investor's position starts to decline as the hedge fund's call option, as well as its put option, become more valuable. The maximum value for the investor occurs at a volatility around $\sigma = 32.5\,\%$. Observe however, that the value is relatively insensitive to the level of $\sigma$, with a minimum value of 1.0016, and a maximum value of 1.0118.

### 5.2.2 Manager Deposit ($c$)

We varied the manager deposit between 1 % and 25 %, while holding all other parameters at their base case values. The results of the sensitivity analysis are shown in Fig. 6.

As would be expected, the value of the investor's position is an increasing function of the manager's deposit. The value of the position is equal to one (break-even point, or 'fair fee point') at around $c = 0.0233$. Any deposit level less than $c = 0.0233$ puts the investor at a disadvantage, and the investor is indifferent to deposit levels higher than 10 %.

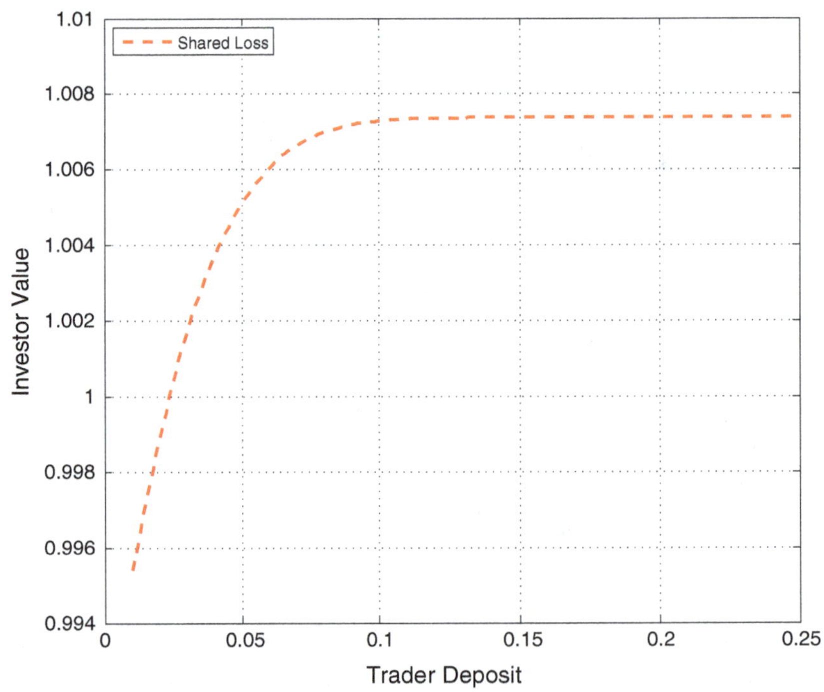


**Fig. 6** Value of the investor's position versus manager's deposit $c$

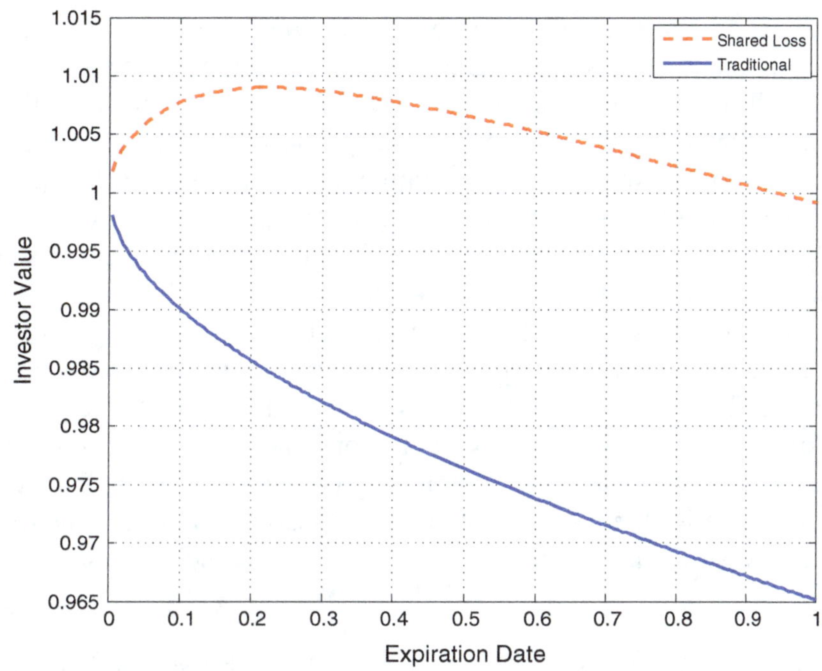


**Fig. 7** Value of the investor's position versus the expiration date $T$

### 5.2.3 Maturity Date ($T$)

The dependence on the time to maturity is of interest specially when adapting the results of this paper to realistic situations. As we mentioned earlier, our mathematical assumption is that fees will be paid at a fixed time in the future. In practice, fees are payable according to calendars agreed between the investors and the manager. In the graphs that follow, we address this by varying the expiration date $T$ from 1 day to 1 year. The results are shown in Fig. 7.

Initially, the value of the position is increasing in $T$, but eventually, it begins to decrease in $T$, as the options given to the hedge fund manager become more valuable. The maximum value of the investor's position occurs at $T$ around one quarter of a year ($T \sim 0.22$).

## 6 Conclusion

The exchange of business value between the manager and the investor is always a complex one: beyond fees paid, there are intangibles the investor gives the manager. An asset management business is valued taking into account many factors, such as track records, years in business, assets under management, the reputation of its investors, and of course fees. In this paper we focus on first-loss fee structures, which are bringing novel points of attention between investors and hedge fund managers in the historical discussions on fair compensation. We focus only on the fee payable by the investor and the guarantee offered by the manager, which is the main novelty in this set up. The main challenge in this new paradigm is to evaluate the value of the guarantee offered by the hedge fund manager in relation to the fee paid by the investor. In this paper, we developed a mathematical approach to compare the two features of guarantee and performance fee from an option pricing perspective. The framework is flexible and can be used for different specific investment settings and can account for slight variations from one fund to another. Our salient leitmotif is: fee agreements must be structured to be attractive to managers so they are willing to participate, and at the same time provide a cushion against losses to the investor. A significant contribution, that sheds light on the road-map and paves the way for deeper investigations, is to see, and more importantly formulate, the underlying fee structure from the lens of option valuation. By employing a risk-neutral framework and options pricing theory, one is able to not only price, but also analyze the sensitivity of the value of the investor's and manager's positions in reference to a set of influential parameters.

**Acknowledgements** We wish to express our gratitude to Sigma Analysis & Management Ltd., and especially to Dr. Ranjan Bhaduri and Mr. Kurt Henry for many endless valuable discussions.

The KPMG Center of Excellence in Risk Management is acknowledged for organizing the conference "Challenges in Derivatives Markets - Fixed Income Modeling, Valuation Adjustments, Risk Management, and Regulation".

**Open Access** This chapter is distributed under the terms of the Creative Commons Attribution 4.0 International License (http://creativecommons.org/licenses/by/4.0/), which permits use, duplication, adaptation, distribution and reproduction in any medium or format, as long as you give appropriate credit to the original author(s) and the source, a link is provided to the Creative Commons license and any changes made are indicated.

The images or other third party material in this chapter are included in the work's Creative Commons license, unless indicated otherwise in the credit line; if such material is not included in the work's Creative Commons license and the respective action is not permitted by statutory regulation, users will need to obtain permission from the license holder to duplicate, adapt or reproduce the material.

## References

1. Banzaca, J.: First loss capital arrangements for hedge fund managers: Structures, risks and the market for key terms. The Hedge Fund Law Report **5**(37), (2012)
2. Carpenter, J.: Does option compensation increase managerial risk appetite? J. Financ. **55**(5), 2311–2331 (2000)
3. Goetzmann, W., Ingersoll, J., Ross, S.: High-water marks and hedge fund management contracts. J. Financ. **58**(4), 1685–1717 (2003)
4. Guasoni, P., Obłój, J.: The incentives of hedge fund fees and high-water marks, forthcoming. Mathematical Finance (2013)
5. He, X., Kou, S.: Profit sharing in hedge funds. www.ssrn.com (2013)
6. Hodder, J., Jackwerth, J.: Incentive contracts and hedge fund management. J. Financ. Quant. Anal. **42**(4), 811–826 (2007)

7. Kouwenberg, R., Ziemba, W.: Incentives and risk taking in hedge funds. J. Bank Financ. **31**, 3291–3310 (2007)
8. Panageas, S., Westerfield, M.: High-water marks: high risk appetites? Convex compensation, long horizons, and portfolio choice. J. Financ. **64**(1), 1–36 (2009)
9. Ross, S.: Compensation, incentives, and the duality of risk aversion and riskiness. J. Financ. **59**(1), 207–225 (2004)
10. WSJ: Calpers to Exit Hedge Funds. http://www.wsj.com/articles/calpers-to-exit-hedge-funds-1410821083?alg=y (2014)

# Negative Basis Measurement: Finding the Holy Scale

**German Bernhart and Jan-Frederik Mai**

**Abstract** Investing into a bond and at the same time buying CDS protection on the same bond is known as buying a basis package. Loosely speaking, if the bond pays more than the CDS protection costs, the position has an allegedly risk-free positive payoff known as "negative basis". However, several different mathematical definitions of the negative basis are present in the literature. The present article introduces an innovative measurement, which is demonstrated to fit better into arbitrage pricing theory than existing approaches. This topic is not only interesting for negative basis investors. It also affects derivative pricing in general, since the negative basis might act as a liquidity spread that contributes as a net funding cost to the value of a transaction; see Morini and Parampolini (Risk, 58–63, 2011, [23]).

**Keywords** Negative basis measurement · Bond-CDS basis · Hidden yield

## 1 Introduction

On first glimpse, it is surprising that investing into a bond and buying CDS protection on that underlying bond, henceforth called a basis package, can earn an attractive spread on top of the risk-free rate of return, as it appears to be free of default risk. This excess return over the risk-free rate is informally called *negative basis*[1]; more formal definitions are given in the main body of this article. [8] has even devoted an entire book to the topic. If, conversely, the cost of CDS protection exceeds the bond earnings, one speaks of a positive basis. In this article, we only speak of negative bases, as fundamentally the concepts of positive and negative basis are simply inverse.

---

[1]Sometimes also called *bond-CDS basis*.;

G. Bernhart · J.-F. Mai (✉)
XAIA Investment, Sonnenstraße 19, 80331 München, Germany
e-mail: jan-frederik.mai@xaia.com

G. Bernhart
e-mail: german.bernhart@xaia.com

© The Author(s) 2016

K. Glau et al. (eds.), *Innovations in Derivatives Markets*, Springer Proceedings in Mathematics & Statistics 165, DOI 10.1007/978-3-319-33446-2_18

The appropriate measurement of negative basis plays an important role with regard to the cost of funding literature, which has become of paramount interest in the financial industry since the recent liquidity crisis. Generally speaking, this stream of literature reconsiders the pricing of derivatives under the new post-crisis fundamentals regarding funding, liquidity, and credit risk issues. Substantial contributions have been made, among others, by [5, 7, 12, 13, 23, 27, 29]. Loosely speaking, most references agree upon the fact that, at least under certain simplifying assumptions (full, bilateral, and continuous collateralization), derivative contracts can be evaluated in the traditional way, only the involved discount factors have to be adjusted by means of a spread accounting for funding and liquidity charges. In particular, [23] show in a simple, theoretical framework that the negative basis is a spread which plays an essential role in this regard. In order to set these theoretical findings into action in the industry's pricing machinery, it is therefore an essential task to establish viable and reasonable measurements for the negative basis. The present article shows that this topic is not only important but also challenging, and contributes a careful comparison of three different measurement methods. In particular, we point out why the most common measurement approaches (denoted by (Z) and (PE) below) are not recommended, and propose a decent alternative.

In the present article, we take the point of view of a negative basis investor whose goal is to detect interesting negative basis positions and to monitor the evolution of such investments over time. Alternatively, consider a bank which has to evaluate its derivative book. As the aforementioned references show that the required discount factors for the pricing algorithms might have to be adjusted by means of the negative basis, one faces the task of measuring this negative basis appropriately. For the effective implementation of these tasks, it is crucial to come up with a reliable and viable, yet reasonable mathematical definition of what the negative basis actually is. Specific focus is put on simple-to-implement approaches that rely on commonly applied pricing methodologies for bonds and CDS, described in, e.g., [18, 25]. In total, we discuss three different measurements (two traditional and one innovative):

- Difference between Z-spread of the bond and CDS running spread, as presented, e.g., in [8], and defined by Bloomberg on the screen YAS.
- Par-equivalent CDS-methodology, as described in the Appendix of [2], who apply this definition for an empirical study, see also [3].
- A hidden yield approach that assumes the risk-free discounting curve to be a reference interest rate curve shifted by the (initially unknown) negative basis.

Important to note is that, according to all these definitions, a negative basis is assigned to a bond, not to an issuer. This means that two different bonds issued by the same company are allowed to have two different negative bases. This viewpoint stands in glaring contrast to some of the more macro-economic considerations carried out in references cited in the next section. CDS protection typically refers to a whole battery of eligible bonds by a reference issuer, and normally the major driver for CDS spreads is considered to be the issuer's default risk. However, some of the deliverable bonds might trade at diverse yields for reasons other than the issuer's default risk—for instance legal issues, liquidity issues, or funding issues, cf. [21] and Sect. 2.

The rest of this article is organized as follows. Section 2 recalls reasons for the existence of negative basis. Section 3 introduces general notations, which are used throughout the remaining sections. Section 4 reviews the traditional methods (Z) and (PE), Sect. 5 discusses the innovative method (HY), and Sect. 6 concludes.

## 2 Why Does Negative Basis Exist?

There are a couple of intuitive explanations for the existence of negative basis, see, e.g., [1, 2, 4, 6, 10, 19, 24, 26, 30]. For the convenience of the reader, we briefly recall some of them in the sequel.

- **Liquidity issues**: Some bond issues are distributed only among a few investors. If one of these investors has to sell her bonds, for instance due to regulatory requirements or demand for liquidity, supply may exceed demand and thus the price of the bond must drop significantly in order for the bond to be sold. At the same time the CDS price might remain unaffected.
- **Funding costs**: From a pure credit risk perspective, selling CDS protection economically is the same risk as buying the underlying bond. However, buying a bond requires an initial investment that must be funded, whereas selling CDS protection typically requires much less initial funding (unless the CDS upfront exceeds the bond price). Therefore, in times of high funding costs there is an incentive to sell CDS rather than to buy bonds, which might lead to an increase in supply of CDS protection, making it cheap relative to bond prices.
- **Market segmentation**: Empirical observations suggest that bond trades sometimes have larger volumes and might be motivated much less by quantitative aspects than CDS trades. Arguing similarly, [6, p. 5, l. 5–7] conjecture that *"market-implied [risk] measures have a stronger impact on the CDS market, while the more easily available rating information affects the bond market more strongly"*. Such instrument-specific differences might contribute to the existence of negative basis.
- **Legal risk**: The bond of the negative basis position might bear certain risks that cannot be protected against by means of a CDS. Examples are certain collective action clauses, debt restructuring events, or call rights for the bond issuer. Such "legal gaps" explain parts of the negative basis.
- **Counterparty credit risk**: A joint default of both the CDS counterparty and the issuer of the bond could lead to a loss for the basis position.[2] These potential losses imply that CDS protection is not 100 % and consequently might contribute to the negative basis, see, e.g., [5, 22].
- **Mark-to-market risk**: The negative basis might further increase after one has entered into the position, due to one of the aforementioned reasons. In this case, one

[2]However, counterparty credit risk can be reduced significantly by a negative basis investor when the CDS is collateralized, which is the usual case.

loses money due to mark-to-market balancing. In theory, one gets this money back eventually, but it might occur that mark-to-market losses exceed one's personal tolerance level during the bond's lifetime. In this case, one has to exit the position and realize the loss. This risk is especially significant if the negative basis position is levered (which has happened heavily during the financial crisis). Part of the negative basis might be viewed as a risk premium for taking this mark-to-market-risk.

Basis "arbitrageurs" are investors that try to earn the negative basis by investing into basis packages. This means that they consider the negative basis an adequate compensation for taking the aforementioned risks. In classical arbitrage theory, their appearance improves trading liquidity. Counterintuitively, however, [9] argue that the advent of CDS was detrimental to bond markets and [20] find some evidence that basis arbitrageurs bring new risks into the corporate bond markets.

## 3 General Notations

All definitions to follow rely on the pricing of CDS and a plain vanilla coupon bond according to the most simple mathematical setup we can think of. This is in order to make the article as reader-friendly as possible; furthermore, we think the setup is already rich enough in order to convey the main ideas. The only randomness considered in the present article is the default time of the bond issuer, which is formally defined on a probability space $(\Omega, \mathscr{F}, \mathbb{Q})$, with state space $\Omega$, $\sigma$-algebra $\mathscr{F}$, and probability measure $\mathbb{Q}$. Expected values with respect to the pricing measure $\mathbb{Q}$ are denoted by $\mathbb{E}$. The default intensity $\lambda(.)$ of the issuer's default time $\tau$ is assumed to be deterministic, i.e. $\mathbb{Q}(\tau > t) = \exp(-\int_0^t \lambda(s)\,\mathrm{d}s)$. Sometimes the function $\lambda(.)$ is constant, sometimes piecewise constant, depending on our application. For example, the computation of a so-called Z-spread requires $\lambda(.)$ to be constant,[3] whereas the joint consistent pricing of several CDS quotes with different maturities requires $\lambda(.)$ to be piecewise constant.

Generally speaking, it is our understanding that a negative basis is a measure for the mispricing between CDS and bonds with respect to default risk alone. This explains why considering the default time as the sole stochastic object corresponds to the most minimal modeling approach possible. Besides the non-randomness of the default intensity, the following further simplifying assumptions are taken for granted throughout:

- We ignore recovery risk: Upon default, the bond holder receives the constant proportion $R \in [0, 1]$ of her nominal. Default is assumed to instantaneously trigger a credit event of the CDS. The bond is assumed to be a deliverable security in the auction following the CDS trigger event, and the auction process is assumed to yield the same recovery rate $R$. Although this is an unrealistic assumption in

[3]See below in Step 3 of Definition 1.

principle (see, e.g., [17]), a negative basis investor can always eliminate recovery risk by delivering his bonds into the auction (physical settlement), in which case he gets compensated by the (nominal-matched) CDS for the nominal loss of the bond.[4] Consequently, our assumption is not severe for the present purpose.
- We ignore interest rate risk: The discounting curve is deterministic and the discount factors are denoted by $DF(t) := \exp(-\int_0^t r(s)\,\mathrm{d}s)$ with some given deterministic short rate function $r(.)$. All presented negative basis figures are measurements relative to the applied short rate function $r(.)$.

Under these assumptions we introduce the following notations:

- $t_j^{(B)}$ denotes the coupon payment dates of the bond.
- The bond's lifetime is denoted by $T$, i.e. $T$ denotes the last coupon payment date, which at the same time is the redemption date. Moreover, the bond is assumed to pay a constant coupon rate $C$ at each coupon payment date.
- $t_i^{(C)}$ denotes the payment dates of the considered CDS contracts, which typically are quarterly on the 20th of March, June, September, and December, respectively, according to the terms and conditions of ISDA standard contracts.[5]
- For a CDS with maturity $T$, the (usually standardized) running coupon is denoted by $s(T)$ and the upfront payment to be made at CDS settlement by $\mathrm{upf}(T)$.
- The <u>e</u>xpected <u>d</u>iscounted value of the sum of all premium payments to be made by the CDS protection buyer (the <u>p</u>remium <u>l</u>eg) is denoted by[6]

$$\begin{aligned} &EDPL(\lambda(.), r(.), s(T), \mathrm{upf}(T), T) \\ &\quad := \mathrm{upf}(T) + s(T) \sum_{0<t_i^{(C)}\leq T} \big(t_i^{(C)} - t_{i-1}^{(C)}\big)\, DF\big(t_i^{(C)}\big)\, \mathbb{Q}\big(\tau > t_i^{(C)}\big) \\ &\quad = \mathrm{upf}(T) + s(T) \sum_{0<t_i^{(C)}\leq T} \big(t_i^{(C)} - t_{i-1}^{(C)}\big)\, DF\big(t_i^{(C)}\big)\, e^{-\int_0^{t_i^{(C)}} \lambda(s)\,\mathrm{d}s}. \end{aligned}$$

- The <u>e</u>xpected <u>d</u>iscounted value of the sum of all default compensation payments to be made by the CDS protection seller (the <u>d</u>efault/protection <u>l</u>eg) is denoted by

$$\begin{aligned} EDDL(\lambda(.), r(.), R, T) &:= (1 - R)\, \mathbb{E}[1_{\{\tau\leq T\}}\, DF(\tau)] \\ &= (1 - R) \int_0^T DF(y)\, \lambda(y)\, e^{-\int_0^y \lambda(s)\,\mathrm{d}s}\, \mathrm{d}y. \end{aligned}$$

---

[4]Interestingly, a mismatch between bond and CDS recovery is often favorable for the negative basis investor, since the CDS recovery rate tends to be lower than the bond recovery, see, e.g., [14]. Thus, it might make sense for a negative basis investor to opt for cash settlement of the CDS and sell his bonds in the marketplace, speculating on a favorable recovery mismatch.

[5]See http://www2.isda.org/asset-classes/credit-derivatives/.

[6]For the sake of notational convenience we ignore accrued interest upon default, which can, of course, be incorporated easily.

- The model price of the bond is given by

$$\begin{aligned}\text{Bond}(\lambda(.), r(.), R, C, T) &:= C \sum_{0<t_j^{(B)}\leq T} \big(t_j^{(B)} - t_{j-1}^{(B)}\big)\, DF\big(t_j^{(B)}\big)\, \mathbb{Q}\big(\tau > t_j^{(B)}\big) \\ &\quad + DF(T)\, \mathbb{Q}(\tau > T) + R\, \mathbb{E}[1_{\{\tau\leq T\}}\, DF(\tau)] \\ &= C \sum_{0<t_j^{(B)}\leq T} \big(t_j^{(B)} - t_{j-1}^{(B)}\big)\, DF\big(t_j^{(B)}\big)\, e^{-\int_0^{t_j^{(B)}} \lambda(s)\,\mathrm{d}s} \\ &\quad + DF(T)\, e^{-\int_0^T \lambda(s)\, ds} + R \int_0^T DF(y)\, \lambda(y)\, e^{-\int_0^y \lambda(s)\,\mathrm{d}s}\,\mathrm{d}y.\end{aligned}$$

# 4 Traditional Measurements

## 4.1 The Z-Spread Methodology

The main idea of the *Z-spread methodology* is to define the negative basis as the difference between (expected) annualized bond earnings and annualized protection costs. This method is described, e.g., in [8]. The negative basis $NB^{(Z)}$ is computed by the following algorithm.

**Definition 1** *(Negative Basis (Z))*

1. A reference discounting curve, resp. the associated short rate $r(.)$, is chosen and used in all subsequent steps, e.g. bootstrapped from quoted prices for interest rate derivatives according to one of the methods described in [15, 16].
2. From a term structure of quoted CDS with different maturities, piecewise constant intensities $\lambda(.)$ are bootstrapped, as described, e.g., in [25]. For this, a recovery assumption is made, i.e. $R$ is model input.[7]
3. Denoting by $B$ the quoted market price of the bond, the bond's **Z-spread** $z$ is defined as the root of the function[8]

$$x \mapsto \text{Bond}(x, r(.), 0, C, T) - B, \tag{1}$$

[7]If CDS prices are quoted in running spreads with zero upfronts, then these quotes typically come naturally equipped with a recovery assumption that is required in order to convert the running spreads into actually tradable standardized coupon and upfront payments. However, after this conversion the recovery rate is a free model parameter.

[8]For a reader-friendly explanation of the Z-spread see [28]. In particular, it is useful to observe that $\text{Bond}(x, r(.), R, C, T) = \text{Bond}(0, r(.) + x, R, C, T)$ for $R = 0$, implying that the Z-spread equals a constant default intensity under a zero recovery assumption.

if existent. In words, the Z-spread is the amount by which the reference short rate $r(.)$ needs to be shifted parallelly in order for the discounted bond cash flows to match the market quote. The root, whenever existing at all, is unique.

4. The (zero-upfront) running CDS spread $s(T)$ for a CDS contract, whose maturity matches the bond's maturity, is defined as

$$s(T) := \frac{EDDL(\lambda(.), r(.), R, T)}{EDPL(\lambda(.), r(.), 1, 0, T)},$$

i.e. the fair running spread when no upfront payment is present.

5. $NB^{(Z)} := z - s(T)$.

Intuitively, the Z-spread $z$ is a measure of the annualized excess return of the bond on top of the "risk-free" rate $r(.)$, whereas $s(T)$ is the annualized CDS protection cost. Hence, $NB^{(Z)}$ equals the difference between earnings and costs (expected in case of survival). If the function (1) does not have a root in $(0, \infty)$, this means that the bond is less risky than the default risk intrinsic in the chosen discounting curve $r(.)$. Especially since the liquidity crisis, when the interbank money transfer ran dry, significant spreads between discounting curves obtained from overnight rates and LIBOR-based swap rates are observed. Consequently, one could recognize, e.g., German government bonds with a "negative Z-spread" with respect to the interest rate curve $r(.)$, which was obtained from 6-month EURIBOR swap rates. For such reasons it has become market standard to extract the "risk-free" discounting curve from overnight rates rather than from LIBOR-based swap rates. Moreover, [19] point out that the difference between bond yields and CDS spreads can depend on whether treasury rates or swap rates are used for discounting. Since negative basis investors are typically trading in the high yield sector, the function (1) normally does have a root in $(0, \infty)$ for several canonical choices of $r(.)$, be it extracted from swap rates with overnight tenor, 3-month tenor, or 6-month tenor. But it is important to stress that all presented negative basis measurements are always relative measures depending on the applied interest rate curve $r(.)$.

The Z-spread methodology has some drawbacks:

- **Imprecision:** Earnings and costs are not measured accurately, but only approximately. The $Z$-spread is only a rough estimate for the expected annualized earnings, and the zero-upfront running CDS spread is also not really tradable, but only a fictitious quantity. Furthermore, the $Z$-spread is earned on the bond value, whereas the CDS spread is paid on the (bond and) CDS nominal, which may result in a nonsense measurement for bonds trading away from par, see Example 1 below. To this end, [10] proposes to replace the $Z$-spread by an asset swap spread. It is possible to define more accurate measurements of earnings and costs taking into account actual cash flows. However, in the present article we do not elaborate on these fine-tunings, since the "earnings and costs"-perspective in general suffers from the following second difficulty.
- **Inaccurate hedge:** The measurement assumes that bond and CDS have the same maturity and nominals and furthermore implicitly assumes a survival

until maturity. Upon a default event the PnL of the position might be considerably different, depending on the timing of the default, see Fig. 1 in Example 1 below. Hence, the assumed CDS hedge cannot really be considered to be default-risk eliminating (it might either profit from or lose on a default event), and consequently the number $NB^{(Z)}$ does not deserve to be called a return figure after elimination of default risk, which the negative basis should be in our opinion.

## 4.2 The Par-Equivalent CDS Methodology

The *par-equivalent CDS methodology* is described in the Appendix of [2]. A similar idea is also outlined in [8, p. 101 ff] and [3]. The negative basis $NB^{(PE)}$ is computed along the steps of the following algorithm.

**Definition 2** (*Negative Basis (PE)*)

1. A reference discounting curve, resp. the associated short rate $r(.)$, is chosen and used in all subsequent steps, e.g. bootstrapped from quoted prices for interest rate derivatives according to one of the methods described in [15, 16].
2. From a term structure of CDS contracts on the reference entity, piecewise constant intensities $\lambda(.)$ are bootstrapped, as described, e.g., in [25]. For this a recovery assumption is made, i.e. $R$ is model input.
3. The (zero-upfront) running CDS spread $s(T)$ for a CDS contract, whose maturity matches the bond's maturity, is defined as
$$s(T) := \frac{EDDL(\lambda(.), r(.), R, T)}{EDPL(\lambda(.), r(.), 1, 0, T)},$$
i.e. the fair running spread when no upfront payment is present.
4. Denoting by $B$ the quoted market price of the bond, a shift $\tilde{z}$ is defined as the root of the function
$$x \mapsto \text{Bond}(\lambda(.) + x, r(.), R, C, T) - B,$$
if existent. In words, the bond is priced with the default intensities $\lambda(.)$ that are consistent with CDS quotes, which are then shifted parallelly until the bond's market quote is matched.
5. A second (zero-upfront) running CDS spread $\tilde{s}(T)$ for a CDS contract, whose maturity matches the bond's maturity, is defined as
$$\tilde{s}(T) := \frac{EDDL(\lambda(.) + \tilde{z}, r(.), R, T)}{EDPL(\lambda(.) + \tilde{z}, r(.), 1, 0, T)},$$
i.e. the fair spread when no upfront payment is present, but now with the shifted intensity rates $\lambda(.) + \tilde{z}$, which are required in order to price the bond correctly.
6. $NB^{(PE)} := \tilde{s}(T) - s(T)$.

The main idea of (PE) is to question the default probabilities bootstrapped from the given CDS quotes, and to adjust them in order to match the bond quote. On a high level, this negative basis measurement is based on the difference between default probabilities that are required in order to match the bond price and default probabilities that are required in order to fit the CDS quotes.

The methodology (PE) has some drawbacks:

- **No link to arbitrage pricing theory:** In our view, there is no convincing economic argument as to why two different survival functions for the same default time should be used. In particular, the method provides no joint pricing model for bond and CDS that explains the negative basis as one of its parameters. The method is "decoupled" from arbitrage pricing theory.
- **No link to "earnings and costs"-perspective:** Unlike the method ($Z$), the method ($PE$) does not have a clear link to an earnings measure above a reference rate, which is what the negative basis is informally thought of.

## 5 An Innovative Methodology

In our opinion, the negative basis should be a spread on top of a reference discounting curve which can be earned without exposure to default risk. This means we question the usual assumption that the applied discounting curve $r(.)$ is the appropriate risk-free rate to be used, because there is actually a higher rate that can be earned "risk-free" (recalling that default risk is the only risk within our tiny model). This motivates what we call the *hidden yield approach*. The negative basis $NB^{(HY)}$ is computed along the steps of the following algorithm.

**Definition 3** (*Negative Basis (HY)*)

1. A reference discounting curve, resp. the associated short rate $r(.)$, is chosen and used in all subsequent steps, e.g. bootstrapped from quoted prices for interest rate derivatives according to one of the methods described in [15, 16].
2. Denote by $\lambda_x(.)$ the piecewise constant intensity rates that are bootstrapped from CDS market quotes, when the assumed discounting curve is $r(.) + x$, as described, e.g., in [25]. The recovery rate $R$ is fixed and chosen as model input.
3. The negative basis $NB^{(HY)}$ is defined as the root[9] of the function

$$x \mapsto \text{Bond}(\lambda_x(.), r(.) + x, R, C, T) - B.$$

In words, $NB^{(HY)}$ is precisely the parallel shift of the reference short rate $r(.)$ which allows for a calibration such that the model prices of bond and CDS match the observed market quotes for bond and CDS.

[9]Lemma A.1 in the Appendix guarantees that this root typically exists and is unique.

The idea of method (HY) can also be summarized as follows: If the risk-free interest rate curve is assumed to be $r(.) + NB^{(HY)}$, then the market quotes for bond and CDS are arbitrage-free (as we have found a corresponding pricing measure). It allows for the intuitive interpretation of the negative basis as a spread earned on top of a reference discounting rate after elimination of default risk. Abstractly speaking, assuming no transaction costs and availability of CDS protection at all maturities $T > 0$ (= perfect market conditions), arbitrage pricing theory suggests the existence of a trading strategy which buys the bond and hedges it via CDS, and which earns[10] precisely the rate $r(.) + NB^{(HY)}$ until the minimum of default time $\tau$ and bond maturity $T$. Since this way of thinking about $NB^{(HY)}$ is its distinctive property and highlights its intrinsic coherence with arbitrage pricing theory, the following lemma demonstrates by a heuristic argument how the rate $r(.) + NB^{(HY)}$ can be earned in a risk-free way.

**Lemma 1** (The rate $r(.) + NB^{(HY)}$ can be earned without default risk) *Assuming perfect market conditions, there exists a (static) portfolio, which is long the bond and invested in several CDS, which earns the rate* $r(.) + NB^{(HY)}$ *until* $\min\{\tau, T\}$.

*Proof (heuristic)* We denote by $\mathbb{Q}$ the probability measure under which $\tau$ has piecewise constant default intensity $\lambda_{NB^{(HY)}}(.)$. We discretize the time interval $[0, T]$ into $m$ buckets $0 =: t_0 < t_1 < \ldots < t_m := T$, but $m$ may be chosen arbitrarily large such that the mesh of the discrete-time grid tends to zero as $m$ tends to infinity. We introduce the following $m + 1$ probabilities:

$$w_j^{(m)} := \mathbb{Q}\big(\tau \in (t_{j-1}, t_j]\big), \quad j = 1, \ldots, m, \quad w_{m+1}^{(m)} := \mathbb{Q}(\tau > t_m).$$

Now let $\tau^{(m)}$ denote a random variable with distribution

$$\mathbb{Q}\Big(\tau^{(m)} = \bar{t}_j\Big) = w_j^{(m)}, \quad \bar{t}_j := \frac{t_{j-1} + t_j}{2}, \quad j = 1, \ldots, m,$$
$$\mathbb{Q}\Big(\tau^{(m)} > t\Big) = \mathbb{Q}(\tau > t), \quad t \geq t_m, \Big(\text{in particular, } \mathbb{Q}(\tau^{(m)} > t_m) = w_{m+1}^{(m)}\Big).$$

Notice that $\tau^{(m)} \approx \tau$ in distribution, with the approximation improving with increasing $m$. In the sequel, we work with $\tau^{(m)}$, assuming that default during $[0, T]$ can only take place at the possible realizations $\bar{t}_1, \ldots, \bar{t}_m$ of $\tau^{(m)}$ in $[0, T]$. We now consider a portfolio of $m + 1$ instruments, namely the bond and one CDS for each maturity $t_1, \ldots, t_m$. We assume that the bond nominal is given by $N_0$. Furthermore, $N_i \in \mathbb{R}$ denotes the nominal of the CDS with maturity $t_i$. Negative nominal means that we sell the bond or sell CDS protection. Let's have a look at the following random variables, which are functions of $\tau^{(m)}$:

[10] By "earning" $r(.) + NB^{(HY)}$ we mean that the internal rate of return of the position is the reference rate $r(.)$ plus a spread $NB^{(HY)}$.

$$V^{(0)}\left(\tau^{(m)}\right) := \left(r(.) + NB^{(HY)}\right)\text{-discounted value of all cash flows from the bond,}$$
$$\text{when default takes place at } \tau^{(m)},$$
$$V^{(i)}\left(\tau^{(m)}\right) := \left(r(.) + NB^{(HY)}\right)\text{-discounted value of all cash flows from the CDS with}$$
$$\text{maturity } t_i, \text{ when default takes place at } \tau^{(m)}, \quad i = 1, \dots, m.$$

All random variables $V^{(i)}\left(\tau^{(m)}\right)$ take on only $m+1$ possible values, since their value on the event $\{\tau^{(m)} > t_m\}$ does not depend on $\tau^{(m)}$ (as there are no cash flows after $t_m$). So without loss of generality we may write $V^{(i)}\left(\tau^{(m)}\right) = V^{(i)}\left(\bar{t}_{m+1}\right)$ for some arbitrary $\bar{t}_{m+1} > t_m$ on the event $\{\tau^{(m)} > t_m\}$. Our goal is to show that it is possible to find a non-zero vector $(N_0, \dots, N_m) \in \mathbb{R}^{m+1}$ such that

$$\underbrace{N_0\, V^{(0)}\left(\tau^{(m)}\right) + \sum_{i=1}^{m} N_i\, V^{(i)}\left(\tau^{(m)}\right)}_{\left(r(.)+NB^{(HY)}\right)\text{-discounted value of outcome}} \equiv \underbrace{N_0\, B + \sum_{i=1}^{m} N_i\, \mathrm{upf}(t_i)}_{\text{initial investment amount}}, \tag{2}$$

where $B$ denotes the market bond price and $\mathrm{upf}(t_i)$ the market upfront of the CDS with maturity $t_i$. This mathematical statement intuitively means that the considered portfolio of bond and CDS earns the rate $r(.) + NB^{(HY)}$ until $\min\{\tau^{(m)}, T\}$ in a risk-free manner, regardless of the actual timing of the default. Now why is this possible? Considering the randomness on the left-hand side of Eq. (2), we actually have $m+1$ equations for the $m+1$ unknowns $N_0, N_1, \dots, N_m$. Rewriting Eq. (2) in terms of linear algebra, we obtain

$$\begin{pmatrix} V^{(0)}(\bar{t}_1) - B & V^{(1)}(\bar{t}_1) - \mathrm{upf}(t_1) & \dots & V^{(m)}(\bar{t}_1) - \mathrm{upf}(t_m) \\ \vdots & & \ddots & \vdots \\ \vdots & & \ddots & \vdots \\ V^{(0)}(\bar{t}_{m+1}) - B & V^{(1)}(\bar{t}_{m+1}) - \mathrm{upf}(t_1) & \dots & V^{(m)}(\bar{t}_{m+1}) - \mathrm{upf}(t_m) \end{pmatrix} \begin{pmatrix} N_0 \\ N_1 \\ \vdots \\ N_m \end{pmatrix} = \begin{pmatrix} 0 \\ 0 \\ \vdots \\ 0 \end{pmatrix}. \tag{3}$$

In order to prove the existence of a non-trivial solution $(N_0, \dots, N_m)$ to Eq. (3), it suffices to verify that the associated $(m+1) \times (m+1)$-matrix does not have full rank. Now here enters the essential heuristic argument: it follows from the definition of $NB^{(HY)}$ that

$$\sum_{j=1}^{m+1} w_j^{(m)}\, V^{(0)}\left(\bar{t}_j\right) \approx B = \sum_{j=1}^{m+1} w_j^{(m)}\, B,$$
$$\sum_{j=1}^{m+1} w_j^{(m)}\, V^{(i)}\left(\bar{t}_j\right) \approx \mathrm{upf}(t_i) = \sum_{j=1}^{m+1} w_j^{(m)}\, \mathrm{upf}(t_i), \quad i = 1, \dots, m,$$

with the approximations becoming equalities as $m \to \infty$. In other words, this means that the rows of the equation system (3) are linearly dependent. Consequently, the associated matrix cannot have full rank and the columns must also be linearly dependent, i.e. there exists a non-zero solution $(N_0, \ldots, N_m)$ of Eq. (3), and hence (2), as desired. Finally, taking a close look at the structure of the involved cash flows, it is obvious that a solution must satisfy $N_0 \neq 0$. Without loss of generality we may hence set $N_0 = 1$ (because if $(N_0, \ldots, N_m)$ is a solution, so is $\alpha\,(N_0, \ldots, N_m)$ for arbitrary $\alpha \in \mathbb{R}$). Concluding, the portfolio we have found is long the bond. □

We present an example that demonstrates how different the three presented measurements of negative basis can be in practice. The specifications are inspired by a real-world case.

*Example 1* We consider a bond with maturity $T = 3.5$ years paying a semi-annual coupon rate of $C = 8.25\,\%$. It trades far below par value, namely at $B = 46.5\,\%$. An almost maturity-matched CDS contract is available at an upfront value of $\text{upf}(T) = 53\,\%$ with a running coupon of $s(T) = 5\,\%$, payed quarterly. This means a nominal-matched negative basis investment comes at a package price of $46.5 + 53 = 99.5\,\%$, and pays a coupon rate of $8.25 - 5 = 3.25\,\%$ until default (however, the bond and CDS coupon payments have different frequencies and payment dates). In the sequel we assume a recovery rate of $R = 20\,\%$, and the reference rate $r(.)$ is bootstrapped from 3-month tenor-based interest rate swaps according to the raw interpolation method described in [15, 16]. Because the bond trades far below par, the measurement (Z) is highly questionable and returns $NB^{(Z)} = -0.42\,\%$, which is clearly not an appropriate measurement. As indicated earlier, improved versions of earnings and costs-measurements must be used in order to deal with such extreme situations of highly distressed bonds, but this lies outside the scope of the present article. The par-equivalent CDS methodology returns the measurement $NB^{(PE)} = 2.29\,\%$, whereas the hidden yield methodology returns the significantly lower number $NB^{(HY)} = 1.18\,\%$. While the authors are not aware of a strategy how to monetize the (PE)-measurement 2.29 %, Lemma 1 provides a clear interpretation for the (HY)-measurement 1.18 % in terms of an internal rate of return that can be earned on top of the risk-free rate, when the negative basis investment is structured as indicated in the proof of Lemma 1.

Now if the described nominal-matched investment seems to earn a rate of 3.25 %, which equals a spread of around 1.75 % above the chosen reference rate $r(.)$ in the present example, why is the measurement $NB^{(HY)}$ so low? Fig. 1 visualizes the discounted value of the sum over all cash flows from the nominal-matched investment in dependence of the default time. For instance, in case of survival until maturity, this value equals approximately 104 %, yielding a return (after discounting) of 5.61 % on the initial investment of 98.39 % (which equals the package price minus accrued CDS coupon, the bond accrued equals zero). Distributed on the 3.5-year investment horizon, this corresponds to a rate of approximately 1.6 % per annum. However, in case of a default just before the first or second bond coupon payment date the

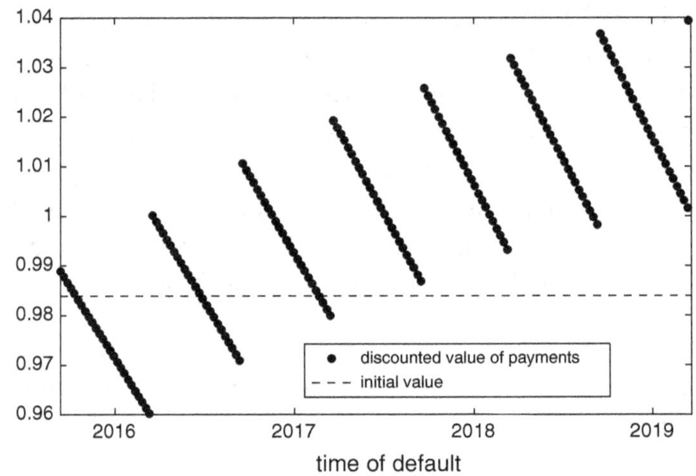


**Fig. 1** Sum over all discounted cash flows arising from the described nominal-matched negative basis investment are depicted, in dependence on the time of default

described negative basis investment faces a loss. The additional short-dated CDS-protection required in order to hedge these potential losses decreases the earnings potential of the investment, which is accounted for in the (HY)-methodology, as explained in the proof of Lemma 1.

## 6 Conclusion

We proposed an innovative measurement for the negative basis, denoted $NB^{(HY)}$. Compared to traditional approaches, it is based on an arbitrage-free pricing model for the simultaneous pricing of the bond and the CDS, which provides a sound economic interpretation. Within a simple model with only default risk being present, the negative basis is perfectly explained as the spread on top of a reference interest rate curve $r(.)$. It was pointed out how the rate $r(.) + NB^{(HY)}$ can be earned without exposure to default risk.

**Acknowledgements** The KPMG Center of Excellence in Risk Management is acknowledged for organizing the conference "Challenges in Derivatives Markets - Fixed Income Modeling, Valuation Adjustments, Risk Management, and Regulation".

## Appendix: The algorithm in Definition 3 is well-defined

The following technical lemma guarantees that Step 3 in Definition 3 admits a unique solution that can be found efficiently by means of a bisection routine.

**Lemma A.1** (Method (HY) is well-defined)

*(a) The function* $x \mapsto Bond(\lambda_x(.), r(.) + x, R, C, T)$ *is continuous.*

(b) *The function* $x \mapsto Bond(\lambda_x(.), r(.) + x, R, C, T)$ *is decreasing on the interval* $[-\inf\{r(t)\,:\,t \geq 0\}, \infty)$.
(c) *We have the lower bound* $Bond(\lambda_x(.), r(.) + x, R, C, T) \geq \frac{R}{1-R}\, upf(T)$.

*Proof* We prove parts (a), (b), and (c) separately.

(a) For fixed $x$, the function $\lambda_x(.)$ is piecewise constant, so actually we only deal with a finite vector of values of the default intensity, depending on $x$. For the remainder of the proof we denote these values by $(y_1(x), \ldots, y_m(x))$. In other words, we observe $m$ CDS maturities $T_1, \ldots, T_m$ and the value $y_k(x)$ is the level of the default intensity on the piece $(T_{k-1}, T_k]$, for $k = 1, \ldots, m$, with $T_0 := 0$. Obviously, the bond price then equals a concatenation of continuous functions if each $y_k(x)$ is continuous in $x$. However, this is guaranteed by the implicit function theorem since $y_k(x)$ is defined as the implicit function yielding the root of a smooth function. Concluding, continuity of the bond price is clear.
(b) In order to see that the bond price is decreasing in $x$, we first re-write it as

$$
\begin{aligned}
\mathrm{Bond}(\lambda_x(.), r(.) + x, R, C, T) = {} & e^{-\int_0^T \lambda_x(s)+r(s)+x\,\mathrm{d}s} \\
& + C \sum_{0<t_j^{(B)} \leq T} \left(t_j^{(B)} - t_{j-1}^{(B)}\right) e^{-\int_0^{t_j^{(B)}} \lambda_x(s)+r(s)+x\,\mathrm{d}s} \\
& + \frac{R}{1-R}\, EDPL(\lambda_x(.), r(.) + x, \mathrm{upf}(T), T),
\end{aligned}
$$

where we have used $EDPL = EDDL$ from the CDS boostrap. This shows that it suffices to check that the function

$$x \mapsto \lambda_x(t) + x$$

is increasing for each fixed $t$, because all summands in the above bond formula are then obviously decreasing.
We proceed with an auxiliary observation. If $\tau_1$ and $\tau_2$ are two positive random variables with distribution functions $F_1$ and $F_2$, satisfying $F_1 \geq F_2$ pointwise on an interval $(T, \infty)$ and $F_1 \equiv F_2$ on $[0, T]$, then $\mathbb{E}[g(\tau_1)] \geq \mathbb{E}[g(\tau_2)]$ for any bounded function $g : (0, \infty) \to [0, K]$, which is non-increasing on $(T, \infty)$. To verify this,[11] define the non-decreasing function $h := -g$ and use integration by parts:

[11]One says that $\tau_1$ is less than $\tau_2$ in the usual stochastic order, and the following computation is standard in the respective theory.

$$\begin{aligned}
\mathbb{E}[g(\tau_1)] &= -\int h\,\mathrm{d}F_1 = -\int_{(0,T]} h\,\mathrm{d}F_1 - \int_{(T,\infty)} h\,\mathrm{d}F_1 \\
&= -\int_{(0,T]} h\,\mathrm{d}F_2 - \Big(h(\infty)\underbrace{F_1(\infty)}_{=1=F_2(\infty)} - h(T)\underbrace{F_1(T)}_{=F_2(T)} - \int_{(T,\infty)} F_1\,\mathrm{d}h\Big) \\
&\geq -\int_{(0,T]} h\,\mathrm{d}F_2 - \Big(h(\infty)\,F_2(\infty) - h(T)\,F_2(T) - \int_{(T,\infty)} F_2\,\mathrm{d}h\Big) \\
&= -\int_{(0,T]} h\,\mathrm{d}F_2 - \int_{(T,\infty)} h\,\mathrm{d}F_2 = -\int h\,\mathrm{d}F_2 = \mathbb{E}[g(\tau_2)].
\end{aligned}$$

Now we proceed inductively over $k = 1, \ldots, m$ by showing that $x \mapsto \lambda_x(t) + x$ is non-decreasing for all fixed $t \in (T_{k-1}, T_k]$, i.e. that $x \mapsto y_k(x) + x$ is non-decreasing. We start the induction for $k = 1$. To this end, recall that $y_1(x)$ is the unique root of the equation

$$EDPL(y_1(x), r(.) + x, s(T_1), \mathrm{upf}(T_1), T_1) = EDDL(y_1(x), r(.) + x, R, T_1).$$

For the sake of a more compact notation we denote the left-hand side of the last equation by $LHS(x, y_1(x))$ and the right-hand side by $RHS(x, y_1(x))$. Furthermore, we denote the value of both sides by $V(x) := LHS(x, y_1(x)) = RHS(x, y_1(x))$. Since all the summands of $LHS$ depend on the function $x \mapsto x + y_1(x)$ in a monotonic way, it is obvious that $V(x)$ is non-increasing in $x$ if and only if the function $x \mapsto x + y_1(x)$ is non-decreasing. Hence, it suffices to prove that $V(x)$ is non-increasing in $x$. To this end, we (obviously) observe with $\varepsilon > 0$ that

$$LHS(x+\varepsilon, y_1(x)) \leq LHS(x, y_1(x)) = V(x), \tag{4}$$
$$RHS(x+\varepsilon, y_1(x)) \leq RHS(x, y_1(x)) = V(x). \tag{5}$$

Furthermore, the function $y \mapsto LHS(x+\varepsilon, y)$ is obviously strictly decreasing. Concerning the right-hand side, we denote by $\mathbb{E}_y[f(\tau)]$ the expectation over $f(\tau)$ when the default time $\tau$ has an exponential distribution with parameter $y$. The function

$$y \mapsto RHS(x+\varepsilon, y) = (1-R)\,\mathbb{E}_y\Big[e^{-\int_0^\tau r(s)+x+\varepsilon\,\mathrm{d}s}\,1_{\{\tau \leq T_1\}}\Big]$$

is non-decreasing on the claimed interval by the auxiliary observation we have derived above (increasing $y$ corresponds to increasing the distribution function of the default time $\tau$ pointwise[12]). We now distinguish two cases:

[12]Here, we have used that the function $\tau \mapsto \exp(-\int_0^\tau r(s) + x + \varepsilon\,\mathrm{d}s)\,1_{\{\tau \leq T_1\}}$ is non-increasing if $x \geq -\inf\{r(t) : t \geq 0\}$.

(i) $LHS(x+\varepsilon, y_1(x)) \leq RHS(x+\varepsilon, y_1(x))$:
In this case $y_1(x+\varepsilon) \leq y_1(x)$, because otherwise we would observe the following contradiction:

$$\begin{aligned} LHS(x+\varepsilon, y_1(x+\varepsilon)) &< LHS(x+\varepsilon, y_1(x)) \leq RHS(x+\varepsilon, y_1(x)) \\ &\leq RHS(x+\varepsilon, y_1(x+\varepsilon)). \end{aligned}$$

This implies that

$$V(x+\varepsilon) = RHS(x+\varepsilon, y_1(x+\varepsilon)) \leq RHS(x+\varepsilon, y_1(x)) \overset{(5)}{\leq} V(x).$$

(ii) $LHS(x+\varepsilon, y_1(x)) > RHS(x+\varepsilon, y_1(x))$:
In this case $y_1(x+\varepsilon) \geq y_1(x)$, because otherwise we would observe the following contradiction:

$$\begin{aligned} RHS(x+\varepsilon, y_1(x+\varepsilon)) &\leq RHS(x+\varepsilon, y_1(x)) < LHS(x+\varepsilon, y_1(x)) \\ &\leq LHS(x+\varepsilon, y_1(x+\varepsilon)). \end{aligned}$$

This implies that

$$V(x+\varepsilon) = LHS(x+\varepsilon, y_1(x+\varepsilon)) \leq LHS(x+\varepsilon, y_1(x)) \overset{(4)}{\leq} V(x).$$

Concluding, $V(x)$ is non-increasing in $x$ and the induction start is finished. We proceed with the induction step, assuming that we already know that $x + \lambda_x(t)$ is non-decreasing in $x$ for each fixed $t \leq T_{k-1}$. To this end, recall that $y_k(x)$ is the unique root of the equation

$$EDPL(\lambda_x(.), r(.)+x, s(T_k), \mathrm{upf}(T_k), T_k) = EDDL(\lambda_x(.), r(.)+x, R, T_k),$$

where $y_k(x)$ enters the equation as the function value of $\lambda_x(.)$ on the interval $(T_{k-1}, T_k]$. The left-hand side of the last equation can be rewritten as follows, using the standard market convention of standardized CDS strike rates $s(T_{k-1}) = s(T_k) =: s$:

$$\begin{aligned} &EDPL(\lambda_x(.), r(.)+x, s, \mathrm{upf}(T_k), T_k) \\ &\quad = EDPL(\lambda_x(.), r(.)+x, s, upf(T_{k-1}), T_{k-1}) + \mathrm{upf}(T_k) - \mathrm{upf}(T_{k-1}) \\ &\quad + s \sum_{T_{k-1} < t_i^{(C)} \leq T_k} \left(t_i^{(C)} - t_{i-1}^{(C)}\right) e^{-\int_0^{t_i^{(C)}} \lambda_x(s)+r(s)+x \, \mathrm{d}s}. \end{aligned}$$

Similarly, the right-hand side can be rewritten as follows:

$$\begin{aligned} EDDL(\lambda_x(.), r(.)+x, R, T_k) &= EDDL(\lambda_x(.), r(.)+x, R, T_{k-1}) \\ &\quad + (1-R)\, y_k(x) \int_{T_{k-1}}^{T_k} e^{-\int_0^t r(s)+x+\lambda_x(s)\, \mathrm{d}s} \, \mathrm{d}t. \end{aligned}$$

Since the values $(y_1(x), \dots, y_{k-1}(x))$ have been determined before, we may subtract the *EDDL* and *EDPL* with maturity $T_{k-1}$ on both sides of the defining equation for $y_k(x)$, simplifying the latter to

$$\begin{aligned}\operatorname{upf}(T_k) - \operatorname{upf}(T_{k-1}) + s \sum_{T_{k-1} < t_i^{(C)} \le T_k} \left(t_i^{(C)} - t_{i-1}^{(C)}\right) e^{-\int_0^{t_i^{(C)}} \lambda_x(s) + r(s) + x \, \mathrm{d}s} \\ = (1-R)\, y_k(x) \int_{T_{k-1}}^{T_k} e^{-\int_0^t r(s) + x + \lambda_x(s)\, \mathrm{d}s}\, \mathrm{d}t.\end{aligned}$$

Again, we denote the left-hand side of the last equation by $LHS(x, y_1(x), \dots, y_k(x))$, and the right-hand side is denoted $RHS(x, y_1(x), \dots, y_k(x))$. Furthermore, we denote the value of both sides by

$$V(x) := LHS(x, y_1(x), \dots, y_k(x)) = RHS(x, y_1(x), \dots, y_k(x)).$$

By induction hypothesis, the function $x \mapsto x + \lambda_x(t)$ is non-decreasing for each $t \le T_{k-1}$. With $\varepsilon > 0$ this obviously implies that

$$\begin{aligned}&LHS(x+\varepsilon, y_1(x+\varepsilon), \dots, y_{k-1}(x+\varepsilon), y_k(x)) \\ &\quad \le LHS(x, y_1(x), \dots, y_k(x)) = V(x), \qquad (6) \\ &RHS(x+\varepsilon, y_1(x+\varepsilon), \dots, y_{k-1}(x+\varepsilon), y_k(x)) \\ &\quad \le RHS(x, y_1(x), \dots, y_k(x)) = V(x). \qquad (7)\end{aligned}$$

Also, the function $y \mapsto LHS(x+\varepsilon, y_1(x+\varepsilon), \dots, y_{k-1}(x+\varepsilon), y)$ is obviously non-increasing, whereas the function $y \mapsto RHS(x+\varepsilon, y_1(x+\varepsilon), \dots, y_{k-1}(x+\varepsilon), y)$ is non-decreasing by a similar argument as in the induction start, namely: the right-hand side has the form[13]

$$\begin{aligned}&RHS(x+\varepsilon, y_1(x+\varepsilon), \dots, y_{k-1}(x+\varepsilon), y) \\ &\quad = (1-R)\, \mathbb{E}_y\Big[e^{-\int_0^\tau r(s) + x + \varepsilon\, \mathrm{d}s}\, 1_{\{\tau \in (T_{k-1}, T_k]\}}\Big],\end{aligned}$$

which is non-decreasing in $y$. Why? Because an increase of $y$ increases the distribution function of $\tau$ pointwise on $[T_{k-1}, \infty)$ but leaves it unchanged on $[0, T_{k-1}]$, and the function $\tau \mapsto \exp(-\int_0^\tau r(s) + x\, \mathrm{d}s)\, 1_{\{\tau \in (T_{k-1}, T_k]\}}$ is clearly non-increasing on $(T_{k-1}, \infty)$ (so that our auxiliary observation above applies). Like in the induction start, showing that $x \mapsto x + y_k(x)$ is non-decreasing in $x$ is equivalent to showing that $V(x)$ is non-increasing in $x$. The remaining proof is now completely analogous to the induction start (this is an exercise we leave to the reader).

[13] Similar as in the induction start, we denote by $\mathbb{E}_y[f(\tau)]$ the expectation over $f(\tau)$ when the default time has piecewise constant intensity with the level $y$ on the piece $(T_{k-1}, T_k]$.

(c) Denoting by $\mathbb{Q}_x$ the probability measure in dependence of the default intensities $\lambda_x(.)$, we have

$$\text{Bond}(\lambda_x(.), r(.) + x, R, C, T) := C \sum_{0<t_j^{(B)} \leq T} DF\big(t_j^{(B)}\big)\big(t_j^{(B)} - t_{j-1}^{(B)}\big)\,\mathbb{Q}_x\big(\tau > t_j^{(B)}\big) + DF(T)\,\mathbb{Q}_x(\tau > T) + R\,\mathbb{E}_x[1_{\{\tau \leq T\}}\, DF(\tau)].$$

We know from the consistent CDS pricing that the appearing expectation can be replaced by the premium leg of the CDS, which allows to be estimated by the upfront, i.e.

$$\mathbb{E}_x[1_{\{\tau \leq T\}}\, DF(\tau)] = \frac{R}{1-R} EDPL(\lambda_x(.), r(.) + x, s(T), \text{upf}(T), T) \geq \frac{R}{1-R}\,\text{upf}(T),$$

which in turn implies the claim.

**Open Access** This chapter is distributed under the terms of the Creative Commons Attribution 4.0 International License (http://creativecommons.org/licenses/by/4.0/), which permits use, duplication, adaptation, distribution and reproduction in any medium or format, as long as you give appropriate credit to the original author(s) and the source, a link is provided to the Creative Commons license and any changes made are indicated.

The images or other third party material in this chapter are included in the work's Creative Commons license, unless indicated otherwise in the credit line; if such material is not included in the work's Creative Commons license and the respective action is not permitted by statutory regulation, users will need to obtain permission from the license holder to duplicate, adapt or reproduce the material.

## References

1. Andritzky, J., Singh, M.: The pricing of credit default swaps during distress. IMF Working Paper 06/254 (2006)
2. Bai, J., Collin-Dufresne, P.: The determinants of the CDS-Bond basis during the financial crises of 2007–2009. Working Paper (2011)
3. Beinstein, E., Scott, A., Graves, B., Sbityakov, A., Le, K., Goulden, J., Muench, D., Doctor, S., Granger, A., Saltuk, Y., Allen, P.: Credit Derivatives Handbook. J.P. Morgan Corporate Quantitative Research (2006)
4. Blanco, R., Brennan, S., Marsh, I.W.: An empirical analysis of the dynamic relation between investment-grade bonds and credit default swaps. J. Financ. **60**(5), 2255–2281 (2005)
5. Brigo, D., Capponi, A., Pallavicini, A.: Arbitrage-free bilateral counterparty risk valuation under collateralization and application to Credit Default Swaps. Math. Financ. **24**(1), 125–146 (2014)
6. Bühler, W., Trapp, M.: Explaining the bond-CDS basis-the role of credit risk and liquidity. In: Risikomanagement und kapitalmarktorientierte Finanzierung: Festschrift für Bernd Rudolph zum 65. Geburtstag, Knapp-Verlag, Frankfurt a. Main, pp. 375–397 (2009)
7. Burgard, C., Kjaer, M.: In the balance. Risk pp. 72–75 (2011)

8. Choudhry, M.: The Credit Default Swap Basis. Bloomberg Press, New York (2006)
9. Das, S., Kalimipalli, M.: Did CDS trading improve the market for corporate bonds? J. Financ. Econ. **111**(2), 495–525 (2014)
10. De Wit, J.: Exploring the CDS-Bond basis. National Bank of Belgium working paper No. 104 (2006)
11. Doctor, S., White, D., Elizalde, A., Goulden, J., Toublan, D.D.: Differential discounting for CDS: J.P. Morgan Europe Credit Research (2012)
12. Fries, C.: Discounting Revisited: Valuation Under Funding, Counterparty Risk and Collateralization. Working paper (2010), available at SSRN: http://ssrn.com/abstract=1609587
13. Fujii, M., Shimada, Y., Takahashi, A.: Collateral Posting and Choice of Collateral Currency. CIRJE Discussion Papers (2010)
14. Gupta, S., Sundaram, R.K.: Mispricing and arbitrage in CDS auctions. J. Deriv. **22**(4), 79–91 (2015)
15. Hagan, P.S., West, G.: Interpolation methods for curve construction. Appl. Math. Financ. **13**(2), 89–129 (2006)
16. Hagan, P.S., West, G.: Methods for constructing a yield curve. Wilmott magazine pp.70–81 (2008)
17. Höcht, S., Kunze, M., Scherer, M.: Implied recovery rates-auction and models. In: Innovations in Quantitative Risk Management. Springer, Berlin pp. 147–162 (2015)
18. Hull, J., White, A.: Valuing credit default swaps I: no counterparty default risk. J. Deriv. **8**(1), 29–40 (2000)
19. Hull, J., Predescu, M., White, A.: The relationship between credit default swap spreads, bond yields, and credit rating announcements. J. Bank. Financ. **28**, 2789–2811 (2004)
20. Li, H., Zhang, W., Kim, G.H.: The CDS-Bond basis and the cross section of corporate bond returns. Working paper (2011)
21. Longstaff, F.A., Neis, E., Mithal, S.: Corporate yield spreads: default risk or liquidity? New evidence from the credit-default swap market. J. Financ. **60**(5), 2213–2253 (2005)
22. Mai, J.-F., Scherer, M.: Simulating from the copula that generates the maximal probability for a joint default under given (inhomogeneous) marginals. In: Melas, V.B. et al.: Topics in Statistical Simulation: Springer Proceedings in Mathematics and Statistics, vol. 114, pp. 333–341, Springer, Heidelberg (2014)
23. Morini, M., Prampolini, A.: Risky funding with counterparty and liquidity charges. Risk pp. 58–63 (2011)
24. O'Kane, D.: The link between Eurozone sovereign debt and CDS prices. EDHEC-Risk Institute Working Paper (2012)
25. O'Kane, D., Turnbull, S.: Valuation of credit default swaps. Fixed Income Quantitative Research Lehman Brothers (2003)
26. Palladini, G., Portes, R.: Sovereign CDS and bond pricing dynamics in the Euro-area. Centre for Economic Policy Research Discussion Paper No. 8651 (2011)
27. Pallavicini, A., Perini, D., Brigo, D.: Funding Valuation Adjustment: A Consistent Framework Including CVA, DVA, Collateral, Netting Rules and Re-Hypothecation. Working paper (2011), available at SSRN: http://ssrn.com/abstract=1969114
28. Pedersen, C.M.: Explaining the Lehman Brothers option adjusted spread of a corporate bond. Fixed Income Quantitative Credit Research, Lehman Brothers (2006)
29. Piterbarg, V.: Funding beyond discounting: collateral agreements and derivatives pricing. Risk, pp. 97–102 (2010)
30. Zhu, H.: An empirical comparison of credit spreads between the bond market and the credit default swap market. BIS Working Paper No. 160 (2004)

# The Impact of a New CoCo Issuance on the Price Performance of Outstanding CoCos

**Jan De Spiegeleer, Stephan Höcht, Ine Marquet and Wim Schoutens**

**Abstract** Contingent convertible bonds (CoCos) are new hybrid capital instruments that have a loss absorbing capacity which is enforced either automatically via the breaching of a particular CET1 level or via a regulatory trigger. The price performance of outstanding CoCos, after a new CoCo issue is announced by the same issuer, is investigated in this paper via two methods. The first method compares the returns of the outstanding CoCos after an announcement of a new issue with some overall CoCo indices. This method does not take into account idiosyncratic movements and basically compares with the general trend. A second model-based method compares the actual market performance of the outstanding CoCos with a theoretical model. The main conclusion of the investigation of 24 cases of new CoCo bond issues is a moderated negative effect on the outstanding CoCos.

**Keywords** Contingent convertibles · CoCo bonds · New issuance

## 1 Introduction

Contingent convertible bonds or CoCo bonds are new hybrid capital instruments that have a loss absorbing capacity which is enforced either automatically via the breaching of a particular CET1 level or via a regulatory trigger. CoCos either convert

J. De Spiegeleer (✉) · I. Marquet · W. Schoutens
Department of Mathematics, KU Leuven, Celestijnenlaan 200B,
Box 2400, 3001 Leuven, Belgium
e-mail: Jan.Spiegeleer@mac.com

I. Marquet
e-mail: Ine.Marquet@wis.kuleuven.be

W. Schoutens
e-mail: wim@schoutens.be

S. Höcht
Assenagon GmbH, Prannerstraße 8, 80333 München, Germany
e-mail: Stephan.Hoecht@assenagon.com

© The Author(s) 2016

K. Glau et al. (eds.), *Innovations in Derivatives Markets*, Springer Proceedings
in Mathematics & Statistics 165, DOI 10.1007/978-3-319-33446-2_19

into equity or suffer a write-down of the face value upon the appearance of such a trigger event.

The financial crisis of 2007–2008 triggered an avalanche of financial worries for financial institutions around the globe. After the collapse of Lehman Brothers, governments intervened and bailed out banks using tax-payers money. Preventing such bail-outs in the future, and designing a more stable banking sector in general, requires both higher capital levels and regulatory capital of a higher quality. The implementation under the new regulatory frameworks like Basel III and Capital Requirement Directive IV (CRD IV) tries to achieve this in various ways, i.e. with the use of CoCo bonds (Basel Committee on Banking Supervision [1], European Commision [2]). CoCo bonds are allowed as new capital instruments by the Basel III guidelines. The Swiss regulators have forced their systemic important banks to issue large amounts of these instruments. Further, the European CRD IV which entered into force on 17 July 2013 enforces all new additional Tier 1 instruments to have CoCo features.

The specific design of a CoCo bond enhances the capital of a bank when it is in trouble in an automatic way. Hence, a loss-absorbing cushion is created with the aim to avoid or at least to reduce potential interventions using tax-payers' money.

The first CoCos have been issued in the aftermath of the credit crisis. In December 2009 Lloyds exchanged some of their old hybrid instruments into this new type of bonds in order to strengthen their capital position after the bank had been hit very hard due to the financial crisis of 2008. Since then a lot of other banks have been issuing CoCos and one is expecting that many will follow in the next years. The market of CoCos is currently above USD 100 bn and is expanding very rapidly.[1]

When an issuer has already some CoCos outstanding and is announcing the issuance of a new CoCo bond, there are at least two opposite forces at work. On one hand, a new issue means that the capital of the issuing institute is strengthened (at the additional Tier 1 or Tier 2 level). Due to the new issue, the losses in case of a future trigger event will be shared over a larger bucket and hence recovery rates are expected to be higher. On the other hand, there are the market dynamics and investors who often prefer to invest rather in the new CoCo than in the older ones. This can be just due to the fact that one prefers new things above old stuff, but also because one believes there is a basis spread to be earned on a new issuance. Some believe a new issuance is brought to the market with a certain discount, to attract investors and to make the whole capital raising exercise a success. Investors then will move out of the old bonds and ask for allocation in the new issue.

In this paper, we estimate the price impact on the outstanding CoCos via two methods. The first method compares the returns of the outstanding CoCo bonds after an announcement of a new issue with some overall CoCo indices. More precisely, we compare the performance with CS Contingent Convertible Euro Total Return index and the BofA Merrill Lynch Contingent Capital index. Here we basically compare the performance of the outstanding CoCos with the general market performance. However such a comparison does not take into account idiosyncratic movements; it

[1]Source: Bloomberg.

basically compares with the general market trend. The issuing company is nevertheless exposed to market dynamics. Its stock price, its credit worthiness etc. can exhibit different timely evolutions compared with the respective quantities of their competitors. This can be especially the case around capital raising announcements since then financial details of the company are published and discussed at, for example roadshows around the new issuance. Therefore, we also deploy a second methodology taking into account idiosyncratic movements. Using an equity derivatives model, we compare the actual market performance of the outstanding CoCo bonds, with a theoretical model performance taking into account idiosyncratic effects, like movements in the underlying stock, credit default spreads or volatilities. The model is derivatives based and is taking as such forward-looking expectations into account.

In total, we investigate 24 cases of new CoCo bond issues. The main conclusion of the investigation is that there is a moderated negative effect on outstanding CoCo bonds. This is confirmed by both methodologies and the impact is an underperformance of about 25–50 bps on average in between the announcement date and the issue date. An extra negative impact of 40 bps was observed in the 10 trading days after the issue.

The analysis in this paper is constrained to CoCo bonds only, but a similar study could be done for other types of bonds as well. A comparative study for corporate bonds was, e.g. done in Akigbe et al. [3], where the authors investigate the impact of 574 outstanding debt issues. The investigation was divided by different reasons of a new debt issue. A significant negative impact on the price of the outstanding debt and equity was observed in case the public debt securities were issued to finance unexpected cash flow shortfalls. No significant reaction was observed when the new debt issues were motivated by unexpected increase in capital expenditures, unexpected increase in leverage or expected refinancing of outstanding debt.

This paper is organized as follows. We first provide in the next section the details of the equity derivatives model. In Sect. 3, we provide details on the data set used and in particular overview the new issuances of a whole battery of issuers that are part of our study. Next, we report on the exact methodology and results of our comparison with other CoCo indices. The final part of that section reports and discusses the results of the Equity Derivatives model. The final section concludes.

## 2 The Equity Derivatives Model

CoCos are hybrid instruments, with characteristics of both debt and equity. This gives rise to different approaches for pricing CoCos. Without considering the heuristic models, two main schools of thoughts exist, namely the structural models and market-implied models. Structural models are based on the theory of Merton and can be found in Pennacchi [4] and Pennacchi et al. [5]. We will apply a market-implied model where the derivation is based on market data such as share prices, credit default spreads and volatilities. The models were introduced in a Black–Scholes framework in De Spiegeleer and Schoutens [6] and De Spiegeleer et al. [7]. Pricing CoCos under smile conform models can be found in Corcuera et al. [8]. Based on the Heston model, the impact of skew is discussed in De Spiegeleer et al. [9]. In De Spiegeleer et al. [10] the implied CET1 volatility is derived from the market price of a CoCo bond. Further extensions and variations can be found in De Spiegeleer and Schoutens [11, 12], Corcuera et al. [13], De Spiegeleer and Schoutens [14], Cheridito and Zhikai [15], Madan and Schoutens [16].

The actual valuation of a CoCo incorporates the modelling of both the trigger probability and the expected loss for the investor. Notice that the trigger is defined by a particular CET1 level or decided upon a regulator's decision. Since these trigger mechanisms are hard to model or even quantify, we project the trigger into the stock price framework as considered in the equity derivatives model of De Spiegeleer and Schoutens [6]. This means that the CoCo will be triggered under the model once the share price drops below a specified barrier level, denoted by $S^\star$. We infer from existing CoCo market data the share price at the moment the CoCo bond gets triggered and we will call this the (implied) trigger level. As a result the valuation of a CoCo bond is transformed into a barrier-pricing exercise in an equity setting.

Under such a framework the CoCo bond can be broken down to several different derivative instruments. In first place, the CoCo behaves like a standard (non-defaultable) corporate bond where the holder will receive coupons $c_i$ on regular time points $t_i$ together with the principal $N$ at maturity $T$. However, in case the share price drops below the trigger level $S^\star$, the investor will lose his initial investment and all future coupons. This will be modelled by short positions in binary down-and-in (BIDINO) options with maturities $t_i$ for each coupon $c_i$ and a BIDINO with maturity $T$ to model the cancelling of the initial value. After the trigger event has occurred, the investor of a conversion CoCo will receive $C_r$ shares. We can model this with $C_r$ down-and-in asset-(at hit)-or-nothing options on the stock. For a write-down CoCo, the investor does not receive any shares and we can just set $C_r$ equal to zero in this case. Therefore, the price of a CoCo can be calculated with the following formula:

$$
\begin{aligned}
P = &\text{ Corporate bond} \\
&-N \times \text{binary down-and-in option} \\
&-\sum_i c_i \times \text{binary down-and-in option} \\
&+C_r \times \text{down-and-in asset-(at hit)-or-nothing option on the stock}
\end{aligned}
$$

Under the Black–Scholes model, we can find an explicit formula for the price of the CoCo at time $t$:

$$
\begin{aligned}
P = &\, N\exp(-r(T-t)) + \sum_{i=1}^{k} c_i \exp(-r(t_i-t)) \\
&-N \times \exp(-r(T-t))[\Phi(-x_1+\sigma\sqrt{T-t}) + (S^\star/S)^{2\lambda-2}\Phi(y_1-\sigma\sqrt{T-t})] \\
&-\sum_i c_i \times \exp(-r(t_i-t))[\Phi(-x_{1i}+\sigma\sqrt{t_i-t}) + (S^\star/S)^{2\lambda-2}\Phi(y_{1i}-\sigma\sqrt{t_i-t})] \\
&+C_r \times S^\star \left[\left(\frac{S^\star}{S}\right)^{a+b}\Phi(z) + \left(\frac{S^\star}{S}\right)^{a-b}\Phi(z-2b\sigma\sqrt{T-t})\right]
\end{aligned} \tag{1}
$$

with

$$z = \frac{\log(S^\star/S)}{\sigma\sqrt{T-t}} + b\sigma\sqrt{T-t} \qquad x_1 = \frac{\log(S/S^\star)}{\sigma\sqrt{T-t}} + \lambda\sigma\sqrt{T-t}$$

$$a = \frac{r-q-\frac{1}{2}\sigma^2}{\sigma^2} \qquad y_1 = \frac{\log(S^\star/S)}{\sigma\sqrt{T-t}} + \lambda\sigma\sqrt{T-t}$$

$$b = \frac{\sqrt{(r-q-\frac{1}{2}\sigma^2)^2 + 2r\sigma^2}}{\sigma^2} \qquad x_{1i} = \frac{\log(S/S^\star)}{\sigma\sqrt{t_i-t}} + \lambda\sigma\sqrt{t_i-t}$$

$$\lambda = \frac{r-q+\sigma^2/2}{\sigma^2} \qquad y_{1i} = \frac{\log(S^\star/S)}{\sigma\sqrt{t_i-t}} + \lambda\sigma\sqrt{t_i-t}$$

where $\Phi$ is the cdf of a standard normal distribution, $r$ is the risk free rate, $q$ the dividend yield and $\sigma$ the volatility.

Applying this equity derivatives pricing model, a CoCo price can be found for a trigger level $S^\star$. However, the other way around is often more interesting. Knowing the market CoCo price, we can filter out an implied trigger $\widehat{S^\star}$ in such a way that market and model price match. Since CoCos of one financial institution with the same contractual trigger should trigger at the same time, their implied trigger levels should theoretically also be the same. Hence the implied barriers give us a way to compare different CoCos in order to detect over- or undervaluation, irrespectively of different currencies and maturities.

Our goal is to compare the actual market performance of the outstanding CoCo bonds with the theoretical model performance. This theoretical price takes idiosyncratic effects into account. Any changes in the actual market performance compared to the theoretical model performance will be described to the effect of the announcement of a new CoCo issuance. The research can also be translated in terms of implied trigger levels. In case the new CoCo does not influence the outstanding CoCo, the implied barrier of the outstanding CoCo should remain constant. Whereas if its implied barrier derived from the market will change, this change will be caused by the new CoCo issuance.

## 3 Measuring the Price Performance of the Outstanding CoCos

### *3.1 New Issuances*

The impact of a new CoCo issuance is investigated on the outstanding CoCos of the same issuing company. The issuers in our study contain UBS, Barclays, Crédit Agricole, Sociéty Général, Deutsche Bank, UniCredit, Credit Suisse, Santander, Rabobank, Danske and BBVA. The effect on the outstanding CoCos is investigated in the period between announcement and issuance of the new CoCo, which are summarised in Table 1. Notice that UBS, Barclays and Crédit Agricole all have

**Table 1** Announcement date, issue date and issue size (in bn) of the new CoCos

| Name | ISIN | Announc. | Issue | Size | Curr. |
|---|---|---|---|---|---|
| ACAFP 6 5/8 09/29/49 | USF22797YK86 | 11/09/2014 | 18/09/2014 | 1,250 | USD |
| ACAFP 6 1/2 04/29/49 | XS1055037177[a] | 01/04/2014 | 08/04/2014 | 1,000 | EUR |
| ACAFP 7 7/8 01/29/49 | USF22797RT78 | 15/01/2014 | 23/01/2014 | 1,750 | USD |
| BACR 7 06/15/49 | XS1068561098[b] | 13/06/2014 | 17/06/2014 | 697.60 | GBP |
| BACR 8 12/15/49 | XS1002801758 | 03/12/2013 | 10/12/2013 | 1,000 | EUR |
| BACR 8 1/4 12/29/49 | US06738EAA38 | 13/11/2013 | 20/11/2013 | 2,000 | USD |
| BBVASM 6 3/4 12/29/49 | XS1190663952 | 10/02/2015 | 18/02/2015 | 1,500 | EUR |
| CS 6 1/4 12/29/49 | XS1076957700 | 10/06/2014 | 18/06/2014 | 2,500 | USD |
| CS 7 1/2 12/29/49 | XS0989394589 | 04/12/2013 | 11/12/2013 | 2,250 | USD |
| CS 5 3/4 09/18/25 | XS0972523947 | 11/09/2013 | 18/09/2013 | 1,250 | EUR |
| CS 6 09/29/49 | CH0221803791 | 20/08/2013 | 04/09/2013 | 290 | CHF |
| DANBNK 5 7/8 04/29/49 | XS1190987427 | 11/02/2015 | 18/02/2015 | 750 | EUR |
| DB 7 1/2 12/29/49 | US251525AN16 | 18/11/2014 | 21/11/2014 | 1,500 | USD |
| RABOBK 5 1/2 01/22/49 | XS1171914515 | 15/01/2015 | 22/01/2015 | 1,500 | EUR |
| SANTAN 6 1/4 09/11/49 | XS1107291541 | 02/09/2014 | 11/09/2014 | 1,500 | EUR |
| SANTAN 6 3/8 05/29/49 | XS1066553329 | 08/05/2014 | 19/05/2014 | 1,500 | USD |
| SOCGEN 6 10/27/49 | USF8586CXG25 | 19/06/2014 | 25/06/2014 | 1,500 | USD |
| SOCGEN 6 3/4 04/07/49 | XS0867620725 | 28/03/2014 | 07/04/2014 | 1,000 | EUR |
| SOCGEN 7 7/8 12/29/49 | USF8586CRW49 | 11/12/2013 | 18/12/2013 | 1,750 | USD |
| UBS 7 1/8 12/29/49 | CH0271428317[c] | 13/02/2015 | 19/02/2015 | 1,250 | USD |

(continued)

**Table 1** (continued)

| Name | ISIN | Announc. | Issue | Size | Curr. |
|---|---|---|---|---|---|
| UBS 5 1/8 05/15/24 | CH0244100266 | 08/05/2014 | 15/05/2014 | 2,500 | USD |
| UBS 4 3/4 02/12/26 | CH0236733827 | 06/02/2014 | 13/02/2014 | 2,000 | EUR |
| UBS 4 3/4 05/22/23 | CH0214139930 | 15/05/2013 | 22/05/2013 | 1,500 | USD |
| UCGIM 6 3/4 09/29/49 | XS1107890847 | 03/09/2014 | 10/09/2014 | 1,000 | EUR |

[a]Incl. XS1055037920
[b]Incl. US06738EAB11 and XS1068574828
[c]Incl. CH0271428333 and CH0271428309
*Source* Bloomberg/own calculations

issued different CoCos on the same day. Since it is not possible to distinguish their influence from each other, these new CoCos are assumed to have one general impact on all the outstanding CoCos of the same issuing company.

## 3.2 CoCo Index Comparison

The first analysis is based on indices as a benchmark to observe a certain impact. It basically compares the returns of the outstanding CoCo bonds after an announcement of a new issue with some overall CoCo indices. More precisely, we compare the performance with the CS Contingent Convertible Euro Total Return index and the BofA Merrill Lynch Contingent Capital Index (whenever the data is available). The methods are explained for one particular new CoCo issuance, namely the USF22797YK86 CoCo of Crédit Agricole. In the end, the overall results and conclusions are shown.

### 3.2.1 Method

In a first step, we analyse the impact of each new CoCo separately on all the outstanding CoCos of the same issuer. The simple returns are derived for the outstanding CoCos during the period between the announcement date and the issue date of the new CoCo. In a second step, we accumulate these simple returns and obtain the returns between announcement and issue date. As an example, the first steps are shown for two outstanding CoCos of Crédit Agricole in Fig. 1.

On each day, we calculate the (equally weighted) average of the cumulative simple returns of all outstanding CoCos. In a last step, we take the difference between these averages and the cumulative returns of the CoCo index on each day between the announcement date and issue date of the new CoCo.

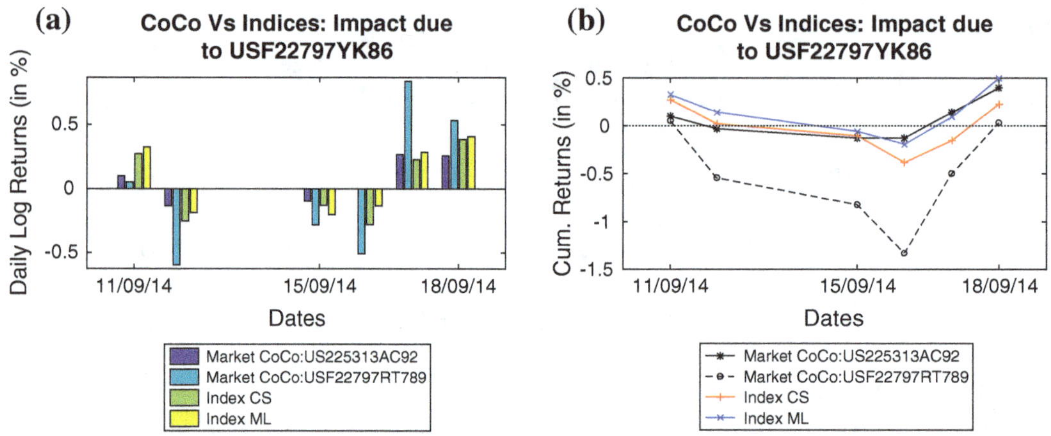


**Fig. 1** Impact of USF22797YK86. **a** Daily returns. **b** Cumulative returns

### 3.2.2 Results

In Table 2, the difference in cumulative returns over the observation period, meaning the period between announcement and issuance, is shown. For some observation periods, the Merrill Lynch index did not yet exist. When the CoCo does show a significant change compared to the global index, we can assume that this change is due to the new CoCo issuance. The averaged difference over all new CoCos analysed is shown in Fig. 2. These averaged differences in cumulative returns are shown for one day until five days after the announcement of the new CoCo and also over the full period as was given in Table 2. As a conclusion, we see that on average the outstanding CoCos get a negative impact of around 25 bps on their return between announcement and issuance due to a new CoCo.

Multiple CoCo indices can be used for this analysis but CoCo indices are relatively new on the market. As such we are obliged to restrict our analysis to indices already available during the period of each analysis. Remark also that we need to handle these indices with care, in the sense that the indices are applied to give a global market view on the CoCos. A point of criticism to this approach can be that the indices are not that representative for the true market. There is also high concentration on some issuers in the indices, e.g. for the ML index the top 5 issuers almost make 50 % of the index (as of December 2014).

Furthermore, this comparison with the general market performance does not take into account idiosyncratic movements but compares with the general market trend. The issuing company is nevertheless exposed to individual dynamics. Its stock price, its credit worthiness, etc. can change differently from their competitors. This can be especially the case around capital raising announcements since then financial details of the company are published and discussed at, for example road-shows around the new issuance. Therefore, we move on to a second methodology taking into account idiosyncratic movements.

**Table 2** Averaged difference in cumulative returns (in %) between the outstanding CoCos and the Credit Suisse CoCo index (left column) and Merrill Lynch CoCo index (right column) over the observation period of the new CoCo

| Issuer | ISIN | CS index | ML index |
|---|---|---|---|
| ACAFP | USF22797YK86 | 0.06 | −0.21 |
| | XS1055037177 | −0.06 | 0.07 |
| | USF22797RT78 | −0.21 | −0.47 |
| BACR | XS1068561098 | −0.25 | −0.12 |
| | XS1002801758 | 0.08 | / |
| | US06738EAA38 | 0.56 | / |
| BBVA | XS1190663952 | −0.51 | −1.18 |
| CS | XS1076957700 | 0.31 | 0.60 |
| | XS0989394589 | −0.28 | / |
| | XS0972523947 | −0.50 | / |
| | CH0221803791 | 1.09 | / |
| DANBNK | XS1190987427 | −1.32 | −2.27 |
| DB | US251525AN16 | −0.13 | −0.29 |
| RABOBK | XS1171914515 | −0.36 | −0.41 |
| SANTAN | XS1107291541 | −1.38 | −1.19 |
| | XS1066553329 | −0.49 | −0.06 |
| SOCGEN | USF8586CXG25 | 0.23 | 0.17 |
| | XS0867620725 | −0.27 | −0.02 |
| | USF8586CRW49 | 1.24 | / |
| UBS | CH0271428317 | −0.46 | −1.01 |
| | CH0244100266 | −0.12 | 0.42 |
| | CH0236733827 | 0.37 | 0.31 |
| | CH0214139930 | −1.15 | / |
| UCGIM | XS1107890847 | −1.75 | −1.48 |
| **Mean** | | **−0.22** | **−0.42** |
| **Std Dev** | | **0.71** | **0.77** |

*Source* Bloomberg/own calculations

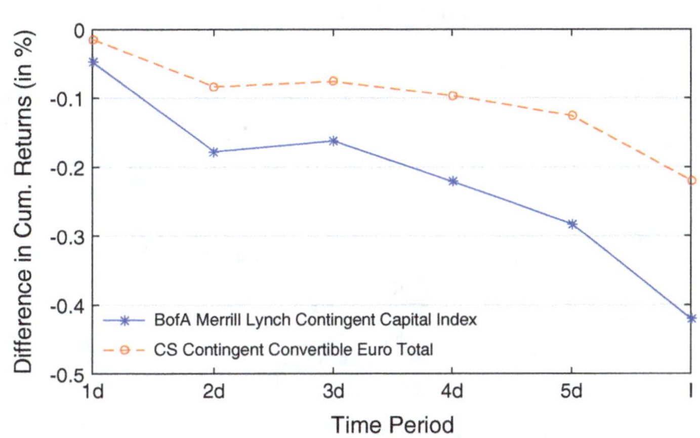


**Fig. 2** Averaged difference in cumulative returns between the outstanding CoCos and the Credit Suisse and Merrill Lynch CoCo index

## 3.3 Model-Based Performance

As experienced by all CoCo investors, the difficulty in these financial products lies in their different characteristics which are hard to compare like the trigger type, conversion type, maturity, coupon cancellation, and so on. However, the implied barrier methodology can be used as a tool to compare CoCos with different characteristics. In this second approach, we will use the implied barrier to derive theoretical values for the outstanding CoCos under the assumption of no impact by the new CoCo issuance and compare them with the actual market values.

### 3.3.1 Method

The implied barrier can be interpreted as the stock price level (assumed by the market) that is hit (for the first time) when the CoCo gets converted or written down. If nothing changes, the market will keep the same idea about the implied barrier level and hence result in a constant implied barrier over time. In other words, when there is no impact due to this new CoCo, no change could theoretically be observed in

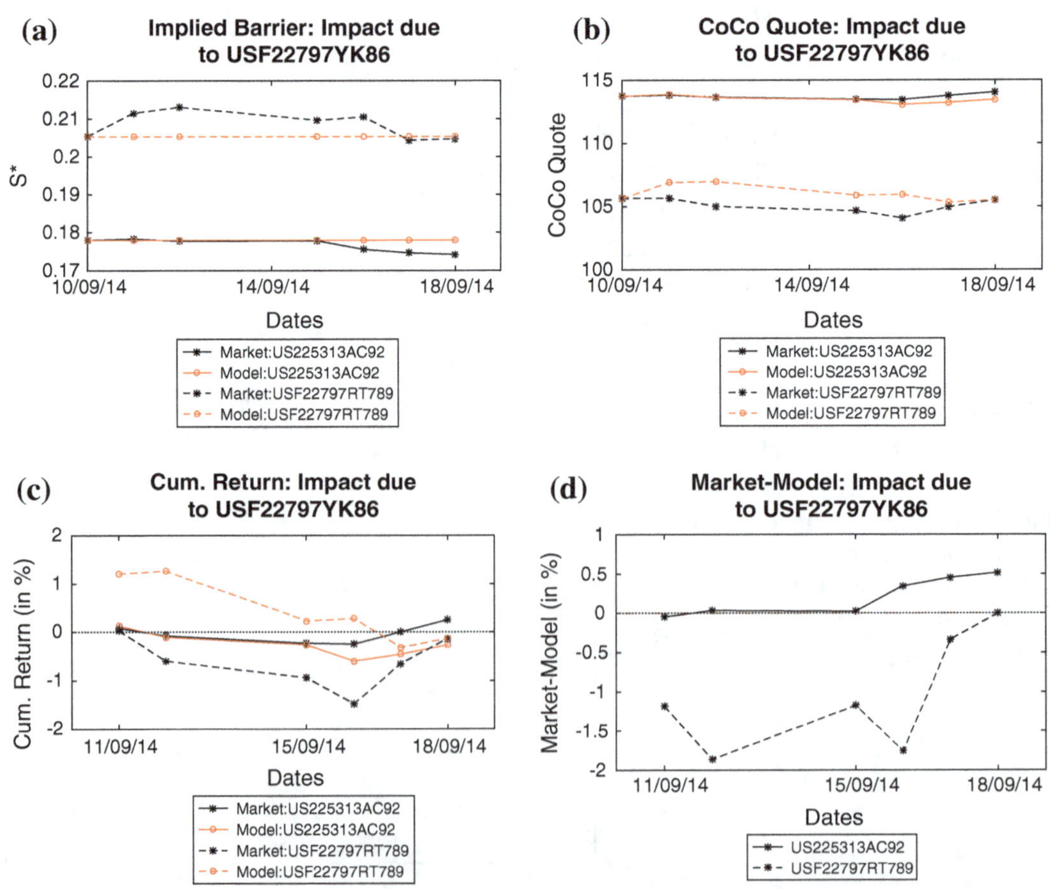


**Fig. 3** Impact of USF22797YK86. **a** Implied barriers. **b** CoCo quotes. **c** Returns compared with announcement. **d** Difference in returns

the implied barrier. As such we can see in the levels of the implied barrier if there is an impact due to the announced new CoCo. This leads us easily to the second approach of our impact analysis. As an example, we show the implied barriers of the two outstanding CoCos of ACAFP from the previous section in Fig. 3a.

As from the previous section, the implied barriers can be translated into CoCo quotes. The theoretical CoCo price does not take any information of a new CoCo issuance into account by assuming a constant implied barrier. These values can be used as our reference. Any change in the market compared with this reference, is then due to the impact of the announcement of a new CoCo issuance. As such we can calculate the theoretical CoCo prices from a constant implied barrier and compare them with the market values. The results of our CoCo examples are shown in Fig. 3b. As a last step, we define cheapness as the difference between the market CoCo return and the theoretical CoCo return until the announcement date. In Fig. 3, the cheapness of the two outstanding CoCos of Crédit Agricole is shown.

**Table 3** Averaged difference between the market and model CoCo cumulative returns (in %)

| Issuer | ISIN | Cheapness |
|---|---|---|
| ACAFP | USF22797YK86 | 0.14 |
| | XS1055037177 | −1.45 |
| | USF22797RT78 | −0.19 |
| BACR | XS1068561098 | 0.17 |
| | XS1002801758 | −0.05 |
| | US06738EAA38 | −0.38 |
| BBVA | XS1190663952 | −1.91 |
| CS | XS1076957700 | 0.12 |
| | XS0989394589 | 0.53 |
| | XS0972523947 | −2.63 |
| | CH0221803791 | 1.44 |
| DANBNK | XS1190987427 | −3.25 |
| DB | US251525AN16 | 0.65 |
| RABOBK | XS1171914515 | 0.31 |
| SANTAN | XS1107291541 | −2.24 |
| | XS1066553329 | 0.07 |
| SOCGEN | USF8586CXG25 | 1.26 |
| | XS0867620725 | −2.31 |
| | USF8586CRW49 | 1.67 |
| UBS | CH0271428317 | 0.71 |
| | CH0244100266 | −1.23 |
| | CH0236733827 | 1.03 |
| | CH0214139930 | −0.89 |
| UCGIM | XS1107890847 | −1.60 |
| **Mean** | | **−0.42** |
| **Std Dev** | | **1.37** |

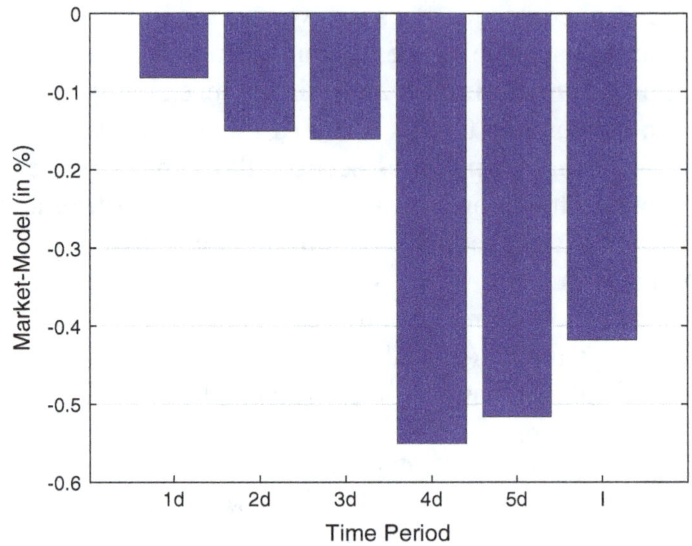


**Fig. 4** Overall difference between the market and model CoCo cumulative returns

### 3.3.2 Results

An overall view is derived for the cheapness by averaging the differences in theoretical and market CoCo prices for each outstanding CoCo during the observation period of the new CoCo. We averaged the differences of all the CoCos on one day until five days after the announcement and also on the issue date of the new CoCo (Table 3).

Clearly, from Fig. 4, on average the cheapness on each day of our observation period is negative, meaning that market price is below the theoretical price assuming no impact. As such we conclude also from this approach that there is a negative impact of about 42 bps on average on the outstanding CoCos when a new CoCo issuance is announced.

## 4 Impact After Issue Date

At this point, we investigated the impact of a new CoCo issuance between the announcement and issue date. In this section, we show the results for a longer observation period. More concrete, both analyses are extended to 10 trading days after the issue date.

From our first analysis, where we compare the outstanding CoCos with the CoCo indices, a downward trending impact is observed in Fig. 5a. The second analysis which compares the market and model prices of the outstanding CoCos is shown in Fig. 5b. In both analyses, the negative impact gets more significant after the issue dates. Hence until 10 trading days after the issue date, there is still a negative impact observable.

**Fig. 5** Impact from the announcement date until 10 days after the issue date. **a** Method 1. **b** Method 2

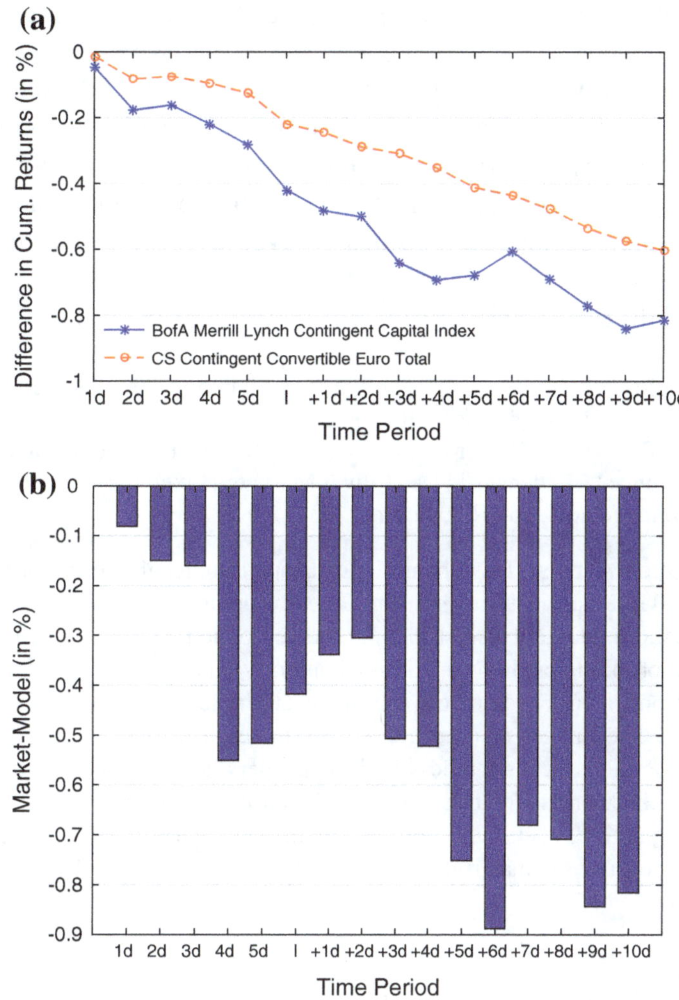


## 5 Conclusion

The price performance of outstanding CoCos was investigated after a new CoCo issue is announced by the same issuer. Based on two approaches, we estimated the price impact on the outstanding CoCos. The first method compared returns of the outstanding CoCos with some overall CoCo indices. As a conclusion, we found that the return of the outstanding CoCos, during the period between announcement and issuance, was slightly lower than the returns of the CoCo indices. There was an underperformance of about 22 bps compared with the Credit Suisse index and about 42 bps with the Merrill Lynch index (although with relative high standard deviations). Since this first study did not take idiosyncratic movements into account, we used also a second method based on the equity derivatives model for CoCos. In this method we compared the actual market performance of the outstanding CoCo bonds with a theoretical model performance taking into account idiosyncratic effects, like movements in the underlying stock, credit default spreads and volatilities. This second approach also concludes that the averaged market returns of the outstanding CoCos were about 42 bps lower than one would expect in case of no influence.

In total, we investigate 24 cases of new CoCo bond issues. The main conclusion of the investigation is that there is a moderated negative effect on outstanding CoCo bonds. This is confirmed by both methodologies and the impact is an underperformance of about 20–40 bps on average in between the announcement date and the issue date. During the period of 10 trading days after the issue date, an extra decrease of 40 bps was observed.

**Acknowledgements** The authors would like to thank Robert Van Kleeck and Michael Hünseler for useful discussions on the topic.

The KPMG Center of Excellence in Risk Management is acknowledged for organizing the conference "Challenges in Derivatives Markets - Fixed Income Modeling, Valuation Adjustments, Risk Management, and Regulation".

**Open Access** This chapter is distributed under the terms of the Creative Commons Attribution 4.0 International License (http://creativecommons.org/licenses/by/4.0/), which permits use, duplication, adaptation, distribution and reproduction in any medium or format, as long as you give appropriate credit to the original author(s) and the source, a link is provided to the Creative Commons license and any changes made are indicated.

The images or other third party material in this chapter are included in the work's Creative Commons license, unless indicated otherwise in the credit line; if such material is not included in the work's Creative Commons license and the respective action is not permitted by statutory regulation, users will need to obtain permission from the license holder to duplicate, adapt or reproduce the material.

## References

1. Basel Committee on Banking Supervision: Basel III: A global regulatory framework for more resilient banks and banking systems. Bank for International Settlements, Dec. 2010
2. European Commision: Possible Further Changes to the Capital Requirements Directive. Working Document. Commission Services Staff (2010)
3. Akigbe, A., Easterwood, J.C., Pettit, R.R.: Wealth effects of corporate debt issues: the impact of issuer motivations. Financ. Manag. **26**(1), 32–47 (1997)
4. Pennacchi, G.: A Structural Model of Contingent Bank Capital (2010)
5. Pennacchi, G., Vermaelen, T., Wolff, C.: Contingent capital: the case for COERCs. INSEAD. Working paper (2010)
6. De Spiegeleer, J., Schoutens, W.: Contingent convertible contingent convertibles: a derivative approach. J. Deriv. (2012)
7. De Spiegeleer, J., Schoutens, W., Van Hulle, C.: The Handbook of Hybrid Securities: Convertible Bonds, CoCo Bonds and Bail-in. Wiley, New York (2014), Chap. 3
8. Corcuera, J.M., De Spiegeleer, J., Ferreiro-Castilla, A., Kyprianou, A.E., Madan, D.B., Schoutens, W.: Pricing of contingent convertibles under smile conform models. J. Credit Risk **9**(3), 121–140 (2013)
9. De Spiegeleer, J., Forys, M., Marquet, I., Schoutens, W.: The Impact of Skew on the Pricing of CoCo Bonds. Available on SSRN: http://ssrn.com/abstract=2418150 (2014)
10. De Spiegeleer, J., Marquet, I., Schoutens, W.: CoCo Bonds and Implied CET1 Volatility. Available on SSRN: http://ssrn.com/abstract=2575558 (2015)

11. De Spiegeleer, J., Schoutens, W.: Steering a bank around a death spiral: multiple Trigger CoCos. Wilmott Mag. **2012**(59), 62–69 (2012)
12. De Spiegeleer, J., Schoutens, W.: CoCo Bonds with Extension Risk (2014)
13. Corcuera, J.M., De Spiegeleer, J., Fajardo, J., Jönsson, H., Schoutens, W., Valdivia, A.: Close form pricing formulas for CoCa CoCos. J. Bank. Financ. (2014)
14. De Spiegeleer, J., Schoutens, W.: Multiple Trigger CoCos: contingent debt without death spiral risk. Financ. Mark. Inst. Instr. **22**(2) (2013)
15. Cheridito, P., Zhikai, X.: A reduced form CoCo model with deterministic conversion intensity. Available on SSRN: http://ssrn.com/abstract=2254403 (2013)
16. Madan, D.B., Schoutens, W.: Conic coconuts: the pricing of contingent capital notes using conic finance. Math. Financ. Econ. **4**(2), 87–106 (2011)

# The Impact of Cointegration on Commodity Spread Options

**Walter Farkas, Elise Gourier, Robert Huitema and Ciprian Necula**

**Abstract** In this work we explore the implications of cointegration in a system of commodity prices on the premiums of options written on various spreads on the futures prices of these commodities. We employ a parsimonious, yet comprehensive model for cointegration in a system of commodity prices. The model has an exponential affine structure and is flexible enough to allow for an arbitrary number of cointegration relationships. We conduct an extensive simulation study on pricing spread options. We argue that cointegration creates an upward sloping term structure of correlation, that in turn lowers the volatility of spreads and consequently the price of options on them.

**Keywords** Cointegration · Futures prices · Commodities · Spread options · Simulation

## 1 Introduction

A distinctive feature of commodity markets is the existence of long-run equilibrium relationships that exist between the levels of various commodity prices, such as the one between the price of crude oil and the price of heating oil. These long-run

W. Farkas (✉) · R. Huitema · C. Necula
Department of Banking and Finance, University of Zurich,
Plattenstrasse 14, 8032 Zurich, Switzerland
e-mail: walter.farkas@bf.uzh.ch

W. Farkas
Department of Mathematics, ETH Zurich, Rämistrasse 101, 8092 Zurich, Switzerland

W. Farkas
Swiss Finance Institute, Zurich, Switzerland

E. Gourier
School of Economics and Finance, Queen Mary, University of London, London, UK

C. Necula
Department of Money and Banking, Bucharest University of Economic Studies,
Bucharest, Romania

© The Author(s) 2016

K. Glau et al. (eds.), *Innovations in Derivatives Markets*, Springer Proceedings in Mathematics & Statistics 165, DOI 10.1007/978-3-319-33446-2_20

equilibrium relations can be captured in economic models by so-called *cointegration* relations.

In this work we employ the continuous time model of cointegrated commodity prices developed by the authors in Farkas et al. [6] in order to conduct a simulation study for assessing the impact of cointegration on spread options. In our model, commodity prices are non-stationary and several cointegration relations are allowed amongst them, capturing long-run equilibrium relationships. Cointegration (Engle and Granger [5]) is the property of two or more non-stationary time series of having at least one linear combination that is stationary.

There is a vast literature on modeling the price of a single commodity as a non-stationary process (see Back and Prokopczuk [1] for a comprehensive recent review). For example, Schwartz and Smith [13] assume the log price of a commodity to be the sum of two latent factors: the long-term equilibrium level, modeled as a geometric Brownian motion, and a short-term deviation from the equilibrium, modeled as a zero mean Ornstein–Uhlenbeck (OU) process. More recently, Paschke and Prokopczuk [11] propose to model these deviations as a more general CARMA process and Cortazar and Naranjo [3] generalize the Schwartz and Smith [13] model in a multi-factor framework.

However, the literature on modeling a system of commodity prices is still quite scarce. Two fairly recent models are proposed in Cortazar et al. [4] and Paschke and Prokopczuk [10], both of which account for cointegration by incorporating common and commodity-specific factors into their modeling framework. Amongst the common factors, only one is assumed non-stationary. Although they explicitly take into account cointegration between prices, the cointegrated systems generated by these two models are not covering the whole range of possible number of cointegration relations, but allow for none or for exactly $n-1$ relations to exist between the $n$ prices. In Farkas et al. [6] we propose an easy-to-use, yet comprehensive, model for a system of cointegrated commodity prices that retains the exponential affine structure of previous approaches and allows, in the same time, for an arbitrary number of cointegration relationships.

The rest of the work is organized as follows. In Sect. 2 we briefly describe the model proposed in Farkas et al. [6] and point out some qualitative aspects regarding the dynamics of the system. Section 3 is devoted to an extensive simulation study focused on computing spread options prices and on assessing the impact of cointegration on pricing spread options. Section 4 is reserved for concluding remarks.

## 2 Outline of the Model

Before proceeding to the simulation study, in this section we present for the sake of completeness, a short description of the model developed in Farkas et al. [6].

Consider $n$ commodities with spot prices $\mathbf{S}(t) = (S_1(t), \ldots, S_n(t))^\top$.

First it is assumed that the spot log-prices $\mathbf{X}(t) = \log \mathbf{S}(t)$ can be decomposed into three components:

$$\mathbf{X}(t) = \mathbf{Y}(t) + \boldsymbol{\varepsilon}(t) + \boldsymbol{\phi}(t), \tag{1}$$

where $\mathbf{Y}$(t) signifies the long-run levels, $\boldsymbol{\varepsilon}(t)$ is an $n$-dimensional stationary process capturing short-term deviations, and $\boldsymbol{\phi}(t) = \boldsymbol{\chi}_1 \cos(2\pi t) + \boldsymbol{\chi}_2 \sin(2\pi t)$ controls for seasonal effects with $\boldsymbol{\chi}_1$ and $\boldsymbol{\chi}_2$ being $n$-dimensional vectors of constants.

The notion of cointegration (Engle and Granger [5], Johansen [7], Phillips [12]) refers to the property of two or more non-stationary time series of having a linear combination that is stationary. For example, if $X_1(t)$ and $X_2(t)$ are two non-stationary processes, one says that they are cointegrated if there is a linear combination of them, $X_1(t) - \alpha X_2(t)$, that is stationary for some positive real $\alpha$. Intuitively, cointegration occurs when two or more non-stationary variables are linked in a long-run equilibrium relationship from which they might depart only temporarily.

Regarding cointegration in the model, we stress that $n$ cointegration relationships are implicitly assumed by (1): the $n$ seasonally adjusted spot log-prices $\mathbf{X}(t) - \boldsymbol{\phi}(t)$ are cointegrated with their corresponding long-run levels, $\mathbf{Y}(t)$, since the linear combination $\mathbf{X}(t) - \boldsymbol{\phi}(t) - \mathbf{Y}(t)$ is stationary.

Secondly, cointegration is allowed to exist between the variables in $\mathbf{Y}(t)$ as well. We denote the number of cointegration relationships between them by $h$, where $h \geq 0$ and $h < n$. The corresponding cointegration matrix is symbolized by $\Theta$, an $n \times n$ matrix with the last $n - h$ rows equal to zero vectors. Each of the $h$ non-zero rows of $\Theta$ encodes a stationary (i.e., cointegrating) combination of the variables in $\mathbf{Y}(t)$, normalized such that $\Theta_{ii} = 1,\ i \leq h$. The total $n + h$ cointegration relationships between the variables in the vector $\mathbf{Z}(t) := (\mathbf{X}(t) - \boldsymbol{\phi}(t), \mathbf{Y}(t))^\top$ can be characterized by the $(2n \times 2n)$-matrix $\begin{bmatrix} \mathbf{I}_n & -\mathbf{I}_n \\ \mathbf{O}_n & \Theta \end{bmatrix}$ where $\mathbf{O}_n$ denotes the zero-matrix with dimension $n \times n$.

The dynamics of $\mathbf{X}(t)$ and $\mathbf{Y}(t)$ under the real-world probability measure is assumed to be given by:

$$d\begin{bmatrix} \mathbf{X}(t) - \phi(t) \\ \mathbf{Y}(t) \end{bmatrix} = \begin{bmatrix} \mathbf{0}_n \\ \mu_y \end{bmatrix} dt + \begin{bmatrix} -K_x & \mathbf{O}_n \\ \mathbf{O}_n & -K_y \end{bmatrix} \begin{bmatrix} \mathbf{I}_n & -\mathbf{I}_n \\ \mathbf{O}_n & \Theta \end{bmatrix} \begin{bmatrix} \mathbf{X}(t) - \phi(t) \\ \mathbf{Y}(t) \end{bmatrix} dt$$
$$+ \begin{bmatrix} \Sigma_x^{\frac{1}{2}} & \mathbf{O}_n \\ \Sigma_{xy}^{\frac{1}{2}} & \Sigma_y^{\frac{1}{2}} \end{bmatrix} d\begin{bmatrix} \mathbf{W}_x(t) \\ \mathbf{W}_y(t) \end{bmatrix}, \tag{2}$$

where $\mathbf{0}_n$ is an $n$-dimensional vector of zeros, and $\mathbf{W} := (\mathbf{W}_x, \mathbf{W}_y)^\top$ is a $2n$-dimensional standard Brownian motion. Furthermore, the matrix $\begin{bmatrix} -K_x & \mathbf{O}_n \\ \mathbf{O}_n & -K_y \end{bmatrix}$ measures the speed by which $\mathbf{Z}(t)$ reverts to its long-run (cointegration) equilibrium level. More specifically, $K_x$ quantifies the speed of mean reversion of the elements in $\mathbf{X}$ around the long term levels in $\mathbf{Y}$. The matrix $K_y$ is an $n \times n$ matrix with the last $n - h$ columns equal to zero vector, such that $K_y\Theta$ is an $n \times n$ matrix of rank $h$. Each of the $h$ non-zero columns in $K_y$ quantifies the speed of adjustment of each element in $\mathbf{Y}$ to the corresponding cointegration relation. The dynamics given by Eq. (2) is "error-correcting" in that a deviation from a given cointegration relation induces an appropriate change in variables in the direction of correcting the deviation.

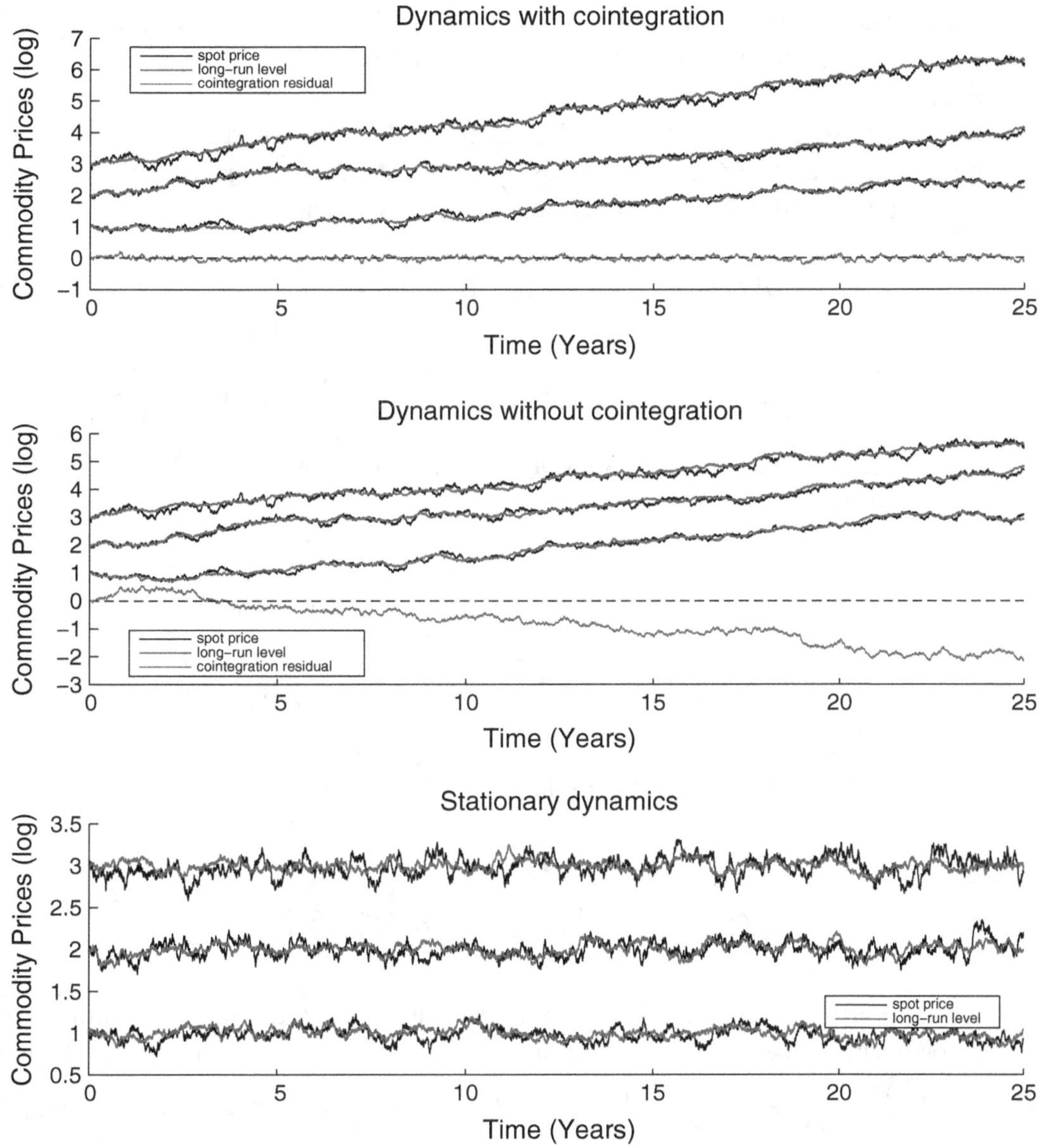


**Fig. 1** Simulated price paths for various choices of the $\Theta$ matrix. *Top panel* prices are non-stationary and there is one cointegration relation. *Middle panel* prices are non-stationary and there is no cointegration. *Bottom panel* prices are stationary

In order to assess qualitatively the role of the cointegration matrix $\Theta$ on the properties of the dynamics of the system, Fig. 1 depicts the results of a simulation of a system of three variables for various choices of the $\Theta$ matrix.

In the top panel of Fig. 1 we assume that there is a cointegration relation and the first line of the $\Theta$ matrix is $\begin{bmatrix}1 & 1 & -1\end{bmatrix}$ and, therefore, the residual of the cointegration relation, $Y_1(t) + Y_2(t) - Y_3(t)$, is stationary. On the other hand, in the middle panel, depicts the case when $\Theta$ is the null matrix and, therefore, the prices are non-stationary and not cointegrated. For example, the residual of the cointegration relation from the previous case, $Y_1(t) + Y_2(t) - Y_3(t)$, is no longer stationary. In fact, there is no stationary linear combination of the long run levels in this case. Moreover, as depicted in the bottom panel, the model also allows for stationary prices, if the $\Theta$ matrix is of full rank.

The characteristic functions of $\mathbf{X}$ and $\mathbf{Y}$ can be readily computed analytically given they are normally distributed since the dynamics of $\mathbf{Z}(t) = (\mathbf{X}(t) - \boldsymbol{\phi}(t), \mathbf{Y}(t))^\top$ is in fact given by a multivariate Ornstein–Uhlenbeck (OU) process:

$$d\mathbf{Z}(t) = [\boldsymbol{\mu} - K\mathbf{Z}(t)]\,dt + \Sigma^{\frac{1}{2}} d\mathbf{W}(t), \tag{3}$$

with $\boldsymbol{\mu} := \begin{bmatrix} \mathbf{0}_n \\ \boldsymbol{\mu}_y \end{bmatrix}$, $K := \begin{bmatrix} K_x & -K_x \\ \mathbf{O}_n & K_y\Theta \end{bmatrix}$, $\Sigma^{\frac{1}{2}} := \begin{bmatrix} \Sigma_x^{\frac{1}{2}} & \mathbf{O}_n \\ \Sigma_{xy}^{\frac{1}{2}} & \Sigma_y^{\frac{1}{2}} \end{bmatrix}$, $\mathbf{W}(t) := \begin{bmatrix} \mathbf{W}_x(t) \\ \mathbf{W}_y(t) \end{bmatrix}$.

At the same time, the vector of spot prices $\mathbf{S}(T)$ can be written as an exponential function of $\mathbf{X}(t)$ and $\mathbf{Y}(t)$:

$$\begin{aligned} \mathbf{S}(T) = \exp\Big\{ & e^{-K_x(T-t)}\mathbf{X}(t) + \psi(T-t)\mathbf{Y}(t) + \left[\phi(T) - e^{-K_x(T-t)}\phi(t)\right] \\ & + \left[\int_t^T \psi(T-u)du\right]\mu_y + \int_t^T \left[e^{-K_x(T-u)}\Sigma_x^{\frac{1}{2}} + \psi(T-u)\Sigma_{xy}^{\frac{1}{2}}\right] d\mathbf{W}_x(u) \\ & + \int_t^T \psi(T-u)\Sigma_y^{\frac{1}{2}} d\mathbf{W}_y(u)\Big\}. \end{aligned} \tag{4}$$

where

$$\psi(\tau) := K_x \left[\int_0^\tau e^{-K_x(\tau-u)} e^{-K_y\Theta u} du\right].$$

Given the affine structure of the model, futures prices can also be obtained in closed form. Under the simplifying assumption of constant market prices of risk, one has that $d\begin{bmatrix} \mathbf{W}_x^*(t) \\ \mathbf{W}_y^*(t) \end{bmatrix} = d\begin{bmatrix} \mathbf{W}_x(t) \\ \mathbf{W}_y(t) \end{bmatrix} + \begin{bmatrix} \boldsymbol{\lambda}_x \\ \boldsymbol{\lambda}_y \end{bmatrix} dt$ where $\mathbf{W}_x^*(t)$ and $\mathbf{W}_y^*(t)$ are standard Brownian motions under the risk-neutral measure, and $\boldsymbol{\lambda}_x$, $\boldsymbol{\lambda}_y$ are the market prices of $\mathbf{W}_x(t)$ and $\mathbf{W}_y(t)$ risks, respectively.

Under these circumstances it can be shown that at time $t$ the vector of futures prices for the contracts with maturity $T$ is given by

$$\mathbf{F}(t,T) = \exp\{\alpha(t,T) + \beta(T-t)\mathbf{X}(t) + \psi(T-t)\mathbf{Y}(t)\}, \tag{5}$$

with $\beta(\tau) := e^{-K_x\tau}$ and with $\alpha(t,T)$ defined by

$$\begin{aligned} \alpha(t, t+\tau) := & \left[\phi(t+\tau) - e^{-K_x\tau}\phi(t)\right] - \left(\mathbf{I}_n - e^{-K_x\tau}\right) K_x^{-1}\boldsymbol{\mu}_x^* + \left(\int_0^\tau \psi(\tau-u)du\right)\boldsymbol{\mu}_y^* \\ & + \operatorname{diag}\left\{\frac{1}{2}[\mathbf{I}_n\ \mathbf{O}_n]\left[e^{-K\tau}\left(\int_0^\tau e^{Ku}\Sigma e^{Ku}du\right)e^{-K\tau}\right]\begin{bmatrix}\mathbf{I}_n \\ \mathbf{O}_n\end{bmatrix}\right\}, \end{aligned} \tag{6}$$

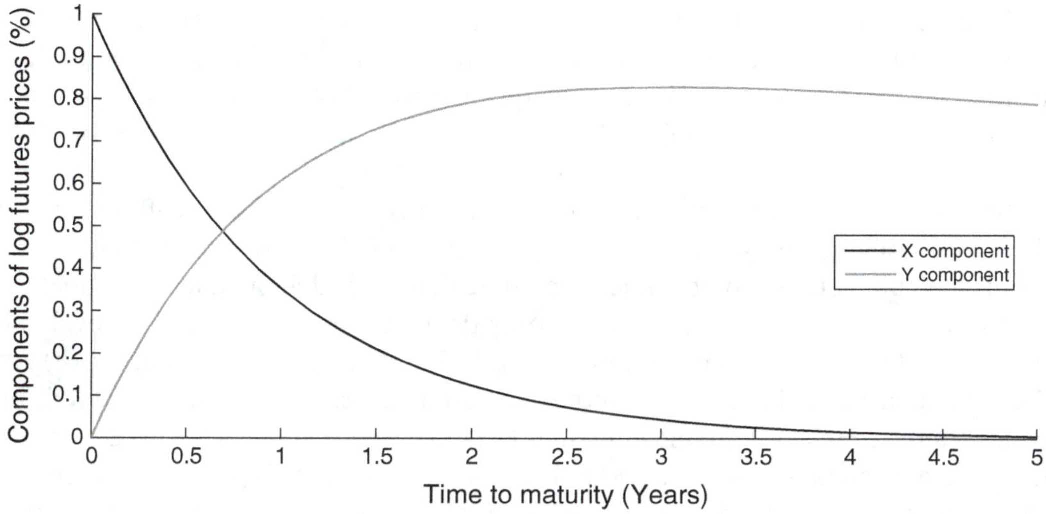


**Fig. 2** The relative contribution of various components to log futures prices

where diag$(A)$ returns the vector with diagonal elements of $A$, and where

$$\boldsymbol{\mu}^* = \begin{bmatrix} \boldsymbol{\mu}_x^* \\ \boldsymbol{\mu}_y^* \end{bmatrix} = \boldsymbol{\mu} + \Sigma^{\frac{1}{2}} \begin{bmatrix} \boldsymbol{\lambda}_x \\ \boldsymbol{\lambda}_y \end{bmatrix}.$$

To better assess qualitatively the impact of the two factors, $\mathbf{X}(t)$ and $\mathbf{Y}(t)$, on the term structure of futures prices, we depict in Fig. 2 the relative contribution of the corresponding two terms in Eq. (5) to the logarithm of the futures prices on one of the commodities in a cointegrated system.

The contribution of the $\mathbf{X}(t)$ component decreases exponentially as a function of time to maturity. On the other hand, the $\mathbf{Y}(t)$ component contributes significantly for higher maturities. Therefore, the two factors capture the short-end and, respectively, the long-end of the term-structure of futures prices.

By Itô's lemma, the risk-neutral dynamics of $\mathbf{F}(t, T)$ is given by

$$\frac{d\mathbf{F}(t,T)}{\mathbf{F}(t,T)} = \left[e^{-K_x(T-t)}\Sigma_x^{\frac{1}{2}} + \psi(T-t)\Sigma_{xy}^{\frac{1}{2}}\right] d\mathbf{W}_x^*(t) + \psi(T-t)\Sigma_y^{\frac{1}{2}} d\mathbf{W}_y^*(t), \tag{7}$$

and it follows immediately that the variance–covariance matrix of returns on futures prices is given by:

$$\begin{aligned} \Xi(\tau) = {} & e^{-K_x\tau}\Sigma_x e^{-K_x^\top\tau} + \psi(\tau)\Sigma_{xy}^{\frac{1}{2}}(\Sigma_x^{\frac{1}{2}})^\top e^{-K_x^\top\tau} + e^{-K_x\tau}\Sigma_x^{\frac{1}{2}}(\Sigma_{xy}^{\frac{1}{2}})^\top\psi^\top(\tau) \\ & + \psi(\tau)\Sigma_{xy}\psi^\top(\tau) + \psi(\tau)\Sigma_y\psi^\top(\tau) \end{aligned} \tag{8}$$

where $\tau = T - t$.

Since the term structure of correlation of futures prices returns plays an important role in the results of the simulations performed in the following section, it is worthwhile to point out some qualitative results about this term structure.

First, Eq. (8) shows that unless $K_x = \mathbf{O}_n$, the variance–covariance matrix $\Xi(\tau)$ depends on $\tau$.

Second, let us consider the case that there is no instantaneous correlation between the shocks driving the dynamics, meaning that $\Sigma_x$ and $\Sigma_y$ are diagonal matrices and $\Sigma_{xy}$ is the null matrix. Moreover, let us assume that $K_x$ is diagonal, meaning that the spot price of a commodity reacts only to its deviation from the long run level and not to deviations of the other commodities. It follows that the first term in Eq. (8) is a diagonal matrix and the next three terms are null matrices. If, in addition, there is no cointegration in the system, meaning that $\Theta$ is the null matrix, then the last term in Eq. (8) is a diagonal matrix since $\psi(\tau)$ is also a diagonal matrix. So, in this case, the variance–covariance matrix $\Xi(\tau)$ is diagonal and, therefore, there is no correlation at any maturity. However, if there is at least one cointegration relation in the system, then the last term in Eq. (8) is no longer a diagonal matrix since $\psi(\tau)$ is not diagonal. Therefore, cointegration induces correlation at various maturities although it was assumed there is no instantaneous correlation between the Brownian motions in the model.

## 3 Spread Option Prices

In this section, we focus on futures prices and prices of European-style options written on the *spread* between two or more commodities, such as the difference between the price of electric power and the cost of the natural gas needed to produce it, or the price difference between crude oil and a basket of various refined products, known as the crack spread. The crack spread is in fact related to the profit margin that an oil refiner realizes when "cracking" crude oil while simultaneously selling the refined products in the wholesale market. The oil refiner can hedge the risk of losing profits by buying an appropriate number of futures contract on the crack spread or, alternatively, by buying call options of the crack spread. Since spread options have become regularly and widely used instruments in financial markets for hedging purposes, there is a growing need for a better understanding of the effects of cointegration on their prices.

There is extensive literature on approximation methods for spread and basket options on two (e.g. Kirk [8]) or more than two commodities, with recent contributions from Li et al. [9] and Caldana and Fusai [2]. However, mostly for simplicity, we relay in this chapter on the Monte-Carlo simulation method for pricing spread options written on two or more than two commodities.

From Eq. (7), it follows that $\mathbf{F}(t, T)$ (conditional on information available up to time $s \leq t \leq T$) is distributed as follows:

$$\mathbf{F}(t,T) \sim \log \mathcal{N}\left(\log \mathbf{F}(s,T) - \frac{1}{2}\int_s^t \operatorname{diag}(\Xi(T-u))du, \int_s^t \Xi(T-u)du\right), \tag{9}$$

where $\operatorname{diag}(X)$ denotes the vector containing the diagonal elements of the matrix $X$. Note that $\mathbf{F}(s,T)$ can be either computed from (5) or observed from data.

The fact that the distribution function of $\mathbf{F}(t,T)$ is known in an easy-to-use and analytic form is one of the key features of the model we employ. It allows us to simulate futures price curves at any time $t$ in the future based on today's curves (time $s$) almost effortlessly. Hence, the price of a call option on the time-$T$ value of a certain spread can be simply obtained by carrying out the following steps:

(i) compute or observe today's futures price curves $\mathbf{F}(s,T)$;

(ii) compute $M$ realizations $\mathbf{F}^{(m)}$ $(m=1,\dots,M)$ of $\mathbf{F}(T,T)$ by sampling from (9) as follows:

$$\mathbf{F}^{(m)} = \mathbf{F}(s,T)\exp\left\{\boldsymbol{\varepsilon}^{(m)}\right\},$$

where $\boldsymbol{\varepsilon}^{(m)}$ is generated from a multivariate normal distribution with mean $-\frac{1}{2}\int_s^T \operatorname{diag}(\Xi(T-u))du$ and variance–covariance matrix $\int_s^T \Xi(T-u)du$[1];

(iii) compute the Monte-Carlo estimate of a call with strike $k$ on the spread

$$\sum_{n=1}^{N} \omega_n S_n(T) \qquad \left(= \sum_{n=1}^{N} \omega_n F_n(T,T)\right),$$

with $\omega_n, n=1,\dots,N$ the weights of each component in the spread, as follows:

$$\frac{1}{M}\sum_{m=1}^{M} \max\left\{\left[\sum_{n=1}^{N} \omega_n F_n^{(m)}\right] - k, 0\right\}. \tag{10}$$

For the sake of clarity we have set the risk-free rate curve equal to zero. We note that the random variables $\boldsymbol{\varepsilon}^{(m)}$ can be simply re-used for pricing spread options with different maturity dates.

In the following we consider a system of three commodities[2] characterized by one cointegration relation with $\Theta = \begin{bmatrix} 1 & -0.4 & -0.6 \\ 0 & 0 & 0 \\ 0 & 0 & 0 \end{bmatrix}$. The rest of the parameters describing the dynamics are $K_x = \begin{bmatrix} 1.5 & 0 & 0 \\ 0 & 1 & 0 \\ 0 & 0 & 0.5 \end{bmatrix}$, $\Sigma_x = \begin{bmatrix} 0.0625 & 0.0562 & 0.0437 \\ 0.0562 & 0.0900 & 0.0262 \\ 0.0437 & 0.0262 & 0.1225 \end{bmatrix}$, $\mu_y =$

[1]Here the technique of antithetic variables is used to reduce the number of random samples needed for a given level of accuracy.

[2]The structure of the parameters is chosen, in a parsimonious manner, taking into consideration the key facts of the empirical study conducted in Farkas et al. [6], where the results provide compelling evidence of cointegration between various commodities.

$\begin{bmatrix} 0.025 \\ 0.025 \\ 0.025 \end{bmatrix}$, $K_y = \begin{bmatrix} 1.5 & 0 & 0 \\ 0 & 0 & 0 \\ 0 & 0 & 0 \end{bmatrix}$, $\Sigma_y = \begin{bmatrix} 0.0225 & 0 & 0 \\ 0 & 0.0225 & 0 \\ 0 & 0 & 0.0225 \end{bmatrix}$, $\Sigma_{xy} = \mathbf{O}_3$. Since $K_x$ is diagonal, each spot price is error-corrected only with respect to deviations from its own long-run level. Moreover, given the specific form of the $K_y$ matrix, deviations from the cointegration relationships between the long-run levels influence only the dynamics of the first spot price. In this respect, the second and third commodities are "exogenous" in that their dynamics is not influenced by the variables characterizing the other commodities. Regarding instantaneous dependence, the shocks driving the dynamics of the long-run factors are not correlated, whereas we imposed positive correlations between the shocks driving the dynamics of the $\mathbf{X}(t)$. More specifically, the instantaneous variance–covariance matrix $\Sigma_y$ for long-run shocks corresponds to an annual volatility of 0.15 for all three commodities. At the same time, the instantaneous variance–covariance matrix $\Sigma_x$ for short-run shocks corresponds to an annual volatility of 0.25 for the first commodity, of 0.30 for the second and of 0.35 for the third and to a correlation coefficient of 0.75 between the first and the second commodities, of 0.50 between the first and the last and of 0.25 between the second and the third. For simplicity, we also assume there is no correlation between the two categories of shocks. Since we focus on the impact of cointegration on spread options, in the following simulations we have set, for illustration purposes, the vector of risk premiums $\boldsymbol{\lambda}_x$ and $\boldsymbol{\lambda}_y$ and the risk-free rate curve equal to zero.[3]

Figure 3 depicts the term structure of correlation, over a period of 5 years, between the returns of futures prices of the three commodities in the system in two cases: the one when the cointegration relation is taken into account and, respectively, the one where the cointegration relation is abstracted from (i.e. $\Theta = \mathbf{O}_3$).

One can observe that, regarding the correlation term structure between commodities 2 and 3, the two curves are identical (Fig. 3, bottom panel). This is not surprising since these two commodities are "exogenous" as explained above and their dynamics is not influenced by the cointegration relation. However, cointegration induces additional correlation when it comes to the commodities 1 and 2 and commodities 1 and 3, as also pointed out at the end of the previous section. In the absence of cointegration, the correlation vanishes after 2–3 years, whereas when the cointegration relation is taken into account the correlation exists also in the long run.

Next, we consider three spreads on two commodities, respectively $S_1(t) - S_2(t)$, $S_1(t) - S_3(t)$, $S_2(t) - S_3(t)$, and one spread on all the three commodities in the system $S_1(t) - 0.5(S_2(t) + S_3(t))$. We assume that at time 0, the two factors are such that $\mathbf{X}(0) = \mathbf{Y}(0) = \begin{bmatrix} 2 \\ 2 \\ 2 \end{bmatrix}$ and, therefore, the current spot prices of all four spreads equal 0. We focus on studying the prices of the at-the-money (ATM) European-style call spread options with up to 5 years to maturity. Figure 4 shows the term structure of

[3]In a real-world application the parameters of the model can be estimated using futures prices data for the corresponding commodities. Given the features of the model one can implement an estimation procedure based on the Kalman filter.

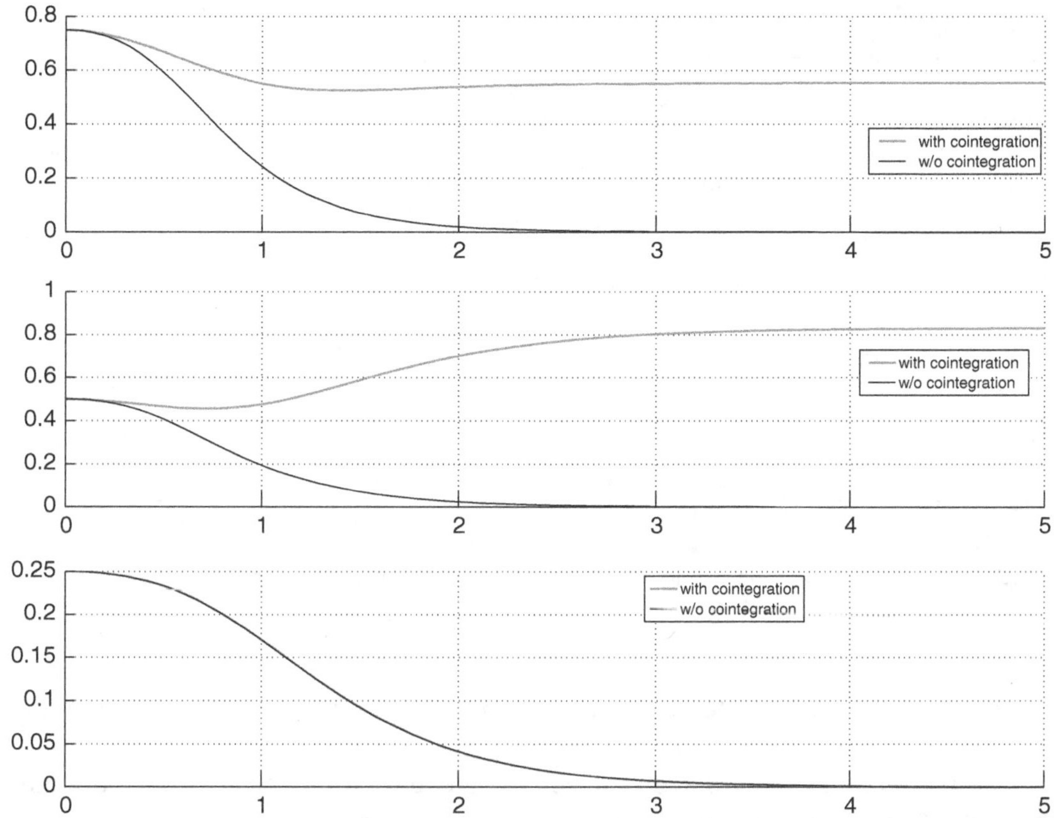


**Fig. 3** Term structure of correlation, over a period of 5 years, between the futures log-returns of three commodities (from *top* to *bottom*: between 1 and 2, between 1 and 3, between 2 and 3)

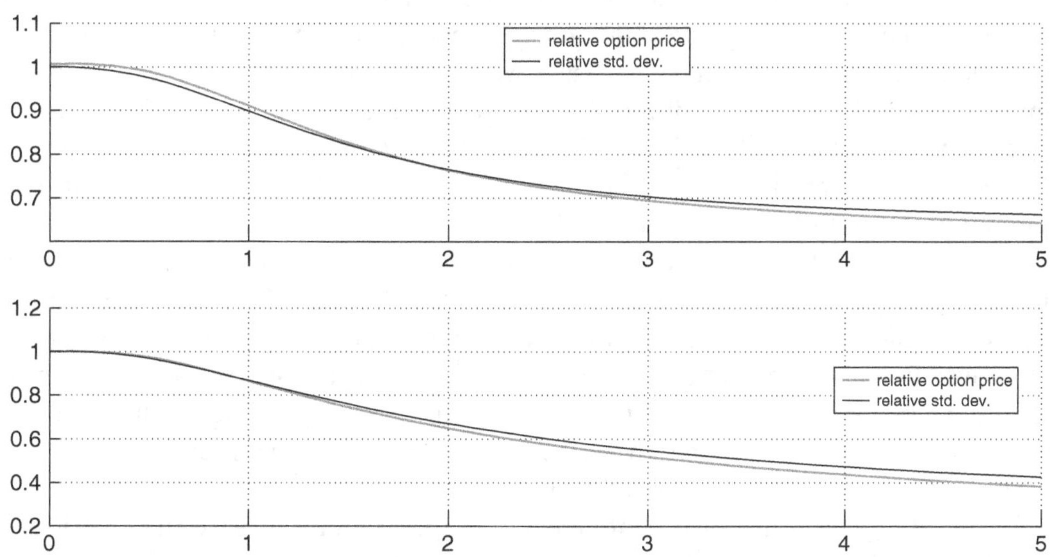


**Fig. 4** Relative ATM call spread option prices with up to 5 years to maturity, and relative standard deviations of the spread distribution at maturities up to 5 years. *Top panel* for the spread $S_1(t) - S_2(t)$. *Bottom panel* for the spread $S_1(t) - 0.5(S_2(t) + S_3(t))$

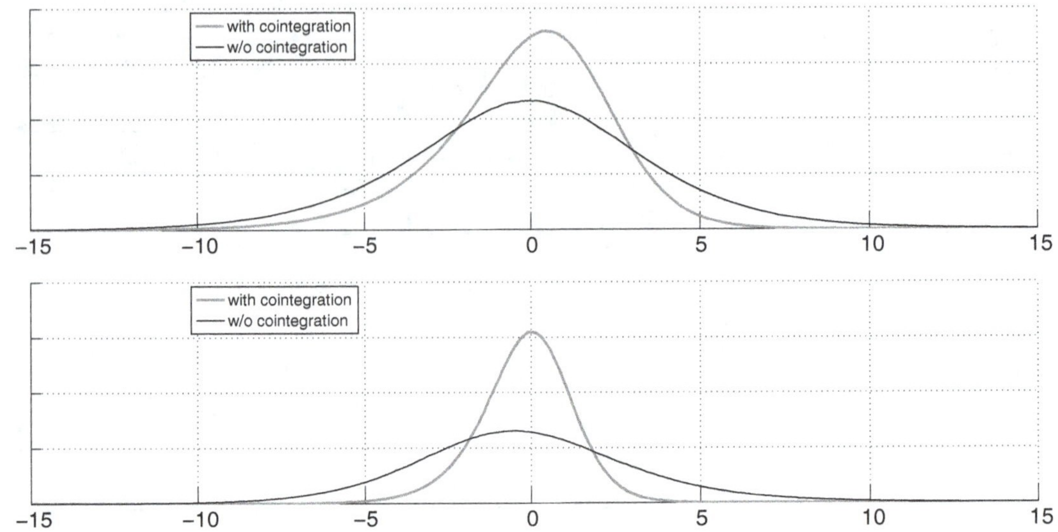


**Fig. 5** The distribution of the spread at maturity (5 years). *Top panel* for the spread $S_1(t) - S_2(t)$. *Bottom panel* for the spread $S_1(t) - 0.5(S_2(t) + S_3(t))$

prices in the case with cointegration relative to the prices in the case the cointegration is not accounted for.[4]

Cointegration has a significant impact on spread option prices, with the price for the call with 5 years to maturity on the $S_1(t) - S_2(t)$ spread being almost 30 % lower in the case with cointegration and for the call on the $S_1(t) - 0.5(S_2(t) + S_3(t))$ spread being almost 60 % lower. This can be explained by the fact that cointegration induces additional correlation that acts to lower the standard deviation of the distribution of the spread at maturity. To give a better grasp of this fact, Fig. 5 depicts the distribution of the spread at maturity in the two cases. We omitted from the figures the other two spreads, because the results for the $S_1(t) - S_3(t)$ spread are similar to those for the $S_1(t) - S_2(t)$ spread, and for the $S_2(t) - S_3(t)$ spread there is, as expected given the "exogenous" nature of these two prices, no difference between the cases with and without cointegration.

If one were to add another cointegration relation to the system, linking the second and the third commodities in a long-run relationship, then the new cointegration relation would affect the prices of the options written on the $S_2(t) - S_3(t)$ spread. Moreover, the new cointegration relation might also affect the option prices written on the other three spreads, the magnitude of this influence depending on the structure of the $K_y$ matrix that captures the strength of responses in various spot prices to deviations in the new long-run relationship.

To have a better grasp of the influence of cointegration, next we run a series of sensitivity analyses concerning the existence of a second cointegration relationship in the system. To account for the new cointegration relation, we assume a new structure

[4]Relative quantities in Fig. 4 are determined as the ratio between the quantity computed with the model accounting for cointegration and the corresponding quantity computed with the model without cointegration.

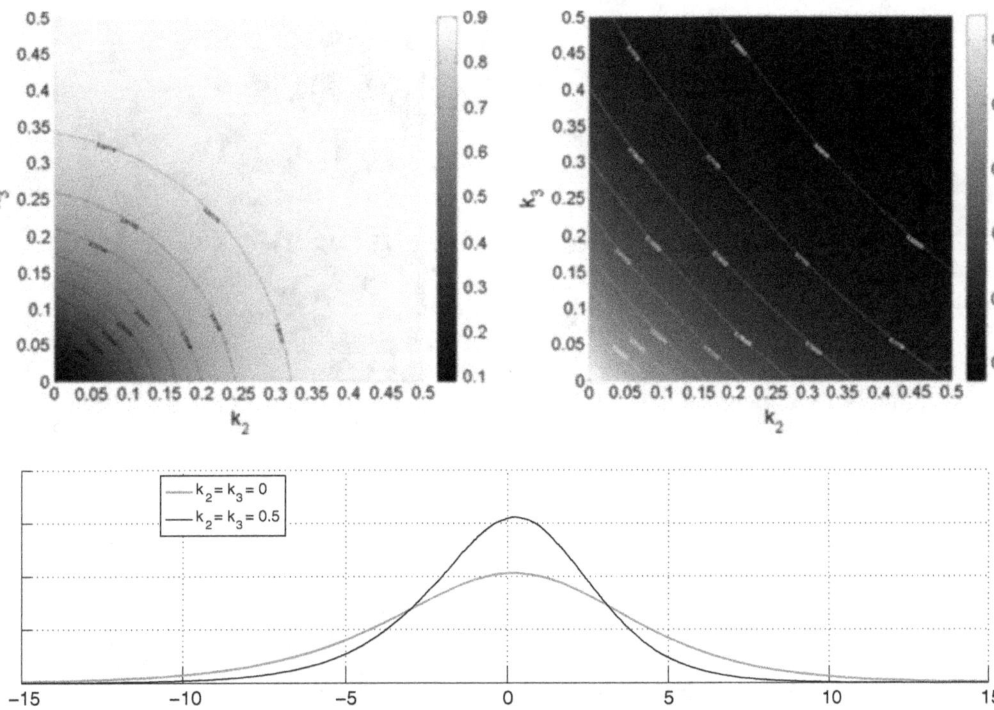

**Fig. 6** The impact of $k_2$ and $k_3$ on the distribution of the spread $S_2(t) - S_3(t)$ at maturity (5 years). *Top left panel* correlation between the futures log-returns of the two commodities in the basket. *Top right panel* relative standard deviations of the spread distribution (the values are normalized by division with the standard deviation in the case $k_2 = k_3 = 0$). *Bottom panel* the distribution for the two extreme cases in the analysis

for $\Theta = \begin{bmatrix} 1 & -0.4 & -0.6 \\ -\theta & 1 & -0.8 \\ 0 & 0 & 0 \end{bmatrix}$ and $K_y = \begin{bmatrix} 1.5 & k_1 & 0 \\ 0 & k_2 & 0 \\ 0 & -k_3 & 0 \end{bmatrix}$, where $\theta, k_1, k_2, k_3 > 0$. The other parameters have the same values as before. We first focus on the impact of the parameters $k_2$ and $k_3$ on the $S_2(t) - S_3(t)$ spread. These two parameters quantify the strength that the second and, respectively, the third commodity reacts to deviations in the newly added cointegration relation. In the extreme case when both $k_2$ and $k_3$ are zero, we are in the same situation as before since the two commodities do not react to deviations. However, with the increase of these parameters the new cointegration relation will start to matter for the dynamics of the two commodities, and will have an impact on the distribution of the spread at maturity. Figure 6 presents the results of the sensitivity analysis when $k_2$ and $k_3$ are varied between 0 and 0.5, with the other parameters kept fixed at a level $\theta = 0.2$ and $k_1 = 0$.

A higher value for the two reaction parameters produces a higher extra correlation induced by the second cointegration relation, which, in turn, is reflected in a lower standard deviation of the distribution of the spread at maturity. Over a 5-years horizon, the standard deviation for the case $k_2 = k_3 = 0.5$ is 32 % lower than in the case the two parameters are equal to zero, and the ATM call price is 35 % lower.

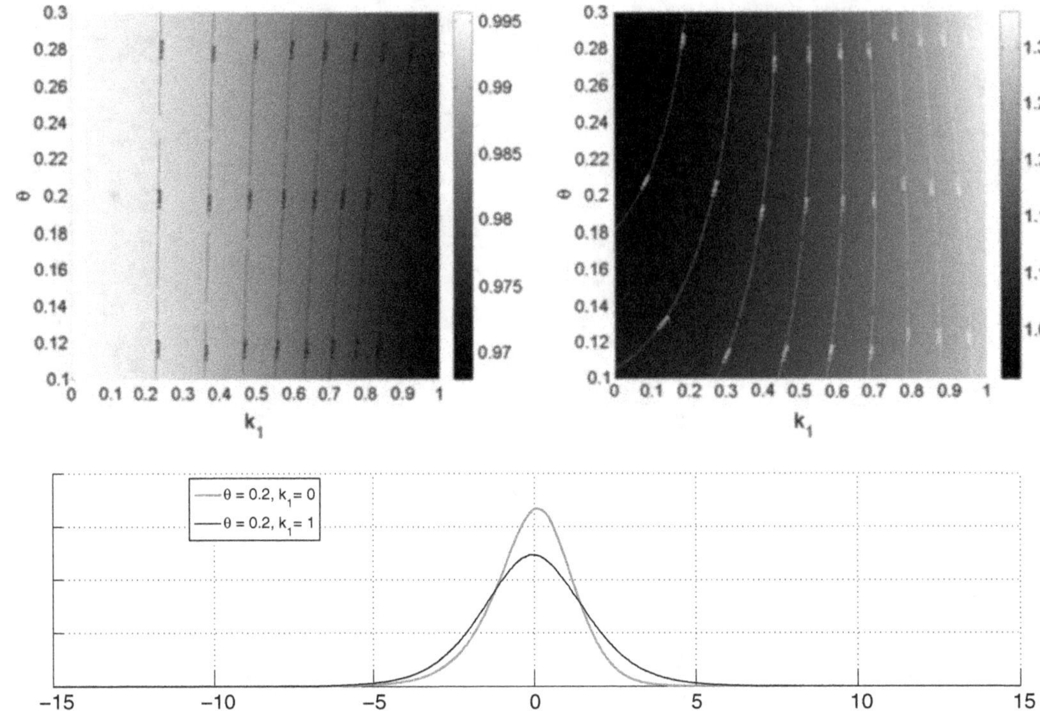


**Fig. 7** The impact of $k_1$ and $\theta$ on the distribution of the spread $S_1(t) - 0.5(S_2(t) + S_3(t))$ at maturity (5 years). *Top left panel* correlation between the futures log-returns of the first commodity and the sum of the other two. *Top right panel* relative standard deviations of the spread distribution (the values are normalized by division with the standard deviation in the case $k_1 = 0, \theta = 0.2$). *Bottom panel* the distribution for two specific cases in the analysis

Next, we focus on the impact of $\theta$ and $k_1$ on the $S_1(t) - 0.5(S_2(t) + S_3(t))$ spread. The parameter $\theta$ is a free variable that determines the second cointegration relationship and the parameter $k_1$ measures the magnitude of the response of the first commodity to deviations from the second cointegration relation. Figure 7 presents the results of the sensitivity analysis when $k_1$ and $\theta$ are varied between 0 and 1 and, respectively, between 0.1 and 0.3, with the other parameters kept fixed at a level $k_2 = 0.25$ and $k_3 = 0.25$. An increase of $k_1$ generates a reduction in the correlation between the components of the spread, showing that the second cointegration relationship has the effect of pulling the components of the spread away from each other. This effect is marginally stronger for the smaller $\theta$. The result of the reduction in correlation is a higher standard deviation of the distribution of the spread at maturity.

For a maturity of 5 years, the standard deviation for the case $k_1 = 1$ is around 33 % higher than in the case the parameter equals zero, and the ATM call price is about 40 % higher. Therefore, the two cointegration relations influence the distribution of the $S_1(t) - 0.5(S_2(t) + S_3(t))$ spread in different directions, the first one generating a reduction, and the second one an increase in the standard deviation. The overall impact depends on the magnitude of the parameters quantifying the responses of the commodities to deviations in the two cointegration relations.

## 4 Concluding Remarks

In this work, we explored the implications of cointegration between commodity prices on the premiums of options written on various spreads between these commodities. We employed the continuous time model of cointegrated commodity prices developed in Farkas et al. [6] and conducted a simulation study for a cointegrated system of three commodities. We calculated the prices of several spread options and found that cointegration significantly influences these prices. Furthermore, we pointed out that cointegration leads to an upward sloping correlation term-structure which lowers the volatility of spreads and therefore it also lowers the value of options on spreads. Although we restricted in this chapter to a simulation study, it is worthwhile to mention that the model can also be estimated using futures prices on various commodities, as shown in Farkas et al. [6].

**Acknowledgements** The KPMG Center of Excellence in Risk Management is acknowledged for organizing the conference "Challenges in Derivatives Markets - Fixed Income Modeling, Valuation Adjustments, Risk Management, and Regulation".

**Open Access** This chapter is distributed under the terms of the Creative Commons Attribution 4.0 International License (http://creativecommons.org/licenses/by/4.0/), which permits use, duplication, adaptation, distribution and reproduction in any medium or format, as long as you give appropriate credit to the original author(s) and the source, a link is provided to the Creative Commons license and any changes made are indicated.

The images or other third party material in this chapter are included in the work's Creative Commons license, unless indicated otherwise in the credit line; if such material is not included in the work's Creative Commons license and the respective action is not permitted by statutory regulation, users will need to obtain permission from the license holder to duplicate, adapt or reproduce the material.

## References

1. Back, J., Prokopczuk, M.: Commodity price dynamics and derivative valuation: a review. Int. J. Theor. Appl. Financ. **16**(6), 1350032 (2013)
2. Caldana, R., Fusai, G.: A general closed-form spread option pricing formula. J. Bank. Financ. **37**, 48934906 (2013)
3. Cortazar, G., Naranjo, L.: An N-factor Gaussian model of oil futures prices. J. Futur. Mark. **26**(3), 243268 (2006)
4. Cortazar, G., Milla, C., Severino, F.: A multicommodity model of futures prices: using futures prices of one commodity to estimate the stochastic process of another. J. Futur. Mark. **28**(6), 537–560 (2008)
5. Engle, R.F., Granger, C.W.: Co-integration and error correction: representation, estimation, and testing. Econometrica **55**(2), 251–276 (1987)
6. Farkas, W., Gourie, E., Huitema, R., Necula, C.: A two-factor cointegrated commodity price model with an application to spread option pricing. Available at SSRN http://dx.doi.org/10.2139/ssrn.2679218 (2015)
7. Johansen, S.: Estimation and hypothesis testing of cointegration vectors in Gaussian vector autoregressive models. Econometrica **59**, 1551–1580 (1991)

8. Kirk, E.: Correlation in the energy markets. In: Managing Energy Price Risk, pp. 71–78. Risk Publications and Enron, London (1995)
9. Li, M., Zhou, J., Deng, S.-J.: Multi-asset spread option pricing and hedging. Quant. Financ. **10**(3), 305324 (2010)
10. Paschke, R., Prokopczuk, M.: Integrating multiple commodities in a model of stochastic price dynamics. J. Energy Mark. **2**(3), 4782 (2009)
11. Paschke, R., Prokopczuk, M.: Commodity derivatives valuation with autoregressive and moving average components in the price dynamics. J. Bank. Financ. **34**, 2742–2752 (2010)
12. Phillips, P.: Error correction and long-run equilibrium in continuous time. Econometrica **59**(4), 967–980 (1991)
13. Schwartz, E., Smith, J.E.: Short-term variations and long-term dynamics in commodity prices. Manag. Sci. **46**(7), 893–911 (2000)

# The Dynamic Correlation Model and Its Application to the Heston Model

L. Teng, M. Ehrhardt and M. Günther

**Abstract** Correlation plays an essential role in many problems of finance and economics, such as pricing financial products and hedging strategies, since it models the degree of relationship between, e.g., financial products and financial institutions. However, usually for simplicity the correlation coefficient is assumed to be a constant in many models, although financial quantities are correlated in a strongly nonlinear way in the real market. This work provides a new time-dependent correlation function, which can be easily used to construct dynamically (time-dependent) correlated Brownian motions and flexibly incorporated in many financial models. The aim of using our time-dependent correlation function is to reasonably choose additional parameters to increase the fitting quality on the one hand, but also add an economic concept on the other hand. As examples, we illustrate the applications of dynamic correlation in the Heston model. From our numerical results we conclude that the Heston model extended by incorporating time-dependent correlations can provide a better volatility smile than the pure Heston model.

**Keywords** Time-dependent correlations · Heston model · Implied volatility · Nonlinear dependence

## 1 Introduction

Correlation is a well-established concept for quantifying interdependence. It plays an essential role in several problems of finance and economics, such as pricing financial

L. Teng (✉) · M. Ehrhardt · M. Günther
Lehrstuhl für Angewandte Mathematik und Numerische Analysis,
Fakultät Mathematik und Naturwissenschaften, Bergische Universität
Wuppertal, Gaußstr. 20, 42119 Wuppertal, Germany
e-mail: teng@math.uni-wuppertal.de

M. Ehrhardt
e-mail: ehrhardt@math.uni-wuppertal.de

M. Günther
e-mail: guenther@math.uni-wuppertal.de

© The Author(s) 2016

K. Glau et al. (eds.), *Innovations in Derivatives Markets*, Springer Proceedings in Mathematics & Statistics 165, DOI 10.1007/978-3-319-33446-2_21

products and hedging strategies. For example, in [3] the arbitrage pricing model is based on that correlation as a measure for the dependence among the assets, and in portfolio credit models the default correlation is one fundamental factor of risk evaluation, see [1, 2, 12].

In most of the financial models, the correlation has been considered as a constant. However, this is not a realistic assumption due to the well-known fact that the correlation is hardly a fixed constant, see e.g. [7, 13]. For example, in many situations the pure Heston model [9] cannot provide enough skews or smiles in the implied volatility surface as market requires, especially for a short maturity. A reason for this might be that deterministically correlated Brownian motions (BMs) of the price process and the variance process are used, as the correlation mainly affects the slope of implied volatility smile. If the correlation is modeled as a time-dependent dynamic function, better skews or smiles will be provided in the implied volatility surface by reasonably choosing additional parameters. Furthermore, compared with the way to extend a model by using time-dependent parameter, e.g., [6, 10] for the Heston model, a time-dependent correlation function adds an economic concept (nonlinear relationship) and its application will be considerably simpler.

The key of modeling correlation as a time-dependent function is being able to ensure that the boundaries $-1$ and 1 of the correlation function are not attractive and unattainable for any time. In this work, we build up a appropriate time-dependent correlation function, so that one can reasonably choose additional parameters to increase the fitting quality on the one hand but also add an economic concept on the other hand.

The outline of the remaining part is as follows. Section 2 is devoted to a specific dynamic correlation function and its (analytical) computation. In Sect. 3, we present the concept of dynamically (time-dependent) correlated Brownian motions and the corresponding construction. The incorporation of our new dynamic correlation model in the Heston model is illustrated in Sect. 4. Finally, in Sect. 5 we conclude.

## 2 The Dynamic Correlation Function

In this section we introduce a dynamic correlation function. Actually, it is in high demand to find such a correlation function which must satisfy the correlation properties: it provides only the values in the interval $(-1, 1)$ for any time; it converges for increasing time. We find the following simple idea: we denote the dynamic correlation by $\bar{\rho}$ and propose simply using

$$\bar{\rho}_t := E\left[\tanh(X_t)\right], \quad t > 0 \tag{1}$$

for the *dynamic correlation function,* where $X_t$ is any mean-reverting process with positive and negative values. For the known parameters of $X_t$, the correlation function $\bar{\rho}_t : [0, t] \to (-1, 1)$ depends only on $t$. We observe that the dynamic correlation model (1) satisfies the desired properties: first, it is obvious that $\bar{\rho}_t$ takes values only in $(-1, 1)$ for all $t$. Besides, it converges for increasing time due to the mean reversion of the used process $X_t$.

Although we could intuitively observe that the function tanh is eminently suitable for transforming value to the interval $(-1, 1)$, one might still ask whether other functions can also be applied for this purpose, like trigonometric functions or $\frac{2}{\pi}\arctan(\frac{\pi}{2}x)$. In theory, such functions could be used for this purpose. However, the problem is whether one can obtain the expectation of the transformed mean-reverting process by such functions in a closed-form expression. Furthermore, our experiments show that the tendency of the function tanh is more suitable for modeling correlations, see [13].

$X_t$ in (1) could be any mean-reverting process which allows positive and negative outcomes. As an example, let $X_t$ be the *Ornstein–Uhlenbeck process* [14]

$$dX_t = \kappa(\mu - X_t)dt + \sigma dW_t, \quad t \geq 0. \tag{2}$$

We are interested in computing $E[\bar{\rho}_t]$ as a function of the given parameters in (2). We compute $\bar{\rho}_t = E[\tanh(X_t)]$ as

$$\bar{\rho}_t = E[\tanh(X_t)] = E\left[1 - \mathrm{e}^{-X_t} \cdot \frac{2}{\mathrm{e}^{-X_t} + \mathrm{e}^{X_t}}\right] = 1 - E\left[\mathrm{e}^{-X_t} \cdot \frac{1}{\cosh(X_t)}\right]. \tag{3}$$

We set $g(X_t) = 1/\cosh(X_t)$. Applying the results by Chen and Joslin [4], the expectation in (3) can be found in closed-form expression (up to an integral) as

$$\frac{1}{2\pi}\int_{-\infty}^{\infty} \hat{g}(u) \cdot E[\mathrm{e}^{-X_t}\mathrm{e}^{iuX_t}]\, du, \tag{4}$$

where $i = \sqrt{-1}$ denotes the imaginary unit and $\hat{g}$ is the Fourier transform of $g$, in this case is known analytically by $\hat{g}(u) = \pi/\cosh(\frac{\pi u}{2})$. Denoting $CF(t, u|X_0, \kappa, \mu, \sigma)$ as the characteristic function of $X_t$, the expectation in (4) can be presented by $CF(t, i + u|X_0, \kappa, \mu, \sigma)$. Thus, we obtain the closed-form expression for $\bar{\rho}_t$:

$$\bar{\rho}_t = 1 - \frac{1}{2}\int_{-\infty}^{\infty} \frac{1}{\cosh(\frac{\pi u}{2})} \cdot CF(t, i + u|X_0, \kappa, \mu, \sigma)du. \tag{5}$$

The next step is to calculate $CF(t, i + u|X_0, \kappa, \mu, \sigma)$. The process $X_t$ is an Ornstein–Uhlenbeck process and its characteristic function $CF(t, u|X_0, \kappa, \mu, \sigma)$ can be obtained analytically, e.g. using the framework of the affine process, see [5]. Then, we only need to substitute $u + i$ for $u$ in the characteristic function of $X_t$ to calculate $CF(t, i + u|X_0, \kappa, \mu, \sigma)$ which is given by

$$CF(t, i + u|X_0, \kappa, \mu, \sigma) = \mathrm{e}^{-A(t) - \frac{B(t)}{2} + iu(A(t)+B(t)) + u^2\frac{B(t)}{2}}, \tag{6}$$

with

$$A(t) = e^{-\kappa t} X_0 + \mu(1 - e^{-\kappa t}), \quad B(t) = -\frac{\sigma^2}{2\kappa}(1 - e^{-2\kappa t}) \tag{7}$$

Finally, the dynamic correlation function $\bar{\rho}_t$ can be computed by

$$\bar{\rho}_t = 1 - \frac{e^{-A(t) - \frac{B(t)}{2}}}{2} \int_{-\infty}^{\infty} \frac{1}{\cosh(\frac{\pi u}{2})} \cdot e^{iu(A(t)+B(t))+u^2\frac{B(t)}{2}} du, \tag{8}$$

where $A(t)$ and $B(t)$ are defined in (7). In fact, $X_0$ in $A(t)$ is equal to $\operatorname{artanh}(\bar{\rho}_0)$.

To illustrate the role of each parameter in (8), we plot $\bar{\rho}_t$ for several values of the parameters. First in Fig. 1, we let $\kappa = 2$ and $\sigma = 0.5$ and display $\bar{\rho}_t$ with different values of $\mu$, which is set to be $0.5$, $0$, and $-0.5$, respectively. Obviously, $\mu$ determines the long term mean of $\bar{\rho}_t$. However, $\mu$ is not the exact limiting value. Considering Fig. 1a where the initial value of the correlation function is 0, we see that $\bar{\rho}_t$ is increasing to a value around $\mu = 0.5$ and decreasing to a value around $\mu = -0.5$ as $t$ become larger, when $\mu = 0.5$ and $-0.5$, respectively. Besides, for $\mu = \bar{\rho}_0 = 0$ we observe that the correlation function $\bar{\rho}_t$ yields always 0 which is the same as constant correlation $\rho = 0$. Now, we set $\bar{\rho}_0 = 0.3$ and keep the value of all other parameters unchanged, then display the curves of $\bar{\rho}_t$ in Fig. 1b.

Next, we fix $\kappa = 2$ and $\mu = 0.5$ and then display $\bar{\rho}_t$ for the varying $\sigma = 0.5$, 1 and 2 in Fig. 2. Obviously, $\sigma$ shows the magnitude of variation from the transformed mean value of $X_t$ ($\mu = 0.5$). In Fig. 2a we see, the larger the value of $\sigma$ is, the stronger the deviations of $\bar{\rho}_t$ is from the transformed mean value of $X_t$. More interesting is that $\bar{\rho}_t$ first decreases until $t \approx 0.25$, then increases and converges to a value, see Fig. 2b where $\bar{\rho}_0 = 0.3$ and $\sigma = 2$.

Again, in order to illustrate the role of $\kappa$, we set $\mu = 0.5$, $\sigma = 2$ and vary the value of $\kappa$, see Fig. 3. From Fig. 3a it is easy to observe that $\kappa$ represents the speed of $\bar{\rho}_t$ tending to its limit. Especially, as we have seen in Fig. 2b, the curve is more

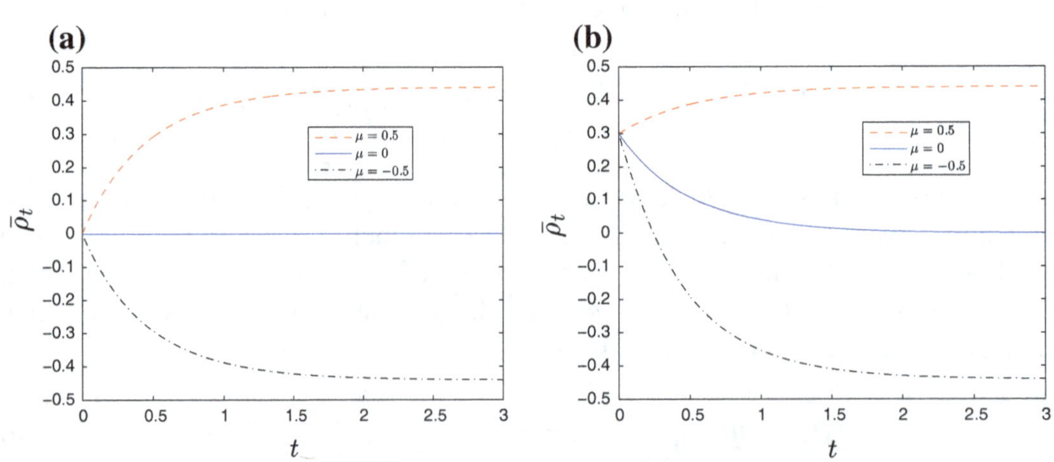


**Fig. 1** Dynamic correlation $\bar{\rho}_t$ for varying $\mu$ ($\kappa = 2$ and $\sigma = 0.5$). **a** $\bar{\rho}_0 = 0$. **b** $\bar{\rho}_0 = 0.3$

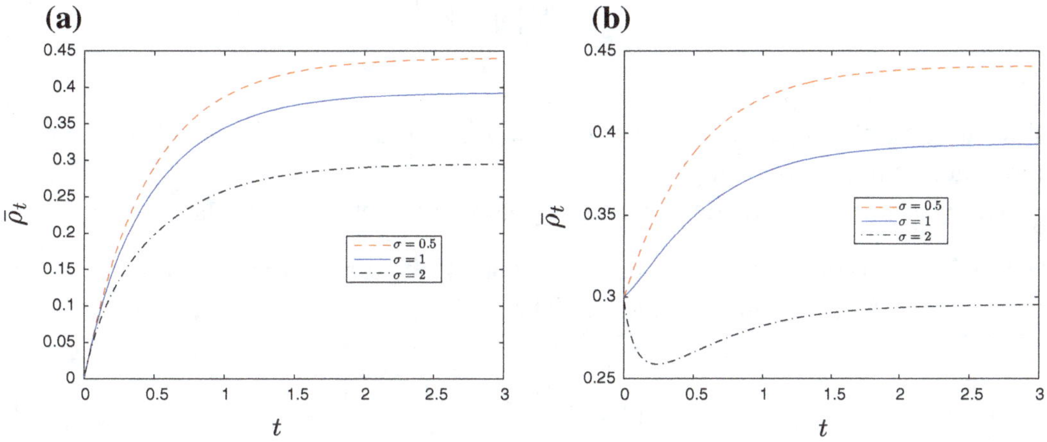


**Fig. 2** Dynamic correlation $\bar{\rho}_t$ for varying $\sigma$ ($\kappa = 2$ and $\mu = 0.5$). **a** $\bar{\rho}_0 = 0$. **b** $\bar{\rho}_0 = 0.3$

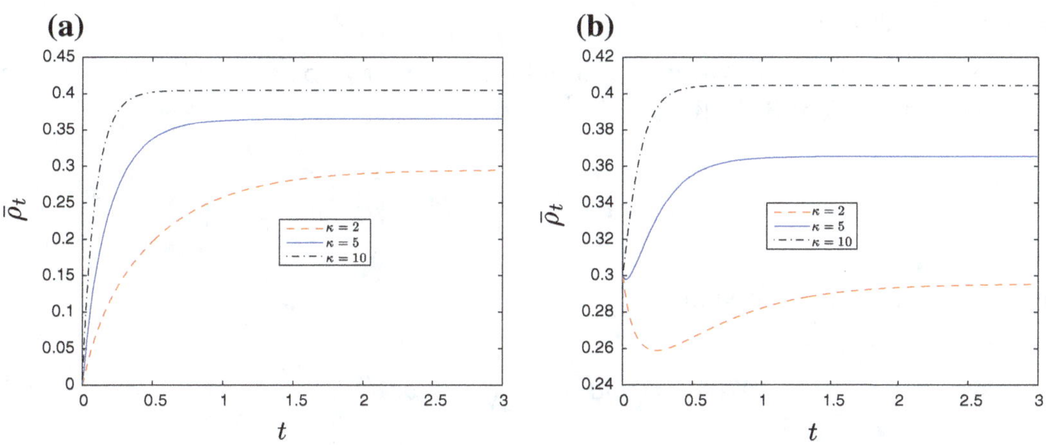


**Fig. 3** Dynamic correlation $\bar{\rho}_t$ for varying $\kappa$ ($\mu = 0.5$ and $\sigma = 2$). **a** $\bar{\rho}_0 = 0$. **b** $\bar{\rho}_0 = 0.3$

unstable for $\kappa = 2$ and $\sigma = 2$ in Fig. 3b. However, if $\sigma$ remains constant while the value of $\kappa$ is increased, we can see that curves of $\bar{\rho}_t$ become more stable and tend straightly to its limit. If one incorporates the dynamic correlation function (8) to a financial model, the parameter $\bar{\rho}_0$, $\kappa$, $\mu$, and $\sigma$ could be estimated by fitting the model to market data.

## 3 Dynamically Correlated BMs and Their Construction

We fix a probability space $(\Omega, \mathscr{F}, \mathbb{P})$ and an information filtration $(\mathscr{F}_t)_{t\in\mathbb{R}^+}$, satisfying the usual conditions, see e.g. [11]. At a time $t > 0$, the correlation coefficient of two Brownian motions (BMs) $W_t^1$ and $W_t^2$ is defined as

$$\rho_t^{1,2} = \frac{E\left[W_t^1 W_t^2\right]}{t}. \tag{9}$$

If we assume that $\rho_t^{1,2}$ is constant, $\rho_t^{1,2} = \rho^{1,2}$ for all $t > 0$, say $W_t^1$ and $W_t^2$ are correlated with the constant $\rho^{1,2}$.

Therefore, we give the definition of dynamically correlated BMs.

**Definition 1** Two Brownian motions $W_t^1$ and $W_t^2$ are called *dynamically correlated* with correlation function $\rho_t$, if they satisfy

$$E\left[W_t^1 W_t^2\right] = \int_0^t \rho_s ds, \tag{10}$$

where $\rho_t : [0, t] \to [-1, 1]$. The *average correlation* of $W_t^1$ and $W_t^2$, $\rho_{Av}$, is given by $\rho_{Av} := \frac{1}{t}\int_0^t \rho_s ds$.

We consider first the two-dimensional case and let $\rho_t$ be a correlation function. For two independent BMs $W_t^1$ and $W_t^3$ we define

$$W_t^2 = \int_0^t \rho_s dW_s^1 + \int_0^t \sqrt{1-\rho_s^2}\, dW_s^3, \tag{11}$$

with the symbolic expression

$$dW_t^2 = \rho_t dW_t^1 + \sqrt{1-\rho_t^2}\, dW_t^3. \tag{12}$$

It can be easily verified that $W_t^2$ is a BM and correlated with $W_t^1$ dynamically by $\rho_t$. Besides, the covariance matrix and the average correlation matrix of $\mathbb{W}_t = (W_t^1, W_t^2)$ can be determined, given by

$$\begin{pmatrix} t & \int_0^t \rho_s ds \\ \int_0^t \rho_s ds & t \end{pmatrix} \quad \text{and} \quad \begin{pmatrix} 1 & \frac{1}{t}\int_0^t \rho_s ds \\ \frac{1}{t}\int_0^t \rho_s ds & 1 \end{pmatrix},$$

respectively.

The construction above could be also generalized to $n$-dimensions. We denote a standard $n$-dimensional BM by $\mathbb{Z}_t = (Z_{1,t}, \ldots, Z_{n,t})$ and the matrix of dynamic correlations $\mathscr{R}_t = (\rho_t^{i,j})_{1<i,j<n}$ which has the Cholesky decomposition for each time $t$, $\mathscr{R}_t = \mathbb{A}_t \mathbb{A}_t^\top$ with $\mathbb{A}_t = (a_t^{i,j})_{1<i,j<n}$. We define a new $n$-dimensional process $\mathbb{W}_t = (W_{1,t}, \ldots, W_{n,t})$ by

$$W_{i,t} = \sum_{j=1}^n a_t^{ij}\, dZ_{j,t}, \quad i = 1, \ldots, n. \tag{13}$$

We can easily verify that $\mathbb{W}_t$ satisfies the following properties:

- $\mathbb{W}_0 = \mathbf{0}$ and the paths are continuous with probability 1.
- The increments $\mathbb{W}_{t_1} - \mathbb{W}_{t_0}$ and $\mathbb{W}_{t_2} - \mathbb{W}_{t_1}$ are independent for $0 \leq t_0 < t_1 < t_2 < t$.
- For $0 \leq s < t$, the increment $\mathbb{W}_t - \mathbb{W}_s$ is multivariate normally distributed with mean zero and covariance matrix $\Sigma : \mathbb{W}_t - \mathbb{W}_s \sim N(0, \Sigma)$ with

$$\Sigma = \begin{pmatrix} t-s & \int_s^t \rho_u^{1,2} du & \dots & \int_s^t \rho_u^{1,n} du \\ \int_s^t \rho_u^{2,1} du & t-s & \dots & \int_s^t \rho_u^{2,n} du \\ \vdots & \vdots & \ddots & \vdots \\ \int_s^t \rho_u^{n,1} du & \int_s^t \rho_u^{n,2} du & \dots & t-s \end{pmatrix}.$$

We call the process $(\mathbb{W}_t)_{t \geq 0}$ *an n-dimensional dynamically correlated Brownian motion,* with the correlation matrix $\mathscr{R}_t$.

# 4 Dynamic Correlation in the Heston Model

As mentioned before, in many situations the pure Heston model has a limitation on reproducing properly a volatility smile. For this problem, several time-dependent Heston models have been proposed for good fitting to implied volatilities, e.g. [6] and [10]. In this section, we show how to incorporate our time-dependent correlation function into the Heston model.

## *4.1 Incorporating Dynamic Correlations*

Heston's stochastic volatility model is specified as

$$dS_t = \mu_S S_t dt + \sqrt{\nu_t} S_t \, dW_t^S, \tag{14}$$
$$d\nu_t = \kappa_\nu(\mu_\nu - \nu_t)dt + \sigma_\nu \sqrt{\nu_t} \, dW_t^\nu, \tag{15}$$

where (14) is the price of the spot asset, (15) is the volatility (variance) and $W_t^S$ and $W_t^\nu$ are correlated with a constant correlation $\rho_{S\nu}$. To incorporate the time-dependent correlations, we assume that $dS_t$ and $d\nu_t$ are correlated by a time-dependent correlation function $\bar{\rho}_t$ instead of the constant correlation $\rho_{S\nu}$. The extended Heston model with dynamic correlation $\bar{\rho}$ is specified as

$$dS_t = \mu_S S_t dt + \sqrt{\nu_t} S_t \, dW_t^1, \tag{16}$$
$$d\nu_t = \kappa_\nu(\mu_\nu - \nu_t)dt + \sigma_\nu \sqrt{\nu_t} \left( \bar{\rho}_t \, dW_t^1 + \sqrt{1 - \bar{\rho}_t^2} \, dW_t^2 \right), \tag{17}$$

where $W_t^1$ and $W_t^2$ are independent. Applying Itô's lemma and no-arbitrage arguments yields [9]

$$\frac{1}{2}\nu S^2\frac{\partial^2 U}{\partial S^2}+\bar{\rho}_t\sigma_\nu \nu S\frac{\partial^2 U}{\partial S\partial \nu}+\frac{1}{2}\sigma_\nu^2\nu\frac{\partial^2 U}{\partial \nu^2}+rS\frac{\partial U}{\partial S} \\ +[\kappa_\nu(\mu_\nu-\nu)-\tilde{\lambda}(S,\nu,\bar{\rho},t)\nu]\frac{\partial U}{\partial \nu}-rU+\frac{\partial U}{\partial t}=0, \tag{18}$$

where $\bar{\rho}_t$ is defined in (8) but with the parameter $\bar{\rho}_0$, $\kappa_\rho$, $\mu_\rho$, and $\nu_\rho$. It is worth mentioning that the market price of volatility risk depends also on the dynamic correlation, which could be written as $\tilde{\lambda}(S,\nu,\bar{\rho}_t,t)$. This means, the price of correlation risk embedding in the price of volatility risk has been considered.

We consider, e.g. a European call option with strike price $K$ and maturity $T$ in the Heston model

$$C(S,\nu,t,\bar{\rho}_t)=SP_1-KP(t,T)P_2,\quad \tau=T-t, \tag{19}$$

where $P(t,T)$ is the discount factor and both in-the-money probabilities $P_1, P_2$ must satisfy the PDE (18) as well as their characteristic functions, $f_1(S_t,\nu_t,\bar{\rho}_t,\phi,t)$ and $f_2(S_t,\nu_t,\bar{\rho}_t,\phi,t)$

$$f_j(S_t,\nu_t,\bar{\rho}_t,\phi,t)=E[\mathrm{e}^{i\phi\ln S_T}|S_t,\nu_t,\bar{\rho}_t]=\mathrm{e}^{C_j(\tau,\phi)+D_j(\tau,\phi)\nu+i\phi\ln S_t},\quad j=1,2, \tag{20}$$

where $C_j(0,\phi)=0$ and $D_j(0,\phi)=0$. By substituting this functional form (20) into the PDE (18) we can obtain the following ordinary differential equations (ODEs) for the unknown functions $C$ and $D$:

$$-\frac{1}{2}\phi^2+\bar{\rho}_t\sigma_\nu\phi i D_j+\frac{1}{2}\sigma_\nu^2 D_j^2+u_j\phi i-b_jD_j+\frac{\partial D_j}{\partial t}=0, \tag{21}$$

$$r\phi i+\kappa_\nu\mu_\nu D_j+\frac{\partial C_j}{\partial t}=0, \tag{22}$$

with the initial conditions $C_j(0,\phi)=D_j(0,\phi)=0$

$$u_1=0.5,\quad u_2=-0.5,\quad b_1=\kappa_\nu+\lambda-\bar{\rho}_t\sigma_\nu \ \text{ and } \ b_2=\kappa_\nu+\lambda, \tag{23}$$

where

$$\bar{\rho}_t=1-\frac{\mathrm{e}^{-A(t)-\frac{B(t)}{2}}}{2}\int_{-\infty}^{\infty}\underbrace{\frac{1}{\cosh(\frac{\pi u}{2})}\cdot\mathrm{e}^{iu(A(t)+B(t))+u^2\frac{B(t)}{2}}}_{:=g(u)}du, \tag{24}$$

with $A(t)=\mathrm{e}^{-\kappa_\rho t}\operatorname{artanh}(\bar{\rho}_0)+\mu_\rho(1-\mathrm{e}^{-\kappa_\rho t})$, $B(t)=-\frac{\sigma_\rho^2}{2\kappa_\rho}(1-\mathrm{e}^{-2\kappa_\rho t})$.

Obviously, (21) and (22) cannot be solved analytically. Therefore, we need to find an efficient way to compute the option price numerically. We firstly generate the

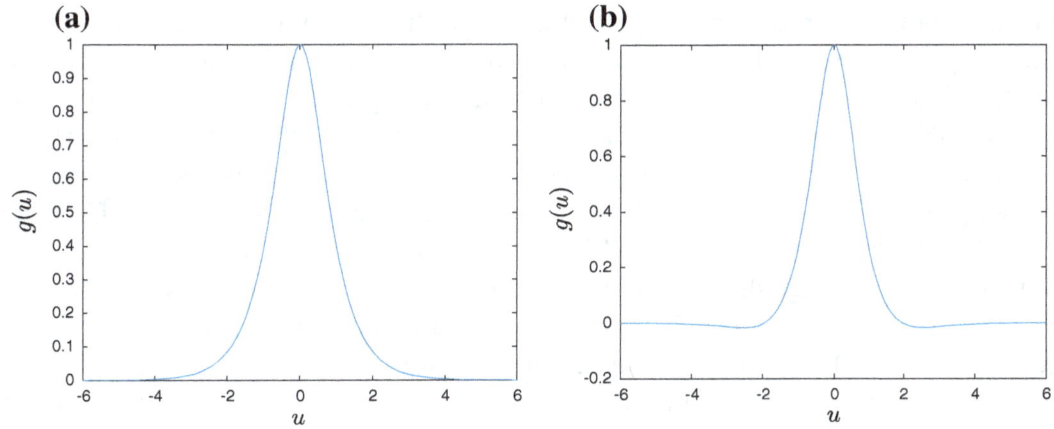


**Fig. 4** $g(u)$ under $\rho_0 = 0.3, \kappa_\rho = 2, \mu_\rho = -0.8, \sigma_\rho = 0.1$. **a** $t = 0.1$. **b** $t = 10$

dynamic correlations using (24). We observe that $g(u)$ is a symmetric function about $u = 0$ and vanishes (approaches zero) for a sufficiently large absolute value of $u$, see Fig. 4. For these two reasons, the numerical integration in (24) is computationally fast. Next we use an explicit Runge–Kutta method, the matlab routine `ode45`, to obtain $C$ and $D$ in (21) and (22) and thus also the characteristic functions (20). Finally, we employ the COS method [8] to obtain the option price $C(S, \nu, t, \bar{\rho})$ in (19). Thanks to the COS method, although we solved that ODE system numerically, the time for obtaining European option prices is less than 0.1 s so that a calibration can be performed. Obviously, the error consists of the error using `ode45` for (21) and (22) and the error using COS method. The detailed analysis of error using COS method has been provided in [8].

## *4.2 Calibration of the Heston Model Under Dynamic Correlation*

In this section we calibrate the Heston model extended by our time-dependent correlation function to the real market data (Nikk300 index call options on July 16, 2012) and compare these to the pure Heston model [9] and the time-dependent Heston model [10].

We consider a set of $N$ maturities $T_i$, $i = 1, \ldots, N$ and a set of $M$ strikes $K_j$, $j = 1, \ldots, M$. Then for each combination of maturity and strike we have a market price $V^M(T_i, K_j) = V_{ij}^M$ and a corresponding model price $V(T_i, K_j; \Theta) = V_{ij}^\Theta$ generated by using (19). We choose the relative mean error sum of squares (RMSE) for the loss function $\frac{1}{M \times N} \sum_{i,j} \frac{(V_{ij}^M - V_{ij}^\Theta)^2}{V_{ij}^M}$, which can be minimized to obtain the parameter estimates

$$\hat{\Theta} = \arg\min \frac{1}{M \times N} \sum_{i,j} \frac{(V_{ij}^M - V_{ij}^\Theta)^2}{V_{ij}^M}. \tag{25}$$

For the optimization we restrict $\bar{\rho}_0$ to the interval $(-1, 1)$ but not the value of $\mu_\rho$. Since it is not the direct limit of the correlation function but the mean reversion of the Ornstein–Uhlenbeck process, thus, it could take any value in $\mathbb{R}$. Our experiments showed, that it is sufficient and appropriate to restrict $\mu_\rho$ to the interval $[-4, 4]$.

We state our estimated parameters and the estimation error for the pure Heston model (abbr. PH), the Heston model under our time-dependent correlations (CH), the time-dependent Heston model by Mikhailov and Ngel [10] (MN) in Tables 1, 2 and 3, respectively. We see that the estimation error using the CH model is significantly less than the error using the PH model and almost the same to the error (sum of errors for each maturity) under the MN model. To illustrate more clearly, for each maturity we compare the implied volatilities for all the models to the market volatilities in Fig. 5. We can observe that the implied volatilities for the CH model are much closer to the market volatilities than the implied volatilities for the PH model, especially the CH model has better volatility smile for the short maturity $T = 1/12$. Compared to the MN model, the implied volatilities for our model are almost the same. However, our CH model has an economic interpretation, namely the correlation is nonlinear

**Table 1** The estimated parameters for the pure Heston model using call options on the Nikk300 index on July 16, 2012 for the maturities 1/12, 1/4, 1/2, 1

| The pure heston model | | | | | |
|---|---|---|---|---|---|
| $\hat{\nu}_0$ | $\hat{\kappa}_\nu$ | $\hat{\mu}_\nu$ | $\hat{\sigma}_\nu$ | $\hat{\rho}$ | Estimation error |
| 0.029 | 4.746 | 0.053 | 1.108 | −0.355 | $1.10 \times 10^{-3}$ |

**Table 2** The estimated parameters for the Heston model under time-dependent correlations using call options on the Nikk300 index on July 16, 2012 for the maturities 1/12, 1/4, 1/2, 1

| The extended Heston model by using our time-dependent correlation function | | | | | | | | |
|---|---|---|---|---|---|---|---|---|
| $\hat{\nu}_0$ | $\hat{\kappa}_\nu$ | $\hat{\mu}_\nu$ | $\hat{\sigma}_\nu$ | $\hat{\bar{\rho}}_0$ | $\hat{\kappa}_\rho$ | $\hat{\mu}_\rho$ | $\hat{\sigma}_\rho$ | Estimation error |
| 0.027 | 5.542 | 0.055 | 1.224 | −0.165 | 5.333 | −0.752 | 0.434 | $2.38 \times 10^{-4}$ |

**Table 3** The estimated parameters for the time-dependent Heston model by Mikhailov and Ngel using call options on the Nikk300 index on July 16, 2012

| The time-dependent Heston model by Mikhailov and Ngel | | | | | | |
|---|---|---|---|---|---|---|
| Maturity | $\hat{\nu}_0$ | $\hat{\kappa}_\nu$ | $\hat{\mu}_\nu$ | $\hat{\sigma}_\nu$ | $\hat{\rho}$ | Estimation error |
| 1/12 | 0.025 | 2.749 | 0.095 | 1.172 | −0.201 | $1.78 \times 10^{-4}$ |
| 1/4 | 0.012 | 2.936 | 0.076 | 0.524 | −0.411 | $2.45 \times 10^{-5}$ |
| 1/2 | 0.011 | 2.890 | 0.058 | 0.592 | −0.430 | $1.14 \times 10^{-5}$ |
| 1 | 0.001 | 2.911 | 0.051 | 0.558 | −0.389 | $4.28 \times 10^{-6}$ |

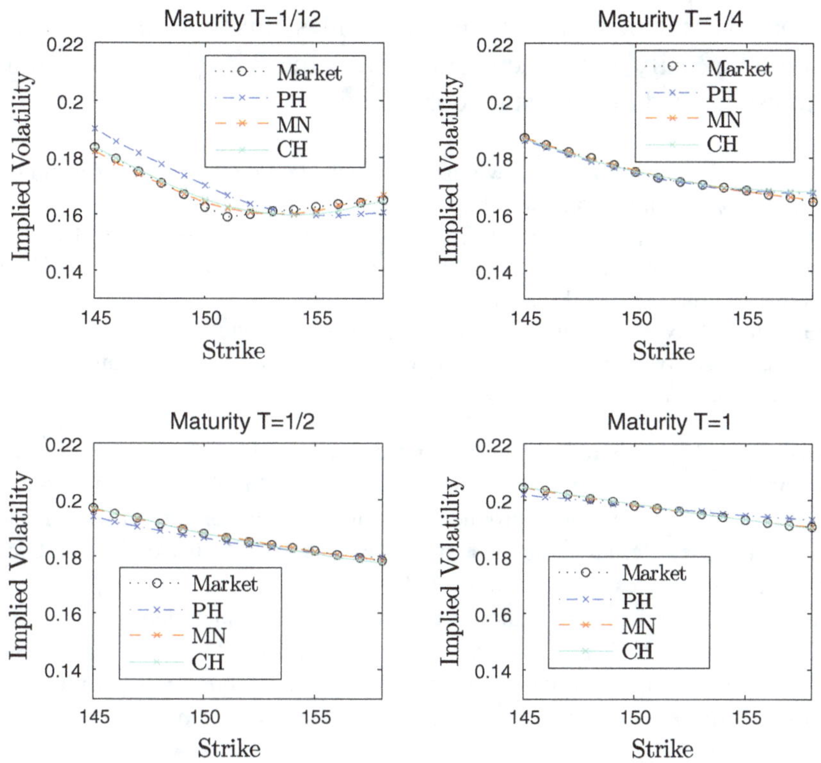


**Fig. 5** The comparison of implied volatilities for all the models to the market volatilities of the call options on the Nikk300 index on July 16, 2012, where the spot price is 150.9

and time-dependent as market requires. We conclude that the Heston model extended by incorporating our time-dependent correlations can provide better volatility smiles compared to the pure Heston model. The time-dependent correlation function can be easily and directly introduced into the financial models.

## 5 Conclusion

In this work, we first investigated the dynamically (time-dependent) correlated Brownian motions and their construction. Furthermore, we proposed a new dynamic correlation function which can be easily incorporated into another financial model. The aim of using our dynamic correlation function is to reasonably choose additional parameters to increase the fitting quality on the one-hand side, but also add an economically meaningful perspective.

As an application, we incorporated our time-dependent correlation function into the Heston model. An experiment on estimation of the models using real market data has been provided. The numerical calibration results show that the Heston model extended by using our time-dependent correlation function provides better volatility smiles compared to the pure Heston model. Besides, this time-dependent correlation function could be easily and directly imposed to the financial models and thus it is preferred to use instead of a constant correlation.

**Acknowledgements** The authors acknowledge the much appreciated inspiration and in-depth discussions with Dr. Jörg Kienitz from Deloitte Düsseldorf, Germany.

The work was partially supported by the European Union in the FP7-PEOPLE-2012-ITN Program under Grant Agreement Number 304617 (FP7 Marie Curie Action, Project Multi-ITN STRIKE—Novel Methods in Computational Finance).

The KPMG Center of Excellence in Risk Management is acknowledged for organizing the conference "Challenges in Derivatives Markets—Fixed Income Modeling, Valuation Adjustments, Risk Management, and Regulation".

**Open Access** This chapter is distributed under the terms of the Creative Commons Attribution 4.0 International License (http://creativecommons.org/licenses/by/4.0/), which permits use, duplication, adaptation, distribution and reproduction in any medium or format, as long as you give appropriate credit to the original author(s) and the source, a link is provided to the Creative Commons license and any changes made are indicated.

The images or other third party material in this chapter are included in the work's Creative Commons license, unless indicated otherwise in the credit line; if such material is not included in the work's Creative Commons license and the respective action is not permitted by statutory regulation, users will need to obtain permission from the license holder to duplicate, adapt or reproduce the material.

## References

1. Brigo, D., Capponi, A.: Bilateral counterparty risk with application to CDSs. Risk Mag. **23**(3), 85–90 (2010)
2. Brigo, D., Chourdakis, K.: Counterparty risk for credit default swaps: impact of spread volatility and default correlation. Int. J. Theoret. Appl. Financ. **12**, 1007–1026 (2009)
3. Campbell, J., Lo, A., MacKinlay, A.: The Econometrics of Financial Markets. Princeton University Press, Princeton (1997)
4. Chen, H., Joslin, S.: Generalized transform analysis of affine processes and applications in finance. Rev. Fin. Stud. **25**(7), 2225–2256 (2012)
5. Duffie, D., Filipović, D., Schachermayer, W.: Affine processes and applications in finance. Ann. Appl. Probab. **13**(3), 984–1053 (2003)
6. Elices, A.: Affine concatenation. Wilmott J. **1**(3), 155–162 (2009)
7. Escobar, M., Götz, B., Neykova, D., Zagst, R.: Stochastic correlation and volatility mean-reversion - empirical motivation and derivatives pricing via perturbation theory. Appl. Math. Fin. **21**(6), 555–594 (2014)
8. Fang, F., Oosterlee, C.W.: A novel pricing method for European options based on Fourier-cosine series expansions. SIAM J. Sci. Comput. **31**, 826–848 (2008)
9. Heston, S.L.: A closed-form solution for options with stochastic volatility with applications to bond and currency options. Rev. Fin. Stud. **6**(2), 327–343 (1993)
10. Mikhailov, S., Nögel, U.: Heston's stochastic volatility model: implementation, calibration and some extensions. Wilmott Mag. 74–79 (2003)
11. Øksendal, B.: Stochastic Differential Equations. Springer, Berlin (2002)
12. Teng, L., Ehrhardt, M., Günther, M.: Bilateral counterparty risk valuation of CDS contracts with simultaneous defaults. Int. J. Theoret. Appl. Financ. **16**(7), 1350040 (2013)

13. Teng, L., van Emmerich, C., Ehrhardt, M., Günther, M.: A versatile approach for stochastic correlation using hyperbolic functions. Int. J. Comput. Math. **93**(3), 524–539 (2016)
14. Uhlenbeck, G.E., Ornstein, L.S.: On the theory of Brownian motion. Phys. Rev. **36**, 823–841 (1930)

www.ingramcontent.com/pod-product-compliance
Lightning Source LLC
LaVergne TN
LVHW080008210926
848481LV00011B/2972